Harvard Guide to Contemporary American Writing

Harvard Guide to Contemporary American Writing.

Daniel Hoffman
Editor

WITH ESSAYS BY

Leo Braudy	Nathan A. Scott, Jr.
Josephine Hendin	Mark Shechner
Daniel Hoffman	Lewis P. Simpson
Elizabeth Janeway	Alan Trachtenberg
A. Walton Litz	Gerald Weales

The Belknap Press
of Harvard University Press   Cambridge, Massachusetts,
and London, England
1979

Library of Congress Cataloging in Publication Data

Main entry under title:

Harvard guide to contemporary American writing.

    1. American literature—20th century—History and
criticism—Addresses, essays, lectures.   I. Hoffman,
Daniel
PS221.H357   810'.9'0054   79-10930
ISBN 0-674-37535-1

Contents

Preface

This book undertakes a critical survey of the most significant writing in the United States between the end of World War II and the end of the 1970s. To describe, anatomize, and judge a literature so vast and so varied in a book of even six hundred pages may seem like trying to stuff a ticking full of feathers into a shoe box. The critic or historian, faced with the individual and particular qualities of works and authors, may be tempted to subordinate these to large general categories and trends; he may be further tempted to emphasize, at the expense of all others, those trends most visible at the time of his writing. Literature during these three and a half decades reflects, indeed often anticipates, the instability and turmoil of a period characterized by the breaking apart of many established institutions and the cultural assumptions upon which they rested. Yet resistance to these deconstructive or reconstructive energies has been strong, in our literature as in our culture. It is the hope of the authors that the chapters which follow will embody a realization of the nature of literature like that voiced in Lionel Trilling's essay "Reality in America" (*The Liberal Imagination,* 1950). In his criticism of V. L. Parrington, whose *Main Currents of American Thought* half a century ago emphasized exclusively the progressive and liberal tendencies in American writing, Trilling reminded us that "a culture is not a flow, not even a confluence; the form of its existence is a struggle, or at least a debate—it is nothing if not a dialectic. And in any culture there are likely to be certain artists who contain a large part of the dialectic within themselves, their meaning and power lying in their contradictions."

Such a dialectic is explored, first, in a survey of intellectual commitments and attitudes during the period, then in an examination of the theories and practices of literary criticism which have accompanied and to some extent even influenced the writing of these decades. Of course, no literary period is actually contained within its historians' bracketing dates. In 1945, where we begin, we find that in middle age and mid-career such important fiction writers as Ernest Hemingway, John Dos Passos, John Steinbeck, William Faulkner, and Richard Wright dominate the scene, as do the poets Robert Frost, Wallace Stevens, T. S. Eliot, Ezra Pound, William Carlos Williams, Marianne Moore, and W. H. Auden. Although the major work of most of these had already been done, all continued both to be productive and to influence their successors. Of these older writers, whether conservative or modernist, we do not attempt full treatment, but try instead to place them before our readers as they appeared at the time to theirs and to the younger authors who either emulated or rebelled against their magisterial presences.

If the beginning of our period is necessarily treated retrospectively, it can hardly be held that our period ends where our scrutiny of its writing stops. Even as we go to press, many of the authors discussed herein are publishing new books without awaiting our commentary. Although we have tried to cover major publications through 1978, we do not offer a terminal date. One aspect of the dialectic evident in this literature is the tendency of many writers to undergo great changes of style and method from one book to another. It would be rash to predict what such quick-change imaginative artists as Norman Mailer, John Updike, or W.S. Merwin may next turn their hands to, as it was unlikely that any such predictions concerning the late Robert Lowell or John Berryman could accurately have foretold their repudiations or innovations. We have endeavored to discuss most authors who have produced a significant body of work and to mention the more promising younger writers.

This *Guide* is not a synopsis of critical or scholarly commentary but a series of original essays by critics especially interested in the subjects and authors about whom they have chosen to write. The general editor of the volume is responsible for its overall design, but within that design the author of each chapter has been free to present his or her own sense of the dialectic perceived in the literature surveyed. It seems preferable that criticism of this kind—especially when it deals with writings as diverse, baffling, and innovative as is much of the literature treated in these pages—be of the sort that Edwin Muir defined (in *The Estate of Poetry*, 1962) as "a helpful intermediary between literature and the reader." One of the values of such criticism, Muir suggests, is "its capacity for admiration . . . A good critic in this style is one who apprehends by a native affinity the virtues of a work of imagination and rejoices in them." The work of such a critic will enrich the reader's experience of the writings with which it deals by revealing their intrinsic shapes while judging their fulfillment of their premises; it will not, however, subsitute a critical analysis for the work itself, recasting the reading of a novel or a poem "into a problem instead of an experience." The criticism of intermediation thus resists becoming "an instrument of power" at the expense of the literature it serves.

The authors of this book hope to have clarified the often unfamiliar designs of contemporary writing for readers who turn to our pages for guidance after having read works which interested but baffled them, and for those who, after reading our pages, will be moved to turn to the writers we have discussed. Although we are aware of serving a possible reference function (and have provided dates of first publication for all works mentioned), we do not intend this guide as primarily a data bank for scholars. We offer it in the hope that it will enlarge the readership of contemporary writing and help to encourage informed discussion of the vital dialectic of themes, forms, and values which that writing embodies.

In organizing this book I am in debt to several friends for advice of various kinds which I have tried to follow whenever possible. Needless to say, any defects herein are attributable to me, while many of the felicities I hope will appear are the fruits of good counsels I received from Ralph Ellison, Alfred Kazin, A. Walton Litz, Richard Ludwig, Theodore Solatoroff, Robert E. Spiller, Helen Vendler, and Robert Penn Warren.

March 1979   Daniel Hoffman

Harvard Guide to
Contemporary American Writing

1

Intellectual Background
Alan Trachtenberg

I N a celebrated essay in 1929, T. S. Eliot wished
to account for what he described as the remarkable "simplicity" and "universality" of the great
medieval poet Dante: the fact that he remains "easy to read." Not
that Dante is by any means a simple or superficial poet; but he is
a uniquely *lucid* poet, a poet of "clear visual images," for whom all
things are so patently meaningful that the very image of them renders
thing and meaning together in one compass. Eliot attributes the
translucence of Dante's verse to the "allegorical method." But more
significant than the method alone was the major historical fact
that lay behind it: the fact that allegory itself was a universal (that
is, European) method rather than "a local Italian custom." In the
transparency of Dante's verse one finds evidence that "he not only
thought in a way in which every man of his culture in the whole of
Europe then thought, but he employed a method which was common
and commonly understood throughout Europe." Unlike the modern
writer, who faces a predicament which Eliot had described in his
famous article on Joyce's *Ulysses* in 1923 as the need to give "a shape
and a significance" to the immense panorama of futility and anarchy
in contemporary life, Dante enjoyed a universally accepted world
view, a philosophy and a theology which held all things together in
one complex and harmonious system.

Whatever the merits of Eliot's placement of Dante in his culture,
the image remains compelling, of a kind of literary Eden, where the
writer could accept a philosophy, be guided by it, and bring it to
a perfect crystallization. The image compels because it serves to

1

define the exactly opposite situation modern writers perceived themselves to be in. Eliot's Dante is at home in his world, as Eliot and his colleagues among the founders of modernist literature and art in the early twentieth century were not. The homelessness, the alienation, of the artist is a basic premise of modernism, of that dominating movement in art and thought which, by celebrating aesthetic and intellectual dissent, unbounded innovation and experiment, indeed often sheer difficulty and opacity, raised the artist's alienation into a first condition of his being an artist at all. Where Dante is "easy," that is, in the very access to his poetry, the modern writer must, according to Eliot, be difficult, difficult and obscure precisely to the degree that the "great variety and complexity" of contemporary life permits him no single intellectual schema.

Describing the "intellectual background," then, of any period of modern writing is a different matter from giving an account of the ideas, the world views, that inform the literature of classical or medieval or early Renaissance times. Modern works of literature—and this is no more or less true for the period under consideration, post–World War II writing in America, than for any other period since the early nineteenth century—are rarely created, and can hardly be read intelligibly, in the light of a single encompassing idea, such as the richly textured and intricate system of Aquinas. The entire relation of works of literature to "ideas" has been conceived of by modern critics as uneasy and by no means obvious. As the critic Lionel Trilling argues in his own excellent contribution to this theme, "The Meaning of a Literary Idea" (1949), a strong suspicion runs through modern culture in America that ideas, insofar as they take the form of abstract thought, represent a threat to the wholeness of life, to the interplay between mind and emotion necessary for a heathy existence and a vital art. Eliot himself expresses one version of this fear when he suggests that thinking by itself, dissociated from feeling, can "violate" a writer's creative capacity; while the cults of spontaneity and irrationalism that have appeared in art and in the general culture since 1945 represent other, more explicitly anti-intellectual versions of this suspicion. And if to a deeply seated tendency in American culture to eschew theorizing as a kind of intellectual disease, one adds the particular revulsion against limiting ideologies in the immediate postwar years, the status of an "intellectual background" to the writing of the period becomes even more doubtful.

Of course, a suspicion or rejection of ideas is itself a kind of idea, itself a feature of the "background" to which particular literary texts provide a foreground. A certain resistance to formal ideas is indeed a trait of much of the writing of the period. But for a period in which the "academic writer" appeared as a major literary-social type, such poses as that of the nonbookish writer seem especially transparent disguises. In fact, never before in American literary history have so many writers, and so many first-rate and major writers, held formal ties with institutions of learning and knowledge: a phenomenon that indicates not only a new ground of acceptance for serious literature, a new audience among college students, but also, at an even deeper level, a new recognition of literature as itself a serious and legitimate form of knowledge—a form, that is, of idea as well as emotion; a form of *thinking* about common existence.

An intellectual history of a period must also be to some extent a social and cultural history: a history of changes in forms of work and play, of private and public life, and in regard to American society in these years, changes in social attitudes toward race, sex, wealth, and poverty—and toward the idea of America itself and its place in the world. An intellectual background has its own background in active human history, and it will be useful at the outset to sketch some of the broader patterns and persisting issues that characterized the postwar decades in the United States.

The Cold War

The years immediately following the Allied victory in 1945 were dominated by international affairs as never before in American history. The war left the United States virtually unscathed (compare its quarter of a million casualties with the nearly twenty million suffered by the Soviet Union) and in sole possession of the atomic bomb, a weapon whose unthinkable scale of destruction was twice demonstrated against Japanese cities in August 1945. Its industrial plant undamaged and much expanded, its agricultural output far exceeding domestic need, the United States emerged as the world's unchallenged superpower, and immediately undertook a program of aid to Western Europe and Japan. The Marshall Plan and the Truman Doctrine of 1947 marked the onset of the Cold War, a state of affairs that colored intellectual, cultural, and political life for most of the period, relenting somewhat only when efforts at détente began in the late 1960s. The Cold War was both a political phenomenon and an emotional one, a state of policy and a state of mind. It was premised on a certain picture of the world, a world divided into two hostile camps: the West, or "free world," led by the United States and protected by its formidable military power; and the East, the USSR, its "satellite" allies, the "people's democracies" of Eastern Europe, and

3

after 1949 the Communist government in China (though relations between the Soviet Union and China had deteriorated to the point of open animosity by the mid-1960s). According to the Western version of this picture—a version held more tenaciously and stubbornly in the United States than elsewhere—the East represented a monolithic and aggressive totalitarianism, and required "containment" in the form of armed bases at the borders of East and West, surveillance in the form of espionage, and military readiness in the form of "collective security" pacts such as the North Atlantic Treaty Organization (NATO) and the South East Asia Treaty Organization (SEATO). And because the enemy threatened "subversion" as much as military aggression, the policy of "containment" included the support of "anti-Communist" regimes, which were embraced as partners in the "free world" whether or not they measured up to the standards of political democracy.

The Cold War represented a degree of political and military involvement in world affairs quite new in American history, though a role as a world power had been developing since the end of the nineteenth century. Events everywhere in the world, in the most remote cities and rural districts, not only were immediately available as "news" (a worldwide instant communications system came into use in the 1960s as one direct result of outer-space technology), but also impinged on the lives of Americans with more force than ever before. Major episodes in the Cold War, some of which threatened actual conflict and contributed to the widespread anxiety about mass destruction, included the Berlin blockade of 1948, the Russian explosion of an atomic bomb in 1949 (which launched an escalating arms race; eventually several other nations tested nuclear weapons, raising the specter of a threat to life from fallout), the building of the Berlin Wall in 1961, and the Cuban missile crisis of 1962. And twice the United States committed troops to actual "hot" wars, in both cases without formal declarations of war: in Korea, from 1950 to 1952; and the much more dramatic and consequential commitment, at one point of more than a half million troops and airpower surpassing that employed in World War II, in Vietnam, from about 1964 to 1973. American casualties in both wars together far exceeded World War II figures.

The Cold War, then, was an inescapable fact of life, implicated as much in the spectacular development of technologies of warfare and of communication and transportation as in the unprecedented concentration of power in government agencies, especially those concerned with military affairs and with espionage. Many Cold War assumptions and the government institutions which embodied them came under sharp scrutiny and attack during the upswelling of opposition and resistance to the war in Vietnam in the 1960s. But throughout this period, and especially from the late 1940s to the middle 1960s, there was no doubt that a Cold War view of the world profoundly influenced the thinking of most Americans. The picture of a world divided between "us," "free" and democratic, and "them," totalitarian and "godless," seemed unshakable, as was the corollary of a need for military strength, preparedness, vigilance. The feeling of a superior virtue threatened by an insidious enemy reached a pitch of hysteria in the 1950s, a time of witch hunts, blacklists, loyalty oaths, charges of "subversion," trials for espionage and treason, and the jailing of Communists and other dissidents on charges of "conspiracy."

But even apart from the more sensational excesses in the name of the Cold War, especially the exploitation of the "internal subversion" fear by Senator Joseph McCarthy in the early 1950s, the Cold War state of mind settled deeply into the intellectual life of the nation. Fundamental criticism of American society, especially from radical perspectives, virtually disappeared from public life in the 1950s, a time described by some critics as an "age of conformity." Many intellectuals and writers who had associated themselves with radical causes and a Marxist point of view in the 1930s either reversed their positions entirely in this period, and appeared now as repentant "anti-Communists," or tempered their former criticisms with a more appreciative and assenting appraisal of the "American way of life." The turnabout owed as much to the widespread loss of belief in Marxism in the face of the Stalinist terror and the general repressiveness of Soviet society (confirmed by Khrushchev himself in his report on Stalin's crimes in 1956) as to external pressures to prove one's loyalty.

A major Cold War consequence for intellectual life was the absolute certainty with which socialism and Marxism were associated with Soviet Russia and with Stalin, national liberation movements and revolutions were linked with "international communism" and "subversion," and domestic dissent from foreign policy and from the values of "big business" was considered proof of disloyalty. For about twenty years after the conclusion of the war, it was common for Americans to read in their newspapers and journals, and hear and see in the mass media, nothing but praise for the "American Way," for the "American Century," typified by an ever-rising Gross National Product, an expanding highway program, and mushrooming suburban shopping malls. It was common to hear America described as a consumer's paradise, a showcase of democratic free enterprise, in which the ubiquitous credit card had wrought a more lasting revolution against class distinctions than any "foreign" ideology could offer. "Freedom" reigned as the rhetorical centerpiece of public discourse. And deviations from the national consensus, either in political views or personal styles, risked the chilling charge of "alien," "subversive," "unAmerican." These were the years, indeed, when the House Committee on Un-American Activities often seemed to rule public life.

What became evident as American cultural life began to emerge from this phase of moralistic and anti-intellectual acquiescence in the middle 1960s was that the presumption of a national consensus had disguised very real divisions and critical social problems. Although a stream of social criticism did appear in the 1950s, it took its themes from the assumption that American society was basically unified and pleased with its material conditions, and focused on issues such as the psychic costs of affluence, or the threat to the individual from the impersonal structures of business corporations and government, or the quality of entertainment produced by the mass media. On the whole, criticism seemed to assume a rather homogeneous, white, middle-class, suburban society—a society of more or less contented consumers who suffered, if at all, from the spiritual malaise of too much consumption. What the Swedish sociologist Gunnar Myrdal named in *An American Dilemma* (1944) as the most flagrant and challenging failure of democracy in the United States, the failure of racial equality, hardly captured the public imagination in these years, when the mass media (including the movies) rarely showed a black face except in stereotypical menial roles. The plight of blacks in the South and in the ghettoes of northern cities did not become prominent, did not enter public consciousness as a potentially tragic rift in American society, until the civil rights movement of the late 1950s, dramatized by the boycotts and marches led by the Reverend Martin Luther King, Jr., and the several ghetto uprisings and riots in the middle 1960s.

The presumption of consensus and homogeneity, of a universal "freedom" available to all in America, was shattered in the 1960s in campus antiwar movements, in urban movements such as the Black Panthers, in efforts to create a "poor people's movement," in the hippie and counter-culture movements of the late 1960s. Whatever the lasting effects of the agitations of the 1960s—and it would seem a decade later that they belonged more to the realm of culture than that of politics, resulting more in an enlarged range of choices in life-styles for middle-class Americans than in visible institutional improvements for racial minorities and the poor, or real changes in the relation of competing groups to the centers of power—whatever the permanent traces, it was unmistakable then that the cultural and intellectual climate of the country had changed dramatically. In part, the change

6

reflected unexpected developments elsewhere in the world, the two most consequential of which were probably the appearance of dissent in Eastern Europe after the death of Stalin (beginning with the violent demonstrations in East Germany, Poland, and especially Hungary in the 1950s and culminating in the "Prague Spring" in Czechoslovakia in 1968), signaling the possibility of a breakup of the grim monolith whose image had served so powerfully to reinforce the Cold War picture of the world; and the sudden appearance of radical youth movements in countries allied with the United States, in Germany and France (reaching a fever pitch of enthusiasm and hope for radical change in Paris, 1968), and in Turkey and Japan, where student movements contributed to the toppling of regimes. Apart from rising protest movements and movements for social justice, notably the women's rights movement, a number of shocking events—the assassination of President Kennedy in 1963, of Malcolm X in 1965, of Martin Luther King in 1967, and of Robert Kennedy in 1968, and the Watergate scandal, which led to the resignation of President Nixon in 1974—fed an undercurrent of doubt, anxiety, instability in the period. The collapse of relations between the USSR and China, and the policy of détente pursued by the American government with both these representatives of noncapitalist systems, further eroded the hold of the dominating Cold War assumptions of the 1950s.

The Intellectual in Postwar Society

Cold War politics often distracted Americans from recognizing that they were embarked on a new journey in their national history, that the most fundamental patterns of life were undergoing rapid and decisive transformation. This is not to say that change rolled uniformly across all levels of society; there had been a notable but increasingly suspect tendency among commentators to take the white urban and suburban middle classes as the typical Americans, the measure of what is "normal." In fact, although a drift toward homogenization of life-styles ("massification," some social scientists call it) is one weighty characteristic of the new society, aggravation of social rifts, of antagonistic cultural interests, is another. As the society as a whole moved steadily toward an urban cultural style, local and regional interests became more stubbornly intense; in one entire school of fiction—the southern school—a rural, antimodern sensibility and traditional customs provided a major literary subject-matter. If the dominant social movements constitute "modernization"—the movements toward more rationalized organization of industry and government, the appearance of "bigness" in all institutions, and with it "impersonality," and a

7

submission of all traditional ways of personal and family and group life to the scrutiny of scientific methods of investigation (sexual behavior is one dramatic and critical example)—then counter-modernism, resistance to the very idea of the modern, provided a not so trivial submotif. It took the forms of racism and sexism, resistance to redressing racial injustice and to granting full equality to women, and also emerged in the idea of the generation gap, with its implied pitting of "up-to-date" youngsters against stodgy, conservative oldsters. The cries against big government, big business, big labor, also carry imputations that older ways were better, healthier, more "American," and modern ways somehow offensive, threatening, dehumanizing.

The process of forging a modern society, in which rational calculations increasingly control decisions about public and private life, did not begin in the postwar era. In many ways, the period marked a resumption of the course of American development first crystallized in the 1920s, then stalled and detoured and corrected through the Great Depression, the New Deal, and the war (itself a kind of solution to the economic failures of the depression): a resumption, that is, of the breakup of genteel attitudes toward sex, a dissolution of "small-town" values, and the consolidation through electric and electronic media of a national popular culture. The 1920s was the first era of "mass culture" in America, and the concept of mass culture, as we shall see, informed virtually all of the significant thinking about American society and culture, about self, soul, and God, in the postwar period.

But who performed this thinking, and under what circumstances? The category of intellectual, of those persons devoted to a "life of the mind," to disinterested, speculative, and critical thought, itself underwent subtle alterations in this period. And we miss a large piece of the intellectual background unless we consider the intellectuals themselves in their self-perceptions and their new roles.

Two phenomena seem uppermost: first, the continuing process, begun early in the century, of the integration of intellectuals into the formal institutions of American society, especially government, universities, and the media; and second, at the same time, a growing sense of discomfort at the very process, a feeling, especially on the part of politically dissident intellectuals, that integration threatened loss of independence, a worry that social acceptance with its rewards of status and material well-being betokened an inner surrender of that edge of skepticism and discontent that gave the intellectual his raison d'être in the first place. Creativity thrived with alienation, some postwar writers insisted—or at least they held that the condition of alienation which had played a nurturing role in fostering modern art, literature, and thought was too precious a heritage to sell for an academic chair or a government post.

The overlapping of these two phenomena—the acceptance of social acceptance and the dissent from it—appears in a 1952 *Partisan Review* symposium, "Our Country and Our Culture." Twenty-five prominent intellectuals—mainly literary critics but including several sociologists and anthropologists and a philosopher—were invited to respond to the proposition that "American intellectuals now regard America and its institutions in a new way." Until recently, the editors wrote, America was regarded as hostile to art, to culture, to independent thinking. Since the war, however, and since the sour outcome of the affair of many intellectuals with Marxism in the 1930s, "the tide has begun to turn, and many writers and intellectuals now feel closer to their country and its culture." American democracy has "an intrinsic and positive value" which "represents the only immediate alternative as long as Russian totalitarianism threatens world domination." With very few exceptions (including Irving Howe, Norman Mailer, and C. Wright Mills), the contributors agreed with the general estimate that conditions have improved for the life of the mind, and that no major social problems remain—no problems except the problem of "mass culture" itself: the worry that the "domination" of politics by the "masses" creates a "new obstacle" for the intellectual, the obstacle of a "mass culture" which converts art into commodity, excludes "everything which does not conform to popular norms," and threatens the very continuation of "high" culture.

Norman Mailer found a "shocking" assumption in the symposium, that "society is too difficult to understand," and the sociologist C. Wright Mills noted "a shrinking deference to the status quo." Moreover, Mills and Irving Howe both detached themselves from the view that political democracy is responsible by itself for the tawdriness of "mass culture"; it is "capitalist commercialism which manipulates people into standardized tastes," wrote Mills, to which Howe added that both democracy and "mass culture" have so far been "known to us only in the corrupting context of capitalism." These dissenting voices implied a role for the intellectual as a critic of the social and economic, as well as the cultural, status quo: a role that entailed an effort to grasp the society in its entirety, to seek a critical point of view, and to resist pressures to abandon any ideological perspectives. The dissenters—and Howe expanded his argument more fully and richly in his essay "This Age of Conformity" (*Partisan Review,* 1954) —clung to an ideal of intellectual opposition, a challenge to wealth,

9

to power, to what Howe described as American capitalism's "claim to a unique and immaculate destiny."

These minority voices in the 1950s seem now to have anticipated the revival of radical social criticism and socialist polemics (the latter still an inconspicuous trickle in the currents of American thought) in the 1960s and 1970s. But the prevailing voices at the time proposed a less embattled, less morally insisting, and more detached, more easily accommodating role for thinkers. The sociologist Daniel Bell, in *The End of Ideology* (1962), and the historian Richard Hofstadter, in *Anti-Intellectualism in American Life* (1963), both suggested (though with different notions in mind of a proper role for American intellectuals) that many intellectuals had nurtured themselves on a "cult of alienation" derived from earlier strains and tensions within capitalism. Bell argued that capitalism "is now providing one answer to the great challenge posed to Western—and now world—society over the last two hundred years: how, within the framework of freedom, to increase the living standards of the majority of people and at the same time maintain or raise cultural levels." The theory of "mass society," with its excessive fear of big organizations and anonymity, was no more than "an ideology of romantic protest against contemporary life," a surrogate for an outmoded *political* protest. Instead, Bell proposed, intellectuals might better devote themselves to the making of "empirical" visions of utopia. The function of intellectuals in the new America was, in short, to write scenarios for the furtherance of a basically sound and admirable society.

Although exact correlations between ideas and social change are difficult to establish, Bell's call for an empirical, pragmatic temper— a call for commitment to their society—among formerly alienated and radical intellectuals seems to represent an adjustment to a new social formation: the intellectual with a steady, well-paying, and fairly prestigious job. In *White Collar* (1951), C. Wright Mills commented that "there has arisen a new kind of patronage system for free intellectuals, which at mid-century seems to have effected a loss of political will and even of moral hope." The new patronage system consists of the newly emerged postwar bureaucracies: "The new bureaucracies of state and business, of party and voluntary association, become the major employers of intellectuals and the main customers for their work." Writers, artists, professors now become "employees," "dependent salaried workers who spend the most alert hours of their lives being told what to do." At the bottom of the new situation is a need felt by the new and often competing bureaucratic structures for precisely what intellectuals are equipped to provide: symbols, "distinct forms of consciousness," and justifying myths. Providing answers to "the continual demands for new justifications" required by the new bureaucracies, the intellectual has "joined the expanding world of those who live off ideas, as administrator, idea-man, and good-will technician. In class, status, and self-image, he has become more solidly middle class."

Accurate or not in all its details, Mills's analysis does disclose a pattern woven into the texture of intellectual life through much of the period under consideration, a pattern which helps account for many of the themes, the tone and the rhetorical emphases, of intellectual work. It should be noted, however, that although social engagement diminished as a preoccupation of thinkers in these years, conservative political ideologies did not gain much currency. While it is accurate to speak of a conservative "mood" in the 1950s, the prevailing political outlook among intellectuals remained "liberal." The fervor of anticommunism may have driven some to embrace the conservative outlook of the *National Review* (Max Eastman, John Dos Passos, Reinhold Niebuhr, James Burnham, and Will Herberg are among the ex-radicals who made this turn in the postwar years), but the formal conservatism of Russell Kirk and Peter Viereck found only a small audience. Conservative premises—such as the valuing of tradition, hierarchy, orthodoxy, and religious mystery, and suspicion of the idea of progress, of human perfectability, of man's "natural" goodness — found significant echoes, however, in the literary world, where, as Irving Howe commented in a 1954 essay, "Original Sin" enjoyed high prestige.

The Sociological Imagination: Diagnoses of American Character and Behavior

In 1959, the British scientist and novelist C. P. Snow published a small book whose title immediately gained currency as a topic of controversy. *The Two Cultures and the Scientific Revolution* argued that a significant gap had opened in Western societies between scientists and humanists and that a hazardous failure of communication existed between the two groups. He charged the upholders of "traditional" culture with not only an "unscientific flavor" but a dangerously "antiscientific" point of view, and called for serious educational efforts to inculcate a better appreciation of the sciences. The challenge to humanism was taken up by the British literary critic F. R. Leavis, and a controversy raged regarding the relative virtues of science and humanism as modern outlooks. The furor did not survive the early 1960s, and its simplifications may now strike us as archaic. However,

11

the phrase "two cultures" continues to sound one of the dissonant notes of contemporary life: if our age takes its character from the unprecedented rate of social change in modern societies (let alone the widening chasm between "developed" and "undeveloped" nations), and if modern societies owe their high social velocity to the extremely rationalized and efficient application of scientific research to technology (the "scientific revolution"), then ignorance of the languages and procedures of science is tantamount to ignorance of modern life.

The word *scientific* itself has won a privileged place in modern life (an accretion of prestige which has its start at least as early as the seventeenth century), and it is perhaps both a substantiation of the "two cultures" argument and partly a refutation of it that among the most vigorous and influential academic disciplines in the postwar era have been the social sciences. A mark of the growing acceptance of their importance to human thinking has been the recent absorption of social sciences into the traditional humanistic fields: the influence of linguistics, anthropology (particularly since the theoretical studies of Claude Lévi-Strauss), and psychoanalysis on the study of literature is a prime example. C. P. Snow himself conceded that a "third" culture might exist among social scientists. Certainly no survey of the intellectual life of the recent period can neglect the influence of the efforts to think scientifically about man in society and in relation to himself, an influence which is felt throughout intellectual life. More an outlook, a *way* of thinking, than a body of ideas, science may provide a rough modern equivalent to the unified world view which Eliot noted in Dante's culture.

As an outlook rather than a fixed system of postulates, science covers a multitude of enterprises. It happens that the social sciences currently in favor among literary humanists are those more concerned with abstract accounts of behavior than with concrete behavior in history. In the period as a whole, however, the discipline in which scientific method and traditional humanistic values have come together most fruitfully is unquestionably sociology. As a field of research into contemporary life, as an academic (and theoretical) discipline, and as a popular mode of writing, sociology impresses itself on the period with more force than any other discipline: not only in the form of certain specific interpretations of American life and its rapid changes, but also as a mode of thinking. In *The Sociological Imagination* (1959), C. Wright Mills defined that mode as a way of enlarging the range of significance of individual lives—a way of grasping "history and biography and the relations between the two within society." True, as Mills points out, the field is itself divided between those who propose the "grand theory," those engaged in "abstracted empiricism," and those, like Mills himself, who reach for historical explanations of contemporary social phenomena. True, also, sociological writing, often ponderous and weighted down with jargon, has hardly endeared itself to literary people. Still, the influence of the kind of thinking which seeks for patterns in society, and seeks further to connect various patterns to each other and to changes over time, has been profound.

Measured by its influence, by the authority of its formulation and images, perhaps the major sociological work of the past twenty-five years was *The Lonely Crowd* (1950), by David Riesman (with Nathan Glazer and Reuel Denney). Appearing early in the period, the book established a critical terminology for the analysis of "mass society." Riesman's subject was "the changing American character," and his work proceeded on the assumption that change in character follows changes in social structure, especially in economic patterns. The title alone carried the resonance of his findings: that Americans found themselves in a newly paradoxical situation, a crowd of isolated, disconnected persons. The book's stance was critical, yet it aimed its criticism at the quality of life rather than the economic and social structures that gave rise to the depressing state of dissociation.

Much of the appeal of the book lay in the aptness of its terminology. Riesman hinged his analysis on three pregnant terms: "tradition-directed," "inner-directed," and "other-directed," each of which describes a historically conditioned "social character," which in turn refers to the "organization of an individual's drives and satisfactions—the kind of 'set' with which he approaches the world and people." Tradition-directed behavior, associated with precapitalistic, agricultural, and nomadic societies, approaches the world through well-defined codes (such as etiquette) and through "adaptation, not by innovation." Inner-directed people belong to the era of early capitalism, when production and mobility ruled social life; they are self-governing, equipped with an inner "psychological gyroscope," the better to cope with a world of vast choices. This has been the ruling character-type through most of American history, Riesman argues. The other-directed character, however, has now replaced the older type, as the society has shifted its primary emphasis from production to consumption, from work to leisure. Not a gyroscope but a radar screen is the "control equipment" of this new type, for it takes its bearing not from an implanted code of behavior but from "an exceptional sensitivity to the actions and wishes of others." In a word, the new type of person is a conformist.

13

Riesman is emphatically troubled by the shift from inner- to other-directedness in American life. His alternative is the "autonomous" individual, one who can manage the temptations of a society of consumption, leisure, and "diffuse anxiety," without losing his bearings. Abundance has diminished the hold of the Protestant Ethic, which had stressed the virtue of work, of vocation, of personal goals, without replacing it with any more humanly satisfying ethic than that of consumption itself. Moreover, the "indeterminancy and amorphousness in the cosmology of power" confuses people, leaves them without a clear target of opposition; and without the moral fervor and righteousness of the old individualism, the other-directed person "leaves it to the group to defend his interests, cooperating when called on to vote, to apply pressure, and so on." He is without the ambition, the dedication to self-interest, the seriousness about his vocation that characterized the older America. Moreover, the pervasiveness of material well-being (poverty and racial inequalities play little role in Riesman's vision of the new America) has eroded older notions of an oppressed working class, eliminating that basis of self-definition.

"Most people in America today," Riesman writes, "—the 'overprivileged' two-thirds, let us say, as against the underprivileged third— can afford to attend to, and allow their characters to be shaped by, situational differences of a subtler nature than those arising from bare economic necessity and their relation to the means of production." The possibilities for "autonomy"—Riesman's word for "freedom," for "rational, nonauthoritarian and noncompulsive" choices—are abundant. But other-direction, a powerful cultural force because of its rush in filling the vacuum left by the departing inner-directed type, has produced instead an anxious, uncertain conformist, looking for "adjustment" and taking his cues from advertising, the mass media, mass political parties. A solution lay in cultural innovation, in a revival of "utopian" thinking (found occasionally among city planners), and imaginative uses of leisure. A certain revivalist eloquence, in fact, invades the social scientist's language as Riesman asks at the end, "Is it conceivable that these economically privileged Americans will some day wake up to the fact that they overconform? Wake up to the discovery that a host of behavioral rituals are the result, not of an inescapable social imperative, but of an image of society . . . ?" Not a new society but a new image is called for: "If the other-directed people should discover how much needless work they do, discover that their own thoughts and their own lives are quite as interesting as other people's, that, indeed, they no more assuage their loneliness in a crowd of peers than one can assuage one's thirst by drinking sea water, than we might expect them to become more attentive to their own feelings and aspirations."

The Lonely Crowd spawned a host of works of popular sociology, such as William Whyte's *The Organization Man* (1956) and Vance Packard's *The Hidden Persuaders* (1957) and *The Status Seekers* (1959), works which added catchphrases to the public vocabulary of self-analysis. The "image of society" became a pervasive theme; somehow, if the image of mindless consumerism could be replaced by an image of a full, self-sufficient private life, then self-images might cease to arouse such anxiety. In *The Affluent Society* (1958), the economist John Kenneth Galbraith also wished to rid people of antiquated attitudes born in an age of scarcity, "in the poverty, inequality, and economic peril of the past." The "conventional wisdom" in economic thinking prevents people from realizing the genuine benefits of affluence, from reducing the hours of work, for example, or making work more pleasant, or developing more occupations based on skill and imagination and a qualified education, thus enlarging the "New Class" of leisure-minded people. While admitting that interest in economic inequality had declined, and arguing that an increase in total wealth was now considered a reasonable alternative to a redistribution of wealth, Galbraith did remark upon the contrast between private affluence and public squalor and proposed channeling some of the resources made available by the enormously increased productive capacity of American industry into public works, into renewing cities and improving social services.

The society reported in the sociology of the 1950s is predominantly the society of "most people in America today." Poverty had yet to be "discovered," and while awareness of the costs of continued racial inequality were becoming a nagging public issue after the Supreme Court decision against segregated schools in 1954, it was not until the urban violence of the 1960s that race and poverty fused into a single image of a deprived section of American society. The emphasis upon middle-class Americans appears also in Mills's *White Collar,* which argued that the new forms of the "white collar world" held "much that is characteristic of twentieth-century experience." Like Riesman, Mills observed a major—and catastrophic—shift in American character, from the nineteenth-century individualist, the frontiersman or "ingenious farmer-artisan" to the twentieth-century "Little Man," the "hired employee." Yet the old images persist as "sentimental versions of historical types that no longer exist."

Mills's task in *White Collar* was twofold, to correct the old images by describing the new American world "as a great salesroom, an enormous file, an incorporated brain, and a new universe of management and manipulation," and also to describe this new social and economic and political world "in terms of its meaning for the inner life and the external career of the individual," especially to explain how people have become "falsely conscious" of their real lives. The social problem Mills focused on was the decline of the older middle classes of independent entrepreneurs, manufacturers, and tradespeople, and the rise of a vast new social configuration of technical, managerial, and professional people that now occupied the middle of society. Early in the nineteenth century, 80 percent of the white working population in America was self-employed; the figure had shrunk to 18 percent by the mid-twentieth century. As "hired employees," the new middle class no longer fit the earlier descriptions of hardy individualism and self-motivation. The "new Little Man" was more like a "cheerful robot," with "no firm roots, no sure loyalties to sustain his life and give it a center." And, moreover, he had no set of beliefs, as in the old days, which might make sense of a life of routine and small calculations. "The malaise is deep-rooted," wrote Mills, and his chief concern was political: the pervasive powerlessness that had spread through the middle reaches of the society. Amorphous, helpless, without direction or aim, the new middle class imprinted their character upon American life as a whole. And the picture was worrisome:

> Since they have no public position, their private positions as individuals determine in what direction each of them goes; but, as individuals, they do not know where to go. So now they waver. They hesitate, confused and vacillating in their opinions, unfocused and discontinuous in their actions. They are worried and distrustful but, like so many others, they have no targets on which to focus their worry and distrust. They may be politically irritable, but they have no political passion. They are a chorus, too afraid to grumble, too hysterical in their applause. They are rearguarders. In the shorter run, they will follow the panicky ways of prestige; in the longer run, they will follow the ways of power, for in the end, prestige is determined by power.

It is much the same picture drawn by Riesman, with the menace to traditional democracy more sharply etched.

Mills extended his account of "mass society" in his controversial *The Power Elite* (1956). If the earlier book concerned the formation of a new kind of "masses," this study focused on a correspondingly new formation at the top of society, among the "higher circles." Here he found not a traditional "ruling class," with clear and rationalized goals and ambitions and sets of procedure for ruling, but instead a set of interlocking (and self-perpetuating) "elites," in politics, business, and the military. The people in these circles made the critical decisions affecting the lives of Americans, and the world, and yet Mills found that they too suffered from a modern malaise, a lack of direction, and, most troublesome of all, a failure of responsibility. Centralization of power had created a new giantism, and while the elites were conservative in outlook, the true character of their behavior was irresponsibility: a result of their aloofness from a democratic mandate, their distance from a powerless mass below.

Mills's thesis provoked criticism from the Right and the Left; he offended the popular version of America as a classless society, but also rejected the Marxist notion of an economic "ruling class." Increasingly through the later years of the 1950s, Mills expressed concern over the conservative political drift in the country, and with his view of the impotence of the masses (the "white collar world" also included the powerful trade union leaders) and the arrogant irresponsibility of the ruling elites, he came more and more to place his hope in a revival of radical thinking among intellectuals, as he argued in *The Sociological Imagination*. At the time of his death in 1962, Mills had already begun to embrace the emerging New Left as a sign of new vigor and hopefulness.

While not exhaustive of all problems or all regions of social research, the works of Riesman and Mills typify the classical "sociological imagination," its attempt to make social behavior intelligible by reference to a "whole," to large patterns and structures of society, and to changes within them. Both writers concern themselves with "problems" that have come to be recognized in America as principally the domain of the sociologist: social classes and mobility, the hierarchies of social structure, marriage and family life, population shifts and urban life, wealth, poverty, politics and, to a lesser though significant extent (increasingly prominent in the 1960s), race relations. The effort is to discover regulations, rules, and exceptions ("deviance") within the arrangements that govern social life; and thus the classical form of the "sociological imagination" evokes large structures, institutions, and bureaucracies as explanations for the way individuals behave. The significant increase in sociologists practicing this form of analysis and even a kind of prophecy corresponded to the rise in popular thinking of a feeling of individual loss of power, insignificance, "loneliness," and a buried resentment toward power as such—currents of thought and feeling that appear often in the literature of the postwar era.

Another mode of sociological imagining also appeared in these years, less dramatic in its public impact, but in fact more dramatic (and literary) in its method. The works of Erving Goffman best represent the trend in sociology away from the large explanation and toward a much closer attentiveness to the modes of actual daily behavior. Viewing sociological writing as "dramaturgy," Goffman eschews the familiar large-scale efforts to "explain" by describing how values derive from institutions, and focuses instead on individual "actors," how they fashion and accommodate their "roles" to the "drama" of any given social situation. Using a method of direct observation, as if he were a camera eye which can generalize from its immediate perceptions, Goffman views society as consisting of occasions of interaction, of self-presentation. In books such as *The Presentation of Self in Everyday Life* (1959), *Encounters* (1961), *Asylums* (1961), *Interaction Ritual: Essays on Face-to-Face Behavior* (1967), and *Frame Analysis* (1974), Goffman has concerned himself with disclosing the tacit understandings, the dramaturgical principles, at work in the social life of small, face-to-face groups, in offices and places of work, in asylums, and in public spaces, in conversations and other interactions. How the individual "presents himself and his activity to others, the ways in which he guides and controls the impressions they form of him"— these are Goffman's empirical concerns. Adopting methods of ethnography, Goffman disposes of categories of class and status, or at least subordinates them to the implicit categories of interaction manifest in such social "materials" as "glances, gestures, positionings, and verbal statements." "Facework" is one of his main subjects: the external expressive signs of the individual's adjustment to a situation. Goffman proposes a "sociology of occasions," in which the classical concern with controlling "social relations" is deferred on behalf of analysis of "the syntactical relations among the acts of different persons mutually present to one another." It is not a sociology that results in easily paraphrased theses or generalizations regarding such entities as "American society," but one whose success counts almost entirely on the precision, the subtlety, and the suppleness of the writing. Goffman's power, increasingly acknowledged as unique among sociologists, lies in his almost novelistic brilliance and elegance as a writer. It has even been claimed that while the contemporary novel has tended to explore antinovelistic forms, such as black humor, surrealism, and stream-of-consciousness autobiography, traditional novelistic description and close observation of social interaction have been kept alive in sociological writings like those of Goffman.

Civilization and Its Discontents:
Conflicting Visions of Self and Society

The sociological imagination in these years devoted its attention mainly to the behavior of Americans in the mass; it fostered the idea that society is more than the sum of its parts, that it is a reality in its own right, with discoverable laws and regularities. But the social view of mankind did not have the field of intellectual life to itself; other currents competed with it, though it is difficult to delimit movements of thought with reliable precision. Two other movements are especially noteworthy because they stand at opposite poles to each other and because the issues posed between them also troubled and preoccupied imaginative writers. Both movements presented themselves as based on "scientific" views of mankind; both attempted a direct application of the methods and findings of science to the improvement of human life. Yet they had little else in common, and the deeper conflicts between them can be said to represent a serious chasm within modern thought itself.

Behaviorism claimed that the human being is an organism whose actions can best be understood in light of demonstrable and measurable responses to definite stimuli or signals. Behaviorism seeks to control behavior by controlling environmental stimuli. By contrast, psychoanalysis, itself a much divided field, holds to the belief that human behavior must be understood in light of the individual's personal history, his buried, often forgotten, life experiences. The determining factors in behavior often lie hidden and protected in the unconscious (a faculty or region of mental life even denied an existence by most behaviorists), and only by introspection, by self-examination (in the therapeutic process known as analysis), can the individual attain self-control. For the psychoanalyst, insight precedes and accompanies freedom. For the behaviorist, freedom and liberating insights are illusions; instead, habit formed by conditioning (repeated responses to certain signals) is the basis of human life, and might become the basis of human happiness, in society and in individual life. Both schools of thought are at bottom therapeutic, concerned with the cure of human dysfunctions; and insofar as a sickness of mind and soul also concerns them (as it does especially psychoanalysis), both can be described as partly religious. The sharp, decisive differences between them range from their conceptions of man to their therapeutic methods, behaviorism seeking to modify behavior by external influence, while psychoanalysis is based on the conviction that the individual can find the source of his ills and the key to his cure within himself.

As conceptions or world outlooks, both behaviorism and psychoanalysis, interestingly enough, look with a disapproving eye upon the shape of American life in the years since World War II. In *Walden Two* (1948), for example, B. F. Skinner evokes the memory of Thoreau's famous experiment in abandoning society in order to support and justify the rejection of politics, of conventional careers and vocations, and especially of traditional education, in a fictional postwar utopian colony. The book is a behaviorist tract in the form of a utopian novel, and its impact established Skinner, professor of psychology at Harvard University, as the major public spokesman for "behavioral engineering." Inventor of a teaching machine, a mechanical baby tender (the "air crib"), and the famous Skinner box for experimental research on animal behavior (the findings from which have then been applied to human behavior), Skinner argued through Frazier, the founder and chief Behavior Manager of Walden Two, that postwar society was a mess, typified by the fact that "millions of young people . . . were . . . choosing places in a social and economic structure in which they had no faith." The atomic bomb stood for the gross and frightening discrepancy between mankind's technical capacities and its wisdom. The only solution—and this justifies the utopian community's withdrawal from politics and from economic and social relations with the main society—is to start at the beginning and create a new kind of person. Science cannot be stopped, "but we must build men up to the same level . . . We must reinforce the weak sectors—the behavioral and cultural sciences. We need a powerful science of behavior."

This is precisely what Frazier attempts through "experimental modification" of behavior and the Walden Two Code. The prevailing attitude is resolutely experimental (and thus, in Skinner's view, scientific): "The main thing is, we encourage our people to view every habit and custom with an eye to possible improvement. A constantly experimental attitude toward everything—that's all we need." A certain sinister note intrudes in Frazier's godlike certainty of success and his arrogance of righteousness: "Give me the specifications, and I'll give you the man!" Skinner seems aware of the dangers (or at least his audience's suspicions) of tyranny, even of fascism, in the vast power that Frazier enjoys, but he accepts the risks. The "all-absorbing question of the twentieth century," he writes, concerns democracy and elitism: "what a few men can make of mankind." The book firmly accepts manipulation on behalf of "a society in which there is no failure, no boredom, no duplication of effort." Frazier's methods of control draw purposefully on the techniques of "positive reinforcement," rather than negative punishment. "Our members are practically always doing what they want to do—what they 'choose' to do—but we see to it that they will want to do precisely the things which are best for themselves and the community. Their behavior is determined, yet they're free."

The question of freedom appears at the heart of a book Skinner published in 1971, *Beyond Freedom and Dignity*. Here he boldly and frontally takes on the challenge to behaviorism from what he calls "the literature of freedom" and "the literature of dignity"—from the traditional cultural sources of resistance to any restriction upon the "autonomy" of man. Skinner's tone in this book is that of an embattled reformer, still a utopian thinker offering a key to a better future, "a world in which people live together without quarrelling, maintain themselves by producing the food, shelter, and clothing they need, enjoy themselves and contribute to the enjoyment of others in art, music, literature, and games." His vision of the future resembles that of the antiutopian fictions influential among writers, students, and intellectuals in the postwar years, Huxley's *Brave New World* and Orwell's *1984*, except that Skinner presents the "totally administered society" (in the words of its critics) as positive, hopeful, and truly progressive for mankind. *Beyond Freedom and Dignity* is not, however, a blueprint for such a world; rather, it is an argument against a way of thinking and especially a language of thought which stand in the way of the full realization of man's potential through science and technology.

The embattled air of the book results from Skinner's perception of the strength of his antagonist, the very ideas of freedom and dignity that bolster the notion of man as "autonomous," as consisting of a mind (or soul or consciousness) distinct from and superior to his body. Although in fact behaviorism had already come to dominate certain crucial fields in American life—educational theory (largely through Skinner's influence), advertising, and much of the thinking within corporate structures—Skinner recognized that the full (or utopian) application of the theories and methods of behavior modification through science and technology was impeded by intellectuals, social critics, religious thinkers, and sentimentalists (most of the American population), who worry over infringements upon freedom, dignity, and autonomy. There is no consciousness separate from the experience of the body in a particular environment, Skinner argues; there is only behavior learned through the "contingencies of reinforcement" (based on the human need to avoid "aversive" effects of an environment). "The picture which emerges from a scientific analysis," he writes, "is not of a body with a person inside, but of a body which *is*

21

a person in the sense that it displays a complex repertoire of behavior." The problems of the world (and the book opens with the statement that "things are getting worse") derive not from "crisis of belief" or "loss of confidence" (all terms that assume an "autonomous man"), but from the specific, observable, and measurable behavior these words obscure. The traditional language not only gets in the way of clear vision; it is also pernicious, "to be blamed" for social and personal ills, for "emotional instability." Traditional terms for cognition especially ("discriminates," "generalizes," "forms a concept," "recalls or remembers") are empty; they "do not refer to forms of behavior." It is not "man" (an abstraction) but "the environment which builds the behavior with which problems are solved." Before the way can be cleared for a truly "intentional culture," the abstraction must be abolished: "To man *qua* man we readily say good riddance. Only by dispossessing him can we turn to the real causes of human behavior. Only then can we turn from the inferred to the observed, from the miraculous to the natural, from the inaccessible to the manipulable."

The crux of Skinner's behaviorism is that "a self is a repertoire of behavior appropriate to a given set of contingencies." Thus what we normally (and inaccurately) call a "person" usually refers to several distinct "selves." Against the traditional humanist ideal of a "whole" man, self-knowing and self-controlling, behaviorism sets the image of man as a function of his habits. Of even greater public impact than Skinner in propagating such a view were Alfred Kinsey's two massive statistical works, *Sexual Behavior in the Human Male* (1948) and *Sexual Behavior in the Human Female* (1953), known as the Kinsey Reports. Neither a doctor nor a theorist, Kinsey aimed neither to prescribe nor to cure, but only to count and measure. Originally a biological taxonomist (his earlier work studied the habits of the wasp), Kinsey claimed no more for his ground-breaking (and icon-shattering) studies than that they were detailed "scientific" investigations of sex as *behavior*—not as feeling, as human relation, but as physical activity, as "release" or "outlet." Decidedly antipsychoanalytic in his rejection of the categories of sickness and health—he accepted all human behavior as "natural" and open to controlled investigation —he nevertheless joined Sigmund Freud in the popular mind as one who ripped aside a veil hiding the true facts of sex and its central place in human (and especially American) life.

Kinsey's work gave major impetus to a revolution in sexual attitudes and publicly acknowledged practices, a change in values and behavior so far-sweeping that any account of postwar culture must give it high priority. A greater freedom and tolerance toward sex had already appeared in the 1920s, the great watershed of modern American culture, but now rapid social changes (a greater proportion of young people in the population, a weakening of marital and familial ties reflected in growing divorce rates) and developments in biological and chemical technology (the "pill") contributed to an even more potent assault upon the barriers to sexual freedom. The removal of legal restrictions on pornography made explicitness in sexual matters virtually taken for granted by the 1970s in magazines, film, theater, and imaginative literature.

The growing awareness of (not to say obsession with) sex in advanced industrial societies in the twentieth century owes an incalculable debt to the teachings of Sigmund Freud and the practice of psychoanalysis based upon them. The influence of Freud in America is a complex matter, running as it does in both popular and clinical channels, often at odds with each other. In the popular version, Freud liberated sex from Victorian shrouds and insisted that it be discussed openly as the most frequent source of troubled feelings and compulsive behavior. His name became a password to a previously well-guarded secret: that sex rules behavior, that the Oedipus Complex lies behind almost all human expressions, that mental and emotional health require an end to sexual repression. Such simplifications seriously distort Freud's own teachings and the practices of most of his followers in psychoanalysis. Freud described sex as an instinctual force (libido) which is necessarily at odds with the needs and demands of society, of civilization itself. He built his theories upon the discovery of the unhappy effects (neurosis and psychosis) of civilization's repression of sexual instinct; his aim was to help patients free themselves from the ignorance of sex fostered by bourgeois morality. But he recognized that repression of some sort was essential for civilization, for the achievements of culture, which he claimed owed their energy to a process of sublimation, or rechanneling of sexual energy into art, religion, and thought. Toward the end of his life Freud claimed to have discovered that another powerful force, the death instinct, or Thanatos, stood in deadly conflict with Eros, or the libido, leading to a pessimistic appraisal of man's chances for anything but a provisional, moderate, and compromised happiness.

There is little doubt that the American popularity of Freud's teachings since the 1920's, even in distorted versions, prepared the ground for the—in many ways opposing—influence of Kinsey. The Kinsey Reports gave off a certain aura of scandal; they appeared, after all, at a time when censorship of explicit sexuality in writing and in graphic depiction was still much in force. The ready acceptance of the Reports as "legitimate" products of "scientific" investigation contributed immeasurably to the change in popular values. With his principled indifference to matters of morality, his refusal to judge any human behavior as "unnatural" or indecent, Kinsey, in effect, followed in the footsteps of literary naturalists such as Theodore Dreiser, for whom the "average" counted for more than the so-called normal. "This is first of all," wrote Kinsey in his first book, "a report on what people do, which raises no questions of what they should do." Homosexuality, masturbation, premarital and extramarital intercourse —all practices taboo according to prevailing moral codes—Kinsey disclosed, were far more common than supposed. And why not, he asked? Sexual pleasure is a natural "good," and any form of pleasure (defined as "release" or "outlet") which does not harm another is self-justifying. The more, in fact, the better. An unmistakable hedonism, an "ethic of abundance" (as one commentator puts it), replaces the traditional moral judgments Americans had been accustomed to hearing from public spokesmen on matters of sex.

Kinsey's implicit celebration of "frequency" of outlet follows from his conception of sexuality as no more or less than *behavior,* a natural activity. His method of investigation focuses entirely on acts, and not at all on feelings or attitudes except insofar as they can be described as factors affecting behavior. Love and guilt have no place in his taxonomy. Instead, in pursuit of his basic information—frequency of outlet (how much?) and source of outlet (what kind?)—Kinsey isolated age and social class, along with marital status, religious background, and rural or urban background, as his key "factors." Using a method of direct interview (about eighteen thousand white males for the first Report), Kinsey designated nine categories of "sources of sexual outlet": masturbation, nocturnal emissions, heterosexual petting, premarital intercourse, marital intercourse, extramarital intercourse, intercourse with prostitutes, homosexual outlet, and animal contacts. Although his intention was not in any degree sociological, his work resulted in a striking profile of variety in sexual behavior—variety determined primarily by differences in age and social class. Age emerged as the prime factor determining frequency, and social class as the major influence on choice of outlet, on the kind or style of sexual behavior.

The findings cut through popular stereotypes and challenged moral structures. Adolescence now appeared as the time of greatest sexual energy, and surprisingly more sexual activity than commonly supposed. Yet, with moral and religious restraints upon premarital sex, the young suffered most from social ignorance and hypocrisy. In another bombshell, Kinsey revealed that, far from being a sickness confined to a few, homosexuality was part of the experience of about one-third of the male population (at one time or another). As if preparing the scripts of countless popular novels (of the *Peyton Place* genre) and melodramas, Kinsey showed that religion and marriage counted for much less as influences upon sexual life than need and opportunity. The incidence of sex outside of marriage (like the incidence of teenage sex) flew directly in the face of accepted pieties.

There can be no doubt that Kinsey's influence in "naturalizing" the subject of sex, and thus in contributing to the popular loosening of restrictions, was decisive. He laid the basis for the subsequent laboratory work of William H. Masters and Virginia E. Johnson, whose study *Human Sexual Response* (1966), based on live experiments, created a new, behavioralist school of sex therapy, with the extremely important side effect of establishing the right to orgasm for both women and men. The therapeutic approach, which one often finds mimicked in satiric fiction of the period, rests upon self-control through conditioning and habit, an approach much different from the Freudian goal of insight gained through analysis with the guidance of skilled therapists. Skinner summed up the behavioralist view of psychotherapy as follows: "awareness or insight is not always enough, and it may be too much. One need not be aware of one's behavior or the conditions controlling it in order to behave effectively—or ineffectively . . . constant self-observation may be a handicap . . . Self-knowledge is valuable only to the extent that it helps to meet the contingencies under which it has arisen."

Perhaps the leading figure in the postwar period associated with the Freudian commitment to insight and self-knowledge, and thus to the beleaguered humanistic ideals, is Erik Erikson. A practicing therapist as well as a prolific (and notably elegant and graceful) writer, Erikson concerned himself chiefly with developing a central issue in Freudian psychoanalysis, namely, the problem of ego identity. This issue, upon which modern fiction has thrown important light in its own concern with "heroes" and "antiheroes," appears in Erikson's work in two related emphases, upon childhood as the critical period of ego formation, and upon the life history, or the psychobiography, in which personal experience interacts with the larger culture and the historical moment to produce a specific character or identity. Learned in anthropology, history, and literature, Erikson moved beyond the clinical and technical limits of psychoanalysis proper in his writings, addressing readers concerned with broad questions of selfhood, history, and culture. In his varied works, psychoanalysis appears as a supple and humane method of disclosing common cultural and psychic patterns of growth in what Erikson calls the "life-cycle." In his studies of childhood, of youth and identity crises, and in his psychohistories, Erikson has given prime emphasis to the idea of "maturity," to the achievement through insight and self-awareness (antithetical to the environmental reinforcements of behaviorism) of a state of being "tolerant of differences, cautious and methodical in evaluation, just in judgment, circumspect in action, and . . . capable of faith and indignation."

Although Erikson cannot be considered a social critic, properly speaking—it remained for other, more radical interpreters of Freud to fuse psychoanalysis and cultural politics—his work responds to the felt urgencies of society and culture in the postwar years. He very much stresses "self" in the theme of "self and society," but like the anthropologists Ruth Benedict and Margaret Mead (upon whose work he draws, along with that of other cultural anthropologists), he focused on problems very much in public attention, those associated with the "youth crisis" after the war—problems such as juvenile delinquency, child-rearing difficulties, generational conflicts, and the centrality of ego identity in the life cycle. One of his earliest essays, "Ego Development and Historical Change," stated the program he chose to follow: "Men who share an ethnic area, an historical era, or an economic pursuit are guided by common images of good and evil. Infinitely varied, these images reflect the elusive nature of historical change; yet in the form of contemporary social models, or compelling prototypes of good and evil, they assume decisive concreteness in every individual ego's development. Psychoanalytic ego psychology has not matched this concreteness with sufficient theoretical simplicity." Erikson tried to achieve this simplicity of theory and concreteness of analysis in his early, and perhaps still most influential, book *Childhood and Society* (1950). This book combines theory (on "infantile sexuality" and on "eight ages of man") with studies of concrete life histories in different cultural settings—those of American Indians (showing the influence of anthropology on Erikson's method) and white middle-class and working-class Americans—and two studies of historical figures, Hitler and the Russian writer Maxim Gorky, anticipating Erikson's later full-length studies of Luther and Gandhi. Throughout, Erikson stresses a view of man directly at odds with the behaviorist definition. He speaks of "wholeness" as "a sound, organic, progressive mutuality between diversified functions and parts within an entirety"; of the importance to wholeness in the adolescent of "a progressive continuity between that which he has come to be during the long years of child-

26

hood and that which he promises to become in the anticipated future";
of the adult ego's "need . . . to experience fate as something which
he chose and in which he was active" (leading often, especially in the
experience of fascism in the 1930s, to an identification with one's
authoritarian persecutors). The emphasis lies upon individual growth
and responsibility: "to be a person, identical with oneself, presupposes
a basic trust in one's origins—and the courage to escape from them."

If for Skinner identity is a false problem, no more than "the identity
conferred upon a self . . . from the contingencies responsible for the
behavior," for Erikson identity is the key problem in individual life:
"the capacity of the ego to sustain sameness and continuity in the face
of changing fate." This definition of the problem inspired one of the
major undertakings in cultural psychoanalysis in the period, *Children
of Crisis* (1967), Robert Coles's multivolume study of the life histories
of children under various conditions of social deprivation and stress.
Two of Erikson's own subsequent books have had a different kind of
effect, on the study and writing of biography (an increasingly popular
literary genre in the 1970s) and of history. In *Young Man Luther*
(1958) and *Gandhi's Truth* (published in 1969 and dedicated to the
memory of Martin Luther King), Erikson explored the confluence of
the psychic and the historical in the development of two prominent
figures in world history: both men emerging from personal crises to
become spiritual leaders of reform. The first is a study of youth, the
second of middle age, and both are at the same time studies and vindi-
cations of psychoanalysis itself, testimonies to the humanist vision of
maturity proposed by Freud. Freud appears in each work in comparison to the crises and resolution in the lives of each subject. The first
is a study of "the powers of recovery inherent in the young ego," the
ability shared by Luther and Freud to free themselves from older
authority, to discover and publish new insights about human experience. The second is, in effect, Erikson's own "re-discovery" of psychoanalysis, as he puts it, "in terms of truth, self-suffering, and nonvio-
lence." The book is a personal revaluation of "an affinity between
Gandhi's truth and the insights of modern psychology," and thus a
treatise on the psychic and historical roots of one of the major political
forces in the postwar era, nonviolent resistance.

Critics of Society: Alienation and Erotic Pastoralism

Somewhere beyond both the scientific social reconstruction proposed
by behaviorism and the image of "maturity" embedded in the ego
psychology of Erikson and others lies the more radical, and for many
young people and writers in the 1960s more appealing, idea of a total

transformation of society and culture, a "liberation" of mankind from all psychic and social repressions. The works of the British anti-Freudian psychoanalyst R. D. Laing have been influential in shaping this deep current of dissatisfaction with any external authority (whether it be behaviorist managers or the very idea of "maturity"). Exploring the way a person deals with his self through interaction with others, Laing proposed that definitions of abnormality, of schizophrenia and madness in general, were themselves social products and instruments of oppression. In *The Divided Self* (1969), *The Politics of Experience* (1967), and other writings, he brought together insights from existentialism, phenomenology, and Marxism, and offered radical alternatives to thinking about madness and to therapy, such as the therapeutic community in which the distinction between the sane and the insane, the patient and the therapist, might be overcome. Insanity, he argued, might very well be a state of health in a mad world.

The notion that society itself resembled a madhouse has had a durable career in modern writing. In contemporary America, the idea owes many of its features to a group of German thinkers, exiles and immigrants from nazism, whose theories and methods were formed in their attempt to understand the phenomenon of authoritarianism in Germany. As a school of thought (loosely considered), they had in common the intellectual effort to integrate the teachings of Freud and Marx, to combine psychology and sociology into a holistic analysis of modern industrial society (of which America seemed the most complete example and thus most accessible for study) and a program for radical change. A commitment to radical politics, to socialism, characterized this group before the war. Afterward, perhaps out of frustration, they tended to abandon political hope on behalf of what seemed a deeper, more authentic kind of rebellion: personal liberation. Man's erotic nature came to seem the best hope for resistance to the encroachment of an ever more potent and insidious (because tolerant) authoritarianism. What one commentator has called a "party of eros" emerged in this period as a distinct alternative to a radical politics which had floundered.

German immigrants who settled in the United States either permanently or temporarily in the 1930s and 1940s included Wilhelm Reich, Erich Fromm, Herbert Marcuse, Max Horkheimer, and T. W. Adorno. Of this group, Reich and Marcuse found the largest American audience, many of their ideas having engendered responses and echoes in the work especially of Paul Goodman, Norman Mailer, and Norman O. Brown. Reich notably appealed to writers and social critics in search of a position after the collapse of radical politics after the war.

An analyst who broke with Freud over politics in the 1920s, he was a member of the Communist party for a short time in the 1930s, hoping to persuade both Marxists and psychoanalysts that their ideas and programs were incomplete without those of the other group. Society was sick as well as unjust; its sickness resulted from the repression of sexuality (man's basic instinctual life, or "nature"), which its economic system (the class system of capitalism) found necessary in order to win the acquiescence of the people it exploited. Reich's thinking tended toward simple oppositions; the instincts represent health, repression represents disease. Class society upheld itself in an authoritarian social order which must squelch "any natural life-manifestation." Like Fromm and others of the so-called Frankfurt School who bent their efforts in the 1930s to explain the phenomenon of German mass support for Hitler, Reich looked for signs of the internalization of authoritarian class structure within the psyche. Borrowing from Marx, they argued that society reproduces itself in psychic forms. Character structure reproduces and thus supports social structure, Reich argued, branding the bourgeois patriarchial family as authoritarian, "the factory of reactionary ideology and structure." Against the protective "armor" erected by the typical authoritarian character to fend off temptations from without and inducements toward free libidinal behavior from within, Reich posed the ideal of the "genital character," of potency and ability to achieve satisfactory orgasm, the key to "health." Thus Reich's therapeutic program, for society at large as well as individuals, called for the liberation of instinctive life, or "nature," against "culture," or organized repression.

In relation to Freud, Reich represents what Philip Rieff in *The Triumph of the Therapeutic* (1966) calls a revision away from the rigors of analysis toward the ecstasy of release, of personal transformation (rather than self-management), and finally of salvation. A religious and prophetic tone appeared in Reich's work in his later years in America—the years of most direct influence upon such writers as Norman Mailer and the Beat writers. He came to associate libidinal energy with a cosmic force—the orgone energy—and to claim that his theories about the proper unblocking of this energy, through a therapeutic breaking down of character armor, might lead to a cure for such physical disorders as cancer (for this claim, Reich was jailed in the 1950s by the Food and Drug Administration, and died in prison). In his writings about the "emotional plague" of modern capitalist and repressed society, one can find a source for much of the literary imagery of the "sick society" pervasive in these years. The curious mixture of a biophysical system and a religious rhetoric lost Reich much of his standing in the psychoanalytic community by the time of his death; but his earlier (and consistent) emphasis upon the need for both a cultural and a sexual revolution in order to accomplish the mutual goals of radical politics and psychoanalysis, and his vision of ideal communities of self-regulating "genital characters" living together in work-democracies, continued to draw eager readers and followers.

Although critical of Reich's simplifications and of his resolute optimism, Herbert Marcuse also sought a marriage of Marx and Freud, and also came to envision an erotic in lieu of a political revolution. A philosopher and social theorist rather than an analyst, Marcuse came to Freud from Hegel and Marx, with his commitment to "liberation" ("the complete and free realization of the whole human being in his social world") already formed. First and foremost, Marcuse was and remained an exponent of "critical theory," the effort to explain the "totality" of man's existence "in terms of his social being." His subject has not been sexuality or erotic liberation per se, but, instead, the conditions of life and the possibilities for happiness in advanced industrial capitalist societies. Through his writings, Marcuse has stood firmly against what he considered "one-dimensional," or narrowing, views of man, such as positivism, empiricism, and strict behaviorism. In *Eros and Civilization* (1955), Marcuse took the erotic to mean more than physical sexuality alone, to include also a fully sensuous (and predominantly aesthetic, pleasurable) experience of reality. Adopting the Freudian idea of a conflict between the pleasure principle and the reality principle (which he redefined as the performance principle), Marcuse argued that capitalist society required a subjection of pleasure as long as scarcity of resources prevailed. With alleviation of economic scarcity, the repressive structures are no longer viable, yet they continue, to the harm of Eros, "the builder of culture." Thus advanced societies, with America as the archetype, embody a paradox: increased abundance and satisfaction of material needs, along with increased repression in the form of external controls and administration. But Marcuse looked forward to an imbalance, in which technological advances would simply render obsolete the repressive structures, allowing the erotic nature of man (seeking gratification rather than, as in capitalist ideology, domination) to emerge and develop new forms of sensuousness, or of integration of mind and body. Although the connection between sheer sexuality and what Marcuse called the erotic (or "self-sublimated sexuality") remains a tricky point in his argument, it is clear that he, too, foresaw less hope in the conventional politics of opposition than in the making of counter-cultures.

A deepening pessimism regarding the likelihood of liberation and

30

genuine happiness appeared in Marcuse's most popular book, *One Dimensional Man* (1964). A complex argument, the book made its impact largely through the central insight that American capitalism had preempted all traditional modes of opposition simply by tolerating them, that tolerance had itself become a form of repression. Most disheartening for the radical critic was the observation that even art and sexuality, the two most promising avenues of liberation, had been absorbed by the intricate, all-devouring system of consumer capitalism —had become "cogs in a cultural machine . . . entertaining without endangering." Allowing a "repressive desublimation" of sexual energy, the system found that it could coopt its rebels by giving them a margin for acting out a harmless and empty freedom. Much of the book is devoted to an analysis of the modes of thinking in modern American society, of advertising discourse, scientific discourse, and linguistic analysis. Here Marcuse found that a repressive ideology governed even formal modes of thought, and that science and technology, based as they seem to be on a domination of nature, are also inherently repressive. What is considered "rationality" in the society is, in effect, a form of adjustment, a way of closing down serious opposition, of holding human beings in a one-dimensional frame, disallowing the "transcendence" that accompanies genuine liberation. Marcuse found no glimmer of hope anywhere; the working class especially, the traditional hope of radical politics, seemed irremediable in its conformity and compliance, its acceptance of consumerism as its goal, and its blindness to its real state of one-dimensionality. If hope appears, it is only in the total negativity of enlightened critics, and the total rebellion (erotic in nature) of young dropouts and experimental, rebellious artists. In his subsequent writings, Marcuse placed greater emphasis on the aesthetic basis of liberation, establishing the "aesthetic" as a social and political category. Looking for models of a new social order, Marcuse turned his attention to an account of the "new sensibility" necessary for social change. Many commentators have found that his later thought tends to conflate art and politics, and to open the door to an elitism of an enlightened minority, in the name of "progress in the consciousness of freedom."

Without pretending to much hopefulness, Marcuse called for a revolution in consciousness that might eventually change the entire society. Paul Goodman also cast a critical eye on the larger society, the "great state" of postwar America, but he then turned more hopefully to small communities, "intentional" groups that might, in their own interaction, solve some of the bigger problems in microcosm. Bigness itself looms as a foe to freedom and to social health in Goodman's thinking. A non-Marxist critic, he fashioned his own position from sundry influences—from the utopian and anarchist traditions of Proudhon and Kropotkin, the American pragmatists William James and John Dewey, from the British educational innovator A. S. Neill, from Gestalt psychology, and from Freud and Reich. Like Reich, Goodman tended to equate the natural with the good and the moral, and society with irrationality. Many of the ideas in his writings are those familiar among the "party of eros" in the period. His unique contribution lay in his emphasis upon voluntary action to form small communities, and to propose "practical" (often shockingly simple) solutions to everyday problems of bigness, such as traffic, and shopping, and larger problems of war and peace. In *Communitas* (1947), written with his architect brother, Percival, Goodman advocates several traditional goals of anarchism, such as decentralization, an integration of workplace and living space, "mutual aid," and "continuous group psychotherapy." The book is both utopian (in its vision of total change in the living environment) and practical (in its many detailed plans for small-scale but consequential changes in urban design). Regional planning, such as the Tennessee Valley Authority (TVA) project in the 1930s, and intentional communities, such as the kibbutzim in Israel and Neill's famous "progressive" school at Summerhill, serve as models of new community forms.

Goodman made his greatest impression as a critic and a presence in the rebellions of the sixties. He gave voice to the sense of powerlessness and to what he considered a dangerous cynicism, among the young in that decade and earlier, and attempted to foster a thinking about alternatives (such as the "free university" movement, in which he was a major influence). *Growing Up Absurd* (1960), his most prominent work of social criticism, called attention to the subculture of dropouts, Beats, and delinquents among the young in the Eisenhower years, and then analyzed the causes of this national malaise in the failure of society to provide an image of a meaningful future in the form of authentic vocations, significant social roles, attractive adult models. The book's force lies perhaps less in its formal analyses than in its voice of compassionate discontent and its unusual civic responsibility. The social system has alienated itself from natural human need; thus the youth "problem" represents deeper problems coming home to roost. The adult world offers a corporate rat race, the "apparently closed room"; and the young rebels are merely acting out "a critique of the organized system that everybody in some sense agrees with." Absurdity is the condition that arises from violating human needs—needs for good work, roles one can respect, a sense of genuine belonging to a community.

If Marcuse argues on behalf of "society," Goodman on behalf of "community," Norman O. Brown stands as an advocate of the individual by himself, in opposition to culture as such. Mankind and culture are antithetical: this is the apparently simple (but in fact quite complex, subtle, and erudite) message of *Life against Death* (1959), Brown's widely read and discussed venture into the "psychoanalytical meaning of history." In this book and in *Love's Body* (1966), Brown turns Freud's insights about repression against his high regard for civilization, and races beyond psychoanalysis, indeed beyond politics and existing cultures, toward myth, religion, and "the resurrection of the body." Brown bypasses the critique of industrial and corporate society in the work of his fellow post-Freudians, Marcuse and Goodman, and focuses intensely on the human condition as such, first in history and culture, and eventually (in his more prophetic writing in *Love's Body* and later) in its pure existential state. In Brown's thinking, the erotic emerges as entirely self-sufficient, and as the only salvation: for the enemy is no longer society as it is presently constituted, no longer capitalism, total administration, bigness, and alienation, but the repression of sexuality that man blindly brings upon himself.

Man represses himself primarily by his fear of death, his refusal thereby to accept his own naturalness. The very condition—mortality—which allows the body to serve as the means (and end) of pleasure implicates man in natural process, which includes death. His fear of death makes man "the neurotic animal," unable to live in his body with ease. *Dis*ease is the human condition in history; witness the monuments, the statues, the cities and their towers, the works of art which man sets against the fact of dying, in an effort to perpetuate himself. This is the insight of Freud's which Brown explored and finally transcended in *Life against Death*: that neurosis was the penalty for civilization. The critique is far-reaching. So far from calling for greater sexual freedom, Brown sees genital sexuality as itself a product of repression; the true erotic condition is that of the unrepressed infant: "polymorphously perverse," taking erotic pleasure across its entire body. Genital specialization is itself a mark of repression for the sake merely of procreation, the furtherance of civilization. It represents a surrender of the pleasure principle to the reality principle. Not orgasm itself but a total eroticizing of one's relations with the world is the sole solution to man's disease of separateness from the world's body, and from his own. Not a social revolution but a vast transformation in human consciousness can liberate man, and the course lies open before each individual. Brown did include a brilliant social-psychoanalytic discussion of money and anality in *Life against Death,* linking "filthy lucre" with the "excremental imagination," and capitalism with sublimation. But the guilt-producing repressions and lust for domination in the Protestant Ethic could be overcome only individually, through a radical break with the dualisms that set man against himself, his body against his soul, his life against his death. The task of abolishing repression, sublimation, aggression, and guilt belonged to each person, and was well within reach. Brown's prose often resounds with apocalyptic chords as he proclaims the imminence of a New Man. In *Love's Body* especially, with its mythopoetic and nondiscursive method, Brown appears as a prophet of a new mystical eroticism, drawing on religious, prophetic, and philosophical works throughout the world (the book is in part a collage of quotations and commentary). No longer the basis for a revolutionary criticism of a specific culture, that of America in the twentieth century, the erotic in Brown's vision is nevertheless the last resort of mankind against the violation by rationality, science, technology, and all forms of escape from self and domination of others.

New Worlds of Science and Technology

Prophets of technology and science, often visionary in their projections of a possible future, were themselves hardly quiescent in these years. Although they lie somewhat outside the main interests and preoccupations of most writers, science and technology engendered a meaningful body of writing, of ideas and controversies that touched the life of literature and of the mind in important ways. In many ways, the inherent conflict between religion and science embraced the many troubling issues that engaged writers and readers of literature in their everyday lives. The sense of an awesomely widening gap between faith and reason, between a commonplace educated sense of the world and the arcane understanding of processes and system in science and technology—the gap also between the technical capacities of science and the moral comprehension and social wisdom of most people—lay at the bottom of virtually all prominent issues in the realm of thought since the explosion of the first atomic bomb over Hiroshima in 1945.

That explosion and its unprecedented destructiveness had seemed to many people the most dire of warnings—not only about the now unthinkable horrors of modern warfare, but also about science and technology themselves. A fearsome vision of a science loosened from the hold of humane ends, a runaway science and technology subjugating rather than serving mankind, had appeared in nineteenth-century literature in Mary Shelley's story of a scientist, Dr. Frankenstein, who had exceeded the normal limits of research and experiment and produced a living monster who then turned murderously against his maker. Rapid advances in scientific research and technological application in industry, communications, and transportation had been accompanied in the nineteenth and early twentieth centuries with two simultaneous effects: undeniable improvement of living conditions (more goods, more ease and convenience of travel and communication), and equally undeniable social dislocation (more poverty, more pollution, more class conflict). The Frankenstein image seemed clutched in a struggle with a happier image of a benign and serviceable science. After World War II, the rate of technological change seemed to rise exponentially, perhaps given an enormous boost by the mobilization of scientists and technologists in the war effort; and one breakthrough after another in fields previously thought to be the exclusive domain of the science fiction writer jolted the public, with mixed effects of bewilderment and delight. Most spectacular of all were the orbital space flights and the moon landing of 1968, but also impressive were the technologies which made the space program possible, in cybernetics and automation, and the only slightly less sensational discovery in the life sciences of DNA (by James Watson and others in the early fifties) and the experiments since in manipulation and control of genetic data (especially "cloning"). The unimaginable seemed to become real—space exploration holding promise of man's actually penetrating in person beyond the solar system and perhaps solving the mystery of the origins of the universe, just as men had "broken" the genetic code in laboratories.

Of course, scientific experiment and technological change continued in virtually every other field touching the material aspects of human life, from the fight against disease (the polio vaccine, for example, and advances against cancer) to new forms of energy (nuclear, solar), from the achievements of new levels of speed in air travel (the supersonic transport) to a new immediacy in communication (satellite television and telephones). Taken in mass, the new discoveries and new applications seem to bury the Frankenstein myth once and for all; an infinite extension of man's rational control of nature, his ability to anticipate and to devise solutions for any difficulties thrown up by nature or by man himself, seemed a plausible promise. On the other hand, the old fears also found new justifications: the threat of supermechanized warfare persists, dangers to the ecosystem from overmechanization and pollution provoked anxious warnings from ecologists, and vastly more intricate specialization raised even more pressing concerns about social and political control of decision-making processes.

In the shadow of The Bomb, and in the face of such far-reaching discoveries and changes in technology, the question of "science and human values" took on a special urgency in the postwar years. Humanists, scientists and technologists joined public debates, symposia, and publications; a new field, "futurology," attracted academics and scientists. Figures such as J. Bronowski, James Bryant Conant, René Dubos, Jacques Ellul, Sigfried Giedion, and Lewis Mumford bent to the task of interpreting the new era of laboratories and machines, seeking grounds of reconciliation between the new sciences and traditional humanistic and religious values, or, as in some cases, prophesying a likely doom if the present course of technological thinking is not altered. Mumford's voice was one of the most urgent, and his intimations of the dangers in what he called "the myth of the machine" were among the most dire. Cultural historian, critic of literature and architecture, and social philosopher, Mumford launched his distinguished career in the 1920s; his first book dealt with the history of utopian literature and experiments, and the problem of the physical environment in relation to human culture has remained a central concern. In *Technics and Civilization* (1934), he formulated what has remained a consistent approach in his work: the study of the development of technology in relation to culture, to the shape of cities, the tone and quality of the physical environment, and the forms and spirit of art and thought.

More than anyone else writing about the machine in history Mumford has insisted on the priority of culture and the necessity of seeing the machine not as an independent force but as a feature of culture as a whole. Tracing the changes in technology (from tool to machine) through several cultural phases (eotechnic, paleotechnic, and neotechnic), Mumford pointed out that the machine tended more and more to displace human activity and to stamp its mold (in the form of mechanization) upon human behavior and thought. "We have merely used our new machines and energies," he wrote in the 1930s, "to further processes which were begun under the auspices of capitalist and military enterprises; we have not yet utilized them to conquer these forms of enterprise and subdue them to more vital and human purposes." Still, he offered an essentially hopeful vision of human societies, through democratic socialist planning (with an emphasis upon the organic wholeness of regions), mastering their technologies.

In his writings since World War II, Mumford has added an emphasis of serious skepticism. The tendencies have been toward increased mechanization of thinking and feeling, increased hardening into formulaic, machinelike solutions to problems of design and planning. More authority has been turned over to machines themselves, with human desire relegated to a subordinate role in decisions. Thus the new situation struck Mumford as critical in the extreme. "Like a drunken locomotive engineer on a streamlined train," he wrote in the fifties, "plunging through the darkness at a hundred miles an hour, we have been going past the danger signals without realizing that our speed, which springs from our mechanical facility, only increases our danger and will make more fatal the crash." The danger signals appear in the ruthless assault against older urban forms, against the natural environment, and also in cultural behavior, in a celebration of the irrational in the arts, violence in the popular media, and military might in nationalistic propaganda. The simple steam- or electricity-driven machine has given way to "mega-machine," the giant all-devouring system, in the form of government or business bureaucracy, or vast computerized electronic structure. This image of a huge and largely invisible mega-system found echoes in much of the literature of the period as well, particularly in the novels of Thomas Pynchon and the writings of Norman Mailer. Mumford described such a development, and scored the "mis-direction" of modern life, in his major postwar books, *The Myth of the Machine* (1967) and *The Pentagon of Power* (1970). Mega-technics, he argued, gave rise to terrible new prospects of authoritarian control: "the dominant minority will create a uniform, all-enveloping, super-planetary structure, designed for automatic operation. Instead of functioning actively as an autonomous personality, man will become a passive, purposeless, machine-conditioned animal, whose proper functions . . . will either be fed into the machine or strictly limited and controlled for the benefit of de-personalized, collective organizations." Mumford now argues that such a prospect derives from the fact that the mega-machine itself derives from a feature of human life, from the culturally based conception of man as worker, as technician, as opposed to another conception of man as organism, really at home in nature and in harmony with his own natural functions. The triumph of the machine and the frightening future it foretells represent the historical triumph of a one-sided image of man himself.

Mumford's fundamental view of technology as a product of human culture and thus expressive (in the manner of works of art) of a human content, however mangled the human form might be within it, was widely shared by other historians and critics of the inhumane uses of technology (in warfare, in political control, and in mass media).

Jacques Ellul represents yet another view of the situation. In *The Technological Society* (1964), this French Catholic sociologist concerns himself less with history than with the nature itself (philosophically speaking) of technology. He identifies "technique" as a mode of behavior in its own right, and attributes to it the character virtually of a Calvinist God, as a determining, pervasive, and irresistible force. It is also invisible, and thus all the more pernicious. Technique, Ellul argues, is the entire "ensemble of practices" by which man uses resources to achieve ends. The definition exceeds the usual notion of either "machine" or applied sciences; it precedes and transcends both machines and science, which in fact are no more than servants of technique. As a method for rational solution of problems, technique pervades all of existence; Ellul speaks of a "characterology of technique," whose major feature is "standardization." With what he calls "the technical revolution" in modern times, technique no longer operates within larger structures which might resist its ultimate reduction of life to method; instead, the "calculus of efficiency" has now conquered all other structures, ruling out spontaneity and imaginative effort. In its present stage, technique is self-perpetuating; human intervention no longer matters. The rate of growth is exponential, and its direction irreversible. Human choices are severely constricted; man faces a network of interlocking techniques with a life of their own. Moreover, the network is global; technique disregards cultural and ideological differences; all parts become interchangeable, just as all modern cities begin to resemble each other, products of the same universal and universalizing technique.

Ellul's view is, as Mumford comments, a fatalistic determinism. Technique has become autonomous in all modern states, reducing differences between capitalism and socialism to insignificance, taking over economic development and social control even without the awareness of rulers that they themselves are being ruled. Not only large systems but everyday life and its environment have also been transformed, denaturalized by technique. Technique imposes geometry upon nature, angled forms against the curving, unpredictable landscape. And workers less and less have direct physical contact with raw materials, with the simple facts of nature which technique transforms into products for use. In its reshaping and restructuring of human life, in its subtle encroachment into all realms of life, and notably in its political manifestation in propaganda, which diminishes the power of thinking independently, Ellul's "technique" is a profoundly totalitarian force. Ellul foresees a "monolithic technical world," an "unfamiliar universe" that cannot be resisted (technique simply *absorbs* its opposition by imposing its own methods upon dissent) except "by an act of freedom, of transcending it." "How is this to be done?" he asked in his foreword to *The Technological Society,* and replied, "I do not yet know."

Another voice prominent in the period did carry a message that sounded promising to many. Marshall McLuhan took a position radically at odds with Ellul's fatalism; while he too assumed a technological determinism, he reveled in the new world of machines, especially electronic machines used in communications. The "media" were McLuhan's province, and by his own somewhat oracular and cryptic style as well as his arguments, he established himself for a time in the 1960s as a prophet of the electronic age. Although McLuhan often seemed more of a "pop" cultural critic than a historian or philosopher of science and technology, he did propose a systematic accommodation to new technologies; he argued not only for their inevitability but for their beneficial cultural consequences. Rather than the traditional humanistic "criticism" of a Mumford or an Ellul, McLuhan proposed a study and an acceptance of the effects of the new electronic media. The term "media" refers to all technologies which serve as "extensions of man"—an argument he makes in his most influential book, *Understanding Media* (1964). A medium is not only a device of communication but a structuring of the senses and the mind; the automobile is as much a medium as television. McLuhan distinguished between the older mechanical media (printing is the archetype), which were typographic, linear, uniform, and repeatable, and the new electronic media, which are immediate, simultaneous, and all-involving. The older media were based on sequences, on fragmentation, and they entailed specialization; the new media offer a reintegration, virtually a new religious harmony. Rather than being simply extensions of the body, better enabling us to accomplish tasks in the physical world, instruments such as television actually "outered the central nervous system itself, including the brain," definitively altering patterns of perception and the entire relation of man to world. This, argues McLuhan, is the true revolution of our times, a "retribalizing" of the world, the making of a "global village," all parts in simultaneous and immediate contact with all others. "The computer," he writes, "promises by technology a Pentacostal condition of universal understanding and unity."

As a prophet of a new cultural order, McLuhan insisted on a new truth, couched in the aphorism "The medium is the message." The "personal and social effects of the media" lie not in their content—the actual programing of television—but in their structure, their electronic form. "The effects of technology," he writes, "do not occur at the level of opinions or concepts, but alter sense ratios or patterns of perception steadily and without any resistance." The "total involvement in all-inclusive *nowness*" of television has nothing to do with the specific program or literal message; as medium, it is itself the determining and shaping message, and the effect is a new cultural consciousness. Moreover, the new is the better, for the old "linear man" was full of narrow prejudices, derived from his commitment to logical sequence, while the new man is open to the world without linear (and traditionally humanistic) prejudices. The new consciousness can find pleasure and profit in its involvement with all products of the media, such as advertisements, comic strips, commercials—into which, McLuhan insists, go "more pains and thought, more wit and art" than into the older forms such as books, newspapers, and magazines. The highest effect of modern technology, then, has been to shift consciousness away from its reliance on written words, on reading, and on the concomitant practice of thinking in logical sequence.

McLuhan's arguments and prophecies stirred wide controversy, but his viewpoint was shared in details if not in its more speculative (and oracular tone) by other writers, such as Harold Innis (from whom McLuhan developed certain basic concepts of media), Walter Ong, S.J., and R. Buckminster Fuller. Although not directly tied to media as such, the new field of systems design (or systems analysis) also presupposed a new kind of thinking based on electronics. Systems engineers are concerned with the actual construction of new environments, new systems (traffic control, for example), new worlds of organization and communication. Linked to "futurology" (the effort to forecast the future by extrapolating from present conditions), systems designers are by and large strictly technicians whose aim is to solve problems—the disposal of waste products, the creation of new transportation systems, the anticipation of new weapons and the military and diplomatic problems they imply—by seeing them in their full complexity, within total systems. The field itself arose from one of the most intricate and astonishing of the new technologies developed after the war: that of computers. The electronic brain emerged as the underlying instrument of all sciences and technologies in this period—and it came as well to pervade everyday life, not only as an instrument (by the 1970s pocket calculators made it possible for every person to possess his own computer), but also as a system of centralized information storage and record keeping. The implications of electronic storage banks which can retrieve information with the speed of light and make calculations in fractions of a second that would occupy many human minds over immeasurably longer periods of time staggered the imagination of many writers (science fiction writers were the first to seize on the literary possibilities of computer technology), and raised agitating questions of social policy and control.

By and large technicians (technologists, planners, designers of systems) have chosen not to appear before the public as articulators of their principles and their procedures. A major exception is R. Buckminster Fuller, who better than anyone else in these years represented a bridge between the nineteenth-century inventor and tinkerer (in the mode of Thomas Edison) and the new breed with their computers and game plans and visionary systems. Inventor of the geodesic dome and a variety of building schemes for enclosing space and making it livable in new, more efficient ways, Fuller appealed especially to young people in the 1960s searching for alternative conceptions of the application of advanced technology to communal life. Fuller was the period's archutopian in the realm of engineering and systems design. He proposed an elevated mode of thinking about immediate physical and social problems, a mode that begins with the ecosystem and works its way into details. He popularized the image of "spaceship earth," an image of the earth as man's present (though not necessarily permanent) life-support system. "Everything we need to work with is already around us," he wrote, "although most of it is initially confusing. To find order in what we experience we must first inventory the total experiences, then temporarily set aside all irrelevancies. I do not invent my thoughts. I merely separate out some local patterns from a confusing whole." Though Fuller's inventions—the geodesic dome, the six-sided "dymaxion" house (prefabricated and delivered by helicopter, with a bathroom without plumbing), and the "dymaxion" automobile, which looked like a dolphin and moved on a rotational wheelbase—have the appearance of eccentricities, and have so far lacked popular appeal, his ideas, expressed in numerous books, articles, and lectures, have given the period a living image of what a consciously planned technological future might look like. His platform has been "a comprehensive anticipatory design science," the only realistic alternative, he argues, to outmoded practices in politics as well as in machine design and construction. The rich playfulness of his mind, as in his proposed game, "Making the World Work," accounts for much of his appeal and his persuasiveness. Man can now determine his own evolution, Fuller argues in a vein that reveals the antitheocentric character of technological thinking, but first he must overcome the individualistic, competitive, nationalistic behavior that inhibits creative application of science—"livingry" must replace "killingry" as the chief concern of science and politics.

Fuller falls into the category of technologist rather than pure (or theoretical) scientist in that he deals in tangibilities; his purpose is to make visible either in fact or in imagination the new possibilities in the reorganization of matter opened by theoretical science and mathematics. Underlying his thought, however, is a set of assumptions about the world as invisible and as arcane to the layman, as the spiritual realm of religion. The world of Fuller is very much a world fashioned by the theories of quantum physics and Albert Einstein, a world of dynamic motion, fluidity, constant change, and relativity. The four-square world of Newtonian physics represents one of the conceptual barriers, in fact, that Fuller rails against—the notion of "permanence as normal," for example, or the notion that a house must be a point fixed in space, made of weighty materials in compression. "Ephemeralization" is Fuller's term for one of the principles of technology, that more can be accomplished with less. The principle not only reverses conventional thinking about construction; it also points to a significant fact in modern science, that its objects seem more and more to lie in the realm of ephemeral experience, of subatomic particles or black holes in space, where discoveries hold startling prospects for changes in the material realm. It is this apparent leap between the invisibilities of the scientific enterprise and the visible world constructed by modern technology that has characterized the cultural and spiritual dilemma posed by science to many concerned minds.

Einsteinian physics worked an intellectual revolution early in the twentieth century, the reverberations of which still made themselves felt in the post–World War II era. The new scientific-technological field that perhaps best represented a post-Einsteinian frame of mind was cybernetics, or information theory. Founded on the electronic computer, cybernetics concerned itself with the theoretical issues involved in the control of machines by machines, with a range of applications from automation in industry and communications to ground control of space flights and exploration. The theory conceives of the machine as a surrogate brain, only vastly more efficient, rapid, and comprehensive than the human brain. In this field, the threat of Frankenstein seemed most plausible, and the challenge to the traditional Judeo-Christian idea of God the creator most stark. One of the founders of the field, the mathematician Norbert Wiener, addressed himself in several works, notably *The Human Use of Human Beings* (1950), to the social and ethical issues raised by this intricate and complex technological system about to saturate the public (and eventually to infiltrate the private) realm.

Wiener located the theoretical origins of cybernation in a phenomenon that had intrigued many literary minds from Henry Adams early in the twentieth century to Thomas Pynchon and others more recently, the phenomenon of entropy. Entropy is the tendency, described in Newton's Second Law of Thermodynamics, of any closed system to lose energy, to run down. Another way of describing it, writes Wiener, is through probability theory: the probable answers to a given set of questions in a given world increase as the world grows older. Probability theory itself represents a great revolution in modern physics, which "now no longer claims to deal with what will always happen but rather with what will happen with an overwhelming probability." The picture of a fixed stable world is no longer tenable. "The world as it actually is is replaced in some sense or other by the world as it happens to be observed." With quantum physics, chance and contingency have entered the world-picture, and information theory is a response to this development. For in the midst of an entropic universe, man represents an "enclave" of opposite tendency, a tendency for "organization to increase." This tendency flows from the fact that man receives and acts on information taken in by his senses, a procedure that assumes a healthy disequilibrium between man and environment. And machines, too, can "resemble human beings in representing pockets of decreasing entropy in a framework in which the large entropy tends to increase." Cybernetics, the movement and control of information through a system by machines, thus serves as an antientropic force, a model for maintaining the stability of a system. The critical feature of such machine-systems, or "life-imitating automata," is their ability to respond to the outer world, "to record the performance or non-performance of their own tasks." This is called feedback, "the property of being able to adjust future conduct by past performance." And this function requires "central decision organs which determine what the machine is to do next on the basis of information fed back to it, which it stores by means analogous to the memory of a living organism."

It is the analogy to a "living organism," to man himself, that raises the fears of a Frankenstein, a golem, and Wiener evokes these fears in order to allay them. Not that he is complacent about the wisdom or usefulness of cybernetics; he recognizes the danger that decisions turned over to machines might not be what mankind wants or needs. But control does rest with the human agent, if he will accept it: "For the man who is not aware of this, to throw the problem of his responsibility to the machine, whether it can learn or not, is to cast his responsibility to the winds, and to find it coming back seated on the whirlwind." The biblical metaphor in this sentence is a telling mark of Wiener's ultimate purpose, to reconcile the advances of science with the traditional ethical views of religion. The book is laced with religious allusions and examples (he prefers, for example, to think of the machine in light of the Augustinian rather than the Manichean idea of evil), and it concludes with a call for an intelligent "faith in science." In *God and Golem, Inc.* (1964), he comments on "certain points where cybernetics impinges on religion," drawing analogies between religious questions of knowledge, power, and worship and the moral implications of machines that can learn and can reproduce themselves. While Wiener's reflections upon the crossroads where religion and science meet have had little impact upon religious thought, they do reflect a current of thinking in the culture at large, a long-standing concern (reaching back at least to the trial of Galileo) with the apparent conflict in the world views of church and laboratory. Wiener represents not a resurgence of piety among scientists but a continuing sensitivity —manifest also by Werner Heisenberg in an essay written in 1973, "Scientific and Religious Truth"—to the relevance of the two pursuits to each other: the scientific pursuit of the truth of nature and the religious pursuit of ethical truth, "the basis of the communal life of men" (in Heisenberg's words). Whether these two kinds of truths might survive side by side remained a fundamental question of the era.

The challenge of science to the Judeo-Christian world-picture accelerated with the discoveries and breakthroughs of the period. The challenge lay both in the ethical dimension—issues of control of technology, decisions in medicine regarding life and death (including the anxious question of abortion), questions concerning the limits of research and experimentation (in biology especially, in regard to cloning)—and in the cosmological. The point of conflict between theology and science is sharpest and most critical in the realm of theory known as cosmology. While religion had preserved as dogma its story of the beginning and the ending of things, astronomy, starting with the great Copernican revolution, opened these ultimate questions to speculation based upon detailed observations of the skies. In the postwar era, the enormous advances in the technologies of observation—the radio telescope, penetration of the atmosphere by space modules— coupled with new explanatory theories regarding matter itself, have placed astronomy (or the new field of astrophysics) once more in a position of the highest authority regarding such questions. Perhaps the ultimate modern science in the sense that its subject is nothing less than the universe itself, its genesis (and the genesis of life), the nature of its time and its space, and the composition of its matter, astrophysics has disclosed newly perceived phenomena and has offered an array of new theoretical explanations on top of those already developed earlier in the twentieth century, adding quasars, pulsars, quarks, radio galaxies, black holes to the established images of an expanding universe originating in a "big bang," and the curvature of space. From the birth of the cosmos to the death of stars, modern astrophysics has propounded a set of images and terms that resemble, as one commentator puts it, "precursors of conceptual revolutions."

"Theoretical cosmology," writes the astronomer George Gamow, "attempts to correlate the observed facts about the universe at large with known physical laws and to draw a consistent picture of the universe's structure in space and its changes in time." The word *picture* is revealing, for it suggests a major point of convergence between scientific cosmology and religion: both offer images and metaphors as names for phenomena which are not directly perceivable by the unaided eye, or if perceived, cannot be accounted for by existing knowledge. Of course, the convergence does not dissolve the fundamental chasm between a picture based on faith and one based on exact observation and mathematical reasoning. From the point of view of the public, however, the field of theoretical cosmology seems to have assumed the function previously performed by religion, of ministering to the existential insecurity of mankind by providing explanations of origins, ends, and the true nature of things. In the postwar era, the explanatory picture changed dramatically, though so far not fundamentally. The notion of an expanding universe, energized in its flight through a curved space by an initiating explosion (now placed at about eighteen billion years in the past) within a substance composed of particles of matter and of light (radiation), is effectively the picture still in place. What caused the initial explosion—the question which seems to preserve some validity for the idea of a divine First Cause—remains a challenge to research and speculation. But it seems clear that with all its recent imagery of cosmic violence, of blazing nuclear infernos at the heart of stars, of exploding supernovas and stars collapsing into ultradense objects which no longer emit light (black holes)—and with its seeming mysticism of space-time folded within itself, of matter joined to antimatter and black holes to white holes—theoretical cosmology continues to underscore the redundancy of an idea of God and the self-sufficiency of natural explanations. Nevertheless, mankind's picture of itself and its place within the universe seemed very much in agitation during these years, with the prospects of startling new discoveries in space exploration—such as evidence of extraterrestrial life and perhaps intelligence, and further light on cosmic processes and thus on cosmic destiny—that might even more radically upset the long-dying image of a God who governs man's destiny, nature's, and the nation's.

The State of Religious Thought

The demise of the belief that America had special providential claim as "God's country," the "nation with the soul of a church," is perhaps the most significant event in the realm of religion in these years, an event with far-reaching cultural consequences. It is fair to say that American religion in these years offers more of a sociological than an intellectual interest, though this is not to undervalue important currents of serious thought and reflection, provoked as much by intensifying social problems in the sixties as by the more enduring philosophical challenge of science. Much of the religious thought was devoted to a reflection upon religion itself, upon the state of religious establishments, upon the unmistakable revival of measurable piety in the immediate postwar years and through the 1950s, and the critical, perhaps decisive, shifts in behavior and moral values that burst upon the scene in the 1960s. Corresponding shifts of emphasis among Christian and Jewish theologians appeared in the midst of social turmoil, but no major commanding voice in theology had emerged by the end of the 1970s; with some modifications and revisions, Christian theology continued to draw upon the intellectual capital of the Neo-Orthodox movement of the thirties and forties.

Neo-Orthodoxy, represented in America especially by Paul Tillich and Reinhold and H. Richard Niebuhr, was a complex and heterogeneous movement, a subtle form of modernism within Protestantism, the dominant religious affiliation among Americans. It emerged in Europe between the world wars as a "crisis theology"; and, most notably in the teachings of Karl Barth, it aimed its polemic against theological (and political) liberalism, its faith in progress, its easy sentimental confidence in man's goodness. It was primarily a movement among Protestant intellectuals, sophisticated, erudite, and cultivated church thinkers who did not shrink from secular modernism, from science, Marxism, existentialism, and radical social criticism. Its primary emphasis—important to grasp for an understanding of the literary climate in America just after the war—was upon the inescapable predicament of isolation, loneliness, and vulnerability faced by man in nature and in history. Reviving interest in nineteenth-century writers like Kierkegaard, Dostoevsky, and Nietzsche, the Neo-

Orthodox theologians stressed (in Kierkegaard's words) the "infinite distinction" between time and eternity, between man and God. Liberalism revealed itself in their eyes as facile optimism, and this perception led to a new concern with biblical exegesis and with the mission of the church in the face of existential human despair. Simply to give comfort no longer seemed the churchly mission; instead it was to teach men (in Tillich's influential concept) "the courage to be." Tillich was especially influential in defining the issues and setting the tone for American Neo-Orthodoxy, with his ranging speculative mind, his ontological as well as ethical interests, and his assimilation of elements of Marxism and existentialism. Rather than obedience to a moral code, or the legalism of giving evidence of faith in good works, Tillich and others proposed a situationalist ethic based on an existential, tragic sense of life. Standing alongside Tillich, the Niebuhr brothers, especially Reinhold, added a renewed emphasis upon the social gospel, transformed now along the lines of newly affirmed Christian (rather than secular) values.

Tillich, the Niebuhrs, and others continued to publish and to exert a major intellectual influence immediately after the war; though the range of their influence was restricted to theology students and disillusioned Marxist and liberal intellectuals, their role in preparing for the radical changes in the religious scene in the sixties was significant. The period of their greatest currency among church and secular intellectuals corresponded, ironically enough, with a period of revived religious interest of a sort they viewed with suspicion, if not alarm. Church membership and affiliation rose to unprecedented heights, and although serious theology also flourished under the impetus of Neo-Orthodoxy, fundamentalism and a liberal "civil religion" experienced the most striking resurgence. Civil religion stressed the "Americanness" of any religious belief; as the theologian Will Herberg put it, the "American way of life" was "the characteristic American religion, undergirding life and overarching American society." In these years of the Cold War, of suspicion of domestic criticism and cultural difference, religious belief and affiliation became a touchstone of proper loyalty and character. No worse charge could be leveled against atheism than that it was "un-American." Religion guaranteed patriotism, and also "peace of mind," perhaps an even greater motive than the political one. Religiosity flourished in the fifties, with figures like Norman Vincent Peale offering nostrums like his best-selling book, *The Power of Positive Thinking* (1952). Exploiting the mass media as religious figures had never done before, Peale, Monsignor Fulton J. Sheen, and revivalist Billy Graham reached millions with their messages of hope through either a fusion of faith and science or, as in the case of Graham, a return to the true, literal faith. Altogether, the religious scene in the fifties seemed clearly more a phenomenon of a culture in transition than a serious intellectual revaluation of the place of faith in modern life. As the historian Sydney Ahlstrom put it, "the so-called revival led to a sacrifice of theological substance, which in the face of the harsh new social and spiritual realities of the 1960s left both clergy and laity demoralized and confused."

The revival itself showed definite signs of decline by the end of the fifties, in time for a new and much different upsurge of religious energy in the coming turbulent decade. The changes reflected events and developments global in scale—Pope John's reforms in Catholicism in 1958, for example—but also particular American tendencies, such as the militant role of churches, black and white, in the civil rights movement in the South, the emergence of Martin Luther King, Jr., as a major spokesman for a renewed sense of social justice in Protestantism, the election of a Roman Catholic to the presidency in 1960, and perhaps most decisive of all, the vast popular outcry of moral concern with the war in Vietnam, in which church leaders often played a conspicuous role. But coincident with what appeared to be a renewed activism after the conformity and compliance with a conservative political mood in the fifties was a new set of challenges to the authority of traditional religious and supernaturalistic explanations. The most profound of these was the emergence of a radical theology, a direct challenge to dogma and accustomed church practice. Another kind of challenge which deserves some mention before a discussion of the radical currents was the diffusion in the late sixties and seventies of counter-cultural religious ideas and practices, betokening a cultural phenomenon of still unmeasured and indeterminate scope.

Partly in response to the new findings of astronomy, partly in response to the apparent deterioration of the authority of such traditional institutions of stability as the family, established churches, universities, and government, the recent period has witnessed an outbreak of fascination with, if not outright belief in, various versions of occultism and a revival of astrology, demonology, magic, and other mystagogic beliefs. Much of this flurry has a science fiction and futurist cast, linked to notions of extraterrestrial communication and UFOs. In another vein, but also within the sphere of the nontraditional and noninstitutional, is the popularity of Eastern religions, with roots in the Orientalism of the Beat movement in the fifties, but now taking on a particular cultist aspect, as among the followers of numerous gurus such as the Korean Reverend Moon. Young followers of Buddhist groups and the "Jesus people" with their unique blend of communal-ism and fundamentalism also contributed to a cultural moment of severely fragmented supernaturalist beliefs and cultist practices, which may (or may not) reflect a deep-seated change in the entire status of religion in the culture. Whatever tidings such phenomena bring to American society, it is clear they represent a fairly widespread disen-chantment with the traditional forms and dogmas of Judeo-Christian-ity. In any case, they manifest a degree and scale of religious (and cultural) pluralism never before so prominent in American life.

The challenge from radicalism has a weightier intellectual substance and is more relevant (so far) to those writers, such as Flannery O'Con-nor, John Updike, Walker Percy, and others, who have concerned themselves with religious matters. This has taken the form of a call, initiated by the German theologian who died at the hands of the Nazis, Dietrich Bonhoeffer, for a "secular interpretation" of the Christian message, a new language and action of concern and intervention within the worldly structures of human society. The movement often went by the name of "God is dead," the line from Nietzsche revived by such writers as Gabriel Vahanian in *The Death of God: The Culture of Our Post-Christian Era* (1961), Bishop J. A. T. Robinson in *Honest to God* (1963), and Harvey Cox in the widely read *The Secular City* (1965). The common theme was a need to demystify and demythologize the gospel, a need for new forms of relevance and commitment. While the precise nature of what was called for in the way of religious be-havior was often unclear and diverse, an unmistakable point of this movement was its resolute criticism of sanctimonious liberalism, hypo-crisy, and the popular pieties of civil religion. The movement was rooted in the intellectual rigor and speculative freedom of Neo-Or-thodoxy; in fact, it must be seen as an outgrowth of the seminal ideas of Tillich, Niebuhr, and others. Some of the new theologians, like Harvey Cox, combined a renewed and militant social activism with an openness to non-Christian religions and to secular creeds such as Marxism and various forms of socialism. The sociological questioning of the historical role of Christianity, as in the works of Max Weber, and of the structure of the contemporary church, as offered by Peter Berger, also appealed to the new radicals and set the questions they argued the church must confront. Changes within the liturgy and a new emphasis upon the creativity of ritual and liturgical forms also ac-companied the "God is dead" movement. Revision of sexual attitudes, particularly toward the ordination of women, is another indication of the depth and breadth of the changes sweeping through the churches.

We are still too much in the midst of these changes to venture an estimate of their meaning for American cultural, intellectual, and literary life. Perhaps Sydney A. Ahlstrom is correct in describing the recent period as the end of the Puritan era in America and the beginnings of a new and radical pluralism (*A Religious History of the American People,* 1972). It is clear, whatever the future holds, that no comprehensive religious synthesis, such as that which supported Dante in the fourteenth century, has emerged as an utterly persuasive world view for writers and readers. The report from religion, as from sociology, psychology, and science, is very much of a time in transition, a time of change, sudden and disconcerting, and surely a time that holds promise of more difficulty, more challenge, and more conflict. It is likely, too, that the intellectual world within which contemporary writing finds its themes and its orientations will continue to provoke artists to extremities of experiment and expression, in search of appropriate styles and forms. Whether the imaginative writer will continue to hold his place of authority against the new media and against the cosmic fantasies fulfilled by reality itself also remains to be seen. As the Catholic theologian Teilhard de Chardin wrote, "not a thing in our changing world is really understandable except in so far as it has reached its terminus."

2

Literary Criticism

A. Walton Litz

RITING an essay on American literary criticism since 1945 is like writing a brief guidebook to a continent. All one can hope to do is indicate the major landmarks and lines of communication, the large contours of an immensely complex landscape. Inevitably, some of the most interesting features will be omitted; and inevitably, the description of the landscape will depend on the writer's point of view. Criticism can never be wholly disinterested, although it often makes that claim, and histories of criticism are equally personal. So it seems best to begin with a polemical argument, a personal sketch of the development of American literary criticism since World War II, which can then be fleshed out through discussion of individual critics and methodologies.

The general trend of literary criticism since 1945 has been from consensus to diversity, from the dominance of formalistic criticism to a bewildering variety of criticisms which seek to move "beyond" or "against" formalism. In various subtle ways American literary criticism has followed the course of our political and cultural history, responding to the national movement from a broad postwar consensus into a time of divisions and uncertainties. To gain a measure of the changes wrought by the last thirty years, one has only to look at the monumental two-volume *Literary History of the United States*, published in 1948, and imagine the difficulties involved in repeating that work today. The contributors to the *Literary History of the United States* were a mixed lot, ranging from H. L. Mencken to R. P. Blackmur, but their essays rest easily side by side: there is a consistency and self-confidence in their critical attitudes and their evaluations of the major writers that could not have been achieved even a few years later. If the *Literary History* were rewritten today, its frankly elitist view of our literary past, which emphasizes the major writers in the Puritan tradition, would have to be revised radically to accommodate our new awareness of the importance of popular culture, minority writers, and general ethnic and regional diversity. But the difficulty would not only stem from these necessary adjustments in content and emphasis; it would come from differences in critical method which are so deep as to make a national enterprise such as the *Literary History of the United States* almost impossible today. The *Literary History* reflects an unusual period in our cultural life when a consensus in historical scholarship was reinforced by an emerging critical orthodoxy, and to understand that orthodoxy—which was called among many things the "New Criticism"—we need to know something of its origins.

Taking the long view, we can say that the New Criticism attempted to harmonize some of the most powerful shaping forces in Romantic and post-Romantic art. One of these was an emphasis on the autonomy or self-sufficiency of the work of art, a notion implicit in the Romantic aesthetic and more systematically developed by the Symbolists of the late nineteenth and early twentieth centuries. According to this theory, the poem possesses a truth of internal coherence, not of correspondence to external reality, and must be examined as an independent verbal structure. As E. M. Forster put it, speaking of the world of modern art: "We have entered a universe that only answers to its own laws, supports itself, internally coheres, and has a new standard of truth. Information is true if it is accurate. A poem is true if it hangs together. Information points to something else. A poem points to nothing but itself. Information is relative. A poem is absolute." This is an assumption which with subtle modifications pervades the literary criticism of T. S. Eliot, especially the essays of *The Sacred Wood* (1920), and underlies the early criticism of I. A. Richards and William Empson, with its stress on the detailed analysis of verbal complexity. Implicit in this obsession with linguistic complexity is a belief that the "value" of a work of art depends on its ability to balance or reconcile complicated and often conflicting qualities. This Coleridgean faith in the synthesizing power of the poetic imagination lies behind a famous passage in Eliot's essay on "The Metaphysical Poets" (1921). "When a poet's mind is perfectly equipped for its work, it is constantly amalgamating disparate experience; the ordinary man's experience is chaotic, irregular, fragmentary. The latter falls in love, or reads Spinoza, and these two experiences have nothing to do with each other, or with the noise of the typewriter or the smell of cooking; in the mind of the poet these experiences are always forming new wholes."

Such a view of the poetic process naturally leads to a high appreciation of irony, wit, and symbolic complexity, rather than the more transparent products of lyric expression or personal reflection. Eliot's early preference for Metaphysical poetry of wit and irony, and his counterbalancing devaluation of the Romantics and Victorians, inevitably affected the received view of literary history, and merged neatly with his notion—most fully developed in "Tradition and the Individual Talent" (1919)—that the movement of literary history is a dynamic transaction between past and present, with each new work of art subtly altering our vision of the past. Joyce's *Ulysses* must be read with Homer's *Odyssey* in mind, but it also conditions and permanently alters our reading of the Greek epic. Therefore, the ideal critic must have "a perception, not only of the pastness of the past, but of its presence; the historical sense compels a man to write not merely with his own generation in his bones, but with a feeling that the whole of the literature of Europe from Homer and within it the whole of the literature of his own country has a simultaneous existence and composes a simultaneous order."

By 1941 the influence of Eliot, Richards, and Empson had become so powerful and pervasive that John Crowe Ransom could canonize their achievements under the title *The New Criticism* (1941), while the working methods of the movement had already been fully developed in the early essays of R. P. Blackmur, especially those of *The Double Agent* (1935). At the center of this "practical" New Criticism lay the act of explication or close reading, the detailed analysis of language and structure. This method, as practiced by Blackmur and his most able contemporaries, such as Allen Tate, Robert Penn Warren, and Cleanth Brooks, displayed few of the mechanical or restrictive characteristics it was later to take on in the hands of less able writers. Their model was T. S. Eliot, who in his early essays had allowed his point of view and that of his subjects to emerge gradually and subtly from his comments on particular passages. Eliot believed that the ideal critic possesses not a set of rigid theoretical assumptions but a coherent "sensibility" or "point of view," a sensibility which evolves out of long meditation on the literary tradition and which informs and unifies everything the critic does. At its best, New Critical explication is not neutral dissection of the text but an act of indirect moral and aesthetic judgment, the two inseparable from each other. Commenting on "Explication as Criticism" in *The Verbal Icon* (1954), W. K. Wimsatt summed up this most vital aspect of the New Criticism: "it is possible to conceive and to produce instances where explication in the neutral senses is so integrated with special and local value intimations that it rises from neutrality gradually and convincingly to the point of total judgment. It is important to observe that in such instances the process of explication tends strongly to be not merely the explication of the explicit but the ex*plicit*ation of the implicit or the interpretation of the structural and formal, the truth of the poem under its aspect of coherence." In the best of the New Criticism, all of the pejorative overtones of the term "formalism" disappear, and the critic gives a sense of the poem's larger contexts while never losing sight of its formal details.

The flexibility and subtlety of the best New Criticism resulted from its radical pragmatism. Its finest practitioners were poets as well as critics, and the movement developed naturally out of the long English and American tradition of the poet-critic, who thinks of criticism as an adjunct to creation and is always willing to modify his theories in the light of new works. Eliot, for example, never thought of his early notions about "tradition" and poetic language as immutable truths. Instead, they were based upon discoveries he had made while forging his own modern style, and were designed to have an immediate impact on the course of contemporary verse. *The Sacred Wood,* with its radical revisions of literary history, was never intended to reflect the full range of Eliot's taste and reading, nor was it conceived as a definitive statement; it embodied a specialized view of the past which Eliot thought most relevant to the problems of contemporary poetry. All critical ideas and practices are post facto, they come after the poem, and the ideal critic stands ready to modify his views in the presence of the "really new" work, just as Eliot had to reconcile himself to the new and troubling energies of Joyce's *Ulysses.* The New Criticism was, in a very real sense, invented to explain the new poetry of the modernist writers. When R. P. Blackmur wrote to Wallace Stevens in 1931, telling of his excitement over William Empson's *Seven Types of Ambiguity,* he knew quite well that Empson was describing qualities of poetic language that Stevens had consciously exploited for many years. The best of the New Criticism was always marked by an openness to new literary experience, and by an awareness of the limitations of the critic when faced with the order and intensity of a great poem. One lesson of Richards's *Practical Criticism* (1929), as Lawrence Lipking has pointed out, is that we do not criticize the poem, the poem criticizes *us,* making us healthily aware of our insincere emotions and faulty techniques. The humility and humanity of the finest New Criticism is best summed up in Part V of Eliot's "East Coker," where Eliot speaks of his own career as a poet-critic:

> And so each venture
> Is a new beginning, a raid on the inarticulate
> With shabby equipment always deteriorating
> In the general mess of imprecision of feeling,
> Undisciplined squads of emotion. And what there is to conquer
> By strength and submission, has already been discovered
> Once or twice, or several times, by men whom one cannot hope
> To emulate—but there is no competition—
> There is only the fight to recover what has been lost
> And found and lost again and again: and now, under conditions
> That seem unpropitious. But perhaps neither gain nor loss.
> For us, there is only the trying. The rest is not our business.

The spirit of this passage, which is the spirit of the greatest English and American criticism, was to disappear gradually from the New Criticism in the years after World War II, and to reappear only fitfully as other critical approaches asserted their claims.

The decade after 1945 might best be described as the "institutionalization" of the New Criticism. Attitudes and tentative generalizations were exalted into dogmas, and a new orthodoxy was established. This tendency is clearly reflected in two highly influential essays by W. K. Wimsatt and Monroe C. Beardsley, "The Intentional Fallacy" (1946) and "The Affective Fallacy" (1949), both reprinted, along with other valuable essays on critical method, in Wimsatt's *The Verbal Icon*. As Cleanth Brooks observed in 1962, looking back over the history of the waning New Criticism: "We have been witnessing a strenuous attempt to focus attention upon the poem rather than upon the poet or the reader." In the two essays by Wimsatt and Beardsley, this emphasis is given legislative force. They used the term "intentional fallacy" to characterize that criticism which seeks to explain a work of art in terms of its origins in the artist's conscious "self," often relying upon the writer's explicit statements of intention. The "affective fallacy" describes those critical methods which try to measure the effect of the poem on the reader. Between these two invalid and dangerous approaches lies the true object of criticism, the poem itself in all its linguistic and structural complexity. This bald statement does not, of course, do justice to the arguments of Wimsatt and Beardsley, which are conducted with great intelligence and sophistication. Nonetheless, the impact of the two essays—and especially their prescriptive titles— was anything but subtle. The slogans "intentional fallacy" and "affective fallacy" soon became fashionable, and took on the authority of scientific laws. It is easy to understand why Wimsatt and Beardsley, still faced with the old-fashioned biographical scholarship and "impressionistic" criticism against which the New Criticism had reacted, adopted a dogmatic strategy; but the long-range effect of their essays was to rigidify the New Criticism and rob it of some of its saving pragmatism.

Another institutionalizing impulse came from the publication in 1949 of *Theory of Literature,* by René Wellek and Austin Warren. This learned and highly influential survey of the various methodologies of literary study is mainly devoted to an anatomy of the "extrinsic" and "intrinsic" approaches to literature. The chapters on "extrinsic" methods ("Literature and Biography," "Literature and Psychology," "Literature and Society," "Literature and Ideas," "Literature and the Other Arts") are mostly given over to the limitations of these "extra-literary" methods, while the chapters on "intrinsic" approaches are fuller and more enthusiastic. Although acknowledging the relative or partial quality of any one critical reading, Wellek and Warren insist that there is a substantial element common to all readings, and claim that our best access to this common center is through close study of the work's formal structure. The arguments of Wellek and Warren are complex and qualified, but their persistent slighting of "extrinsic" methods served to reinforce the more narrow formalistic tendencies of the New Criticism. Widely read in colleges and universities, *Theory of Literature* had a profound impact on a whole generation of teachers and students.

But it was *Understanding Poetry,* an anthology with elaborate commentary compiled by Cleanth Brooks and Robert Penn Warren, that did the most to popularize the New Criticism. First published in 1938 and later revised, *Understanding Poetry* was the handbook for two generations of American students of literature, holding a commanding place well into the 1960s. "Bliss was it in that dawn to be alive, / But to be young was very Heaven!" Wordsworth's youthful enthusiasm over the French Revolution could not have exceeded the joy of discovery felt by countless students when they first picked up *Understanding Poetry.* No one brought up on Brooks and Warren can ever forget the excitement of following the editors through their close analyses of individual poems, or the even greater excitement of using their models as a basis for new readings. By making two generations of students more attentive to the text itself, more aware of nuance and ambiguity, Brooks and Warren performed a major service to literary study. The present decline in the skills they fostered may well turn out to have profound and detrimental effects on future scholarship and criticism.

We tend to forget today how late the study of English and American literature entered our colleges and universities, and for how long after that introduction it was dominated by purely historical and philological concerns or by impressionistic methods. Works such as *Theory of Literature* and *Understanding Poetry* helped to give the study of literature the central position it now occupies, for better or worse, in American academic life.

In the end, *Understanding Poetry* fell victim to its own success and even contributed to the decline of the methods and values it promoted. By simplifying the working procedures of the New Criticism and presenting them in textbook form, Brooks and Warren did more than focus the reader's attention on the poem as an "organic system of relationships"; they programmatically excluded all consideration of historical, sociological, and biographical contexts, leaving the poem naked on the page, and led many students to believe that any naive but sincere response could be turned into valuable literary criticism if clothed in the language of formal analysis. In addition, the choice of poems, with its emphasis on seventeenth-century wit and modern irony, on the dramatic rather than the lyric, canonized that highly specialized view of the literary tradition that T. S. Eliot had created in response to his personal needs and those of his contemporaries. A generation had to pass before the nineteenth-century precursors of the modern writers could receive a proper new assessment, and much of the blame for this can be attributed to the attitudes enshrined in *Understanding Poetry*. For all its pedagogical virtues, *Understanding Poetry* accelerated the movement toward rigidity and dogmatism that would be one source of the New Criticism's undoing.

There were other factors which led to the decay of the New Criticism, even at the moment of its greatest influence and popularity. Since it had been created largely to explain and justify the radical achievements of the modernist writers, the feeling of contemporary urgency and relevance declined as those writers receded into literary history. At the same time, many readers and critics became restive with a method which (at least in its debased form) attempted to legislate away many of our natural reactions to literature, minimizing the contributions that knowledge and experience can make to literary study. If a poem can be satisfactorily analyzed as an isolated artifact, with minimal reference to historical and cultural forces, then a brilliant undergraduate can produce just as impressive a "reading" as the critic who has lived with the poem for many years (*Seven Types of Ambiguity*, perhaps the most dazzling example of such close reading, was written while Empson was an undergraduate at Cambridge). Furthermore, our instinctive needs to see a work of literature in relation to the man and moment that created it cannot be suppressed for long, no matter how many "fallacies" are invoked, and the growing popularity of literary biographies during the late 1950s and early 1960s may be interpreted as a reaction against the cultural and human thinness of much New Critical writing. Finally, and most disabling of all, the New Criticism was a method best suited to the short poem, not to narrative or drama. It could treat the language and form of local passages with great sophistication, but was less successful in handling the larger architectural problems of plot and character development. *Understanding Fiction* (1943), by Brooks and Warren, is far less effective than *Understanding Poetry* because the structural difficulties posed by fiction are constantly dissolved into image patterns or linguistic rhythms. The basic assumptions of the New Criticism logically led to an exaltation of the poetic or "Jamesian" novel, with its controlled point of view, since such novels are more amenable to the techniques of poetic analysis. At the same time, the New Criticism was ill at ease with the typical eighteenth- or nineteenth-century novel, that "loose and baggy monster," and the preference for a focused "poetic" novel promoted methods and value judgments which simply could not do justice to the range and elasticity of prose fiction.

Even in its heyday after World War II, the New Criticism was not without powerful opponents. Yvor Winters, whose most influential work of the 1930s and 1940s was collected in 1947 under the title *In Defense of Reason,* wrote from a viewpoint largely at variance with the developing New Criticism. He rejected the notion of aesthetic autonomy, the belief that the internal order of a work of art is the prime object of criticism; he deplored the reliance of most modern poets on a logic of images or feeling, rather than a rational argument; he distinguished sharply between traditional irony, which is a means for defining emotion, and "Romantic" irony, which he took to be a mask for self-indulgence or sentimentality. Like Irving Babbitt, whom he closely resembles, Winters regarded Romanticism as a distorting force in modern literature, and rejected those beliefs in the sanctity of individual or spontaneous feeling that he detected at the heart of most modern works.

In contrast to many of his contemporaries, who found a positive value in paradox or in the ironic balancing of opposite and discordant feelings, Winters argued that poetry must have a rational, paraphrasable statement that can be judged on moral grounds. Using Eliot as his chief target, Winters claimed that modern poetry expresses emotion without judging it: that the typical modern poem, such as *The Waste*

Land, has a form which reflects the intensity and confusion of life without bringing it under moral control. According to Winters, such verse exhibits the fallacy of "expressive, or imitative, form: the procedure in which the form succumbs to the raw material of the poem." This emphasis on judgment from the standpoint of an external moral order (in Winters's case a conservative and Catholic order) often led to didacticism or outrageous exclusions, but his powerfully argued opposition to the major tendencies in contemporary criticism caused many other critics to reexamine their premises and sharpen their arguments. R. P. Blackmur called Winters a necessary member of the "loyal opposition," and this "loyalty" is reflected in Winters's constant attention to details of poetic language. The moralistic passages of *In Defense of Reason* alternate with perceptive readings of individual poems and brilliant statements on poetic meter. Even in his last work, *Forms of Discovery* (1967), Winters's savage distortions of the English poetic tradition are redeemed by his careful scrutiny of the relationship between form and meaning. Winters did not wish to move beyond formalism, but tried instead to place formal analysis under the guidance of a moral vision that transcends literature.

Other members of the loyal opposition to the New Criticism were the "neo-Aristotelians," a group of scholars and critics at the University of Chicago who did their major work in the 1940s and early 1950s. The best of their work was collected in 1952 as *Critics and Criticism, Ancient and Modern,* edited by R. S. Crane, who was the leading figure in the movement. Solidly academic in orientation, at a time when the New Criticism had not yet become the orthodoxy of the academies, the Chicago critics were often thought of as opponents of the New Criticism, enlisting scholarly methods in a war on those who would treat the poem as a timeless artifact without historical context; but this view is too limited and too partisan. The ideas of Crane and his group may be viewed as complementary to those of such critics as Empson, Brooks, and Blackmur. In contrast to the "monism" of many of his contemporaries, Crane saw himself as a "pluralist," trying to recognize the virtues of different critical and scholarly methods and their appropriateness to the literary problem at hand. In the analysis of prose fiction, for example, Crane's emphasis on the Aristotelian elements of action, plot, and character, which were often disregarded by the New Critics, had a salutary effect, leading ultimately to Wayne Booth's *The Rhetoric of Fiction* (1961), a work which decisively altered the major trends in criticism of the novel. Crane's aim, contrary to the polemics of the time, was not to denigrate the New Criticism but to enlarge it, to prevent literary criticism from lapsing "into contentment with simple and easy procedures and a narrow range of questions and distinctions." He wished to place literary criticism in the larger context of the "humanities," and to revive methods (such as those of the Aristotelian tradition) which could supplement current practices. The title of his 1953 collection of lectures and essays, *The Languages of Criticism and the Structure of Poetry,* sums up his major concern: to bring the whole range of critical languages to bear on the problems of formal analysis.

One sign of the New Criticism's growing parochialism was its identification with the academic world and its separation from the less tidy world of the reviewer or man of letters. The variety of interests and procedures displayed by that archetypal American man of letters, Edmund Wilson, is a reminder of how much the New Criticism excluded as it hardened into orthodoxy. Although none of Wilson's essays has the classic dimensions of the best essays by Lionel Trilling or Blackmur, his total achievement is marked by a force of personality and an openness that are truly liberating. Much of his best work belonged to the years before World War II, but throughout the Cold War and its aftermath he remained what he had once called Hemingway, a "gauge of morale," the one critic who most consistently reflected the complex cultural life of his time. In the essays of *The Triple Thinkers* (1938) and *The Wound and the Bow* (1941) he had managed to bring together in a literary context those twin obsessions of the 1930s, Freudianism and Marxism, but he was never imprisoned by these doctrines and remained open to new experience. In his postwar reviews of contemporary literature and his excursions into American history, such as *Apologies to the Iroquois* (1960) and *Patriotic Gore* (1962), Wilson followed the "idea of what literary criticism ought to be" announced in the dedication to *Axel's Castle* (1931): "a history of man's ideas and imaginings in the setting of the conditions which have shaped them." His writings are a constant reminder of how much literary criticism stands to lose when it neglects the traditional role of the man of letters.

By 1953 the poet Randall Jarrell could complain, in *Poetry and the Age,* that he was living in an "age of criticism," where the main job of the critic—"simply to help us with works of art"—had been obscured and criticism had become a nearly autonomous activity, with many students preferring a "reading" of *King Lear* or *The Turn of the Screw* to the works themselves. Jarrell's tone would have been even more shrill if he had written the essay a few years later, since the last quarter-century has witnessed an increase in theoretical speculation and abstract discussion unprecedented in the history of English or

American literary criticism—a decisive and perhaps permanent shift away from the pragmatic poet-critic and toward the theoretical critic, who often draws his models from other disciplines. Before the mid-1950s practice had always weighed more heavily than theory, and a poet-critic such as John Berryman could move easily through the 1930s and 1940s feeling unthreatened by any "school," content to work from instinct and need rather than theory. Looking back over his early career in 1970, shortly before his death, Berryman could say: "I think my critical practice has attached itself to no school, though it was influenced in its inception by T. S. Eliot, R. P. Blackmur, Ezra Pound, and William Empson . . . My interest in critical *theory* has been slight." This is the classic stance of the English or American poet-critic, who seeks—in Wallace Stevens's words—"to discover, not impose," who believes that literary criticism is a post facto process, in which the critic generalizes upon the shape of what has been written and is always responsive to the needs of contemporary writers. Whereas the continental practice has often been to create a theoretical model out of an alliance with philosophy and aesthetics, and then fit literature to that model, the traditional English and American habit has been to work from a fluid and pragmatic sense of literary reality. It may be argued against this view that critics such as Coleridge or Emerson or Pater often worked from preconceived theory, but in general the style of Anglo-American criticism has been tentative and unsystematic. Over the past twenty-five years, however, much of the best American literary criticism has been aggressively "continental" in both source and method. Partly this has been the result of a lack of major, revolutionary writers who could demand the critic's attention and force him to come to terms with their untidy accomplishments. Without a Joyce or a Pound or a Stevens to be assimilated, criticism itself has become creative and self-sustaining, with critics more aware of each other than of the achievements of contemporary poets, novelists, and playwrights. Randall Jarrell's vision of an "age of criticism," which seemed somewhat exaggerated and even petulant in 1953, is more compelling today: "Criticism, which began by humbly and anomalously existing for the work of art, and was in part a mere by-product of philosophy and rhetoric, has by now become, for a good many people, almost what the work of art exists for: the animals come up to Adam and Eve and are named—the end crowns the work."

We can begin to measure this shift from "practical" to "theoretical" criticism, from literary study as devotional practice to literary study as a theology, through two major publications of 1957: *Literary Criticism: A Short History,* by William K. Wimsatt and Cleanth Brooks, and

Northrop Frye's *Anatomy of Criticism*. Admittedly an argumentative history, written from a definite point of view, the *Short History* makes the "contextual" close analysis of the New Criticism seem the natural outgrowth—even the culmination—of the history of English and American literary criticism. The chapters on critics before the twentieth century were written by W. K. Wimsatt, and in his early sections on Plato and Aristotle he sets up a dialectical movement which becomes a recurrent pattern in the tracing of later criticism. The major emphasis in the *Short History* is upon the English poet-critics and the evolving notions of poetic diction and poetic truth that resulted from their constant attempts to reform literature. More theoretical and philosophic "continental" influences are considered where appropriate, but the focus of the *Short History* is firmly upon practical matters. In the chapters on Coleridge, for example, his philosophic and theological interests are given far less emphasis than his speculations on Wordsworth's poetry and the problems of poetic diction. The chapters on twentieth-century criticism, by Cleanth Brooks, follow the New Critical themes of his own earlier works, such as *Modern Poetry and the Tradition* (1939) and *The Well Wrought Urn* (1947). Brooks is most sympathetic to a poetics of irony, which sees the individual work as a tensional union of competing forces, and he writes most compellingly of that "contextual" criticism which probes this ironic balance through close analysis of language, imagery, and local structure. He is less well disposed toward psychological, mythic, and archetypal criticism, being more interested in the uniqueness of the work of art than in its place in a family of types or kinds. He is resistant to all criticism which tries to impose "extra-literary" values and methods. The emphasis is finally upon the work of art as an independent structure.

The last chapter of *Literary Criticism: A Short History,* written by Wimsatt, goes beyond Brooks's summary accounts of modern criticism to provide an almost metaphysical rationale for the New Criticism in its most liberal and subtle forms. This essay, like the late essays of R. P. Blackmur, belongs to what Walter Jackson Bate once called the "autumnal mood" of the New Criticism, where the formal study of literature reaches out toward larger cultural and ethical relevance. Wimsatt finds in the unifying power of irony or paradox that ability to unite form and spirit, to make the concrete universal, which is a literary counterpart to the religious concept of Incarnation. In this epilogue Wimsatt places the theories of Richards, Eliot, and their followers in a line of argument initiated by Coleridge in Chapter XIV of *Biographia Literaria,* where the reconciling power of the imagination is seen as an analogue to divine creation.

The poet, described in *ideal* perfection, brings the whole soul of man into activity, with the subordination of its faculties to each other, according to their relative worth and dignity. He diffuses a tone and spirit of unity, that blends, and (as it were) *fuses,* each into each, by that synthetic and magical power, to which we have exclusively appropriated the name of imagination. This power, first put in action by the will and understanding, and retained under their irremissive, though gentle and unnoticed, control (*laxis effertur habenis*) reveals itself in the balance or reconciliation of opposite or discordant qualities: of sameness, with difference; of the general, with the concrete; the idea, with the image; the individual, with the representative; the sense of novelty and freshness, with old and familiar objects; a more than usual state of emotion, with more than usual order; judgement ever awake and steady self-possession, with enthusiasm and feeling profound or vehement; and while it blends and harmonizes the natural and the artificial, still subordinates art to nature; the manner to the matter; and our admiration of the poet to our sympathy with the poetry.

This passage, first quoted in connection with wit and irony by T. S. Eliot in his seminal essay on Andrew Marvell and later discussed by I. A. Richards, may be considered the sacred text of modern formalist criticism, justifying the claim that the most profound of human paradoxes can be uncovered through rigorous analysis of a particular poetic context. Wimsatt's epilogue to the *Short History* makes a third-generation, more humane, more "Arnoldian" stage of the New Criticism seem the inevitable future, toward which the whole history of English and American literary criticism has been tending. Wimsatt believes that "poetry is truth of 'coherence,' rather than truth of 'correspondence,' " and that the job of the critic is to explore the formal coherence of image and metaphor; but he also believes that there is a close internal relationship between "form" and "tension of values and emotions."

Such tension can occur at structural levels or in local detail of symbols and metaphors. It can be read as metaphoric meaning here and there in poems or as metaphoric character or dimension extending all through poems and constituting their very "imitative" relation to the world of reality which with their aid and in them we come to know. For excellent reasons the *discordia concors* of the metaphysical metaphor or simile has seemed to some critics of our generation the very type and acme of the poetic structure. Such a figure is at least a small-scale model, a manageable miniature, in which a critic may more or less readily scrutinize certain features: the non-literal confrontation of vehicle and tenor, the pull of opposite values and feelings . . .

For Wimsatt this tensional union of the general and the concrete in the particular contexts of poetry has moral implications, and fits most comfortably into "the vision of suffering, the optimism, the mystery which are embraced in the religious dogma of the Incarnation." Like the Eliot of *Four Quartets,* Wimsatt turns easily from the words of poetry to the Word of Christian theology.

Although Wimsatt's final chapter is moving and persuasive, it can be seen from the perspective of twenty years as truly an "epilogue," speaking more of the past than the future. The future belonged to different critical approaches, and the schematic, "structural," value-free work of Northrop Frye, with its dazzling ability to include and classify all literary productions, can be taken as prologue to the last twenty years. *Anatomy of Criticism* (1957) had its origins in Frye's earlier study of William Blake, *Fearful Symmetry* (1947), and resulted from his desire to understand the general structures of such highly patterned works as Spenser's *Faerie Queene,* Blake's prophetic books, Joyce's *Finnegans Wake,* and the "seasonal" long poems of the later Wallace Stevens. Like Stanley Edgar Hyman or Richard Chase (whose *Quest for Myth* appeared in 1949), Frye was deeply influenced by modern anthropological studies of myth and ritual, which provided a new language for classifying literary works and therefore could counter the New Critical bias against criticism by type or genre. The larger contributions of the *Anatomy,* and of Frye's subsequent works, will be touched on later in this chapter. For the purposes of the present argument, it is enough to note that Frye's aim is "structural" in a sense very different from Wimsatt's use of that term, a sense closer to that found in the phrase "structural linguistics" or in the "structural anthropology" of Claude Lévi-Strauss. That is to say, Frye is most interested in the relations *between* literary phenomena, not in the phenomena themselves: his criticism is focused on the structural patterns that unite a large work or bind together many diverse works into a type or genre. *Anatomy of Criticism* is a product of vast learning, containing references to literally hundreds of literary works, but they are deliberately not discussed in any detail. Frye is interested in "groups" or "families" of literary works. He feels that the study of genres has advanced very little since the time of Aristotle, who approached poetry "as a biologist would approach a system of organisms, picking out its genera and species, formulating the broad laws of literary experience, and in short writing as though he believed that there is a totally intelligible structure of knowledge attainable about poetry which is not poetry itself, or the experience of it, but poetics." Aiming to induce this "poetics" from the whole range of literary phenomena, Frye constructs his theories of symbols, myths, and genres, constantly classifying and schematizing. The chief object of his scrutiny is the "literary archetype," which differs from the archetypes of psychological or anthropological criticism in that it is "an element of one's literary experience as a whole," not a recurrent pattern in the individual mind or the racial consciousness. Poems are made out of other poems, literature feeds upon itself according to its own laws; and Frye is determined to systematize this other world, this "second nature" which is our total literary experience.

Anatomy of Criticism represents in many ways a profound interruption of the Anglo-American critical tradition. The customary functions of the great critics from Johnson to Eliot, "discrimination" and "judgment," are deliberately overturned. Frye is not interested in the qualities which make works of art different from each other, but in those qualities which make them look the same. Works of widely different value can live comfortably in the same sentence, because they share structural similarities. In a perceptive early review of the *Anatomy,* the English critic Frank Kermode pointed out that although Shakespeare's *Othello,* the opera *Otello,* and the "bloody little story" by Cinthio from which they derive are radically different in form and quality, Frye would be content to show how they resemble each other. In fact, Frye specifically rejects the traditional metaphor of the "critic as judge," leaving matters of judgment to the book reviewers. He shares with his modern predecessors a post-Romantic view of the poem as an autonomous organism, which exists independently from the intentions of its creator: "the poet, who writes creatively rather than deliberately, is not the father of his poem; he is at best a midwife, or, more accurately still, the womb of Mother Nature herself: her privates he, so to speak. The fact that revision is possible, that a poet can make changes in a poem not because he likes them better but because they are better, shows clearly that the poet has to give birth to the poem as it passes through his mind. He is responsible for delivering it in as uninjured a state as possible, and if the poem is alive, it is equally anxious to be rid of him, and screams to be cut loose from all the navel-strings and feeding-tubes of his ego."

Commenting in the *Short History* on an earlier version of this bizarre analogy, which appeared in Frye's "My Credo" (1951), Cleanth Brooks said that in Frye's world the critic actually becomes "the midwife and nurse, who ties off the cord, tells the mother the infant is a boy or girl, washes it up for presentation to the outside world, and presumably gives it an anthropological classification and takes its Bertillion measurements." If the poet is the partly unconscious source of the poem, the critic takes on the exalted role of conscious custodian and classifier. Unlike the traditional poet-critic, who was assumed to have special authority because of his intimate knowledge of the creative process, Frye's ideal critic takes his authority from his familiarity with other disciplines and makes claim to knowledge beyond that of the poet. "In short, is the aim to make criticism a purely descriptive, value-free social science?" asked Brooks when confronted with "My Credo." The answer of the *Anatomy* is, to a large extent, "Yes."

If *Anatomy of Criticism* is a major work of enduring importance, as I believe it to be, then it is the first great work of English or American literary criticism not produced by a practicing artist, and signals a decisive turn toward the continental model. The critic is no longer the servant of the artist but a colleague, with his own special knowledge and powers. Northrop Frye is a writer of great humanity and culture, and these qualities shine through even the most schematic parts of the *Anatomy*; but he provides a system which tempts the critic to interpose himself between the artist and the audience as an independent creative force. *Anatomy of Criticism* is itself a high work of the organizing imagination. As Frank Kermode said in his 1958 review, "it would be reasonable to treat this as a work of criticism which has turned into literature, for it is centripetal, autonomous, and ethical without, I think, being useful." Kermode is here employing "useful" in the sense of the critic who patiently analyzes and explains, conscious of the individuality of the literary work and the practical needs of the reader. Like every admirer of the *Anatomy*, Kermode has been influenced by it, and his own recent work has tended toward more "structural" interests. But the fact remains that Frye made extravagant claims for criticism that were relatively new to the Anglo-American tradition, and delivered a system which—when manipulated by less subtle minds—tended to homogenize literature and give the critic a spurious authority.

As the monolithic social and political attitudes of the 1950s gave way to the diversity and conflict of the 1960s, literary criticism also lost its monolithic appearance. In spite of his many radical departures from the New Criticism, Frye had retained in the *Anatomy* many of the "Symbolist" assumptions about the autonomy of the work of art and its need to be described in literary terms: his theory of archetypes may be seen as a purely literary application of the archetypal theories developed by the anthropological critics (especially the followers of Sir James Frazer) and Jungian psychologists. But other critics were less suspicious of "extraliterary" approaches, and the critical landscape of the 1960s was marked by a number of attempts to align literary study with other disciplines. By 1967 the Modern Language Association could give this new historicism academic sanction by publishing a collection of essays, under the editorship of James Thorpe, called *Relations of Literary Study: Essays on Interdisciplinary Contributions.* The essays in this collection represent a new (or rather renewed) spectrum of interests: "Literature and History," "Literature and Myth" (by Northrop Frye), "Literature and Biography," "Literature and Psychology," "Literature and Sociology," "Literature and Religion," "Literature and Music." The formalist critics of an earlier generation had reacted against the narrow concept of literary criticism which emphasized source studies, philology, or naive biographical analysis and substituted "the history of ideas" or "the life of the artist" for the work itself. During the heyday of the New Criticism, many scholars and critics had continued to use and refine "extraliterary" methods, but often with a sense of being outside the critical establishment, and it was not until the end of the 1950s that such work regained theoretical respectability. In effect, another period of social crisis and cultural anxiety brought to the surface the concerns of the 1930s, when Marxism and Freudianism had been uneasily joined as the twin enemies of repression, but these concerns took new forms.

Any chapter heading in *Relations of Literary Study* could provide a rubric for tracing the interactions between criticism and society in the 1960s, but "Literature and Psychology" provides the neatest paradigm. Frederick Crews, the author of this chapter, began his critical work in the late 1950s as a student of the New Criticism, and his brilliant collection of parodies, *The Pooh Perplex* (1963), displays an ironic and detached attitude toward all critical dogmas. In the early 1960s, however, Crews adopted the language and techniques of Freudian criticism, and produced a psychoanalytic study of Nathaniel Hawthorne, *The Sins of the Fathers* (1966). This study shows Crews, like so many critics of his generation, reacting against such artificial restraints as the "intentional fallacy" and the "affective fallacy," seeking to restore the full range of our literary responses. As Crews put it in 1966, "the literary work which is completely free from its biographical determinants is not to be found, and in many of the greatest works—the prime example is *Hamlet*—unresolved emotion and latent contradiction are irreducibly involved in the aesthetic effect. To appreciate why there are gaps in the surface we must be prepared to inspect what lies beneath them." In other words, Crews joins with the early Eliot in finding "gaps" in *Hamlet,* but instead of discussing Shakespeare's failure to attain formal objectivity, he is interested in probing the psychological motives for doubt and conflict.

Crews's 1967 essay "Literature and Psychology" reflects both the enthusiasm and the impatience with opponents that characterize a new believer. But as the decade rounded to a close, and Crews became deeply involved in the New Left movement and resistance to the Vietnam war, his feelings about psychoanalytic criticism became more qualified. His humane good sense was offended by the fashionable blend of Marxism and Freudianism (as in Herbert Marcuse) that seemed to justify all adolescent forms of rebellion without touching the serious reasons for social and cultural discontent. Crews emerged from this period of social activism with a more chastened and complex view of psychoanalytic criticism, which insists on its permanent usefulness while acknowledging the dangers of reductionism and self-indulgence. He is especially suspicious of the confessional tendencies in some recent psychological criticism, such as that of Norman N. Holland, whose progress from *Psychoanalysis and Shakespeare* (1966) and *The Dynamics of Literary Response* (1968) to *Five Readers Reading* (1975) has been a movement toward a more aggressively affective criticism, where the reader's individual response is the object of psychological analysis. It is almost as if Holland had returned to the methods of I. A. Richards's *Practical Criticism* (1929), but without Richards's desire to rationalize individual responses through a common understanding of the poetic context. In his recent collection of essays stretching from 1967 to 1975, *Out of My System* (1975), Crews provides an intellectual autobiography which not only documents his new and more compromised view of Freudian methods but gives a sensible and humane account of the social pressures that affected the responsible critic during those chaotic years.

In contrast to Holland's psychoanalytic analysis of reader response, Stanley Fish has tried to develop a more open method in which every reader becomes an author. Beginning with his early study of Milton, *Surprised by Sin* (1967), Fish placed more emphasis on the temporal experience of reading than on that spatial apprehension of the finished work which lies at the heart of formalist procedures. In his 1970 essay "Affective Stylistics: Literature in the Reader" and in subsequent works, Fish has claimed that the subject of criticism should be "the developing responses of the reader in relation to the words as they succeed one another in time." His method is admirable in that it frees the reader and the text from any kind of psychological determinism, focusing on the "specifically human activity of reading." By resisting the notion of a completed spatial form which can only be analyzed in retrospect, Fish has escaped the static and dehumanized nature of so much formalist criticism. But his method ultimately leads to a creative relativism in which one reading is much like another in value, uncontrolled by the intentions of the author or the conditions of his age. Fish may find this world of multiple and self-confirming readings "creative" and "liberating," but many others will miss that drive toward a center of generally accepted meanings which is the essence of historical and formalist criticism.

Another trend of the 1960s was the increased attention given to prose fiction. The inherent bias of the New Criticism toward novelists (such as James and Joyce) whose works demand close linguistic analysis found a major corrective in Wayne Booth's *The Rhetoric of Fiction* (1961). Following the example of R. S. Crane and the Chicago critics, Booth makes broad generic distinctions and tries to judge each kind of fiction by its own standards. His work began as a reaction against those formalist critics who insisted on taking the novel as a poetic construct, who assumed an absolute value in the unified "point of view," and who denigrated those fictions where the "telling" is overt and the author stands in direct rhetorical relationship to his audience. Although weak in its treatment of some modern works, Booth's study is masterly in its handling of authorial "distance" and its attack on what the New Critics called "the heresy of plot." By enlarging our sense of the many ways in which prose fiction can be criticized, Booth also enlarged the accepted "great tradition," returning the earlier eighteenth-century and Victorian novelists to a central position denied them by the rigorous formalist critics.

A second major study of fiction that had a liberating impact was *The Nature of Narrative* (1966), by Robert Scholes and Robert Kellogg. Greatly indebted to Frye's *Anatomy* and especially to his theory of fictional modes, Scholes and Kellogg present the modern novel not as a sophisticated organism which has evolved from more primitive forms, but as simply one more kind of "narrative." The genealogy of the novel constructed by Scholes and Kellogg served, like Booth's *Rhetoric of Fiction,* to break down the orthodox assumption that one kind of fiction (which we might call "Jamesian") merits special status and consideration. Like the work of Frye, their broad classifications expanded our sense of what the literary "text" can be, and provided a view of fiction which cut across the normal distinctions between poetry, epic, and the novel.

The changes in critical emphasis which took place in the decade after Frye's *Anatomy* are summed up in three documents of 1965–1966: Susan Sontag's *Against Interpretation and Other Essays* (1966); J. Hillis Miller's "The Antitheses of Criticism," general reflections on the Yale Colloquium on Literary Criticism held in spring 1965; and Geoffrey Hartman's crucial essay which gave its title to his later collection, *Beyond Formalism: Literary Essays, 1958–1970*. Sontag's essay "Against Interpretation," in its wild oscillations between revolutionary slogans and conventional remarks on the need for more attention to "form," looks forward to the late 1960s and backward toward the New Criticism. Her fundamental point is one that the best New Critics would have applauded: interpretation based on content or a search for the author's intentions is stultifying and distorting. "What is needed," she claims, "is more attention to form in art. If excessive stress on *content* provokes the arrogance of interpretation, more extended and more thorough descriptions of *form* would silence. What is needed is a vocabulary—a descriptive, rather than prescriptive, vocabulary—for forms. The best criticism, and it is uncommon, is of this sort that dissolves considerations of content into those of form." This unexceptional appeal for flexibility and tact is then followed by a scarcely avant-garde list of the best critics, including Panofsky, Frye, Erich Auerbach, and Walter Benjamin. But the tone of the essay runs counter to this moderation, with calls for an "erotics of art" and wistful glances at that lost paradise before the fall into interpretation when we could confront art directly with an innocent eye. In this regard, "Against Interpretation" points forward to the ambivalences of the late 1960s and early 1970s, when serious social criticism and literary commentary became entangled with a new hedonism and anti-intellectualism.

Geoffrey Hartman's title sounds much like Sontag's, but he is out for bigger game in a more serious manner. Having already shown a mastery of formalist analysis in his early work on Wordsworth and Hopkins, Hartman takes as his target not formalism per se but explication, the precritical act of close analysis which had long since become ritualized in America's schools and universities.

There is good reason why many in this country, as well as in Europe, have voiced a suspicion of "Anglo-Saxon formalism." The dominion of Exegesis is great: she is our Whore of Babylon, sitting robed in Academic black on the great dragon of Criticism, and dispensing a repetitive and soporific balm from her pedantic cup. If our neo-scriptural activity of explication were as daring and conscious as it used to be when Bible texts had to be harmonized with strange or contrary experience: i.e. with history, no one could level this charge of puerility. Yet our present explication-centered criticism *is* puerile, or at most pedagogic: we forget its merely preparatory function, that it stands to a mature criticism as pastoral to epic.

Hartman's essay is really a call to move beyond explication to a more profound formalism, which can give free play to critical intuition (our accumulated literary wisdom) and a sense of history. He is equally critical in laying out the limitations of Cleanth Brooks, with his exegetical procedures, and Georges Poulet, with his antiformalist stance. Poulet and the other critics of the "Geneva School" had a large influence in the 1960s on American critics such as J. Hillis Miller, but Hartman can find little satisfaction in a criticism which turns away from the work's objective qualities and seeks to recreate the consciousness of an author or a literary period. In its uneasiness with current formalist procedures and its simultaneous unwillingness to abandon the formalist position, Hartman's essay clearly reflects the ambivalence of a new generation of American critics.

J. Hillis Miller's account of the 1965 Yale Colloquium on Literary Criticism begins in this fashion:

> This Colloquium testifies to an important shift of focus in American literary criticism. The temper of the conference can be accounted for partly by the topics chosen for papers and partly by the fact that so many of the participants are European-trained or teach in departments of romance language or of comparative literature. Even so, the new orientations of the Colloquium have significance for American criticism generally. A few years ago one would have expected an American colloquium on literary criticism to be a dialogue between our native formalism and other approaches. Quite recently, for example, Professor Murray Krieger described present-day literary criticism in America in terms of a conflict between a fading "new criticism" and the archetypal approach. The latter is, for Krieger, the most viable alternative. At the Yale Colloquium, however, neither the new criticism nor archetypal criticism figured centrally, in spite of the fact that there was a paper on the work of Northrop Frye. There was hostility to neither, but a sense that their lessons can be taken for granted. For most of the participants part of the impetus for the next advances in literary study will come from one form or another of European criticism. Assimilating the best recent continental criticism, American scholars may come to develop new forms of criticism growing out of American culture as well as out of the encounter with European thought.

Miller's summary has turned out to be only partially prophetic. Much

71

of the best American criticism of the last decade or more has come from encounters with European thought, but its relation to "American culture" has been much more problematic. American criticism in the 1940s and 1950s was dominated by conservative, southern writers, and could have been accused of both parochialism and a reactionary political-social bias. Recent criticism, on the other hand, seems often to be operating in a cultural vacuum, with little revelance to any of the major movements in American cultural life. The pragmatic nature of our native critical tradition has proved resistant, even antagonistic, to the theoretical aims of much European criticism, with the result that there has been a split between the theoretical critics (who claim to seek a nonelitist audience) and the criticism written for general readers and students. Criticism was not less affected than other cultural activities by the disruptions of the Vietnam years, often (as we shall see later in the case of Lionel Trilling) with tragic results. At a time when left-wing activists were calling for the overthrow of a "counter-revolutionary" curriculum based on elitist masterpieces, any attempt to focus on style or form was viewed by some as a deliberate act of oppression, diverting the reader's consciousness from political implications. In this charged atmosphere American culture revealed once again its inability to produce major literary critics with a deep understanding of social processes. Wilson and Trilling carried on their work, but they were somewhat removed by age and past experience from the contemporary scene. Alfred Kazin and Irving Howe, heirs of an earlier left-wing tradition, did fine work in preserving a cultural perspective, and remained open to the achievements of young writers. The essays in Kazin's *Contemporaries* (1962) and Howe's *The Critical Point* (1973), as well as Kazin's later study of the novel from Hemingway to Mailer, *Bright Book of Life* (1973), reveal a resistance to narrow fashions and a willingness to talk plainly about the social implications of avant-garde experiments. Along with Leslie Fiedler, whose *Love and Death in the American Novel* (1960) had combined archetypal with social criticism, Howe and Kazin sought to maintain a balanced view of modernist writing and the postmodernist reactions. Their attention to the novel, a form often shunned by more systematic criticism, reflected the seriousness of their engagement with contemporary culture. But Kazin and Howe and Fiedler were not able to attain the commanding position of the English social critic Raymond Williams, and the 1960s produced no literary spokesman in the sense that Edmund Wilson had been a spokesman for the decades from 1920 to 1950.

The strain of these years told on even the most fastidious of critics, as Hartman's essay of 1970, "Toward Literary History," clearly shows. In the spirit of the time, Hartman proclaims the death of "high culture," which has been hastened to its end by social change and by the democratization of the literary text (Frye, for example, had broken down the barriers between popular and highbrow art by stressing structural connections and abolishing value judgment.)

> We look back at Pound and Eliot, at Bridges and Yeats, and we realize that their elitist view of culture is dead. Though their art aimed for the genuine vernacular, it could not resist the appeal of forms associated with high culture, forms that remained an 'ideological' reflex of upper-class mentality. To purge this ideological stain, and to rescue art from the imputation of artiness, the writer had to become his own enemy. Today all art stands in a questionable relation to elite modes of thought and feeling. But while the artist moves closer to self-criticism, the critic moves closer to art by expanding the notion of form until it cannot be narrowly linked to the concerns of a priestly culture or its mid-cult imitations.

Moving from this assumption (which seems far less secure now than it did in 1970), Hartman reviews what he takes to be the strengths and inadequacies of four approaches to form and literary history: Marxism, Frye's theory of archetypes, and "two kinds of structuralist theory, that of C. Lévi-Strauss, and that of I. A. Richards and the Anglo-American critics." Hartman is especially acute in his comments on Frye, showing that he has produced a system which is not truly comparative, since it ignores national or ideological differences and depends on a purely literary framework in which diverse works can exist easily side by side. "The shift in linguistics from individual languages (or sign systems) to language in general (or semiotics) and from there to structures of the mind parallels Frye's shift from the individual work of art to literature as a totality and from there to a 'verbal universe' which exhibits archetypes basic to science as well." According to Hartman, Claude Lévi-Strauss differs from Frye in that he deals with "real social problems," and it is this historical consciousness that Hartman wishes to infuse into literary criticism.

Hartman reserves his harshest comments for the "unity or reconciliation" discovered in the work of art by the New Critics, claiming that the leading terms of the by now "Old Criticism"—unity, complexity, maturity, coherence—are "code words shored against the ruins." His argument is subtle and sophisticated, if perhaps based on too immediate a sense of a culture under stress, but when the time comes for Hartman to produce his answer, he sketches a theory of the national spirit, of Genius and *Genius Loci,* which is both vague and speculative. Moreover, the writing in this essay and others of the time—unlike Hartman's earlier writing—is marked by carefully sprung colloquialisms ("hang-ups") and ponderous witticisms ("Apollo retrieved his garland by hobnobbing with hobgoblin") which mesh uneasily with the generally academic style and point toward the excesses of Hartman's later essays.

At least on the level of theoretical speculation, American literary criticism since 1970 has been dominated by Hartman and his Yale colleagues Paul de Man, J. Hillis Miller, and Harold Bloom, and we will do well to explore their ideas and vocabularies, since their work has contributed in large measure to the current split between theoretical criticism and the daily business of literary study, as carried out in the classroom, the more popular literary journals, and traditional works of scholarship and particular criticism. Miller, de Man, and Hartman differ in many ways, but they have in common an admiration for continental critics (especially Jacques Derrida) and a sense of literary criticism as a dialogue among critics. Their work is one result of the shift toward theory already charted, and of the historical fact that we are not confronted with contemporary writers of such overwhelming power that they command the critic's attention. The result (Coleridge without Wordsworth?) is a self-regarding criticism that can easily become an end in itself. These critics share a delight in word play and linguistic high jinks which is straight from France, from the world of Derrida and Jacques Lacan, and this explains the curious feeling of déjà-vu that pervades much of their work. Official French literary criticism never experienced *Seven Types of Ambiguity,* and was untouched by the linguistic experiments of Joyce and his imitators a half-century ago. As a result, France is only today catching up with the verbal play of modernism. It is no accident that Joyce's *Finnegans Wake* is presently a cult text of French avant-garde criticism. Although it is written in a form of English and stubbornly refuses to yield its secrets to those without a profound knowledge of the English language, *Finnegans Wake* appears to many French critics to be an international polyglot text, the ideal testing ground for a criticism of creative word play. Partly under the spell of this French criticism, and partly out of a desire to make criticism a "creative" presence, the new equivalent to Arnold's Culture, some of the Yale critics—for all their learning and brilliance—have constructed verbal systems so remote from the experiences of the average intelligent reader as to be separate worlds, which demand special glosses and commentaries.

In a survey of recent American literary criticism published in the

New Republic in 1975, J. Hillis Miller briefly surveyed the works of more conventional critics and then turned from these critics, who remain "mostly innocent, whether innocently or not, of any continental tinge," to consider that large body of "the most significant Anglo-American literary criticism," which "would have been impossible without the continental 'influence.'" The last paragraph of his essay deserves quotation, since it represents much contemporary criticism that is engaged in a search for absolutes.

> Hartman, Bloom and de Man are members, in fact, of a new group of critics centered at Yale. These critics are by no means unified in their methodological commitments. They share questions rather than answers, but draw strength, often by opposition, from one another's example. To this group may be added Jacques Derrida, who now presents a seminar at Yale in the early fall of each year. The fundamental issue at stake among the members of this group is the question whether the "cure of the ground" which Stevens demands of poetry and of discourse about poetry is to be a "grounding," a making solid of the foundation, as one 'cures' a fiber-glass hull, or whether the ground is to be cured by being effaced, made to vanish, as medicine cures a man of disease by taking it away. As Stevens says, the rock is air, "nothingness," "the dominant blank, the unapproachable." Is a "cure of the ground" the clearing away of the ground, leaving nothing to stand on, or is it a securing of the ground, making it firm, so one can build on it? Space limitations forbid exploring this difference now. It must suffice here to say that the difference generates the inner drama or *polemos* of contemporary criticism, for example that among the members of the Yale group.

Miller's use of Wallace Stevens is typical of this criticism, and it is always the Stevens of *The Necessary Angel,* who in his essays and lectures of the 1940s sought to construct a theoretical ground for his great last poems of seasonal change. Like Stevens, these critics are pressing toward the "central," toward some master theory, but without taking into account Stevens's admonition in *The Necessary Angel*: "The adherents of the central are also mystics to begin with. But all their desire and all their ambition is to press away from mysticism toward that ultimate good sense which we term civilization." Too much contemporary criticism resembles the ideas of Wallace Stevens when they have been abstracted from his poetry, taken from a context rich in its involvement with the particulars of time and place. The "mysticism" is seldom counterbalanced by a feeling for our common experience, "that ultimate good sense which we term civilization."

Perhaps the most commanding figure in recent American literary criticism is Harold Bloom, whose revisionary judgments and theory of "influence" became a centerpiece for discussion in the mid-1970s. Bloom possesses all the necessary talents of the great critic: a deep knowledge of the literary past, a phenomenal verbal memory, and a passionate commitment to literary study. He believes, with Wallace Stevens, that "words of the world are the life of the world," and it is this energy of belief that makes his writing so compelling. Bloom was taught by the masters of the New Criticism, but his temperament early led him to an appreciation of Romantic visionary poetry, and his first works—*Shelley's Mythmaking* (1959), *The Visionary Company* (1961, a companion to the Romantic poets), and *Blake's Apocalypse* (1963)— represent an attempt to come to terms with the mythopoetic qualities of the major Romantic poets. During the 1960s, however, Bloom came to feel that he could not do justice to these poets and their inheritors without creating a new frame of reference, moving beyond the assumptions and terminologies of his early models, M. H. Abrams and Northrop Frye. His massive study of Yeats (1970), which emphasizes Yeats's Romantic and mystical affinities at the expense of his modernism, revealed Bloom in a state of intellectual transition, determined (like Blake) to create his own system rather than be enslaved by another man's. In the studies following *Yeats,* especially *The Anxiety of Influence* (1973), *A Map of Misreading* (1975), *Poetry and Repression* (1976), and *Wallace Stevens: The Poems of Our Climate* (1977), Bloom has developed a theory of literary influence which traces recurrent patterns of anxiety and evasion in the literary works of the past two centuries. Briefly stated, Bloom believes that no writer since Milton has been able to maintain the easy attitude toward literary precursors that marked the classical and Renaissance worlds. The willing "imitation of models" has given way to anxiety in the face of past achievements, and the modern poet, haunted by his "belatedness" in the sequence of literary history, is faced with the choice of ignoble submission or agonized resistance. "Weak" poets succumb to the tradition, while "strong" poets do battle with their literary ancestors and, through a ritual of conscious and unconscious "misreading," assert their own identities by deforming the achievements of their predecessors. In this view of literary history, the archetypal "strong" poet is Milton, who did battle not only with Homer and Virgil but with his greatest precursor, the Author of Scripture; and the archetypal "weak" poet is T. S. Eliot, who in *Four Quartets* makes an accommodation with the past through humility, affection, and love. Hence Bloom's notorious judgments on Eliot, which go far beyond any response to his particular achievements. When Bloom states, as he did in 1977, that Eliot is the most overrated writer of the twentieth century, his remarks must be read in the context of *The Anxiety of Influence* and *A Map of Misreading*: "Most overrated: T. S. Eliot, *all* of him, verse and prose; the academy, or clerisy, needed him as their defense against their own anxieties of uselessness. His neo-Christianity became their mask, hiding their sense of being forlorn and misplaced. His verse is (mostly) weak; his prose is wholly tendentious." This passage is aimed at a "straw man," at an exaggerated assessment of Eliot's importance now twenty years out of date; it must be read as a strident defense of Bloom's theory of literary influence, which is most explicitly and powerfully challenged by the Eliot of *Four Quartets*.

In order to analyze the struggle between the would-be poet and his strong precursors, Bloom has developed a set of rhetorical terms that apply both to the progress of the poet and to the structure of individual "crisis" poems, such as Wordsworth's Intimations Ode and Yeats's "The Wild Swans at Coole." It is this private vocabulary—*clinamen, tessera, kenosis, daemonization, askesis, apophrades,* and their later refinements—that has offended so many readers, who often argue that Bloom is describing in a willful and unnecessarily obscure fashion problems that have been known to generations of critics. It has long been recognized that the writer's relationship to the past underwent a radical transformation in the late seventeenth and early eighteenth centuries. Edward Young, in his *Conjectures on Original Composition* (1759), complained that "great models *engross, prejudice, and intimidate,*" and since the time of Young the poet's sense of anxiety or inadequacy in relation to his predecessors has been a constant theme. Walter J. Bate's *The Burden of the Past and the English Poet* (1970), which appeared in the same year as Bloom's *Yeats,* explores the "accumulating anxiety" which accompanies the question "What is there left to do?" and opponents of Bloom often contrast Bate's elegant and understated work with *The Anxiety of Influence,* implying that Bloom's rhetoric is an unnecessary exercise in ego gratification. Yet there can be no doubt that Bloom's recent criticism has changed our ways of reading in a manner that Bate's scholarly monograph never could have; and if we value Bloom's work, we must accept his bizarre vocabulary as a personal necessity, just as we must accept the eccentricities of *A Vision* if we are to understand how Yeats came to his major poetry. In reading Bloom's recent works we are left with a question posed by much contemporary criticism: is the critic's role as a creative force, a rival to the poet himself (Bloom concludes *The*

Anxiety of Influence with a poem of his own), worth the inevitable distortions and pretensions? Must we "misread" in order to survive?

The answer to this question must be "Yes" if we accept the view of literary history put forward on the first page of *A Map of Misreading*: "there are *no* texts, but only relationships *between* texts. These relationships depend upon a critical act, a misreading or misprision, that one poet performs upon another, and that does not differ in kind from the necessary critical acts performed by every strong reader upon every text he encounters . . . As literary history lengthens, all poetry necessarily becomes verse-criticism, just as all criticism becomes prose-poetry." This vision of the critic's role flatly denies the traditional belief that the critic is always "belated": it implies a different relationship between critic and poet, just as Bloom's relationship to his admired contemporaries A. R. Ammons and John Ashbery—that of a powerful coequal—differs from the relationship of Arnold to Wordsworth or Eliot to Dante. Whether this movement of the critic to center stage is the inevitable product of a historical process, as Bloom's references to Vico and Nietzsche and Freud imply, or whether it is a temporary aberration which will be corrected by the next generation of truly "strong" artists, is a question that only time can unravel.

The major characteristic which separates Bloom from contemporary literary theorists is the range and effectiveness of his commentaries on particular poems. He has always claimed that his aim is "not another new poetics, but a wholly different practical criticism," and his recent books—especially the studies of Yeats and Stevens—are filled with individual readings of central poems which decisively alter our received ideas. Whether these readings are achieved in spite of the "theory of influence" and its rebarbative language, or whether they could not have been arrived at without the support of that theory, is a problem that may never be resolved. Meanwhile, we should be grateful for the readings themselves.

The foregoing sketch of American literary criticism since 1945, like all schematic accounts, is highly selective, and omits many works that later generations will consider the real triumphs of the period. I have passed over the great achievements in literary biography, such as Richard Ellmann's *James Joyce* (1959) and Leon Edel's *Henry James* (five volumes, 1953–1972), which have reached a wider audience than any theoretical criticism because they combine the insights of the literary historian and psychological critic with the methods of the traditional novelist. One might even say that as the novel has become more hermetic, concerned with structures rather than character, and as criticism has become more self-regarding, literary biography has captured the audience once held by the nineteenth-century novelists and essayists. I have also omitted the many excellent works of particular social criticism, such as those of Alfred Kazin, Leslie Fiedler, and Irving Howe; works of critical synthesis, such as E. D. Hirsch's *Validity in Interpretation* (1967); and the many great works of historical scholarship that have made the last thirty years a golden age of American scholarship. It may well be that M. H. Abrams's *The Mirror and the Lamp* (1953) and René Wellek's *A History of Modern Criticism* (five volumes, 1955–) will outlast most of the works mentioned in the preceding pages. Most regrettable of all, I have had to omit such impressive figures as Hugh Kenner and Kenneth Burke, whose criticism is *sui generis* and does not fit easily into any pattern of historical development. The title of Kenner's recent study of modern American poetry, *A Homemade World* (1975), might be applied to the accumulated writings of both Kenner and Burke. Each critic has tried in a personal, "do-it-yourself," quintessentially American way to create a "homemade world" that will compel assent through its efficiency and practicality. In his two most satisfactory works, *A Grammar of Motives* (1945) and *A Rhetoric of Motives* (1950), Burke assimilated the terminologies and methods of a wide variety of critical approaches, his ideal being a closed system in which we can easily move from one set of terms to another. Combining the insights of psychoanalysis and theology, of conservative New Critical theory and radical political analysis, Burke produced a critical machine which infuriated his contemporaries because of its eclectic nature, but which has appealed to a later generation because of its constant reliance on principles of structure. In fact, Burke can be viewed as an idiosyncratic forerunner of much recent "structuralist" theory, with the difference that beneath his polysyllabic prose there lies a deep fund of common sense. Burke is always interested in process, in the Aristotelian entelechy, and his works are best understood as a reservoir of provisional theories and insights, not the "closed" system they appear to be.

From the beginning, Hugh Kenner took as his unquestioned model the view of literary history put forward by Pound and Eliot in their early essays, and he therefore became the ideal interpreter of the modernist tradition. His studies of Pound, Joyce, Eliot, and Beckett culminated in *The Pound Era* (1971), which might be considered the "official" history of the modern writers as Pound or Eliot would have wished it to be written. As the title indicates, Kenner has not been touched by recent revisionist criticism, which has tended to produce

79

a more complicated view of the early twentieth century, with Pound and Eliot and Joyce less dominant in their influence. Kenner operates in the world of those Pound canonized, and consequently every anecdote or gesture concerning that small group takes on symbolic significance. Kenner and Burke have this in common: a genius for discovering hidden relationships, and a conviction that any relationship, once discovered, must have crucial importance. Kenner and Burke have immense talent, but this talent is not always controlled by a sense of proportion. Each creates a "homemade" world that delights us with its intricacy and order; but these worlds often seem idiosyncratic and obsessive, not easily joined to the world in which we imagine our social lives.

In his constant job of analysis, comparison, and evaluation, the literary critic finds himself poised between two worlds. One world, as Northrop Frye describes it in *The Well-Tempered Critic* (1963), is "the world in which our imaginations move and have their being while we are also living in the 'real' world, where our imaginations find the ideals that they try to pass on to belief and action, where they find the vision which is the source of both the dignity and the joy of life." The task of the critic is to chart this world while keeping us constantly aware of the "real," to remember—in Wallace Stevens's words—that most of the time "One walks easily / The unpainted shore, accepts the world / As anything but sculpture." A persistent tendency in recent American criticism has been to make unnecessary choices between these two worlds, either to treat literature as a self-sufficient "second nature" or to judge it entirely by extraliterary standards. The "perfect critic" will always avoid such choices, and if we look to American criticism since 1945 for approximations of this impossible ideal, three figures stand out: Frye himself, R. P. Blackmur, and Lionel Trilling. Having accomplished in *Anatomy of Criticism* the "pure" exercise of locating autonomous literary works in a variety of archetypal structures, Frye proceeded in his later writing to the more Arnoldian function—already adumbrated at the end of the *Anatomy*—of establishing a cultural context for literary criticism. Since he believes that "in a modern democracy a citizen participates in society mainly through his imagination," Frye has a deep belief in the formative and educational powers of literary study, and the challenges to traditional education which marked the 1960s caused him to reexamine and refine his conception of literature's social value. In the essays of *The Critical Path* (1971), Frye uses his "mythic method" to isolate two cultural myths, the "myth of concern," with its conservative emphasis on social cohesion, on what we hold in common, and the "myth of individual freedom." Frye finds a necessary tension between these "closed" and "open" attitudes, although his own temperament inclines him toward the "myth of individual freedom"; and out of this tension between concern and freedom "glimpses of a third order of experience emerge, of a world that may not exist but completes existence, the world of the definitive experience that poetry urges us to have but which we never quite get." This ideal world, which we can never quite attain because of our social lives, provides a constant example of the reconciliation of opposites that is an ethical goal.

Although *The Critical Path* is filled with references to the actual events of the late 1960s, Frye's conclusions seem curiously abstract and remote from that time and place; his persistent urge to generalize always smooths over particular social concerns. We must never forget that the title of Frye's greatest work is *Anatomy of Criticism*, not *Anatomy of Literature*, and that he believes all literary study is a transposition of literature into criticism. A more profound sense of cultural involvement is found in the later works of R. P. Blackmur. Having come to maturity in the *anni mirabiles* of modernism, 1921–1925, Blackmur was instinctively in touch with the best literature of his generation, and it is not surprising that his criticism of the 1930s contains near definitive statements on the art of Yeats, Eliot, Stevens, Cummings, Pound, and Marianne Moore. He began to write literary criticism at precisely the time when "close reading" became the dominant mode of literary analysis, and his essays of the 1930s (collected in *The Double Agent* and *The Expense of Greatness*) are models of the genre. Each essay strikes toward the essential qualities of the writer under consideration, so that each remains exciting and authoritative after nearly half a century. It is safe to say that no critic of the 1930s has worn so well.

But Blackmur was never content with the dogmas of the New Criticism, and in the 1940s his work on the great modern novelists—especially James, Dostoevsky, and Joyce—broadened the scope of his criticism. In the last fifteen years of his life (he died in 1965), Blackmur made his peace with Matthew Arnold, and combined social commentary with formal analysis in a subtle prose that makes the two inseparable. Speaking once of Allen Tate's confident discussions of vanished political and moral certainties, Blackmur said that "they have the force of virtual existence because he has experienced their need." Blackmur himself had such a need for cultural stability: like Henry Adams, the American writer he most closely resembles in temperament, he felt deeply the effects of social confusion; but unlike Adams, he believed that he could embody some idea of cultural wholeness in his personal sensibility and style. The essays of *The Lion and the Honeycomb* (1955), *Eleven Essays in the European Novel* (1964), and *A Primer of Ignorance* (1967) manage to trace in broad terms the decline of bourgeois humanism while giving full weight to the individual details of each work under consideration. Brimming with what Henry James called "felt life," they brilliantly affirm that criticism can do justice to literature's special status while maintaining our sense of its relationship to other forms of knowledge.

More even than Frye and Blackmur, Lionel Trilling saw literature as social action, the expression and ultimate critique of our common life. Like Edmund Wilson, whom he resembles in important ways, Trilling was a "man of letters," committed to an audience larger than the circle of professional critics, and like Wilson he was an heir of nineteenth-century historical scholarship, fascinated by the dynamic exchanges between culture and personality that produce the representative work of art. Both Wilson and Trilling were interested in the energy that flows from art into society, not just in the social forces that determine literary form. Both reacted against the determinism of old-fashioned historical study, but both wished to preserve the best in historicism. They knew that we can never fully recapture the life of another age, that something essential in culture—its vibrant details, its unstated assumptions—must be forever lost in time. We can never recover the full sense of Shakespeare that the Elizabethan audience had, but neither can we make Shakespeare wholly our contemporary unless we have a taste for farce or caricature. The historical imagination is an accommodation between past and present. Wilson and Trilling had this in common: they shied away from the notion of the autonomous work of art, and from the kind of criticism that is concerned only with formal qualities. They could not conceive of a satisfactory method of literary study which did not involve the moral, social, and historical dimensions of literature.

Looking back over Trilling's full career, we see that it is marked—like that of all major critics—by a deep consistency which did not prevent him from responding alertly to political and social change. When we read the best of Trilling's essays, we are immediately aware that they are "of that time, of that place," yet concerned with permanent problems of literary and social life. His early studies of Matthew Arnold (1939) and E. M. Forster (1943) led to his lifelong admiration for the nineteenth-century liberal imagination, which held that the "self" was defined through integration with society, and this theme is examined in the magisterial essays of *The Liberal Imagination* (1950) and *The Opposing Self* (1955). Typical of Trilling's method is his famous essay "Freud and Literature," which attempts a balanced assessment of literature's relationship to psychoanalysis (the moral would seem to be that Freudian theory owes more to literature than it can ever repay). With characteristic elegance and precision, Trilling lays bare the inadequacies in Freud's early theory of the artistic process, only to affirm the immense value of "his whole conception of the mind . . . which makes poetry indigenous to the very constitution of the mind." Like all Trilling's best essays, this one reflects an admirable sanity and centrality of purpose. We feel that the critic is speaking of what matters in our common experience, and giving literature its proper place as only one of many social activities, but perhaps the one most concerned with the formation of our moral lives.

The major limitation in Trilling's criticism is its deliberately restricted subject matter. Like the early Blackmur, he is preoccupied with the "modern," with those writers and works of the nineteenth and twentieth centuries that have shaped our contemporary sensibility. But within this area of the "modern," no recent American critic has ranged farther or with a more liberal spirit. Trilling's famous essay "On the Teaching of Modern Literature," collected in *Beyond Culture* (1965), testifies to the intellectual vigor and moral force that he brought to his subject. All our talk about education is disguised autobiography, and in this essay Trilling movingly recounts how his teaching of modern works soon extended beyond the literary work as "a structure of words" to a consideration of "the poet's social and personal will." In his best criticism, Trilling is always attentive to the internal and external realities of art, and this dual approach stemmed from his belief that the "self" which sincere art embodies must be defined in relation to social and moral contexts. Thus his last work, *Sincerity and Authenticity* (1972), written against the background of uncontrolled self-expression and social chaos in the late 1960s and early 1970s, maps a historical movement from the responsible to the irresponsible self, and is tinged with an almost tragic sense of loss—the loss of that glory of the "modern spirit," the individual who can balance his inner needs against his external responsibilities. The cultural scene has changed dramatically in the few years since *Sincerity and Authenticity,* and in ways that Trilling could scarcely have foreseen; but criticism is always in need of the double commitment to internal and external realities that his finest essays exemplify. They remain with us as reminders of what literary criticism can be, and of how much we stand to lose when it becomes an end in itself.

3

Realists, Naturalists, and Novelists of Manners
Leo Braudy

BORN with the modern age, novelists have always been entrepreneurs of order, impresarios
each promoting a personal vision of the world.
World War I marks a decisive change in the ways those visions could be
expressed. Two pressures especially transformed the legacy of nineteenth-century fiction. Formally, the close attention to language and
sensibility heralded by the novels of Joyce, Proust, and Woolf redefined
what it meant to tell a story, while socially and politically the war
brought a new awareness both of America's place in the world and of
the complex variety of the American people. Parochialism both abroad
and at home was crumbling under the impact of unprecedented events,
and a new literature that challenged traditional expectations of both
form and content was being born.

The American tradition in fiction had always been at once more
panoramic and more personal than either the English or the French.
Although after World War I American fiction might still take cues
from the masters of the nineteenth century or such early twentieth-
century writers as Edith Wharton, Theodore Dreiser, and Sinclair
Lewis, it was now faced with the task of being large and capacious at
a time when the public world seemed in danger of becoming too complicated for any one person to understand, let alone encompass. From
Sir Walter Scott onward, novelists had explored the place of individual
action amid the pressures of historical forces and sweeping public
events. Through the early twentieth century writers could still retain
a belief in the scrutability of historical forces, although even Marxist
categories fumbled with the slippery enormity of World War I. In-

creasingly through the 1930s history seemed to have no controls, no inner logic to be perceived, and therefore no way to adjust its demands to those of the individual, or, in literary terms, to adjust the demands of form and story to the demands of character and sensibility.

Barely twenty years after World War I, World War II furnished events and movements of men and materiel that made Stendhal's vision of Fabrizio at Waterloo or Tolstoy's of Prince Andrei at Borodino seem like triumphs of the human spirit and understanding. It was a mobilization of American resources that was incomparably more vast than any that had preceded it, more inspiring, and perhaps more daunting to writers who sought to create from it their own shapes and stories.

The threat to personal order had come from history, a history that swept us first into World War I and then into World War II and out again, victorious—but unsure. Many popular novels helped combat this underlying helplessness in the face of events by portraying worlds in which personal choice and action counted. Historical fiction especially had been a feature of best-seller lists since the late 1930s and would remain there until the 1960s, when its dramatizations of will and power were gradually replaced by the thinly disguised celebrity-novels of Harold Robbins, Jacqueline Susann, and others. Until then, novelists such as Kenneth Roberts, Samuel Shellabarger, Thomas B. Costain, F. Van Wyck Mason, Frances Parkinson Keyes, Taylor Caldwell, Frank Yerby, and Lloyd C. Douglas wrote of worlds historical and quasi-historical, where individual assertion was again possible, where excitement and adventure rather than frustration and death were the result of an encounter with history. To swashbuckle with Charles II, to march in the ranks under George Washington, or to die for Christianity were only a few of the vicarious possibilities, and all was not total fantasy, since the authors prided themselves on the scrupulosity of their research and their vivid shaping of retrieved detail. The utopians, whether communist, socialist, or capitalist, may have demanded that the past be plowed under to nourish the growth of the future. But popular novelists such as these cultivated the past as a source of individualist values—a fictional place of pastoral refreshment for Americans who lived in a society increasingly technological, grand, and anonymous.

Since the past was over, there was a greater chance that it might be understood. So in the 1950s the American Civil War, long before its centennial, became the theme of many best sellers, in both fiction and nonfiction, allowing contemporary political conflicts between North and South over integration, industrialization, and Americanism to be comfortably displaced into a reconstruction of nineteenth-century social detail and battlefield strategy. The onset of Cold War paranoia, the dogged effort to root out heresy of all sorts, might therefore have sprung from a nostalgia for the simpler political and historical patterns of World War II, when everyone worked together with a common purpose. But after the enforced coherence of the war (and its professed moral goal) had disappeared, the search for fictional and personal order became more troubling and inconclusive for writers unwilling to embrace the pieties and purities that characterized the public world of the 1950s.

Although the terms "realist" and "naturalist" might be applied to novelists of the interwar period without too much distortion, they therefore become much more restrictive by the time of World War II and the postwar period. The writers I shall survey here have no easy affiliation by which we might know them, nor any explicit polemic that binds them together. My task has been less to apply the right term than to create or reveal a set of relationships, a preliminary map that may help to locate some of the writers who lived and worked in a period marked by experimentation and exploration, even in the works of those who seem most traditional. History itself was such a forceful presence to many of these writers that the funneling of them into timeless critical categories seems less important than tracing the new highways and shunpikes of their journeys. The critical language can be only a simple backdrop for what actually happened.

These worries about the terrain ahead, where to turn and what features to note, reflect one dominant urge of twentieth-century American literature—the effort to take the measure of the country itself. Some novelists might see America spread in its variety from shore to shore; others might choose a special group, a microcosm of the whole. The fascination with differences is more easily expressed in the naturalistic sweep through social classes and across continents, while the patterns of stability yield their secrets to the perceiver of manners and social nuance. But at the heart of both kinds of novels is a polemic about America, and both will usually build their worlds from a pattern of observed detail that can only be called realist. It is this impulse toward a total vision of America that becomes most embattled in the postwar period, as more and more novelists take on the role of documenting the special place of minority and private perception in American society—exploring and often romanticizing the soul-quickening virtues of the Jewish, southern, black, or woman's experience, while allowing the reader to become part of those experiences with their full shares of social despair and individual energy.

New social worlds were being brought into American fiction, just as they were being brought into American culture. But often ignored in such imperatives was the earlier effort to create a novel that could span the variety of America. How American novelists responded to the postwar world might therefore first be charted by considering four writers who began their careers in the 1920s and 1930s: John Dos Passos, James T. Farrell, John Steinbeck, and Ernest Hemingway.

Born in 1896, John Dos Passos established his reputation with such novels as *Three Soldiers* (1921), *Manhattan Transfer* (1925), and the three volumes later collected in 1937 as *U.S.A.—The 42nd Parallel* (1930), *1919* (1932), and *The Big Money* (1936). Although he was a member of the "lost" generation of American expatriates in Paris in the 1920s that included Ernest Hemingway and e. e. cummings, Dos Passos's literary inclinations were always less toward personal and poetic expression than toward the social panoramas that were to become typical of the fiction of the 1930s. His best novels approached such massive subjects as World War I or World War II through a dazzling array of rhetorical techniques that included prose poems, documentary collages, and biographical essays on notable figures— all linked by a detached, often ironic, narrative of the destinies of fictional characters whose lives invariably intersected with every major national and international event of the years the novel covered. As John O'Hara sought to make himself a Balzacian secretary to the social history of his generation, so Dos Passos seemed bent on being a Zolaesque observer or moral witness to all of twentieth-century American history. His world is a world of palpable immediacy, attuned to the latest in materialism and communication, infused with an energetic assemblage of detail that forces the reader to pay critical attention to all the competing ways information is being thrown at him. The result, in *Manhattan Transfer* and *U.S.A.* most strikingly, is an uplifting vitality and an enthusiasm for the complexity and variety possible in the world. Always incredibly prolific, Dos Passos wrote a tremendous amount of general reportage and travel literature as well, presenting himself, as he did in his fiction, as the model of the interested, sympathetic, but finally detached observer—the quick study who in a week or a month could catch the essence of a profession or a culture, the American novelist as all-embracing as the country itself.

World War II for Dos Passos, as for Hemingway and others, seemed to offer the opportunity for the kind of detached involvement that had been possible in World War I, and Dos Passos, again like Hemingway, became a combat journalist. But the strain was beginning to show.

In the 1920s and 1930s, Dos Passos's special brand of individualism, what he later called his "allegiance" to "an imaginary republic," could find easy affinities with either the struggling left-wing politics of union agitation or the effort to free Sacco and Vanzetti. But its essentially personal anarchism balked more and more at what Dos Passos perceived to be the deadeningly organized quality of American life. Younger writers might be inspired by the camaraderie and social fluidity that World War II made possible; but for Dos Passos the war was a corporate suffocation of individual valor that reflected the suffocation of individual idealism wrought by Roosevelt's New Deal. The trilogy called *District of Columbia* (1952)—which includes *Adventures of a Young Man* (1939), *Number One* (1943), and *The Grand Design* (1949)—is a typically multifaceted study in disillusionment: the ideals of communism giving way to the reality of party politics; the democracy of populism turning into the fascism of demagoguery; and the promise of Roosevelt and the New Deal smothered by the red tape of Washington bureaucracy.

Perhaps this disillusionment was the offspring of the romantic streak that also marks Dos Passos's work. His political idealism seemed to evaporate whenever its cause was successful or its heroes came to power. Since history worked through individuals and individuals were being shunted aside, his novels more and more strenuously attacked any ideological "grand design" that either left out individuals or promoted a few at the cost of the many. Unfortunately, as his spleen against the direction of American history and politics grew, his characters became more and more passive instruments of his own polemic purposes. "Satire as a Way of Seeing" is the title of a late Dos Passos essay (published in *Occasions and Protests*, 1964), and it may be most interesting (some might say most charitable) to see many of Dos Passos's postwar novels as primarily satiric. Dos Passos may therefore be less a realist trying to express the complex factuality of America than a naturalist whose tendency to heighten social reality shades into a satiric vision resembling that of Hogarth, Smollett, or Dickens. In the postwar period his refusal to adopt a distinctive authorial voice, his disintegration of narrative into documentary and pseudo-documentary fragments, expressed not the exuberant variety of his earlier works but a splenetic lashing out in all directions. Like Gulliver, his travels had led him to assume an almost impossible purity, more misanthrope than militant, abstractly involved with an individualism he perhaps unwittingly denied to his characters.

In his own way Dos Passos was reacting to the crisis of male individualism that preoccupied American culture in the years following

World War II: all that training, that power, that energy, now not only without a cause in which to put it to use, but also with an injunction that it was irrelevant. His nonfictional writings increasingly returned to the period of the American Revolution and especially to the character of Thomas Jefferson in an effort to define the national and personal values he believed were so quickly disappearing. But in his novels he continued to restage his own progress through the twentieth century, though without the passionate involvement that had so authoritatively shaped his earlier work. Among his novels of this period *Midcentury* (1961), a *U.S.A.*-like chronicle of the growth of labor unions and the subsequent loss of rank and file integrity, is the most ambitious, although perhaps *Chosen Country* (1951) best retains the undeniable power of his vision. After *Midcentury* Dos Passos wrote no more novels, but continued his interest in history, especially that of the American revolutionary period and now also that of Portugal—the country of his family roots. For the first time, as well, in a literary career marked by his unwillingness to use his own experience except emblematically, Dos Passos in the years before his death in 1970 began to publish his letters and, in 1966, an autobiography, *The Best Times,* which focused on his relation with his father and his fascination with travel. Consonant with its title, however, *The Best Times* ends in 1936.

Dos Passos's first novels had dealt with the impact of Europe and World War I on an America just emerging from the nineteenth century. But the first novels of James T. Farrell, only eight years Dos Passos's junior, were clearly products of the depression. With his prolific and concentrated integrity, Farrell took as his subject the Catholic working class and lower middle class of Chicago, essentially as it existed in the twentieth century before World War II. In novel after novel he has explored its intricacies through the prisms of different characters, all usually caught in a fatal movement toward frustration and despair. Like Dos Passos, Farrell frequently uses the trilogy or tetralogy format to imply a perspective that goes beyond the confines of a single novel to create a necessarily incomplete work, whose sprawling shape is a mirror of or rival to life itself. While the three volumes of Dos Passos's *U.S.A.* may draw on the Cubist effort to see from many different directions at once without treating any particular angle as privileged, Farrell's capacity to spawn novels in series involves an effort to capture the infinite minutiae of details that surround the chronological growth of his characters, so that nothing remotely relevant will be missed.

Farrell's first and most notable works were the novels constituting *Studs Lonigan: A Trilogy* (1935): *Young Lonigan: A Boyhood in*

Chicago Streets (1932), *The Young Manhood of Studs Lonigan* (1934), and *Judgment Day* (1935). Through his unadorned prose Farrell captured the wandering mind of Studs as he grows up on the South Side of Chicago, struggling against the pressures of his family, his Catholic background, and the harshnesses of city life. *Young Lonigan* especially was so graphic for its time and so uncompromising in its realism that it was first advertised as a case history suitable for purchase by social workers, lawyers, sociologists, and other interested professionals. Farrell, in his personal synthesis of Theodore Dreiser and the James Joyce of *A Portrait of the Artist as a Young Man,* had introduced to American literature an urban language as violent and vital as that picked up on the frontier by Mark Twain. Essentially, it was a male language, a working-class language, the language of sports and the poolroom, delivered in a clipped, direct, bleak style that often made Hemingway's similar adaptations seem mannered.

Indebted explicitly to Zola, Dreiser, and Tolstoy, Farrell's aesthetic materialism produces a mixture of sympathy and condescension similar to that which permeates the novels of Dos Passos, O'Hara, Nelson Algren, and Mary McCarthy. The novelist is defined as a reporter, bringing new people and new places into the dead house of literature, to restore its importance and its relevance. But the novelist is also kept, in a Flaubertian way, outside the narrative, as a "literary" impediment to the truth he wishes to convey. In part, this separation of novelist from narrative is a response to the obtrusive Victorian novelist, who was constantly pointing a finger and articulating a message. The new reportorial detachment aimed to ensure that the faults were specifically perceived to exist in the structure of society itself. Where the nineteenth-century naturalist or realist may have conveyed an assured fatality, the more politically conscious writers of the twentieth century wanted to keep the path open to reform.

But form is more than just a stylistic choice. It also contains a necessity that must be fought with rather than ignored. Too often the great American naturalists and realists, enamored with the sincerity of their plain style, failed to appreciate that the magisterial Flaubert also identified himself with Madame Bovary or that the fact-seeking Zola also questioned the ability of his journalistic method to discover anything like the total truth. Farrell, like Dos Passos, was constantly restaging his own initiation and those of his friends into a world they never made. One would think that if a character could not be free of the oppressive environment of the modern world, at least he might display a personal autonomy that reflected the imaginative empathy of his creator. But when society and the pressure of environment are made so totally responsible for the shape of individual character, the only options open to the overseeing novelist seem to be either a withdrawal into satire (as in the later Dos Passos) or a repeated plunge into despair, as the eternal cycle of idealism and disillusionment is portrayed once again.

Farrell's own inclination seemed toward the comforts of repetition. After the war, he published another trilogy (*Bernard Clare*, 1946; *The Road Between*, 1949; *Yet Other Waters*, 1952) that deals with the career of a gradually disillusioned writer and Communist, and bears comparison with Dos Passos's *District of Columbia*, although without its political sweep. Farrell's later novels do show an increasing interest in the dynamics of personal relations, especially bad marriages, but the original bite of his style is almost gone. Still, Farrell maintains the standard of quantity he had first tapped in the early 1930s, lately discovering an autobiographical stream as well: for one book he has visited Israel, and in another he describes his lifelong involvement with baseball. In 1963, at the age of fifty-nine, he published *The Silence of History*, the first of a projected twenty-nine-volume series of novels. But despite his energy, in the 1970s Farrell still remains a figure of the 1930s, and one revisits even his new work for nostalgia rather than discovery.

John Steinbeck, who was born in 1902, might have been as angry as Dos Passos or Farrell at the way the roar of twentieth-century history has drowned out the softer rhythms of human nature. But his own work stands generally to one side of great events, and his ideals, perhaps because they have less to do with the uses of power, remain less tarnished than theirs by frustration or bitterness. Writing out of a setting in northern California where the main occupations are agriculture and fishing, Steinbeck rarely separated his politics from his feeling for nature. Historical time is not as important as the cycles of the growing season, and evil is the interruption of nature, when land is expropriated, when people are thrown off their farms, when bosses of any sort refuse the fruits of labor to those who earned them. The land and the people are what basically exist and what must remain.

This attachment to nature ensures that Steinbeck builds his works from a rich variety of observed detail. But it also leads him to shape his stories more like myths or fables than realistic novels. Detail is infused with almost symbolic significance, and the relation between characters verges on the allegorical. In his two most overtly political novels, *In Dubious Battle* (1936) and *The Grapes of Wrath* (1939), Steinbeck plays between the personal lives of his characters and their larger significance. *In Dubious Battle* especially experiments with the

91

intersection between the realistic and the symbolic. The story of a fruitpickers' strike in the Imperial Valley of California, *In Dubious Battle* clearly shows that proletarian fiction is rooted in an ideal pastoral world of instinctive brotherhood. The forces that are attempting to crush the workers are not merely self-interested; they are unnatural. In *The Grapes of Wrath,* similarly, the dispossession of the Joads from their native Oklahoma may seem to be a result of the dust storms, but is more directly caused by the profiteering of the banks that own the land and cannot wait for the natural balance to be restored. Through alternate chapters Steinbeck interweaves the personal story of the Joad family's journey to California with the larger statistical and documentary reality of all those like the Joads adrift in the America of the middle 1930s. Unlike the somewhat impersonal characters of *In Dubious Battle,* the Joads retain their individuality even while they also serve as emblems of what is happening all over the country. The juxtaposed chapters may sometimes be awkward, but they finely embody a simultaneously documentary and heroic view of experience, portraying a world in which one person's problems are part of a larger pattern that yet can be altered by the force of human will.

Steinbeck's fascination with biology and nature might make him a naturalist, but his insistence on will and the power to change one's destiny severely qualifies any fatal gloom that naturalism might imply. What primarily diverts his political impulses, however, is his general suspicion of power. In three novels written over almost a twenty-year period—*Tortilla Flat* (1935), *Cannery Row* (1945), and *Sweet Thursday* (1954)—he celebrates the layabouts and good fellows of Monterey, who are less interested in accomplishing anything than in creating a community of friendship and spirit. To the myth of American success and achievement Steinbeck opposes a myth of high-minded failure. But too often his style and his stories convey a sentimental whimsy, akin to that of his fellow Californian William Saroyan, that undermines the anarchic values he attempts to celebrate. Only his script for Elia Kazan's *Viva Zapata!* (1952) preserves a powerful ambivalence about the relation of ideals and political authority, perhaps because Marlon Brando's performance in the title role contains a dynamism often lacking in Steinbeck's novelistic characterizations.

Many of Steinbeck's works were written as plays or became plays later (including *Of Mice and Men,* 1937, and *The Moon Is Down,* 1942), and their ritual quality often was served better on stage than in his fictions. In 1941, along with the marine biologist Edward F. Ricketts, he wrote *Sea of Cortez,* a strange but perhaps appropriate combination of a journal of a voyage down the California coast with a detailed description of the marine invertebrates they observed along the way. The book is noteworthy because its structure reflects Steinbeck's difficulty in making just that fusion in his novels between the impressionistic empathizing *amateur* and the objective observer and categorizer. Awarded the Nobel Prize in 1962, Steinbeck became increasingly uneasy with the direction of his own work and increasingly unsure of the sources of his authority. In *The Short Reign of Pippin IV* (1957), he told the story of a bored Cincinnatus who could hardly be bothered with being king of France. *The Winter of Our Discontent* (1961) unconvincingly bemoaned a fatal loss of ideals, just at the dawn of the Kennedy era. In the last two books published before his death in 1968, Steinbeck, like so many other novelists with roots in the land, affirmed that the literary quest for the essence of a place leads directly to a quest for the essence of America. In *Travels with Charley: In Search of America* (1962) and *America and Americans* (1966), Steinbeck gave his final pictures of the diversity and community his novels so often tried to express.

Much more than either Dos Passos, Farrell, or even the celebrity-conscious Steinbeck, Ernest Hemingway from the beginning of his career seemed determined to create as much an image of himself outside his work as a style inside it. Born in Illinois in 1899, Hemingway, in his novels and short stories of the 1920s and 1930s, established his reputation by showing how a new subject matter—personal, physical, emotional—could transmit its energies (nonliterary by nineteenth-century standards) through a newly honed, newly spare style, based on the rhythms of speech, journalistic prose, and the vivid precision of Imagist poetry. In these early works Hemingway seemed simultaneously able to be as direct as Jack London and as sensitive as Sherwood Anderson without (as yet) taking on either London's literary self-importance or Anderson's sentimentality. As if in answer to Dostoevsky's or Conrad's fear of the disease of thought, Hemingway created a world in which narration, his own voice, was a standard of extrapersonal purity against which his characters were to be measured. Craft, the solitary profession of writing, constituted a subduing force, a metaphysic of expertise. What a writer, what a person, *knew* could hold off the darkness of historical chaos and personal moral confusion.

The new literary sensibility Hemingway heralded was one of a personal isolation and honor that wrapped its individuality around itself like a banner in the face of the (eastern) social worlds of James, Wharton, and even F. Scott Fitzgerald. Unmoved by the encyclopedic methods of the naturalist novel of the 1930s, Hemingway wrote a fiction of sensibility caught in history, not philosophical in the European mode that Norman Mailer, Saul Bellow, and others were to introduce to postwar fiction, but ruminative in the older American tradition of London, Frank Norris, Stephen Crane, and the other journalists *manqués* and sportswriters from whom Hemingway had sprung. Its tone was aphoristic and folkwise, frightened of nothing but the charge of pretension.

So quickly celebrated, Hemingway by the 1950s began to inhabit his own style as if it were a classicism to which he could refer without the need to justify it anew. *Across the River and into the Trees* (1950) was attacked at the time and later for turning what had been a self-conscious purity into an unwitting self-parody. But in the face of the more massively diagrammatic and ambitious works of the period, *Across the River and into the Trees* preserves a quietly resonant refusal to gain imaginative control by detailing and thereby exhausting a world. "Who should ever discourage a liar," ponders the Colonel, the hero of the novel, "unless he is giving you co-ordinates?" To underline the point, another character in the novel, to one side of the aged Colonel and his nineteen-year-old lover, is an acned American writer, constantly taking notes and consulting his Baedeker in the observing-without-experiencing manner Hemingway hated. The Colonel at fifty is filled with wounds and memories. He has made mistakes, but he has fully experienced his life and, like the fisherman in *The Old Man and the Sea* (1952), he does not feel the need for possessions to prove it. Hemingway's own disgust with the voyeuristic and passive life implied by writing seems apparent in the Colonel's assertion that he is not and could not be a writer. His profession is that of soldier. Like Aeschylus, whose epitaph reports that he fought at Marathon but is silent about his authorship of the *Oresteia* or any other plays, Hemingway opposes experience to writing; he condemns any writing that even threatens to substitute itself for the immediate apprehension of life and feeling. The greatest virtues are directness and simplicity—the hallmarks of Hemingway's definition of style as "grace under pressure." In the Colonel's life that style must face its natural enemy, the decay of the body, the end of love, and so the Colonel presses himself against the body of his young lover desperately (a favorite word in the novel), to feel the hardness of the embrace, the taste of blood in the kiss that is the evidence of a feeling that goes beyond the trivially tender.

In the 1920s and 1930s Hemingway had helped spawn a generation of tight-lipped sentimentalists who tried as much as possible to bridge the irreducible gap between writing and action. But after the war his importance became more iconographic than exemplary, the Great

Writer who fished with the famous, winner of the Nobel Prize for Literature (in 1954), the individualist institutionalized by the constant repetition of his grizzled image on magazine covers. In both *Across the River and into the Trees* and the posthumous *Islands in the Stream* (1970), Hemingway refers to Dante, "the great Florentine egotist," who demonstrated the connection between a heightened sense of self and the ability to accomplish great work. But what may have intrigued Hemingway more was the way Dante could be both inside his greatest work as the ignorant pilgrim and outside it as the professional poet. Hemingway, like many modern writers, often turned up in the reverse situation, manipulated by his public in strange revenge for the power his books had over them. The Colonel could die at the end of *Across the River and into the Trees,* but Hemingway lived on, to be prematurely embalmed in his legend, his last work published in *Life* magazine. In his most compelling works, Hemingway's characters, like his style, had a precision of being, a punctiliousness of self, far from the postwar degeneration of that hard-boiled elegance into the brand-name "taste" of Ian Fleming's James Bond, the civil servant who kills with government approval. But Hemingway too had become an advertised image, and his death by suicide in 1961 may have announced how much the victim of that image he was. Whatever formed the integrity of his characters had turned into a system of empty gestures, a costume available to all who had the price. Only his posthumous memoir *A Moveable Feast* (1964) retained some of his old vitality, now spiked with a surly vengeance, in its evocation of the Paris of the 1920s, when the world had seemed more open.

For many younger writers, Hemingway's career furnished an emblem of the writer's life, with the glory to be gained and the losses to be avoided, even as it attempted to bring together the oddly assorted values of public acclaim and a kind of footloose, jaundiced individualism, mediated by an increasingly self-conscious invocation of the writer's "profession." Important branches of Hemingway's heritage are represented in the works of James Jones, Nelson Algren, Norman Mailer, and Gore Vidal; it would seem to be impossible for any American male novelist of the postwar period to escape his influence entirely, so thoroughly had he made war and masculinity two of his most important themes. But each of the novelists I have named, as well as many others, bends also toward other strong influences—Algren toward Farrell's urban realism, Mailer toward Dos Passos's synoptic sweep, Vidal toward his own special amalgam of social comedy, historical reconstruction, and sexual science fiction. Typically, the Hemingway influence takes the form of nostalgia for a world where individual effort counted. Vance Bourjaily, for example, in *The Violated* (1958), *The Man Who Knew Kennedy* (1967), or *Brill among the Ruins* (1970), translates Hemingway's concern with craft and personal testing into the kind of densely detailed naturalistic world so often called "brawling" or "tumultuous" by postwar blurb writers. The model situation for masculine testing is the hunt, the trial by nature. The outcome is usually tragic or at least melancholic. Matching the nostalgia is a cynicism about the possibility for self-definition and affirmation in the materialistic world of postwar America. The war had been won, but what had been lost?

The career of James Jones expresses with a barely controlled intensity the checkered fortunes of the Hemingway heritage in the world of postwar disaffection. Jones is not very interested in a well-wrought literary style. He has said that he learned he was a writer in 1942, when he read Thomas Wolfe's *Look Homeward, Angel* in the Post Library at Schofield Barracks, Hawaii, and his literary self-image owes much as well to Jack London, the prototypical knockabout American novelist, for whom authenticity of experience superseded concern about literary style or construction. But, like Hemingway, Mailer, Algren, Vidal, John O'Hara, J. P. Marquand, and a fascinating variety of other postwar novelists, Jones is obsessed by professionalism—what is truly rewarding work and how can it best be appreciated? In postwar American society the increasing demand for the writer to come forward personally both answered Jones's desire for recognition and contradicted his belief that true professionalism is a stylish anonymity and the best work is appreciated by only the select few.

Jones's career is a model of these conflicts. In his first novel, *From Here to Eternity* (1951), both he and his characters constantly refer to "The Profession"—the peacetime army in the months before the Japanese attack on Pearl Harbor on December 7, 1941. The army infuses every conversation and every incident; as in the priesthood, while individuals might be hated, the system itself is loved, because it affords a hierarchy, a backdrop of meaning for men who otherwise feel utterly will-less and lost. Jones's two heroes are Robert E. Lee Prewitt, the twenty-one-year-old miner's son from Harlan County, Kentucky, and Milton Anthony Warden, the thirty-four-year-old top sergeant. Although Prewitt, because he refuses to go out for the regimental boxing team, is the butt of "The Treatment" administered by Warden, the two men share an affinity that goes beyond their particular place in the system of the army. Both are varieties of the outsider, Warden through his cynicism about the fallible men who fill the places in the army's grand plan, Prewitt through the absolute integrity that refuses to allow him to do anything that could possibly be considered playing the odds, cutting corners, or finding an angle. Warden has psyched out everything, but Prewitt believes that psyching out the world is not manly. Warden considers himself to be "the instrument of a laughing Providence," while Prewitt's sense of himself comes only when he fights against fate.

From Here to Eternity first sounds the theme of a universal blankness to any assertion of human will that Jones will explore through all his novels: "the overpowering injustice of the world he could not stomach nor understand nor explain nor change." But Jones's role in the novel is not to analyze, predict, or shake his head sadly. Instead of speaking as a narrator whose sweep rivals that of God or History, Jones's voice inhabits his characters, remaining close and sympathetic to their every word and thought. In place of the stark elegancies of Hemingway, Jones's soldiers speak and are spoken of in an unsure, tentative language, infused sometimes with ambiguous meaning, sparked often by a surprising wit, without any illusions about the relation between directness of language and directness of feeling. The reader is less an invited guest at the theater of fate than "you," who remembers, who has had similar experiences, a male reader certainly, but one raddled by uncertainties, drawn equally to Prewitt and Warden, to the one's ideal integrity and the other's ideal cynicism.

In this world shadowed by fate, politics, and the large movements of social institutions, Jones is drawn especially to the effort to make human connections, and some of his most powerful scenes are discussions in which two people break through to each other, "touch another human soul and understand it." In the nature of this world, the encounters are usually between men, for this is "civilization, where men are men . . . and women hate them for it, and they hate the women for not loving it." But many of the encounters are also between men and women, principally between Warden and Karen Holmes, with whom he is having an affair, Karen Holmes, whose most contemptuous characterization of her Regular Army Captain husband is: "You sound like a page out of Hemingway."

Until Pearl Harbor, the moment of History, arrives, the peacetime army can be a refuge alike from both women and politics, the two clearest threats to masculine will and personal control. Even the almost ideal relation between Warden and Karen Holmes must end, in part because of the onset of war, but in part also because she wants him to become an officer, a social insider. The theme of retreat from both society and the control of women has been a staple of American literature at least as far back as James Fenimore Cooper. In much of the fiction influenced by or set in the war, it takes on a new intensity. Philip Wylie's *A Generation of Vipers* (1942) and *Opus 21* (1949), for example, popularized the term "Momism" and detailed its crippling effect on American masculinity. In the introduction to "The Tennis Game," one of the stories collected in *The Ice-Cream Headache and Other Stories* (1968), Jones alludes to the "male masochism of which there seems to be a great deal in my generation . . . brought on of course by mothers like the mother in the story." Prewitt may rail at the historical fate and social hierarchy in the face of which "a man himself is nothing," but he absolves the army of blame, for it preserves a psychic comfort, a home away from women, moms or otherwise, whose presence might shred the frail carapace of masculine self-containment and security.

Jones's career might in fact be described in terms of two themes: novels about war and novels about being a writer. The first—*From Here to Eternity, The Pistol* (1959), *The Thin Red Line* (1962)—are contained, intense, and resonant; the second—including *Some Came Running* (1957), *Go to the Widow-Maker* (1967), and *The Merry Month of May* (1971)—are usually diffuse, self-important, and despairing. Jones's wrestling with his muse, with his materials, and with the whole process of novel writing has less to do with the familiar modernist theme of the writer who refers to his own act of creation than with the gloom of the male writer, in part the legacy of Hemingway, who fears that his writing debars him from the companionship of other men and even from masculinity itself. No wonder then that writing must be celebrated as a profession, when the fear is that it may not be even men's work, certainly not a satisfying fellowship like the army, but more often a fatal combat, carried on in the presence of more enemies than friends. *Some Came Running* opens with Dave Hirsh's return to his hometown in Illinois, after years of first being in the army, then in California, writing two novels. His fantasy that one had to have new and strange experiences in order to be a writer has evaporated, and Dave has come back to Parkman to discover the stories that before he had been unable to see at home. With him, like an emblem of promise, he carries his Viking Portables of Fitzgerald, Hemingway, Faulkner, Steinbeck, and Wolfe.

But *Some Came Running* is less about the material of small-town American life than about the search for that material and the struggle to subdue and express it. Plot for Jones must always therefore give way to character and its obsessions. At the center of such obsessions, the emblem of all human frustrations, is the writer, with his desperate need for both self-exposure and self-protection. For Dave, as well as for

Jones, writing with its self-conscious discipline and detachment seems fatally opposed to the naturalness and sincerity they seek: "He was a writer, and so he didn't—couldn't live . . . You had to be every-body, and every-thing [to be a writer], and hence you were no-body, and no-thing." When one can no longer participate, even vicariously, in history, what is there left to do but spin works from one's insides, without caring in what warped form they may emerge? Outside of war, romantic self-consciousness and realist selflessness collide; the loss of external compulsion reveals the actual amorphousness of individual perception and will. The real hero of *Some Came Running* is not Dave, but Dave's gambler friend, Bama Dillert, the stylish cynic, who, like Warden, intuitively works the angles because he has the artist's sensibility without the artist's need to express it.

The style of sincerity, the unpremeditated, uncompromising statement, can shade at one end into muteness and at the other into self-display. Jones's war novels subdue the ego as his peace novels depict its frantic assertion. Both are oddly mixed critiques of and homages to Hemingway, whose shotgun suicide so strangely resembles that of Bloom in *From Here to Eternity*, with its combination of self-importance and self-hatred, the joy and fear of knowing oneself only in public. Men, says Jones, will continue to make up fictions about themselves to order and justify their lives, but what, he wonders, about the writers, who consider themselves superior because they make up fictions about many men, women, places, and things, yet are twice-deluded by the semblance of meaning and the semblance of emotion?

From his earliest works, then, Jones wrestles with that crippling paradox that steals through so much postwar American fiction—the writing that celebrates the superiority of those who do not write. Norman Mailer, in *Advertisements for Myself* (1959) and *The Armies of the Night* (1968), brandishes a double image of himself as both writer and experiencer in a virtuoso effort to escape the same imprisoning perception. Jones, in his impassioned and less literarily self-conscious way, flounders with more clumsy integrity, and with more loss. His last novel, *Whistle* (1978), was to end his war trilogy, but was unfinished at his death. Completed by Willie Morris from Jones's notes, *Whistle* continues Jones's fascination with "the company," now returning to the United States to wait out their healing in army hospitals, still involved in a dependence on each other that goes beyond the details of individual friendship. Once again, women both define and threaten their relationship: "Cunt had broken the centripetal intensity of the hermetic force which sealed them together in so incestuous a way. Their combat. Cunt vs Combat." Caught between women and the army, where is a man to go? Beyond one striking scene in *From Here to Eternity,* Jones shows little, for example, of Mailer's interest in the political implications of war and the forces it releases. His combat is more primordial, and by *Whistle* time has almost run out.

Whistle is set in the last years of World War II, but it reflects the moods of the post Vietnam era. For his dramatization of man's irrelevance to the operations of the universe, Jones has no handy philosophical category like Albert Camus's "Absurd," and his fatalism in his later novels rarely allows more than the grimmest humor to lighten its gloom. Joseph Heller, in *Catch-22* (1961), could take much of the same material of helplessness and turn it into a backdrop for eccentric self-assertion. If Heller might be considered a Jones without a tragic sense (or distrustful of it), Jones might be a Heller without detachment (or scornful of it). But both immeasurably helped change the American attitude toward war. The Vietnam war has produced more powerful memoirs than powerful fiction, in part because the myth of male camaraderie that could sustain writers like Jones had lost its power. So too the sex war that enabled the myth to survive mutated into the self-conscious parody and polemic of Mailer's *The Prisoner of Sex* (1971) and the apocalyptic fantasy of Thomas Berger's *Regiment of Women* (1973). One of the few distinguished novels of Vietnam, Robert Stone's *Dog Soldiers* (1974), is less about the war than about its effect on the United States. Its one admirable character dies essentially for his effort to uphold a tattered loyalty to his "buddy."

A less despairing conclusion to Jones's own career might be found in the memoir *Viet Journal* (1974) and *W.W. II* (1975), an illustrated history of World War II art for which he wrote the text. In both he speaks in a voice reminiscent of that in his war fiction, a much more personal voice than that of Dos Passos or Hemingway in their combat reporting. Its tones may be a dramatization of that place where the sociology and the aesthetic of fiction meet in the character of the novelist. In the epilogue to *Viet Journal,* one of the best pieces of writing in these two books, Jones returns to Hawaii, on the way back from Vietnam, to revisit the places he wrote about in *From Here to Eternity,* unsure whose memories and actions he is reliving: "I no longer knew whether Prewitt had done it, or I had."

The macho desperation of so many of Jones's characters, like its surrealist equivalent in Mailer's *An American Dream* (1965), springs from a refusal of narrative detachment, a radical subjectivity that seeks extreme situations to feel itself more keenly. So much postwar fiction seems powered by a half-articulate feeling that the war had not solved all it claimed to have, and that in its wake had come a world few wanted and few enjoyed. A fine melancholy of mingled nostalgia and loss threads through the stories of John Horne Burns's *The Gallery* (1947), set in wartime Italy. In his next novel, *Lucifer with a Book* (1949), a soldier returns to teach in a New England prep school only to discover the deeper corruption at home. If the war had been fought to preserve the American way of life, who would fight the war against selfish American prosperity?

Still another new battleground was the war between the sexes, where female sexuality furnished the crucible of tempering or destruction for a masculine sense of self that arose from the necessity of combat, a personal fate that could be grappled with and subdued. In Jones's peacetime novels, the iconography of family and male-female difference appears again and again: the antisexual but art-nurturing mother, the weak father, the sexual and supportive dream wife. So, for example, in *Some Came Running*, Dave Hirsh wants to write a "comic combat novel" (a phrase Jones later uses to refer to *The Thin Red Line*), and he is encouraged by Gwen French, a teacher at Parkman College who is writing a book about Dave and his friends: a case history of the writer in America focusing on the direct association of aesthetic and sexual failure. Only the woman as friend, as equal, the woman "like a man," can supply support and refuge from the eternal war.

These themes of sexual and social combat were not without a political dimension, and their roots ran deep into postwar popular culture. The great popularity of detective fiction in the period, for example, indicates how the historical moment could give new relevance and energy to a preexisting literary form, concentrating and distilling the frustrations of the culturally displaced ex-soldier into a general attack on the greed and false corporate values of postwar society. Dashiell Hammett had established the metaphysic of the detective for American eyes in a number of short stories and only four novels, written in a brief space of years in the high depression—*The Dain Curse* (1929), *Red Harvest* (1929), *The Maltese Falcon* (1930), and *The Glass Key* (1931). The style was spare, and the central character, the almost nameless Continental Op, was a blunt counterpunch to the rebellious elegance of forebears like Poe's Dupin or Sherlock Holmes. Raymond Chandler, in such works as *The Big Sleep* (1939), *Farewell, My Lovely* (1940), and *The Lady in the Lake* (1943), elaborated Hammett's vision of the detective pulling apart the delicate stitchwork of a venal society by creating Philip Marlowe, a moral knight *manqué* fallen into the corrupt present to chastise and punish. The rich were generally the villains, but the tones of Marlowe's character included a heroic purity that allowed the reader to be absolved merely for listening to his voice. Hammett's Continental Op worked in a long-fallen world; it was Chandler who first sounded the possibility that personal morality was essentially antisocial. Since society was built on a continuous round of greed and exploitation, the detective, as its anatomist, had to remain pure, although unillusioned. Hammett's jaundiced view of society (he had been a Pinkerton operative himself) had obvious connections with his left-wing politics. But Chandler's Marlowe was a moral loner and the implications of his critique were much more apolitical.

In the postwar period, Mickey Spillane and Ross Macdonald restored the political implications of the detective's position without allowing the reader the moral absolution of nostalgia, perhaps because by the 1950s personal morality and political withdrawal were themselves acquiring the dimensions of a political position. The heroes of Spillane and Macdonald may fall into mawkishness or bombast, but their force remains. In great part, the legacy they have inherited from World War II is the need, so akin to that in the more "serious" novel, to make personal sense of a world that seems to have gone crazy. What was definitely not possible was any corporate politics, right or left. The detective hero of the 1950s was alone, either defiantly, like Spillane's Mike Hammer, or melancholically, like Macdonald's Lew Archer. Spillane's first novel, essentially a rewriting and updating of *The Maltese Falcon,* announces its view in its title—*I, the Jury* (1947). In it, and five subsequent novels (including especially *Vengeance Is Mine!* 1950, and *Kiss Me, Deadly,* 1952), Spillane took his hero on a trail of revenge against anyone he thought was a threat to individuality and the masculinity that was its most dominant metaphor. Hammer's barely hidden weakness, his fear of psychic or physical castration, is the necessary foundation for his aggression, for the same reasons that he drives a Chevrolet with a Cadillac engine inside. Sex and violence are the main instruments of Hammer's quest, powering his rage against a world that he believes has robbed almost everyone else of the ability to fight back. As Hammer threads his personal path amid the police, the government, and the criminal gangs, he considers all but a very few friends to be actual or potential enemies. Neither assimilated nor reconciled, beholden to no etiquette but his own, he is the crude, direct underman who defends us against all those forces, public and criminal, that would manipulate us for their own gain.

Lew Archer, the detective hero created by Ross Macdonald in *The Moving Target* (1949), is more literary in his tastes than Mike Hammer, and so more apt to muse on fate and the past than to create a political philosophy out of the individualist fantasies of the present. In part, Archer owes his special sensitivity to the fact that his creator placed him in the hastily thrown up world of California and the West Coast rather than in the grimy eastern cities of Spillane and Hammer. Attuned to history as much as to action, Archer is more fascinated by the past patterns of relationship that erupt into the present than by the immediacies of violence and personal confrontation. Like other American naturalists, both Archer and Hammer pride themselves on their ability to know all the parts of town and country. But Macdonald explores what Spillane essentially disregards: the intricacies of family and the gradations of social class. Thus Spillane's hero seems to spring from Hammett and Hemingway, while Macdonald's Archer owes his lineage to Chandler and Faulkner.

The attraction of the figure of the American detective is due less to the interest in crime or in puzzle solving, than to the feeling that another America of family and friends and trust between strangers has been lost and that the only guardians of its empty treasury are these tender, armored professionals of loneliness. In his novels of the 1950s, Macdonald is still too much enthralled by the traditional detective plot and the traditional movement toward clarity and solution. But such novels as *The Drowning Pool* (1950), *The Ivory Grin* (1952), and *The Galton Case* (1959) point toward the more haunting novels of the 1960s—*The Zebra-Striped Hearse* (1962), *The Chill* (1964), *The Far Side of the Dollar* (1965), *Black Money* (1966)—in which the detailed observation of manners and social milieu combines with a powerful perception of the basic human patterns that lie beneath them. So the solution to the mystery in Spillane's novels is an explosion of the false façades of the world, a demolition, after which there is nothing, while the solution in Macdonald's novels is the revelation of a web of feelings and events that has been repressed, less an attack against the social fates than an effort to give them their due. Archer's sympathetic separateness ensures that the prime emotion in Macdonald's novels is nostalgia for the same values whose loss prompts Spillane to rage. Both Macdonald and Spillane place a great weight on memory, and so many of their villains are people who willfully refuse to remember.

Yet forgetting the past and embracing the future could be profitable. The camaraderie of World War II marked an efficient acceptance of the heterogeneity of American life, that amalgamation of peoples now bent on a single goal. The economic period that followed the war assured the newly assimilated a more accessible array of pleasures and comforts than had been previously thought conceivable by a majority of Americans. But the boom was inextricably tied to maintaining a high level of defense spending in the new holy war against Russia. The conservatism of the 1950s therefore goes hand in hand with the great postwar consumer society, the proliferation of the suburbs, and the expanding number of things to buy. The newly prosperous emerged from the slums and decayed neighborhoods of the cities and moved to the suburban tracts that surrounded the cities, replacing the extended families and communal ideals of the past with the nuclear families and institutional ideals of an upwardly mobile, competitive future.

The 1930s retained a hope: the Joads of John Steinbeck's *The Grapes of Wrath* (1939) would finally settle down and start a farm because of their indomitable will. But many of the postwar inheritors of Steinbeck's tradition were not so optimistic about either the future or the panacea of prosperity. It would be the novelists of manners who would explore most fully the difficulties of success in America. But the novelists in the naturalisic tradition of the 1930s turned away from the emerging classes to write instead of Americans who would never be successful, whose lives were doomed from the start. In the midst of efforts to define a "pure" Americanism, they celebrated those left out. The dispossessed of American society, who lived the nightmare rather than the dream, became more symbolically important in a postwar world that seemed so filled with consumer riches for everyone. In part, the message came proudly from the legacy of Walt Whitman. Whether "they" were the Chicago South Side junkies and petty criminals of Nelson Algren, the Monterey barflies and layabouts of Steinbeck, the angry blacks of James Baldwin, the dropouts of Jack Kerouac—if you didn't know them, you didn't know yourself. Like their predecessors in both Europe and America, such novelists aimed to shock the public into facing a previously ignored social reality. But it was a task made more difficult by the triumphs of Rooseveltian liberalism. While novelists explored the lives of the unassimilated, the reading public tended to perceive them as "problems" that social engineering would easily solve: the "problem" of juvenile delinquency, or drugs, or bigotry existed because prosperity, progress, and assimilation were not yet complete. Popular "social" novels like Laura Z. Hobson's *Gentleman's Agreement* (1947) unwittingly fed the complacency by suggesting that we should not be anti-Semitic not because anti-Semitism was wrong but because the supposed Jew might actually be a WASP reporter out to trick us. Guilt may be a mighty motive. But each novelist in his own way had to face and subdue the paradox

104

implicit in celebrating losers to the precarious winners who joined book clubs to read about them.

Both the novels of Nelson Algren and his attitude toward the role of the writer in American society brilliantly exemplify the lapses and strengths of traditional naturalistic fiction in the postwar period. Only somewhat younger than Steinbeck, Farrell, and Dos Passos, Algren lived in a small apartment on the South Side of Chicago, from which he viewed the dispossessed and disaffected, mainly Eastern European Catholics, of his neighborhood. In his best works, his eye sharply notes every detail and nuance of the ragged, depressed milieu of his characters, while his tone embodies a poetic despair that all their efforts to get a little ahead in love or money will be fatally squashed by the world, which will allow them no escape. Often their doomed lives seem less the fault of society or environment than a fact of nature. Frankie "Machine" Majcinek, the hero of Algren's most successful novel, *The Man with the Golden Arm* (1949), is renowned in the neighborhood for his ability to deal cards, the "golden arm" that ensures him a job in the best card games. But Frankie, through his own nature, his bad luck, and even the desire and energy that gives him his stature, winds up dead at thirty—his good looks, his strength, his sensitivity worth nothing against this blank world. Frankie Machine, like almost everyone else in Algren's novels, carries some nickname or epithet with him like a battered escutcheon, the last remnant of a lost individuality. Although the chivalric suggestion may have its roots in Joyce's effort to show the epic grandeur of the everyday, Algren emphasizes its mock-epic and melancholic side: through these conmen, grifters, pimps, whores, and thieves flows the last thin blood of heroes who in another world performed grand and glorious actions, their sphere now shrunk to a few garbage-strewn back alleys and streets.

Algren gives the nineteenth-century romantic and naturalist fascination with the outsider and the disinherited a particularly urban tone of comic pessimism. Like Farrell and Dos Passos, he has philosophical affinities with the Marxist critique of capitalist social structure. But in the postwar period, as the war turned from hot to cold, and action was thwarted more often than expressed, any political energy in the naturalist novel seemed similarly short-circuited, sidetracked, or rerouted. The assumption of naturalism was that the writer stood outside his work, a kind of God, contemplating with sympathy the futile struggles of his characters. But when the writer also sought to express compassion and some political conclusion—the situation was bad, it should be changed—the form frequently bent under the weight of romantic idealism or sentimentalizing. *Somebody in Boots* (1935), Algren's first novel, perfectly captures the aimless outrage of characters for whom the author is the only spokesman. There, and in his best works, Algren's delicate sense of the day-to-day life of his characters mingled with his belief in the writer's necessary opposition to society to yield a need to remain outside, to embrace disinheritance, so that one's sensibility might truly develop.

Dos Passos had said, "most of all *U.S.A.* is the speech of the people," and in Algren's novels—as in the works of Farrell and Steinbeck or in such ghetto fiction as Henry's Roth's *Call It Sleep* (1935)—the one inalienable possession of the dispossessed is their vivid, living language. But if the only triumph possible in Algren's novels is a triumph of language, of speech, of invective, then the only real success is the author, who creates from the garbage a poem of despair. Even when the observing author asserts his identification with his subjects and their world, the naturalist attraction for implacable forces dictates their dooms. He writes about their deaths, but they die. So Algren cautiously treads the line between celebrating the speech of the semiliterate and sentimentally condescending to their bombastic efforts to create a language of self-importance. If his own voice is often reminiscent of the gallows humor of Céline or Genêt, at other moments the treacly sounds of Damon Runyon predominate.

Algren's special sensitivity to the conflict between the writer outside, who shapes the novel, and the writer inside, who sympathizes with the characters, is bodied forth in *The Man with the Golden Arm* by the character of Record Head Bednarik, the cynical-sentimental interrogating cop who knows everything about everyone who appears before him in the lineup, standing on the edge of jail or death. Cursed by his knowledge, "trapped between the hunters and the hunted," he equally understands and scorns both the lost in front of him and the outsiders from fancy neighborhoods who have come to gawk. The writer's perspective, his special way of seeing the world, has become more important than the political implications of what he sees. In later works Algren explicitly argues the need for the writer to remain hostile to his society, for without that conflict there is no creativity and no energy. Like the writer, Bednarik is an emblem of the individual in America, working but alone, compromised but not co-opted.

In his isolation Bednarik has still managed to remain sensitive to social forces. Algren's hero in *A Walk on the Wild Side* (1956) is Dove Linkhorn, a hillbilly conman/Candide, whose adventures in the South of the 1930s are a less scabrous version of Henry Miller's comic picaresque. Both figures have their attractions, but too often in Algren's later works the only sensibility he recommends is his own, a flailing irritation without either the irony of Mailer or the evasive elegance of Hemingway. Disgusted with writers like Mailer for being public performers, Algren himself, cast as the untamed Novelist, does only his own inept version of their performances. *Who Lost An American?* (1963) exhibits a paranoia about the New York control of literary success, while *Notes from a Sea Diary: Hemingway All the Way* (1965) interweaves a defense of Hemingway's works and personal nature with a trip around the world. Hemingway's secret, says Algren, was his actual lack of interest in money; and he was nothing like "the bloody adventurer" whom Algren believes was created by *Life* magazine. Yet Algren never faces Hemingway's willingness to acquiesce in the images with which others draped him, whatever they had to do with his personal nature.

One way out of the conflict between the naturalist view of the writer as an invisible God and the postwar pressure on the writer to be a public figure was a deeper experimentation with the first-person voice, where the writer could doff the protection of third-person detachment to define himself more directly as an outsider. A stronger influence on this self-definition than Hemingway, in both style and subject matter, is Henry Miller. Born in 1891, Miller might seem to be part of the same literary generation as Dos Passos, Farrell, Steinbeck, and Hemingway. But although his two most important works, *Tropic of Cancer* and *Tropic of Capricorn* were published in Paris in the 1930s (1934 and 1939), because of their heavy sexual content they were not published in the United States until the early 1960s, when Miller's work became the leading battlefield in the war over "pornographic" literature, and his role in American cultural history generally overshadowed his place in American literature.

Perhaps the emphasis was suitable, since Miller's "autobiographical romances" (as he called them) constantly proclaimed the writer as the model "new man," as much for the sensibility he displayed as for anything he actually wrote. In the Paris editions of *Cancer* and *Capricorn* brought back clandestinely by GIs after the war, readers found a celebration of what Miller described as an American evangelist's vision of the individual, distinctly at odds with the heavy historical fates and corporate organization in which the returning soldiers found themselves. An American innocent never foreseen by Henry James, Miller discovered in the bohemian world of Paris, where he lived for most of the 1930s, a vantage point from which to view America. Not a writer who likes to stand outside his work, Miller is his own favorite character, a first person Odysseus/Don Quixote, dedicated to "the recording of all that which is omitted in books" (*Cancer*). In one guise

Miller is a Studs Lonigan with energy, in control of his own language and wedded to his own perspective above all, creating a flow of images, adventures, scenes, rhapsodies, and sketches of eccentric characters that have little connection in the usual sense of plot but much in his own often infectious tone and combined self-mockery and self-assertion.

After the depiction of his life in Paris in *Cancer,* Miller in *Capricorn* and in the subsequent trilogy *The Rosy Crucifixion* (*Sexus,* 1949; *Plexus,* 1952; *Nexus,* 1959), as well as in much of his other writing, moved backward to explore his boyhood and growing up in Brooklyn. Constantly in these books, he is on the verge of writing, of becoming the writer that he wants to be. Around him history may be moving forward, but his exploration of his personal history (or "romance") moves backward as Miller attacks facts and the politics they imply in order to celebrate what is beneath and beyond them: "One can't make a new heaven and earth with 'facts' " (*Capricorn*). Unlike the Englishman George Orwell, one of Miller's first and still most acute critics, who in *Down and Out in Paris and London* (1933) sought to understand what it means to be marginal and poor, Miller finds in his past ghetto and present bohemian life a source of exuberance, change, and discovery. His attack on comfortable American values yields not despair (or even hope, he would say) but a grandiose release of energy that ought to change the world: "I will give you Horatio Alger as he looks the day after the Apocalypse, when all the stink has cleared away" (*Capricorn*).

Miller is less interested in justice than in freedom, and freedom is the combined right to live and write as one pleases. Sex is so central to his work because it expresses the individual will he values so highly. Sex and language are both acts of subversion and revenge—ways of getting back at a world that has deprived men of will. Miller's work is Rabelaisian in the sense that it is more about language than about things, more about the act of naming than the act of defining. His sensuous memory, his literary allusiveness, the metamorphic quality of his writing—all illustrate his greater affinity with Whitman, French symbolist poetry, and the Surrealists and Dadaists than with the novelists and story tellers of either America or Europe. His catalogues of the sights, sounds, smells, touches, tastes, and ideas of his world tumble more than they tick.

The extreme gestures of Miller's writing and self-dramatization stand in high contrast to the massing of order that characterizes more politically and socially oriented writers. What is most appealing in his work comes from his willingness to discover the clown in the artist. Detachment never seems to be a virtue for him, especially literary detachment, and the frequently comic situations he finds himself in spring from his own willingness to become the innocent but greedy butt, the literary dynamiter willing to blow himself up as well, if it makes a good show. *Cancer* and *Capricorn* keep the show moving briskly. But with *Sexus* Miller's Emersonian platform style has begun to take over, sermons amid the sex, without the incantatory flow of the earlier works. In this and many of his later works, especially the short pieces in *The Air-Conditioned Nightmare* (1945), there is much of the old wit and energy, but popular and critical success has otherwise succeeded in turning the old literary bridge-burner into a comfortable pontificator.

Yet Miller's legacy was strong, especially his emphasis on the personalized narrator and his effort to include as much of experience as he could. Jack Kerouac, whose writing shows affinities to Algren and other poetic naturalists, adopts Miller's first-person vulnerability in his most important novel, *On the Road* (1957), when he presents himself clearly as the author, the one who observed and wrote it all down. Kerouac's first novel, *The Town and the City* (1950), had presented a much more traditional naturalistic picture of growing up that drew especially on the style and sensitivities of Thomas Wolfe. But already the seeds of change were present. Like many other novels of the early 1950s—Norman Mailer's *Barbary Shore* (1951), John Clellon Holmes's *Go* (1952), Chandler Brossard's *Who Walk in Darkness* (1952), and William Burroughs's *Junkie* (1952)—*The Town and the City* sought to bring a new kind of character into literature, akin to the alienated detective, a disaffected, escaping young man, sometimes a veteran, sometimes not, for whom the boom world of the 1950s promised nothing but emptiness and who looked instead for a new rebirth of the arts, a commingling stimulated by drugs, presided over by jazz, but expressed in language.

A few years later, in Kerouac's creation of something like the final version of *On the Road* in a three-week typing session with a roll of teletype paper, he had discovered a form to fit the events he wished to depict rather than one that would impress them into preexisting plots and situations. The looseness of the narrative drew for its strength not on the synoptic vision of Dos Passos, the encyclopedic playfulness of Melville, the detached ironies of Algren, or the total immersion of Farrell. Rather, like many another novel of the postwar period, it hearkened more to the picaresque, to the odyssey through a society rather than a submission to it. But Kerouac is the picaró who watches and remembers much more than he acts, as if, instead of having Sancho Panza for his companion, Don Quixote had Cervantes himself, pen in hand, more willing to be driven than to drive. Kerouac does not brood over his scenes; he is there inside them. By including himself as a character and thereby individualizing his own perspective, Kerouac can more easily celebrate the autonomy of characters like Dean Moriarty, the hero of *On the Road,* who, unlike Algren's fated losers, embodies the new values for which Kerouac is searching.

Kerouac's characters are less washouts and misfits than self-conscious dropouts who have decided to create themselves in their own terms, hearkening back to a more individualist and personal America, far from the faceless present. Between the publication of *The Town and the City* and that of *On the Road,* Kerouac wrote in whole or in part almost all the works that were published in later years (up to and after his death in 1969), weaving a poetic, harsh, loving, and surrealistic tapestry of his own life and the lives of his friends, as they attempted to create a fabric of relationship across the United States, an extended family of people like themselves, linking and relinking in endless car trips and visits. Despite the melancholy that runs through Kerouac's works (with the notable exception of *The Dharma Bums,* 1958), the onward rush of his narrative, what he called "spontaneous prose," carries a message of continuity through the most disastrous and most ecstatic experiences. His friends, his characters, are people on the fringe, dopesters, drifters, who yet create a community between themselves that is warm and nurturing, unlike the constant battle and competition of Algren's more urban world. On the road Kerouac can connect without the oppressive compulsions of urban life or literary tradition. His direction is away from New York, and toward the west, less bent on asserting the Second or another City than on discovering an alternate way of being, into which American romantic primitivism and Oriental mysticism carry potent streams. Literarily, his narrative drive toward connection and family expresses a detachment without condescension. He would become a midwife at the birth of another culture, constantly puzzled or bemused at what through his works he brought into being. Kerouac had turned naturalist observation of the underside of social life into a statement about the more deeply felt lives of the people who either have not succeeded or do not want to succeed in the terms available to them. If naturalism, in Zola's sense, shared a politics with the scientific socialism that wanted to raise the low, lower the high, and democratize society, Kerouac's naturalism, tinged with romantic, mystical, and surrealist urges, reversed the standards and looked for its values in everything society had left behind.

International literary modernism has often been characterized by its preoccupation with its own structure, language, and self-conscious place in artistic tradition. In contrast, as the postwar period was making clear, the American novel, however it might borrow modernist techniques, still would concentrate its powers on the effort to bring a nonliterary or even an antiliterary reality into the novel's special perspective, to renovate more by the disruption of content than by the self-consciousness of form. In Europe, rebellion might still be carried on through the aristocratic manipulation of aesthetic forms, although the work of Céline, Genêt, and the rediscovery of Sade were defining another tradition. But in America writers sought to discover and portray varieties of human nature beyond those that could be encompassed by bourgeois comforts or definitions of society. Whether through the moral conscience of Steinbeck, the grim pessimism of Algren, or the run-on elation of Kerouac, the observing novelist searched for new energy in the American places traditional literature had usually left dark. Kerouac could date the inspiration for his new writing style from a long letter sent to him by the unlettered Neal Cassady (the original of Dean Moriarty and later the bus driver for Ken Kesey's Merry Pranksters). But Kerouac and other novelists avoided a romantic homage to the nonliterary life of action and energy (as well as its implicit condescension) by identifying themselves with a first-person teller who was not the hero of action, but the hero of contemplation. The actions of the maniacally disruptive individualist Randle MacMurphy in Kesey's *One Flew Over the Cuckoo's Nest* (1962) are watched and recorded by the stolid Chief, whose only defense against being imprisoned in the insane asylum has been to pretend catatonia. All the repressive weight of the institution falls, of course, on MacMurphy, and finally the Chief smothers the lobotomized MacMurphy and makes his escape—into an uncertain future, since the only individualism possible still seems to be the coolness of keeping your counsel.

How then to choose between cool contemplation and unreflective action? In an oddly similar way, the narrator of John Rechy's *City of Night* (1963) maintains an almost icy, detailing calm amid his world of transvestites, thieves, murderers, and other habitués of downtown Los Angeles. The urban novel had gradually given its imprimatur to an almost sociological urge to catalogue the human discrepancies between American myth and American reality. Its hidden message proclaimed that if the atypical was central, then perhaps the "deviant" part of each of us might offer salvation in the conformist wilderness. In the 1930s, realist and naturalist fiction could explicitly support a liberal or radical critique of American society. But, as the ministrations of the New Deal and the mobilization of resources prompted by the war changed the shape of that society, the politics of urban naturalism shaded toward the anarchic, and its formal procedures moved from third person to first person. In the 1950s especially such anarchism could be left or right in political complexion, until the more personally oriented politics of the late 1960s forged a new political coalition. But throughout the early postwar period an exalted sense of profession that went beyond mere expertise and into sensibility became an essential part of the writer's image before the world.

The one writer of the war generation who most elaborately attempts to mediate all these influences while he remains open to the strongest trends of postwar culture is Norman Mailer. Born in 1923, a year younger than Kerouac, Mailer began his career in *The Naked and the Dead* (1948) as an imitator and extender of Dos Passos, although, in the manner of the second generation, he did not change older forms so much as he was self-conscious about their application. At least until *The Prisoner of Sex* (1971), Mailer's career forms a continuing meditation on the varieties of postwar novelistic style that orchestrates the synoptic naturalism of Dos Passos, the hard-edged neighborhood fatalism of Farrell, and the mythic natural rhythms of Steinbeck into concert with the quintessentially postwar motif of the writer as a special person with a special mission. Hemingway's careful fiction of the isolated writer-hero becomes in Mailer's work the writer-hero as weathervane in the winds of culture—focal point for Mailer's special combination of modernist stylistic self-consciousness and naturalist political self-consciousness.

"The end of epic" could be a chapter in the history of postwar fiction, as the generation of war novelists wondered if peace would ever furnish so grand a theme as war. Such a chapter might begin with the young Mailer, in the days after Pearl Harbor, "worrying darkly," as he writes in *Advertisements for Myself* (1959), whether the great war novel would come out of the European or the Pacific theater of operations. He decided that it would be European, but then himself set first a short story ("A Calculus at Heaven") and later *The Naked and the Dead* in the Pacific, because, in his Jamesian phrase, he did not have the "sense of the past" necessary to write about "the culture of Europe and the collision of America upon it." The product therefore as much of Mailer's literary aspirations as of his actual experiences, *The Naked and the Dead* appeared almost, as it were, on schedule, the first war novel to be a great critical and popular success. It was a vast fabric of American diversity pitched on a Pacific island, with no real central character, certainly no hero, and a plot that focused less on the war with the Japanese than on the metaphysical-political conflict between the liberal Lieutenant Hearn and the conservative General Cummings, fought under the shadows of the constantly encroaching, blinding jungle. The action is pseudo-historical—the effort to capture the island of Anopopei in the Philippines—but the novel is so concerned with the interplay of the lives of the men that public history seems actually more suspended than fatally rushing onward. Much time is spent arguing about strategy, going on missions, and thinking about the past. When the battle is won, it happens by accident. The grand strategy of General Cummings is not useless, but its intricacies and its intellectual power seem primarily to be human ways of taking up time, while nature and chance bring in their revenges.

After the narrative sweep of *The Naked and the Dead,* Mailer's later work becomes much more personal, and many would say that he had somehow reneged on his early "promise." But already in *The Naked and the Dead* the naturalist assumption of interpretive authority was being undermined. Certainly it conveys even more palpably than do the works of Dos Passos that the author knows many things about America. But the Mailer behind the novel is not the same kind of authority as Dos Passos. Through a variety of techniques—straight narration, playlet interludes, biographical sketches—Mailer infuses Dos Passos's affinity for detail with an empathy for character that creates a new synthesis between the detached naturalist Author and the involved participant. Even in this early work, Mailer's metamorphic quality, his potential to become all of his characters, contributes an emotion that was often lacking in Dos Passos. Their different aims have conditioned the result: Dos Passos was putting together a total American experience of which his readers were in great part unaware, while Mailer, with World War II as his magazine, was constructing a coherence for new experiences, information, and impulses that his audience was struggling to make sense of as well.

One problem in reading *The Naked and the Dead,* the result of Mailer's double allegiance to the first and third persons, is the frequent difficulty of telling which is the thought or image of the author and which of the character. In *Barbary Shore* (1951), his second novel, he shifts decisively to the first person. The narrator has lost his memory. He can no longer tell fact from fiction, memory from imagination: "Probably I was in the war," his only proof a scar on his head that seems to be a war wound. Set in a rooming house in Brooklyn, *Barbary Shore* is more the stuff of political allegory than of history, and it argues the interrelation of the political and the psychological, the irrelevance of history that is not personal. Increasingly, Mailer was becoming fascinated by the psychology of politics, or, as he explained in an article written in the early 1950s, the effort to build a bridge between Marx and Freud. More and more, he explored the same themes of violence, competition, and assertion that had been present in *The Naked and the Dead,* but now in a context of peacetime impotence, where sensibility and emotion were constantly being brought into question by a Cold War America in which only efficiency and demonstrated competence mattered. Too much of a romantic finally to accept the cool professionalism of Jones, Mailer still embraced the image of the writer as outsider, and after censorship problems with *The Deer Park* (1955), brought out his most resonant challenge to the gray-flannel anonymity of the 1950s—*Advertisements for Myself* (1959). The method was again a descendant of Dos Passos's naturalist pastiche. But the tone was defiantly personal, as Mailer feathered together fiction, political essay, poetry, literary criticism, and autobiography to present himself, the working writer, model 1959. Conscious of what he considered to be Hemingway's inability to control the growing gaps between his public, personal, and professional selves, Mailer sought to control their interplay, not by a Baudelairean nakedness but by the subtly calculated medium of "advertisements"—a necessary schizophrenia for the novelist that he had predicted in his 1952 short story "The Man Who Studied Yoga." In American terms the formula might be considered a way to avoid both F. Scott Fitzgerald's searing self-exposure in "The Crack-up" (1936) and Hemingway's own sternly elegant displacement in *Across the River and into the Trees* (1950). Impersonation, especially the self-conscious creation of "Mailer," allowed an escape from the Hemingwayesque trap of the expectation of others.

Once again, Mailer seemed to sniff something brewing in American life, and his willful splitting of himself into public and private versions was aptly suited to explicate the confusions of style and self that preoccupied the 1960s. Holding them together was an increasingly baroque and insinuating style that was almost the diametrical opposite of either the straightforward word-object clarity of Dos Passos and Farrell or the pared-down nuances of Hemingway—so distrustful had Mailer become of the ease with which they expressed their knowledge. His own vision of America became increasingly enveloped in a personal mythology of disease and paranoia that was purgeable only through writing that suited the work to its subject instead of imposing a falsely clarifying vision. *An American Dream* (1965) outraged many critics by its seemingly autobiographical fantasies. But after *The Naked and the Dead* Mailer never again wrote in anything resembling a third-person narrative, tying his decision specifically to the belief that the kind of assurance that sat behind the third-person narratives of a writer like E. M. Forster was no longer possible in postwar America. *Why Are We in Viet Nam?* (1967) reworked Hemingway and Faulkner's theme of the hunt into a book-length monologue by a young Texan, whose fundamentally nineteenth-century moral values are overlain with all the slogans, symbols, and icons of American popular culture. *The Armies of the Night* (1968) completed Mailer's defection from or his growth out of his naturalist past by being both first person and third person at the same time—a retrospective look at the 1967 Pentagon March, through the eyes of "Mailer," half in league with and half dubious about the effort of the marchers to make their individual voices heard in protest against the war. "History as a Novel" and "The Novel as History" were the subtitles of its two sections, and in his later work, as well as in the three films he has made, Mailer has constantly pointed to the ways in which factuality and history need the shaping power of imagination to make them "real."

The dream of community that had inspired the Popular Front—and the literary methods of Dos Passos and the Mailer of *The Naked and the Dead*—had been replaced first by the enforced order of the World at War and then by the annihilating torpor of postwar Togetherness. The popular propaganda of the Cold War quieted national anxieties by asserting or implying that everything truly American was the same as everything else: the system was fine, only individuals were wrong. In such a world the virtuoso accumulativeness of naturalism had nothing to do except go on the road, turn inward, or paint the world in broader strokes than ever before. Mailer's concentration on the writer's style as the image of the individual contemplating the complexity of American experience coincides with the rediscovery of the power of picaresque intimacy by postwar writers otherwise as disparate as Kerouac and Saul Bellow (in *The Adventures of Augie March*, 1953). The romantic, first-person perspective might hope to balance or at least find a refuge from the growing pressure of inhuman events. But in other hands, by the late 1950s and early 1960s, naturalist fatality had become paranoid surrealism, drawing on the facts of national life and the clichés of popular culture to create a world where technology, politics, and history had run wild and the only possible humanism was gallows humor. Mailer himself had worked the vein, most deeply in *An American Dream*. But his own politics finally had a streak of practicality that issued, however eccentrically, in journalism, reportage, and a fascination with the mystery of public personality (for example, in his books on Muhammad Ali, 1971, and Marilyn Monroe, 1973). In the complementary urge, more akin to science fiction than to picaresque adventure, the naturalist contemplation of History was not personalized but expanded into the realm of apocalyptic fantasy, where everything was fatally connected and everything fatally explained. While some novelists took up the special problems of groups and others investigated the daily life of particular worlds and places, the paranoid novel created order through mockery and exaggeration, exposing in its satire the anonymity and inhumanity to which its readers were too easily getting accustomed. History was no longer a pattern of factually and philosophically analyzable causes; it was a nightmare, an allegory of good and evil, a metaphysical comic book.

In the 1920s film, in the 1930s radio, and after the war television bound together the country in an electronic web of overlapping cultural loyalties. The naturalists of the 1930s often similarly worked to create a total vision of America. But their descendants in the 1950s, 1960s, and 1970s seemed to be bent on trying to pry themselves loose from the enveloping embrace of the media and their jovial paranoia. Then the individual might have wanted in; now he wanted out. And the clearest way out was to create the most overarching vision. With his special focus on the situation of the black in America, Ralph Ellison in his prophetic *Invisible Man* (1952) helped create a style in which surrealism and naturalism mingled to portray an America gone mad. In this world of paranoid connection and impersonal power, the imagination of the individual is the last refuge of will. History was up for grabs—to be made fantastic, to be flattened out, to be invaded and reshaped as the novelist desired. American newspaper editorials and many popular magazines in the 1950s scored easy points in the Cold War by attacking the Russian effort to "rewrite" history. But many American novelists, and many members of groups left out of the Cold War consensus, felt equally dispossessed by the official American view of the past. The answer was a personal retreat that could turn into a literary weapon. "Serious" history and "serious" fiction were the prime enemies, and so the novelists moved closer to the realm of popular culture, absorbing its vitality and variety into a self-created coherence that mocked official order even while pushing it to absurdity.

Already in 1959 Richard Condon had published a terrifying forerunner of later efforts to struggle against the enclosures of history. *The Manchurian Candidate,* his second novel, parodied the McCarthy period and virtually every political event of the last ten years through the story of a Congressional Medal of Honor winner who had been turned into an assassin by Chinese Communist brainwashing. For Condon, typically, there is no escape; America is a madhouse in which only the most insane assume power, high office, and fame. In his best works —*The Manchurian Candidate, Some Angry Angel* (1960), and *Winter*

Kills (1974)—Condon has a controlled corrosiveness that levels every-thing in its sights. His style is naturalism gone mad—true details in absurd patterns that convince by their maniacal ability to precipitate solidity from the haze of stories, rumors, half-truths, and myths that were beginning to pass for reality in America.

Not as jagged in his rage as Condon, Thomas Berger began his career as a satiric naturalist of the older style with the World War II novel *Crazy in Berlin* (1958) and its sequel *Reinhart in Love* (1962). But with *Little Big Man* (1964), he reached out to try to encompass an older America, to discover where the myths finally ran down. The sup-posedly tape-recorded reminiscences of Jack Crabb, a 114-year-old Indian scout, *Little Big Man* somehow manages both to satirize the Old West and to create a nostalgia for its clear and uncomplicated values. We are there, as if in a historian's reconstruction, yet with the full knowledge and therefore the distance of what happened after-ward, filtered through the cynical-sentimental tones of Jack Crabb. Like Condon and others, Berger uses popular forms as a way of in-dicating the failure of the elitist and modernist vision of the world. As Mailer tries to end naturalism, Berger seeks to end the western, the detective novel, the science fiction novel, the hard-boiled depression novel—to show where and why the myths no longer work.

In the works of Mailer, Condon, Berger, and Kurt Vonnegut, Jr., the mythic quest, the rite of passage that has been a part of American literature since the time of James Fenimore Cooper, is absorbed into the realm of fantasy and dream. The rewards that American society hands out to those who achieve are shown to be corrupt and tainted, and the assumption that the shape of society should be imitated by the shape of fiction is attacked for its implication that society is either logical or immutable. So naturalism is rejected by its own stylistic heirs. The natural heir of the naturalist *manqué* Mailer is the natu-ralist gone manic Thomas Pynchon, who in *The Crying of Lot 49* (1966) defines America as part mysterious inheritance, part Jacobean revenge tragedy, and in *Gravity's Rainbow* (1973) mocks the naturalist project by making much of World War II seem to be a conspiracy against the sanity of one Tyrone Slothrop. From *The Naked and the Dead* to *Catch-22* to *Gravity's Rainbow* echoes the cry of battered in-dividualism: "Someone out there is trying to kill me."

Perhaps the most striking image of the novelist trying to escape from History by turning to the methods of a pseudo-historian appears in E. L. Doctorow's *Ragtime* (1975), a novelized version of early twen-tieth-century, principally American, history that centers less on a hero than on a kind of master of ceremonies, the magician and escape artist

Harry Houdini. In a previous novel, *The Book of Daniel* (1971), Doctorow had created a plausible but fictional biography of Daniel, whom he supposes to be the older of the two boys orphaned on June 19, 1953, when Julius and Ethel Rosenberg were executed as spies. For many who had come of age in the 1950s, the Rosenberg case held a fascination beyond the questions of guilt and innocence that preoccupied the lawyers, the politicians, and the journalists. If the Rosenbergs were guilty of spying, there was a justifiable paranoia loose in America, dictated from Russia; if they were innocent, there was still a paranoia loose, but perhaps dictated from America. Two ordinary people had been caught, wittingly or not, in the rush of international politics, where beliefs, sincerity, and personal will existed only at the whim of History. Doctorow's *Book of Daniel* preserves a realism of plausible detail in its effort to recapture the times and, through Daniel's own effort, to explain what happened. Yet finally it creates history as much as it explores it, or, rather, creates history in order to explore it.

To mess with History threatened the postwar novelist with either annihilation by its God or assimilation to its evil purposes. How then to speak for the underdog and for the order at the same time? More influenced than Doctorow by the novel of apocalypse, Robert Coover in *The Public Burning* (1977) uses the Rosenberg trial and the career of Richard Nixon as the documentable center of a sweeping Brueghel-like vision of all of 1950s culture. To rely on the novelist's imagination would seem to be a self-indulgence when the ever-filling memory banks of historical fact might demand a mastering selection and coherence. But for Doctorow as much as for Coover, that imagination could find an order that in other, more public, hands would become intolerable. In *Ragtime* Doctorow uses a structure reminiscent of Steinbeck's *Grapes of Wrath* or a compressed *U.S.A.*, focusing first on the meaning of public events and then on the fortunes of several distinct persons, some fictional and some historical, whose lives impinge upon or help create those events. In all his characters exists the desire to explore, to understand, and thereby to be free. But Doctorow, like a vaudeville Zola, allows only the barest of compensations for the sin of being involved in public events. Once History is joined, after one yields to the urge to perform, there is no escape, even for the escape artist Houdini, whose art, although it offers a model of freedom to the less free, is actually another form of confinement.

The uncertain situation of the traditional naturalist novel in the violent and History-ridden America of the 1960s may most clearly be reflected in the career of John Gardner. His first novel, *The Resurrection* (1966) is an effectively told story of family and feeling in the mode of James Agee's *A Death in the Family* (1957). But Gardner is also a professor of Middle English literature, and many of his later novels, especially the popular *Grendel* (1971), ambitiously attempt to infuse the patterns of ancient myth and ritual with the ironic intelligence of the present. In part, Gardner represents the new academic novelist, continuing a professional career of criticism and translation while in his fictions he is intent on identifying himself with the alien and unassimilated man from the outside who has been so strong a presence in American literature.

Yet Gardner's most explicit sources are not Cooper, Hawthorne, or Melville but the Middle English and classical works he admires and often imitates in pastiches of poetry, dialogue, and narrative. In the face of the depredations of History, Gardner implies that the only real truth may be found in the rhythms of myth and ritual. Like Steinbeck, Gardner is drawn especially to the stories of King Arthur and the Knights of the Round Table, the thin edge by which civilization defines its victory over nature. Again like Steinbeck, Gardner illustrates the writer's special moral mission by his ability to penetrate the lives of small-town characters and layabouts. Whether the violent Grendel or the peaceful Sunlight Man of *The Sunlight Dialogues* (1972), Gardner's heroes stand like the holy fools or urban gurus of Steinbeck and Algren—figures of the writer who wants acceptance only on his own terms, without being sure what they are. Too often, though, Gardner's literary self-consciousness blunts his moral concerns. Although *The Sunlight Dialogues* takes place in upstate New York during the 1960s, its situations and characterizations have little edge, their tones and voices more impersonated than felt. In *Nickel Mountain* (1973), however, Gardner embraces his strengths with less premeditation. Subtitled "a pastoral novel," it is closer to the rhythms of nature and character than his earlier works, because it avoids their constant sonority. But his next novel, *October Light* (1976), interweaves this attractive domestic mood with sections from a novel of sex, violence, and philosophical discussion (akin to *An American Dream*) that is being read by one of the characters. Once again, Gardner reaches restlessly for the easy solutions of pastiche, his folksy highstyle thinly binding together the relaxed natural humanism of a Steinbeck with the pompous moral assertions of a mythic didact. Finally Gardner seems more convinced by his own virtuosity than by the truths of his stories and characters, and his effort to reconcile myths of community and myths of isolation holds little of the animating conviction of, for example, Gabriel García Márquez's powerfully imagined *One Hundred Years of Solitude* (1970). Perhaps I am saying only that Gardner is a typical American novelist of his period. His recent critical work, *On Moral Fiction* (1978), in which he condemns his contemporaries and trumpets himself (with a select few), conveys his uncertainty about what he is trying to do. His career, at least so far, seems easier to map in terms of its voraciously absorbed precedents than to assess in terms of its genuine achievements.

Gardner's exploration of myth as a refuge from history, like those carried on by Robert Coover in *The Public Burning* and such earlier, more realistic works as *The Origin of the Brunists* (1966) and *The Universal Baseball Association, Inc., J. Henry Waugh, Prop.* (1968), attempts to restore the losses of will with the balm of the creative imagination. As the anxieties of the characters in the novels of Hemingway, Jones, and others make clear, that imagination was often implicitly if not explicitly defined as masculine. The personal residue of the historical experience of World War II, those paradoxes that attracted many writers, simultaneously seemed to glorify and to diminish the individual male ego, so stimulated to achieve and so doomed to fail. Mailer's explicit manipulation of the division between private and public self indicated the need for a way out of the social expectations for male behavior that World War II had helped embed in American culture. Gore Vidal, who also began his career as a war novelist, has taken another way, to question finally the idea of masculinity itself and to tie sexuality even more firmly than does Mailer to the theme of will and action in history.

Vidal's career, since the publication of his first novel, *Williwaw* (1946), when he was nineteen, has embodied perhaps the most concerted effort of any postwar novelist to establish himself as a "man of letters" on the European model, equally at home in a variety of forms—novels, essays, plays, screenplays. Expectations for Vidal were high, as they were for so many of the young war novelists, and his own hot-house beginning may have caused his public self-creation to lag somewhat behind the creation of his works. In that interaction between working author and public person that Mailer has made so central to his career, Vidal works with a certain clumsiness and ineptness, his mandarin narcissism an intriguing contrast to Mailer's struggling self-obsession. Mailer, from *The Naked and the Dead* on, is essentially an intellectual, oratorical and (if I can say it descriptively) a wordy writer, while Vidal's language is much closer to that of Hemingway, a plain style of flatly resonant significance. Mailer values the tumble of language; Vidal's natural mode of expression is the witty, succinct phrase, the conversation-stopping quip or putdown, the irony that allows him to draw back and assess all that has passed and find it wanting. Even in his most fantastical works, such as the marvelous *Myron* (1974), the extravagances are delivered deadpan.

In his novels the irony shading to bitchiness that so relentlessly striates Vidal's essays has become an instrument of virtue. There his style implies the ability to perceive beyond the commonplace, to be disinterested, to be involved but aware, talking while listening. The true homing ground of Vidal's imagination lies eccentrically but comfortably in the place where science fiction and history meet, where the lost chances of the past and the possibilities of the future can finally be given life. Only in these two places can the imagination be set free from the tyrannies of the present, for the present seems infinitely restrictive, tedious, and fallen to Vidal, coming to life only with the prospect of violence. Like Tennessee Williams, with whom he collaborated on the script for *Suddenly, Last Summer* (1959), Vidal is preoccupied with the necessary failure of any urge to perfection or recaptured innocence. Against the day-to-day boredom of society, the spasm of sex and the gesture of violence are the only resources the individual has—sex, violence, and, of course, the act of writing. So many of Vidal's novels translate this theme into a push-pull between a strong father and a weak son, weak because his powers are so dependent on those of his father. The fathers experience the emotions and the events of history; the sons can only observe, narrate, and survive. The grandeur has passed, and even when heroic actions are accomplished, they will be obscured and the heroes never given proper credit.

For Vidal, the place of true passions and true values is always in the past, and the best of his characters call on the past to restore the present. Three of Vidal's most successful and impressive works—*Julian* (1964), *Burr* (1973), and *Myron* (1974)—are preoccupied with this effort to reclaim for the present a vital past in which character could grow instead of being thwarted. Like Mailer, Vidal both applauded the personal energies released in the 1960s and was appalled by what he considered to be their refusal to know the past. The history that crushes individuals, implies Vidal, is not the abstract force of the naturalists, but a consciously manipulated plan. Both Julian the Apostate and Aaron Burr are the victims of conspiracies by the historically "successful" forces to ignore or obscure their characters and importance. As Mailer implies in *The Armies of the Night*, the perspective of the novelist must correct the overdetermining patterns of the historian, the sly apologies for tyranny. For Vidal, the Christians who assassinated Julian and the Virginia Junto that tried to get rid of Burr represent the interests of selfish men pretending they embody historical necessity, a totalitarian politics out to stifle the great originals. Character is the essential human mystery. History is merely the efforts of mean men to take power, while they sonorously assert moral motives. Julian the Apostate seems to echo Vidal himself when he says, "That is why Hellenism must be restored: to instill again in man that sense of his own worth which made civilization possible."

In *Julian, Burr,* and *Myron* Vidal retains a faith in the autonomy of individual action, whether in personal relations or in history. To enter the past in fiction is often to enter a fatal world. Everything has already happened. Because we know the outcome, the scope of human will has become almost comically narrow. But Vidal uses history to restore will and personality rather than submerge it in the surge of historical rhythms. Vidal's particular mythology often sets character in a family context—especially the competition between brothers or the relation of father and son—while Mailer's portrayal of competition, as in *An American Dream,* sketches the Oedipal drama in comic-book tones. But both celebrate an individuality and personal voice that tries to stand against the impersonal patterns of History. Mailer replaces the naturalist God of History with the constant interplay between himself as actor and as observer. Vidal is at once more detached and more preoccupied with his own view, celebrating an aristocracy of sensibility constantly thwarted and ignored by those mere whores after fame, the statesmen and politicians. After the political isolation of the 1950s, the Kennedy presidency (1960–63) seems to have inspired both Vidal and Mailer to believe that their particular sensibilities could be effectively translated into politics. Both ran unsuccessfully for office, Vidal for Congress in 1960 and Mailer for mayor of New York in 1969.

From their earliest literary works, both Vidal and Mailer reached out to redefine the scope of will, rejecting American imperial politics and the assumptions about masculinity that so often accompany it. They sought to give a political edge to the sense of personal isolation in an overstructured America that runs through the novels of Spillane, Jones, Bourjaily, and so many others—to bring the loner into the system and thereby change it. But loners and systems are necessarily at odds, and Vidal, like Mailer, gets more literary capital from the anomalies of his position than any reconciliation could possibly give. A central expression of Vidal's changing view of himself as a writer appears in *Two Sisters: A Memoir in the Form of a Novel* (1970), whose subtitle inverts that of John P. Marquand's *The Late George Apley: A Novel in the Form of a Memoir* (1937), which itself had inverted George Santayana's *The Last Puritan: A Memoir in the Form of a Novel* (1935). At the time when the news of the novel was still the "nonfiction novel" (such as Capote's *In Cold Blood*, 1965) Vidal in *Two Sisters* created a work in which the lines of fiction and memoir, novel and play, experience and expression, are constantly crossed and recrossed. The result is less successful than suggestive, a storehouse of themes and techniques to be developed rather than magisterially delivered. In the 1950s three arch detective novels (written under the pseudonym of Edgar Box) and a group of distinguished plays and screenplays set the stage for Vidal's more complex later work, and the way *Two Sisters* connects formal self-consciousness with the psychology of role playing demonstrates the distance Vidal has traveled from the spare directness of his early fiction.

An important aspect of Vidal's later work is his preoccupation with the theme of celebrity, as if fame could supply the power that the individual has otherwise lost. Interestingly enough for a story about the symbiosis between twins, *Two Sisters* is almost a gloss on *Washington, D.C.* (1967), a more conventional dynastic-satiric novel of life in the high political society of the capital from the 1930s to the 1960s. The Siamese relation seems crucial. If Vidal leans toward the naturalists in his grapplings with History, he leans also toward the novelists of manners in his preoccupation with the determining effect of family. He has lavishly praised Louis Auchincloss (who has a family relation to him) as a great original, the only American novelist who knows and writes about what happens in the world of high society and money. Yet it seems less the theme of money or society that attracts Vidal to Auchincloss than an elusive but substantial authenticity. In a world of Hemingway-imitators and Fitzgerald-imitators, Vidal has written, "certainly no one was himself—but then selves are hard to come by in America . . . [Auchincloss] was simply himself, and so odd man out to the young counterfeiters."

Vidal's own effort to avoid counterfeiting (and perhaps his fear of falling into it unawares) seems most successful after *Julian* through his intricate interweaving of historical reconstruction and historical fantasy: Myron/Myra Breckinridge, the bisexual fantasist who is trying to change the history of America by turning a flop Maria Montez film into a success; Charles Schuyler, the narrator of *Burr*, who is trying to change the nature of America by making her real hero Burr rather than Jefferson. *Julian, Burr*, and even the perfunctory *1876* (1976) attempt the synthesis of action and history in the serious tones of the historical novel, while *Myra Breckinridge* (1968) and *Myron* (1974) express the dilemma in a comic mode. So too the same body alternately contains the assertive, world-historical Myra and the passive, dowdy Myron—neither totally in control, neither whole without the other.

Similarly, when the temper suits him, Vidal has become either the outsider or the insider. With the popular success of *Myra, Burr,* and *1876,* this Myra/Myron perspective has turned him toward essayistic celebration of himself and occasionally Saul Bellow as great writers for a mass audience, while he attacks John Barth, Donald Barthelme, and others for writing a "new academic novel" suitable only for explication by the elite intelligences of the university. Yet Vidal himself has lived in Italy off and on since 1965, the patriotic expatriate, affirming his status as an American writer by his separatist fascination with America.

The mystery of character for Vidal is inextricably related to the mystery of sexuality. He shares with Mailer, Jones, Kerouac, and many other novelists of the postwar period an inclination to find the clearest incidence of repression in the way society limits an individual's efforts to discover the shape of his sexuality. Sexuality had always been a central theme in realist and naturalist fiction because it constituted the unspoken and unspeakable secret; all an author had to do was allude to it and he seemed to have left the world of manners and a more demure literary tradition behind. It could become a subject of metaphysical speculation in postwar fiction because the new social freedoms brought about by World War II had also helped ease the restraints on sexual reference, sexual language, and sexual incident in literature: sex in literature was authentic, it was true to "real" experience, and it no longer needed to be confined to the pages of underground or "difficult" novels like *Ulysses* (itself only free of banning since the Wolsey decision of (1936). Henry Miller's sexually explicit novels would not be freely published in the United States until 1962, when Grove Press won its case to prevent censorship of *Tropic of Cancer.* But years before, in *For Whom the Bell Tolls* (1940), Hemingway had supplied an evocative dignity for sexual language by using the word *obscenity.* A publisher's somewhat comical timidity forced the appearance of *fug* all through *The Naked and the Dead* (1948). But three years later, in *From Here to Eternity,* James Jones was explicit both about the language and about its metaphysic: " (you shy away from the Word, don't you?)." Saying, writing, printing *fuck* could be a source of assertion and strength for the novelist even while sexuality might be a burden for his characters, for sexual scenes and sexual references allowed the loss of control and the dip into untapped energy without which art was impossible, yet with which life became more chaotic and disrupted.

Such hard-won freedom, of course, became easily imitated. Through the 1950s underground and aboveground best sellers overflowed drugstore shelves and conditioned the American reading public to an increasing sexual explicitness that existed in odd symbiosis with the stifled political life of the period—perhaps the American version of a Soviet cultural politics that also preserved a strict chastity about personal behavior. With their first-person emphasis, Kerouac, Mailer, and others were exploring Wilhelm Reich's theory that sexual freedom could be at the root of both psychic renovation and social change. But the more traditional use of sexual reference in literature had been satiric, to deflate social or individual pretension. There, once again, the writer's freedom was often linked to or depended upon the character's confinement. So too in many sexually "free" novels of the postwar period, especially those with the greatest popular success, sexuality was the finally unveiled truth before which all the characters, from the highest to the lowest, were helpless. The great master of this theme in the postwar period was John O'Hara.

O'Hara, in many aspects of his fiction, stands between the novelists of urban milieu and the novelists of manners. Similar to Farrell in age and religion, but, like Sinclair Lewis, the son of a small-town doctor, O'Hara set most of his novels and short stories in a medium-sized Pennsylvania town he named Gibbsville, roughly based on the Pottsville where he had grown up. O'Hara's first book of short stories is called *The Doctor's Son and Other Stories* (1935), and although he left Pottsville for New York in his early twenties, something of the doctor's son remains in his perspective—coldly observing all the classes of his hometown, with the intricate details of their lives and relations with each other, from the angle of their physicality, the blood and bone beneath the masks. Sex is central to O'Hara's vision because his universe revolves according to iron laws of human causality. Everyone manipulates or wants to manipulate everyone else, and a frequently repeated moment in O'Hara's work occurs when all of a sudden a character learns the foul, trivial way that others think of him, overhears exactly how he is at their mercy and how unwittingly he has placed himself there, usually by the uncontrollable eruption of his desires. Everyone in Gibbsville, and any other place O'Hara writes about, talks constantly of two subjects, sex and social distinctions, and the narrator is the expert on both, simultaneously a condescending God and an intimate confidant, encompassing both the invisible pattern and the secret eruptions. Through the intricate gradations of status, he searches for the false step, the slip, that will catapult someone outside the fold, with no hope of ever reentering.

Gibbsville was the setting of O'Hara's first novel, *Appointment in Samarra* (1934), the story of the last few fateful days in the life of

Julian English, a young Cadillac dealer from an important local family headed by a doctor father. Like many later O'Hara characters, Julian has a special sensibility that by its intensity, its integrity, or its willful blindness to small-town standards of success is unappreciated until it finally bursts out in a reckless, unredeemable gesture. Julian English commits suicide for little reason, as it turns out—while his creator channels his own rebellion into a devastating critique of the social codes that have stifled so much potential energy. So the paradox rises again: successful authors, doomed characters. O'Hara's sympathies seem more divided than those of Algren or other chroniclers of the fatally dispossessed, perhaps because he shares the dilemma of his status-conscious characters, so pressed between the standards of society from without and their tumultuous impulses from within. Throughout his career O'Hara's moral condemnation is leveled against the stifling town. But he remains captivated by the infinite patterns of that stifling. In *Main Street* Sinclair Lewis remarks that "the greatest mystery about a human being is not his reaction to sex or praise, but the manner in which he contrives to put in twenty-four hours a day." What might be O'Hara's riposte to Lewis on the question of a writer's knowledge and where the most crucial secrets may be found appears in a short story entitled *Andrea* (published in *Waiting for Winter*, 1966) when one character defines a confidant: "There are two things I can't discuss with anyone but you, my sex life and my ambition."

The essential conflict in O'Hara's world can be neatly characterized by the titles of two postwar novels, both owed to Alexander Pope, *A Rage to Live* (1949) and *Ourselves to Know* (1960)—action with its faults, introspection with its passivity. Increasingly after World War II, O'Hara returned to the Gibbsville setting for both his novels and his short stories. In *A Rage to Live,* for example, Julian English has a flirtatious dance with Grace Tate, recounted almost fifteen years after O'Hara had recounted Julian's last days and death. In part, the impetus for O'Hara's elaboration of the Gibbsville setting may have come from William Faulkner's Yoknapatawpha County, whose family and historical structure had been made more explicit in Malcolm Cowley's *Portable Faulkner* (1946), for which Faulkner had furnished a genealogy. But O'Hara's world has little of Faulkner's mythic resonance; his taste is more for tragical satire. And while Faulkner's sense of the difficulty of telling a story straight allows his characters a kind of willfulness, O'Hara (or one of his biographical narrators) coolly arrays a world within which characters follow less their own dooms than those their Author has meted out for them. O'Hara's essential message is that social surfaces are a lie, but a lie that it is fatal to contradict. His specialty is the moment when the shell of civilized discourse and behavior cracks and the inner beast emerges. People exist most keenly at the extremes of either society or skin, and there is little scope for individual will in either realm. The characters who succeed are those who know their own limits, although O'Hara so intricately constructs them for us from their actions and their social relations that they often seem invariable, without an inner life, dissectable in terms of clubs and schools and physical urges, but finally unknowable. Even so, O'Hara attacks the psychological penetration that other authors call on to help present their characters. He is a historian, a chronicler: "There is here, in the biography of Joe Chapin, nothing that could not have been seen or heard by the people whose lives were touched by Chapin's life. Whatever he thought, whatever he felt has been expressed to or through someone else, and the reader can judge for himself the truth of what the man told or did not tell" (*Ten North Frederick,* 1955).

In his early works O'Hara was fascinated by the exclusivities of American life and created a novelistic voice to bridge those gaps. But by the postwar period more and more of O'Hara's characters have become fatally imprisoned in his own desire to amass, define, and fictionally freeze forever the past he lived through. Many times, usually in the short stories, he can convey the searing strangeness of other people's pains and desires. But too often he presents the lives of his characters as only puzzles to be solved. Throughout his career O'Hara was accused of a snobbery obsessed by minute distinctions. Yet it is the flatness and repetitiousness of his moral generalizations that are finally more destructive to his imaginative impact. All his characters become typical, because all that he wants to know about them is their typicality.

It may have been the final joke of the God O'Hara liked to call "The Supreme Ironist" that the writer who wanted to be remembered as the accurate chronicler of his age should make a deeper mark as a cantankerous public figure, remembered more for his pretension than for his achievement. Although some of his short stories did retain his old focusing power, the increasingly didactic and assertive novels testified to a feeling, often expressed by O'Hara in print, that he was not getting his due as an important writer. In part, his fatally ordered works elaborated a ferocious revenge (tinged with envy) on the weak and ineffectual rich who were so often their central characters. With sex as its main dissecting tool, the method was easily adopted by writers whose instincts for both profession and doom were less finely honed than O'Hara's, such as Grace Metalious (*Peyton Place,* 1956), Harold Robbins (*The Carpetbaggers,* 1961), and Jacqueline Susann (*Valley of the Dolls,* 1966).

O'Hara's sense of being embattled in an America of frowning critics and illiterate readers owed something not only to the first glimmerings of the postwar celebrity culture but also to the demands of the special kind of fiction he practiced. A realistic portrayal of milieu, when taken from a detached perspective, might seem unavoidably pessimistic. But when the writer was close at hand, either inside the novel or outside, satire was close as well. O'Hara's satiric edge, like that of Dos Passos, came from his impersonal perspective, and so his fatalities seemed embedded in the structure of the universe itself. But for a writer like Mary McCarthy, who was as fascinated by the infinite facts of social life as was O'Hara, the inclusion of a personal speaker, a character not identifiable with but certainly similar to her own, changed the focus from cosmic forces to the more immediate failures and successes of individual taste. The writer's revenge, instead of being on an entire social world, was taken on individuals, and so the standard of perception was also palpably her own.

Mary McCarthy first began making her appearance through essays and short stories in *The New Yorker, The Southern Review, Partisan Review, Harper's Bazaar,* and other magazines that had since the 1920s been one of the main proving grounds for American fiction. Many of them were based in New York, and they often displayed variations of the New York sensibility, either in setting or in perspective. By the 1970s *The New Yorker* was one of the few that remained active and demanding in its search for quality short fiction, and it had already long since branched out into more regional and even foreign work by writers such as Peter Taylor, Anne Tyler, Ann Beattie, Santha Rama Rau, and Sylvia Townsend Warner—an expansion that provides an emblem of the gradual decentralizing of American culture that characterizes the post-Vietnam period.

But when Mary McCarthy began publishing, New York was still the center, since the 1880s the heir of Boston as the hub of American culture. Like many out-of-towners, McCarthy brought to New York a special sensibility, hers the uprooted (and orphaned) midwestern Catholic turned literary and political sophisticate. Even though she was hardly either a self-advertiser on the scale of Mailer or a self-abnegator such as Salinger or Pynchon would be, McCarthy nevertheless set part of the pattern for the interplay between autobiography and fiction that became part of the novelist's ideological traveling kit in the 1950s. In her short stories and novels she displayed and articulated the sensibility that she represented in person—the New Woman of the 1930s and 1940s, politically aware, sexually adventurous, infusing culture with a special brand of American energy that no longer drew on European patterns, however much it might be aware of the validity of European ideals.

In *The Company She Keeps* (1942), McCarthy viewed this New Woman in the character of Margaret Sargent through first-person, third-person, and even one second-person narrative ("You would go to bed with him finally, but it would not last long, because you had both been compromised at this dinner party and you had both understood this and understood each other"). Images of theater and being on stage abound in the novel's pages. The McCarthy behind the heroine sardonically presents the McCarthy who is the heroine through an array of details, political arguments, aesthetic decisions, and personal choices. In their sheer density these would become such a hallmark of McCarthy's style that in 1960 she would publish a theoretical essay entitled "The Fact in Fiction," which argued that the basic nature of the novel was its empirical truth, its mosaic of sheer factuality. But in *The Company She Keeps* McCarthy kept her facts to a penumbra around Margaret Sargent. Their importance lies less in their brute "truth" than in the way they capture what was significant for Margaret and her New York intellectual world, the play of ideas as much as the resonances of the everyday. With the armature of Margaret's self-awareness and the imitative self-awareness of her own style, McCarthy conveyed an involved mockery that in her later novels moves more firmly into satire and even caricature. The simultaneous fear of exposure and the need to be onstage yielded a novel about a character akin to but not the same as the author, unblinkingly observed because neither author nor character could be let off without blame. In these early works McCarthy's social observation could be both trenchant and humane, even when, as in "The Friend of the Family" or "The Man in the Brooks Brothers Shirt," the type may have vanished into history.

Her next novel, *The Groves of Academe* (1952), deals with a common theme of the films and fiction of the 1950s, the pretended political problem that is actually a personal problem, here a teacher fired for incompetence who asserts that he has been done in for being a Communist. But the penetrating, even humanizing mockery of McCarthy's earlier works has begun to change into something much more exaggerated. After years of writing criticism, mainly of the theater (collected in *Cast a Cold Eye*, 1950), McCarthy lets loose with cascading lists, almost absurdist arrays of facts that seem intended to anchor the reality of her theme, yet actually caricature it into disembodied allegory: "She dressed in jerseys and wool shirts and brogues, wore a boyish haircut and necklaces of turquoise or Mexican silver, was fond of tea, little Cuban cheroots, Players, English Ovals, candied ginger, and so on." Description shades easily into prescription, and no character has the self-awareness to emerge from his or her intricately embroidered costume of being. The legacy of her upbringing, as McCarthy remarks in *Memories of a Catholic Girlhood* (1957), was self-awareness, for the lack of self-awareness ensured mediocrity, the unwillingness to believe that one was worth puzzling over. Yet when self-awareness loses its guard of irony, the world abruptly flattens. So intent is McCarthy on re-creating the factual atmosphere around her characters that she prematurely embalms them. Thus the psychological and formal necessities of her fiction make her more sensitive to the Machiavellian than to the spontaneous, more attuned to premeditation than to autonomy. In *The Groves of Academe,* as in her essays on fact in fiction, McCarthy demonstrates her belief that the characteristic mode of the novel is "gossip and tittletattle." But she had moved to the big city too quickly to know the small-town secret that trivial things become important when everyone has something to say about them.

Fiction, McCarthy argued, was an aid to memory, and the past would become more real when frozen in the amber of narrative—warts, flies, and all. Her facts were less the chunky substance she admired in Balzac or Tolstoy, Dreiser or Dos Passos, than a kind of mulch, which, like a ferocious lawnmower, she chewed up from the surrounding countryside and redeposited in a thin but pervasive layer to enrich the growth of her fiction. In *The Group* (1963), her first popular success, the lawnmower has lost its human guide. *The Group* has not one central character but six—a group of Vassar girls, class of 1933, whose destinies are traced until the early days of World War II. Their characters are complicated, but predetermined, like good recipes, each except one a possible emblem of American experience, New York variety, in the 1930s. Lakey, the exception, preserves her mystery by going to Europe, as if McCarthy could express this one character's more complex inner life only by her absence. None of "the group" has any self-consciousness (except Lakey, who has only that). But the arch tone of the narrative supplies enough self-consciousness for all, as well as the rationale for their interconnection, through a short-story structure that focuses on each in her turn. In fact, McCarthy has retreated to a comfortably wry place from which she can contemplate the frailties of her youth and turn the 1930s into a box

130

of properties in which attitudes, objects, and emotions all tumble together with equal emphasis. At times, McCarthy's facts do have a life
of their own, an intellectual sensuosity that binds the bricolage of
observation and research. But too often they have only the realism
of an inventory. Without her acute sense of the ways people behave
in public and their self-conscious dramatizations, her characters give
only thin blood to her cultural statistics.

McCarthy and O'Hara, politically in opposing camps, the left-wing
critic and the right-wing journalist, nevertheless find a kinship in the
cold detachment with which they view the societies they make their
subject matter. They, at least, have escaped to tell the tale. The loss
is in the complexity of character. Detail shades into satire just as
detachment invites a fatalism of plot and characterization. The ra-
tiocination of emotions, the intricate dissection of motives, becomes
much less appealing when it is too clearly preordained, an expression
of the author's mind rather than the character's will. In *The Group*
the play of ideas abounds—politics versus aesthetics, the spirit versus
the letter, character versus form. But the method and tone of the
novel side with form against feeling. In 1961 McCarthy moved to
France with her husband and remained in residence there until the
late 1970s. Her most recent novel, *Birds of America* (1971), maintains a long-distance effort to understand the America of the 1960s.
Its title, however, reflects the cataloguing mood she values so highly,
and her more recent works have been frankly moral-reportorial.

Randall Jarrell's *Pictures from an Institution* (1954) seems to counter McCarthy's *The Groves of Academe* and its satiric picture of
cloistered academic life by drawing on resources of character and empathy rather than detail and detachment. McCarthy's big-city eye
looked disdainfully at the professors who thought so hard about everything while they unconsciously gave themselves away with every gesture, piece of clothing, or favorite popular song. In Jarrell's novel
Gertrude Johnson, a novelist who knows all the facts, comes to Benton,
a small elite woman's college, and proceeds to write a novel about
her experiences there, or rather a novel about several of the people
she knew and some she did not know, all caught in an intricate, plum
pudding plot. In part, Jarrell's novel is a severe critique of the novelist who cannibalizes every human situation to advance her work:
"Gertrude was never polite to anything but material." But Jarrell,
a poet and critic now writing fiction almost out of self-defense, also
presents an alternative to McCarthy's method through his effort to
restore a human nature to *Academe*'s otherwise denatured academic
types. Unlike McCarthy's butterflies, constantly being pinned against

131

the wallboard of her sensitivity, Jarrell's characters tend to evade Gertrude's efforts to define them. When she does "capture" them, Jarrell implies, she is lying, as she lies when she asserts there is a plot in the world. "Nothing ever happens at Benton," his narrator says in response to Gertrude's description of her novel. The refusal of plot, the acceptance instead of only the momentary glimpse implied by the "pictures" of the title, is the polemic of the imagist against the empiricist. The frequent allusiveness of Jarrell's poetic prose stands in high contrast to McCarthy's precise ticking-off. His fascination is with the unique nexus of every character's nature rather than with the precisions of material existence that preoccupy McCarthy and O'Hara. Gertrude's great strength in the novel is her belief in her ability to explain—a trait that links her with McCarthy, O'Hara, and all the great naturalists and realists of the 1920s and 1930s. But Jarrell seems more in sympathy with the line from Gide that Norman Mailer uses as an epigraph to *The Deer Park* (1955): "Do not understand me too quickly."

Because they try to convey a familiar world, realists, naturalists, and novelists of manners all piece together facts to construct that world. However their standards and assumptions might differ, they are therefore similarly involved in the problem of *knowing*: what the character (and perhaps the reader) must know in order to survive and prosper; what the novelist must know in order to convince the reader that the novel's world is "real." Both the naturalists and many of the realists, with their commitment to the objectivity of detail and the irreducible truth of materiality, imply or assert larger than human forces. But the novelists of manners tend to be more involved with characters who are less completely describable and therefore less restricted. Even Gertrude Johnson is allowed to be complicated in Jarrell's *Pictures from an Institution,* despite the single-noted way she would like to see other people.

The naturalistic novel therefore tends toward the reality of detail, fact, and empirical nuance, while the novel of manners tends toward the reality of psychological nuance and the varieties of human communication. The novel of manners focuses especially on a settled, geographically limited world. Unlike the sweeping works that try to encompass all of American possibility through multiple heroes or an omniscient movement through the intimate lives of a variety of people, the novel of manners limits its sphere and makes up in intensity what it lacks (or refuses to indulge) in generalization. In the novels of Henry James, Edith Wharton, Sinclair Lewis, F. Scott Fitzgerald, and John O'Hara, sensibility often lives in thwarted isolation. Following their lead, the novelists of manners often set their scenes in small-town America or in the upper-class enclaves of big cities. Their theme was the life of class, usually observed without the brooding fatality of O'Hara or the world-historical implications of Dos Passos.

Competition therefore would seem to be a keener issue for the naturalist and the omniscient realist than for the novelist of manners because they labor to assert individuality in the face of Fate or History—even though that individuality may be a clearer possibility for the novelist (as a detached, aware consciousness) than for the character (who still remains subordinate to the novelist's vision). The consumer acquisitiveness of postwar society had only emphasized this thematic conflict. There was greater comfort available than ever before, but the possibility of self-definition seemed even more remote. Partly in the grip of nostalgia for the brotherhood of the war and partly in an attempt to seek the margins where frontier traits might be discovered again, the postwar novel sought out testing situations, where the paradoxical reward was an acceptance by the group that affirmed one's ability to go it alone. The archetypal setting is, of course, the hunt, the testing in nature. But works with this motif also bear close affinities with the seemingly more settled worlds of the novelist of manners, where testing takes place in urban settings, amid the pressures of business and profession. The testing there might seem less stripped, but it is no less decisive. Just as the novel of the dispossessed might disclose the etiquette of self-preservation, so in the novel of manners, the dog is never far beneath the skin. All struggled with the standards of the group; the difference lay in how that group was defined. Even as the realists and naturalists create characters who often turn out to be rejected by History, the novelists of manners, because they are more interested in the shape of individual lives than in the frailties of individual will, often stay outside or aslant from great events, allowing their characters freer play to invent an ideology of their own. But the basic similarity remains: the act of fiction making demands a solitary sensibility speaking to another solitary sensibility. On one side, then, any theoretical, philosophical, or intuitive belief in mass or scientific meaning is eroded by a sensitivity to individual nuance, while on the other, a frequently attacked social conservatism cannot avoid a similar commitment to the individual sensibility, no matter how doomed or destroyed.

The most consistently popular and perhaps the best-selling of the novelists of manners in the postwar period was John P. Marquand, who also wrote under the name John Phillips. Born in 1893, Marquand began writing costume dramas and adventure fiction in the 1920s, often publishing in popular magazines. In the 1930s he continued his writing of adventures with several set in the Far East, as well as a series of spy tales featuring a Japanese detective named Mr. Moto that begins with *Thank You, Mr. Moto* (1938) and ends with an oddly timed fourth volume, *Last Laugh, Mr. Moto* (1942), set, however, before the alliance between Germany and Japan. In the midst of these popular genre works came Marquand's first great critical success, *The Late George Apley* (1937), an often melancholic satire of life in Boston from the late nineteenth century to Apley's death in 1933. The narrator is the ingratiatingly obtuse Ralph Willing, who assembles letters, conversations, and Apley's own writings and reminiscences to portray a proud son of an upright and idealistic Boston, even while Marquand's ironic and parodic vision shows it to be a stultifying, repressive, and finally a soul-destroying place. In a pattern that Marquand was to follow closely in many of his later works, he simultaneously satirizes the values that shaped Apley and then demands that we respect Apley for acquiescing to them.

It may be difficult now to understand how *The Late George Apley* and Marquand's subsequent Boston novel, *H. M. Pulham, Esquire* (1941), shocked the city that was their setting. At our distance the satire has dated more quickly than the things and people satirized, and Marquand's point of view may seem as self-satisfied and unreflective as what he is mocking. It is Marquand's realistic depiction of this world of enclosure that still retains some power, rather than the particular judgments he makes on the varieties of its blindness. Marquand's master is explicitly Sinclair Lewis, but Marquand remains less an expounder or expander of Lewis than a domesticator of Lewis's harsh yet humane perspective, turning satire into parody and characters into types. By choosing so often, in *Apley* and later, to score off the imperceptions of a first-person narrator or a self-deceived central character, Marquand misses Lewis's feeling for the awkwardnesses of human connections and his ability to see beyond the momentary easy ironies of parochial fatuousness. Outside the limited social world of Boston, Marquand implies, perhaps in a greater commitment to the imagination, there is freedom—a naivete that, for example, Lewis dismisses in *Main Street,* when Carol Kennicott realizes that escape is only another illusion and that the real challenge is changing oneself. After Marquand, no American novelist would treat the old nineteenth-century Boston world with as much seriousness and lend it as much power until Thomas Pynchon, in *Gravity's Rainbow* (1973), traced universal paranoia to the influence of the New England sensibility.

134

Apley may worry that his life was lived in a circle, but Pynchon widens that circle to the entire world—wherever you go, it's still Boston. Marquand recognized the materialist values, but retained only a tinge of a materialist critique, perhaps because as an author he became too accepted himself. Lewis, who had the ravaged face of the perpetual outsider, could never have sat as comfortably on the board of the Book-of-the-Month Club as did Marquand (from 1944 to his death in 1960), his smoothly patrician cheeks encouraging young writers to come forward and achieve "swift accumulation of renown."

Apley had established Marquand's talent for a social comedy of manners with an ironic tone that promised larger meaning. As he became more popular, Marquand turned out almost a novel a year, written in a smooth, unremarkable style, whose main quality was a kind of ease and evenness of texture, with little, for example, of O'Hara's brooding presence behind it or little of James Gould Cozzens's vexed intricacy within it. Retrospect was his great theme, whether the looking backward of a man at the end of his life or the looking backward of a family into its genealogy, the connections that precluded rather than encouraged feeling. Each novel, carefully built around a group of well-researched and well-organized facts, was eagerly accepted by a reading public as fascinated by the details of industries and professions as they were by the details other authors furnished about sexual encounters and ghetto life. One telling feature of Marquand's novels is the way he so elaborately makes the obligatory "purely coincidental" statement before the novel begins. He supports the lack of resemblance between his characters and living people with such ferocity not because he is sailing too close to a *roman à clef,* but because he believes as an axiom of his craft that fiction should deal in generalizations: "Living men and women are too limited, too far from being typical, too greatly lacking in any universal appeal, to serve in a properly planned piece of fiction." So satire defeats psychology in the name of universality.

Such novelistic precepts strangely contradict the themes of novels like *Apley, Pulham, Melville Goodwin, USA* (1951), *Sincerely, Willis Wayde* (1955), or *Women and Thomas Harrow* (1958)—all of which, despite differences in setting, are concerned with lives limited and frustrated because a choice to be atypical has not been made. This contradiction between Marquand's principles and his actual themes intriguingly mirrors the nods of his characters toward rebellion while they finally accept what John Bunyan would call Worldly Wisdom: an individualism clearly in accord with convention.

From his position promoting fame and wealth to young writers,

Marquand became an emblem himself of the trap of popular success, like his characters, never quite able to discern the line between self-sufficiency and self-deception. Once again, as in the novels of Hemingway, Jones, Mailer, and so many others, the central value is professional craft. *Melville Goodwin, USA* appeared only a year after *Across the River and into the Trees* (1950) and echoes its respect for the professional soldier, the man whose individuality is clearly delineated against a faceless organization, the man who stands ready to define himself in action, even though the virtuous theater for such action has vanished. After the adventure of his early works, and the exuberance of his satires, Marquand's final works seem more bitter: the success is less satisfying, the materialism more grating. His characters are moved only by memory: the present is repellent and difficult. Even in success, his characters remain on the outside, often in some area of writing or show business, not hostile, as O'Hara would be, but benevolently and weakly resigned. At his best, Marquand presents this weakness directly. But his favorite device of the flashback affirms that his characters, unlike Carol Kennicott, will never grow. Marquand's flashback is his version of O'Hara's omniscience or Dos Passos's documentary technique, forever an inhibition to characters who must re-remain types instead of people.

Louis Auchincloss, almost twenty-five years Marquand's junior, brings to the novel of manners a less hearty, less directly satiric, but more literarily aware sensibility. Unlike the mainly professional writers who are his contemporaries, Auchincloss also holds a full-time position as a partner in a Wall Street law firm. Since his first works, he has been drawn particularly to the world where law, finance, and family intersect, usually among the very rich, the descendants of Edith Wharton's and Henry James's people. Auchincloss enriches these settings with an interest in history, genealogy, and class that in one essay he finds typical also of Marcel Proust, whom he calls the greatest writer about society a society ever produced.

Auchincloss is a strangely mixed writer, often appealing, yet frequently pedestrian, who will produce a vivid characterization or a passionate scene just after he has seemed to be most safely self-limiting. Essentially, he is a craftsman, with all the faults and virtues that term implies. His plots are often as patterned as the Oedipal romances of Ross Macdonald: a young man, generally contemptuous of class, rises to the top; he is ruthless and lacks a sense of family, which, more than money or genealogy, is the real cohesion of class. Whether the young man succeeds (as in *Portrait in Brownstone*, 1962) or fails (as in *A World of Profit*, 1968), the plot resolution is usually less important than the opportunity it gives Auchincloss to fashion a chronicle of years and generations, with all the nuances of relationship and manner such a chronicle can contain. Auchincloss's New York is a closed world whose seemingly well-polished surface masks an overwhelming desire to win at almost any cost. Auchincloss's moral and novelistic alternative to this competition is survival and the view over time. Like Marquand, although with less broad comedy, Auchincloss will juxtapose the same character at different stages of life and will expect thereby (and sometimes get) a residue of richness and resonance from the juxtaposition: the handsome young cousin becomes the fat middle-aged alcoholic; the mousy daughter matures into the witty matriarch; the distinguished professor was once the obnoxious agnostic. In the moment, fatal steps may occur, rash mistakes may be made; but if family persists, there will be a moral evolution. Genealogy does not determine character in Auchincloss's world, but family can support it, because society has no real rules or standards of continuity. "Why should [society's] rules be defined in any way other than by a list of exceptions to them?" he asks in his essay on Proust, and concludes later: "The rapidly fluctuating nature of society makes it a perfect theme in a book about time."

At his most compelling, Auchincloss seems split between the attractions of stability and the attractions of energy, the old families and the new achievers. Like Marquand, he is drawn to an aristocracy of individualism that he sees reflected all too dimly in the contemporary upper-class world, although it may appear with startling vividness in the guise of the boorish immigrant entrepreneur. But finally, in the present, energy and moral stature rarely meet in the same person. In *The Rector of Justin* (1964), Auchincloss's most popular and most critically successful novel, the narrator, Brian Aspinfall, approaches with due deference and self-abnegation the massive task of writing the biography of Frank Prescott, the headmaster of the private school of the title. In the process of putting together the man Prescott from the memoirs and memories of friends, enemies, and relatives, Aspinfall discovers the story of an egoism that contrasts sharply with his own passivity and lack of personal assertion. The men of the past may have been warped, but they were grand, and they seem grander still in the petty world of the present, where there are no giants, only upstarts. Like Aspinfall, Auchincloss is fascinated by the old individualistic figures and the more open world that allowed them scope. Only the novelist's eye, the innocent "silent watcher" at the center of the hurricane, remains to tell the tale, beacon in a storm of "romantic egoists" (the title of an Auchincloss short-story collection of 1954).

The writer is a survivor, but the writer has also come too late for grandeur; the individualism he expresses is much punier than the individualism he celebrates. In the novels of immediacy, adventure, and testing—such as those by Mailer, Hemingway, Jones, and Spillane —this paradox of postwar literary masculinity is often expressed by a simultaneous assertion and undermining of the first person or the hero. Auchincloss's version is closer to that favored by Gore Vidal, Marquand, and Thomas Berger in *Little Big Man*: the story of a dynamic, attractive central character or characters, told by a weak, ineffectual, often self-deceived narrator, a hero-worshiper who demonstrates that although history passes and great men meet with destruction, the normal, the unassertive, the bystander, always escapes the conflagration. This narrator, or distancer, through whom we enter the story, is less energetic than "aesthetic," avoiding the strenuous world to live primarily by the keener perceptions and sensibility it takes to tell the tale. Many novelists of the individual leave a clue to their ideals in the real historical figures they constantly refer to. Dos Passos never tired of Jefferson, while Vidal celebrates Aaron Burr, Jefferson's arch-antagonist. Perhaps, then, Auchincloss's interest in how the writer's gift for social nuance might be translated into temporal power may be bodied forth in his devotion of biographical studies to both Edith Wharton (1971) and Cardinal Richelieu (1972). But Auchincloss's medium is language, and he frequently compares writing to law as ways of interpreting the world. Finally, he never dares more than he can do. As one of his characters says of another who was in Paris in the 1920s and knew everyone, painted, wrote, but never quite succeeded in creating anything of value: "His candor had too little egotism; it was the candor of good manners and not of self-revelation."

One variety of the novel of manners focuses on those classes, the upper classes, who have manners innately and after whom manners are modeled. Another takes a broader canvas and is fascinated by the way different groups have evolved different modes of daily relationship. Still another expands the importance of manners to the structure of society itself, implying that to know and be aware of manners is to know and be aware of the most powerful forces in American life. Norman Mailer once remarked that we all constantly write and revise a vast social novel in our minds in order to make sense of what we see and hear. The one novelist who has perhaps come the closest to getting that novel down on paper is James Gould Cozzens. Cozzens wrote his first novel, *Confusion* (1924), as a Harvard undergraduate. His first critical successes were two shorter works, *S. S. San Pedro* (1931) and *Castaway* (1934), the first a Conrad-like exploration of men at sea in close quarters (akin to Vidal's *Williwaw*) and the second a Kafkaesque parable of a mad Crusoe figure, "Cain, his prototype," reduced almost to animal status as he fights for his life in a deserted department store. In the end, like Poe's William Wilson, he finds that the man who threatens him and whom he has killed is himself.

The implication of *Castaway* that personal failure is a conspiracy from within in an alienating materialistic society seems less a main theme of Cozzens's career than a cautionary undertone. Cozzens's later work at its best depicts the minute gradations of feeling by which people create a life for themselves in a world of others. His three most powerful novels—*The Just and the Unjust* (1942), *Guard of Honor* (1948), and *By Love Possessed* (1957)—are intricate fabrics of relation in which there is no single line of plot but a constant filiation. Attacked violently in the 1950s by such critics as Dwight Macdonald for what was considered a conservative and bourgeois point of view, Cozzens in retrospect seems less conservative than nonideological, so bound is he into the daily lives of his characters. That he chooses to focus on small-town lawyers (*The Just and the Unjust, By Love Possessed*) or soldiers on the home front (*Guard of Honor*) seems due less to his political prejudices than to his aesthetic preoccupations. Unlike Sinclair Lewis, whose Carol Kennicott turns back to her straitened small town because it is the only life she has, Cozzens dramatizes the complexity and stature possible in small-town life, where passions need neither money, status, nor romantic adventure for their intricate theater.

Cozzens may be as preoccupied by small-town social patterns as is O'Hara, but he escapes O'Hara's cool sociological anatomizing because his voice is less moralistic than nuanced; he is an observer of verbal scene and atmosphere who stands back to let his characters create their own meaning. The effect, of course, is as much a fiction as that created by the all-powerful tones of O'Hara. But the implication is very different: Cozzens allows his characters to have reasons he does not know or anticipate. His central characters, such as Abner Coates in *The Just and the Unjust* or Arthur Winner in *By Love Possessed*, have an unpatterned combination of faults and virtues that allow them to seem real. *By Love Possessed* especially is that rare best seller that contains at once the pride and emptiness of American life. Like the macho artists of James Jones, the conservative professionals portrayed by Cozzens have been imagined so fully that his affirmations and his criticisms are inseparable.

Alexander Pope is often cited by both O'Hara and Cozzens, and the difference in their invocation of a writer who in their day was considered the paradigm of aesthetic order offers a key to the different ways they view the small towns that are their most constant scene. Whereas O'Hara's fictions often seem reducible, like Pope's *Essay on Man,* to morals and maxims, Cozzens's are like Pope's *Moral Essays,* less interested in abstract themes than in the mystery of the individual. As we progress through each novel, we begin to tag and generalize about the characters, getting involved with their problems, making mistakes in our assessments as they make mistakes about each other. But these mistakes, as Cozzens presents them, are not cosmic ironies that point us toward the author or encourage us to muse on the deficiencies of human understanding; they are the normal mistakes of living. Like Henry James and Ford Madox Ford, especially the Ford of *Parade's End,* Cozzens is fascinated by the way manners exist, not as a timeless pattern of social order or a clue to behavior and destiny, but as a series of accommodations created by individual men and women for their own survival.

The attack on Cozzens for his cultural conservatism may reveal the basic aesthetic bias of the liberal critics of the 1950s toward the naturalistic wanderer of the 1930s, although they were hardly so comfortable with the appearance of his descendants in the works of Kerouac, Algren, or Mailer. Whereas naturalistic assumptions place us, with the writer and often with his central character, outside the social institutions that seem designed to repress the individual, novels of manners more often deal with the ways institutional dictates are translated into livable private standards. So the naturalistic novelist tends to make himself into a figure at least as important as what he writes about, while the novelist of manners tends to recede, to undermine his authority and let his characters speak for themselves.

Novels of manners generally seem conservative in surface implication because, by limiting themselves to a smaller world, they often take on the values of that world (although they may satirize them), and are therefore less interested in the possibility of escape, the existence of other standards and values. But the great novel of manners, even as it delves into the nature of its special milieu, as it illustrates and even accepts the values of that milieu, also creates a separate, totally imagined place, in which the author is felt not as a shaper of events and characters, but as an observer, a mediator. The greatest achievement of a novel of manners is to create not a didactic etiquette but a picture of possible human interactions, including the darker, erosive forces that undermine the sunny assertions of stability.

Yet since the novel of manners always contains some assertion of the need for manners—whether they are acquired or innate, which are best and how they are best shown—the novelist of manners cannot remain recessive or invisible for long. If the naturalistic novelist contemplates History and makes decisions about fate and order, the novelist of manners is at least equally intent on teaching the reader how to live. In the novels of Marquand, Auchincloss, and Cozzens, the designated hero is often a lawyer, a member of a profession that held a definite sway over the national imagination in the 1950s—in the revival of Faulkner's lawyer-hero Gavin Stevens; in the courtroom dramas of such popular novels as *Trial* (Don Mankiewicz, 1955), *Compulsion* (Meyer Levin, 1956), and *Anatomy of a Murder* (Robert Traver, 1958); in the lawyers turned politicians of *Advise and Consent* (Allen Drury, 1959), and in the courtroom films of Alfred Hitchcock and Otto Preminger. Around the figure of the lawyer could coalesce the dark atmosphere of trial and inquisition that pervaded postwar American political life. The structure of law, that narrowing corridor of factual and verbal logic, seemed to lead to a clear moral choice: guilty or not guilty? Until the 1960s and 1970s when movie stars, comic-book superbeings, and other mythic figures threatened to crowd out more accessible models of behavior and understanding, the lawyer-hero and the writer-hero occupied an important place in the spectrum of postmartial heroism. The writer-hero depends on his sensibility, but the lawyer-hero is hampered by it. He avoids what Cozzens in *The Just and the Unjust* calls "that egotism of confidence in one's ability and one's resulting right, which can never be shown safely, since it entrenches on every other man's ego"; he avoids it because "his profession had taught him to curb the impulse to blurt out what was on his mind."

But far from seeing his lawyers ideally, Cozzens is also aware of the trap of being only "professionally just" and its inhuman pride in detachment. The need to subordinate individual to institution is much less compelling for him than it is for an anti-intellectual writer like Herman Wouk (*The Caine Mutiny*, 1951), who devotes a large proportion of his thematic space to attacking the excesses of literary sensibility that are unfounded in tradition (*Marjorie Morningstar*, 1955; *Youngblood Hawke*, 1962). Truth for Cozzens comes just as often from impulse as from fact or law. And it is difficult to dissociate his flexible sense of human possibility from a sensitivity to language itself—its allusive meanderings rather than its unilateral affir-

141

mations. In *By Love Possessed* Cozzens's style, often baroque and referential in his early works, has become even more complicated, in odd affinity with Mailer's or Faulkner's entwined ruminations and in sharp contrast to Hemingway's elegant or Jones's blunt directness.

Unlike Mailer or Vidal or Hemingway, Cozzens successfully avoided or failed to embrace any public position as a literary figure. Whatever his personal conservatism, through his work runs a distrust of the great and of the desire to be great, the absolute egotism that turns people into leaders. At the army post of *Guard of Honor* there is a constant one-upping and one-downing in which each confrontation exacts its expenditure of ego. As in *The Just and the Unjust*, but with more intensity, Cozzens here looks at a male professional world of rules, complete with all the nuances and exceptions that are available to those in the know. But Cozzens's goals in his army are not the self-affirming ones of Hemingway, in which identification with the hero and irony about the hero go hand in hand. Cozzens accepts the structure of the world without accepting the need to play its game. Explanations are proffered only to be undermined; plots appear only to be anticlimactically yanked offstage. "In any human situation," he says, "even the simplest, there are more variables than any human mind can properly take account of"—even the human mind that created the novel itself.

One virtue of the novel of manners is that the place, the milieu, can be a source of coherence for a loosely connected group of incidents. The reader moves through the work, seeing the same spots from different angles, coming on the same characters through different doorways. The chronicle history of manners allows what is often a collection of short stories to radiate along the years, by the simple expedient of making all the characters related. When those years correspond to an important chunk of the American past and those characters participate, however peripherally, in the stuff of history books, then manners can stand alongside naturalism in its claim to explain and express America.

Such dynastic family narratives, in the looseness of their construction, often show affinities with the more experimental fiction being written after World War II, in which the traditional concerns of plot and causal structure were being disjointed in the interests of either character or the metaphysic of an author's personal style. In as many ways as possible, the old clarity of narrative line was being undermined, and with it the rational, even fatalistic universe it implied. With the collapse of traditional order, every writer was at least more free to create whatever confusion he liked. One approach was the detachment and coolness that mark the fictions of writers like O'Hara and Auchincloss. But for John Cheever the settled tones of the novel of manners could be the frame for a vision of everyday life that was anything but normal.

Cheever's first two books, published ten years apart, were collections of short stories—*The Way Some People Live* (1943) and *The Enormous Radio* (1953). *The New Yorker,* where all of them were first published, had been from the 1930s on under continual political attack for the style of its short fiction. *The New Yorker* story, to the extent that it was a recognizable form, attempted to crystallize a moment of feeling in all its personal and social dimensions, often without any political or historical elements at all. It was focused and limited, a matter of nuances, a briefly glimpsed scene. A writer like John O'Hara, whose novels were so filled with detail, in his *New Yorker* short stories often dramatized situations where feelings became totally oblique, narrator and reader sitting silently while the characters groped fruitlessly for control. Revelation came through incident rather than verbal texture or explicit characterization. The mood was less often one of clarity than one of impotence and misunderstanding.

In this atmosphere of uncertain implication, John Cheever's characters are equally groping. But his narrative tone is much more sympathetic and all-embracing than the coolness of O'Hara or McCarthy. Cheever is less intent on exposing, in a Menckenesque satire, the fatuities and self-deceptions of his suburban New York and Connecticut world than he is on understanding the compromises and the repressions of what might be called the upwardly dispossessed, whose very material success has removed them from all that is really vital in life. Cheever's narratives often contain moments of violence or sexuality in which the characters finally reach some buried or thwarted core of self. But he sets their realizations, if such they are, in a comic or ironic ambiance that baffles any energy they may have released.

A frequent theme of 1950s fiction was the depression at the top. William H. Whyte's *The Organization Man* (1956) furnished sociological documentation, and such novels as Sloan Wilson's *The Man in the Gray Flannel Suit* (1955) and Cameron Hawley's *Executive Suite* (1952) dramatized the paradox: freedom lay in the poverty-stricken, war-torn past; repression and corporate backstabbing in the affluent present. The price paid for success was the loss of self-restraint, each achievement of security and status demanding even greater personal or moral abasement. Cheever, however, never quite sought to dramatize the New York business world. He picked up his characters at the train station, focusing on the melancholy that set in after self-interest and achievement had brought them to suburbia. In the supposedly bright and open suburbs, Cheever found a vein of fantasy, gothicism, and allegory—witches who lived down dark streets in coastal Connecticut, love affairs with solutions out of Ovid, fatalities in which pettiness was transformed into myth. Where only sociology or satire had been before, Cheever, in such stories as "The Swimmer" and "Metamorphoses" (in *The Brigadier and the Golf Widow,* 1964) mined a potential for mania in the heartland of ordinariness and conventionality that seemed to spring from the land itself. Perhaps necessarily, such an epiphany-seeking vision expressed itself best in short stories or in some striking, almost incantatory sections of his novels. As keeper of the mysteries of place, Cheever could be loose even while his characters tied themselves in knots. His own story telling, for example, in his first two novels, *The Wapshot Chronicle* (1957) and *The Wapshot Scandal* (1964), is picaresque and happenstance, even as the fates he depicts grow narrower and narrower. Like the symbiotic attachment of the two main characters in *Bullet Park* (1969), Hammer and Nailles, Cheever's sense of connection owes more to the spirit of language than to the rhythms of history. The mood, as in the irresolutely plotted *Falconer* (1977), is more important than the matter, the denial of authorial "authority" (with its nod to Yeats) now a settled conviction.

Close to Cheever in his fascination with the verbal shapes of mood, and in his way as much a cult figure as a literary one, is J. D. Salinger, whose short stories had begun to appear in *The New Yorker* some time before the publication of his first and only novel, *The Catcher in the Rye* (1951). The hero, Holden Caulfield, who tells the story of three days in New York after he decides to quit prep school, could pass for a somewhat younger, much more privileged combination of Sal Paradise (the Kerouac character) and Dean Moriarty in Kerouac's *On the Road.* The publication of *Nine Stories* (1953) further solidified Salinger's critical and popular reputation as spokesman for another postwar variety of disengaged seriousness, bordering in one direction on whimsy and in the other on mysticism. In them he perfectly caught the mood of the disaffected middle-class teenagers of the 1950s who couldn't quite let go, but also didn't want to join in. Slowly awakening to the cheats of the adult world, they chose not to create anything more for themselves or others than a separate peace (in the title of John Knowles's Salingeresque 1960 prep school novel). But the celebrity of Salinger's work—the reception his audience gave to the sensibility he crystallized in his playful-serious style, his jaundiced observation of detail, and his perfect capturing of the rhythms of overeducated conversation, circa 1950—combined with his own reticence to turn him into the vanishing man of American letters. Feted as a master by critics and cultists alike, Salinger has since published in book form only two other works—*Franny and Zooey* (1961), and *Raise High the Roof Beam, Carpenters; and Seymour: An Introduction* (1963), each composed of two long stories that, in Salinger's own version of the 1950s dynasty novel, extend the chronicles of the Glass family, who had first appeared in *Nine Stories*. The main character, Buddy Glass, a writer, is preoccupied with his dead guru-brother Seymour, whose suicide had taken place in the 1948 story "A Perfect Day for Bananafish."

If the *New Yorker* story could be accused of a certain incompleteness, a hovering effect that promised more in atmosphere than it delivered in substance, then Salinger was the perfect *New Yorker* writer, whose promise and celebrity delivered less and less. But what could satisfy the expectations Salinger's work had created for his audience? The self-involvement of the Glass family and Salinger's preoccupation with them, the increasingly heavy shadow of death and spirituality over his work, seemed to imply a better world where writing itself might disappear. If writer's block, that paramount literary topic of the postwar years, could be made a theme in itself, as both form and content, Salinger had done it. His works grew increasingly gnomic and involved with wisdom literature, as Mailer in his infinitely more garrulous way became intrigued during the same period with the brevity and suggestiveness of Martin Buber's *Tales of the Hasidim*— a tantalizing literature of psychological nuance and moral suggestion rather than an aggressively clarifying literature of plot, observation, and moral analysis.

John Updike, born in 1932, is younger than both Cheever and Salinger, although he shares so many of their preoccupations and interests that they together form a kind of *New Yorker*-nurtured triumvirate. But Updike's literary nature is much more assimilative than distilled, and his urge to push into new literary spaces gives his work a scope and complexity (or at least a variety) that contrasts strongly with the purity and single-mindedness of his colleagues. Unlike Cheever or Salinger, Updike is not solely associated with one particular geographic or social milieu. His early works are set in and around the town of Olinger, Updike's name for Shillington, Pennsylvania, not very far from O'Hara's Gibbsville (Pottsville). But with *Couples* (1968), the scene switches to Tarbox in Massachusetts, parallel with Updike's own move to Ipswich.

As prolific a novelist and man of letters as the postwar period can offer, Updike began his outpouring of fiction, poetry, short stories, and essays with a volume of poetry, *The Carpentered Hen* (1958), and a novel, *The Poorhouse Fair* (1959). *The Poorhouse Fair, Rabbit, Run* (1960), *Of the Farm* (1965), *Couples* (1968), and *Rabbit Redux* (1971) may be his most memorable novels, but Updike has so consistently created his own world that his other works, especially the short-story collections *Pigeon Feathers* (1962), *The Music School* (1966), and *Museums and Women* (1972), also contain many pleasures and moments of illumination.

The Poorhouse Fair inaugurates Updike's career of calculated eccentricity by taking as its setting an old-age home in the somewhat distant future, viewed during a traditional holiday weekend when the residents make a feeble, inconclusive protest against the well-meaning but essentially abstract liberalism of the new director. In contrast, *Rabbit, Run* focuses on Harry "Rabbit" Angstrom, a former basketball star in the Biff Loman mold, whose life has been one downhill slide since the triumphs of high school; his only decisive act in the drifting stability that seems to be his destiny is to desert his wife and young children and, once again, aimlessly run. Common to both novels, and to all of Updike's fiction, is a referential and evocative prose that enwraps its traditionally realistic or naturalistic subjects in a web of allusion and nuance that often oddly suits both the scenes Updike depicts and the minds of the characters he inhabits. In *The Centaur* (1963) Updike makes this disparity his central structure, adroitly moving between the story of Peter and George Caldwell, teacher-father and student-son, and their mythological parallels in the story of Chiron the centaur and his student Prometheus.

Updike wrote *The Centaur* at about the same time that Cheever was investing his suburban side streets with witches and wood nymphs. In the immediate postwar period, Arthur Miller in *Death of a Salesman* (1949) had raised the possibility of tragedy outside its traditional upper-class setting. In the early 1960s Updike and Cheever responded to the Kennedy world of stylization and gesture by exploring either an older mythological backdrop against which their "normal" characters could move or a new mythology that was potential in the characters themselves. Both writers are aware that to invoke the shadow of myth always risks the unwanted possibility of mock-epic and parody. So Cheever seems content to invest his world with only the suggestion of larger, magical, forces. But Updike, through his much more elaborated and therefore more self-indicating prose, continually risks deflation and a misanthropic interpretation of the world he otherwise spends much loving care in detailing. In his short stories, with

146

their concentrated moments of illumination, the richness of Updike's prose works in his favor. But in his novels it seems less integrated, too often taking on a separate life of its own. His interests are so wide, his sense of the possibilities of language so playfully acute, that what in his writing is rich and complex, in his characters may appear trivial and diffuse. In great part his constant subject has been a middle class that is trying to change its mind without changing its comforts, and that mind is so well-stocked with contemporary allusion and cant that the effort of Updike's style simultaneously to imitate and to judge often flounders in a sea of its own devise.

Nowhere does this happen so decisively as in *Couples,* in which Updike details the intertwined sexual and emotional lives of a group of friends in Tarbox. More and more in Updike's novels sexual explicitness begins to take a counterweighting place to intelligence or knowledge, as if the explicit "knowingness" of his style were attempting to search out its own denial in the wordlessness of the flesh or the determined, direct flatness of sexual language. *Couples* marks as well Updike's increasingly explicit fascination with religious and doctrinal language; a Calvinist irony creeps into the animistic lusciousness that had before invested each person, place, or thing with a life and history of its own. Sexual and doctrinal language in the later Updike reach out to each other for definition, just as his earlier, more poetic, style played against the details of naturalistic setting. Pleasure, Updike implies, especially aesthetic pleasure, needs a limit to shape it. Sexuality then becomes sacramentalized, a lovely intricate ritual, as much verbal as physical, far indeed from the bestial darkness it invoked for O'Hara and so many of his generation. Cheever appreciates these moments as well, when sexuality and religion meet in a self-conscious alliance that allows carnal sin to be the opportunity for infinite gradations of moral discovery, transforming the seemingly bland stage of suburban infidelities into a minefield of moral adventures and metaphysical choices. Updike's novels and stories may be poetic, but his poetry tends to be comic. Once again, the tension may be the game: to be impeccable while still sinning.

More than most novelists of the postwar period, Updike meditates about literary tradition and continually experiments with his own place in it, not only through the variety of forms he has used but also through the different fictional shapes he has given his own voice and nature, not in the explicit self-impersonations of a Mailer but in a series of performances all his own. In *Rabbit Redux,* for example, Updike experiments with a Dos Passos–like view of the conflagrations of the 1960s through their effect on one person, the Rabbit Angstrom of his earlier novel, now thirty-six, still adrift, but yet alive to change. In *Bech: A Book* (1970) Updike assumes the voice of a Jewish novelist on a tour of Eastern Europe for the State Department. In *Buchanan Dying* (1974), a play, he tries his hand at a psychological-historical fiction akin to that of Vidal's *Julian* or *Burr*, although with the specific overtones of the Pennsylvania setting of so much of his earlier fiction. In *A Month of Sundays* (1975) he plays yet another role, speaking in the voice of the Reverend Thomas Marshfield, whose musings run quickly to his problems with sexuality and religious belief.

Yet, as I have pointed out, however diverse the literary interests of the novelists of manners, they are attracted to professionals: Hemingway's soldiers, O'Hara's doctors, Marquand's businessmen, Cozzens's lawyers, Updike's ministers. As usual, when such attractions become more explicit, they are often less powerful, and *A Month of Sundays* in its purification of Updike's themes seems aimed more toward his explicators than his readers, although, like all his work, it has the charm of a writer committed to writing as a special way of engaging the world. Through all his role playing and gropings, his acts of homage and irony, Updike, like so many of the writers I have discussed, and the many more I have not, offers, not without some diffidence, his prose style, his etiquette as a writer, as a model of perception and sensitivity. As politically and morally involved as the naturalists and realists of the 1930s were in their way, Updike is yet a prime representative of a vision that considers sensibility to be the necessary forerunner of politics. However writers vote, or whatever petitions they sign, this vision seems inextricable from the deepest inclinations of their minds and hearts.

Updike, like Cheever, O'Hara, Cozzens, and Auchincloss, pitched his literary camp in the eastern United States. The tendency of the novelists of ambition after World War II to use a New York setting for their work, no matter where in fact they had come from, reflected a centralizing of book and magazine publishing in the city, a centralization of the readership of fiction, and the rise of a generation of Jewish and black novelists who spoke specifically out of an urban experience. In this postwar mythology of New York as the center of American culture (as opposed to its real position as the center of the publicity of American culture), the writers who drew for their strength on regional rather than ethnic roots were often considered eccentrics or sports. But, by the 1970s, the national mood of decentralization and the defusion of New York's central importance in all but the performing arts accompanied a flow of energy back into a newly strong and diverse American culture. In many areas there was, of course, more standardization than ever before. But in the arts individual expression maintained and expanded its force. This new map beyond the interstates is only gradually taking shape. But my survey would not be complete without paying tribute to at least one regional writer who can sit as parent to the new mood, where naturalist diversity and sweep are combined with the sense of nuance and empathy typical of the novel of manners.

Drawing on a heritage that includes Sinclair Lewis and Willa Cather, Wright Morris has worked primarily out of his native Nebraska, with occasional novels set elsewhere, but all infused with a sense of movement, of in-betweenness, that is alien to either the settled worlds of the eastern suburbs or the tumultuous ambitions of the crowded ghettoes. "The city" for his characters is not New York but Chicago, and his novels bear more kinship to those of Dreiser, Farrell, and Algren than to anything in either East Coast naturalism or the proletarian writers. Morris's first novel, *My Uncle Dudley* (1942), lays out some of the basic landmarks of his world: the older man on the road, usually in a car, going from some new place (here Los Angeles) so some older place (here Chicago)—a sardonic comic picaresque, in which the generations mix and mingle under the American sky, but without the epic pretensions of Steinbeck's Joads. Unlike Algren's downtrodden, Morris's characters hardly ever break out into violence (exceptions occur in *In Orbit*, 1967). At most, they muse, and Morris's own tone is bemused, comic verging on satiric, shading in his later works more and more toward the grotesque. The texts of his novels are less stories than portrayals of characters through a minute attention to the things of their world, the moment to moment fleetings of their minds, the underground thoughts that rarely if ever reach the surface. He creates what he has called "a fiction inhabited by people with a love of the facts . . . speaking up for people who would rather remain silent." Since the people would not speak, their things would speak for them; their facts, as Morris says, would become artifacts.

In 1946 Morris published *The Inhabitants,* a combined photograph and text work about the meaning of America that in form recalled James Agee and Walker Evans's collaboration, *Let Us Now Praise Famous Men* (1941), with its evocation of the bare, beaten dignity of southern farm life. But Morris's photographs are almost empty of people. His camera chronicles their places, not them, and his accompanying text contains not Agee's proletarian pastoral, but a harsh, melancholic humor, a documentary lyricism reminiscent of Farrell or Hemingway. Morris's photography is crucially related to his fiction because it furnishes a model of disjunctive intensity, the capture of a moment in time. With the same intensity, Morris's characters meet on the road or in deserted places, their minds reflecting the fractions of personal acquaintance they have of each other, the glimpses of their homes and how far they have come since. Because so many of his novels take place on a single day (one is even called *One Day*, 1965), the artificial frame of time itself can make an end to the actual endlessness of events, thoughts, and things.

Two photographs in Morris's second book about his early life in Nebraska and Chicago, *God's Country and My People* (1968), are devoted to books. One shows a shelf of old library books, with the most worn among them the novels of Sinclair Lewis; another is a photograph of the first page of *Babbitt*. John Dos Passos thought that Sinclair Lewis was too condescending to the people of the plains he depicted in his novels. But Lewis remains a strong influence on novelists like Morris, who attempt to combine a naturalism of observation with a sensitivity to both the psychology and the etiquette of social relations. Such a fascination with moments of emotional intensity, the wanderings of minds and bodies through a timeless landscape, makes Morris's fiction somewhat puzzling to anyone looking for the obvious significance of the themes of "classic" fiction. Often, it is true, his submersion in the minds of his characters and the details of their lives becomes an end in itself, so that the novels seem like swatches cut off an endless bolt of prepatterned cloth. But in his best novels, his sensitivity to the moment interweaves delicately with the theme of perception itself, the effort of the mind to overcome the separations between people that sight has created. *The Field of Vision* (1956) and *Ceremony in Lone Tree* (1960) both focus on Tom Scanlon, an old man who tells stories to keep alive an Old West and a sense of past purpose that has been a myth even for him. Even though Morris can be ferociously opposed to symbols himself, he allows his characters a freedom to think and interpret as they will. Each novel has its external events, but in the separate minds of the characters there is a heat, a pressure, and an irreducible aloneness that gives story itself a new meaning. The effect is like overlapping negatives. Fleeting thoughts echo from mind to mind, unhampered by the seeming solidity of time and history, what is actually happening or what is actually there. Perhaps Morris leaves people out of his photographs and allows them to bulk so large in his fiction because he believes that seeing people is the least of their reality, while seeing things tells all.

I have mentioned Morris's photographic tribute to Sinclair Lewis because one continuing thread in the many breaks from tradition that characterize the writing of fiction after World War II has been the sense of continuity and dialogue with the writers of the past, who were themselves transforming nineteenth-century traditions. World War I had helped or forced writers to remake the received shapes of fictional writing and subject matter. The global organization of World War II even more clearly pitted novelists against politicians and the generals as shapers and explainers of the world. No matter how unobtrusive the method or how narrow the subject matter, the novelist of ambition could not help implying that he was describing, even in miniature, an essential part of human experience.

While the kind of novel I have treated here tends toward the traditional in subject matter and method, its affinities with other, less traditional, kinds of fiction, are clear. The naturalism of Dos Passos and the early Mailer flow easily into the apocalyptic fantasies and language games of Ellison, Condon, Vonnegut, Barth, and Pynchon. When Jewish and black novelists explore the drawbacks and privileges of their ethnic perspectives, Steinbeck, Algren, and Kerouac, who also identified the writer with the outsider, can be counted as spiritual kindred. The vexed question of masculinity, so elaborated by Hemingway, Jones, and the war novelists, finds its appropriate response, if not solution, in the growing volume and self-consciousness of women's literature. The sense of region and family roots in the novels of manners may be most complexly expressed in the fiction of the South.

All these associations are, of course, as rough as using your thumb to determine mileage on a road map. What does hold them together is the map itself, the constant theme of the writer contemplating and trying to express, if not understand, the complexity of America. In this contemplation only literary terms like "realist," "naturalist," "romantic," or "novelist of manners" can be constant, because they exist not in time but in the classroom. Traditions live when writers use them, and the greater the writer, the more transformed and perfected will be the tradition. The American novel, unlike the more single-minded novelistic traditions of other countries, is absorptive and pluralistic. Even at its most verbally self-conscious, it maintains an effort to confront the entire country and to respect its spaces and the differences of its peoples for the opportunity they allow to build and to create. Sinclair Lewis's vision of Carol Kennicott gazing at the prairie beyond Main Street can therefore stand as both my prologue and coda:

Here—she meditated—is the newest empire of the world . . .
What is its future? she wondered. A future of cities and fac-

tory smut where now are loping empty fields? Homes universal and secure? Or placid châteaux ringed with sullen huts? Youth free to find knowledge and laughter? Willingness to sift the sanctified lies? . . . The ancient stale inequalities, or something different in history, unlike the tedious maturity of other empires? What future and what hope?

Carol's head ached with the riddle.

Hers would not be the last.

4

Southern Fiction
Lewis P. Simpson

I thirst to know the nature and power of time
ST. AUGUSTINE, *Confessions*

IN his classic essay of 1935 "The Profession of Letters in the South," Allen Tate refers to the "peculiarly historical consciousness" of the twentieth-century southern novelist, which has made possible the "curious burst of intelligence that we get at a crossing of the ways, not unlike, on an infinitesimal scale, the outburst of poetic genius at the end of the sixteenth century when commercial England had already begun to crush feudal England." Identifying the motive and the subject of the contemporary novelist of his region with the seventeenth-century transition to modernity—the time of the final defeat of the corporate community of Christendom by the emergent forces of science, finance capitalism, and individualism—Tate suggests that we discover a parallel between the southern writer and Marlowe or Shakespeare. We may of course find an even stronger parallel between Tate's contemporary and the first modern novelist, Cervantes. In *Don Quixote*, not only does Cervantes, like Shakespeare in *Hamlet* or *Richard III*, dramatize the psychic consequence of the shift in the Western apprehension of existence from the traditionalist to the historical mode; but, unlike Shakespeare in his treatment of Prince Hamlet or King Richard III, Cervantes in the tale of the Knight of the Sad Countenance elaborates and diagnoses the consequence. Detailing the intricate experience of individuation—comic, pathetic, tragic—which occurred when the forces of history began to break up the society of assigned status, Cervantes, by embodying the seventeenth-century vision of the crossing of the ways in a form which grew out of complex needs of the vision itself, created both the chief subject of modern

153

literature and its appropriate form. The novel entered into literature as no mere reflection of the crossing of the ways. It embodied the phenomenon of the crossing as the literary myth of modern history. The novel became a primary scene of the self's emergence as a historical entity and a primary registration of its struggle to define its existence, pulled on the one hand by the will to autonomous meaning in the present and on the other by the recognition of its origin in the fragmentation of social order and community.

While such a sense of the function of novel is definable in the stories of Ernest Hemingway, F. Scott Fitzgerald, and John Dos Passos, the consciousness of history and self in the southern novelists is fundamental. They are students of—meditators on—history as the necessary mode of the modern existence. Indeed, southern men of letters have been so ever since the colonial settlement, when, unable like their New England contemporaries to refer the contingencies of history to the revealed mission of a chosen people, they began to know history as the shaping pressures exerted by adventitious commercial imperatives. They were especially aware of the expedient character of an economic and social novelty, African chattel slavery. Like the rise of tobacco smoking in Europe, to which it became inextricably linked, the enslavement of Negroes bore no relation to an Anglo-Saxon society of hierarchy and tradition. Its casual introduction into the American colonies represented the capricious character of modern history as it began to center in a world marketplace. Transforming a historical accident which had become an economic necessity into a providential act, the southerners defended slavery as their "peculiar institution," and southern men of letters attempted to devise a historical schema which would incontrovertibly justify its singularity. This meant, as Henry James says in *The American Scene* (1907), that the southern literary mind placed itself under the interdiction of a self-interpreted "new criticism" of history.

For thirty years before the Civil War and for as many more following it, the South's obsessed self-interpretation of modern history repressed the participation of the southern literary mind in the civilizational drama of the past in the present, of self and history. After World War I this drama broke out of its imprisonment in the narrowly historicist cast of the southern literary mind. A larger vision of southern history was slowly opening to writers in the South even before World War I occurred. But in the illumination of this cataclysm, the War for Southern Independence and the South's defeat, the darkness of Reconstruction and the ironic rise of a materialistic New South, appeared as vivid symbols of the southern participation in the final act of the dramatic transit in Western civilization from the traditionalist to the modern society. With the force of a revelation, the southern literary mind discovered itself: it was the modern literary mind, possessing in the history of its own world a powerful version of the myth of modern history, and potentially possessing the visionary powers of Proust, Mann, and Joyce. Mark Twain and George Washington Cable, and even Thomas Nelson Page, had had glimpses of the possibilities open to a novelist who, sympathetically yet ironically, grasped the southern situation in its world-historical context. Bringing into focus the history, and the historical aftermath, of a slave society at once novel and anachronistic—a society which had attempted at the same time to become a modern nation-state and a replication of a patriarchical community, a major supplier of raw materials to the world industrial machine and a pastoral retreat from it—southern novelists of the 1920s and 1930s realized the possibilities of the South as a representation of the crossing of the ways. They created in the southern novel a compelling drama of self and history—one, notably in the works of William Faulkner, suggesting the range and depth of *Remembrance of Things Past, The Magic Mountain,* and *Ulysses.*

When the second phase of the world wars of the twentieth century —the massive conflict known as World War II—terminated in 1945, the modern literary subject, the myth of the past in the present, lay in the cultural debris. The atomic explosions over Hiroshima and Nagasaki had blown the past out of the present, rendering obsolescent the vision of the crossing of the ways. Novelists must now define the drama of world and self beyond the crossing. The common theme of the American novel, southern or not, became a quest to define a vision of the self's being in a posthumanist, post-Christian society; in short, in a postmodern world. In this world the southern novelist has struggled to confront the meaning of a vision of existence no longer assuredly historical. His resistance to the decline of the equation between self and history has provided a continuity between the southern novel as it was before and as it has been after World War II. It has also provided a continuing distinction between the work of the southern novelist and that of the nonsouthern novelist. To put this in a somewhat paradoxical yet more definite way, the southern novelist has resisted the effort of the postmodern self to close history in the self by denying its own historical character. The nature and quality of this resistance, and its apparent tendency to lapse, will be discussed in the following commentary on the course of southern fiction since the end of World War II.

From fifty to seventy-five novelists and short-story writers could appropriately be considered in the discussion.[1] But among the southern novelists of the last thirty years only three stand out as major figures in contemporary American and world letters: William Faulkner, Robert Penn Warren, and Eudora Welty. Although no more than half of Faulkner's work was done in the period after 1945 and Warren's and Welty's writings began to appear before this date (in Warren's case well before), we find in these three writers the essential course of southern fiction in the post–World War II age. Their careers at once represent the continuing achievement of the southern movement in fiction and imply why, for all its busyness and its gestation of many novelists, the movement after 1945 is marked by numerous other careers that seem uncertain in direction and fragmentary in accomplishment. While the obvious reason would seem to be that writers like Flannery O'Connor, William Styron, Walker Percy, and Reynolds Price have been circumscribed by the necessities of deference and imitation (O'Connor's statement about Faulkner is famous: "Nobody wants his mule and wagon stalled on the same track the Dixie Limited is roaring down"), the post-1945 careers of Faulkner, Warren, and Welty suggest that all southern novelists of the past three decades, of whatever fame, have experienced in the common loss of the southern literary subject a more inhibiting force than literary competitiveness. At the same time the achievement of Faulkner, Warren, and Welty, viewed individually or collectively, indicates as well that to an appreciable degree the writing of fiction in the South has retained its autonomy within American literature by making the very loss of its subject its subject.

Although not the whole of it, Faulkner's achievement as a novelist is singularly marked by the creation and marvelous peopling of a mythical county in north Mississippi called Yoknapatawpha, of which the county seat is Jefferson. The task of making this world (which has its real counterpart in Lafayette County, Mississippi, with its county seat of Oxford, where Faulkner lived most of his life) occupied Faulkner from 1925 until his death in 1962. The major portion of the task was accomplished in the seven or eight years during which he published *Sartoris* (1929), *The Sound and the Fury* (1929), *As I Lay Dying* (1930), *Sanctuary* (1931), *Light in August* (1932), and *Absalom, Absalom!* (1936). (The first Yoknapatawpha novel, *Sartoris*, was an abridged version of a work called *Flags in the Dust*, now available

1. The careers of black writers associated with the South are considered in Chapter 7 of this volume.

in an edition published in 1973.) Two other Yoknapatawpha novels appeared before 1945: *The Hamlet* (1940) and *Go Down, Moses* (1942).

The world which takes shape in these eight novels, the first cycle of the Yoknapatawpha saga, is a Balzacian representation of southern history. But it is more profoundly the embodiment of Faulkner's imagination of history and myth as modes of human existence. Nothing else like it appears in American literature, or for that matter in world literature. Faulkner created Yoknapatawpha, he said, in toil and sweat—and, as he also indicated, in moments of inexpressible exaltation. Yet in spite of his intense devotion to it, Faulkner's possession of his world weakened as he grew older. The reasons for his lapsing hold on it existed to a degree in personal circumstances. His family responsibilities were heavy. To meet them he spent a good deal of time working as a Hollywood hack. This necessity probably aggravated his strong tendency to alcoholism, as did a painful spinal injury. Still, the declining power of Faulkner's vision of Yoknapatawpha may be ascribed more to literary than to personal problems. Although his declaration that he wrote unaware that anybody might read him is a gross overstatement, there were undoubtedly periods in his best years when the pressure of his vision was so intense, as in the writing of *The Sound and the Fury,* that he was oblivious of either publishers or public. By the time he reached his middle forties, these periods seem to have become infrequent. Faulkner attempted to deceive himself into believing that he had become a more consummate artist. He was, he explained to a correspondent, becoming more like Flaubert and no longer "banged" it on like an apprentice paper hanger. Actually, Faulkner did not gain in artistic control with advancing years. Taking the turn expected of the literary artist in middle age, he simply became more philosophical about his art. But, it is important to realize (and the same point may be made about Robert Frost, T. S. Eliot, and, in a more rarefied but important sense, Ernest Hemingway), the crisis of middle age in Faulkner is associated with his recognition of the diminishment of the fundamental modern subject, the literary myth of modern history. Even as World War I heightened the dialectical play of the crossing of the ways in the American literary imagination, it forecast the decline of this tension.

The poignant relinquishment of the classical-Christian amalgam—of a mythic, traditional, and ceremonial world—is the underlying subject of Faulkner's largest non-Yoknapatawpha work, *A Fable* (1954). Begun in 1944, this novel occupied him for ten years. Often counted as his one genuine failure in fiction, *A Fable* is nonetheless of crucial significance in the Faulkner canon. A work that may seem to intervene in the development of Faulkner's world, it is in truth an essential demarcation of a first and second cycle of Yoknapatawpha tales, the second cycle consisting of *Intruder in the Dust* (1948), *Requiem for a Nun* (1951), *The Town* (1957), *The Mansion* (1959), and *The Reivers* (1962). In the first cycle of Yoknapatawpha stories, Faulkner's treatment of the drama of myth and history is oriented toward the deprivation of the past in the present and is always inclined toward history as the controlling force of existence. His vivid images of the futility of the struggle against history are unforgettable: Quentin Compson in *The Sound and the Fury* wrecking his watch; Boon Hogganbeck at the end of "The Bear" desperately trying to reassemble his rifle (a machine-age tool of death made with interchangeable parts) so that he can kill the cavorting squirrels; Will Varner at the beginning of *The Hamlet* sitting in his flour-barrel chair in front of the ruins of the Old Frenchman's place; Flem Snopes at the end of *The Hamlet* riding by contemptuously with Eula Varner, his earth-goddess bride, on their way to Jefferson. But Faulkner refused to seal his vision of the human struggle in images of history's inexorability. Running counter to the deterministic pattern in the Yoknapatawpha tales is a developing myth of man as a creature of history who yet transcends his history. Although it is implied as early as the Dilsey section of *The Sound and the Fury,* the Faulknerian myth of man is not deliberately formulated until *A Fable.*

The conception of *A Fable* would appear to have been triggered by an idea for a movie script passed on to Faulkner by a producer. But the way in which he seized on the notion of a story based on a legend about the French Unknown Soldier of World War I suggests that it answered to a deep urging in his imagination. He wanted to bring into full focus his conception of man as a creature who has created his nature as a human being by telling stories about himself: a creature who is, in the entire sense of the term, a *fabulous* being. The relationship between man the fabulist and civilizational meaning was a question Faulkner had dramatized in *The Wild Palms* (1939). He had broached it also both in *The Hamlet* and *Go Down, Moses.* In *A Fable* he conceived a mighty effort to come directly to it in a stylized, philosophical, allegorical fable of epic proportions. The endeavor was bolder than, if not as successful as, Milton's attempt to write the epic of the fall of man; for Milton worked with a received myth to justify the ways of God to man. Faulkner, having no received myth, sought to justify the ways of man to man by a mythic construction of his own devising. He envisioned the justification as being the intervention in history of the son of man bringing the message that man has the capacity as man to spiritualize his own history.

Based on a radical adaptation of the pivotal story of the Christian myth, the events of the Passion Week, *A Fable* has as its informing idea the use of the sacred myth as a means of bringing into focus the mystical humanism which in Faulkner's work so far had developed as an uncertain foil to the ruthless historicism of modernity, the culmination of which Faulkner locates in World War I. Yet the idea in *A Fable* is not brought into focus. Faulkner encountered a dilemma: man cannot fulfill the meaning of the Passion Week because he cannot confer grace on himself. Possibly Faulkner had come to the point in the development of his art and craft when he was willing to risk a more or less literal equation between the Passion of Christ and the passion of art. He had suggested in his second novel, *Mosquitoes,* that the modern world has the impulse to make art not merely a means to grace but the source of grace. Had Faulkner succumbed to the dangerous illusion that the literary artist can confer grace on man? If Faulkner felt the appeal of such artistic arrogance, it was a response to what he had found out in writing the Yoknapatawpha stories: at stake in the dialectic of myth and history is whether or not the mythic capacity of the imagination must be absorbed in the commitment to a historicist materialism. Through the power of the literary artist Faulkner endeavors in *A Fable* to construct a mythic paradigm of man's imaginative capacity to transcend fact in passionate dreaming. His intention is not to elevate a contrived myth above all other myths. What he sets out to do is to make a modern myth of man to be placed in the "firmament of man's history"—the firmament being a compound of other self-consciously devised literary myths and the classical Christian mythology in general. Conforming the history of World War I to his poetic revision of its actuality, Faulkner, like Virgil or Milton, aims at a fresh differentiation of myth from history. He seeks to make the mythic sensibility alive in the present.

This motive becomes plain in the section of *A Fable* detailing the story of two horse thieves. Apposite to the story of the Corporal's (the son of man's) incredible passion for peace among men, the improbable tale about the unnameable desires and dreams of a groom, a Negro preacher, and a stolen horse rises above the "mere rubble of the past" to become a part of the living "firmament of men's history."

But *A Fable* fails in its larger purpose: to place the story of the Corporal in the firmament of history. For having no resource in the grace of God, but relying on the assumption that man as literary artist has the capacity not only to revise the history of World War I but to

159

revise the transcendent mystery of the Passion Week, Faulkner could not identify the power of artistic conception with the lowly Corporal and so had to assign it to the champion of man's Faustian power, the dark angel, Satan. The identification is murky, and Faulkner seems not to have thoroughly comprehended it himself. But it is clear that, although he insisted on a reductive, mechanical interpretation of *A Fable* as a representation of man's conscience, Faulkner unequivocally intended that Satan—in the guise of the Marshal, commander-in-chief of the Allied forces (also called the Old General)—be the dominant figure in the novel. When a student at the University of Virginia expressed puzzlement about how the Old General (Satan) could be the father of the Corporal, Faulkner said: "That was a part of Satan's fearsomeness that he could usurp the legend of God. That was what made him so fearsome and so powerful, that he could usurp the legend of God and then discard God. That's why God feared him."

The Christ who is crucified in *A Fable* is conceived by Faulkner to be the son of man because he is the son of Satan. His mutiny against war and the martyrdom that follows are strangely unconvincing. Against the background of "the vast and serene and triumphal and enduring Arch [of Triumph]," the Corporal's protest hardly persuades us that the part of man's conscience which says "I'll do something about it" actually can do or even wants to do anything about it. In the "trinity of man's conscience" (a term Faulkner uses elsewhere instead of "trilogy of man's conscience"), the voice of the Runner is subordinate to the voice of the Old General: "This is terrible but we can bear it." The Old General personifies the attributes of man most celebrated by Faulkner, the strength to endure his fate as the creature of his own history and pride in the capacity to endure. The most eloquent and persuasive rhetoric in *A Fable* is the Old General's. It is his (Satan's) apology for man that, in the Temptation scene, strikes the truest note in the story:

> "I dont fear man. I do better: I respect and admire him. And pride: I am ten times prouder of that immortality which he does possess than ever he of that heavenly one of his delusion. Because man and his folly—"
>
> "Will endure," the corporal said.
>
> "They will do more," the old general said proudly. "They will prevail."

Knowing what will happen in history, the supreme general knows the futility of the myth of sacrifice the Corporal is engaged in making. "Remember whose blood it is that you defy me with," he tells the

Corporal. The Old General is indeed the ruler of this world. And in *A Fable* there is no other: no City of God, only the City of Man. In its overall effect the novel—abounding in the paradoxes and ironies of man's dualities—does not sustain the vision of a duality in which mundane history exists beneath a glorious humanistic firmament of history. Faulkner does not fulfill the promise of distinguishing a transcending humanistic myth from history. On the contrary, he not only accepts the fall of man from the mythic mode of being into the historical mode of existence but concludes that the modern literary imagination cannot reverse the fall. Its only mode, Faulkner admits, is history. Man's ironic immortality is the untranscending, unending succession of individual mortal lives in human society; history is the idiom of existence.

The stories of the second Yoknapatawpha cycle bear on the unrealized motive of *A Fable*: the literary artist's deliberate construction of a myth of man, which, transcending the historicity of man's condition, affords a vision of his responsibility for history.

Intruder in the Dust dramatizes the irony of the tension between myth and history in a detective-story plot about the threatened lynching of Lucas Beauchamp, a dignified old Negro (who has white blood, being the grandson of Lucius Quintus McCaslin). Sixteen-year-old Chick Mallison, nephew of the lawyer Gavin Stevens, is indebted to Lucas for having four years earlier saved him from drowning. Chick, with the aid of a friend, Aleck Sander, and an elderly spinster, Miss Eunice Habersham, violates a grave in an attempt to prove that Vinson Gowrie, the white man Lucas is supposed to have shot, could not have been killed by a bullet from the Negro's pistol. When instead of the body of the presumed victim, they uncover that of another white man, they initiate a series of discoveries leading to the arrest of the real murderer, Vinson Gowrie's brother, and the freeing of the innocent Lucas. As the events develop, Chick faces the dilemma of whether or not he is betraying his own class by trying to repay his obligation to Lucas. At the end of the story, the youth, now entering into manhood, decides that he has earned the right to be at once a proud member of his class and its moral critic. His moral autonomy parallels the independence which Lucas quietly but firmly displays in his relation to the community, white and black. In spite of its rational examination of the southern heritage and its emphasis on a reasoned apprehension of morality in the southern community—especially on the part of Chick, who contrasts with Ike McCaslin and his rejection of his heritage in *Go Down, Moses*—*Intruder in the Dust* is pervaded by the suggestion that moral problems are so imbedded

161

in their dense historical context that they are virtually closed to rational perception. In a striking meditation toward the end of the novel, another key passage in Faulkner, Chick thinks of his identity with his native people and recalls one of his Uncle Gavin's eloquent homilies on the South:

> It's all *now* you see. Yesterday wont be over until tomorrow and tomorrow began ten thousand years ago. For every Southern boy fourteen years old, not once but whenever he wants it, there is the instant when it's still not yet two o'clock on that July afternoon in 1863, the brigades are in position behind the rail fence, the guns are laid and ready in the woods and the furled flags are already loosened to break out and Pickett himself with his long oiled ringlets and his hat in one hand probably and his sword in the other looking up the hill waiting for Longstreet to give the word and it's all in the balance, it hasn't happened yet, it hasn't even begun yet, it not only hasn't begun yet but there is still time for it not to begin against that position and those circumstances which made more men than Garnett and Kemper and Armstead and Wilcox look grave yet it's going to begin, we all know that, we have come too far with too much at stake and that moment doesn't need even a fourteen-year-old boy to think *This time. Maybe this time* with all this much to lose and all this much to gain: Pennsylvania, Maryland, the world, the golden dome of Washington itself to crown with desperate and unbelievable victory the desperate gamble, the cast made two years ago.

Chick finally refers his participation in the history of Jefferson to the stasis of the actor's role. Although the actor has only partial control of his part, he plays a role to its assigned completion. What Chick Mallison learns from Gavin Stevens is confirmed through his experience of the ordeal of Lucas Beauchamp. The individual participates in the community of man, which is the community of history.

This is also what Temple Drake Stevens learns from Gavin Stevens (her husband's uncle) in *Requiem for a Nun,* although her education in history is a good deal more complicated than Chick's. In this novel (a cross between a play and a novel, but with its lengthy historical interludes more nearly a novel), Faulkner intends to invest Temple with a soul. She requires one. More bleakly and succinctly than any other work by Faulkner, the first novel about Temple registers the historical exhaustion of the classical-Christian civilizational ethos: at the end of *Sanctuary* the "all-Mississippi debutante, descendant of long lines of statesmen and soldiers high and proud in the high proud annals" of her state, is left stranded in a world utterly depleted of the moral and ethical drama of the past in the present. To repair her condition, Faulkner invents a redemptionary scheme not unlike that of *A Fable* but more bizarre in its effect, since it is accommodated to a realistic rather than a fabulous story. The sacrificial act, the center of the novel, is performed by Nancy Mannigoe, Temple's maid, who has a lurid past as a whore and dope addict. Temple employs her because she still longs for her own lurid past. To prevent Temple from returning to her former ways, Nancy murders Temple's baby. Her act is inspired by her newfound trust in God and is motivated by her more or less inarticulate but conscious desire to redeem Temple from her life in death. Temple's response makes up the burden of the story.

Condemned to hang for her act, Nancy cannot, like the Corporal in *A Fable,* be taken as a symbol of the Christ legend secularized. Describing Nancy as a nun and the bride of Christ, not as the daughter of man, *Requiem for a Nun* projects the Christian story as, conceivably, historical reality. At the same time the novel-play subtly qualifies Nancy's faith by associating it with the mythic compulsions of the human imagination as these are represented in the eloquent historical prologues to each of the three acts. The prologues stress the relation of Yoknapatawpha's history to man's propensity for mythmaking—so "vast, so limitless" in its power "to disperse and burn away the rubble-dross of fact and probability, leaving only truth and dream." In contrast, Nancy's act in murdering Temple's baby is reminiscent of the Hebraic-Christian imperative to fulfill history through blood sacrifice. Both Gavin Stevens and Nancy serve as interpreters of the murder, leading Temple toward the acceptance of Gavin's dictum: "The past is never dead. It's not even past." The past is real, not myth and dream: accepting this as truth, Temple comes to life as a living human soul. But whether the soul has a resting place without a literal faith in a transcendent nontemporal heaven thereupon becomes Temple's anguished question. Resisting Nancy's simple admonition, "Believe," Temple reflects the Shakespearean mood at the crossing of the ways. "What about me?" she asks. "Even if there is one [a heaven] and somebody waiting in it to forgive me, there's still tomorrow and tomorrow. And suppose tomorrow and tomorrow and then nobody there, nobody waiting to forgive me—."

Temple's several allusions to Macbeth's lament upon the suicide of Lady Macbeth lead us back to *The Sound and the Fury,* and suggest to us that Temple's equivocal fate may be compared with that of Candace Compson, Quentin's sister and Faulkner's favorite among his female characters. Five years before he published the continuation of

Temple's story, Faulkner went back to pick up Caddy's in a genealogical commentary he prepared on the Compsons (published in *The Portable Faulkner*, 1946). This account of Caddy records the discovery of her photograph in a picture magazine of the World War II era. She is standing beside a gleaming sports car with a Nazi staff general, her face "hatless between a rich scarf and a seal coat, ageless and beautiful, cold serene and damned." Caddy's fate defies the past in the present; for, however it has been given to her, she knows the secret of human history: the endlessly repetitive acts of the human heart in conflict with itself do not transcend time. This is a knowledge Satan (the Old General in *A Fable*), or a goddess or a demon, may possess with impunity, but a human being who has it is doomed. And Caddy was "doomed and knew it; accepted the doom without either seeking or fleeing it." In the terrible detachment and passivity of her sealed knowledge, she is free, not from history, but from a pathetic submission to her historical creaturehood. Yet in her transcendence of the anguish of the historical condition of being, Caddy can suffer no redemption; her fate is ironically symbolized by her association with the grossly willed attempt of the Nazis to usurp the ground of history —the human heart in conflict with itself; she is in total captivity to history. The best and bravest and loveliest of the Compsons, Caddy is the only one of them irrevocably damned.

Paradoxically, as she emerges in her interpretation in the Compson genealogy, Caddy has claim to being the chief figure in Faulkner's resistance to history. Her inner knowledge of desire and shame, love and hate, endurance and pride not only embodies the doom of the Compsons and that of the South, but prophesies the historical doom of modern man. In the grandeur of her acceptance of history as fate Caddy asserts the possibility of a tragic victory over it, and indeed almost joins the modern sense of the tragic as resistance to the pitiless historicism of human existence to the sense of tragedy at the core of the Greek mythic sense, resistance to foreknown and implacable fate. Still, Caddy's very uniqueness is additional testimony to the frustration of Faulkner's half-formed desire to transcend the historicity of the modern condition of man. The other two characters in his works envisioned as superior to history, Flem Snopes and Eula Varner in *The Hamlet*, are reduced to roles in the pathos of history in *The Town* and *The Mansion*. In fact, the definition of history as the pathetic deprivation of the mythic existence—a description of history intimated in *A Fable* and more definitely implied in *Requiem for a Nun*—is the shaping theme even of the first novel of the Snopes trilogy. *The Hamlet* depicts a rural people, largely ignorant of art and literature, who seem to be the unconscious embodiment of pastoral myth; and yet, their very presence on the landscape is the result of the modern historical conquest of the American continent. The Frenchman's Bend "peasants" (as Faulkner in historical jest calls these children of frontier wanderers) live a parody of the pastoral mode. As the intertwined legends of Flem and Eula unfold, the parody is at times boisterously comic, at other times merely sad. Flem is a demon, or at least a demonic presence, in his utter obsession with money. Eula is a pastoral goddess. Neither has any sympathetic connections with those around them. Flem is so separated from the community by his shrewd rapacity that (in a dream sequence) Ratliff, the pragmatic but sensitive sewing-machine salesman, recounts a tale about how Flem usurps the dominion of the Prince of Darkness. Eula's "entire appearance suggested some symbology out of the old Dionysic times— honey in sunlight and bursting grapes, the writhen bleeding of the crushed fecundated vine beneath the hard rapacious trampling goat-hoof."

When in the course of his progress to wealth the impotent Flem acquires Eula as his bride, he takes on the historical character of the bourgeois financier and Eula becomes the unfaithful bourgeois wife. Nevertheless, Flem and Eula are indelibly marked by their origins in Faulkner's predilection for myth. Unlike Caddy, whose displacement from conventional life is the badge of her historical origin, Flem and Eula are immersed in conventional existence, but never lose the signs of their beginnings in Faulkner's fascination with satyrs and fauns, demons and goddesses. Undoomed by the conflicts of the human heart, they exist in a curiously ambivalent relation to the historical motives that provide the context of their lives. Striving to make them vulnerable to the force of warring human passions, Faulkner is uncertain of their strengths and fallibilities. He makes them convincing neither as displaced creatures of myth nor as creatures of a historical society. Eula commits suicide in *The Town*. Ostensibly, she is obedient to social convention, wanting to save her daughter Linda from the knowledge that Flem is not her father; but, as Ratliff discerns, she kills herself to escape the town's efforts to reduce her to human status. A displaced goddess has had enough of her isolation in human history. Flem, also having had enough, in the last volume of the trilogy sits in his lonely mansion apparently waiting for his cousin Mink to come and kill him. When Mink shows up with a rusty pistol that misfires and has to be recocked, Flem makes no gesture to save himself and dies when the pistol fires on Mink's second try.

In a prefatory note to *The Mansion*, Faulkner remarks that between the initial conception of the Snopes story in 1925 and its completion in 1959 he "learned . . . more about the human heart and its dilemmas." What he learned confirmed what he had already grasped by 1925, namely, the assimilation of the mythic consciousness by the modern historical sensibility. In the course of the three volumes of the Snopes trilogy the dialectical tension of myth and history progressively diminishes. Eula's sexuality, symbol of the life force of cosmological myth, becomes entrapped in common human attitudes toward love and its passions. Flem's impotence, which has set him apart from the general community of men, becomes an emblem of his pathetic humanity. Yet the more compassionate attitude toward the Snopes on Faulkner's part does not make them redemptive figures. To be sure, pathos and suffering in the Snopes trilogy never seem quite real. The drift of the stories of Flem, Eula, Linda, and Mink is toward the somber pronouncement of the pervasive moral nihilism in human affairs made by Stevens and Ratliff at the end of *The Mansion*. This represents an attitude implicit in Faulkner's concern for the loss of the transcendent reference of myth.

> "There aren't any morals," Stevens said. "People just do the best they can."
> "The pore sons of bitches," Ratliff said.
> "The poor sons of bitches," Stevens said.

In his last look at Yoknapatawpha, *The Reivers*, Faulkner becomes distinctly sentimental. Dramatizing the passage of the child into manhood—as he had in stories about Quentin Compson, Ike McCaslin, Chick Mallison, and Gavin Stevens—Faulkner once again treats a situation in which a social drama originally controlled by myth and tradition undergoes a frustration in modern historical society. He had begun, in fact, to fear that society as a meaningful structure is being lost, and with it the capacity of human beings to make a mythic structure of existence. When he read J. D. Salinger's *Catcher in the Rye* in the 1950s, he was astounded at Holden Caulfield's situation. Holden fails of acceptance into society, Faulkner commented, not because he fails to be "tough enough or brave enough or deserving enough," but because he has no society and thus no human race to be accepted into. Contrasting Huck Finn to Holden, Faulkner pointed out that Huck is kicked around a good deal but that he knows he is growing up in the human race. In *The Reivers*, subtitled *A Reminiscence*, Faulkner gives a nostalgic version of the Huck Finn story. Lucius Priest, the narrator, relates the events of a period during 1905, when, in his eleventh year, he comes into the prospect of manhood. Sparked with autobiographical elements, *The Reivers* concludes the Yokna-patawpha saga with an at times realistic but generally affectionate celebration of a past that has no present. *The Reivers* is a subtle, final relinquishment of the literary myth of modern history.

In contrast to Faulkner's effort to establish a generalized relation between a myth of man, compounded of Greco-Roman and Hebraic-Christian elements and modern history, Robert Penn Warren has endeavored to realize a more specific goal: to discover the connection between the self and American history. Attached to the Enlightenment idea of America as the liberation of the self, yet ironically fully attuned to the biblical interpretation of self and history, Warren is basically Hebraic and Christian rather than classical in his outlook. How fully he represents that singularly American mixture of Augustine, Calvin, and rational doubt or agnosticism so distinctly present in Hawthorne, Melville, and Mark Twain is succinctly indicated in his austere summary definition of "self" in his recent essay on *Democracy and Poetry* (1975): "in individuation, the felt principle of significant unity." By "significant unity" Warren means "two things: continuity—the self as a development in time, with a past and a future; and responsibility—the self as a moral identity, recognizing itself as capable of action worthy of praise or blame." Comprehending the literary myth of modern history as the self's experience in American history, Warren is sharply aware that the national self-definition originated in an abstract promise—an idea about the individual human being's capacities for freedom, equality, and happiness that presented itself to the founders of the Republic as an embodiment of truth in history. Ever aware that American history has taken the ironic form of a perpetual series of attempts by the free and equal individual to incarnate the truth of the nation in the solitary self, he has made the search of the American for moral and spiritual meaning in unique selfhood the rich substance of his novels. That (with the exception of Adam Rozenweig in *Wilderness*, 1961) he has depicted this seeking largely through fictive southerners is less fundamentally owing to the accident of Warren's birth than to his conviction that the questing for an American selfhood assumes its most intense and complex meaning in the historical situation of the individual in the South.

We may follow Warren's hunt for the American self through an interesting series of protagonists, including Percy Munn in *Night Rider* (1939), Jerry Calhoun in *At Heaven's Gate* (1943), Jack Burden in *All the King's Men* (1946), Jeremiah Beaumont in *World Enough and Time* (1950), Amantha Starr in *Band of Angels* (1955), Brad Tolliver in *Flood* (1964), Murray Guilfort in *Meet Me in the Green Glen* (1971), and Jed Tewksbury in *A Place to Come To* (1977).

Percy Munn and Jerry Calhoun are emotionally limited characters. But in his delineations of both Warren anticipates the complex exploration of the drama of self and American history represented in the story of Jack Burden. Although *All the King's Men* has been widely interpreted as being primarily the story of Willie Stark, dictatorial governor of a southern state bearing a resemblance to the Louisiana of Huey Long, the novel is clearly Jack Burden's story. Told by Jack as narrator and commentator, it is an explicit effort to write the myth of the historical self in America. Its structure grows out of Jack's retrospective endeavor to relate and to analyze in detail the events in the three stages of a quest to establish his significant identity in history. His retrospection includes accounts of the entanglement of his life in the lives of Anne Stanton, his childhood sweetseart; Sadie Burke, Willie's tough secretary; and Tiny Duffy, Willie's lieutenant. Of still greater importance in Jack's strivings to perceive himself are (besides Willie) the Scholarly Attorney, Jack's presumed father, who devotes himself to writing religious tracts; Judge Irwin, his real father, the aristocrat and gentleman, whom Jack in the role of historical researcher for Willie exposes for his part in a long past criminal act; Adam Stanton, Anne's brother, a skilled surgeon, the man who kills Willie; and one dead man, Cass Mastern, a Confederate soldier who died of wounds suffered in the Battle of Atlanta but who leaves as his memorial a packet of letters chronicling and interpreting his misdeeds and his redemption. The letters are of no historical importance in the usual sense put prove to be crucial to Jack's salvation. In the first phase of his quest for self, Jack is in "hiding from the present." A graduate student in history, he has the letters of Cass Mastern in his dingy apartment, where he broods on them without understanding that they bear upon his condition. He tries to be an ironic idealist, assigning individuals to categories like the Scholarly Attorney (Ellis Burden) or the Friend of His Youth (Adam Stanton). Later, after his experience of life has become more complicated, the "Brass-Bound Idealist" is altered into a naturalist of sorts, an advocate of the philosophy of the Great God Twitch. Either as idealist or as naturalist, Jack tries to represent life to himself with a false detachment—seeing it, we might say, as a horizontal series of people, brutal in its necessity but meaningless. Slowly prepared in his emotional and intellectual flounderings for a deeper, more comprehensive understanding, Jack discovers the vertical dimensions of history when, after Judge Irwin's suicide, he learns that the Judge is his real father. He realizes the self's incarnation of time. At the end of his story, Jack Burden, the "student of history," has witnessed "the terrible division of the age" in Willie ("the man of fact") and Adam ("the man of idea") and has perceived that their doom was not dictated by the Great God Twitch but by their living "in the agony of will." He is able to say with Hugh Miller, once Willie's subservient Attorney General but now also morally awakened: "History is blind, but man is not." He is prepared to go with Anne out of his father's house "into the convulsion of the world, out of history into history and the awful responsibility of Time."

Warren would seem to have presented in Jack's story a myth of the historical self redeemed. But it is doubtful—and this uncertainty may defy Warren's intention—whether anyone in Jack's story becomes a unified sensibility save Cass Mastern. That "one can only know oneself in God and in His great eye" is the vivid deduction Jack draws from his study of Cass's life. Although he confirms his interpretation of Cass in his own life, is Jack healed of the terrible division of his age—of the terrible division of America? The Scholarly Attorney, dying at the end of the novel, dictates to Jack his final insight into truth: "The creation of evil is . . . the index of God's glory and His power. That had to be so that the creation of good might be the index of man's glory and power. But by God's help. By His help and in His wisdom." When Ellis Burden asks Jack if he believes this, he says he does, not wishing to trouble the sick old man. Later he thinks, "I was not certain but that in my own way I did believe what he had said." *In my own way:* Jack still opposes his will to the search for truth in its wholeness. Although he does not realize it, this is the condition on which he accepts his responsibility for time. The historical self seeks to define itself through its own resolution of the dialectic of the age. An eminently self-conscious modern literary intellectual, Jack is not able like Cass or the Scholarly Attorney to assent to the biblical resolution of the dialectic of self and history in the wholeness of God's incarnation in human history. For all his attraction to the biblical God, Jack comprehends God as but a spiritual essence in history. While the account of his redemption to historical responsibility is often interpreted as a modern exemplum, in failing to acknowledge the mystery of Christ in history, Jack remains in the grasp of self-will. How he ultimately may construe his answerability to history is left a question. He offers no more than the potentiality of investing the modern historical self with a spiritual body, and of keeping the soul open to history and history open to the soul.

Warren has continued to believe in the possibility of a responsible historical self. But he has done so with great difficulty. In the five most substantial novels of the seven he has written since 1946, he has sounded the depths of the self's solitude in America but without creating another protagonist like Jack.

Jeremiah Beaumont, whose story is based on Warren's fictional transformation of a historical murder case, the famous "Kentucky Tragedy" of 1825, arrives at a knowledge of what he is guilty of and what he must seek expiation for: "It is the crime of self, the crime of life. The crime is I." Jeremiah never glimpses the God of Cass Mastern. He cries out mournfully: "There must be a way I have missed . . . There must be a way whereby the word becomes flesh. There must be a way whereby the flesh becomes word. Whereby loneliness becomes communion without contamination. Whereby contamination becomes purity without exile." In Jeremiah the likelihood of the self's incarnating meaning is lost; in the terrible division of the age as presented in *World Enough and Time,* the dialectic of self and history disappears. To a degree *Band of Angels, Flood,* and *Meet Me in the Green Glen* may be read as moving toward a restoration of this dialectic in Warren's vision. In these novels Warren appears to accept the conquest of the self by history but, in accepting this, to propose that the frustration of the historical self may be resolved in the emergence of the self as an existential entity. The protagonists of both *Band of Angels* and *Flood* make a progress of sorts from a state in which they are isolated in history to one in which their reality as individuals opens to them. Amantha, who, reared in luxury as a white girl, discovers that she is in truth of mixed blood and consequently a slave, speaks at times with much insight into the nature of her relation to history. "You live through time, that little piece of time that is yours," she remarks in a well-known passage, "but that piece of time is not only your own life, it is the summing-up of all the other lives that are simultaneous with yours. It is, in other words, History, and what you are is an expression of History, and you do not live your life, but somehow your life lives you, and you are, therefore, only what History does to you." But Amantha asks, "How do you know how you yourself, all the confused privateness of you, are involved with that history you are living through?" Eventually she seems to come to terms with history, yet, remaining more an idea than a genuinely realized person, she is not convincing in her privateness and tends to be simply the narrative voice of her story rather than its embodiment. Brad Tolliver, a novelist and screenwriter, is a larger and more impressive character than Amantha. When he returns to his hometown in Fiddlersburg, Tennessee, he has long been in a psychic condition similar to the state of abnormal historical consciousness which Kierkegaard so deplores. "For him History was merely what happened, no matter how blank the happening. In a kind of grim humor he thought of himself as one of those muskrat-skinners of long back, of his great grandpa's time, who had peered out of the willows to watch the squat, improbable-looking ironclad gunboats of General Grant puffing and clawing their way southward, upriver, out of nowhere, toward nowhere. Yes, for him—out of nowhere, toward nowhere—that was History. But for the people around him now History was a train that arrived on time, or only a little late. He was in awe of them."

"Out of history into history"—this is history for Jack Burden. "Out of nowhere, toward nowhere"—this is history for Brad Tolliver. Even in Jack's worst times he does not experience Brad's despair of history. The Great Twitch concept of history is a construct based on a feeling for the drama of self and history. Brad has so subjectified history in the self that, having no sense of this drama, he suspects that he has no story at all. Working on a movie script about the life of Fiddlersburg, shortly to be abandoned and flooded by the waters of a manmade lake, Brad tries to dramatize his solitariness as part and parcel of the historical condition of the South: "The Confederate States were founded on lonesomeness. They were all so lonesome they built a pen around themselves so they could be lonesome together." Yasha Jones, the movie producer, understands Brad's alienation, for he has grasped the existential meaning of the human heart as an ethical reality. "To give the impression of the mysterious inwardness of life," Yasha tells Brad, should be the intention of the movie about Fiddlersburg. But Brad continues in the "sin of the corruption of consciousness," until he arrives at the moment "in his inwardness" when he admits, *"I cannot find the connection between what I was and what I am. I have not found the human necessity."* At the conclusion of *Flood* there is the chance that Brad may move out of nowhere toward a Kierkegaardian differentiation of the ethical existence. In his experience of Fiddlersburg, the town has become something more than a metaphor of his angry loneliness. Seeing it for the last time, he thinks, *"There is no country but the heart."*

In the succession of his novels from *All the King's Men* to *Flood*, Warren's search for the responsible historical self tends to be altered into one for a version of self derived from an apprehension of the inwardness of responsibility. The ethical self, if it can be realized, would resist the collective loneliness that Warren increasingly recognizes as the historical condition of man by responding to the community of

171

selves. As Warren acknowledges in *Democracy and Poetry*, the thought of Martin Buber has influenced his changing perception of self-responsibility. "The idea of responsibility," Buber contends, "is to be brought back from the province of specialized ethics, of an 'ought' that swings free in the air, into that of lived life. Genuine responsibility exists only where there is real responding." Although Jack Burden becomes empathetically involved with the reality of others, he responds primarily to the "ought" incumbent upon a secularized Calvinist. Jeremiah Beaumont suggests a less hopeful state of self-knowledge than Jack. Unable to separate the self from the "ought"—from dedication to fulfilling the self's idea of what the "ought" should be —he is cruelly separated from "the warm world and its invisible fluids by which we live," and goes in agony and bewilderment on his destructive way. Brad Tolliver undergoes a somewhat different development. He has at least entered into an initial experience of the "lived life." Consequently, it might seem that Brad is a logical prophecy of a Warren hero who will succeed in becoming existentially responsible. Yet the lawyer Murray Guilfort in *Meet Me in the Green Glen* responds negatively to a felt identity with other selves. Discovering, in an experience of the inwardness he has so long avoided, that a world "full of people" who move across it "as though they knew what it meant" *must* mean something, he numbly protests, "But nobody told me." In terror of his incapacity he kills himself. In *A Place to Come To*, Jed Tewksbury (like Brad Tolliver a literary intellectual from a small southern town, although unlike Brad he is poor white in origin) realizes in retrospection that, in a life replete with associations with others (in Jed's case there are two marriages and two passionate extramarital affairs), he has failed to experience the reality of other persons. His isolation promises some remedy in his discovery that selfhood is never fulfilled in the closure of history in self-consciousness—in the self-willed moment of perception between "pastlessness and futurelessness." The self's fulfillment is exemplified in the life of his ignorant mother, who has lived in the "blessedness" of the response to specific human connections in time.

Against the power of modern history to effect the simultaneous quantification and subjectification of the individual existence, and thus to create a condition of alienation unknown to men before, Warren has attempted to envision the counterpower of the durable moral force exerted by responsible self-perception. If the attempt has been awkward and oftentimes murky, it is partly owing to Warren's subordination of his talent as a storyteller to his philosophical bent. It is more owing to the fact that the attempt involves the uncertain conflict between the self-awareness and the historicism of the modern consciousness. Warren points to the St. Augustine who says he is a question to himself, not to the St. Augustine who resolves the question by saying, "It is I who remember in my memory, and understand in my understanding, and will in my will." Warren's struggle has been to keep the self open to history and history open to the self.

Neither the tension between myth and history in Faulkner's stories nor that between history and existence in Warren's describes the motivation of Eudora Welty's stories. While the drama of resistance to history is the subject of her major novels—*Delta Wedding* (1946); *The Golden Apples* (1949), a unified collection of episodes that, like Faulkner's *Go Down, Moses,* compose a novel; *Losing Battles* (1970); and *The Optimist's Daughter* (1972)—she has approached the subject through celebrations of the resistance family and/or community enclaves offer to historical change. With unequaled fictional art and with delicate, incisive social perception, she has created a loosely chronological saga of self and collective memory in the twentieth-century South.

Superficially considered, postbellum southern literature indicates that the literary survival of the Old South took the form either of a criticism of slavery or else of a purely reverential regard for the past. But the writers associated with the region that fought a long war to nationalize the most complex experience of community and selfhood yet undergone on the American continent did not entirely yield their imagination of the past to oversimplified interpretations. Mark Twain, Thomas Nelson Page, Joel Chandler Harris suggest how memory, searching the drama of the antebellum southern experience, molded itself into a construct of cultural will, or a metaphysics of survival. Looked upon with mingled piety and irony, the southern past assumed in the literary imagination—and to an undeterminable extent in the general southern imagination—the aspect of a past alive in the present, of a culture of memory struggling against modern history. Eudora Welty's saga of southern memory is based on her subscription, on the one hand, to memory as a necessary mode of survival; and, on the other, to the realization that the survival of the mode of memory itself depends on the passionate self-consciousness with which it is apprehended as a way of life.

Welty's essay "Some Notes on Time in Fiction" (1973) sets forth her formative attitudes toward memory: "Remembering is so basic and vital a part of staying alive that it takes on the strength of an instinct of survival, and acquires the power of an art. Remembering is done through the blood, it is a bequeathment, it takes account of what happens before a man is born as if he were there taking part. It is a physical absorption through the living body, it is a spiritual heritage. It is also a life's work." The work of memory, Welty points out, preeminently demands the novelist, whose vocation is to discover "a way to make time give back all it has taken, through turning life by way of the memory into art." Her specific example in this part of her argument is Proust, but the point she makes is that "most novels reflect that personal subjective time that lived for their writers throughout the writing." The novel is "time's child." More than Warren, and more consistently than Faulkner, Welty sees modern history not as the passing of days and years (as a calendar chronology reminiscent of cosmological time) but as a clock chronology—at once an irreversible, ongoing measurement of time and its ruthless fragmentation. Memory, she implies, responds not to myth and tradition (attuned to the cosmological vision of time as a great cyclical motion) but to time as the insistent ticking of the clock. Memory is the response to an ephemerality unknown before the ticking clock. The dominion of memory, Welty discerns, has been the special province of the novelist, who comprehends the novel as "fictional time." A clock that can be run backward as well as forward, not merely telling time but penetrating it, the novel incarnates the artist's power to reorder and interpret clock time by the force of the imagination. But in Welty's novels this power is imaged not in a Proustian figure of the highly self-conscious artist, but in a community of twentieth-century Mississippians. With no aspiration to transform life into art, through memory to make time give back all that has been lost to it, they simply live in a continuity with the antebellum defiance of the clock. The old southerners, whose presence is constantly felt in Welty's portrayal of their descendants, made their kingdom in a raw frontier world. In the midst of the Mississippi wilderness they willed the recovery of mythic and traditionalist qualities and values. Their descendants, the Mississippians of Welty's tales, are the last artificers of memory. Their community redeems the lonely individuation in time proclaimed for each person by the clock, but it is on the verge of its appointed doom in history.

Telling the story of a week in the life of the Fairchilds of Shellmound in 1923, *Delta Wedding* forebodes this doom. Living in a world which has ceased to represent the reality of the past in the present, the Fairchilds preserve the art of community; but with memory lapsing into the memory of memory, they do so in a fantasy life, as in a dream. How perilously close they are to the rending of their illusion and to the exposure of their essential loneliness and anxiety is delicately evident in Laura McRaven, a cousin from Jackson, who has intimations of the real world. The knowledge of reality does come to Virgie Rainey in *The Golden Apples,* a more complicated treatment of the relation of memory, time, and the art of living than *Delta Wedding.* The "bad girl" of the little Delta town of Morgana, principal setting of *The Golden Apples,* Virgie has taken piano lessons from Miss Eckhart, Morgana's only artist. Miss Eckhart has persisted in trying to teach Virgie because she knows that Virgie is her sole pupil with the potential to play Beethoven. But the willful girl has refused to be obedient to the discipline of the metronome. At length in her frustration Miss Eckhart sets fire to a house where Virgie is making love to a sailor. Virgie's escape under the eyes of the town ends her association with her music teacher but not her feeling for the metronomic beat of life. She comes to see "things in their time like hearing them." Many years later, recalling a painting on Miss Eckhart's wall, Perseus with the head of the Medusa, Virgie thinks of the sword cutting off the Medusa's head in "three moments, not one. In the three was the damnation—no, only the secret, unhurting because not caring in itself—beyond the beauty and the sword's stroke and the terror lay their existence in time—far out and endless, a constellation which the heart could read over many a night." As Virgie's heart reads the Perseus story, the collectivity of memory which is Morgana and the personal recollection of her relation with Miss Eckhart coalesce as an emblem of the relationship between art and life: "In Virgie's reach of memory a melody softly lifted, lifted of itself. Everytime Perseus struck off the Medusa's head, there was the beat of time, and the melody. Endless the Medusa, Perseus endless." We last see Virgie, now in her forties, sitting under a big tree with an old black woman, who is a chicken thief. They listen to the October rain falling like the "world beating in their ears." Beyond the beat of the world Virgie hears the movement of the constellations far out in time: "the running of the horse and bear, the stroke of the leopard, the dragon's crusty slither, and the glimmer and trumpet of the swan." Wanderer beyond the confines of Morgana's ritualistic preservation of the identity with the past, an outsider who is yet an insider, Virgie is privy to the knowledge of the artist: the power of the human imagination to redeem the isolation and transience of the self from the magnitude of time and space. Her austere vision of the great mythic memorialization of the story of existence in the wheeling firmament contrasts with the narrow, protective culture of the memory the townsfolk have erected against history. It contrasts too with the vision Cassie Morrison has in the first story in *The Golden Apples*: Virgie and Miss Eckhart as "human beings terribly at large, roaming on the face of the earth . . . like lost beasts." Virgie and Miss Eckhart, and not less Beethoven and the old black chicken thief, are identified with the stories of the beasts symbolized in the constellations wheeling in the far spaces of time and thus with the capacity of the storyteller's, the artist's, imagination to make an order of time.

The relation of memory to the southern structure of community is developed in a northern Mississippi setting in *Losing Battles*. A quite different world from the Delta, the northern section of Mississippi —specifically in the novel the northeastern hill country—is described as it was in the age of the Great Depression in the 1930s. In this place and time live the numerous members of the Renfro-Vaughn clan. Their community, called Banner, is dominated by the presence of Granny Vaughn, the clan's ninety-year-old matriarch. The novel depicts a family reunion held on Granny's "birthday Sunday" during a late summer of the thirties. Much of the novel comes to us through the "great hum of the reunion"—the playful repartee and joking and, most of all, the storytelling—during one night and into the following day. Out of all the talk a tangled situation develops, revolving around the long battle between the numerous tribe of Granny Vaughn and the just deceased Miss Julia Mortimer, the hard-willed teacher and founder of the Banner School, who had devoted her life to trying to change the future. Although the people of Banner are a crude lot compared with the residents of Shellmound or Morgana, we discover in the reunion a secret, artful resistance to history similar to that of the Delta enclaves. Indeed, the Banner residents are more aware of the encroaching outside world than those of Shellmound and Morgana. Miss Julia is its highly articulate messenger. *Losing Battles* affirms, to be sure, a vision of transcending community; but it is that of human hearts and wills engaged in the "lonesomeness and hilarity of survival." The ironic tone of *Losing Battles* implies an intensification of Welty's focus on the decline of memory and the isolation of self.

In her next novel, *The Optimist's Daughter*, Welty virtually makes the attrition of memory an overt theme. The story centers on the last days and funeral of Judge McKelva of Mt. Salus, Mississippi, a community the Judge served faithfully in something like the spirit of the New South movement. The conflict between his youthful second wife, Fay (who in the old unfavorable sense of the term is "common"), and his daughter, Laurel McKelva Hand, mature, well-educated Chicago designer, is the chief element of the plot. As she tries to unravel the motive of her father's second marriage, Laurel is led to ponder the meaning of the relationship between her dead parents. The problem is complicated by the question of the meaning of her own marriage, a short, intense connection ended abruptly by Phil Hand's death in World War II. "What burdens we lay on the dying . . . ," Laurel thinks, "seeking to prove some little thing that we can keep to comfort us when they can no longer feel—something as incapable of being kept as of being proved: the lastingness of memory, vigilance against harm, self-reliance, good hope, trust in one another." Against Fay, the dispossessor, who is invulnerable to past and present alike, Laurel has no real defense. She can only call on her renewed vulnerability to memory, the "somnambulist" coming "back in its wounds from across the world." Laurel has no shared memory like the people of Shellmound, Morgana, and Banner; nor does she have, like Virgie Rainey, a heroic vision of the self's loneliness. Although she realizes after a night-long, agonized meditation that the past may assume wholeness in the memory of the single heart, and this gives her courage and hope, it is clear that the conclusion of *The Optimist's Daughter* signifies the death of the southern community of past and present.

When we extend the discussion of southern fiction in the last thirty years beyond its massive substance in Faulkner, Warren, and Welty to other southern novelists, we can single out for discussion those who most vitally and fully represent the shift from the portrayal of the dialectical drama of history and myth to the depiction of a drama involving a quest for the basic existentialist condition of being. This shift is foreshadowed, as has been indicated, in Warren and Welty; they incorporate it in, or at least accommodate it to, the dialectical drama. On other serious and highly talented southern novelists the shift has seemingly made demands they cannot effectively meet. Their careers, fragmented or erratic in contrast to those of Faulkner, Warren, and Welty, appear to represent the literary expense of seeking to transcend the dialectical relationship of past and present. At the same time they seem to illustrate the fact that the novelist is never more obedient to historicism than when he seeks to transcend it.

It is important in this connection to call attention to the work of three post–World War II novelists whose origins are contemporary with those of Faulkner, Warren, and Welty: Andrew Lytle, Caroline Gordon, and Katherine Anne Porter. In these writers (none of them prolific since 1945), the quest for the absolute takes the form of an emphasis on the Christian myth of the fall and redemption of man. Using James's *The Turn of the Screw* as allusory frame but not as interpretive reference in *A Name for Evil* (1947), Lytle employs Henry Brent as the first-person narrator of the story of Brent's contention with the demonic presence of a Confederate ancestor whose absorption in himself mirrors Henry's own moral condition. The situation symbolizes the evil of the self's attempted arrogation of the world to its will. This monstrous evil, Lytle indicates, hid itself in the New World man's presumptively good but arrogant dream of acquiring dominion not only over nature but over the self. In *A Name for Evil,* the past destroys the present, fulfilling a pattern of damnation implicit in the secularization of the Western mind. Lytle's *The Velvet Horn* (1957) pursues the same theme in a still more involved representation of the Christian myth. As Thomas H. Landess has pointed out, this intricately designed novel is about "the responsibilities of the blood." Unlike Warren's Jack Burden, who speculates that blood sacrifice may be necessary for salvation yet remains a humanist, Lytle's Jack Cropleigh makes a sacrificial death to fulfill the Christian myth.

Caroline Gordon (whose conversion to Roman Catholicism is of prime significance in her stories written after World War II) suggests a great deal about the sensibility both of Lytle's stories and of her own—*The Strange Children* (1951), *The Malefactors* (1956), and *The Glory of Hera* (1972)—in the epilogue to the last-named work. It is St. Augustine's remark in the *Confessions*: "My ignorance was so great that these questions troubled me. I did not know that evil is nothing but the removal of good until finally no good remains." *The Glory of Hera,* a telling of the myth of Heracles as an archetype of the myth of Christ, is informed by the conviction that men share a universal or collective inner mythos of truth and righteous action. This truth, as St. Augustine says, is corrupted by puritanical judgments based on a false regard for particular manners and codes as sacrosanct. Caroline Gordon, like Lytle, expresses the faith that in the universal absoluteness of his fall, man has not fallen out of sacramental wholeness of being save when "through self-willed pride" he has devoted himself to a part of life "under the false assumption that it is the whole." This kind of fragmentation is puritanism: the desire to separate out and glorify in its purity one element of a complex tradition. The puritanism of history and science are linked by Lytle and Gordon to the self's negation of family and society, which in effect is a negation of the gift of God extended to man in his fall from innocence, the gift of community.

The community of man and its bearing on the fall is brought to a climax as a subject of the southern novelist in Katherine Anne Porter's *Ship of Fools* (1962). It is not a convincing climax, partly because the novel reduces the fall of man to a strongly particularized historical image—the North German Lloyd *S. A. Vera,* en route from Veracruz, Mexico, to Bremerhaven, Germany, August 23–September 17, 1931. Intended to be directly reminiscent of *Das Narrenschiff* (1494), by Sebastian Brant, the novel offers the *Vera* as a "simple almost universal image of the ship of this world on its voyage to eternity." But the *Vera* is something else. Her passengers, officers, and crew are minutely specified representatives of Western civilization in the twentieth century. An effort, like Faulkner's *A Fable,* to transform the modern historical consciousness into mythic consciousness, *Ship of Fools* is a brilliant failure. No novel of the present century more forcefully illustrates the defeat of the mythic and allegorical impulse by historicism, and the difficulty the modern literary imagination has in getting out of history into anything else but history. The modern ship of fools sails not into eternity but into the Nazi dream of the thousand-year Reich, a complete gnostic assimilation of eternity to history.

The movement out of history toward the absolute is more precisely illustrated in the stories of three southern Roman Catholics whose careers began in the 1950s and 1960s: Flannery O'Connor, Walker Percy, and John William Corrington. What Percy says of Flannery O'Connor's motive characterizes all three: an interest in "ultimate things." Central among these things is the question of what the self may be. Is the self the "soul"? To explore the nature of the self's being, O'Connor, Percy, and Corrington—largely rejecting myth and tradition, history and memory as modes of being—construct special, basically grotesque, versions of contemporary man in the setting of the American South. While their stories resemble dialectical or allegorical dramas about the modern effort to attain spiritual reality, they violate and, in violating, transcend dramatic decorum. They are more nearly daring metaphors of the self's (the soul's) longing for being. As O'Connor declares in "The Nature and Aim of Fiction", the artist must "intrude upon the timeless, and that is only done by the violence of a single-minded respect for the truth."

Although an adherent of a faith which has stood on a reverence for tradition against Protestant literalism, O'Connor feels that in order to break through historicism to the timeless she must display a grotesquery of the self (soul). She commits violent acts of imagination, more to be associated with the psychology of the southern Bible belt than with a religion disciplined by hierarchy and maintained by the orderly process of the confessional. Profoundly aware that it is the sense of existential reality rather than of historical literalism which characterizes the southern biblical mode, O'Connor concentrates on situations in which an individual faces the apocalyptic intensity of the existent moment. The individual is a basically simple person, non-intellectual, spiritually blinded by pride. The pride may be that of smug social status, as in the case of Mrs. Turpin in "Revelation," who, standing by the "pig-parlor" on her farm, has a vision of the apocalypse of grace. In *Wise Blood* (1952), the novel about Hazel Motes, who founds the Church without Christ, pride in human self-sufficiency (in the wisdom of the human blood) leads to a lurid sequence of events that reach an apocalyptic climax when Hazel blinds himself with wet lime. *The Violent Bear It Away* (1960), O'Connor's only other novel, is a more complex rendition of the same subject, the danger of pride in the self's ability. No scene in O'Connor is more memorable than the final one in this story, the account of young Tarwater's burning of the woods and his acceptance of the divine mission handed to him by the old Tarwater. The boy has a vision of his great-uncle's partaking of the loaves and fishes; and smearing his face with dirt from the prophet's grave, he leaves the burning woods to move "toward the dark city, where the children of God lay sleeping."

Tarwater finds himself in the separation of the prophets from temporality. His discovery of himself may be associated with O'Connor's idea that the southern Catholic novelist descends within himself to find his region and discovers that the South insists on a prophetic resistance of the self to modern history. Nothing is more instructive in Flannery O'Connor's own comments on writing fiction than her interpretation of the southern writer's connection with the "blessing" of the Civil War: "In the South we have, in however attenuated form, a vision of Moses's face as he pulverized the idols . . . The writer operates at a peculiar crossroads where time and place and eternity somehow meet. His problem is to find that location." In the direct correspondence between the southern situation and the Old Testament prophetic history, O'Connor implies, the southern writer's capacity for prophetic insight is at one with a violent and transcendent country of truth—a South which is a landscape of eternity. Although she has a keen sense of place and writes at times with a genuine feeling for the language and humor of her region, she has no basic regard for mundane place in history or for the pieties of memory and tradition. In her stories the sense of the past in the present is abrogated.

Preceded by his studies in science and medicine, a long period of inquiry into the writings of Kierkegaard, Marcel, Sartre, and other existentialist philosophers, as well as by his conversion to Catholicism, Walker Percy's novelistic intrusion upon the timeless is more uncertain than Flannery O'Connor's. When we compare Percy with O'Connor we must take into account his rearing, particularly the period when, following the deaths of his parents, he went to live in the Delta community of Greenville, Mississippi, home of his second cousin, the poet-planter William Alexander Percy. Here the young Walker Percy (who refers to his cousin as "Uncle Will") was at the heart of the Mississippi world Eudora Welty transforms into a culture of memory. The character of this world in its bearing on the future novelist is revealed in William Alexander Percy's autobiography, *Lanterns on the Levee* (1941). In his first two novels—*The Moviegoer* (1961) and *The Last Gentleman* (1966)—Walker Percy's characters reflect the sensibility of the Delta people. Unlike Flannery O'Connor's characters, they have a societal context and awareness; yet like hers they are an odd assortment of marginal grotesques, whose motives are developed primarily within the drama of a quest for salvation. In fact, Percy's protagonists—intellectually aware of their grotesqueness and agonizingly self-conscious—run the risk of being emblems of Kierkegaardian philosophy. Yet although he approaches the novel with the motive, and to some degree, the manner of the phenomenologist, and even though he deprecates the southern strategy of surviving through memory as an impediment to the self's being, Percy has not separated his imagination as a storyteller from the southern community of memory and its fate in the modern world. For this reason he is far more successful than Flannery O'Connor in depth and delicacy of character depiction.

Binx Bolling in *The Moviegoer* and Williston Barrett in *The Last Gentleman* not only suggest the aura of ineffable loneliness associated with the modern experience of radical individuation; they embody the experience through their participation in a specific society which is experiencing the loss of the illusory image of its history. Aunt Emily in *The Moviegoer*, like William Alexander Percy, is a conscious keeper of the southern culture of memory. Her advice to Binx is that he "act like a soldier." But Binx has come too late into the world for the Stoic salvation (which was discovered by the Roman culture of memory). He conceives that he is living "in the very century of merde, the great shithouse of scientific humanism where needs are satisfied, everyone becomes an anyone, a warm and creative person, and prospers like a dung beetle, and one hundred percent of people are humanists and ninety-eight percent believe in God, and men are dead, dead, dead; and the malaise has settled in like a fall-out and what people really fear is not that the bomb will fall but that the bomb will not fall." Feeling that "he knows nothing" and has "nothing to do but fall prey to desire," Binx would live in the comfortable solitude of a beast. Still, he makes a kind spiritual pilgrimage of life, and he learns

181

something about his condition. Eventually, he is on the verge of making the leap into faith. The pilgrimage of Will Barrett is more enigmatic, his eventual fate less predictable. His connection with memory is one rooted in positive terror: an integral awareness of the doom of his own family, which has so internalized the conflict between the culture of memory and modern history that his father has killed himself. The "last of his line," Will is subject to recurrent periods of amnesia: "Much of the time he was like a man who has just crawled out of a bombed building. Everything looked strange." In his spiritual pilgrimage from New York back to his native South and eventually out into the West, this hysterical youth misses the meaning of God's grace at the moment when he has a genuine opportunity to grasp it. He is left open to the possibility of learning the "great secret." But, ironically, being open to possibility is Will's greatest difficulty. Percy's description of the cultural trauma which is the psychic heritage of the educated southern youth like Will derives, we must feel, from Percy's own descent into the self: "What happens to a man to whom all things seem possible and every course of action open? Nothing of course. Except war. If a man lives in the sphere of the possible and waits for something to happen, what he is waiting for is war—or the end of the world."

In Percy's third novel, *Love in the Ruins: The Adventures of a Bad Catholic at a Time Near the End of the World* (1971), the waiting time is almost over. But the setting of this novel, the South after American scientific-technological humanism propelled by its goal of the "good life" has collapsed in a hideous parody of itself, requires a strongly satirical manner and a decided stylizing of characters. Even though the satire is telling, history does not happen in the future; and in spite of the fact that like all good futuristic novels *Love in the Ruins* is really about the present, it smacks of an evasion of historical reality. The culture of the future is as illusory as the culture of memory. In fact, it is more so. One cannot fail to see that although Percy had no intention either in *The Moviegoer* or in *The Last Gentleman* of writing a "southern novel," Binx Bolling and Will Barrett, especially the latter, convincingly exemplify an ambient tie between the southern culture of memory and the modern self's salvation from the modern malaise. The recovery through the grace of God of the wholeness of self is credible as a possibility inherent in the southern sense of the past; the tendency to survive by remembering keeps open the relation to an older religious consciousness. But the protagonist in *Love in the Ruins,* Dr. Thomas More, seems so far divorced from the past that his return to the traditional acts of confession and penance is less convincing than his attachment to his "lapsometer"—"the first caliphor of the soul and the first hope of bridging the dread chasm that has rent the soul of Western man ever since the famous philosopher Descartes ripped body loose from mind and turned the very soul into a ghost that haunts its own house".

The ambiguity of More's situation is not, however, a violation of Percy's intention in *Love in the Ruins*. This is to dramatize the situation he describes in his essay "A Novel about the End of the World": "The psychical forces presently released in the postmodern consciousness open unlimited possibilities for both destruction and liberation, for an absolute loneliness or a rediscovery of community and reconciliation." This either/or situation in the postmodern consciousness —distinguished from the "old modern consciousness" in that it expresses an intense escalation of the capacity both for catastrophe and for hope—is more succinctly and graphically presented in Percy's fourth novel, *Lancelot* (1977). In this story, cast in the present, Percy focuses completely on the specific place in which the confrontation of psychical forces occurs, the "individual consciousness of postmodern man." The novel takes the form of an implied dialogue between Lancelot Andrewes Lamar, Louisiana aristocrat and member of the bar (who in his youth has been a football star and a Rhodes scholar) and Percival, a psychiatrist-priest and boyhood friend. Save for Percival's rather enigmatic "yes" and "no" answers to a series of questions put to him by Lancelot at the end of the story, Lancelot is the sole direct speaker. But Percival, whose presence is both real and symbolic, speaks through his relation to Lancelot. Whether Lancelot's lurid tale of his destruction of the house of Lamar is a tale told by a madman or by the only sane person in the world is left up to the reader to decide. Lancelot presents the drastic issue: either the Sodom the nation has become will rediscover the transcendent classical-Christian ethos of the West or it will yield to the iron discipline of a new prophet. This may be Lancelot himself, who says, "I am my own instrument." The closure of history in the self has left no way open for salvation save self-will. When Nietzsche perceived this, he proclaimed the superman. Lancelot is less perceptive than Nietzsche, but he is less despairing. He tells Percival that he will "wait and give your God a chance." The hope in *Lancelot* is that the prophet has not yet quite proclaimed the self as God.

Confidence in the possibilities of history is more positive in the stories of John William Corrington than in Percy's. As a matter of fact, Corrington harks back to a vision of history proclaimed by the defeated South: history must be an overriding scheme of justice. Varied approaches to this theme are to be found in his novels and short stories. We may note particularly *And Wait for the Night* (1964) and *The Upper Hand* (1967), his first two novels, and such short fictions as "The Lonesome Traveler" (in the collection of stories entitled *The Lonesome Traveler,* 1968) and "The Actes and Monuments" and "Pleadings" (in the collection entitled *The Actes and Monuments,* 1978). The last two stories reflect a deepening regard for the subject of history and justice. This has been attendant upon Corrington's formal studies in law (he holds a law degree from Tulane University Law School and is a practicing attorney in New Orleans) as well as his extensive readings in philosophy, history, and science. "The Actes and Monuments," an impressive tour de force in the grotesque and the absurd, brings into persuasive focus a southern metaphysic of "grace as history transcendant."

It may be highly significant that the two strongest voices (aside from those of Faulkner, Warren, and Welty) in post-1945 southern fiction so far have been O'Connor and Percy, both writers of intense religious commitment. But strenuous religious commitment is not generally characteristic of the southern novelists who have emerged in the past thirty years. They display a diversity of vision, talent, interests, and achievement.

In some instances they have followed the multiple ways of the man of letters, and (perhaps unendowed with the great energies of a Warren) have allowed the writing of fiction to assume a smaller role in their careers than they may have intended. This may be true of the novelist-poet-critic Marion Montgomery. Like Warren a writer with a decided philosophical bent (though with a marked Anglo-Catholic coloration), Montgomery shows a strong novelistic imagination in *The Wandering of Desire* (1962), *Darrell* (1964), and *Fugitive* (1974). But in his storytelling he is more inclined than Warren to subordinate the novelist to the cultural critic. Another notable, and more extreme case, of the southern novelist who has given divided attention to the novel is that of Shelby Foote. After a series of five remarkable novels—*Tournament* (1949), *Follow Me Down* (1950), *Love in a Dry Season* (1951), *Shiloh* (1952), and *Jordan County* (1954)—Foote turned for the next twenty years to the composition of the "American Iliad," his three-volume *The Civil War: A Narrative* (1958, 1963, 1974). He has recently turned once again to the novel in *September, September* (1977), a dramatic story set in the time of the school desegregation crisis in the South. Other southern novelists of the past two or three decades who have given important yet less than full attention to the novel include Walter Sullivan (*Sojourn of a Stranger,* 1957; *The Long,*

Long Love, 1959); David Madden (*The Beautiful Greed,* 1961; *Cassandra Singing,* 1969; *Brothers in Confidence,* 1972; *Bijou,* 1974; *The Suicide's Wife,* 1978); and George Garrett (*Cold Ground Was My Bed Last Night,* 1964; *Do, Lord, Remember Me,* 1965; *Death of the Fox,* 1971). Sullivan has occupied himself with provocative, somber evaluations of the twentieth-century southern novel and modern literary art (*Death by Melancholy,* 1972; *A Requiem for the Renascence,* 1976). Madden has been attracted by many interests, including popular literature and film. *Bijou,* his most substantial novel to date, focuses these interests in the story of Lucius Hutchfield, a young usher in a movie theater, who aspires to be a writer and finds an idol in Thomas Wolfe. Garrett also has followed varied interests, including film and Elizabethan history. His major work, *Death of the Fox,* a convincing fictional reconstruction of the life of Sir Walter Raleigh, bears obliquely on the history of the South.

Several novelists who began their careers writing stories about their native South have been diverted not simply from fiction to other forms but from the southern scene. Prominent among these are Elizabeth Spencer and Shirley Ann Grau. After writing three substantial novels depicting the Mississippi Delta world—*Fire in the Morning* (1948), *This Crooked Way* (1952), and *The Voice at the Back Door* (1956)—Spencer turned to Italian settings in *The Light in the Piazza* (1960) and *No Place for an Angel* (1967). In *The Snare* (1972) she returns to a southern setting (New Orleans) but not to a definable southern theme. Grau began her career with vividly depicted southern scenes in *The Black Prince and Other Stories* (1955), *The Hard Blue Sky* (1958), and *The House on Coliseum Street* (1961). She took up the southern themes of race and family in *The Keepers of the House* (1964). But in *The Condor Passes* (1971) the southern emphasis lapses, and in *Evidence of Love* (1977) it disappears. Yet departure from southern settings and subjects has not become an established trend on the part of storytellers native to the South. Madison Jones, Jesse Hill Ford, Ellen Douglas, and Berry Morgan are among natives who have been consistently faithful to their homeland. Jones has written six highly crafted novels—*The Innocent* (1957), *Forest of the Night* (1960), *A Buried Land* (1963), *An Exile* (1967), *A Cry of Absence* (1971), and *Passage through Gehenna* (1978). The last is based on the crossing of the ways in the rural world of Tennessee, where physical and psychic violence are linked in the residual Calvinistic vision of its people. Ford, another Tennessean, has written his strongest novels in *The Liberation of Lord Byron Jones* (1965) and *The Raider* (1975), the first a story of contemporary theme (racial segregation), the second a story of the Civil War in Tennessee. Douglas, whose home is in the Mississippi Delta, is concerned in *A Family's Affairs* (1962), *Black Cloud, White Cloud* (1963), and *Where the Dreams Cross* (1968) with the ironic displacement of southern values in the present day, a theme somewhat modified in *Apostles of Light* (1973), a novel about the universal problem of aging in contemporary society. In *Pursuit* (1966) and *The Mystic Adventures of Roxie Stoner* (1974), Morgan, yet another Mississippi writer, has (under the collective title "Certain Shadows") inaugurated a sensitive multivolume representation of the decay of family and community in the South. This subject has lent itself especially well, it should be noted, to the talents of southern short-story writers. In portraying the critical moment when an ordinary person has an inner revelation of the fallibility of social order, Peter Taylor (*Collected Stories*, 1969) is unsurpassed. His range is small: the intimacies of historical displacement in twentieth-century upper-middle-class families of the urban South, his locale in particular being Nashville, Tennessee. Charles East (*Where the Music Was*, 1965), like Taylor, has a gift for conveying, within the miniature scope of the short story, the unobtrusive but resistless destruction of accepted reality by historical actualities.

All of the writers just mentioned illuminate the southern novelistic perspective on the theme of self and history, as do numerous others: Harris Downey, James Agee, William Humphrey, Guy Owen, William Goyen, Sylvia Wilkinson, Joan Williams, Barry Hannah, James Whitehead, Robert Canzoneri, and Wilma Stokeley. The list can be augmented. But if we seek the post-1945 southern novelists (other than the major trio or the Catholic group) who most clearly see the spiritual identity of the self against the persistent intimation of its historicity, we discover Carson McCullers, William Styron, Reynolds Price, and Cormac McCarthy. With no calculated, or for that matter, probably no conscious intention of doing so, each one of these novelists suggests a paradoxical but existentially logical resolution of the dilemma of the self in history.

Carson McCullers's first novel, *The Heart Is a Lonely Hunter* (published in 1940, when she was twenty-three years old, and her best work) is a prescient anticipation of this resolution, as are her second and third novels—*Reflections in a Golden Eye* (1941) and *The Ballad of the Sad Café* (1951). The three stories together offer a striking confirmation of McCullers's intuition of an estrangement of the self which cannot be defined in the normative terms of social alienation. The definition McCullers sought eludes her in *The Member of the*

Wedding (1946), as the brilliant portrayal of Frankie becomes diminished by pathos. With this novel McCullers virtually exhausted her insight into the self's loneliness in time. Her last novel, *Clock without Hands* (1961), is a botched effort. McCullers began her work with the idea that "consciousness of self is the first problem the human being solves," but in her stories she is never at rest with her own dictum. She sees the problem of self-identity as less and less susceptible of solution. By implication, she asks if the self is definable as an entity. Is the self an abstraction of the human consciousness? Which is another way of asking if the self has become a casualty of history.

The protagonists in Styron's chief novels—*Lie Down in Darkness* (1951), *Set This House on Fire* (1960), and *The Confessions of Nat Turner* (1967)—are, it is not too rash to say, all versions of self-identity in extremis. In each novel we witness the life of a person who has lost the anxious, even desperate, yet preserving sense of identity conferred by self-awareness of alienation. Styron dramatizes the anomalous self blindly seeking its apocalypse in the murder of what it cannot name. All the historical signposts dissolving, including those of the family relationship, Peyton Loftis in *Lie Down in Darkness* kills her nameless self, tortured in her last moment by the one token of identity that remains to her, her repressed passion for her father. Cass Kinsolving in *Set This House on Fire* may have a better time of it, in that by divorcing himself completely from his place of birth he undergoes a kind of regeneration; but it amounts to not much more than a rather fuzzy notion of the self as a true homeland. Nat Turner, the best known of Styron's protagonists and the most controversial, is created in a novel that, Styron says, is a "meditation on history." The meditator in the novel is not Styron but Nat. A chattel slave who not only has learned to read and to write but has acquired the complex literary sensibility of the white man's world, Nat tells his own story, eloquently contemplating the origins, progress, and bloody resolution of a rebellion against his condition. But in recording his life, Styron's Nat makes the story of an old slave uprising a paradigm of the modern self's apocalypse. Styron depicts Nat as having absorbed the style of thought and emotion, the messianic longings and loneliness, of his masters—who are not less the contemporaries of Hegel and Kierkegaard, of Emerson and Poe, than they are Styron's (and our) contemporaries. Nat not only anticipates but epitomizes the contemporary self in its intricate, total captivity to the idiom of the self. Against the modern self's captivity by history nothing avails, Kierkegaard says, save a whole sacrifice of self to faith. But Styron's Nat has no vision of the self transcended. His deepest motivation lies in his grounding in the author's romantic existentialism. Nat's mission ends in a vision of an ecstatic, onanistic union with his beloved, Margaret Whitehead, adolescent daughter of the master class—which is at the same time his union with Christ. His meditation on history finds its resolution in a version of the Tristram and Iseult or the Romeo and Juliet story. Early emblems of the modern self's rebellion against the self's absorption in the modern society of history, such romantic love stories discover the self's salvation in narcissistic sexual rapture. Styron's Nat Turner dies in the ironic belief that the self can be liberated from historical circumstance by slavery to self-fulfillment. In the solipsistic, romantic idiom of his meditation on history he terminates history in a pathos of self.

A similar sense of pathos is suggested in Reynolds Price's stories. Of his first two novels—*A Long and Happy Life* (1962) and *A Generous Man* (1966)—Price has said, "What I have chronicled is my own world, that world which has seemed to me . . . to exist *beneath* the world perceived by other people, that world which seems to impinge upon, to color, the shape of the daily world we inherit." The elusive nature of the self's connection with the forms and institutions of society demands, he says, their "reinvention" in the memory of the literary artist, so that when the ghosts return they do so in their corporeal dimensions. Seeking to portray society as essentially a dimension of the self, Price strives to envision self as its own entity. But burdened with a sensitivity to memory like Eudora Welty (a writer he much admires), Price (like Hemingway, another writer he admires) cannot separate the self from its embodiment in time and place. The tension in his stories between the self and the aura of the myth of the past in the present becomes more involved in his third novel, *Love and Work* (1968); and in *The Surface of Earth* (1975) it becomes thoroughly enigmatic, if not hermetic, in quality. A huge chronicling of the lives of two families, the Mayfields and the Kendals, during the years 1903–1944, *The Surface of Earth* is set in North Carolina and Virginia. Realistically detailed, slow, almost lethargic, the novel records the stories of lives that never rise above the ordinary in social stature or personal achievement—of lives that frequently seem dreary. The inner intention of the long recording is not only to celebrate the self's capacity to survive, but in doing so to comprehend, especially in the never-ending urgency of its need for love, its sacramental identity. Rob Mayfield, the ne'er-do-well son of Eva and Forest Mayfield, discerns "the constant promise that the skin of a body, of maybe the earth, was only the veil of a better place where the soul would be borne. A sheltered bay." His parents, he decides, "intended his life," and "they met in him, only place on earth." In spite of its scope in time and its assemblage of characters, its appearance as a big family novel, *The Surface of Earth* is a lyrical rather than a novelistic expression. Almost secretly commemorative, it identifies the southern culture of memory with the secrecy of the self. Without intending to do so, Price effects a virtual closure of the southern mode of memory and history in the self's dominion.

But no twentieth-century southern writer has created a novel which emblematizes the tendency to resolve history in the self with the chilling precision of Cormac McCarthy's *Child of God* (1973). In this and two earlier novels—*The Orchard Keeper* (1965) and *Outer Dark* (1968)—McCarthy, who grew up in rural Tennessee, employs as his setting the harsh and poverty-ridden southern mountain country. Dealing with a world in which survival from one day to the next is often the primary concern of the inhabitants, McCarthy centers his attention not on sociological or economic but on psychic survival. His protagonists, loners who traffic with evil as they move about a landscape still retaining more than a semblance of natural beauty, are figures in a grotesque pastoral. The detritus of a pioneer stock stranded by history in the mountains, they represent the inversion of the Jeffersonian self-subsistent yeomanry. Lester Ballard, who dies in Knoxville at the state hospital for the mentally ill, is one of them. Isolated by his ignorance and crudity from whatever community there is about him, Lester is dispossessed of his father's land at a sheriff's auction, during which he is slugged with an ax. Later he has an accidental encounter with a local whore. Falsely accused of rape, he is jailed for a time but is soon released. When he finds a couple dead of carbon monoxide poisoning in a parked car, he assaults the corpse of the girl and carries her to an abandoned cabin he uses as his home. The rest of the story is taken up with the murders Lester commits and his preservation of the corpses of his victims in a cave. There are no comments in the novel about Lester's motives, save one or two that seem to be authorial: "He is small, unclean, unshaven. He moves in the dry chaff among the dust and slats of sunlight with a constrained truculence. Saxon and Celtic bloods. A child of God much like yourself perhaps." It is also said of Lester, "Were there darker provinces of night he would have found them."

The dark narcissism of Lester Ballard has an important antecedent in the bizarre career of Sut Lovingood, the creation of the nineteenth-century Tennessee humorist George Washington Harris. Just below the surface of Sut's often boisterous accounts of semifrontier life in

Tennessee lies Harris's sense of the terror of individualism in American history. In a democratic solitude of the self Sut pleasures himself in aggressions—often either overtly or symbolically sexual—against others. Plainly willing to destroy everyone else for the sake of his own pursuit of happiness, Sut is singularly obedient to a major modern historical imperative: the emancipation of the self, at any cost, from the community of past and present. The ultimate expense of this liberation—which follows the logic that history reaches its goal and its termination in the perfection of individual freedom—is not only the imprisonment of self in self but the closure of history in the self.

Lester has another significant antecedent in the various necrophiles who appear in Edgar Allan Poe's stories, no instance being more compelling than Roderick Usher in "The Fall of the House of Usher." The deep vault of the gloomy mansion where Usher places his living twin sister in the tomb anticipates Ballard's cave of moldering female corpses. In the case both of Usher and of Ballard, the history of a family, and in a larger sense of a society, ends in an individual locked in the psychopathology of loneliness. Whether or not *Child of God* represents the decisive inclination of southern fiction since 1945 it is impossible at this point to say. About all that can be said with assurance is that since the southern novel has adhered closely to the novel's origin in modern historicism, the southern novelist's imagination of the self's condition waits upon further revelations of the congruence of self and history.

5
Jewish Writers
Mark Shechner

We have been devoted to words.
Even here in this rich country
Scripture enters and sits down
and lives with us like a relative.
Taking the best chair in the house . . .
　　　LOUIS SIMPSON, "Baruch," in *Searching for the Ox*　(1976)

The Jewish Era

TO try to be cogent on the subject of Jewish writing in America at a time when a coherent and identifiable Jewish culture and religion have effectively ceased to exist except in special enclaves is to confront such ambiguity that one must be wary of all tidy definitions of Jewish group identity. Neither "Jewish writer" nor "Jewish fiction" is an obvious or self-justifying subdivision of literature, any more than Jewishness itself is now a self-evident cultural identity. Such writers as Norman Mailer, Bernard Malamud, Joseph Heller, and Cynthia Ozick would seem to have little in common as writers or as people that would support inferences about a shared heritage or tradition, and little common apprehension of the momentous events of recent history to justify any sweeping definitions of a Jewish historical sense or sensibility. All the same, since we want to talk about a historical fact that is everywhere acknowledged—the many ranking American novelists who happen to be Jews or, to put it more prudently, of Jewish descent—it is not unreasonable to invoke "the Jewish writer" as a convenient shorthand for a feature of the literary census that we want to examine but are not yet prepared to define.

For though terms like "Jewish fiction" and "the Jewish novel" are not useful as either literary categories, like "the Elizabethan sonnet," or national catchalls, like "the Russian novel," they do merit a place in *social* history. The most accessible collective facts about Jewish novelists in America are demographic: their sheer numerical presence

191

among the ranks of American novelists and their insistent upward mobility through them. Not only are so many American novelists Jews, more or less, but the work of these writers includes some of the most acclaimed fiction written in this country since World War II. The postwar era has seen Saul Bellow, Norman Mailer, Isaac Bashevis Singer, Philip Roth, and Bernard Malamud take their place among the most celebrated of our writers, and to mention them together is to be conscious of both their place in our literature and the enormously varied terrain they occupy collectively. And to their names can be added others from that vast penumbra of Jewish fiction writers who have also earned some measure of national recognition since the war, including Herbert Gold, Mark Harris, Stanley Elkin, E. L. Doctorow, Joseph Heller, Leonard Michaels, Irvin Faust, Arthur Miller, Grace Paley, Tillie Olsen, Cynthia Ozick, Meyer Levin, and Irwin Shaw. Whether this entry of the Jews into American fiction constitutes a literary movement is uncertain, and such things at any rate defy precise definition, but it surely qualifies as a social movement that has had enormous literary consequences.

The presence of Jewish writers and intellectuals in American letters was apparent early on in the century, for the production of imaginative literature—fiction, poetry, drama—was one expression of the political and cultural ferment in progress among the Eastern European Jews during the great immigration of 1881–1924. But though the immigrant generation produced a small bounty of "American" books, of which Mary Antin's *The Promised Land* (1912) and Abraham Cahan's *The Rise of David Levinsky* (1917) are the best known, its language was essentially Yiddish, with infusions of Russian, Polish, Rumanian, and Hungarian, and its literary and cultural life a thing apart. Between the world wars, however, the first American generation made an auspicious debut into American fiction, which can be measured, at least quantitatively, by the brimming, thirty-five page roster of Jewish-American writers compiled in 1939 by Joseph Mersand in *Traditions in American Literature: A Study of Jewish Characters and Authors*. But what the reader of Mersand or other prewar bibliographies (for example, those that appeared from time to time in the *American Jewish Yearbook*) will notice is how few of these Jewish writers now seem to warrant more than historical or ethnographic recognition. After Cahan, Anzia Yezierska, Henry Roth, Daniel Fuchs, Michael Gold, and Meyer Levin (who is still going strong), the ranks thin out noticeably, and we do not recognize in these bibliographies a single novelist who exercised any lasting influence upon American writing. In retrospect, only Nathanael West (born Nathan

Weinstein), whose Jewishness was hard to locate, has left a mark on our fiction. Despite the many Jewish writers to enter American literature in the 1920s and 1930s, the emergence of Jews as major contemporary writers had to await the 1940s, when a prevailing fiction of documentary realism and proletarian romance, produced by the likes of Cahan, Fuchs, Gold, Howard Fast, and Albert Halper, gave way to the subtler and more evocative writing of Delmore Schwartz, Saul Bellow, Isaac Rosenfeld, and Norman Mailer, and a significant advance in articulateness, power, and modernity appeared to be at hand. It was largely in the ten years between 1945 and 1955 that the Jewish writers in America came forward as the producers of and spokesmen for an influential, modern literature.

Though the sociology of the mass entry of Jews into American letters is complex, two historical conditions for it stand out. First, the Jews came to America as they were emerging from a traditional way of life that stressed the rigorous spiritual authority of the Bible, the moral authority of an extensive legal and ethical code, contained in the Talmud and its commentaries, and the democracy of learning. The general correlation between class and learning that characterized most Western cultures through the end of the last century never held true for the Jews; despite their often crushing poverty, the immigrants brought with them a rich tradition of literacy and scholarship and the beginnings of a secular fiction that needed only translation into modern terms to gain entry into American writing. "We have been devoted to words." Whatever else the Jews did, be it in Judea or Canaan or Egypt or Spain or Poland, they were devoted to the reading and writing of books.

The second point, amply illustrated by Irving Howe in his *World of Our Fathers* (1976), is that the great immigration was itself the expression of a cultural revolution in full career throughout the Jewish world. From the eighteenth century onward, successive waves of Hassidic enthusiasm, Enlightenment liberalism, Zionism, trade unionism, and socialism had swept through the rural villages (*shtetlach*) and urban ghettoes of Eastern Europe, undermining the traditional life of stoic pietism and stirring the Jews to restless self-scrutiny and revolt. Among the first- and second-generation Jews in America, the traditional reverence for learning easily detached itself from the holy books to become a free-floating receptivity to new ideas and moral challenges. In our time, when the restlessness and passion of the Jewish transformation from a medieval to a modern people have largely subsided, it is difficult for us to appreciate the enormous vitality that was set loose by this break with tradition and the overnight emergence of the Jews from centuries of semifeudal isolation into the tumultuous modern world.

Among the intellectuals of the second generation, the messianic flavor of traditional Judaism was often transformed by the poverty of ghetto life and the Jewish encounter with radical ideas into a secular revolutionism, for which Marx, as often as not, provided the text and the Russian Revolution, for a time, the example. But secular bookishness and the pursuits to which it attached itself led also to the public library and to American and English literature. Bookish and impecunious boys who, two generations before, might have pored over their Talmuds in the bleak synagogues of the Russian-Polish border, or who, a generation later, would have debated the economic interpretation of history or the fate of Western man in the ghettoes of Vilna or Bialystok or the cafés of East Side Manhattan, by the twenties and thirties had discovered Twain, Melville, and Hawthorne, and even, pursuing the vectors of the language back to their origin, the treasury of English literature and culture. "One hot June afternoon in 1934, deep in the depression," recalls Alfred Kazin in his memoir, *Starting Out in the Thirties* (1965), "I had just completed my college course for the year and was desolately on my way home to Brooklyn when a book review in the *New York Times* aroused me. I was just nineteen years old, my briefcase full of college essays on Henry Vaughan, T. S. Eliot, Thomas Traherne, John Donne, and other Anglo-Catholic poets who had come into fashion, and I had no prospects whatever." Kazin's own first book, *On Native Grounds* (1942), an examination of the American realist movement in fiction, gave voice to the impulse to merge with the history that is built into the new language and its literature, as did Lionel Trilling's early avowals of Anglophilia, *Matthew Arnold* (1939) and *E. M. Forster* (1942); Philip Rahv's endorsements of Henry James and Nathaniel Hawthorne; Delmore Schwartz's enthusiastic encomia on T. S. Eliot as a modern culture hero; Irving Howe's books on Thomas Hardy, William Faulkner, and Sherwood Anderson; and Leslie Fiedler's later summing up of his own intellectual "heritage," *Love and Death in the American Novel* (1960). Even when placing themselves in opposition to America's politics or declaring themselves alienated from its social life, the second-generation intellectuals were poised to champion its literature and affirm its rebels, such as Thoreau, Poe, and Whitman, or even such Tory expatriates as James and Eliot, as spokesmen for *their* dreams. Though it was not until the 1950s that they publicly pledged allegiance to "our country and our culture," the way had been prepared twenty years earlier by the separate peace they had made with American literature.

A certain line of influence may be traced to the Yiddish linguistic and cultural renaissance, which occurred during the late nineteenth century and laid the groundwork for a secular, imaginative Jewish fiction even before the emigration to America. In the waning years of the nineteenth century there emerged in Europe and America a flourishing Yiddish press, theater, literature, and scholarship, urged on by the promptings of cultural nationalism and the various brands of labor socialism, which elevated Yiddish from the position of a despised popular jargon to that of a respected and resourceful language. Although the Yiddish revival was doomed from the start in America, as it would soon be in Europe and Israel, its accumulated momentum was transferred into the English language, in which those of its old projects congenial to new developments could go forward, including the formulation of a modern and secular Jewish imagination.

From the viewpoint of American literature, what counted was the special affection with which the second-generation intellectuals and writers adopted the English language, an affection their grandparents had seldom displayed for Russian and Polish. Of course, English was thrust upon the Jews by a public school education dedicated to the effacement of differences, but to see the adoption of English solely as a form of assimilation is to mistake for mere convenience what was often a fierce embrace of a language rich in expressive resources and literary possibilities. It was not simply to gain access to the American mainstream that the Jews pursued English so strenuously, but to release mute and long-suppressed yearnings into the world of articulate desire.

Thus Jewish fiction in America arose in an interregnum between the experience of the Old World, where the Jews were hemmed in by poverty and exclusion but united by traditions and a sense of common destiny, and their full participation in the New. By and large, the values of this fiction have been neither traditionally Jewish nor comfortably American; it has tended to speak for those ironic middle grounds that are illuminated by the light that fulfillments shed upon hopes, and real fates upon millenarian destinies. The novel itself is well suited to such hybrid views, being in its very essence a hybrid form: a commercial arm of the visionary life, a bargain struck between imagination and business. It is our leading forum of the mind in which one can be both a philosopher and a celebrity, a sage and a success, as Norman Mailer is usually busy reassuring himself. If the best-seller lists just now yield the highest return on such visions, the

Nobel Prize—to Saul Bellow and Isaac Bashevis Singer—would appear to be their ultimate sanction.

Fiction in the Wake of Socalism

The major Jewish writers of the postwar era have all been acutely attuned to political history and to its characteristic modern themes: war, brutality, depression and unemployment, the implications of money, class, and ideology, and, especially, the individual sentiments and sensibilities that grow out of such a history. The horror of the recent past stands behind all postwar Jewish-American fiction, even if something commonly known as "sensibility" is what frequently comes forward. The Jewish writers who have done their major creative work from the forties through the present either started out in the thirties or took their cues from the decade that was marked by the Great Depression, the rise of fascism, the final collapse of the Russian Revolution into Stalinist terror, and the Spanish Civil War. To such a prelude the 1940s added the world war itself and the slaughter of Europe's Jews, devastating finales to an era that Isaac Rosenfeld called "an age of enormity." The fiction written by Jews in the next three decades shares a common patrimony of disaster, and the writers, different as they are, have all been obliged to make artistic capital out of a shared sense of loss and deracination.

Though the conflicts and fears that underlay the emerging Jewish writing went deeper than what is commonly implied by the failure of socialism, I have come to think of that writing as fiction in the wake of socialism, since a good many Jewish literary careers were hatched in the socialist incubator and enlivened by its warmth until events drove them out. If we look upon socialism as a vision of historical possibility rather than a body of formulas about money, power, class, and production—that is, as sentiment rather than doctrine—we may understand how an entire generation of Jewish intellectuals could have been attached to it and could have defined a common destiny in relation to it. Socialism was to many of them what agrarianism was to southern writers in the 1930s: a sentimental myth devoid of specific content around which they could rally forces against contemporary conditions. While some Jewish intellectuals knew their Marx and their lessons in dialectics—the young Sidney Hook comes to mind— most avowed socialism as an unspecified vision of a collective future, a projection forward of warm memories of Old World *Gemeinschaft* and more current experiences of organized mutual aid: a father's labor union, an uncle's burial society, the family itself. Kazin has observed of his own youthful socialism, in *Starting Out in the Thirties,* that it "did not require any conscious personal assent or decision on my part: I was a socialist as so many Americans were 'Christians': I had always lived in a socialist atmosphere." By 1940, such a socialism, as common as air and as familiar as horseradish, was in retreat, and six years later it was only a family heirloom for all but a residual core of leftists who had locked themselves into embattled and isolated positions. Between 1936, when the Moscow Trials and the Spanish Civil War began, and 1946, when the world war came to an end, a world of political assumptions went out of existence, and the Jewish writers were presented with a clean cultural slate. For them the task of making culture had to be started from scratch.

In fact, I mean to propose that a renaissance in the literal sense of the word did take place among Jewish writers after the war and that the death of several lines of historical continuity to which they had been attached was not only the background of their writing but its very raison d'être. Since the traditional materials from which an intellectual identity might be formed were in shambles, the writers who emerged on the scene were orphans from tradition, each responsible for his own identity. Marxism, which had formerly offered both a world view and an aesthetic, was in ruins; Yiddish culture, which had long been in decline in America, was wiped out altogether in Europe and along with it those vestiges of traditional Jewish life that might have supported an alternative vision to the prevailing American world view; and the new era of American prosperity and acquisition lacked at first any claims on the allegiance of intellectuals who had only yesterday championed the Marxist prognosis that the state would soon wither away. Thus it is that so many heroes of the new fiction are orphans or characters whose pasts have been repressed beyond recall, or men who have changed their names, or, like Saul Bellow's Joseph in *Dangling Man* (1944), representative symbols shorn of family names entirely. The most poignant cases of dispossession come later, though they bear the earmarks of the postwar dilemma: Daniel and Susan Isaacson of E. L. Doctorow's *The Book of Daniel* (1971), who are literally orphans of history, their parents having been executed as Communist spies. In light of this history, one might expect some of this literature to be militantly particularist and Zionist, taking cues from that other momentous Jewish rebirth, the founding of Israel in 1948. But the fiction reflecting the Zionist impulse among American Jews turns out to be surprisingly small and largely concentrated in the writing of Meyer Levin, whose novels and autobiographical books, especially *My Father's House* (1947), *In Search* (1950), *The Obsession* (1973), *The Spell of Time* (1974), *The Settlers* (1972), and

The Harvest (1978), are the most developed expression of that tendency.

The disarray into which the Jewish intellectual was thrown has all
the earmarks of a modern dilemma: disillusionment with ideology
and politics, isolation both from one's own past and from an increasingly affluent society, and an inhibition about embracing America.
Like Norman Mailer's Sam Slovoda in the story "The Man Who Studied Yoga" (collected in *Advertisements for Myself,* 1959), "He is
straddled between the loss of a country he has never seen, and his repudiation of the country in which he now lives." As Irving Howe put
it in a *Commentary* article in October 1946, with himself in mind as
a typical case, "For the kind of contemporary intellectual of whom
we write, *it is difficult to be a Jew and just as difficult not to be one.*
He is caught in the tension resulting from conflicts between his society and his tradition, his status and his desires; he suffers as a man,
intellectual, and Jew." We have heard such laments at other times
from other quarters, for this is almost a formula for what we have
now come to think of as The Modern Condition. Its symptoms are
alienation, a sense of hanging on at the margins of one's national, not
to say, human, community, a feeling of expendability, and, not
atypically, a corresponding intellectual pride: a desolate moral preeminence. So it is no surprise that what began to emerge into the intellectual culture of the 1940s is something we recognize as a conventional modernism, and by that decade such a phrase was not at all a
contradiction.

Modernism may even be viewed as the escape clause in the cultural
contract drawn up by the independent left-wing intellectuals in the
late 1930s under the aegis of the *Partisan Review,* allowing them to
take part in the postwar world of capitalism triumphant without abandoning the stance of radical opposition. *Partisan Review,* which was
a rallying point for independent leftists after 1937, was founded on a
program of radicalism in politics and avant-gardism in literature, despite the appearance of such profound contradiction between the two
that made it anathema to more rigorous Marxists, who could scarcely
see beyond the angry redundancies of agit-prop art. An added difficulty in arranging the marriage was the plain fact that some of the
leading modernists of the 1920s and earlier turned out to be reac-
tionaries in the 1930s: Eliot, Pound, Yeats, Lawrence, and Wyndham
Lewis, to name several of the most prominent. And yet it was the very
improvisational assertiveness of the blend, the intuitive faith in the
spiritual compatibility of radical politics and adventurous writing,
that gave strength to the *Partisan* synthesis and set it apart from the

sterile agendas of dogmatic, usually Communist, publications such as the *New Masses.*

Partisan's position in the intellectual culture of the 1940s made it the staging ground for a new literature after the war, for it was the bridge between an American and a European intelligentsia and thus an importer of continental attitudes and ideas. It published new translations of Franz Kafka as though he were a contemporary, published portions of T. S. Eliot's *Four Quartets,* launched into prominence such young poets as Delmore Schwartz, Robert Lowell, and Theodore Roethke, and brought together the critical voices of W. H. Auden, Edmund Wilson, Stephen Spender, Philip Rahv, Meyer Schapiro, Isaac Rosenfeld, George Orwell, Sidney Hook, Mary McCarthy, and Nicola Chiaromonte, creating in the process a community of awareness that was at once American, international, Jewish, cosmopolitan, left, and libertarian. If cosmopolitanism is, as the wisecrack goes, the Jewish parochialism, there are few richer examples of what such a parochialism could be than the *Partisan Review* of the 1940s, with its editorship divided between Jews (Philip Rahv and William Phillips) and Yalies (Dwight Macdonald, George L. K. Morris, and F. W. Dupee) and its intelligence partaking equally of Trotsky and Kafka, dialectics and *Weltschmerz.* Its successes were born of its editors' stubborn loyalty to their ambivalences and their refusal to let their ideological adventurism harden into doctrine.

Out of this high-octane mixture of militancy and depression came the distinctive voice of Saul Bellow, whose writing first appeared in *Partisan* in the early 1940s. It is not amiss to see Bellow's conspicuously literary cast of mind, his Hegelian preoccupation with contradiction and synthesis, and his unembarrassed pursuit of culture as expressions of *Partisan Review*'s ghetto cosmopolitanism and even, in the long run, its ultimate justification. A poor Jewish boy from the Montreal ghetto and the Chicago West Side, Bellow invented a literary voice that brought Chicago street lingo into the high culture of *Mitteleuropa,* making it sound as though the ghetto quite naturally educated its children to absorb the full range of European experience, even if that style meant the occasional confusion of *Geistesgeschichte* with inside dope, to be lectured upon from the side of the mouth.

One way to see what the modern element of this writing was is to recall these auspicious first sentences: "There was a time when people were in the habit of addressing themselves frequently and felt no shame at making a record of their inward transactions. But to keep a journal nowadays is considered a kind of self-indulgence, a weakness, and in poor taste. For this is the era of hardboiled-dom." Here, in Bellow's first novel, *Dangling Man* (1944), we find the dominant tone of the emerging fiction in a nutshell: its privatism, its aggressive interiority, its prevailing tone of aloofness tempered by depression, its intimations of spiritual orphanage. Such moodiness has nothing in it of the robust optimism of the 1930s, which, despite the depression, had turned down-at-heels American writers into spokesmen for bright industrial futures. It is a more continental attitude, redolent of political disillusionment and personal ennui, and drawing its world view from Sartre and Camus and, behind them, the masters of psychological estrangement: Dostoevsky, Kafka, Proust, and Rimbaud. But here too is a modern attitude with one eye on Jewish tradition, for *Dangling Man* is very much an indoor book, a study in confinement: "In my present state of demoralization, it has become necessary for me to keep a journal—that is, to talk to myself—and I do not feel guilty of self-indulgence in the least. The hardboiled are compensated for their silence; they fly planes or fight bulls or catch tarpon, whereas I rarely leave my room." The explicit allusion is to the Hemingwayesque code of action and taciturnity, the code of the outdoors, which in the 1930s was shared in common by the proletarian novel, with its contempt for "bourgeois subjectivity" and its lets-roll-up-our-sleeves-and-get-down-to-work approach to problems; the detective story, with its rough and ready versions of masculinity; and all the pervasive realisms, socialist and documentary, that took so grim a view of conditions and therefore so stern an attitude toward responsibilities.

The new literature was one that called attention to what it could no longer use: all forward-looking social theories and those principles of literary representation that had gained currency under the umbrella of progressive thought. Reality now outflanks all efforts to capture it. To be sure, this "existential" pose struck by Bellow's Joseph, who is an updated version of Kafka's Joseph K. and Dostoevsky's underground man, was a rejection not of Marxism alone but of all rationalized materialisms, socialist and capitalist alike, and along with them the belief that reality can be fully understood, human conduct explained, and improved futures realized.

The postwar "end of ideology" that is already in sight in *Dangling Man* can be blamed, at this point, not on the comfort of the intellectuals—the leisure of the theory class, as Daniel Bell called it (*The End of Ideology: On the Exhaustion of Political Ideas in the Fifties,* 1960) —but on their grief. *Dangling Man* and the books that take up its mood constitute a literature of mourning, behind which lie losses that are rarely expressed but everywhere understood. Joseph rarely leaves his room because he finds little to leave it for; he inhabits a depleted universe or at least one whose blandishments are so tainted that they must be turned aside. Thus he refuses work, rejects family aid, chases away friends, and neglects both his wife and his mistress. He is literally a penitent; in his isolation he mortifies his senses and grieves secretly for deaths he cannot name or number and therefore cannot openly mourn. Only twelve years later does Tommy Wilhelm of Bellow's *Seize the Day* (1956), an updated Joseph whose emotions are blocked by nameless aggressions, finally burst into tears at the funeral of a complete stranger, thereby working through, in a sense, an extended sorrow that had first expressed itself in *Dangling Man* but did not ripen until the later book.

The extent to which Joseph's mourning captured a mood prevalent in intellectual circles may be seen in the proliferation of moody, dangling heroes introduced into our literature by Jewish writers in the postwar decades, when words like *alienation, victimization,* and *marginality* became popular definitions of the Jewish sensibility and the Jew became a stand-in for something known as "the universal estrangement of man." Among the early postwar books and plays to strike the note of isolation and drift were Isaac Rosenfeld's novel *Passage from Home* (1946) and his short stories, collected posthumously in *Alpha and Omega* (1966); Lionel Trilling's *The Middle of the Journey* (1947); Delmore Schwartz's stories in *The World Is a Wedding* (1948); Arthur Miller's *Death of a Salesman* (1949); Paul Goodman's *The Break-up of Our Camp* (1949); Norman Mailer's *Barbary Shore* (1951) and *The Deer Park* (1955); Bernard Malamud's *The Natural* (1952) and *The Assistant* (1957); Herbert Gold's *The Man Who Was Not with It* (1956); and Bellow's subsequent novels, especially *The Victim* (1947) and *Seize the Day* (1956). In the 1940s, the Great Depression gave way to the depression of the intellectuals, which was all the more poignant for being so wholly out of phase with the American economic and spiritual boom. Later on, "after alienation," as Marcus Klein has put it (*After Alienation: American Novels in Mid-Century,* 1964), the alienated Jewish hero maintained a vestigial presence as an older, grayer, and more embittered ghost of history in Edward Lewis Wallant's *The Pawnbroker* (1961), Bellow's *Mr. Sammler's Planet* (1970), and Isaac Bashevis Singer's *Enemies, A Love Story* (1972). Their refugee heroes, Sol Nazerman, Artur Sammler, and Herman Broder, respectively, are survivors in name only; their new lives in America are versions of death-in-life, behind which lie wishes to have the whole business done with.

Although "conditions" remain as vital to the new writing as they had been to the fiction and drama of the thirties, they no longer attract the rhetoric of material oppression and social injustice, except from stubborn holdouts for solidarity like Howard Fast or from Norman Mailer, who, as Leslie Fiedler once remarked, discovers everything twenty years late. That rhetoric has largely given way to the language of neurosis and alienation: the central issue is no longer labor against capital but the incapacities of the human heart. And art, no longer a weapon, now becomes a diagnosis. The novel remains as devoted as ever to circumstantial realism—Henry James's "solidity of specification"—and with even greater fidelity than before, but the urban panoramas we now get are subtly dematerialized and turned into symbols of psychological disorder: they become inner landscapes. In the name of sensibility, the novelist sharpens his focus on life and reads its attributes as "objective correlatives" rather than as the data of class conflict and capitalist oppression. Compare the opening composition of place in Michael Gold's *Jews without Money* (1930) with a similar cityscape from Saul Bellow's *Seize the Day* (1956):

> I can never forget the East Side street where I lived as a boy. It was a block from the notorious Bowery, a tenement canyon hung with fire escapes, bed-clothing, and faces. Always these faces at the tenement windows. The street never failed them. It was an immense excitement. It never slept. It roared like a sea. It exploded like fireworks. People pushed and wrangled in the street. There were armies of howling pushcart peddlers. Women screamed, dogs barked and copulated. Babies cried.

> Most of the guests at the Hotal Gloriana were past the age of retirement. Along Broadway in the Seventies, Eighties, and Nineties, a great part of New York's vast population of old men and women lives. Unless the weather is too cold or wet they fill the benches about the tiny railed parks and along the subway grating from Verdi Square to Columbia University, they crowd the shops and cafeterias, the dime stores, the tea-rooms, the bakeries, the beauty parlors, the reading rooms and club rooms.

The telling differences here are not the levels of style and talent at work or the obvious distinctions between a rough evocation of poverty and a lyric of the higher dissatisfactions but the sharply opposed conceptions of reality itself. For Gold, reality is a function of money and class; these Jews of his are first and foremost people without money: in a word, masses. Bellow's Jews, by contrast, are subject to influences more global *and* more particular, of which money is just one. Not incidentally, some of them have already made it and are now clipping their coupons, so that the impact of money on their lives is no longer an attribute of class but one of character. Class, indeed, has even come to mean character: Tommy Wilhelm's father, Dr. Adler, has "class"; Tommy lacks it entirely. In a middle-class fiction, that is, a fiction of uptown tea-rooms as opposed to downtown fire escapes, *culture, character,* and *manners* replace *environment* as the focal points of interest. Tommy Wilhelm, like Kirby Allbee of *The Victim,* may be as desperately unemployed as anyone in a Gold novel, but no blueprint for social reorganization follows upon the fact. To prewar Jewish writers life was harsh but its meaning always clear: money. After the war, as circumstances grow less exigent, the meaning of life grows more obscure. In the midst of opportunity, the Jewish writers are busy inventing the likes of Tommy Wilhelm, Kirby Allbee, Morris Bober and Frank Alpine *(The Assistant)*, Charles Eitel *(The Deer Park)*, and Willie Loman *(Death of a Salesman)*, who manage to fail on their own, according to formulas which touch not only on the injuries of class or the failures of politics but also on the deeper and more inaccessible mysteries of the human condition.

Making It in America, or Horatio Alger Meets Gimpel the Fool

This movement must be seen against the backdrop of the wholesale assimilation of the Jews into middle-class America and the emergence of America itself as a prosperous consumer society. It might have been expected that success as a social fact, if not as a moral dilemma, would assume important dimensions for Jewish writers and that the conflicts attendant upon the Americanization of the ghetto Jew, examined as early as 1917 by Abraham Cahan in *The Rise of David Levinsky,* would emerge into prominence. For the intellectuals were experiencing their own rise into importance: marginal critics, sociologists, and writers who had previously lived by their wits suddenly found themselves the recipients of foundation grants, publishing contracts, lecture dates, and professorships, often enough at institutions that not long before scarcely would have dreamed of allowing a Jew, let alone a tainted Jewish leftist, to join their faculties. Delmore Schwartz's sojourns at Harvard, Princeton, and Syracuse were suddenly not so atypical. During the postwar flowering of philo-Semitism, as Leslie Fiedler once put it *(No! in Thunder,* 1960), Zion briefly became Main Street.

What was so surprising, then, about Norman Podhoretz's *Making It,* published in 1967, was not that it celebrated the pleasures of that brave new world in which a boy from Brooklyn could find himself in uptown Manhattan, sipping martinis and having fun, but that the celebration came so late, twenty years or more after so many others had taken the first intoxicating sip. *Making It* was startling after making it in most of its familiar forms—having a portfolio, living in the east nineties, publishing in *The New Yorker,* dictating taste—had ceased to startle anyone. But as a book, it was something else, a *succès de scandale,* rivaled in the 1960s only by Philip Roth's *Portnoy's Complaint* (1969) for the opprobrium it brought down on its author's not-so-unsuspecting head. For *Making It* was and remains the only Jewish novel after the war, or, to my knowledge, before it, whose hero is allowed to achieve social success without paying a moral price. Ostensibly just a memoir, *Making It* is, in its way, a novel as well, the imagination of a life in terms of a significant moral pattern: the pattern of the traditional bildungsroman or, to keep cultural lines straight, the "up from the ghetto" book. Its myths cannot be separated from its recollected facts, which are recollected according to their place in the myths, and the plot is racy and tight. But for a Jew it is an unconventional plot indeed, because the hero rises from humble origins and keeps rising—that's it: no backtracking, short-selling, stock-taking, nostalgia for the slums, moral crisis, or comeuppance. As moral patterns go, this one is distressingly linear: the retribution and guilt that eventually catch up to the overreacher in proper moral fiction never arrive. Only the Jewish hero arrives, just as real Jews have been doing throughout their term of occupancy in America.

> I am a man who at the precocious age of thirty-five experienced an astonishing revelation: it is better to be a success than a failure. Having been penetrated by this great truth concerning the nature of things, my mind was now open for the first time to a series of corollary perceptions, each one as dizzying in its impact as the Original Revelation itself. Money, I now saw (no one, of course had ever seen it before), was important: it was better to be rich than to be poor. Power, I now saw (moving on to higher subtleties), was desirable: it was better to give orders than to take them. Fame, I now saw (how courageous of me not to flinch), was unqualifiedly delicious: it was better to be recognized than to be anonymous.

Podhoretz, also a bookish boy and one of those famous A+ students we have learned to put up with in Jewish fiction, cannot help seeing the literary situation involved, viewing himself in the light of those French novels in which a young man from the provinces—a Rastignac or a Julien Sorel—comes to Paris to make his mark. But it is not Balzac or Stendhal who wrote this script but Horatio Alger, for nothing could be more American than this success story, even if, as the age demands, the talents needed for this particular climb are no longer hard work, thrift, responsibility, and plain dealing, but literacy, shrewdness, circumspection, and timing. *Making It* is a fable for the managerial age, in which success is not the owning of one's own business but acceding to the editorship of *Commentary*.

It is little wonder that the book provoked such outrage when it appeared, for if success is not quite the "dirty little secret" Podhoretz had made it out to be—and how, in 1967, could it have been *that?*—it was nonetheless anathema to the myths of humility rewarded and ambition chastised that Jewish fiction writers had drawn upon ever since Sholem Aleichem, and the book was consequently read as an assault on the moral economy of the intellectual community to which it was addressed.

Thus the book was to measure the distance between the Jewish intellectuals and the world of practical accommodations, since what Podhoretz had done was to announce in print what the better part of the Jewish middle class had long since announced in the manner of life it had assumed. As editor of *Commentary,* Podhoretz was lining up with his readers, particularly with a new class of readers with whom he had come to identify, thereby demonstrating how far both he and *Commentary* had come from being satellites in the *Partisan Review* orbit, and how far also Jewish moral mythology had come from the days when the Jewish hustler had to be taken to task for his conniving in such books as *The Rise of David Levinsky* (1917), which remains the classic formulation of the literary attitude toward money, and Jerome Weidman's *I Can Get It for You Wholesale* (1937), Budd Schulberg's *What Makes Sammy Run?* (1941), and Mordecai Richler's *The Apprenticeship of Duddy Kravitz* (1954). Success and moral convenience had joined hands at last.

Since the belated rise of secular, imaginative literature among the Jews, fiction has become a marshaling point for the currents of myth that flow through the Jewish community and represent the Jews to themselves, and it is noteworthy that in fiction the inevitable conflict between success and innocence is normally still settled on the side of innocence, if not in jackpots for the meek then in spiritual bankruptcies for the ambitious. Long after the eminent Jewish lawyer, entrepreneur, and power broker have become American commonplaces, and the magnates of *Our Crowd*—Seligmans, Loebs, Kuhns, Guggenheims, and Bambergers—have ascended from men into symbols, *dos kleyne mentchele*[1] and his cousins-in-failure, the victim, the dangling man, and the shlemiel, continue to carry the day in American Jewish fiction.

1. *Dos kleyne mentchele* (1864), or "the little man," is the title of Mendele Mocher Sforim's early novel of life in the Jewish *shtetlach* of Eastern Europe.

Two recent books identify the shlemiel as the figure who has most consistently represented the Jew to himself in modern times, from the Yiddish story to the modern novel, from Sholem Aleichem's Menahem Mendl (*The Adventures of Menahem Mendl,* 1969)[2] and Isaac Peretz's Bontsche the Silent (*Selected Stories,* 1974) to Philip Roth's Peter Tarnopol (*My Life as a Man,* 1974), Bellow's von Humboldt Fleisher (*Humboldt's Gift,* 1975), and Woody Allen's Woody Allen. Both Ruth Wisse, in *The Schlemiel as Modern Hero* (1971), and Sanford Pinsker, in *The Schlemiel as Metaphor* (1971), argue convincingly that the shlemiel may be found everywhere in Jewish literature with his heart-warming antics and his bitter resentments, his will to virtue and nose for disaster, his frustrated liberal humanism, and his secular canonization as saint of missed opportunities.

Though he is the stock in trade of all the major Jewish writers save Mailer, who displays a preference for his antitype, the bully, the shlemiel has a special place in the stories and novels of Bernard Malamud, where the idea of circumstantial failure as spiritual success is the very bedrock of Jewish moral insight. But Malamud's shlemiel, through drawing on traditional sources, is a unique figure who has little about him of the comic, the warm-hearted, or the *gemütlich*—little that reflects a communal life. His defeats do not become victories through irony or resilience or insight into his predicaments, and he is part of no community that can absorb and justify his failures by participating in his impotence. More often than not, he is an isolated American type: a drifter, an orphan, a writer, or a deracinated intellectual in flight from the past and in search of a new life, which turns out, when found, to be a life of physical constraints and moral double-binds. Pursuing his dreams, he encounters his nightmares as the past he thought he had left behind reappears as his future, the repressed unexpectedly returned. The antihero's new life offers not freedom but trial, in which he acquits himself, if at all, by boning up on the ethics of his predicament and "converting," as Frank Alpine, the Italian grocery clerk, does quite literally at the end of *The Assistant* (1957), when he has himself circumcised and becomes a Jew. Suffering, as Iris Lemon instructs Roy Hobbs, the baseball hero *manqué* of *The Natural* (1952), "makes good people better."

Wherever Malamud's alienated hero finds himself—Kiev, Rome, Brooklyn, or Cascadia, Oregon, or Center Campobello, Vermont—he is still in the ghetto, psychologically bound to whatever he had sought

2. Menahem Mendl is Sholem Aleichem's classic figure of the *luftmensch,* literally "air man," the marginal Jew whose luck and dreams constitute his only visible means of support.

to flee and learning to settle for a modified imprisonment and a course in the requirements of civilized life: conscience, responsibility, mercy, love, and delayed gratification. He learns, in other words, to be a liberal. The characters who pass muster by these lights, like Frank Alpine of *The Assistant,* Seymour Levin of *A New Life* (1961), and Yakov Bok of *The Fixer* (1966), are grim heroes of conscience, while those who fail, like Roy Hobbs and the antagonists of *The Tenants* (1971), Harry Lesser and Willie Spearmint, are object lessons in calamitous egotism. More than one critic has pointed out just how Christian these figures in the Jewish carpet may appear.

What renders moral education problematic for Malamud's characters, as well as for his readers, is that Malamud expects his heroes to take instruction in cooperation and humility in a world in which other values, like narcissism, self-interest, or David Levinsky's brand of social Darwinism, are likely to be more appropriate. In a world in which the ethics of *Gemeinschaft* are impractical, Malamud punishes his characters for harboring attitudes and enacting desires that many of us will regard as reasonable. Thus the instructional side of his fiction may seem arbitrary to a modern reader who holds no particular brief for complex sexual scruples or endlessly delayed gratification or Malamud's versions of ethical responsibility: being humble, observing your limitations, or owning up to your Jewishness. Not everyone is ready to concede that Roy Hobbs, Malamud's imperfect natural, should not have an eye for fancy women or not want to be the greatest hitter of all time. Nothing intrinsic to the morality of baseball calls upon him to acknowledge the deeper resources of his humanity, his *menschlichkeit,* as some critics now call it. Ted Williams was never struck down by fate for failing to tip his cap to the Red Sox fans. Nor is there any plain moral reason basic to the codes of Brooklyn or the ethics of the grocery business why Frank Alpine should be so inspired by the example of Morris Bober's immolation behind the cash register that he should eventually desire that very fate for himself, and should even, at the cost of his freedom and his foreskin, turn himself into a ghetto Jew. The lessons drawn in both books seem artificially applied; they appear to come from outside the fictions in which they operate and to skew them in the direction of allegory, in which the crucial conflicts belong not to the characters, but to the author.

Over the years, Malamud's staunch adherence to a claustral and depressive vision has tended to shift our focus from the common sentiments for which he once seemed to speak to those personal struggles his books now apparently express. True, novels such as *The Natural* and *The Assistant* and the stories in *The Magic Barrel* (1958) and

Idiot's First (1963) did speak for a certain mid-century climate of opinion and did appeal to principles of reading that have since passed out of vogue. Their persistent tone of admonition, their apolitical appeals to the individual best self, their blending of Yiddish dialect into medieval fertility myth in celebration of Judeo-Christian solidarity, and their wealth of reference to T. S. Eliot, Jesse Weston, Wagner, *Parsifal,* and the Bible now look like habits of thought peculiarly suited to an era that placed a premium on symbolism and orthodoxy. It is significant that the start of the Kennedy era in 1961 saw the publication of *A New Life,* in which Malamud announced his readiness to cast off stodginess and to mount a critique of intellectual and political reaction, specifically at Oregon State University, which he himself was just leaving for yet a newer life at Bennington College. By 1966, *The Fixer* appeared to be all for revolution—in czarist Russia, at any rate—and though its hero, Yakov Bok, is less a revolutionary than a conscientious objector, bombs nevertheless fly through the air on his behalf.

But in later years, though Malamud has tried to maintain an air of currency in *The Tenants* (1971), which is ostensibly about the black-white *Kulturkampf* in New York City, his voice has become increasingly private. In the wake of *Pictures of Fidelman* (1969), *The Tenants, Rembrandt's Hat* (1973), and *Dubin's Lives* (1979) Malamud sounds less than ever like a moral Everyman and more like a driven and eccentric writer. At times the civilized skin of his writing, its campaign for the whole checklist of humanist virtues for which Morris Bober had once been the spokesman, wears thin, and conflicts and anxieties that had previously been held in solution by the skillful application of narrative techniques and mythic frameworks come forward as open violence that quite overwhelms all moral implications and literary meanings. Earlier antagonists, like Seymour Levin and Gerald Gilley (*A New Life*) or Frank Alpine and Morris Bober, may have wished to do away with each other but always wound up striking civilized, if bitter, *modi vivendi,* substituting mannered hostility for physical assault. But the main characters in *The Tenants,* Harry Lesser and Willie Spearmint, who share an abandoned tenement while trying to complete their novels, just smash each other to bits, and Malamud apparently wants us to conclude that both get what they richly deserve.

The Tenants, whose ostensible message is mercy but whose innermost emotion is pure rage, highlights a long-standing discrepancy in Malamud's books between their didactic lessons and their deeper emotional ground rules: those dialectics of transgression and retribution that put his characters through their paces. A striking example is the early story "The Lady of the Lake," which, like most stories in *The Magic Barrel,* is either a working paper for *The Natural* and *The Assistant* or a recent aftershock. In that story, Henry Levin, a young Jewish clerk who is "tired of the past," goes to Italy and, to conceal his identity and play up his readiness for sexual adventure, calls himself Henry Freeman. And on an island in Lake Maggiore he discovers nothing less than the girl of his dreams, Isabella del Dongo, whom he takes for Italian nobility and pursues in the full awkwardness of his shlemielhood, while she puts him off with coy appearances and disappearances, distant unbuttonings and rebuttonings, and the repeated question, "Are you a Jew?" Of course not, he reiterates, until finally, in exasperation, he exclaims, "How many no's make never? Why do you persist with such foolish questions?" What happens next is absolutely spectacular: "Because I hoped you were. Slowly she unbuttoned her bodice, arousing Freeman, though he was thoroughly confused as to her intent. When she revealed her breasts—he could have wept at their beauty (now recalling a former invitation to gaze at them, but he had arrived too late on the raft)—to his horror he discerned tatooed on the soft and tender flesh a bluish line of distorted numbers." Stunned as he is, and unmasked as a fool even as she is unbodiced as a Jew, Levin/Freeman stares and gropes and stutters his retractions, and in a final spasm of desperate hunger lunges forward toward those retreating breasts: "He groped for her breasts, to clutch, kiss or suckle them; but she had stepped among the statues, and when he vainly sought her in the veiled mist that had risen from the lake, still calling her name, Freeman embraced only moonlit stone."

The lesson of this parable, that *you should never lie about your Jewishness because if you do the woman of your dreams will pass you by,* dissolves in absurdity and non sequitur as soon as it is thought about. As instructional homily, "The Lady of the Lake," with its superimposition of Arthurian myth upon holocaust terror, has all the moral trenchancy of "Cinderella"; what adventure-bound tourist at the shores of Lake Maggiore would glance up from his *Guide Michelin* for even an instant to ponder its warning? Or what Jewish boy, to put this in perspective, would become the better man for having such instruction in his head? As imaginatively realized situation, however, this story is potent stuff, rich in conflicts and implications that go quite beyond what its pedestrian moralism will comprehend.

"The Lady of the Lake" is a particularly straightforward rendition of a basic Malamudian story: sex denied and the denial moralized. Levin/Freeman, like Roy Hobbs, Frank Alpine, and numerous figures in the short stories, yearns for what he may not have or, since this dilemma is instructional, what might have been his had he played his cards right. But it need not be moral dereliction that intercepts pleasure: when fulfillment threatens, any intervention will do: the hero may have second thoughts and lose his appetite, or succumb to an irruption of conscience or disgust, or find himself outmaneuvered by some rival on the road to release. To be tricked into self-betrayal by a Jewish princess, or shot down in a hotel by a maniacal temptress (*The Natural*), or put down by Helen Bober as an "uncircumcised dog" (*The Assistant*), or put off by a nubile temptress who at the point of consummation suddenly loses control of her bowels (*Dubin's Lives*) are only some of the more spectacular possibilities.

These tales of prurience and responsibility derive their power and interest from their underlying sense of sexual deadlock, out of which come those stunning, final tableaux in which the ambiguities of a story are framed and held fast. One thinks of Freeman clutching his moonlit stone, or Leo Finkle ("The Magic Barrel") rushing forward, bouquet in hand, to meet the girl of *his* dreams, who stands awaiting him under a lamppost, smoking. Indeed, where emotional symmetries are not meticulously adjusted and artistically controlled, we can get mayhem instead of epiphany, as we do in *The Tenants*. But in the novels, generally, the stalemate is grudgingly lifted and the hero released into a future that looks like an even more insidious form of entrapment. Frank Alpine becomes a Jew and a grocer and elects to wait, in perpetuity we suspect, for the love of Helen Bober and a run on milk; Yakov Bok is led away to a trial of uncertain outcome (though we know that his real Russian prototype, Mendel Beiliss, was acquitted); Seymour Levin drives off into the Oregon sunset, unemployed, out of prospects and illusions, and encumbered by Pauline Gilley and her three children; William Dubin leaps out of his lover's bed, and races home to attempt love with his wife while he still has an erection.

What is best about Malamud when he is at the top of his form are his intuitions about the unfulfilled life and his epiphanies of disappointment and loss: his frozen moments of the sinking heart. He is par excellence the writer of the half-life, the shabby region of mediocre attainment between pure wish fulfillment and total disaster, and he has perfect pitch for the language of poignancy and loss. He is also most spokesmanlike when drawing that life of quiet desperation which he sometimes places in the thirties but which is really a permanent feature of our national existence and the emotional underside of our prosperity. But poignancy is a small note on which to found a literature; it does not lend itself readily to sustained effects. As a result, Malamud's stories are generally more moving than his novels, and the novels more convincing in their momentary touches than in their sustained architecture.

Malamud's reluctance to serve up happy endings could be taken for moral realism of a sort, the sober assessment that life is tough, especially for a Jew, and moral compromise the essence of maturity. What removes this sobriety from realism but places it in the mainstream of Jewish sentiment is its puritan bias, which attaches personal fate to sexual conduct. Those Malamud heroes who suffer from history commonly encounter it through a woman, and their new lives are characteristically erotic quests that lead them to keyholes, transoms, and other furtive blinds for the ogling of their dream women. But the gap between their arousal and their fulfillment is never closed, leaving a space between hope and attainment in which their strange destinies can unfold. Sexual agony is Malamud's stock in trade. It is not, however, the standoff between the pleasure and reality principles that sets the moral curve of his fiction but the ambivalence of appetite itself; his characters are disappointed *because* they desire, and where they fail they do so because their desire either sabotages itself or is undercut by Malamud's own distaste for achievement.

Dubin's Lives would appear at first glance to violate the Malamudian rule, and to have substituted sexual gratification for the customary pangs of regret. In a brave, Lawrencian moment, the aging biographer, William Dubin, announces his creed of life to Fanny Bick, with whom he is about to embark upon an affair. "If you don't live life to the hilt, or haven't for whatever reason, you will regret it—especially as you grow older—every day that follows." Such resolve sounds like the anthem of the midlife crisis. But the breakthrough represented by the subsequent affair is illusory, since living life to the hilt quickly becomes a moral burden that presents its own constraints and obligations. If anything, Dubin suffers more for his victory over late middle age than he had for merely harboring secret yearnings. Through the gradual dissolution of his marriage, the alienation of his children, impotence with his wife, writer's block, and a failing memory, Dubin pays richly for his furtive delights, as his misery increases in direct proportion to his pleasures. Sexual liberation, it turns out, means no less turmoil than restraint. The Malamud hero suffers either way.

Malamud is a leading figure among the Jewish writers who specialize in ambivalence, and his conflicting cultural perspectives have led to the creation of improbable worlds. He has drawn heavily upon folkloric sources for his characters and situations while at the same time keeping an eye on modern life. He is both an inventor of sexual romances and a gloomy interpreter of modern experience. The same dialectic may be found in Saul Bellow's writing, though there it seems the product of skillfully effected mergers that make it appear to arise neither out of the exigencies of culture nor out of the primal interior world of conflicts and anxieties, but out of his sensibility—the negotiating agency of his talent. But with Malamud we feel ourselves in the company of two writers: one who is responsible for the textures, the local realities, the English Departments and grocery stores that he portrays so well, and another who supplies the plots, the predicaments, the titillations, the fables, the moral ferocity, and, not incidentally, the dramatic tension. Little wonder, then, that his books seem so ambiguous, like real ghettoes with imaginary Jews in them.

Because Gimpel the Fool is our ranking shlemiel in contemporary Jewish fiction we might expect a comprehensive review of Isaac Bashevis Singer's work to turn up a multitude of comic failures or secular saints whose irony or wisdom or hidden sanctity elevates them above the press of circumstances or the disasters of their own contrivance. But that is not at all the case: Gimpel turns out to be a special event in Singer's fiction, an experiment in Yiddish iconography that is never repeated in its pure form. Not that failure and weakness do not abound in his books: victims, neurotics, *luftmenschen,* and self-made failures, of whom the shlemiel is a special incarnation, turn up everywhere, but they are created according to different moral rules. Singer's characters are not primarily instructional types—emblems of racial durability or beacons for moral navigation—but revelations of the providential in human affairs and the weird proclivities of human desire. Like all Jewish writers, Singer is drenched in considerations of conscience, responsibility, and love, but his moral sympathies are far more diffuse than Malamud's. Whatever strictness of conscience he may have acquired as the son of a Hassidic rabbi in Warsaw (see his *In My Father's Court,* 1966) has been tempered by his experiences as an uprooted intellectual in Warsaw and New York.

Singer is not essentially American in his national identifications, though by now that is a matter of choice rather than provenance. In labeling him we are obliged to transpose the terms around the cultural hyphen and call him an American-Yiddish writer, for though he has lived here since 1935 he continues to write exclusively in Yiddish, though his readership in that language has virtually died out, and to take for his subject a life that disappeared almost two generations ago in the crematoria at Auschwitz.

A look at other emigré writers in our century, including Conrad, Joyce, Beckett, and Nabokov, invites the conclusion that ultimate choices of subject and language, though perhaps abetted by circumstance, are finally matters of irrational preference or, as Singer might say, of passion. From the start, Singer's life in America has been deeply committed to the Yiddish language and Yiddish culture. For years after having come to America at the urging of his brother, the novelist I. J. (Israel Joshua) Singer, he worked as a journalist and fiction writer for Abraham Cahan's *Jewish Daily Forward,* the most influential of New York's Yiddish-language dailies, where he first published many of the stories and sketches that were later translated and assembled into his early novels, memoirs, and recollections. Unlike Conrad and Nabokov, geniuses of adaptation who readily mastered new languages and the patterns of experience they reflect, Singer has been more the exile, like Joyce, turning a confirmed separation into an imaginative embrace of what has been lost, and casting his thoughts back upon his own past and beyond, upon the history of the Jews. Even though Singer has made the switch in recent years from the *Forward* to *The New Yorker* and adopted New York locales for some stories and even a novel, *Enemies, A Love Story,* the haunted world of Yiddish Poland maintains its grip on his imagination. "It strikes one as a kind of inspired madness," says Irving Howe. "Here is a man living in New York City, a sophisticated and clever writer, who composes stories about Frampol, Bilgoray, Kreshev *as if they were still there*" (*Decline of the New,* 1970).

The place held by "Gimpel the Fool" in our image of Singer has a good deal to do with the way both Gimpel and Singer were brought to the attention of American readers by Saul Bellow, who translated the story for *Partisan Review* in 1953, when Singer was known to scarcely anybody but the aging readers of the *Forward.* In 1953, Bellow himself, having just completed his most decidedly "American" novel, *The Adventures of Augie March,* was casting about for new sources of character and mood, and apparently found in Yiddish writing some of the direction he sought. The figure of Tommy Wilhelm, who appeared three years later in *Seize the Day,* looks remarkably like a graft of such figures as Gimpel and Sholem Aleichem's Menahem Mendl onto the "masochistic character" of Wilhelm Reich's *Character Analysis,* from which Bellow was also taking instruction in the 1950s; and there are signs throughout *Seize the Day* that the little society of elders in the Hotel Gloriana is to be understood as a contemporary updating of ancestral social arrangements, the *shtetl* raised to the order of a retirement community. In all, I think Gimpel's prominence may be credited to the American writers who took him up in later decades and turned him into Tommy Wilhelm, Eugene Henderson, Moses Herzog, Frank Alpine, Seymour Levin, Alex Portnoy, Yossarian (who in an early draft of Joseph Heller's *Catch-22* [1955] is Jewish), and Stern (Bruce Jay Friedman's *Stern*, 1962), rather than to anything he did on his own, which was just, after all, to be the perfect fool.

This is not to say that defeat, disaster, and righteousness are not on Singer's mind, for he has embroidered the edges of the shlemiel tradition with such experts in fiasco as Yasha Mazur (*The Magician of Lublin*, 1960), Lucian Yampolski (*The Manor*, 1967), Herman Broder (*Enemies, A Love Story*, 1972), and those many characters who trudge disconsolately through his seven volumes of published short stories. But these failures are not in the main sentimental or moral heroes, and neither pride nor shame attaches to a behavior that is not freely come by but is the unfolding of inexorable inner laws. "There are people who must hurt themselves," observes a character in *The Manor*. "It's hard to understand why they do it." The answer is partly that it is in the blood and partly that it is the inscrutable design of providence. For such people, destiny is character. Their fates are beheld not in pathos but in amazement.

Out of his apparently inexhaustible fund of tales and yarns Singer has published to date (1978) seven volumes of collected stories, eight novels, four contributions to an autobiography, and a host of children's books. The stories are collected in *Gimpel the Fool* (1957), *The Spinoza of Market Street* (1961), *Short Friday* (1964), *The Seance* (1968), *A Friend of Kafka* (1970), *A Crown of Feathers* (1973), and *Passions* (1975). The novels are *The Family Moskat* (1950), *Satan in Goray* (1955, though first published in Warsaw in 1935), *The Magician of Lublin* (1960), *The Slave* (1962), *The Manor* (1967), *The Estate* (1969), *Enemies, A Love Story* (1972), and *Shosha* (1978). The autobiographical writings include two collections of sketches whose contents partially overlap—*In My Father's Court* (1966) and *A Day of Pleasure* (1969)—and two longer, sustained efforts which are apparently episodes in an even larger project: *A Little Boy in Search of God* (1976) and *A Young Man in Search of Love* (1978).[3] One has to marvel at the fact of it: nineteen books in English—not including

3. All dates given for the publication of Singer's books refer to the first English publication in book form. Since all of Singer's books and stories were written originally in Yiddish, and since many first appeared serially in the *Jewish Daily Forward* years before book publication, their actual publication history is often exceedingly complex.

children's books—the first of which, *The Family Moskat,* did not appear in English until Singer, born in 1904, was forty-six years old.

The novels, by and large, appear to be linked by a grand design and may be read as chapters in a continuous *roman fleuve.* They trace the history of the Jews from their villages and ghettoes in Poland to New York's West Side, beginning with the devastating Chmielnicki pogroms in the seventeenth century—in *Satan in Goray* and again in *The Slave*—and leading to the eve of the holocaust, in both *The Family Moskat* and *Shosha. Enemies, A Love Story* picks up the drama in America with the bedraggled lives of the emigré survivors in New York City. Thus Singer follows the Jews from disaster to disaster, from Chmielnicki to Hitler, depicting the three hundred years in between as a tormented interregnum for a nation in exile, intent upon survival but ultimately waiting for the end. And that end is prefigured in the very events which open the chronicle: the seventeenth-century Cossack raids and the wave of Sabbatian messianism that followed them. All the historical novels, except *Satan in Goray,* were written after the holocaust and all their characters are endowed with their author's knowledge: they live in the shadow of his melancholy. "Death is the Messiah," declares Hertz Yanover at the end of *The Family Moskat.* The novels as a whole are as austere and joyless as the history they reflect.

To read Singer's novels and stories side by side is to come into touch with two very different kinds of imagination. On the one hand we have dynastic sagas like *The Family Moskat, The Manor,* and *The Estate,* attempts to do *Buddenbrooks* in Yiddish, immersed in history, taking long views, and sounding the note of what one critic has called "real magnificence"; on the other are stories consistent in scale with small lives and intense passions. The novels tend toward the melodramatic, yoking Byzantine plots to simple and predictable moral codes, which may be due to their place and method of publication and Singer's need to maintain continuous episodic levels of action while providing constant moral assurance. But in Singer's writing, the grander the sweep, the narrower the imaginative angle; he gains freedom to invent by turning his back on history, verisimilitude, probability, and propriety. He is a fabulist and master of the short form, and has acknowledged his preference. "In a short work you can concentrate on quality. In a large novel, you give only essentials. In short stories you elaborate."

Like Malamud, Singer is also a moralist against his own imagination, but where Malamud wants to moralize his characters' deep yearnings so that their failures take on ethical coloration, Singer usually keeps his fantasies and his scruples separate, letting the novels, except the first and most extraordinary, *Satan in Goray,* do the moralizing, thereby freeing his stories to explore the demonic. Another way to see this is to observe that Singer has made a compact with his energies, which expresses itself in his indefatigable literary output, even into his seventies. But only in the stories does that energy seek its own level of fantasy and pull free from the simple rhythms of temptation and renunciation or transgression and atonement that dominate the longer novels. The stories achieve a certain imaginative purity that way, pushing through the novels' conventional codes of conduct toward whatever lies on the other side. Hints of what that might be can be found at the beginning of Singer's career, in *Satan in Goray,* in which the frenzy of Sabbatian antinomianism that sweeps through the village of Goray sparks an orgy of license in which all that had previously been prohibited becomes mandatory: "The young men who studied together in the study house were up to all kinds of evil. They would climb into the women's gallery in the middle of the day, committing pederasty with one another, and sodomy—with the goats. Evenings they went to the bathhouse and, through a hole they had bored in the wall, watched the women purifying themselves. Other young scholars even went off to observe the women tending to their bodily needs."

Here, and in many of the stories that speak for his wilder side, Singer gives voice to that special alloy of sex and violence that is the underside of strict observance, and fashions a Yiddish Gothic whose occasional pleas for restraint or severe chastisement of sinners are only quaint footnotes to the main attraction: the lurid details of transgression itself. Before destroying his orgiasts or setting them to penitential labors, Singer puts them through their paces and indulges their passions, which often boil over into madness or demonic transformation. "The reader," observes one critic, appalled at what happens when Singer cuts loose, "may well wonder what ever happened to the Torah."

Yet it is this consistent involvement with those passions that are banished from conventional morality that is most intriguing in Singer and distinguishes him from the classic Yiddish writers: Mendele Mocher Sforim, Sholem Aleichem, and Isaac Peretz. Like Steven Marcus's "other Victorians," Singer is the other Yiddishist. Not only does he deal with sex openly, if in grotesque and distorted images, but he embraces the whole eroticized shadow world of demons, dybbuks, evil eyes, Cabalism, telepathy, and madness, those spiritualized accompaniments of forbidden sexual desires. Story after story about love or marriage turns on a supernatural point: a telepathic signal, a demonic possession, a spiritual transmigration, an instant of uncanny prescience. It is as if the demonic universe were a metaphor for the unconscious itself, and cabalism and mysticism primarily forms of erotic inquiry. As Herman Broder, the emigré hero of *Enemies, A Love Story*, puts it so vividly. "In the beginning was lust. The godly, as well as the human, principle is desire. Gravity, light, magnetism, thought may be aspects of the same universal longing. Suffering, emptiness, darkness are nothing more than interruptions of a cosmic orgasm that grows forever in intensity."

The demonic element in Singer's stories is the perfect vehicle for a tormented and ambivalent sexuality, since the demon lover, who turns up nearly everywhere, is a fantasy that allows erotic wishes to be entertained even while responsibility for them is denied; we say we are bewitched. In "The Black Wedding" (*The Spinoza of Market Street*), the spinster Hindele is married against her will to a young Hassidic rabbi, Reb Simon, only to learn that he is a demon and the wedding ceremony a rite of desecration. That night, "Hindele felt herself lying in blood and pus. The one who had raped her snored, coughed, hissed like an adder. Before dawn a group of hags ran into the room, pulled the sheet from under her, inspected it, sniffed it, began to dance." And the schoolteacher Mark Meitels in "The Witch" (*Passions*) is enchanted by his inept and misshapen student Bella, who has put a curse on his wife and a deadly blessing upon him. After a night of passionate love making in which Mark, despite deep loathing for his monstrous lover, has pledged to run off with her, he finds himself sexually enthralled and unable to let go. "He couldn't wait to get to the bedroom and pushed her down on the rug—a witch drenched in blood and semen, a monster that the rising sun transformed into a beauty." Such sexual monstrosity is not so rare in the fiction of conventional moralists, for the grotesque is what the imagination produces when sex as such is granted entré only through the back doors of horror and disgust—when it can be shown to be loathsome.

The full measure of this imagination has yet to be taken, in part, I suspect, because Singer's position as the last major Yiddish writer throws a haze of light nostalgia over his work. That haze is a smoke-screen, behind which lies a harsh, fierce, and singular imagination; and what it lacks in breadth of ideas or sympathies—for the range of experience it can entertain is very narrow—it makes up for in relentlessness and invention. One obvious way to approach this imagination is to consider the historical conditions for it, to regard Singer's warlocks, dybbuks, and demons as stylized ways of talking about the ghosts of the recent Jewish dead. This view of Singer gains support from *Enemies, A Love Story*, whose hero, Herman Broder, is a holocaust survivor and postwar emigré in New York, stymied by the past and circling around in a universe of lost connections. Ghostlike, the past returns in the form of a wife who had supposedly perished in the death camps but turns up in New York to complicate an already unhinged life. But even *Enemies* demonstrates that urgent turn toward the pornographic that dissolves the social and historical textures of the survivors' experience into a familiar melodrama of erotic roulette. Through a combination of carelessness, fate, and self-destructiveness, Broder is obliged to choose among several women who are competing for his affections (like Yasha Mazur of *The Magician of Lublin* and Aaron Greidinger of *Shosha*), and eventually picks, as Singer would have him, the one who will destroy him. It is not that Singer misapplies history so much as that, as a novelist, he places it at the service of the mythologizing portions of his imagination. And *Satan in Goray*, written in 1933, is evidence of a proclivity for the lurid already formed and in place some years before the war.

Though Irving Howe has honored Singer by calling him a modern writer, there is far more reason to see him as a throwback, a link to the pagan animism of the European Middle Ages. He has stayed closer than any American writer I can think of, Jewish or otherwise, to the folk roots of narrative and, correspondingly, to the primitive regions of his own imagination. Unlike such contemporaries as Bellow, Roth, and Mailer, who are modern precisely in their struggles to cast off excess civilization in an effort to make contact with repressed images and feelings, Singer has always stayed in touch, and his loyalty to Yiddish is a commitment to the memories and emotions that are available to him only through the *mamaloschen,* the mother tongue. In *In My Father's Court,* he recalls that, as a boy, he would spend hours outside his father's study with his ear to the door, listening in wonder at the stories being told within by petitioners for justice at the rabbinic court. In his stories, his ear is still poised at the door for those random slices of Yiddish life, even if he is prone to retell them in his own violent and metaphysical idiom, so redolent of cabalism and sex. It is in this buried life that his uncanny energy is rooted, and in his realization that he is the last literary witness to a lost world and therefore under an urgent obligation to get it all on record while he remains alive. The achieved record thus far is not the *life* of the *shtetl* as Sholem Aleichem has given it to us with his characteristic detail and sympathy, or as Singer's older brother, Israel Joshua, so faithfully portrayed it in his memoir, *Of a World That Is No More* (1946, translated 1970), but its *imagination,* the pagan imagination of rural Poland, that tribal side of European Jewish life that all the

218

Torahs and all the Talmuds and all the great rabbis from Vilna to Warsaw never wholly suppressed. Though Singer's career comes at the end of the Yiddish line, his voice belongs to the very beginning, as though he were the ancestor, not the descendant, of Mendele, Peretz, and Sholem Aleichem.

Manners, Morals, and the Novel, Revisited

There is a famous passage in Lionel Trilling's essay "Manners, Morals, and the Novel" (*The Liberal Imagination,* 1950) in which he declares a true fiction of manners to be impossible in America because the texture of American social life is too thin to grant manners (defined as "a culture's hum and buzz of implication") more than passing interest in our lives. Recalling Henry James's observations on the thinness of American social institutions, Trilling agrees that there is "no sufficiency of means for the display of a variety of manners, no opportunity for the novelist to do his job of searching out reality, not enough complication of appearance to make the job interesting." He sets writers like Dreiser, Dos Passos, and Faulkner (who gets passing marks, though he is unfortunately a provincial) against Balzac and Flaubert, to point up the differences between the social textures of a new, open, and mobile society and one that is traditional and class-bound. And though he concedes that "life in America has increasingly thickened since the nineteenth century," Trilling contends that "it has not . . . thickened so much as to permit our undergraduates to understand the characters of Balzac, to understand . . . life in a crowded country where the competitive pressures are great, forcing intense passions to express themselves fiercely and yet within the limitations set by a strong and complicated tradition of manners."

When first made in 1947, these strictures had a certain cogency and pertinence in a literary environment where young writers, laboring under the shadows of Hemingway and an impoverished, brute realism on the one hand and the native American proclivity for romance on the other had to fight clear of the American taste for literatures of raw experience and psychological or ideological romance to discover fresh ways to imagine society. Certainly, recent shifts in the literary climate would seem to have taken up the challenge of Trilling's criticism, for we now do have, after our fashion, a fiction of manners, despite the somewhat exaggerated poverty of our institutional lives. For our social experience does not lack for codes of propriety and decorum or subliminal signs of caste, place, and breeding, nor does our literature now lack a fiction that wants to exploit them and to employ "a culture's hum and buzz of implication" to express social nuances that are incapable of being "fully phrased and precisely stated."

Of course, I mean largely the novels of Saul Bellow, whose instinct for the textures and habits of urban life sets him apart from all other American writers, past and present, except Henry James and, perhaps, Scott Fitzgerald, and it is telling that both James and Bellow share a feeling for the velleities of manner and gesture best cultivated by a mind that lives in two cultures and purchases its ease by keeping its discriminations alert. Bellow, born in Quebec, the French-speaking province of Canada, to Yiddish-speaking parents who had only recently fled from Russia, has taken up a literary position that had previously been held by a patrician and Anglophile Bostonian, for it is a feature of the modern Jewish experience that learning to live *between* worlds may be the price of surviving *in* any one of them. As immigrant, emigré, displaced person, or holder of dual citizenship, the Jew finds the correct interpretation of foreign signs a vital part of his daily routine, and has been obliged historically to turn the hyphen in his identity into the cutting edge of a sharp sensibility. Such habits of irony and wariness that may come of the shuttling between worlds and languages breed natural forms of anthropological wonder; amphibians that they are, Jews are experts in incongruity. "Orpheus, the son of Greenhorn," Bellow calls his Von Humboldt Fleisher. "He brought Coney Island into the Aegean and united Buffalo Bill with Rasputin." Bellow himself, born into a Russian, Yiddish, French, English, cosmopolitan world—a ghetto with certain unique international features—is currently our most noted fieldworker in American manners, with a degree in anthropology to lend formal credentials to his native intuitions.

In addition to Bellow, we have both Philip Roth, who is a genuine novelist of manners and a master of the incongruous, and, in his maverick way, Norman Mailer, who has sometimes gone about the investigation of American manners, largely in his political journalism, with a rough and ready insight. At fainter levels of hum and buzz, there is the Jewish-Irish J. D. Salinger, whose novels are all about "manners," albeit crudely defined as forms of dullness and masks for social fraud.

Bellow's genius for portraying manners, especially in three books, *Seize the Day* (1956), *Herzog* (1964), and *Humboldt's Gift* (1975), did not emerge all at once, but has evolved slowly as he has discovered the dimensions of his talent and voice. He has never been a social novelist as such, and although the derelictions of modern society are now an almost obsessive theme in his writing, he can still be regarded as a social writer only if the term is properly hedged with provisos and qualifications. He was originally, and remains primarily, a novelist of mood and character and the conflict between them. Mood is a given, a fact of life beyond the reach of conscious will except under special therapeutic arrangements, as in *Henderson the Rain King* (1959) and the play *The Last Analysis* (1964). It sprouts up involuntarily from the unconscious like fierce, tropical foliage; it is incorrigible. But character is a stance, the human face one turns toward the implacable, be it the decline of civilization or the rush of one's own emotions. In this particular version of psychological fiction, character is the style with which one moves along the axial lines of an emotion or, as the case may be, across its grain. It is invariably the dialectic of feeling and character that creates the tension in Bellow's novels, from the style in which Joseph gives in to his depression in *Dangling Man,* turning an involuntary petulance into a principle of aloofness, to Augie March's discovery that elation is a form of patriotism and Von Humboldt Fleisher's way of implicating all of history in his intolerable manic and depressive moods. Indeed, Von Humboldt Fleisher, the manic-depressive poet of *Humboldt's Gift,* goes to the heart of Bellow's "case"; his ineluctable cycles sum up the larger swings of emotion that set the tone for Bellow's entire fiction.

Bellow's books can be sorted generally into depressive books (*Dangling Man,* 1944; *The Victim,* 1947; *Seize the Day,* 1956; *Mr. Sammler's Planet,* 1970) and expansive ones (*The Adventures of Augie March,* 1953; the play *The Last Analysis,* 1964; *Herzog,* 1964; *Humboldt's Gift,* 1975), whose roughly alternate publication dates suggest an intention. Much can be made of Bellow by reading the ebullient *Augie March* as an answer to the gloomy *Dangling Man* and *The Victim,* and *Seize the Day* as a withdrawal from *Augie March*'s immoderate joy, and so on. But too much emphasis should not be placed on these moods as such, since it is the struggle to come to grips with them that ultimately counts in these books. Bellow is a moralist, and his heroes' ability to face up to what is given, historically or psychologically, is usually the moral point of each book. One measure of Von Humboldt Fleisher's failure is his compulsion to let the world in on his pathology, implicating everyone in what is involuntary within himself, as he rather grandly understands. "When a Manic Depressive escapes from his Furies he's irresistible. He captures History. I think that aggravation is a secret technique of the Unconscious. As for great men and kings being History's slaves, I think Tolstoi was off the track. Don't kid yourself, kings are the most sublime sick. Manic Depressive heroes pull Mankind into their cycles and carry everybody away."

Bellow's dilemma as a novelist remains: what to do with the world while aggrandizing the emotions. The solutions have largely been catch as catch can, no two books going about it in just the same way, and some even demonstrating mid-course deflections of stylistic trajectory that correspond to deeper changes of purpose. Generally, each of Bellow's characters carries the stamp of his modernity within him, in the form of his brand of desperate ennui, making the circumstantial world unnecessary, except as a climate or tone or overall condition. The war, the holocaust, the decline of the West, are the very thematic heart of three books—*Dangling Man, The Victim,* and *Mr. Sammler's Planet*—but they are interior realities at best, whose influence upon the emotions of the heroes of these books is their point of entry into the fiction. The chronic depressions shared in common by Joseph, Asa Leventhal, and Artur Sammler reflect a repressed rage toward history that has no means of venting itself. Lacking the emotional means to run amok or the cultural climate in which doing so is a recognized form of "growth" (though Eugene Henderson is "cured" by roaring like a lion), these men settle for being out of sorts, and the world, in answer to their testiness, seems a bleak and degraded place, as in *The Victim*: "Already, at half-past seven, the street looked deadened with heat and light. The clouds were heavily suspended and slow. To the south and east, the air was brassy, the factories were beginning to smolder and faced massively, India red, brown, into the sun and across the hot green netting of the bridges."

We hardly know what we are seeing here: Asa Leventhal's *Weltschmerz* or an industrial sunrise, and the difference hardly matters. Leventhal's hidden rage is known through its projections: Kirby Allbee, who haunts Leventhal like an eerie embodiment of his unconscious, and the city itself, with its stifling, brassy air and smoldering factories, like so many smoldering hearts. Here is reality done up as a dream, in a style of realism that takes its principles more from *The Interpretation of Dreams* than from *Middlemarch* or *Sister Carrie.*

In *Augie March* this depression is turned inside out and Augie himself created as an improbably robust American, an urban Huck Finn who out-Hucks Huck for sheer adventurousness and can barely contain himself when the adrenalin is on tap. Correspondingly, his Chicago is a runaway inventory of buoyant particulars, whose very enumeration announces the victory of American get up and go over brooding, Jewish, *foreign* habits of thought. Augie's classmates at the city college constitute a veritable democratic vista: "In the mixture there was beauty—good proportion—and pimple-insolence, and parricide faces, gumchew innocence, labor fodder and secretary forces, Danish stability, Dago inspiration, catarrh-hampered mathematical genius; there were waxed-eared shovelers' children, sex-promising businessmen's daughters—an immense sampling of a tremendous host, the multitudes of holy writ, begotten by West-moving, factor-shoved parents. Or me, the by-blow of a traveling man."

Different as they are, both *Augie March* and *The Victim* embody the same relationship of mind to matter: that the mind is the handiwork of history and circumstance or that reality is a psychological arrangement—half created as it is perceived. Either way this is a statement of equivalence or mirroring, and where it is subtly applied, as in *The Victim,* the urban landscape speaks for the mind in its hidden aspects. Kirby Allbee is a part of Leventhal unknown to Leventhal himself. Where the principle of mirroring is crudely applied, as in *Augie March* and *Mr. Sammler's Planet,* reality is little more than a justification for mood: America jumps or New York City stinks.

But in *Seize the Day, Herzog,* parts of *Humboldt's Gift,* and some of Bellow's best stories, such as "Leaving the Yellow House," "Looking for Mr. Green," and "The Old System" (all collected in *Mosby's Memoirs and Other Stories,* 1968), the world is known by its own logic and weight, ripeness and plenitude. For example, as Madeleine Pontritter, soon to be Madeleine Herzog, does her morning toilette prior to leaving for work, Moses Herzog sits along the side of the tub, clad only in his trench coat, and watches in amazement as she assembles her public face and adult character with swift and expert assurance: "First she spread a layer of cream on her cheeks, rubbing it into her straight nose, her childish chin and soft throat. It was a gray, pearly bluish stuff. That was the base. She fanned it with a towel. Over this she laid the makeup. She worked with cotton swabs, under the hairline, about the eyes, up the cheeks and on the throat. Despite the soft rings of feminine flesh, there was already something discernibly dictatorial about that extended throat. She would not let Herzog caress her face downward—it was bad for the muscles."

It is traditional to suppose that such a scene is the standard exposé of feminine artifice that we are familiar with in the literature of misogyny, from Swift and Pope through T. S. Eliot, but here too is Herzog the city boy suddenly become the Columbus, or, better, the stout Cortez, of the boudoir, gazing in wild surmise at the secrets of eros and authority in culture—the beguiling sideshow of style among the *haute bourgeoisie.* Since *Herzog* is not a simple fiction of *contemptus mundi,* as I think *Sammler* is, Bellow is not just taking his shots at Madeleine, though his malice is hard to miss: she *is* dressing to kill. But what is an urbane fellow like this Moses Herzog expected to admire: Levis and sandals? This is Chicago! Such a description, indeed, reads less like a denunciation of Madeleine than a celebration of the rites of civilized taste and allure, with this very Moses the celebrant. Madeleine may well be a Golden Calf, but the more maternal and thoughtful Ramona Donsell, in whose bed Herzog later finds solace from the rigors of his divorce, is anything but an artless woman in her spike-heeled shoes and black lace underthings. For what a man like Herzog is finally in search of is not a girl just like the girl who married dear old dad—though deeper probing might prove otherwise—but a fuller communion with his own vanities, even if he should die of them. If vanity is finally Herzog's downfall, it is also his raison d'être; he *is* a sport.

This is not to say that all here is just so much admiration of the rich and spoiled, or a delightful inventory of what Revlon hath wrought among the Michigan Avenue shopping class, for Bellow's fiction of manners is a true anthropology: a study of tribal (in this case leisure-class) rites as they express primitive and universal human urges. Madeleine's toilette and Herzog's rapt attention to it describe a genuine ritual; Madeleine is painting her face, just like the Balinese or the Arnhem Landers or the People of Kau. That is the point that sets Bellow, as an American, apart from British or continental novelists of manners: the inexorable drift of the eye from the social fact to its psychological import and, often enough, to what is most primitive beneath what appears most socialized—the dog beneath the skin.

In the books from *Henderson* on, Bellow has often invoked the primitive—when he has not been reaching out toward the infinite—and achieved some of his best insights and effects by playing off the civilized against the archaic, or offering his own well-turned prose in homage to the primal and unmannered. In *Humboldt's Gift,* the Russian steambath on Divison Street in Chicago seems a relic of some Pleistocene habitat, a steaming diorama of existence at the very dawn of man: "The patrons of the Russian Bath are cast in an antique form. They have swelling buttocks and fatty breasts as yellow as buttermilk. They stand on thick pillar legs affected with a sort of creeping verdigris or blue-cheese mottling of the ankles. After steaming, these old fellows eat enormous snacks of bread and salt herring or large ovals of salami and dripping skirt-steak and they drink schnapps. They could knock down walls with their hard stout old-fashioned bellies. Things are very elementary here. You feel that these people are almost conscious of obsolescence, of a line of evolution abandoned by nature and culture."

As Marcus Klein has pointed out (in *After Alienation*), Bellow's heroes are often Nietzscheans who tend to resolve the tension of competing claims by raising the metaphysical ante and sailing past all contradictions. Here and there, Wilhelm Reich, Sigmund Freud, and Rudolf Steiner turn up alongside Nietzsche as launching pads for such transvaluation of social values, pointing Bellow beyond the cluttered surfaces of urban reality as well as beneath them. Thus his characters experience a gap between the level of their desires and that of their experiences, and the books, in attempting to keep in touch with both, wind up dividing their attention between disparate worlds. *Humboldt's Gift* is our only American novel about poker and the afterlife. All Bellow's novels since *Henderson* are instances of a social fiction in struggle with the conditioned nature of our social existence, in which Bellow gives evidence of wanting to give over the world of circumstances for biological or interstellar prospects. His heroes suffer from chronic vertigo under the pull of such divisions. Moses Herzog survives his flight into ultimate visions through the support of an indulgent woman and generous brothers, while Von Humboldt Fleisher destroys himself in his passion to circumvent the ordinary in the name of his capitalized abstractions: "Poetry, Beauty, Love, Waste Land, Alienation, Politics, History, the Unconscious." Somewhere between the two, Artur Sammler and Govinda Lal's innocent longings for the moon in *Mr. Sammler's Planet* are only the feckless woolgathering of literary intellectuals.

As a literary resource, Bellow's Chicago is much like Dickens's London or Joyce's Dublin, not only an intimate locale or colorful backdrop but an ultimate city, the very idea of one, a superorganic region that shapes the character of its citizens and presses upon them a collective identity. "I am an American, Chicago born," announces Augie March, and we know immediately that he is a Chicagoan, that is, a tough cookie who appreciates fine things. This is, after all, the city of Max Factor and his brother Jake, "The Barber," Factor: the cosmetician and the gangster. But what is missing from Augie's Chicago, as it is missing from Joseph's or Herzog's or Charlie Citrine's, is politics. There is no real politics anywhere in Bellow's writing, unless we want to count the nonfiction report from Israel, *To Jerusalem and Back* (1976), however prevalent may be its appurtenances and by-products, such as money, position, and influence, and the visible forms of its invisible presence: its police, its courts, its lawyers. For one finds little recognition in Bellow's books that Chicago or New York or America has anything to do with power. The best measure of this absence is a comparison of his later urban novels with Norman Mailer's contemporaneous journalism, notably *The Armies of the Night* (1968), *Miami and the Siege of Chicago* (1968), and *St. George and the Godfather* (1972). Mailer's Chicago, in *Miami and the Siege of Chicago*, richly imagined in its own right, is an intensely political place, for it is Mayor Daley's Chicago during the 1968 Democratic convention. Of course, power, specifically the potency and charisma possessed by men of position and wealth, has always been the center of Mailer's gravitational field, and he is bound to register its effects wherever he is. And yet, insofar as power has everything to do with the character of a nation or a city, we cannot help noticing Bellow's shyness about it. Both *Miami and the Siege of Chicago* and *Mr. Sammler's Planet,* though very different kinds of books, are ostensibly reports on the culture and politics of the late sixties, though read together they seem to describe life on different planets in alien galaxies. Their discrepancies reflect the differences between a mind like Bellow's, nurtured on Hegel and Schopenhauer and the world as will and idea, and a concrete mind like Mailer's, nurtured on Marxist visions of the world as power and property. "Politics is property" is the theme of *Miami and the Siege of Chicago,* and Mailer notes, reflecting on an earlier tour of Chicago's nauseating slaughterhouses, that "Chicago was a town where nobody could ever forget how the money was made." Though the show of money is everywhere in Bellow's Chicago, a mythic city suspended somewhere between divorce court and the New Jerusalem, no hero of Bellow's, except Asa Leventhal in *The Victim,* ever does a day's work, though many wind up in uneasy intimacy with conspicuous consumers and name-brand merchandise. As reporters, Bellow and Mailer could not be more different: the one is an expert in décor and a curator of the evanescent and the other a connoisseur of the brutal, which is another way of calling Bellow an Augustan and Mailer a Romantic.

The impressions that Bellow collects and savors through the prehensile grasp of "sensibility," a finely tuned apparatus of visual and intellectual radar, Mailer gathers by way of "instinct," as though each has given the task of testing experience to a different portion of the sensory equipment. Mailer, being nearsighted, or so he says when the world slips out of focus, has assigned the job of being the soul's antenna to the nose, an altogether cruder instrument of moral discrimination than Bellow's eye or Roth's ear, though not without its own brands of finesse. Just as his first apprehension of funky Chicago was the rare stink of the slaughterhouses, his report on the first manned moon flight, *Of a Fire on the Moon* (1970), takes off from the failure of the Manned Spacecraft Center in Houston and its WASP personnel to emit any scent at all, filling him with an instinctual dread ("It was part of the folklore of New York," he jokes, "that the Wasps were without odor"). "They had divorced themselves from odor in order to dominate time, and thereby see if they were able to deliver themselves from death!" These people are a world apart from Chicago's Ukrainians, Poles, and Slovaks—they eat packaged beef and vote Republican —and Mailer is a fish out of water among them, as would be Saul Bellow or Mayor Daley.

This intuitive, visceral distrust of the dominant technological culture and its achievements, coupled with an admiration for and desire to come to an intimate knowledge of its power, has been the prevailing note of Mailer's thought from the beginning, though in his early books, that is, those issued before 1957, when he published the manifesto "The White Negro," he explained that distrust in more formal, political ways.

Just after the war, as a rebellious young intellectual and independent Marxist, Mailer came on the scene as a writer of intermittent genius and, more consistently, of unfulfilled promise. His initial literary ambition was to become a major American novelist, a younger Hemingway, and his first three books were novels of a conventional sort, done with varying degrees of power and skill: *The Naked and the Dead* (1948), *Barbary Shore* (1951), and *The Deer Park* (1955). *The Naked and the Dead,* published when Mailer was just twenty-six, was a virtuoso performance by so young a writer, and brought him enormous popular as well as critical acclaim. Against all the counsels of the Jewish literary superego, which he was prepared, in any case, to reject, he was a *success.* (But then, to be an antitype and speak for the all-American "other" within has always been Mailer's special gimmick.) Though the book now seems something of an artifact, overburdened with philosophical longeurs, a shallow psychology, and a primitive cinematic realism appropriated from Dos Passos, it is nevertheless remarkable for its sheer ambition and sustained energy of performance, as well as for those insights into power and the American obsession with it that have become the trademarks of Mailer's thought. *The Naked and the Dead* is a study of power at two levels: the irrational brutality of organized destruction and the sexual ferocity of the masculine contest, the *mano-à-mano*. When all the thematic and formal accoutrements of the great novel and the ideological baggage of the major statement are cut away, what remains of *The Naked and the Dead* is a book about destruction: the slaughter of enemy troops in the era of the body count, the decimation of a reconnaissance patrol in an absurd, Ahabian quest, and, at the center of focus, the killing of Lieu-

227

tenant Hearn, Mailer's spokesman for liberalism, by two stronger men: General Cummings, a closet homosexual whose love has been spurned, and Sergeant Croft, whose authority over his platoon has been threatened.

Mailer has never been able to shake this fixation on power and competition, and through all his subsequent ideological meanderings and psychological conversions, he has returned to it time and again, like a plow to the furrow, deepening the groove, perfecting it, then circling back. In a sense, his career has gone forward by standing still. Just as it is said of Bellow that all his books can be called *Dangling Man,* so all Mailer's might be entitled, if not *The Naked and the Dead,* then *The Armies of the Night,* or, as Robert F. Lucid entitled his anthology of Mailer's writings, *The Long Patrol* (1971). The military remains Mailer's favorite metaphor, standing for organized, national violence and collective repression, just as the boxing ring has come to symbolize for him, as it did for Hemingway and James Jones, all that stands opposed to the psychology of the regiment: physical grace and courage, independent will, and the swift violence that clears the air. One might even think at times that it was Mailer, not Jones, who wrote *From Here to Eternity,* the postwar novel of a boxer who is crushed by the collective power of the army.

Barbary Shore, by contrast, is a rough-hewn Marxist tract with underdeveloped overtones of perverse passion and sexual blockage. If it ultimately fails both as a novel and as an argument, that is largely because Mailer himself had no clear view of the forces he was grappling with. *Barbary Shore* is really two books in one: a straight Leninist thesis on imperialism as the last stage of American corporate capitalism and a more tentative statement about sexual failure as a byproduct of garrison-state politics. But having no calculus for mapping the connection (a calculus he explicitly called for in his essay "The White Negro"), and no literary formula for bringing such grand theses to life in the Brooklyn rooming house to which all action is confined (shades of *No Exit* in Brooklyn), Mailer quickly fell into his worst posture, that of the pamphleteer, and talked his subjects to death. But as an incomplete and tormented book, *Barbary Shore* casts light on the psychological pressures that were driving Mailer to write even as they were undermining his fiction. For it is a desperate book whose conflicts cannot be contained by the formal limits of the conventional realism to which Mailer had at that time subordinated his talents. Later, in *The Deer Park,* we watch Charles Eitel, blacklisted and blocked screenwriter, work desperately at a screenplay he cannot complete. "No matter how he tried, and there were days when he drove himself into exhaustion, sitting before his desk twelve and fourteen hours, the work would always turn into something shoddy or something contrived, into something dull, into something false." That, clearly, was Mailer himself, battling against his own resistances while writing both *Barbary Shore* and *The Deer Park*.

The Deer Park does manage to bring Mailer's sexual theses into the open as political accusations and to yoke his imaginative powers, as if for the last time, to the formal conventions of dialogue, plot, and character that the particular traditions of progressive realism to which Mailer had allied himself called for. For all its inconsistencies of rhythm and tone and its unsolved formal problems, such as what to do with its stick-figure of a narrator, Sergius O'Shaugnessy, *The Deer Park* is Mailer's only extended work of fiction to take up the human cost of politics with any dramatic credibility. Eitel's failures as a writer and as a man, we understand, are to be chalked up to his predicament as a blacklisted writer. The book is also Mailer's only successful, extended piece of sexual fiction, and the affair between Eitel and Elena his only convincing love story. Much of the strange and anguished quality of honesty-in-avoidance that distinguishes Mailer's writing since *The Deer Park* has to do with his inability to face up one more time, without posturing and gimmickry, to those mysteries of sexual and emotional failure that he had begun to explore in that book. Indeed, it is the very fascination with success and the refusal to give any credit to failure that set Mailer apart from other Jewish writers (making him presumably more "American") and have prevented him from realizing some of his own best intuitions about the deeper ironies of the American dream.

To this inventory of Mailer's fiction can be added a handful of stories, including two fine ones—"The Time of Her Time" and "The Man Who Studied Yoga" (both to be found in *Advertisements for Myself,* 1959)—and two subsequent fatuous and overblown novels that have to be regarded as cavalier exploitations of a reputation for adventure and risk: *An American Dream* (1965) and *Why Are We in Vietnam?* (1967). Whatever acclaim Mailer now enjoys as a writer and celebrity has little to do with this fiction, which hardly earns him any preeminence in his generation of postwar novelists, among whom are Gore Vidal, Vance Bourjaily, James Baldwin, William Styron, James Jones, and Truman Capote.

The books, or rather the public performances, for which Mailer is largely known and valued are his miscellaneous collections of jottings, speeches, lectures, and manifestoes, including *Advertisements for Myself, The Presidential Papers* (1963), *Cannibals and Christians* (1966), and *Existential Errands* (1972), and his journalistic reports on the state of the nation and its culture (that is, its politics, boxing, rocketry, and sex), most notably *Armies of the Night, Miami and the Siege of Chicago,* and *St. George and the Godfather.* But among them must also be counted such indeterminate grab bags of insight, potboiling, and sheer swindle as *Of a Fire on the Moon, The Prisoner of Sex* (1971), *Marilyn* (1973), *The Fight* (1975), and *Genius and Lust: A Journey through the Major Writings of Henry Miller* (1976). So connected are these books in theme and style that we scarcely think of them as books at all so much as instances of a public voice with which we are thoroughly familiar though seldom at ease, a voice so fantastic in its familiarity that we are always brought up short by the hints of strangeness in the articulation of the commonplace. It is the voice of a theatrical desperado, at once pugnacious and discriminating, resolutely anti-intellectual and slyly bookish, despairing of American politics but enamored of the centers of power. How American! Bellow might almost have invented this real-life Augie March, this sensitive tough guy who rolls his shoulders and stalks his own shadow—or the shadow of Hemingway—jabbing and sniffing with all the real mock pugnacity of a peacock in courtship.

To interpret the whole career as an exercise in consistency, one would have to note that at the bottom of all concerns is the obsession with power, usually at the point of conjunction between sex and politics where policy melts into potency and the arms race abuts the presidential orgasm. The cardinal points of such an imagination are energy, competition, power, and repression, energy being the highest human good, and power, insofar as it is collective, fearful, and aligned against the anarchic potential of the individual will, the totalitarian principle in public life. But seen in a different light, power is also the great alluring mystery, attractive enough to entice Mailer to run for mayor of New York in 1969 but repellent enough to cause him to scuttle his own campaign. Such ambivalence is more or less what can be expected of a mind nurtured intellectually on Marx and Wilhelm Reich but drawing its deeper nourishment from the demotic Nietzscheanism of James Jones and Sonny Liston.

For Mailer, as for Roth and Bellow, it is the clash of psychological forces at the pressure points of character that determines our stance toward politics and sex. Each writer possesses a typology of character, a theory of energy and resistance whose intricate calculus can be read upon the body, making appearance an index to the whole moral life. What each practices in his way is a medieval craft, physiognomy; you may know the man by his physical signs: an offset nose, a pasty complexion, a wide mouth, a hitch in the stride. Mailer's particular genius as a political reporter has been a talent for measuring the climate of politics by diagnosing its cast of characters, pressing mannerisms into service as ultimate, telltale manners. The most startling and effective example of this is probably the Reichian description, in *St. George*, of Richard Nixon's character armor and the battle between body and mind evident in Nixon's gesture and gait that is expressive of his whole, cluttered emotional life.

> He must be obsessed with the powers he could employ if his body could also function intimately as an instrument of his will, as intimate perhaps as his intelligence (which has become so free of the *distortions* of serious moral motivation), but his body refuses. Like a recalcitrant hound, it refuses. So he is still trying out a half dozen separate gestures with each step, a turn of his neck to say one thing, a folding of his wrist to show another, a sprightly step up with one leg, a hint of a drag with the other, and all the movements are immediately restrained, pulled back to zero revelation as quickly as possible by a brain which is more afraid of what the body will reveal than of what it can discover by just once making an authentic move which gets authentic audience response.

Nearsighted or not, Mailer sees all right with his glasses on. But is Nixon really like this, this Pinocchio of a politician, and what of the various McCarthies, McGoverns, Rockefellers, and strange, misshapen Republicans who spook up Mailer's Republican conventions like ten thousand phantoms at the Miami opera? Are they *really* like that? Well, *they are now!* More than anyone, even Hunter Thompson or Theodore H. White, it is Mailer who has invented what remains of these people when the issues have receded and the struggles are forgotten. We remember, however, Mailer's versions of them, in part because they are so sharply drawn and in part because they seem so richly deserved. These are portraits of the moral life made visible in the flesh, and if they ultimately seem to be cartoons in prose, we might remember what another caricaturist, Philip Roth, has said of the technique, that "distortion is a dye dropped onto the specimen to make vivid traits and qualities otherwise only faintly visible to the naked eye" (*Reading Myself and Others*, 1975).

Philip Roth is another forward scout in that American wilderness where caste and class throw shadows over love and sex, but because his senses are uniquely balanced, what he sees is not half so telling as what he hears: his moral sense is the ear. In Roth's sixth and best novel, *My Life as a Man* (1974), Peter Tarnopol's failures at love become a community problem that attracts commentary like a Talmudic text. Dr. Spielvogel, who volunteered only a punch line in *Portnoy's Complaint* (1969), is back with a published article on Tarnopol's aggression and narcissism, "Creativity: The Narcissism of the Artist," which he hopes to present as a general theory of art. Peter's wife, Maureen, threatens to publish an exposé of the creative imagination at home, "Dressing Up in Mommy's Clothes," while Peter himself ponders his misadventures in two "useful fictions": "Salad Days" and "Courting Disaster (or, Serious in the Fifties)." These, in turn, draw comment from two figures out of J. D. Salinger: Lane and Frances Coutell, who are the Franny Glass and her unctuous Yalie boyfriend of *Franny and Zooey*. The ironic flavor of this critical enterprise—assembling a casebook on Tarnopol—is best captured by Peter's brother Mo, whose reaction to Peter's useful fictions and less useful experiences is also an ingenious footnote to the Jewish novel: "What is it with you Jewish writers? Madeleine Herzog, Deborah Rojack, the cutie-pie castrator in *After the Fall,* and isn't the desirable shiksa of *A New Life* a kvetch and titless in the bargain? And now, for the further delight of the rabbis and the reading public, Lydia Zuckerman, that Gentile tomato. Chicken soup in every pot, and a Grushenka in every garage. With all the Dark Ladies to choose from, you luftmenschen can really pick 'em."

Except for the slightly overemphatic voice, which is unmistakeably Roth, this might be Bellow, for *My Life as a Man* is, like *Herzog*, an ironic refraction of domestic crisis through competing points of view, which are never resolved but simply added up. But, although Roth resembles Bellow in certain formal inclinations—his sharply delineated local milieus, his ear for fancy street talk, his affection for exaggerated instances of American culture, and his general sense of fun—certain interior dimensions of his work recall Malamud, as *The Great American Novel* (1973), Roth's heavy-handed parody of *The Natural,* seemed to suggest and a subsequent essay, "Imagining Jews" (*Reading Myself and Others),* has since confirmed. Younger than the other major Jewish writers, Roth has felt the need to establish his credentials by taking a stand on cultural myths to which his predecessors had already laid claim, including the myth of what he calls "ethical Jewhood," the belief that the Jewish character is one that places a premium on generosity, abstinence, concern, responsibility, and civilization, a view for which Malamud's early books spoke with gloomy confidence. A look at Roth's own early writing, the stories in *Goodbye Columbus* (1959) and the novels *Letting Go* (1962) and *When She Was Good* (1967) explains why he later seized upon Malamud as a surrogate for aspects of his own moral imagination, for as Roth now understands it, this early fiction is committed to principles of renunciation and deep concern that he had associated at the time both with Jews and with Henry James and the duties of the civilized life. Of the gray and depressive background of *Letting Go,* the University of Chicago in the 1950s, Theodore Solotaroff has observed (in *The Red Hot Vacuum and Other Pieces on the Writing of the Sixties,* 1970): "It was a time when the deferred gratifications of graduate school and the climb to tenure and the problems of premature adjustment seemed the warranty of 'seriousness' and 'responsibility': those solemn passwords of a generation that practiced a Freudian/Jamesian concern about motives, pondered E. M. Forster's 'only connect,' and subscribed to Lionel Trilling's 'moral realism' and 'tragic sense of life.' In contrast to today, everyone tried to act as though he were thirty."

It was under the auspices of such literary versions of moral accountability that Roth initially set up shop as a specialist in frustrated longings and paralyzed wishes, and although he has subsequently reversed his stand on renunciation, his books remain supersaturated with sex and scruples and evidence that violence may be the chief byproduct of love. Although all the Jewish writers have seen action on the front lines of sexual mayhem—Norman Mailer unpacks the combat ribbons with each new book—it is Roth and Malamud who most insistently rehearse their puzzlement over sex and carry on the quest for meanings and solutions. That sex should turn out to be a sticking point for many Jewish novelists may be because the Jewish family takes so little account of it that every son and daughter is obliged to discover it on his or her own, in the pioneering spirit of adventure and foreboding. It is one of the incongruous and seemingly retrograde points of Jewish modernism that so many of its spokesmen in this age of Beckett, Burroughs, and Genêt still come urgently forward to testify on issues of pleasure and duty that had presumably passed out of the picture with Matthew Arnold, John Stuart Mill and Cardinal Newman.

Roth's modernity and those features of his work that distinguish him *as a writer* lie not in his current resistance to conventional sentiments but in his strategies of fictional attack. The erotic yearnings and inhibitions that give rise to Malamud's fiction or, for that matter, Bellow's and Singer's, have been turned by Roth into the very topics of his investigation. In *Portnoy's Complaint* (1969), hard-core fantasies and textbook explanations frantically leapfrog each other as Alex Portnoy the interpreter exerts himself to keep up with Portnoy the patient, whose story he is trying to pin down. Since *Portnoy,* the thrust of Roth's serious books has been inward, toward the center of conflict itself, in an effort to sort out the elements of the deadlock that stymies all his characters. Here is a career that, with the aid of psychoanalysis, bears some resemblance to a case history: first the symptomatic books, then the diagnostic ones. As I argued in an earlier essay on Roth's fiction *(Partisan Review,* 1974):

> The early books . . . with their repressed and driven characters, constitute a fiction of failed renunciation. Their heroes are all characters who repress desires that, as we might expect, refuse to go away and keep returning in the form of compulsive and irrational behavior. In *Letting Go,* the mutual renunciation of Gabe Wallach and Libby Herz (based on their mutual reading of *A Portrait of a Lady*) is prelude to six hundred pages of indecision (his), neurasthenia (hers), confusion, and sudden, irrational tantrums (theirs). In *When She Was Good,* the praise accorded to Willard Nelson in the very opening sentence tells us exactly what is wrong with him. "Not to be rich, not to be famous, not to be mighty, not even to be happy, but to be civilized—that was the dream of his life."

Portnoy's Complaint, which appeared two years after *When She Was Good* (and, indeed, began to appear serially the very same year), is a complete turnabout, a "breakthrough" novel in which psychoanalysis makes its debut as both narrative setting and source of interpretations; and emotions that had formerly been held in check or isolated as symptoms are brought forward and given voice. It is a spectacularly Freudian novel, a no-holds-barred confession of masturbation, filial impiety, failure in love, taboo violations of every minor sort (Jewish literary rebels commit only victimless crimes), and the presentation of guilt as the slapstick of the superego. Its winning blend of cultural rebellion, raunchy humor, boyish hijinks, and textbook psychoanalysis was sufficient to gain Roth a mass audience and a movie contract, but not the universal approbation of either literary critics or Jewish parents, who peered uneasily past the spirited antics to the free-wheeling aggression beneath. But what saved the book from mere petulance were the seriousness of the research into troubled emotions, the apparent candor of the confessions (in which certain critics and Jewish "leaders" were quick to spot the "Jewish self-hatred"), a documentary intelligence that took copious notes on Jewish culture while taking shots at its representatives, and an ambiguous tone that stood somewhere between *ressentiment* and comedy, aggravation and surrender. Roth's agitated equipoise spoke for a capacity to withdraw from his emotions at the point of greatest angst and to have fun with shame, sexual confusion, and a hopeless bondage to childhood, even while performing a frantic exorcism.

In the books since *Portnoy,* the elements of breakthrough and liberation have been either played up or attenuated, but always, at some point, in focus: *Our Gang* (1971), a malicious and overwrought satire on Richard Nixon and his White House mafia; *The Breast* (1972), a Kafkaesque parable on entrapment in which an English professor turns into a giant female breast and learns to "adjust"; *The Great American Novel* (1973), a long, free-associative routine on the subject of baseball and anti-Communism, which is alternately dull and hilarious; *My Life as a Man,* Roth's most ambitious book after *Letting Go* and a bitter summary of the theme of female power and male submission that has haunted his books from the beginning; and *The Professor of Desire* (1977), a celebration of erotic and emotional recovery—in brief, a novel of convalescence. Roth has also published his collected essays on literature and culture in *Reading Myself and Others* (1975), which show him to be a canny interpreter of the intricate emotional dynamics of modern lives and Jewish novels, his own included.

Though Roth is our leading psychological novelist, there is really nothing new in his way of bringing psychoanalysis into the fictional medium, except the relentlessness with which he has pursued his libidinal mysteries from *Portnoy's Complaint* through *The Breast* and *My Life as a Man.* For these books are also conventional novels, and the conception of narrator as patient is not just a way of gaining access to remote corners of the will but also a way of employing flashbacks, digressions, and epiphanies to get around the constraints of the well-made plot without floating off into the sea of experimental fiction. Most important is the effect of the psychoanalytic setting on Roth's language, giving him, as Solotaroff has put it, "the freedom and energy of language to sluice out the material: the natural internal monologue of comedy and pain in which the id speaks to the ego and vice-versa, while the superego goes on with its kibbitzing." To think of Roth is to call to mind distinctive strategies of approach and delivery: a voice that is knowing, desperate, witty, and aggressive, and a capacity for listening to the world and mimicking its language. The memorable features of *Portnoy,* when the *Kulturkampf* has been assimilated and the jokes, accusations, and "points" have grown hazy, are its timbre, pace, and rhythm, its tone of controlled hysteria, its resources of humor, and the clarity of its impressions. And what remains fresh in "Goodbye Columbus," long after the adolescent love story has lost its grip, is the rhetoric. Recall the dead-hour lament of Leo Patimkin, Brenda's penurious uncle, who had married badly and then failed, as a traveling lightbulb salesman, to get in on the general rush to the suburbs: "Look at me . . . I sell a good bulb. You can't get the kind of bulb I sell in the drugstores. It's a quality bulb. But I'm the little guy. I don't even own a car. His brother, and I don't even own an automobile. I take a train wherever I go. I'm the only guy I know who wears out three pairs of rubbers every winter. Most guys get new ones when they lose the old ones. I wear them out, like shoes. Look . . . I could sell a crappy bulb, it wouldn't break my heart. But it's not good business." It is not so far from the sodden intimacies of Leo Patimkin, whose instinct for comedy is submerged beneath his self-pity, to those desperate monologues of Alex Portnoy, in which the humor has worked itself free of pathos and claimed its own voice.

In both cases an entire culture is summoned to the bar of one man's torments. Indeed, Leo Patimkin, Alex Portnoy, David Alan Kepesh (*The Breast* and *The Professor of Desire*), Nathan Zuckerman, and Peter Tarnopol are all, as they see it, victims of circumstance, and their complaints are rich in circumstantial evidence. The documentary texture of Roth's books seems like a marshaling of evidence in the preparation of a case—against mothers or wives or the fifties or, at the point of deepest analytic penetration, against the heroes themselves. Roth and his stand-ins are always alert for signs of contradiction, incongruity, and distorted emphasis that indicate hidden motives or crimes. Such habits of listening are common to psychoanalysts and lawyers alike, who are obliged to listen hard and get it right, but they also belong to comedians, for whom frustration, conflict, and the pitched battle of the emotions yield, not pathos, but material. If the early Roth was especially attentive to *Civilization and Its Discontents,* the later has taken his cues from Freud's *Jokes and Their Relation to the Unconscious.*

The situations that arise out of unrelenting interior conflict, in or outside of savage marital strife, may be comical or grim, but at their most interesting are comically grim. When the superego relents and the call for judgment backs off a few notches, anything is grist for the comic mill, and the worse the predicament the better the joke. Recall Alex Portnoy's fantasy of disaster after failing with Bubbles Girardi and then ejaculating in his own eye, thereby, as he imagines it, blinding himself for life: " 'Tap, tap, tap, it's just me, Mother—this nice big dog brought me home, with my cane.' 'A *dog*? In my house? Get him out of here before he makes everything filthy! Jack, there's a dog in the house and I just washed the kitchen floor!' 'But, Momma, he's here to stay, he has to stay—he's a seeing-eye dog. I'm blind.' 'Oh my God! Jack!' she calls into the bathroom. 'Jack, Alex is home with a dog—he's gone blind!' 'Him, blind?' my father replies, 'How could he be blind, he doesn't even know what it means to turn off a light.' "

This is as funny as it is outrageous; everything is tossed into the comic pot: a mother's fastidiousness, a father's chronic distress over his bills and his bowels, and an inept son's genius for imagining the worst. Yet these jokes are also the only known instances, at least in fiction, of stand-up patter being delivered from a couch, to an audience that is not rolling in the aisles but listening with the third ear and patiently taking notes. For this humor has welled up from the deepest regions of the unconscious and comes wrapped in all the primal terror that attends desperate joking. Roth's comedy often sounds like this, poised between calamity and absurdity. But then, following Freud on such matters, Roth is no longer inclined to render unto comedy that which belongs to comedy or unto sobriety that which belongs to sobriety, and has concocted instead a chilling humor, whose deeper purposes are ambiguous but whose technical ingenuity is sometimes spectacular. He is a master of spinning a joke out relentlessly until he has laid bare its infantile factors.

Much of Roth's effort since *Portnoy's Complaint* has been given to finding common ground between the ironic and the driven parts of himself, and the difficulty of striking such emotional balances is surely one reason that it took him some seven painful years to write *My Life as a Man*. That is as long as Joyce needed to write *Ulysses*, although Roth periodically took time out for forays into extravagant satire and comedy, such as *Our Gang* and *The Great American Novel* and the story "On the Air" (*New American Review*, 1970), as though he could turn out quality handiwork only so long as one foot were pumping away on the comic treadle. *My Life as a Man* is a balancing act in which Roth brings the playfulness and rebelliousness of *Portnoy* to bear upon the grim domestic world of *Letting Go*, not by harmonizing his contradictions into a placid self-acceptance but by keeping them alive and being morose and ironic by turns. In *My Life as a Man*, Roth's attitudes are unstable in ways that ring true to the ear as well as to one's own sense of experience. He seems to round up his conflicting moods and distribute them to different chapters or characters, employing in the novel techniques of irony and "splitting" that are more commonly found on the stage.

If *My Life as a Man* is less available than *Portnoy*, it is because its mixed styles and shifting perspectives reflect a thick infolding of intentions, level upon level, something like overdubbing in the recording of music. But for that reason the book seems to me to strike deeper emotionally than *Portnoy,* whose formulas for the origins of Alex Portnoy's distress come down to a handful of theories from Freud, Otto Fenichel, and other convenient sources, brilliantly applied though they may be. *My Life* seems almost to retreat to the earlier uncertainties of "Goodbye Columbus" and *Letting Go* and to indicate that the truth, if one exists, lies beyond the scope of psychoanalysis in its customary forms. Only these doubts are now held at higher levels, having transcended the provisional certainties of *Portnoy.* The very point of Tarnopol's disagreement with Dr. Spielvogel over the latter's "interpretation" of his unpredictable sexuality is that there are no privileged explanations of authentic mysteries, only points of view. Tarnopol is a character, not a case. Thus Roth, committed as ever to psychoanalysis but disabused of the libidinal commonplaces of *Portnoy,* managed in *My Life as a Man* to free himself to invent the world as he went along and, through the play of perspectives of which psychoanalysis was just one of many, to produce the most richly exploratory and densely textured of all his books.

By contrast, *The Professor of Desire* (1977) is a mopping-up operation, a recapitulation of used themes at reduced levels of urgency. It is a novel of convalescence: David Alan Kepesh (the same as in *The Breast,* but a different man for all that) has experienced the same bleak marital strife and abysmal self-doubt as have Paul Herz of *Letting Go* and Peter Tarnopol. Only Kepesh survives, at least in *this* book, emerging from divorce sufficiently intact to take a chance on love (with plenty of professional support, to be sure) and, *mirabile dictu,* to make a go of it. We know what subsequently happens to him in *The Breast,* though this book has its own upbeat view of things and does not appear to point the way to Kepesh's eventual catastrophe. But Roth does not render recuperation all that convincingly, and the novel turns out to be a fairly uninspired piece of emotion recollected in tranquillity, capped off by a paean in praise of mature love, in this case with the soothing, doting, large-breasted, maternal Claire Ovington, a woman so physically endowed and temperamentally serene that Kepesh himself, with his Kafkaesque nightmares and blockages, can scarcely believe his luck, or make us believe it, for that matter. Kepesh's Jewish imagination, like Roth's, keyed to disaster and prone to be sentimental about failure, has trouble rising to rapture, and never quite clicks into gear with this material. Perhaps this book is a boundary marker for Roth's talents, an indication of what his imagination can*not* encompass, for there does not seem to be enough aggression or despair or irony in Kepesh's predicament to bring into play Roth's full talent, a talent so completely geared to doubt, apprehension, and incipient panic that it appears to be the imaginative equivalent of Georg Simmel's definition of a highly developed culture: a crisis constantly held back.

For Roth, as for Mailer and Bellow, manners are the signs of energies in collision deep within the psyche. Like so much emotional lava, they well up involuntarily from our centers of being and express our most intimate relations to our instinctual lives. Such manners are what an older generation of psychoanalysts called symptoms. And it is here, I think, in this attention to the symptomatic life, that these writers are most profoundly linked as moderns, all being psychoanalytic realists, interpreters of the social life under the glow of the psychic. What they have accomplished collectively without harboring any intention toward teamwork is to invent a writing that harnesses the resources of realism *and* the fiction of manners *and* the psychological novel, and that shuttles between levels of reality, from the social to the repressed, without seeming to violate any intrinsic boundaries. If this writing appears to give priority to the inner world as the primary reality in which significant meanings originate, it is not at the expense of the social life but to its advantage, for under the auspices of the unconscious, the "real" world seems richer, stranger, and more interesting than ever.

Such writing is not definably Jewish in ways that prior generations of Jews would have recognized: its orientations are neither Talmudic nor Yiddishist nor socialist nor messianic. But this psychological realism, drawing energy from therapeutic ideas on the one side and social ones on the other, does represent a stage in the evolution of a brand of urban self-consciousness for which Jewish writers just now are the leading spokesmen, and it traces a line of sensibility that arose in the 1940s in the attempt to bring literary modernism into line with progressive ideas. Yet it is a sensibility that, for all its ideological origins, withholds commitments. The impurity of its origins and the indeterminacy of its allegiances, however, constitute its strength; it is ideally suited to the expression of extremes of thought as well as extremes of doubt, that is, to modern states of informed confusion. Psychologically, this sensibility stands at the boundary between outer and inner worlds, just as it seems, stylistically, to accommodate both realism and interior monologue, as though in acknowledgment that to be both Jewish and modern—in America, at any rate—is to be a bridge between worlds and to be required, above all else, to keep the traffic flowing.

6

Experimental Fiction
Josephine Hendin

POSTWAR experimental fiction may be seen as a search for ways to deal with the violence, brevity, and rigidity of life. It carries to great extremes the themes of combativeness, fragmentariness, coolness, and meaninglessness that are the marks of modern fiction. It may originate in the modernist sense of life as problematic, but unlike the great experimental fiction of the 1920s, it does not lament the brokenness of experience as a sign of the decline of Western civilization. Instead it offers an acceptance of dislocation as a major part of life and perhaps a hope that the displacement of traditional ideals might permit new ways of dealing with the human situation.

The postwar experimental writer tries to see man differently. The modernist experimental hero was shaped by the humanistic ethos—political, religious, anthropological, and psychoanalytic—sensitively and succinctly described by Irving Howe in the title essay of *Literary Modernism* (1967). The experimental hero of the postwar period is shaped by the concern with functioning and behavior that spawned and accelerated the growth of ego psychology in the 1940s, 1950s, and 1960s, and is characteristic of an age of increasing technological sophistication. Only a few experimental writers use explicitly technological imagery to describe people; only the most extreme prefer the assembly line and the computer to organic images for the processes of birth and thought. In only the most radical experimenters is the mind equated with the cyberneticist's feedback mechanism, responding to changing external conditions. But virtually all experimental fiction is concerned with the mechanism and conduct of the individual's

240

mind and life, with the search for a different adaptation, an angle of vision, a mode of feeling or behavior which will alter the protagonist's condition.

Innovative in neither style nor form, postwar experimental fiction uses modernist or standard literary devices to conduct its own experiments with human subjects. For example, the great experimental writers of the modernist period, influenced by Freud and Jung, were fascinated by the subconscious forces that motivated behavior. They used the stream-of-consciousness style to reproduce the actions of memory, to expose the connective tissue of human life, binding generations and binding man to his own past, and to show the repetitive, archetypal unity of character beneath the swarm of impressions that flicker across the mind. Postwar fiction exploits the phenomenological aspect of the stream-of-consciousness style, using it to capture a variety of images and impressions without locating those impressions in a character stabilized by the forces of memory and attachment. The stream-of-consciousness style, for the postwar experimental writer, is used to express discontinuity.

Experimental man's life is ruled by fragmentation of personality. John Barth, for example, parodies Sartre's idea that man can create himself and is the sum of his choices by satirizing personality as a set of movable blocks and momentary structures. He adopts a vision of man as an actor in search of the right role. For Kurt Vonnegut, character may be a physiological accident. As he puts it, "We don't care about your childhood. Tell us about your blood chemistry." Through maximizing emotional disconnection from himself, the character may hope to distance himself from a legacy of pain. In many experimental novels, character and emotion are consciously and self-consciously cut up or manipulated to distance the hero from fear, anger or despair.

In the manipulations of experimental fiction, literary devices frequently serve as psychological defenses. Fragmentation of character and narrative often serve as devices for allaying anxiety. By disassembling the jigsaw puzzle of values, mores, and personality, a character can take refuge from the whole picture in its parts. Donald Barthelme's remark "only trust the fragments," and Thomas Pynchon's advocacy of the "forcible dislocation of self" reflect the use of fragmentation and alienation as defenses against painful confrontations. The character who can change roles at will, who has minimal memory of or attachment to his past, his nation, or others emerges in many novels not as an antihero but as a wry "ideal," a shock-resistant man.

Experimental fiction uses standard literary devices to achieve unconventional effects. Irony has become the dominant comic style. Irony yokes unlike things and by force of the tension between truths, or between what is true and what is not, both mirrors and organizes conflict, undercutting the emotional impact of each term of its equations. In effect, it makes contradiction a part of perception. Paradox, which may be the dominant intellectual style of much postwar fiction, can also be a technique for giving opposites equal weight. In the experimental novel such techniques are used to challenge traditional distinctions between weakness and strength, good and evil, truth and falsehood, the victim and his oppressor. Parody may help a novelist and his characters contain, control, and organize emotions or situations. Pastiche may express a sense of the interchangeability of experience.

Although the concerns of experimental fiction receive a distinctive elaboration in American fiction, they are not limited to the United States. The work of the South Americans Jorge Luis Borges and Gabriel Garcia Marquez, of Robert Musil in Germany, of Anthony Burgess and the concrete movement in England, and of the *nouvelle vague* and the *roman nouveau* in France—to name only a few experimental writers or movements—suggests that the concerns of experimental fiction are worldwide in scope and significance. Nor can our own writers be considered the most extreme reporters of personal crisis. Alain Robbe-Grillet, for example, in "A Future for the Novel" (1965) rejects what he calls "the world of depth signification." Susan Sontag's *Against Interpretation,* while drawing on a similar, phenomenological vision of art, is careful not to rule out subjective reactions or human emotions as significant.

Experimental writing in America is colored by social and cultural factors. The novelist's perception of human relations as power relations, his fascination with the survival of the individual, not only has obvious links to our past literature, but also mirrors the intellectual concerns of the postwar period. The great expansion of sociology in the 1950s and 1960s illustrates our interest in devising operational explanations for how people live with each other. Our economy also helped shape experimental heroes and heroines. Just as the expansion of industry after the Civil War spurred the creation of the financiers and businessmen who once filled our literature, so the emergence of an enormous middle-class after World War II helped shift the drama in fiction from the quest for great wealth or the plight of the very poor to the emotions of the middle class and its dropouts in a time of relative affluence. With few notable exceptions, our literature is marked by the sense of personal crisis that may be distinctive of a culture in which increasing consolidation of economic power and estrangement from political process throw the individual back upon himself. The drama of power and vulnerability, once played out in our literature on a social and economic stage, fills the arena of personal relations.

It is impossible to know for sure whether or not the experimental writer intends to provide a mirror of personal crisis and defenses against it. What we can know for sure is that his texts exist and contain as situations, as themes, as represented emotions, explorations of the problematic and its alternatives. The unconventionality or darkness of experimental fiction has led some to condemn it as nihilistic or despairing. Yet to do so may be to miss the significance of such attitudes in the text and in the novelist's attempt to describe and integrate experience.

In the best experimental fiction even nihilism can have a raison d'être, providing, in the Aristotelian sense, catharsis. Pessimism may serve a moral purpose as an indictment of an undesirable status quo, or it may have a protective function as a defense against unrealistic hopes. What may seem to the casual observer to be only negativism may be, on closer inspection of the text, part of the novelist's attempt to achieve unconventional effects. Experimental fiction admittedly leaves out much of the joy and nobility which exist in the real world, but all art involves exclusion; no single work of art tells the whole truth about all experience. Experimental fiction exaggerates, dramatizes, and probes the problematic. It provides a vision of people under pressure, of desperate measures, of sometimes horrendous solutions, of necessary attempts.

This essay is critical and interpretive rather than structural or formalistic in approach. It aims to suggest the variety of experimental perspectives, to focus on the writer's attempt to reinterpret our relation to ourselves and each other, and to elucidate the many adaptive and maladaptive attempts of the novelist and his characters to deal with experience. Writers who would not usually be considered experimental, such as Norman Mailer or J. D. Salinger, are included to illustrate the development of experimental themes or to sharpen our understanding of them. The discussion of novels by theme is not an attempt at classification, but a means of focusing attention.

Experimental fiction reflects a persistent process of personalization. Aggression, as an emotion and as a theme, beginning in the late 1940s with descriptions of violence in war, developed in the postwar period into a literature of emotional combat, of drug addiction, sexual humiliation, and crime that has affected even our traditional writers.

Passivity, once the mark of the antihero's victimization, emerges in experimental fiction as a coping device. Aestheticism, once the refuge of the artist who might declare with Villier de L'Isle D'Adam, "Living? Let the servants do it for us!" has been altered by a sense of the inescapability of personal turmoil. Surreal novels and cerebral ones whose images are drawn from technology and science offer a behavioristic vision of people struggling to express and control their vulnerabilities.

There is, of course, a wide range of literary merit among the writers discussed. From a new writer of the first magnitude like Thomas Pynchon to the excellence of John Barth, John Updike, or Flannery O'Connor, through the talented and competent novelists who form the majority of those discussed, to eccentrics like William Burroughs, who, despite the excitement of his style, remains unreadable to all but the most determined, the spectrum of talents and abilities is full. Given the determined quirkiness of experimental fiction, I have chosen to eschew the usual literary comparisons and judgments and to let each writer speak as an individual voice for the experimental spirit.

At the core of the postwar experimental novel is a vision of all relations as power relations. Where the novels of the 1930s frequently saw people as victims of the depression or of economic exploitation, the postwar novel sees people caught up in a psychological drama of power and vulnerability. The dénouement of this drama will determine not merely financial security but, more significantly, a sense of self-worth.

Fascination with aggression and submission is a legacy of World War II. Norman Mailer's brilliant *The Naked and the Dead* (1948) dealt with the fight, in World War II, for an imaginary Pacific island, Anopopei. Using the traditional framework of the naturalist novel, he wrote of jungle warfare in terms of the Darwinian fight for survival, virtually depoliticizing the war between the Japanese and Americans to personal issues of ambition, appetite, and individual strength. Mailer explodes political issues by returning war to issues of need.

General Cummings, who heads the American forces on Anopopei, judges the worth of a man by the swiftness with which he translates his anger into an act. Cummings believes the war will not be won by anything but the swiftness with which the enlisted man translates his hatred of his own officers into murderous rage toward the enemy. As he tells his soft-hearted orderly, Hearn, "If you're holding a gun and you shoot a defenseless man, then you're a poor creature, a dastardly person. That's a perfectly ridiculous idea, you realize. The fact that you're holding a gun and the other man is not is no accident. It's a product of everything you've achieved; it assumes that if you're aware enough, you have the gun when you need it." The drama of the novel comes from the indecision over seizing or using power experienced by Lieutenant Hearn, the Harvard man who is uncomfortable with his own aggression and who argues that the war will be won by the persistence of ethical ideas.

War is the metaphor for the world as combat. In *The Naked and the Dead* the fight between the protofascist and the liberal, the man at ease with his aggression and the one driven and drawn by his sympathies, seems fixed. Hearn falls victim to his illusions about himself as, incurring Cummings's anger, he is sent to head a platoon on a mission with minimal chance of success. He finds in leading his platoon a sense of the joy of command, remaining oblivious to the resentment and malice of the sergeant who has previously led the platoon, whom he now outranks, and who arranges to get Hearn killed to restore his own command.

Mailer personalizes large-scale violence, putting it in the perspective of distorted human appetites. The purpose of Mailer's strong men is "to achieve God." "When we come kicking into the world we are God, the universe is the limit of our senses. And when we get older, when we discover that the universe is not us, it's the deepest trauma of our existence." Mailer's aggressive men kill to repair the trauma of their own vulnerability, their own sense of smallness. Crofts, the instrument of Hearn's death learned a crucial lesson as a boy in Texas when, hesitating to shoot a deer he had tracked, his father shot it first, claimed it, and jeered at him. The man who hesitates is humiliated.

The postwar experimental novel has an acute sense of cruelty and powerlessness as flip sides of the perception of all relations as power relations. This vision would be explored by the traditional writer James Gould Cozzens in *Guard of Honor* (1948) in terms of the code of career officers confronting enlistees who do not share their values; by James Jones in *From Here to Eternity* (1951) in terms of the stratification of the regular army that helps crush sensitive men; and by Joseph Heller in comic terms in *Catch-22* (1961). There all power and all evil are external. The villain is the army, which tries to close all escapes with red tape; Heller's hero, Yossarian, is the man who tries to open them up.

The largest impact of the perception of all relations as power relations is felt outside of war novels, in the internalization of violence and impotence that has become pervasive in recent fiction. In Malcolm Lowry's *Under the Volcano* (1947), one man's alcoholism and stupefaction are made to stand for the impact of fascism on the individual mind. In Nelson Algren's *The Man with the Golden Arm* (1949), the sense of social oppression and humiliation is imprinted in the life of a junkie. Where the novel of oppression in America used to tell the story of social injustice, the postwar experimental novel increasingly speaks of individual men attempting to cope with the violence around them and in themselves.

War as a state of mind, as a constant craving for power, encouraged a literature based on a sense of male combativeness and carrying into peacetime the vision of power relations as a matter of life and death. This literature of disgust caught both the aggression and humiliation of life and the attempt to escape them through narcotics. William Burroughs wrote in *Junkie* (1953), "Junk is not a kick, it is a way of life." The relation between addict and pusher could be used as a model of all relations, the dependent man and the controlling one each completing the other. The body, not the nation, was the arena for a power play resolved only through the sensation of peace produced by heroin.

Originating in the widespread use of painkillers in the war, addiction was a new theme in American fiction. The addict, emerging in Nelson Algren's *The Man with the Golden Arm,* and in William Burroughs's experimental novels, was a new figure in literature, an oppressed character who was a social victim and who also oppressed himself by his need for heroin; a sufferer who took the drug to take the edge off his own violence. Unlike the novel of the depressed 1930s, the postwar novel of the oppressed explored the violence of the *victim,* virtually doing away with the "noble sufferer," his ancestor as a heroic type. Because the body was the arena of the power play between addict and pusher, what protest existed in such novels was predominantly interior, chaotic, reflecting the disorder in an individual mind more than the disorder of society.

William Burroughs's cut-up or fold-in method (take a page or tape, cut it into pieces, and paste or splice together in any order except the original one) is meant to blur the lines between personality, society, and politics. In Burroughs's novels the enemy is one's own needs and emotions externalized as the other guy, the system that inflames self-hatred, the world that exerts power over how one feels about oneself. In *Naked Lunch* (1959) Burroughs politicized heroin addiction as the mold of all addictions—of governments to power, of men to cruelty. In his later novels sex was the model for every kind of con-

246

flict or degradation. Passion comes from demon bacteria, "virus powers," who tempt strange, homosexual men with "Johnny Yen," "the boy-girl god of sexual frustration from the terminal sewers of Venus." His characters tell of beautiful boys who turn into monsters, of lust leading to degradation, of men being violated by men who are not even people, but mutants whose "penis had absorbed the body," leaving only "vestigial arms and legs."

Naked Lunch, Soft Machine (1966), and *The Ticket That Exploded* (1967) are filled with people locked destructively together. Lovers are spliced in a parasitic bond. In *Nova Express* (1964) the universe is this principle of devouring appetites. Two astral bodies are typical. Mr. Bradley and Mr. Martin are stars, locked together by gravitational forces. Mr. Bradley, a small dense blue star, pulls fuel from Mr. Martin, a large red one, and grows brighter while Mr. Martin is diminished. "First it's symbiosis, then parasitism," comments Burroughs on love. In *Nova Express* wars of sex and politics are waged in outer space. In *Soft Machine* they occur in the ancient past: a Mayan peasant is so bitterly used by a high priest that the tyranny of office reverberates with sexual cruelty. But the intercourse of stars or the degradation of a Mayan are more than parables for love or tyranny. Events like these reflect the process by which Burroughs's characters disown what happens to them, where it happens, and what they feel. In the recesses of hallucination they symbolize their rage away, move out into space or back in time, but always away from their own fury.

But Burroughs's people cannot fully escape their own violence. Hatred and self-hatred loom large in Burroughs's many images of homosexual lovers who know that "murder is never out of his eyes when he looks at me" and "murder is never out of my eyes when I look at him." In *Wild Boys* (1971) Burroughs himself emerges in his "Venusian" hates, no longer the victim but the master of those "virus-gods" that infect people with the love-and-need disease. Burroughs is unmistakable as the Mayan superpriest, "The Incomparable Yellow Serpent" who is a demon artist. He controls everyone by "singing the pictures" that fill their minds and patterns their actions. He "shifts from AC to DC as a thin siren wail breaks from his lips. Pictures crash and leap from his eyes blasting everyone to smoldering fragments. DEATH, DEATH, DEATH. When comes such another singer?" demands Burroughs.

The images that spring from the pages of Burroughs's novels are clearly meant to kill. Burroughs has always written of life as controlled by self-images, by "sets" of behavior programed or taped into consciousness. But he has usually not written from the point of view of the filmmaker. *Wild Boys* is clearly meant to be a movie of the wild mind of Burroughs, "Billy B. St. Louis Encephalitis," who records the "1920 St. Louis boyhood of Audrey," whom everyone humiliated because he "looked like a homosexual sheep-killing dog," and who went to "kindergartens like mental homes." In fantasy films of the future, wild boys vindicate Audrey by erasing the word *mother* from the blackboard. More than cinematic in style, the novel works toward a statement of life as movie, of people as moviegoers—the spectators of their own lives—and of both life and film as products of Maya, the force of illusion that shapes all visible forms.

Burroughs's heroes are "wild boys," "a whole generation . . . that felt neither pleasure or pain." Wild boys live in an emotional nowhere with no "emotions oxygen." They have no memory because they have no past—some of them are born through a process of replication in which they spring full-grown from another man, vibrate into life, and immediately begin having anal intercourse with their creator without desire or loathing. In these surreal scenes Burroughs tries to purge all the old self-images from memory, all the hates that fester in his characters' minds. In Burroughs's filmland memory and emotion can be exploded away. When one man begins to remember "the pawn shops, the cheap rooming houses, the chili parlors," he detonates a "film grenade" and "explodes the set." The "boys" end the novel by wishing the world dead and then watch the screen explode in moon craters and boiling silver spots. They see "dim jerky stars blowing away across the empty sky." Having turned the world to ashes, "wild boys smile."

Writing in *The Nation* in 1964, Alexander Trocchi remarked, "There is no more systematic nihilism than that of the junkie in America." In the novel, the world of the addicted, the pill popper, the barbiturate abuser, where men live by the law of the junkie jungle—steal from him before he steals from you—is a continuing metaphor for the bitterest possible version of the American drama of power and vulnerability. In the 1950s Burroughs's fiction produced the shock it was intended to produce, becoming the subject of censorship hearings and clearly meant to appeal to the underground avant-garde of the time. But the sense of rage of those at the bottom apparently spread.

In Robert Stone's *Dog Soldiers* (1974), Converse, a journalist for a pornographic newspaper in California, wants to write about a pure subject. He goes to Vietnam in search of one, but finds the only pure thing there is heroin. Hicks, a career Marine turned pusher, perceives the army and the police in America as part of the same corruption. As he lies dying in an American desert, his heroin having been stolen by a policeman who shot him so he could sell the heroin himself, Hicks thinks: "You know what's out there? Every goddam race of shit jerking each other off. Mom and Dad and Buddy and Sis, two hundred million rat-hearted cocksuckers in enormous cars. Rabbits and fish. They're mean and stupid and greedy. They'll fuck you for laughs. They want you dead. If you're no better than them, you might as well take gas. If you can't get your own off them, then don't stand there and let them spit on you, don't give them the satisfaction." Heroin is the symbol of a corrupt society; it is peace, currency, and poison. It stands for American destructiveness, greed, and vulnerability.

Stone's renegades are mirror images of the system they hate. They are out to outdo the system at its own game, however outmatched they may be. Their goal is not change, but exploitation and vindictiveness. In *A Hall of Mirrors* (1966) Stone offers a vision of America cast in the mold of southern boss politics. Rheinhardt, the hero, is a musician who unaccountably gives up a promising life as a concert clarinetist playing the music he loves to drink and drift. As a musician, while playing Mozart he felt like God, but his need to feel omnipotent is a trait Stone both attacks and admires. America shapes dropouts, in this novel, in its image. Rheinhardt runs from ambition but not from his need for power. He runs from the competitions he cares about, and is successful in, to become an announcer for a racist radio station. He does not escape his need to be on top; he only helps crush other people fighting for life.

Having spent all his money during an alcoholic binge, Rheinhardt is glad to be the announcer who fulfills his boss's desire for a pattern in the news which reveals the work of the red menace, the rising discontent of blacks, and the danger caused by Yankee liberals. Your bosses are "sub-human cruds," remarks one of Rhinehardt's neighbors. "You talk like an extremist," Reinhardt said. "You're not seeing the Big Picture. Speaking as a broadcaster it's my opinion that there is a deep confusion in the popular heart and mind. The pop heart and mind demand assurance. Unusual times demand unusual hustles. The explanation number is very big. My conscience is clear," Rheinhardt said, "it's bone dry."

Rheinhardt is rude to a civil rights activist whose own vulnerability has brought him nervous breakdowns in the past and who feels a close kinship to the suffering of blacks. Stone seems to imply that people are destroyed by the sufferers of the earth; they cannot change injustice, all they do is magnify their own pain. Rheinhardt's goal is invulnerability. His drinking and pot smoking bolster a personality already striving to feel nothing. It is his quality of being above caring that make him attractive to those who have suffered. His lover is Geraldine, a pretty girl from Appalachia who has lost her husband through violence and her baby to poverty and disease. Her face was scarred in a barroom by a man who did not like something she said. She adores Rheinhardt. "You're so wild and you don't have nothin' to do with anythin' . . . I need you, love, I really do." Rheinhardt, who is determined not to get too involved with this woman he lives with, says, "You must be out of your mind. I don't say things like that to you, why do you say them to me? Man that's an obscenity—if somebody ever tells you Geraldine, that they need you you tell them to buy a dog."

People who need, who care, do not survive in Stone's America. The novel's climax is a giant rally sponsored by the local political boss and rigged to turn into a race riot which will arouse positive sentiment for his repressive programs against the interests of poor blacks. By the time it erupts, Rheinhardt is so stoned all he can think about is the wonderful greenness of the grass on which people are about to be trampled to death. Called upon to quiet the mob, he speaks from the podium: "Americans, our shoulders are broad and sweaty but our breath is sweet. When your American soldier fighting today drops a Napalm bomb on a cluster of gibbering chinks it's a bomb with a heart. In the heart of that bomb, mysteriously but truly present, is a fat old lady on her way to see the World's Fair. This lady's innocence if fully unleashed could defoliate every forest in the torrid zone. This lady is a whip to niggers." The riot goes on; the civil rights activist is about to get blown up. Geraldine, also stoned, tries to make her way to Rheinhardt, but cannot. She is arrested by two policemen who see she is stoned and, finding a gun in her bag, send her to jail, where she hangs herself.

"No help" is Rheinhardt's lament for Geraldine's death. Although he is more moved than he wants to be by her suicide, he says over and over, "I'm alive, baby. It was you who died. Not me. I don't need you. How could you think that. You know . . . I mean . . . it was no great passion, Geraldine. It's me that is going to have the next drink not you. That's what No Help means. Once more . . . One more time. I'm a survivor. I love you baby—no help."

In Stone's novels, drugs are the metaphor for the corruption of the system, the individual's need for release from his own aggression, and his fear of intimacy. The unequivocal equation in Burroughs's novels of heroin with subjugation—the use of the drug which symbolizes total dependency—is underlined by his use of characters who remain on the bottom of the social ladder. In contrast, Stone's middle-class heroes have fragmented their dependency on drugs. They take a variety of barbiturates and use heroin when it is available or, like Rheinhardt, go from alcohol to marijuana. They also have other options, moving more freely through the establishment world. Rheinhardt's best friend, a phony preacher, makes money on the Bible circuit and gets rich on "the religious hustle," while Rheinhardt makes money by doing his racist radio show. The incorporation of drugs into the modes of social exploitation in these novels of the early sixties and seventies is one sign of the internalization of social despair. The nihilism once characteristic of underground fiction concerned with drugs has begun to appear in novels dealing with middle-class life in mainstream America. The soft addictions (alcoholism, marijuana, barbiturates) reflect an effort to withstand the anger stirred up in a world where people are seen only as winners or losers.

Tom Wolfe's remarkable work of imaginative reportage, *The Electric Kool-Aid Acid Test* (1968), dealing with novelist Ken Kesey's acid commune, was also a documentary of the will to believe that happiness was converting experience into a series of wonderful, dissolving images. In such experiences one could break the determinisms of personality and involvement. This effort in the sixties reflects the determination to play out the drama of power relations as chaotic theater, in Rashomon scenarios where it is scarcely decipherable whether the hero is a victim or an aggressor. Kesey, in Wolfe's book, rules over his group, called "The Merry Pranksters," dispensing LSD as he sees fit. What anger the Pranksters have toward society is expressed theatrically through outraging the world of "Mom and Dad and Buddy and Sis."

Drug literature, from the heroin novel of the 1950s to today's novels, reflects an attempt to resolve the anger and pain inherent in the vision of life as a power struggle. Drugs may be used to take the edge off violence and humiliation (Burroughs); drugs may be a wedge against the hero's caring about anyone but himself, or a buffer against intimacy (Stone). Politicized in the tribal quality of the commune, they may define a way of life. But they are, of course, only one way of dealing with experience.

The experimental richness of postwar fiction lies in the variety of adaptive devices used to minimize feelings of violence, humiliation, and vulnerability. A primary defense against perceiving oneself as a victim is not to put the pieces of experience together, to fragment

251

feeling and act, reality and perception, so that there is no possibility of seeing anything whole. Where the modernist writer saw brokenness as a mark of the fall from tradition and order, the postwar novelist employs it as a switch to turn off pain, a way of returning to the innocence of an unfinished canvas. The hero, like the schizophrenic wise men in R. D. Laing's psychology, can be self-consciously refusing to connect the pieces of his personality.

Been Down So Long It Looks like Up to Me (1966), by Richard Fariña, a talented jazz musician who was killed at the age of twenty in a motorcycle accident, playfully offers a hero who is determined to be invulnerable. He boasts that he has no "valency," no connection to anyone. Bonding is chemical bonding for the man who takes so much opium he has to carry around an enema bag, who prefers to "bang" women rather than know them and arrives in "Corinth," a college town, after a trip west in search of hash and wisdom from an Indian shaman. In his detachment, presumably, lies his extraordinary belief in his own innocence. His name is Gnossos but he calls himself Pooh Bear, and his best friend Heffalump, names out of A. A. Milne's children's stories. When these two swipe nativity groups one Christmas, they proceed to dump two Christ children down a gorge and lose the head of the Virgin Mary in the street. Are suffering and vulnerability out, or are idealizable women gone? In this new kind of innocence, violence does not count because it occurs when people are "high" and detached.

Novels of aggression are increasingly also novels of social detachment. Where Tom Wolfe's nonfiction novel described the social hostility of the Merry Pranksters as an LSD joke, Truman Capote's sober *In Cold Blood* (1965) explored such hostility in the wider context of the hidden conflicts in the American heartland. Dealing with the murder by two drifters of a family in the Plains town of Holcomb, Kansas, *In Cold Blood* explored violence in terms of the pathology of a single downtrodden, crushed, and damaged outcast who murdered not for profit or even for fun, but because of his extraordinary self-absorption. Perry Smith, who inflicts the first wounds, is aware only of the pain in his crippled legs as he kills, a pain which stands for all his psychic wounds and which he scarcely relieves in the act of murder. Social injustice, of which his childhood and life could be an example, is narrowed to the power play in progress in his mind, his dim sense that to avoid remaining a cripple he must become a fury.

The brief popularity of the "nonfiction novel" may be due to our fascination with the self-absorption of people who act out, as theater or as violence, the aggressive dramas in their own minds and who perceive their victims as spectators or assistants. Norman Mailer's *The Armies of the Night* (1968), while about a significant social event, the Pentagon March of 1967, nevertheless was most concerned with the theatrical elements of the protest, the pot-smoking audience, the mystics who tried to levitate the Pentagon, the sheer mass of people who turned the march, for Mailer, into a circus or a football game in which he could make his "linebacker's run" to get arrested by the police. The nonfiction novel reflects the extent to which we may externalize ourselves, becoming moviegoers to ourselves or to the political drama of power and vulnerability.

The growing sense of virtually all relations as power relations has touched novelists with traditional concerns. Joyce Carol Oates uses ideas associated with naturalism—the determinisms of heredity and environment—to achieve a new purpose: to show the breakdown of social and psychological continuity. Violence in her novels is accepted, legitimized, and even idealized. *Them* (1969) deals with aggression as the result of prolonged frustration and powerlessness. In this novel, which climaxes with the Detroit riots of 1967, Oates describes the conflict between social classes as a conflict of generations. Loretta and Howard are children of the working poor, unable to achieve their parents' idealized goal of lower-middle-class stability. But they accept their lot, Howard immersing himself in alcohol and taking his failure out on his wife, and Loretta accepting her husband's brutality for what it is and going on to other men.

What happens to their offspring? Their children do not perpetuate such passivity or acceptance of failure. Their son, Jules, failing, like Howard, to change his life through work, finds an outlet for his bitterness in fascination with social protest and violence. He is adopted by radical university professors and becomes a kind of hero because of his bitterness. His sister, Maureen, lacks her mother's sensuality but learns how to use sex for profit. She inveigles a middle-class man into an affair and into leaving his wife and children to marry her, although she has little feeling for him. Maureen and Jules are burnt-out cases who find in the destruction of their capacity for hope and affection the will and determination to force others to notice them. Jules's rhetoric of violence redeems the violence done to him by life; Maureen's guiltless exploitation of her husband ensures, she hopes, that she will not live her mother's life.

John Gardner's major works are traditional in form, but innovative in their concern with the dislocation of men who attempt to be heroic in the old sense in current times. *Nickel Mountain* (1973) and

The Sunlight Dialogues (1972) are pastoral novels which explore the downfall of men who attempt to play the knight-in-armor whose life is service to a lady. They protect their women, but are finally done in by these creatures, who, only appearing helpless, turn out to be wolves in sheep's clothing. Joseph in *Nickel Mountain* marries a girl pregnant with another man's child and loves the child as his own. He finds himself virtually ousted from the modest diner he owns by his wife, who, coming of age, turns out to be an ambitious business-woman. The Sunlight Man marries an ethereal creature who turns out to be capable of violent, insane rages. Devoting his life to her cure, he is rewarded by her setting fire to his office.

Gardner's most experimental novel is *Grendel* (1971), an adaptation of the Beowulf legend told from the monster's point of view. Gardner projects a twentieth-century psychology of the alienated into Anglo-Saxon myth. His Grendel is an amiable nihilist, a literal monster who possesses the gifts and grace of a man but is an outcast wishing he could believe in civilization and order. He tests his belief in change and chaos as the rulers of all things against King Hrothgar's belief in his Hall as a pinnacle of civilization. Laying waste to Hrothgar's Hall, his warriors, and his priests, Grendel nevertheless is always waiting to be converted from his bitterness and his loneliness. And certainly the only relief from loneliness for him is the arm-to-arm combat he has with Hrothgar's men. A meditation, written in spectacular prose, *Grendel* calls into question the unlovability of the hero as killer, negator, and scourge.

The experimental novel is frequently a debate, an argument over the meaning of life, love, good and evil. William Gass's *Omensetter's Luck* (1966) is a densely written meditation on the impact of a man of peace, large of soul and expansive in emotion, on other, "more modern" people. In this novel of the politics of emotion in a small town, Brocket Omensetter drives into Gilian, Ohio, one day in the 1890s with his wife and children. People seem to know instinctively that he has a special relation to the universe. Grace and peace seem to flow through him; he is in harmony with everything and makes most people feel good just to be near him. His goodness arouses the envious hatred of the Reverend Jethro Furber and his landlord, Henry Pimber, whose combined malice foments trouble and finally drives Omensetter out. His fabulous peace, his "luck," deserts him through their intervention. Complacency is restored when Omensetter is gone. The town returns to its normal despair. Gass, a professor of philosophy, has written a novel of crucifixion in terms of small-town America, projecting into a turn-of-the-century situation a modern sense of exile.

Flannery O'Connor took the traditional concerns of southern fiction and exploded them in a new direction. She saw with alarm that the South was becoming less "Southern," was "losing its many faults and few virtues," but she may not have realized that she herself would contribute to the process of change she condemned. Those familiar characters of southern fiction, the one-horse farmer, the outlaw, the itinerant workman, appear in her stories and novels; concern with fundamentalist religion, the distrust of intellect and abstraction Robert Penn Warren sees as a southern trait, and the world of violent contrasts—filled with men doing violence to each other and the land—are there. But O'Connor used them, unlike Faulkner or William Styron, not in the service of the southern myth of the fall, but as gateways to a world without myth. While other southerners sought to expand the dimensions of emotion, O'Connor used convention and tradition to heighten the constriction of her characters.

O'Connor's stories show no revelation of subtle states of mind, no psychological analysis, and no interior monologue. Like one of her characters, O'Connor does not care about the "underhead"; she shows no stream of consciousness but instead simplifies complex feelings and objectifies psychological states.

In "The Life You Save May Be Your Own" (1953), Shiftlet is a one-armed drifter who comes upon a mother and her deaf-mute daughter on an isolated farm. The mother feels she can get him to marry her daughter, Lucynell, and run the farm by offering him her old car to repair and giving him a place to stay. He repairs the car, works on the farm, accepts the money to marry Lucynell, goes off with her in the car and marries her. He abandons her in a roadside restaurant. He does not feel anger toward his mother-in-law or guilt over leaving his defenseless wife in a strange place; instead, he becomes furious at a hitch-hiking boy because the boy ran away from his mother. O'Connor's characters are, in a way, so estranged from emotional life that they feel their emotions do not belong to them. They seem to belong to someone else, a stranger who is nevertheless oddly familiar, a double who in some way recapitulates their own experience.

Writing within an older literary framework of traditional symbols, O'Connor often begins with a symbol which flattens out as the story progresses. In "The River" (1955) Mrs. Connin and the little boy she is caring for go to the river to a healing. The preacher uses the metaphor of baptism as admission to the visible church of Christ. The child, unhappy and neglected by everyone, takes him literally. He goes into the river and "intended to keep on going this time until he found the Kingdom of Christ in the river." What he may find there is his death. The story closes with the preacher's fear that the child has drowned himself, the awareness that his metaphors of Christ's healing river are rooted in literal death.

The crucifixion that is real to O'Connor is the one a freak, misfit, or abandoned child lives out every day. She was a victim of lupus, a degenerative disease that had killed her father in three days and that afflicted her from the time she was twenty-four until her death at thirty-nine. Her stories of the uprooted ("The Displaced Person," 1954), of the crippled ("Good Country People," 1955; "The Lame Shall Enter First," 1962), of the psychically wounded ("Revelation," 1964) may originate in her immediate realization of the physical facts of life as determining and dominating emotional life. The body, weakened by illness, accident, or simply time, is, in her work, a universal symbol of both human limitation and pride. O'Connor's heroes and heroines do not want to be other than they are, do not want to be whole or understood. The mothers, authorities, social workers who try to "help" or who demand they analyze themselves, think about their situation, or accept pity, only render them impotent and furious.

O'Connor's most violent people have been so crushed by life that they suffer passively the world that judged them destructive or "different." O'Connor, daughter of a genteel family who wrote distinctly ungenteel books, knew what it meant to be "different." She covered her anger with politeness and wrote about people who did the same. In "A Good Man Is Hard to Find" (1953), the Misfit, an escaped murderer, enters into a polite conversation with a grandmother, apologizing for not wearing a shirt before a lady, while he has her son, daughter-in-law, and grandchildren murdered one by one. The grandmother, wishing to save herself and absorbed by him, calls him one of her babies, after he speaks of his confusion over whether Christ raised the dead and of his belief that there was no finer woman than his mother. When the grandmother reaches out to console him, he replies by shooting her in the chest. In O'Connor's "Revelation" (1964), Mary Grace tolerates her mother in polite silence as she maligns her daughter to another woman, Mrs. Turpin. Mary Grace grows furious toward Mrs. Turpin, who functions in the story as her mother's double. She hurls a book at Mrs. Turpin, then crumbles, clinging to her mother. Violence toward a stranger lets many "misfits" express their fury and remain detached from its source at the same time.

O'Connor's leveling impulse may be seen as part of the demythologizing effect of postwar fiction. O'Connor created a remarkable art.

She wrote in praise of a hard coolness about the human predicament. She celebrated the emotional coldness that freed her characters from an agony of human needs, ties, and longings. As her hero Parker in "Parker's Back" (1965) tattooed a portrait of Christ on his back so he would not have to come face to face with his own sense of crucifixion, so O'Connor would prevent her people from confronting their own agonizing rage. If they do not find joy in their estrangement from their own feelings, they find an ignorance of themselves that is the closest they will get to happiness. O'Connor took from them memory, the inner life that would have engulfed them in guilt or fear. She helped them to fulfill dreams of revenge or revolt and to live on the surface of life.

The fiction discussed so far helps us understand what a sense of vulnerability means in concrete terms. In much of our fiction it means characters who avoid the threat of humiliation by striving for an unambivalent combativeness they see as a human ideal. The attempt to cope with the emotions stirred up by violence drives other characters to drugs or psychological detachment. The sense of being personally overwhelmed makes many characters see social problems as personal crises resolvable only through a hard and hardening acceptance of life as an experience of force or submission. Novels of aggression may document a process of internalization in which the once large social canvas of the traditional novel is reduced to a mental image in an individual mind, a tableau of private, inner conflict into which the traditional struggle of man with society is compressed. But internalization of conflicts is only one way in which writers have attempted to contain and control aggression as a human fact and a literary subject.

In an experiment in values, some writers have attempted to reduce the trauma of either violence or humiliation by blurring the differences between winners and losers. In this experiment, all evil and all anger are not internalized but externalized. The hero becomes concerned with avoiding rather than confronting what he perceives to be unbeatable situations. In contrast to the novel of aggression, these are novels of passivity.

Kurt Vonnegut, Jr., uses the immense canvas of intergalactic space to magnify the pointlessness of human effort in any direction. In his science fiction novel *The Sirens of Titan* (1959), Salo, a friendly Tralfamadorian "machine," is trapped on a satellite for lack of a part for his spaceship. He cannot continue his mission of delivering a message to every planet in the universe. Through his plight, Vonnegut reveals that the rise and fall of Earth's civilizations was only a factor in a complicated Tralfamadorian plan to bring Salo the part he needs to fix his ship and continue his mission. What is the message he brings? A single dot, which in his language means "Greetings!" Vonnegut's message is that we on earth suffer and strive for the smallest possible point, for nothing. And there is no possibility of altering our fate.

In human terms, Vonnegut's pessimism adds up to a vision of people doomed by a programing they cannot resist or change. In *Cat's Cradle* (1963) Felix Hoenikker, father of the A-bomb, also fathered three unhappy children. He leaves them his last discovery, a chunk of ice-9. Derived by restacking water molecules, an ice-9 chip dropped in water sets up a chain reaction that freezes all the water around it to an ice unmeltable below 114 degrees Fahrenheit. Touched to the lips, it freezes the blood and kills; dropped into the sea, it can end the world. Hoenikker's children split the chunk in three, put their chips in thermos jugs and literally take on their father's destructive bent. They cannot help being stacked for disaster. Angela, the oldest, who mothers the family after their mother dies, is a lonely, forlorn girl who dropped out of school and whose only amusement is playing the clarinet to records; Frank, a mechanical genius, is wanted by the police; Newt, the lovable youngest, is a midget. Ice-9 brings each of them the promise of happiness and power, the chance to trade a death-heritage for happiness. All they want is to be normal. But through their simple desire, the world ends.

Vonnegut makes a mock religion out of pessimism. Bokonon, Hoenikker's black counterpart, tries to save the island of San Lorenzo from poverty and disease but fails to accomplish anything by social reform. He then invents a religion of scaled-down aspirations which is the equivalent of ice-9, conferring emotional coldness. When the world freezes over, Bokonon's step-daughter steps out of her shelter to look for other survivors and finds masses of ice-9 suicides arranged around her father's note explaining that they have died on his advice. Having been summoned to explain the meaning of the frozen seas, he told them, "God is trying to kill you . . . Have the good manners to die." Mona, his step-daughter, burst into "laughter, touched her finger to the ground, straightened up, and touched the finger to her lips and died." All science and religion seem to confer is the ability to suffer and die without caring.

Passivity, acceptance, resignation, and denial are offered as solutions in Vonnegut's novels to the sense of helplessness life engenders. *Slaughterhouse-Five or the Children's Crusade* (1969) deals with the dislocation between one's life and one's feelings through a violent

258

juxtaposition of science fiction and realism. In the Dresden fire-bombing in 1945 Vonnegut and other POWs spent the night in a meatlocker well beneath the earth and survived the firestorm that exploded above them. This real event is Vonnegut's most perfect symbol for the way many of his characters survive by burying themselves.

Billy Pilgrim, the novel's hero, is a POW who has always been a POW; by World War II he is a casualty for the second time. His Great War began in childhood in the YMCA, when his father "told him he would learn to swim by the method of sink or swim." His "father was going to throw Billy into the deep end of the pool and Billy was going to damn well swim. It was like an execution. Billy was numb as his father carried him from the shower room to the pool. His eyes were closed. When he opened his eyes, he was on the bottom of the pool. He lost consciousness, but the music went on. He dimly sensed that somebody was rescuing him. Billy resented that." Billy never gets angry at his father for throwing him in or taking him out. He is one of Vonnegut's many crucifieds who fight brutality by shutting it out of mind, burying themselves at the bottom of the pool, bottom of the earth, bottom of the universe. Billy does not fight back in war; he gets unstuck in time and space and lets his mind float free.

Vonnegut's orchestration of World War II with science fiction flights to Tralfamadore juggles public catastrophe with personal anguish as it develops a working defensive system against pain in all its intensities. What barricade against a city's destruction? When the guards emerge from the meatlocker and see their incinerated city Vonnegut has them draw together "like a silent film of a barbershop quartet." Vonnegut writes them dumb. And dumbness is precisely Vonnegut's solution. Like Bokonon, he tells you to go dead to the fact that the past is the destruction you have known, the present the violence you see, and the future the holocaust to come.

Spacing out is Vonnegut's answer to death, war, human glaciers. In Vonnegut's many descriptions of Pilgrim's trips to Tralfamadore, space-time travel is the ultimate withdrawal, the burial of suffering in meaninglessness. When you look at life from Tralfamadore, its wins and losses do not count. Tralfamadore provides not merely the vantage point *sub specie aeternitatis,* but the chance to see life in the context of intergalactic pointlessness.

The themes of detachment and meaninglessness are celebrated in Vonnegut's fiction as devices for diminishing the emotional charge of painful experience. Similarly, in a popular novel such as R. A. Heinlein's *Stranger in a Strange Land* (1961), the hero, who is an American raised on Mars by Martians, has perfected the ability not to tolerate strong feeling. "How can these human brothers suffer intense emotion without damage?" he asks in disbelief, before he "discorporates," detaches himself from his body and his too-intense emotions.

Novels of passivity refuse to believe in the traditional American values of effort, perseverance, and striving. In Richard Brautigan's lyric stories *Revenge of the Lawn* (1971) can be found cautionary tales, warnings against trying to be the old-time, hard-working American hero. "Corporal" is a touching account of humiliation at the heart of an American dream of success. A poor schoolboy during World War II yearns to be a general in a paper drive his school organizes like a "military career." He scrounges for scrap after scrap of paper, hoping to bring in enough to spiral from private to general. But after an incredible effort, he finds all his work will make him no more than a corporal. (Only kids whose parents were rich enough to have cars and to know "where there were a lot of magazines" get to be officers.) Crushed and humiliated, he takes his "God-damn little stripes home in the absolute bottom of (his) pocket . . . and enter[s] into the disenchanted paper shadows of America where failure is a bounced check or a bad report card or a letter ending a love affair and all the words that hurt people when they read them."

Suffering makes Brautigan's people gentle and cold. The evanescent *In Watermelon Sugar* (1968) describes appetitive America as a fantastic ruin where there are mile-high remains of skyscrapers, books, remnants of technological achievements, and ghosts of appetites which do not exist in the new world, iDEATH. This iDEATH is a commune in which the assertive "I," the ego, is subordinated to the harmony of a group in which nobody competes with anyone else, sexual jealousy is taboo, and nights are lit up by sugar lanterns in the shape of a trout and a child's face. Only misfits fall in love or become possessive of a beloved. In *Trout Fishing in America* (1967) Brautigan's luckiest character is the Kool-Aid wino, a poor kid who is thrilled even by the Kool-Aid he must ration so sparingly that he has to dilute it in a gallon, instead of a pint, of water. The people who survive in Brautigan's books are in control of their appetites but out of control of their illusions, able to make the dream of fullness, sweetness, and peace do the work of reality. Brautigan is a spokesman for the disenchanted, seeking to allay anxiety by blurring the distinctions of status, wealth, and ambition which exist in the real world.

Art has traditionally provided an escape from the real world. Yet increasingly writers for whom art is an explicit subject are describing the *difficulty* of escape, and the extent to which the world of "art" is shaped or twisted by the emotions of life. Such fiction tends to focus on the effort and exhaustion involved in trying to escape. Donald Barthelme's best stories, for example, are those most highly charged with a sense of frustration at pursuing an unattainable goal. The stories in *City Life* (1970) pinpoint his themes: the collapse of consciousness, the exhaustion of creative power, impatience with the puzzle of the disassembled personality. "The Glass Mountain" is the story of an artist caught between an exhausting concrete labor, his own anger, and the fury of his audience. The story parodies a fairy tale, partly retold in it, about a youth who must reach the top of a glass mountain to free a beautiful enchanted princess. But Barthelme's hero is a New Yorker painfully climbing a glass mountain on the corner of Thirteenth Street and Eighth Avenue with the aid of two toilet plungers. He wants to free an "enchanted symbol" at the top.

The climber inches along, aware that the mountain is already ringed by corpses of people who have made the attempt and failed. The streets around them are studded with dog droppings and crowded with his audience—passersby who shout obscenities at the climber, wonder who will get his apartment, and make such comments as "won't he make a splash when he falls now." He realizes he will never free the symbol through his labor; only a literal flight of imagination could do it. He borrows a method from the fairy tale he parodies: he seizes the legs of an eagle and is carried above the mountain until, at the proper point, he cuts off the eagle's legs and lands upright on the mountaintop. And he even finds the enchanted symbol. But when he touches it, it changes into "only a beautiful princess." He flings her "headfirst down the mountain" to the cursing crowd, who "can be relied upon to deal with her." Barthelme's artist deals with life in the manner of the crowd below. At the heights and depths there is nothing but frustration with people.

In "Brain Damage" Barthelme suggests an alternative to the vulgar and rarefied forms of rage in imaginative ruminations without belief in imagination's power. Disbelief in art, like pessimism about life, has a particular force for Barthelme. Meaninglessness is Barthelme's answer to the rage of the glass-mountain artist who is always sliding into the fact of his own hate, who cannot find images anywhere that are removed enough from the intimacy even fairy-tale princesses suggest. In droning emptiness and trivial activity Barthelme finds a cure for brain damage (thought and feeling): "The elevator girls were standing very close together. One girl put a candy bar into another girl's mouth, and the other girl put a hamburger into another girl's mouth." Just as concentrating on a candy bar frees the elevator girl from an awareness of highs and lows, so the Winston ad, sung by a passing girl, saves another Barthelme character from falling apart, falling down into his wrath. Anything that produces enough boredom to blot out feeling and ward off the emotions that "damage" the mind stabilizes collapsing personalities. Feeling looms large only in questions between episodes, when "To what end?" and "What recourse?" appear in boldface type. Barthelme's episodes show how to avoid either asking or answering such questions. Emptiness and boredom operate as alternatives to fury and pain. If there is nothing that signifies anything, then feeling and not feeling, having and not having are alike.

Art can be a tool for survival in the hands of a virtuoso writer. The meaninglessness of life or the fragmentation of personality can be as full of possibility as a roulette game for the writer with a pragmatic imagination. John Barth turns our concern with "identity," with the modernist search for who or what we are, into a pure entertainment. The artist can turn up as the man next door who lives by lies, who falsifies what he is to ease the pain of the truth of his life. In *The End of the Road* (1958), Horner, the hero, is Barth's prototype of contemporary man, paralyzed in aimlessness because he feels nothing for anything. Having passed his Master's orals at Johns Hopkins, Horner checks out of his room, for he has no reason to stay in it. He goes to the bus terminal to go anywhere twenty dollars will take him. But while making up his mind where to go, "he simply ran out of motives as a car runs out of gas. There was no reason to go anywhere. There was no reason to do anything . . . except in a meaningless metabolistic sense Jacob Horner ceased to exist altogether, for I was without a character, without a personality: There was no ego; no I." He sits immobilized in the terminal for twenty-four hours. How do you make a self? Barth plays with our ideas of personal crisis by offering a doctor whose therapies are all scenarios.

Unconcerned with emotions, disdainful of introspection, the doctor insists that people require rules, tight formulas, or roles to hold them together. What they need is his "Mythotherapy," which, he says, "is based on two assumptions; that human existence precedes human essence, if either of the two terms really signify anything; and that a man is free not only to choose his own essence, but to change it at will." If Horner cannot exist in and for himself, he can be the parody of another. Play roles, assume masks, insists the doctor. "Don't think there's anything behind them, there isn't. Ego means I and I means ego and the ego by definition is a mask." The doctor's talent is for turning life into drama, for infusing the awareness of fiction into people who could never make it in life, but might thrive as art forms.

Barth's cheeriest spokesman for the glories of detachment, the doctor loves people as protean storytellers, performers who cannot feel a thing. But both Horner's disease and the doctor's cure are defensive maneuvers, designed to block feeling, to deny the continuity of personality, and to focus on the forms of paralysis so that the content can disappear. What that content is is scarcely apparent to Horner, who goes dead to his own depression. But it is ominously suggested in Barth's descriptions of a plaster bust of Laocoon, that Trojan priest to whom Apollo granted knowledge of the contents of the Trojan horse. Driven by love for his people to warn them, killed by a vindictive god whose passion was wide enough to annihilate him and even his innocent sons, Laocoon is the man cursed by knowledge and feeling alike. Horner's bust of Laocoon serves as a fixed point of consciousness, a death mask reminding him that intelligence, involvement, and concern can end in the annihilation of the country you love, the children you want to protect, and the betrayal by the god you have served for a lifetime. Laocoon is the book's tragic presence, an omen that involvement unleashes destruction.

Barth turns *The End of the Road* into a tragi-farce on philosophy and infidelity, a parody of the agitations of love and thought. Horner, newborn mythotherapeutic poet, a pragmatist, neutral before all grand designs, is played off against Joe Morgan, the superrationalist, idealist, and advocate of nothing but absolutes. And between them is the honest, anguished Rennie, Joe's desperately loving wife, who has looked "deep within herself and found nothing," and who clings to all Joe's ideas for wholeness and stability. The *ménage à trois* that ensues rises to a great spoof on self-consciousness of any kind, a parody of people who think they are saved by ideas, but are doomed in Barth's vision of all relationships as deadly. Rennie, made pregnant by either Joe or Horner, cannot endure the possibility of bearing Horner's child and resolves to kill herself. Horner, his disengagement breaking down, frantically gets the doctor to perform an abortion, and in one of Barth's rare queasy scenes he watches Rennie die on the operating table.

Barth's *The Floating Opera* (1956) is about Todd Andrews's decision and indecision on the day he decided to kill himself and changed his mind. No parodist, no mythopoet, Andrews is Barth's attempt at a character riveted in obsessive reasoning, in stating and negating, doing and undoing himself. A lawyer with a legalistic soul, Andrews spends ten years investigating the facts of the day he decided not to die. And the fruit of this "Inquiry is one logical proof whose final term is "There is . . . no 'reason' for living . . . (or for suicide)."

Formalized despair and logic at the edge of craziness permit Barth's characters to spring out as benign, witty presences spinning out their existence on the thin line between paralysis and suicide. Andrews reaches the neutrality of a Horner. But Barth accomplishes a sublime spoof on the whole logical process, the power of mind to syntactify, order, and categorize life into meaning anything at all. For beyond Andrews's survival theorem is Barth's vision of life as broken episode, the floating opera you can watch from a riverbank, never seeing more than the bit played before your particular spot. This sense of life as fragmented, elusive, incapable of arousing any gripping, coherent feeling controls all Barth's realistic work, and informs his conception of character as a compilation of ideas, roles, terms. For Barth the modern world is a game better kept in pieces.

Barth's characters go looking through myth and history for answers to the pain life generates. *Giles-Goat Boy or the Revised New Syllabus* (1966) offers a vision of life as an educational experience. A satire in which life is a college campus, *Giles-Goat Boy* shows a world divided and waiting for the messianic Grand Tutor who can save Studentdom from the Devil as Dean o'Flunks. The world, divided into East Campus and West Campus, is ruled by a computer. Giles is an anagram for Grand Tutorial Ideal, Laboratory Eugenical Specimen. He was fathered by the WESCAC computer and a virgin. He has been raised as a goat among goats by a scientist soured on humankind. He leaves the herd and comes to the New Tammany College, West Campus, to preach the Revised New Syllabus and prove himself as Grand Tutor. As a goat he has lust without introspection, responsibility, or involvement. As a man he has curiosity, ambition, and the capacity to be touched. With a beautiful masochistic girl who needs an answer to her unhappiness, he descends into the innards of the computer. In the belly of the machine they make love, he discovering an ungoatish tenderness, she pleasure. Here the search for controls on aggression and submissiveness ends in the monitor machine. In this overlong novel where the analogy between universe and university is belabored, Barth nevertheless makes an argument for balance, for checks on both aggression and suffering through adopting a "computerized" that is, controlled, less emotional, way of being with each other.

In Barth's brilliant historical novel of colonial Maryland, *The Sot-Weed Factor* (1967), America on the edge of wilderness offers a chance to give all the warring tendencies and conflicted impulses in oneself free play. One balances aggression against civilization by playing all parts. Eben Cooke, sent by his father to the New World to make his fortune, resolves to become Maryland's poet laureate, singing the praises of the new civilization. He is too constricted to be much more than an observer of the wildly entertaining scene of greed, piracy, and prostitution. His former tutor, who plays at different times in the novel the part of pirate, Indian, and English lord, has the key to the kind of multiplicity that permits all of one's wishes to be fulfilled. In this most buoyant and spectacular of Barth's novels, the way to reconcile all opposites is to be everything at once. His peculiar celebration of American multiplicity is a celebration of character as a kind of mobile art.

History is Barth's escape hatch from modern times. The writer who has run out of words and plots wishes, in *Chimera* (1972), a collection of three novellas, "to go back to the original springs of narrative for inspiration . . . And of all the storytellers in the world his very favorite was Scheherazade." What follows is Barth's *Dunyazadiade*, a delightful spoof in which a feminist, Sherry, and her sister plot to castrate and murder the shah and his brother, who have deflowered and murdered the young women of their country. In the story they are persuaded to forgive and forget, to be like the Scheherazade of the Arabian Nights, to make love "as if" they love. Barth pits parody of legend and myth against anger, using emulation of legendary heroines as a force for love.

Barth writes parables protesting the betrayal of beauty by reality, of imagination by human rage. Identityless as the women of the Arabian Nights, his characters are voices for fiction. Moving toward their own survival, against the tide of their malice, or their inability to will or to care, Barth's mythotherapied people nevertheless celebrate the image of heroes and lovers preserved in legend through centuries of frustration.

William Gaddis's *The Recognitions* (1955) shares the tendency to find a form of release in infatuation with preexisting art. Its hero is Wyatt Gwyon, a Yankee who goes abroad to paint, but who expresses his devotion to beauty not by originality, but by becoming a copyist of Flemish Old Masters. Gaddis offers characters who move through life looking for themselves in the mirror images of earlier art, people who seem like print-outs from a Jamesean novel. In *JR.* (1975), the tale of a boy wonder who goes into business and gets rich, Gaddis uses American tough talk and business noise to create the hyped-up effect not only of boyhood, but of ambition and greed. But the self-consciousness with which his characters see themselves as prototypes, representative people, backfires, preventing them from representing anything alive.

When the circumstances of reality are perceived as so predominantly tragic, one may try to change the definition of what is real. The tragic is seen as illusory, and the real is a private dream. The repatterning of the past, or of the present, in line with an individual imagination is, obviously, the protest of the writer persuaded he cannot change the world and determined to change at least his vision of it. A sense of powerlessness before reality becomes for such a writer a catalyst for seeking a world of manageable size, of controllable problems, of puzzles confusing only to others.

Vladimir Nabokov, an aristocrat forced to leave Russia in 1919, revolts against his adversary, "history," by creating an art which is against time. *Ada, or Ardor: A Family Chronicle* (1969) explores the incestuous love of a sister and brother who seem mirror images of each other throughout their fifty-year affair. Their love begins at Ardis Hall—"the romantic mansion appeared on the gentle eminence of old novels"—a place about which Van Veen, the brother, can say, "Nothing in world literature . . . save maybe Count Tolstoy's reminiscences, can vie in pure joyousness . . . with the 'Ardis' part of the book." The world's best fiction becomes the measure of "reality" for Van Veen, who fills his chronicle with literary allusions, puns, and multiple perspectives to which only he has the key. His self-proclaimed magnum opus, "The Texture of Time," is also his weapon against the passage of time. Through him Nabokov not only circumvents the politically tormented time of his youth and his own precarious existence, but returns to the prerevolutionary literature of Chateaubriand, Flaubert, Tolstoy, and Chekhov.

The reliance of Nabokov's art on other literature may seem to connect him to the modernist writers—Joyce or Eliot, for instance—for whom fiction was inextricable from the accumulation of historical matter. Nabokov's reliance on literary allusion, however, is put to a different use, one which links him more to our contemporaries. He uses past literature to obscure the present and replace it, not to heighten the connections or differences between postwar or postrevolutionary life and an earlier time. Incest in *Ada* is the symbol of the self-protective aspect of his use of literary themes of pastoral, youthful, forbidden love. The artist loves only his mirror image and so subjects himself to no frustration or turmoil. He is not changed by love but merely reinforced. In Nabokov's own "revolution," art and literature, playing in one's own mind, can be barricades against the real world.

266

Nabokov can hold the reader spellbound in the grip of his dense and rich narcissism. Writing about himself, he parodies himself, committing literary incest. *Look at the Harlequins!* (1974) pits the "real" Nabokov against Vadim Vadimovitch Naborcroft, an imaginary Russian emigré novelist who wrote a popular book about a nymphet. To see oneself and others in a funhouse mirror is the point of the novel. The title *Harlequins* is attributed by Naborcroft to his great aunt, who said to him when he was a child, moping through the day, "Look at the harlequins. 'What harlequins?' he asked. 'Where?' " "Oh, everywhere, all around you. Trees are harlequins, words are harlequins. So are situations and sums. Put two things together—jokes, images— and you get a triple harlequin. Come on! Play! Invent the world! Invent reality!"

The forms of Nabokov's inventions are designed to confound historical progress. In a fine observation in *The Atlantic* (1974) Page Stegner noted: "Hegel's triadic series was simply an expression of the spirality of all things in relation to time. When the spiral unwinds, things warp into new dimensions—space into time, time into thought, thought, into a new spatial dimension. This spiral unwinding of things is a basic structural design of much of Nabokov's fiction just as the texture of time is a philosophical preoccupation that surfaces in almost all of the longer works."

Nabokov breaks down the reality of all distinctions. In *Harlequins*, burlesquing his own literary career also involves repossessing his past by acts of recapitulation and reinterpretation. Present and past, truth and falsehood are treated interchangeably.

John Shade, another of Nabokov's writers, says in *Pale Fire* (1962), "one should not disregard . . . a person who deliberately peels off a drab and unhappy past and replaces it with a brilliant invention." *Pale Fire* is a curio, satirizing the human race as it divides between those blessed with the gift of invention, those who have no gift and feed on the inventions of others, and the worldly political people whose diversion is power politics and murder. *Pale Fire* consists of a thousand-line poem divided into four cantos and attributed to John Shade, poet in residence at a New England university. Representing those who feed on the inventions of others is the pedant Charles Kinbote, an emigré who is the deposed king of Zembla and who spends his life happily writing a commentary on Shade's work which parodies the style and thought of the most soporific academic writing. While Kinbote writes his exegeses, a secret agent named Gradus makes his way from Zembla to murder him. By mistake, Gradus murders the poet Shade, leaving Kinbote free to belabor Shade's work unhampered by the presence of a living artist. Attempts to politicize *Pale Fire* have resulted in the explanation of this novel as having the moral that modern dictatorships kill poets but spare petty scholars like Kinbote. Yet the novel seems a parable for Nabokov's own art, where artist, pedant, and predator coexist. Shade, Gradus, and Kinbote are aspects of the same personality, suspended in the densely packed sensibility of Nabokov, who is all three.

Nabokov uses ideas of interchangeability, of personality as a mirror-maze, in a curious way. Other experimental writers share the love of breaking down perspectives and distinctions, but Nabokov brings to this mark of experimental fiction a unique touch. In the work of other writers (Vonnegut, Brautigan) the goal of the breakdown is the elimination of individuality and the burdens of selfhood. The objective appears to be consolation achieved through the dissolution of self in the vision of life as impersonal—a molecular flow, a series of masks to be put on and discarded at will. In Nabokov's work, the dissolution of ideas of time, roles, history operates as a curious preservative. Recapitulation of a writer's career gives it a second life; the confusion of time and place pare away extraneous differences to expose one overcharged ego and to reduce all concerns to those of individual need.

Obsession is perhaps Nabokov's unifying theme, the densely focused emotion that unites his poets, pursuers, and pedants. *Lolita* (1958) is the by now legendary novel of a man whose life is his desire for a twelve-year-old nymphet. Humbert Humbert marries the mother of Delores Hayze (Lolita) to be near the girl. Lolita's mother dies, relieving Humbert of the necessity of murdering her, and removing the one obstacle to his possession of the girl. On a trip across America, stopping at many motels, he achieves what he desires. After a while he loses Lolita to another man, whom he later tracks down and kills.

Nabokov uses Humbert to burlesque a certain kind of American lust. Totally ruthless and guiltless, Humbert is frank about what he wants and is concerned only with the tactics he must use to win the girl and not get caught. The grotesque parody of American ambition, the idealization of youth, and the unscrupulous individualism of Humbert certainly justify Alfred Appel's remark that "Lolita succeeds better than any other American novel in underlining the ways in which songs, ads, magazines and movies create and control their consumers." Or, as John Updike said in *Picked-up Pieces* (1975), of Nabokov's treatment of America, "A neurosis is a profounder product of a culture than a theory." Nabokov makes fun of American single-mindedness and concreteness. Murdering her new lover, Humbert regains

Lolita. But by then she is "old" and pregnant. The obsession which is the one trait that distinguished him involves him in death and in the defeat of his dream by time.

To love as Humbert loves is to suffer in concrete terms a kind of "historicity," to be bound into the passage of time. To love a child is to experience time and biology as purely defeating forces. To love no one is preferable. *Pnin* (1957), Nabokov's tender novel of an emigré Russian professor, uses a lovable exile who rents rooms in other people's houses as a figure almost blessed by his detachment. As Pnin remarks, "One of the main characteristics of life is discreteness. Unless a film of flesh envelops us, we die. Man exists only in so far as he is separated from his surroundings. The cranium is a space-traveler's helmet. Stay inside or you perish . . . death is communion." The self-infatuation of many of Nabokov's characters and the doom that affects them as lovers of women not their sisters or other selves may be defensive or cautionary, conveying Nabokov's faith that the safest objects of communion, affection, and thought are within one's own mind.

Both the desire to escape into art and the pull of violence reflect a sense of real life as hardship, competition, and aggression. One of the revolutionary forces in the postwar period is the revolt against adult male life, a revolt that has until recently played a larger role in fiction than feminism. Since novels of manners have been discussed in Chapter 3, only a brief suggestion of relevant changes in mores seems warranted here. Ambivalence about the way men live finds many expressions, but the most radical is an idealization of childhood as in every respect superior to the life a man faces. The idea of innocence has traditionally had overtones of American optimism, but in the novel of the fifties it became tied to pessimism about the possibilities of adult life. J. D. Salinger's *The Catcher in the Rye* (1951) effected the most uncompromising equation between "evil" and adulthood.

In this novel Holden Caulfield rejects all the rites that mark initiation into adolescence and adulthood: graduating from school, sexual involvement, becoming his own big brother. The book spans the time between Caulfield's leaving Pencey Prep after he has flunked out and coming to New York looking for something to believe in—the one teacher he respected, the girl he idealized. He is shocked when the teacher—whom he admired for picking up the body of a boy who jumped from a window without caring about staining his own clothes—makes a homosexual gesture toward him. Coming on the heels of his disillusionment at learning that his romanticized girl friend may

269

have had some sexual experience with another boy, the teacher's gesture shatters Holden. A teenage prostitute who comes to his hotel room depresses him too much even to seem human to him. He goes to his sister Phoebe's school and begins washing obscene graffiti off the walls but cannot keep up with it. Feeling he will disappear each time he steps off a curb, he prays to his dead older brother, Allie, to help him get to the other side of the street and thanks him when he does. The novel ends with Holden hugging his sister Phoebe in the rain.

Holden appears to be totally loving, but he is unable to connect with people, unable to accept them as they are, unable to accept sexuality. The appeal to Allie is an appeal for the perpetuation of his own childhood, for someone who can save him from falling off a curb, and from crossing the line toward manhood. Allie is the father as divine child innocent of sex, of adult standards or demands. For Caulfield as for Salinger, one can preserve goodness by not growing up, but one can achieve this goal only by dying in childhood.

The peculiar pathos of *The Catcher in the Rye* is its belief in both innocence and doom and their connection to a gentleness that has to do mainly with family relations among brothers and sisters. In the Glass stories, Salinger leaves the parents remarkably out of the picture. The Glass children make up a tribal revolt against the rest of the world, seeming to have a monopoly on sensibility, love. The special openness to pain, the use of vulnerability as a kind of sacrament, is given expression in the name of the family, Glass; all of them are mirrors of each other's specialness and fragility. In "A Perfect Day for Bananafish," Seymour Glass, on his honeymoon, calls his wife, who talks on the phone and polishes her nails, Miss Spiritual Tramp of 1948; he walks out to the beach, makes up a charming children's story about bananafish, and drowns himself. Salinger's men are too good for this world. These blessed boys cannot grow up; if they do they kill themselves; if they marry they often find death is preferable. They yearn, as Holden longs for Allie, for the life before puberty, before responsibility.

The sexual revolution in the novel was given an early push in Jack Kerouac's *On the Road* (1957) and *Dharma Bums* (1958), which idealized the lives of men committed to sensation and utterly opposed to any future as husbands or fathers. But by far the finest novelist to deal with complex sexual attitudes and men conflicted by the life custom has prescribed is John Updike. *Rabbit, Run* (1960) and *Rabbit Redux* (1971) shows changes in men and women as husbands and wives, mothers and fathers. In *Rabbit, Run* Momism is flourishing in an American housewife who is controlling, ironic, and relentlessly involved with her son, whose narcissism she alternately wounds and strokes. Rabbit's Pop is a stereotyped, hard-working man who is passive before his wife. They do not reproduce their kind. Rabbit has had a taste of abundance as a high school basketball star. At twenty-six he is married, aged by his heavily pregnant wife, who drinks too much, by his concern for his two-year-old son, by his humiliating job, and by his fear of becoming like his father. He runs away. His sister, Mim, will not be a kitchen martyr. She becomes an efficient manager of people, a call girl who thinks life works best for self-protective independents on a hard-cash basis. These are Updike's new Americans: the man engulfed by self-destructiveness and anger, the woman who is all cool sex.

Updike defines maleness as sexual and economic responsibility for women, and connects the decline of society with the decline of masculinity. *Rabbit Redux* offers an ambitious patterning of social forces that create uncertainty—automation that devalues work, Vietnam protests that devalue authoritative institutions, sexually free wives who help elevate the values of self-expression over self-control and make the working man's pro-war, pro-family, pro-patria values seem outmoded. All these make Updike's men feel obsolete.

At thirty-six, a hard-working linotyper, Rabbit would seem to have become his father. But it is no longer possible to live his father's life. He is replaced at work by a photo-offset machine and in his wife's bed by a man who is an infinitely better lover. Technology has changed his mother's life, too. Old and ill, she is propped up and pepped up by a pill that brings her sexual fantasies she presumably never had as a healthy woman. Is sex the medicine of the sixties? Only for women. For Rabbit there is no tonic for frustration but revenge. He takes in a black nihilist and a girl who dropped out of upper-middle-class life into drug addiction. He lets the man abuse him and takes out his rage passively by letting him kill the girl. His destructiveness and self-destructiveness get his house burned down. Updike brilliantly compresses into the fall of a single house and marriage the war between the sexes, the dissidence between classes and races, the efficiency economy that undermines a man's sense of himself. Houseless, jobless, wifeless, Rabbit crumbles. Giving up on being a father to his son, he goes back to Mom.

What happens to a man's sexual, emotional, and professional life under the pressure of time is the subject of Charles Simmons's *Wrinkles* (1978), a novel which follows a traditional man through innovative times. Simmons explores the experience of Irish Catholics in

New York, providing a portrait of a group and a time through an intensely personal rendering of one man's memories of parents, church, and family. Like James Joyce's *Dubliners,* which progresses from childhood to maturity, and which Joyce thought of as a chapter in the moral history of his race, Simmons's *Wrinkles* addresses what happens to a product of a Catholic education under the pressure of experience. Simmons achieves his result through a series of meditations—on sex, marriage, and work. These highly compressed chains of association take his hero back and forth through time, linking past and present events so precisely that they successfully evolve the man of the 1970s from World War II to a prewar childhood.

Realizing the difficulty of fixing moral values, Simmons shows them as they stretch between conflicting standards. Exactitude about confusion and experience emerges as a major value; the act of signification is made synonymous with the act of description. Setting out with his mass of packaged distinctions, his hero arrives in middle age at a point where all values seem dispersed, unfathomable. Every experience, including his often hilarious sexual encounters, fades according to what seems a law of human entropy. Ideas and affections exist ever-threatened by loss of validity or desire. Human entropy—the running down of interest and appetite—negates most anarchic urges and traditional beliefs, in the novel, but Simmons nevertheless keeps his character's decline in the grip of his self-control. Precision and exactitude are operative, functional values in a world where so many conflicting claims produce a climate of neutrality.

The upheaval in traditional male values in work and marriage has produced heroes who are torn apart by their lives as husbands and fathers. Since the novelists of this dislocation are discussed at length in Chapter 5, only brief mention will be made here.

Norman Mailer's sexual novels, *The Deer Park* (1955) and *An American Dream* (1965) offer characters caught in their own sexual schizophrenia, going from strong, successful women who become symbols of their power, to waiflike, sweet girls who make them feel genuinely strong, but do not satisfy their need for status or acquisition. Charles Eitel in *The Deer Park* is torn between Elena, a beautiful, womanly waif, and Lulu, his ex-wife, a shallow, pretty movie star. Mailer resolves the conflict by marrying a reluctant Eitel to Elena and granting him an extended affair with Lulu. In *An American Dream,* Rojack murders his rich wife and falls for a nightclub singer, who is finally killed because of her attachment to him. He is the death of both women and therefore free of his problem. Even in so traditionally "masculine" a writer as Mailer there is a profound ambivalence about one's life as a man, either as the "protected" husband of a wealthy, powerful woman, or as the protector of a weak and loving one.

Joseph Heller's *Something Happened* (1974) deals with Bob Slocum, a middle-class husband and father who is locked into his own frustrations, unable to feel much for his wife or children and obsessed with his own gratifications. His many affairs usually fail to bring him the pleasure he craves; he ruminates most on the woman he was too inexperienced to pursue when he was seventeen. Stylistic repetitiveness and the heavy joylessness of Slocum prevent *Something Happened* from succeeding as a novel, but it nevertheless develops an emerging theme of postwar fiction: the vulnerability of men to narcissism and to a masochistic preoccupation with what they do not have.

In Philip Roth's *The Professor of Desire* (1977) the hero, Kepesh, is too worn out by his life as a husband to do more than be preoccupied with the highs and lows of his potency and his inability to love any woman. He casts himself as a tragic figure, a male Madame Bovary. Saul Bellow's brilliant *Herzog* (1964) showed a gifted man betrayed by his femme fatale wife, and reacting by learning the benefits of sexual martyrdom: he begins coercing care from all around him. In the emerging fiction of vulnerable men, male characters are playing the roles once assigned to women. Self-absorbed and self-pitying, they practice the politics of helplessness.

The passive hero is an image of our anxiety about ourselves, our ability to shape life. Emerging from the sexual revolution is fiction by women which uses the victimized heroine to launch an assault on helplessness. The trapped heroine may reflect our will to overpower the sense of impotence and helplessness. Feminist fiction runs the gamut from black comedy to novels of manners to a new literature of aggression.

Cynthia Buchanan's brilliant comic satire, *Maiden* (1972), mocks both the old-fashioned romantic and the new woman whose unabashed sexiness makes her look as if she has it made. Her heroine, Fortune Dundy, is a thirty-year-old virgin with inflamed dreams and an impacted maidenhood, a female Don Quixote who is waiting for the perfect man. Her roommate is Biscuit Besqueth, who, fearing her lover will wander, gets a breast lift and paints on her "new high riders" in Day-Glo paint "Hey Daddy, Remember Us?" Through Fortune's idealism and Biscuit's sense of the palpable, Buchanan achieves a wide-ranging satire of American sexuality. Her experimental adaptation of a stream-of-consciousness style encompasses the sounds of the California singles scene, the talk of disc jockeys, and disco music—

the mass of pleas and promises of advertisers who swear to build you up and flatten you out. Her humor is deliciously black in its insistence that love must survive this manipulation, if only as a hope. But the price of Fortune's optimism is her ignorance and virginity.

The disruptions of the 1960s surface in the dislocation of a stable marriage in Paula Fox's *Desperate Characters* (1970), which deals with the tensions in the childless marriage of Otto and Sophie Bentwood. In this beautifully crafted novel, every emotional tie is loosened by the times. The failure of reciprocity in marriage, sex, friendship, business, which is the novel's major theme, is compressed into the betrayal of one simple gesture of kindness. Giving food to a stray cat at the opening of the novel, Sophie is bitten by the animal she strokes and nourishes. In the three days spanned by the story, she realizes, as the slum around her brownstone seems to be pressing in, as partnerships, friendships, and marriages bend under the pressure of inflamed sexual and political appetites, "God if I am rabid, I am equal to what is outside." In the controlled correctness of Sophie's language and marriage, Fox is able to capture the nervousness and anxiety of people who live on a tightrope.

Not an experimental stylist, Joan Didion has nevertheless employed pastiche and montage techniques—laying one scene next to another without apparent connection—to project a woman's dislocation. In *Play It As It Lays* (1970) Maria, her heroine, is divorced from her emotional life, growing weaker and more emotionally dead as her anger mounts. Moving from opulent scenes of Hollywood parties to Maria's emptiness, the novel projects a peculiar American combination of paralyzed nerves and frenetic, aimless movement.

A radical experiment in values and emotions is to be found in Lois Gould's *such Good Friends* (1970) and *A Sea Change* (1976), which deal with women's aggression, both frustrated and released. In *Such Good Friends* Julie Messinger speaks in a slashing, quipping style of her painful discovery, as her husband lies comatose and dying, of his infidelities. She goes on to expose a lifelong habituation to taking a beating from the people she loves. Imprinted in this novel of middle-class mores is a pitch of feeling that shapes it into a harbinger of a female literature of disgust. In *A Sea Change* Gould's characters are personifications of human aggressive and masochistic drives. Her heroine begins the book tied up and being robbed by a black gunman. She ends by being magically transformed into a black man who becomes a rapist. The novel calls into question our ideas of sexual vulnerability and power, while taking a sophisticated look at the feminist cliché that a woman can shed her vulnerability by "becoming" a man.

The most radical feminist visions can be found in science fiction. Joanna Russ's *The Female Man* (1975) is interesting in its conception of a planet for females only but marred by its ungainly style. The beautifully written science fiction novel *The Left Hand of Darkness* (1969) by Ursula Le Guin offers a tender treatment of androgyny in the story of a traveler from an Earth-like planet who discovers a world where there is only one sex, each being possessing the ability to both father and bear children. Since the father of one child may be the mother of several others, there is no differentiation in sexual roles and no inability of people to understand each other because of sexual differences.

In postwar experimental fiction, the situation of women is often not so different from that of men. A feminization of the hero has occurred. The narrow sphere of activity, the family, encircles many male characters, men who can confront disruptions in society only as represented by their irate sisters and wives. The sense of vulnerability distinctive to women in nineteenth-century novels is almost universally shared by current heroes. Women have been taught vulnerability as a means of gaining male protectiveness and other benefits of civilization. Now the male hero also accepts and becomes resigned to his situation in order to resolve tension. What seems, in fiction, to make the sexes coalesce is a common sense of powerlessness.

The images that fill our dreams come from the world we know. Surrealists who have delved into the recesses of consciousness where nightmare is the only reality, and fantasies cannot be distinguished from facts, have nevertheless described a world as familiar as it is strange. They offer a unique perspective on postwar concerns. Political violence and terror turn up as nightmares of persecution, torture, or pursuit. The same novelist may write in an explicitly political context in one book, and in another express his concern with sexual domination and submission. He stretches the concern with aggression and vulnerability which runs through experimental fiction toward the breaking point where images of all oppressions and all repressions flow into each other.

John Hawkes's *The Cannibal* (1949) is a hallucination on the theme of war. Set in World War II, the novel reaches back to World War I and forward to predictions of a third war to create a sense of the cyclicity and inexorability of genocide and murder. This novel of horrendous atmosphere opens with an American in charge of most of devastated Germany riding through his domain on a motorcycle. He carries a sack filled with "unintelligible military scrawls" and has only "hypothetical lines of communication." Intellectual confusion, the ruin of Western culture, the sheer silence through which the American rides and to which he can bring no relief serve to make the country vulnerable to another Hitler.

Zizendorf, the American's antagonist, is a German tyrant who will be the next Hitler and the creator of a third world war. Perceiving that the American is unable to be more than an extension of the devastated world, Zizendorf outdoes him easily and fills the country with his propaganda, his noise. Hawkes suggests that Zizendorf's political "certitude" paves the way for the return of the country to an insane asylum. The asylum, ironically, consists not of the schizoid confusions of the "real" world, but of Zizendorf's authoritarian platitudes.

What is real in Hawkes's novels is terror—as nightmare, hallucination, emptiness. He has praised the novel which can "objectify the terrifying similarity between the unconscious desires of the solitary man and the disruptive needs of the visible world."

The world disrupts by *permitting* the fantasies of fear and ambition, terror and love to see the light of day and become real. In Hawkes's *Second Skin* (1964), to prove his love for his daughter, Skipper submits to her sadistic wish that he have her "long and exotic" name, Cassandra, tatooed on his breast in green. "Green's a bad color . . . Green's going to hurt, lady. Hurt like hell." "The scream . . . that was clamped between my teeth was a strenuous black bat struggling, wrestling in my bloated mouth and with every puncture of the needling—fast as the stinging of artificial bees, this exquisite torture. While the punctures were marching across, burning their open pinprick way across my chest, I was bulging in every muscle, slick, strained, and the bat was peering into my mouth of pain . . . I was resisting, jerking in outraged helplessness, blind and baffled."

In Hawkes's *Lime Twig* (1962) William Hencher's love for his dead mother takes him back to the house they lived in until her death in the London blitz. When he finds Michael and Margaret Banks, who now have the house, his love flames up in a perverted eroticism. He uses her lipstick, lies in the Banks's bed when they are out, makes love to the house, to them, to himself. Banks, who possesses the house, is equally odd. He loves horses, finds images flashing through his mind—"The silver jaw, the enormous sheet, the upright body of the horse that was crashing in the floor of the Dreary Station flat"—and steals a racehorse. He is killed by what he lusts for, throwing himself under the hooves of horses as they turn for the finish line. Hawkes's characters tend to be enamored of forces which are larger than themselves and which excite by terrifying. The position of helplessness and fear is eroticized in Hawkes's grotesque fiction to a way of life. In the surreal fetishism and sadomasochism that mark much of his work, reality becomes divided into the sufferers and inflicters of pain. Skipper in *Second Skin* is only half drawn by suffering; he survives the suicides of those around him. The Zizendorfs and characters like Larry in the *Lime Twig*, who remains at the end in his brass knuckles and bullet-proof vest, are actively determined to be on the giving end of pain.

Ambivalence over suffering and fragility are at the heart of the experimental fiction that opens up life as impulse and emotion. Eugene Wildman's *Nuclear Love* (1972) offers characters who shift in and out of focus toward and away from their recognitions of the incurable unhappiness in all they meet. Wildman opens up a sense of subconscious reality, a world of primal need perceived with striking lucidity: "Most of my life has been spent around underworlds. When you live near the entrance to the underworld, everything in life becomes breakable. There is no difference between glass and emotion. Shelves are a necessity."

In Wildman's *Montezuma's Ball* (1970) Montezuma, playing Aztec basketball, dribbles a ball down a court which expands to include Mexico and part of America. The book beats out the rhythm of flight and pursuit, of blockers and scorers. A group of loiterers, workers, and tourists keep the ball of energy bouncing above and below the level of consciousness. The atmosphere of violence closes in on a couple of tourists looking for a hotel, relief from exhaustion, and escape from a menacing beggar. It troubles a man in Chicago who cannot pay his bills. Characters turn up and disappear; objects—sunglasses, knives, streetlights—light up like flashing signals of emotion pressed into a concrete form and offered as artifacts. Wildman's subject is the energy of the man who knows he will be a victim, but is never sure what form his oppressor will take.

Moving in an opposite direction, Don DeLillo (*Ratner's Star,* 1976), and Joseph McElroy draw images from a controlled and cerebral world, writing experimental literature based on conscious, external experience. The complex plot of McElroy's *Lookout Cartridge* (1974) centers on the mysterious disappearance of a film made by two Americans living in London. In search of a clue as to what their film showed that might have prompted someone to destroy it, Cartwright, one of the filmmakers, reconstructs it in his mind, the images coming to him out of order, altered by memory. But what the novel exposes is the vision of people as lookout cartridges, consciousnesses unaware of what they know, but compelled to decipher what they do know. Drawing on technological imagery, McElroy makes an analogy between faulty equipment and faulty minds, between the collapse of machines and the collapse of nature, the unremembered scene and the blotted-out life, the memory bank of pictures one never sees until some other image calls them to view. McElroy's writing is precise, exact, relying on understatement to achieve surprising effects:

> Like me you have in your head things you may not have exactly seen.
> Like a lookout cartridge.
> Or the Landslip Drive-in Movie, whose monumental screen under clean and clement American stars and in front of you and a hundred other cars without audible warning one summer night began to lower, to tilt back hugely and drop as if into a slot in the earth.
> The image became yours even more surely by disappearing . . . An actress and actor in the corrected colors of the spectrum had been touching each other's colossal faces and their breaths kept coming faster and more intimately loud to bring right into your car this whopping slide of mouths and fingers and nostrils inserted into the night-pines and sea-sky above the locally well known clay cliffs that had just enjoyed their first clear day in two weeks. But not for the first time since before World War II a section of cliff gives way and the famous faces are swept as if by their camera right up off the monumental screen until you have only the upper half of the two torsos thrown onto the remaining upper half of the descending screen as it tilts back toward the sea; and now where's the movie?

The mind is also a lookout cartridge in that it serves as a warning device, a feedback mechanism designed to alter the organism's response to the real world. By appropriating the control and technological predilections of the cyberneticist, McElroy achieves an unemotional statement of his characters' fear that the world is slipping out from under them.

Robert Coover walks the line between reality and nightmare, using surrealism as a form for capturing the dark side of American conviction. In *The Origin of the Brunists* (1966), he focuses on the growth of a religious cult in a small coal-mining town in western Pennsylvania. The lone survivor of a mining accident which kills ninety-seven people spurs the formation of the Brunist cult, whose symbol is a white bird and whose members wear white tunics. A newspaper editor sensationalizes the cult and its belief in the end of the world at a certain date. Coover takes apart the economic situation that produces both unsafe mining conditions and the newspaper's ability to commercialize and spread the cult. He attacks the social organization and sexual morality of a small town swallowing holiness and apocalypse like moonshine. The harsh blend of realism and fantasy, the popularity of a predicted "apocalypse" indict economic and religious values. Coover stretches the naturalistic novel toward fantasy, rendering realistic portraits grotesque in their exaggerated representation of religious faith and opportunism.

Coover's *Pricksongs and Descants* (1969) and *The Universal Baseball Association, Inc., J. Henry Waugh, Prop.* (1968) are concerned with new modes of perception, with the dislocation of time and space, with nonrational behavior. In the former, a collection of stories, Coover develops the use of folktales—Noah's dim-witted brother is a character, a shepherd is pitted against a computer—using simple stories for the complex purpose of dislocating one's reactions. *Universal Baseball Association* deals with contemporary folk heroes—baseball stars—as imagined in the mind of a superfan, J. Henry Waugh, an accountant who dreams over his books by day and comes alive at night, keeping elaborate records of baseball associations which exist only in his dreams. His ability to imagine the camaraderie of men on a team is in bitter contrast to his own lonely life. Through his ability to identify with a young pitching star, he wins himself one great night with a lovable neighborhood woman of easy virtue, making love to her pretending he is the glowing young Damon Rutherford, hero at the mound.

The Public Burning (1977) returns Coover to startling, controversial analogies between nightmare and political life. Set in the first year of the Eisenhower administration, the novel moves from New York to Washington to California to climax in Times Square as the Rosenbergs are found guilty of conspiracy to steal atomic secrets and pass them on to the Russians. They have been sentenced to die in the electric chair. Coover's characters are Uncle Sam (Sam Slick, the wily Yankee Peddler), a superhero; the Phantom, his evil counterpart; and Vice President Richard Nixon, presiding over the Senate, playing golf with Uncle Sam, talking of his early years and linking his success to the lives and deaths of Julius and Ethel Rosenberg. Pulling fact beyond history, Coover paints a stark, bitter picture of one kind of American vindictiveness, of a love of one-up-manship and callous ambition. The "real" characters are distortions of American types: victims, winners, capitalizers on other people's misfortunes.

Politics on the edge of fantasy is also the subject of E. L. Doctorow, whose *The Book of Daniel* (1971), while not explicitly about the

279

Rosenberg case, seems to owe much to it. Set in 1967 between Memorial Day and Christmas Day, the novel deals with Daniel Lewin, a twenty-seven-year-old graduate student and son of Communist Jewish parents who were executed at Sing Sing in the 1950s for conspiring to steal atomic secrets for the Russians. Lewin is writing the book, which is his attempt to discover the truth about his parents and himself, his relation to America and his sister, who is locked in her own despair. Doctorow captures much of the spirit of revolt of the 1960s, the sense of rage and bitterness against government and the experience of America as a personal tragedy.

Doctorow's *Ragtime* (1975), a confection of a novel, lacks the fervor and passion of *The Book of Daniel*. It offers scenes from the life of an upper-middle-class family in New Rochelle engaged in the manufacture of banners and flags. The novel also touches on immigrant poverty and on the oppression of blacks, which leads one black jazz musician, who loses everything because of the suspicion and malice of whites, to seize control of Pierpont Morgan's library. Emma Goldman, the revolutionary, and Stanford White, the architect, turn up and bow out. The middle-class family declines in cohesiveness and wealth and produces one nihilistic son who makes bombs instead of Fourth of July fireworks. The family is finally united by ties of love to an immigrant family, whose fortunes rise as the novel progresses. The novel evokes the atmosphere of a period piece, remaining all surface, offering dazzlingly polished scenes where "real" and imaginary characters are set like mosaics.

Tom McHale is a comic writer whose surreal humor is directed toward blasting standards of value and ideas of right or wrong. In *Farragan's Retreat* (1971) he offers caricatures of what is "expected" of a father in conservative Philadelphia. To appease his superpatriotic brother and sister, Farragan pretends to try to kill his long-haired son, who is a draft evader and the author of a number of affectionate letters to Ho Chi Minh. Against overtones of salvation and grace, this tale of vindictiveness between generations comes down heavily against all traditional family ties.

In *School Spirit* (1976) McHale deals with the adventures of Egil Magruder, a retired prep school football coach who decides at the age of sixty-eight to avenge the death of a boy found in a cafeteria freezer twenty-three years earlier. The boy was the victim of a "prank" perpetrated by three of Magruder's first-string team. An odyssey to Vermont through a series of encounters with a gallery of comic-strip characters, including a squash-playing priest, Magruder's journey to assuage his twenty-three-year-old guilt is as morally suspect as the lives he exposes on his search for the killers.

Crime and punishment are the subjects of Jerome Charyn's explorations of the troubles between generations, the nature of masculinity, and attitudes toward authority in *Blue Eyes* (1975). In this metaphysical thriller Manfred Coen, a New York police inspector, tries to infiltrate a white slavery operation. He loves his father, a suicide; Papa Guzmann, a numbers organizer who befriended him; and Isaac Sidel, a police inspector who adopts him as a protégé. Sidel tries to get Coen to betray Guzmann and adds to the corrupt and tortured feelings that drive everyone in this novel. In the companion novel *Marilyn the Wild* (1976) Sidel is the hero who has to deal with crooks, FBI kibitzers, and unreliable journalists. His daughter, Marilyn, wants Manfred Coen, but Sidel will not help her win her man, preferring to keep Manfred pure for the NYPD. Youth against age and authority and the weird cast of New York types (the novel boasts an albino Negro pyromanic) put Charyn's novel, for all its gross, police-blotter realism, solidly on the side of the surreal. Charyn renders all power struggles as the war between cops and robbers.

A perception of force as the determinant of action and behavior, and a consequent sense of individual impotence, may be at the heart of the variety of experimental literatures in America. From the fiction of aggression, to that of passivity, fragmentation, and escape, to the novel of sexual confusion, pain, and revolt, our experimental literature provides a documentary of American imaginative experience. The writer who deliberately set out to be the historian and cartographer of this journey is also its product. Thomas Pynchon, born in 1938, set out to describe the values of his generation and its despairing belief that the way to reduce anger and pain is to reduce involvement, to model one's self on those smoothly functioning feedback mechanisms bequeathed to our time by cyberneticists.

Technology is commonly blamed as the source of all our woes, our short-circuited relations, our IBM-ized lives. Pynchon created in *V.* (1963) a novel in which technological imagery shapes religious and erotic feelings. A major character in *V.* is the messiah "machine," Benny Profane, a man whose nightmare is that his "clock-heart" and "sponge" brain will be disassembled on the rubble-strewn streets, but whose grace is his ability to be a perpetual-motion man who rolls on too fast to lose his heart or let anyone touch the controls of his mind. The profane Christ is the one who will not get crucified.

Profane's world is no vale of tears. His nativity is on Christmas Eve in the Sailor's Grave Bar, the hip world where every man is a drunken sailor, and women are interchangeable quick lays. Everyone is waiting for Suck Hour, the moment when Chow Down calls the sailors to custom beer taps made of foam rubber in the shape of large breasts. There are seven taps and an average of 250 sailors diving to be given suck by a beer-breast. There is very little nourishment in Pynchon's world. His wise man controls his thirsts. Profane does not really want to turn on anything, even a beer tap. He wants a woman who will not love him but will be a really self-contained machine: "Any problems with her you could look up in a maintenance manual. Remove and replace was all." He gets an erection thinking about the sex money can buy while reading the want ads in search of a job, and notices that his erection traces a line in the *Times*. He waits until it subsides so he can choose the employment agency where it comes to rest. He wants the least exciting job. He has the peace that passeth understanding.

History produced this human yo-yo. Pynchon uses a complex panorama of three generations to develop the changing social and political forces that produced a Profane. But his wacky sewer scenes provide a capsule statement of how three generations differ. Three of *V*.'s characters descend into the urban colon. A Victorian priest moved into the sewers of New York to preach to rats. Does he see people as rats trying to become sanctified? He and his generation could still believe rats had souls. A middle-aged man who lived through World War II goes through the sewer looking for clues to his mother's identity and his own. Life is possible for him only as an endless quest for personal meaning that keeps him too busy to notice the stench. Young Profane, hired to kill alligators, is on the sewer patrol, a job he takes just to earn the money for women and food. He embraces meaninglessness as a value. He makes the directionless flow of sewage wastes his life.

V. herself is female serenity, the clean, eternal balance of emotional control. She absorbs the force of war, of all male thrusts, as erotic curios, and returns them when as mother she abandons, as protectress she corrupts, as lover she murders, as transvestite priest she damns. She is the destructive, indestructible objet d'art who mutilates her body to adorn it with golden feet and a glass eye. She is always young, always fascinatingly beautiful. One man dreams of her ecstatically as a young machine: "At age 76, skin radiant with the bloom of some new plastic, both eyes glass, but now containing photoelectric cells connected by silver electrodes to optic nerves . . . Perhaps even a complex system of pressure transducers located in a marvelous vagina of polyethylene, all leading to a single silver cable to the correct register of the digital machine in her skull." She is Profane's woman, the girl who has lost her virginity to the gear shift of her MG, whose great love is her car or its human equivalent, Profane. V. is a self-contained autoerotic machine. V. is the crucial pivot, the profane fulcrum on which you can survive forever. V. may be vulnerability conquered.

The degree to which men and women want each other to be ever-ready erotic tools, needing neither tenderness nor love, is one sign of sexual hate. Pynchon is saying that men control their destructiveness through Profane-like passivity and disengagement; that women conquer their vulnerability to men, life, and death by becoming virtual automatons who cannot feel a thing. "Keep cool, but care," someone advises. The only way to contain destructiveness is to deadlock coolness and caring.

In war all controls on violence seem to disappear. *Gravity's Rainbow* (1973), Pynchon's novel of World War II, deals with appetites gone out of control in war and in a psychological warfare unit operating in London. In this unit, called "Psychological Intelligence Schemes for Expediting Surrender," it is never clear whose surrender is being plotted because all are busy devouring each other. Why is the world ruled by destructive ambition, or life so dominated by anger?

Pynchon poses his question in a thriller in which the deadliest man in London is the American officer Tyrone Slothrop, a ladykiller. The places where he has gone to bed with his pickups are exactly the spots where the V-2 rockets fall. The psychological warfare unit knows this because Slothrop, who is a member of it, keeps a map, charting with paper stars the places where he has scored. Roger Mexico, a statistician, charts the bomb sites. His map and Slothrop's are identical. Is it the bomb that excites Slothrop or sex that draws destructiveness on the girls? What is the relation between sex and death?

Pynchon's detective team is composed of those we have entrusted with solving problems, the scientists and psychologists. His thriller is a satire on their expertise. Pointsman, a Pavlovian psychologist, believes there is a point, a particular switch in the brain, that turns on sex or death. He tries to find the mystery stimulus that controls Slothrop's "switch" so he can turn off death and win the Nobel Prize. Roger Mexico, the mathematician and statistician, thinks Pointsman is wrong and tells him there is no explanation for the identical graphs for Slothrop's pickups and the bomb sites. "Bombs are not dogs. No link. No memory. No conditioning," he insists. Many other "experts" turn up in the novel, many explanations are offered and refuted. By supersaturation with reason, the novel draws us further toward admitting the failure of reason and science to explain the truths of life clearly or completely.

What Pynchon indicts is the inexplicability and inexorability of aggression, the extent to which it is inflamed only by scientists like Pointsman, who dominate and humiliate men, and who control them through conditioning in order to schematize behavior. Our "conditioners" are not, of course, Pavlovians but our parents and the social and economic institutions which shape how we live. Pynchon indicts the capitalistic urge, the multinational corporation, the mega-cartel as models of America, its allies and enemies, drifting toward centralized wealth and power.

Pynchon indicts the quality of emotional relationships between parents and children through American comic strips. "Perilous Pop," says Pynchon, is the antagonist of every western, every comic strip. He is "every typical American teen-ager's own father, trying episode after episode to kill his son. And the kid knows it. Imagine that. So far he's managed to escape his father's daily little death plot—but nobody has said he has to keep escaping."

Pop and his gang may not kill you, but they kill every emotion that makes life worth living. Slothrop's love-hate affair with the V-2 rocket is the paradigm of his conditioning. The rocket outstrips sound: the noise of its coming rises only after it has already exploded. Before you know what has hit you, you are dead. This is Pynchon's most powerful symbol for the subliminal takeover of your mind. In this novel of sexual and political aggression, every infant has been blasted by the war between his parents, by their resentment of him, and by the society which gears him for a future of assertiveness on demand.

Pynchon seems to believe that America is manufacturing plastic people, people without positive emotional capacities. Slothrop's father sold out his baby boy, Tyrone, not out of malice but out of a concern for a future that was greater than his love for his child. In return for the money to send him through college, he gave the infant Tyrone to a stimulus-response experimenter who measured his reactions by the swiftness of his infant erections. Imipolex-G, a polymer whose every fiber is capable of erection, is the sexiest cloth there is, the mystery stimulus that conditioned infant Tyrone's erections. Pynchon is saying that you are geared to excitement by synthetics, cast into your programing too soon to know what is happening, too ignorant to realize that a father's love for your human possibilities is so meager that he is willing to plasticize you so that, alive or dead, you would get through Harvard.

Pynchon offers comic-strip heroes to rescue such victims from Perilous

Pop. Myrtle the Miraculous is a wonder woman who hates people but adores perfectly functioning robots and machines. Marcel, the mechanical chess player, is the ideal male, a robot tactician. Maximilian, a dropout from the performance ethic, allies himself with "rhythms," all "rhythms," up to and including the cosmic. Slothrop, as adult, is only a "glozing neuter" who can find himself neither as a man of feeling nor as a machine. His fate is simply to run down, ignorant of the purpose or meaning of anything that has happened to him. These are prototypes of the kinds of people Pynchon feels America is producing.

Cold, harsh, exaggerated in his rejection of contemporary values, Pynchon nevertheless puts together the emotional and cultural life of his generation with a brilliance and depth comparable to James Joyce's in *Ulysses*. Although he casts a cynical eye on our time and the historical forces that shaped it, he is a moralist, making precise distinctions between ideals of love and justice and the realities he sees.

Like many other experimental writers, Pynchon challenges the meaning of effort and the value of thought. He judges ideas as ideologies, by the uses to which they are put, and ultimately condemns them as instruments of destructive power. Like other experimental writers, he calls into question the worth of emotion. Unlike experimental writing of the Romantic period, which stressed the ecstatic freedom experienced in charged emotional states, contemporary experimental fiction sees charged emotional states as predominantly painful. It is antiromantic in its emphasis on the limitations and dangers of feeling. The devaluation of emotion as an ideal has altered the nature of heroes and heroines and turned the focus of many novels from enlarging experience to controlling it, from love to devices for managing human contacts.

Fascination with self-protection, which Pynchon takes as an explicit subject, is a recurring theme in experimental literature. It has had an inevitable impact on sexual love and sexual roles. As heroes and heroines search for armature rather than intimacy, they cease to see themselves as husbands, parents, workers or even as traditional lovers. Many heroes are attempting to correct the problems of masculinity by feminization, by playing the passive roles once assigned to women. Although a fully aggressive, assertive woman has yet to appear in the pages of feminist fiction, she is there as an ideal and a hope. How to explain the wish for so large an exchange of sexual roles? Aggression and vulnerability can serve as checks and balances; the aggressor plays the victim rather than unleash or face his anger. The victim attempts to avoid victimization by becoming an aggressor. It would be an oversimplification to say that men and women are only attempting to repair or correct their lives by assuming the role conventionally assigned to the opposite sex. The need to do so expresses a more pervasive and nonsexual need which permeates experimental fiction. This is the wish to divest oneself of known and predictable troubles and situations and to see oneself and one's world differently.

What experimental fiction contributes to us is its perspectives, its faith in possibility. It makes us see in extreme and at times frightening images the impact of the postwar period on our imagination of ourselves at work, in love, and in the recesses of thought.

7

Black Literature
Nathan A. Scott, Jr.

T
HE decidedly ethnic and regional configuration of the American literary scene over the past generation is frequently remarked, and it is surely a primary fact of our cultural life. Such figures as Ellen Glasgow, DuBose Heyward, Stark Young, and John Peale Bishop had, it is true, upheld a vigorous Southern tradition in the decades prior to World World II, but it was not till after the sudden recognition at last in the mid-1940s of Faulkner's towering genius that the Southern vanguard appeared to be bursting outside its previously presumed parochialism, and only then did we feel ourselves all at once beset by a great efflorescence of talent—in criticism (John Crowe Ransom, Donald Davidson, Allen Tate, Cleanth Brooks), in the theater (Tennessee Williams), and most especially in fiction (Katherine Anne Porter, Robert Penn Warren, Eudora Welty, Flannery O'Connor, Peter Taylor, William Styron, and numerous others). Or, again, such writers as Ludwig Lewisohn and Paul Rosenfeld, Henry Roth, Daniel Fuchs, and Nathanael West had tenuously guaranteed a certain Jewish presence in American literary life in the twenties and thirties, but it was only at some no doubt undatable point between (let us say) the appearance of Saul Bellow's *The Victim* (1947) and Bernard Malamud's *The Assistant* (1957) that we suddenly became aware of a huge and extraordinarily vital Jewish movement having very much taken on what Matthew Arnold called "the tone of the center"—by way of critics like Lionel Trilling, Alfred Kazin, Irving Howe, and Leslie Fiedler, and by way of novelists beyond number (Norman Mailer, J. D. Salin-

ger, Philip Roth, Bruce Jay Friedman, Herbert Gold, and a host of others).

Now it is a similar pattern which is presented by the newly vigorous Black insurgency of the present time. Though customarily ignored in the "standard" accounts of the period, two Negro writers of genuine, if minor, distinction—the poet and novelist Paul Laurence Dunbar and the novelist Charles Waddell Chesnutt—had already come forward at the turn of the century. And in the years that immediately followed a sizable number of Negro critics and scholars (W. E. B. DuBois, Benjamin Brawley, Carter G. Woodson, William Stanley Braithwaite, Alain Locke), as well as numerous minor poets (Fenton Johnson, Joseph Cotter, Georgia Douglas Johnson, Alice Dunbar-Nelson, Anne Spencer), were steadily active. Then, stretching from the late 1920s into the middle years of the ensuing decade, there came a bright, happy time of great promise—now much mythicized—when at last it seemed that in the arts and in intellectual affairs one might herald the arrival of (in the phrase forming the title of a widely read anthology edited by Alain Locke)[1] the New Negro. The sudden emergence of an immense number of gifted black writers appeared to augur the inception of a Third Force on the American literary scene, and since—by reason of its closeness to the nerve center of the country's cultural ferment and the hospitality it offered radical movements in Negro life—New York City's Harlem was for this generation of Negro intellectuals a kind of Mecca toward which they gravitated in spirit if not as actual residents, the movement has long been spoken of as the Harlem Renaissance. Nor can its focal role in the formation of a people's sensibility be easily overstressed, for it was in the poetry of James Weldon Johnson and Claude McKay, of Langston Hughes and Countee Cullen and Sterling Brown, that Negro Americans of this century first encountered a large expression in lyric form of their ancestral memories and of the strange, bitter exactions which their fated involvement in the American reality entailed—just as it was in the fiction of Nella Larsen and Jean Toomer, of Claude McKay and Rudolph Fisher, of Wallace Thurman and Zora Neale Hurston that they also found a multifaceted mirror of much that belonged to the concrete actuality of their "ordinary universe"; and, inevitably, the advent of a burgeoning literature so clearly *theirs* was profoundly quickening.

Amongst those whom we associate with the Harlem Renaissance it was Langston Hughes who had the longest productive career, and, by the early 1960s, the impressive accomplishment he had realized over

1. See Alain Locke, ed., *The New Negro: An Interpretation* (New York: Albert and Charles Boni, 1925).

forty years of unremitting work had won a considerable public whose relation toward him was distinguished perhaps most especially by its genial and steadfast affectionateness. But none of the other representatives of the Harlem movement succeeded in making any large impress on the general literary scene. They were, many of them—Weldon Johnson and Countee Cullen particularly—cherished within the Negro community, and, for a brief moment, when black writers and artists were felt to be wondrously strange, they were hawked about by such specialists in exotic *Tendenz* as Nancy Cunard and Carl Van Vechten; but by the major strategists of literary politics—such critics, say, as Edmund Wilson and Malcolm Cowley, or the editors of *The Hound and Horn* and *The Southern Review*—they were simply ignored.

So it was not until the spring of 1940, when Harper and Brothers brought out Richard Wright's *Native Son,* that the work of a Negro writer made, by its appearance, a truly salient event. Within a month after its publication this novelistic account of the violent criminality with which a Chicago Negro opposes an oppressive social order was moving across book dealers' counters all over the land by tens of thousands of copies. It frequently was being said—with an absurdity by which many reviewers in their zeal for a generous liberalism were unembarrassed—that nothing so comparable to the great tragic fictions of Dostoevsky had yet appeared in our literature. And hordes of Wright's readers were enjoying that great thrilling shiver of delight that many had come to find in "the fun-world of proletarian legend," especially when the fun involved the moderately threatening specter of some black desperado venturing an act of resistance.

In one of the stories in his book of 1938, *Uncle Tom's Children,* the husband of a Negro woman who has been seduced by a white salesman says: "The white folks ain never gimme a chance! They ain never give no black man a chance! There ain nothing in yo whole life yuh kin keep from em! . . . Ahm gonna be hard like they is! So hep me Gawd, Ahm gonna be *hard!* When they come fer me Ahm gonna *be here!*" Which is precisely the posture of the demoniac wraith who is the protagonist of *Native Son.* As James Baldwin was perhaps the first to remark, the novel is, however, at every point overwhelmed by the very cancer it wants to cauterize.[2] For from the moment on its first page, when Bigger Thomas is awakened by the *Brrrrrriiiiiiiiiiinnng!* of his alarm clock, until he turns at the end to his Jewish lawyer, Mr. Max, with a "faint, wry, bitter smile" of farewell, *Native Son* is controlled by just those hopeless assumptions about Negro life which elicited its

2. See "Everybody's Protest Novel," *Partisan Review,* 16, no. 6 (June 1949), 578-585.

rage. In taking its measure of Bigger's homicidal malevolence—"inspired in him, woven by our civilization into the very structure of his consciousness, into his blood and bones"—it tells us that to multiply this black *enragé* "twelve million times . . . [is to] have the psychology of the Negro people." And thus, in offering a depraved and inhuman monster as its comprehensive image of the American Negro, it shows itself to be wholly captive to the envenomed abstractions of racial myth. In short, the imagination that we meet here is extremist and melodramatic, feeding on the horrific themes of alienation and violence and abysmal fear. It wants to sound a hue and a cry and to warn of "the fire next time," if black men are not soon granted a decent justice; and its special pathos is a consequence of its being required, therefore, very severely to brutalize its fictional protagonist, in order to make him "hard"—the unhappy result being an image of *la présence noire* that is in no great way removed from the wild and lickerish nigger who inhabits the demented imagination of the racial paranoiac. The logic guiding the novel says in effect that to be black is to be an outsider, in a sociological sense and, even more decisively, in a moral sense as well. It is assumed that the mission of the outsider is, in the manner of Camus' Caligula, to disclose the human City to be something like a jungle where all the disciplines and restraints of civilization are but screens wherewith men seek to conceal the disorder that seethes beneath the surface. And since this is a mission that must often entail some form of terrorism, Wright asks us to believe that the natural life-movement of the Negro who bears the full burden of his situation is toward a great blasting moment of supreme destruction. Bigger Thomas is an inarticulate proletarian who enacts this role unthinkingly —whereas Cross Damon, the hero of Wright's novel of 1953, *The Outsider,* accepts his mission with deliberateness and in the spirit of a kind of inverted messianism, since he is a half-educated autodidact who is drunk with his misconceptions of Nietzsche's *Übermensch.* But both figures aim, as it were, at getting outside of history altogether, through an act of consummate violence: by being "hard," each bursts the belt and wins through at last to the unhistorical realm of the dream—which is of revenge.

Richard Wright was, of course, always impatient with the "proving disciplines" of art. For him the greatest uses of literature were not those by which we distance ourselves from the world in order to contemplate more strenuously its pattern and meaning: they were, rather, those by which we seek a more direct entry into the world for the sake of redeeming it from the brutality and the indecencies by which it must otherwise be overwhelmed. And thus it is a sad irony that his work did in point of fact so often drift toward a definition of man, and particularly of black men, that deeply undercut his intention to make it serve a genuinely humane purpose. As James Baldwin has said, the real tragedy of Bigger Thomas "is not that he is cold or black or hungry, not even that he is American, black; but that he has accepted a theology that denies him life, that he admits the possibility of his being sub-human and feels constrained, therefore, to battle for his humanity according to those brutal criteria bequeathed him at his birth."[3] And it is such a confusion that renders so ambiguous not only Bigger Thomas and Cross Damon but many of the other chief protagonists of Wright's fiction.

Yet, for all the dubieties surrounding Wright's legacy, it *lasts*—for young Blacks of the present time, most especially by way of his two most important novels (*Native Son* and *The Outsider*) and his moving autobiography of 1945, *Black Boy*. And one suspects that the chief reason for the eminence accorded him by the Black insurgency of recent years is that he, more powerfully than any of his predecessors, is felt to have certified and given a large kind of moral prestige to the angers lodged in the hearts of those who have had to endure such cruel disadvantages as the penalties of color have ordained for the American Negro.

It is, however, only in the years since his death (in 1960) that Wright's example has proved to be deeply quickening for Black writers. In his book *The Negro Novel in America,* Robert Bone, in speaking of the novelists who followed Wright in the forties, proposes that they be thought of as forming "the Wright School"[4] of the period; but this, surely, is a sect which is largely an invention of Mr. Bone's. True, when one looks back at the work being produced by Negro writers in those years—when one thinks of Carl Ruthven Offord's *The White Face* (1943), of Chester Himes's *If He Hollers Let Him Go* (1945) and *Lonely Crusade* (1947), of Ann Petry's *The Street* (1946), of Willard Motley's *Knock on Any Door* (1947), of William Gardner Smith's *Last of the Conquerors* (1948)—one cannot fail to be reminded of how tyrannously this literature was dominated by the procedures of documentary naturalism. But their abject surrender to the kind of literary positivism which conceives artistry to be something merely superimposed on the exposition of a subject argues no special role for Richard Wright in relation to these writers: they were simply the natural issue of a generation which supposed that *J'accuse!* could be pronounced

3. Ibid., p. 585.
4. See *The Negro Novel in America,* rev. ed. (New Haven: Yale University Press, 1965), pp. 157-160.

only in the idioms of Dreiser and Farrell, and their general style of work was no whit different from that which one encountered in the fiction of Erskine Caldwell and Ira Wolfert and various others committed to one or another form of special protestantism and representing the tag ends of the naturalism of the 1930s. Nor does Wright's essential spirit—his fierce dudgeon, his grim, implacable stridency—figure very prominently in the work of Negro poets in the forties. Margaret Walker's *For My People,* which in 1942 was the award-winning volume in the Yale Series of Younger Poets, is frequently informed by a stirring racial militancy, but, in its sensitive use of biblical idiom and of the sonorities of traditional Negro pulpit rhetoric, it stands not in the line of Wright but in that of the James Weldon Johnson of *God's Trombones* (1927). Similarly, in her book of 1945, *A Street in Bronzeville,* though Gwendolyn Brooks is in various ways at pains to remind us that a black man who would perform any great service for this Republic must "kick their law into their teeth in order to save them," the predominating tone of her charmingly etched vignettes of the Negro scene in Chicago is that of a relaxed and genial comedienne. Or, again, the poetic work of Owen Dodson (*Powerful Long Ladder,* 1946) and Robert Hayden (*The Lion and the Archer,* 1948) in the forties represents positions quite independently taken. So, however much Wright's early successes may have prepared the way for a new attentiveness where Negro writers were concerned, those who were active in the years immediately following the appearance of *Native Son* do not form any direct and easily traceable line of descent from Wright himself.

Yet, though very gradually doors were being opened, the novel which represents the most impressive work done by any Negro writer in the decade following the first emergence of Richard Wright—William Demby's *Beetlecreek* (1950)—did, by some miscarriage of advertisement, immediately after its appearance slip into an unfortunate obscurity from which, even now, it has not quite been rescued. It is not a book whose weight and range are of the kind belonging to major fiction, but its refusal of the automatisms of racial protest and the cogency of its construction ought to give it pride of place over many less worthy books of its period which have enjoyed much wider currency. It takes us into a small West Virginia town and places two figures in the foreground—an old white man, Bill Trapp, and Johnny Johnson, a Negro boy who is living in the town with his aunt and uncle for the period of his mother's hospital confinement in Pittsburgh. Bill Trapp, who keeps a small farm on the edge of the town's Negro quarter, somehow long ago became disconnected from the world of men and for years has lived as a hermit, a distant and vaguely disturbing presence amongst the townspeople, and one so much a stranger to that sense of self mediated by one's minglings with others that, when he stands before a mirror, he is often uncertain as to whether he is inside the mirror or inside himself. Then one day he catches Johnny and some of his playmates raiding one of his apple trees, and at once the boys, long familiar with his gruff crotchetiness, run shrieking from the yard. But Johnny, having only recently come into the neighborhood and not thinking of him as any sort of misanthropic ogre, remains, and, to his own astonishment, the old man finds himself touched by some sweetness in the boy's "gentle, pear-shaped face." After Johnny descends from the tree, he bids him sit down on the porch of his shack and brings him a cup of cider, and then another and another—by which time the child's uncle, David Diggs, has come to search him out, and he in turn is persuaded by the old man to tarry, over a bottle of dandelion wine:

> They drank; their breaths and sighs were in unison. They stole looks at each other from out of the corner of their eyes. And then the Negro man laughed.
> "So you're Mister Bill Trapp?" he said. "Well, sir, it's a pleasure to be here with you. A real pleasure."

And they sit there on the porch, talking and drinking, till the light fades to near darkness.

The news of Diggs's *causerie* with Bill Trapp quickly spreads through the Negro district, where the event wins no approval, since, there, it is taken for granted that no "peckerwood" is to be trusted. Meanwhile, the old recluse is undergoing a great resurrection of spirit, for the experience of his encounter with little Johnny and with David Diggs has awakened in him, after his long years of isolation, a sense of the necessity of reaching out to touch and to love others. So, diffidently and uncertainly, he begins to try to make contact with his neighbors: he offers a donation to the Negro church's annual bazaar, and he arranges a picnic for the town's children, black and white. But, though his party is a success, its aftermath is a rumor, swiftly bruited about, that he sexually molested one of his little guests. And sentiment becomes greatly inflamed in the Negro quarter, where the people invite one another to reverse the thing and to consider what the consequence would be if "a colored man . . . [had started] all this monkey business with white girls." "His life wouldn't be worth a row of pins," says one—"not one row of pins!"

So it is not surprising that a teenage gang, the Nightriders, should decide that an act of retribution is called for. And Johnny Johnson proves to be their ready instrument. For he is a boy uprooted from his native Pittsburgh, lonely in the setting of his new residence and desperately wanting to be included within some snug community of acceptance in the little world of Beetlecreek; and thus he consents to perform the "courageous deed" which the Nightriders lay down as the prerequisite for his formal admission into their circle. On the night he keeps his appointment with the group in the town's Negro cemetery, the leader says: "You knows this old white man Bill Trapp? . . . Everybody know what would of happened if it had been a colored man did all that funny stuff. Everybody knows, ain't nobody doin nothing about it. The Nightriders want action! To test whether you worthy of 'comin a member of the Nightriders, we hereby charges you to go out to Bill Trapp's shanty and burn it to the ground! Bring forth the gasoline!" But not only is Johnny thereby committed to arson: after the shanty is enveloped by flames, as he stands looking at the spectacle, transfixed with horror at the thought that Bill Trapp is caught within the burning house, the old man suddenly appears beside him and says sadly, resignedly: "What have you done, Johnny?" Then the boy's chagrin and his guilt and his fright bring all at once a spasm of utter hysteria: "His fist closed tighter on the handle of the gasoline can and he felt his arm swinging out in a high swooping arc. And he heard a dull clang. And he felt Bill Trapp become limp. And he saw him fall to the ground." And thus the last state of things involves not only a ruined house but the death of a man.

There is much else, of course, that is happening in the novel, so much indeed (particularly in the matter of a revived affair between David Diggs and his college sweetheart, Edith Johnson) that Demby is finally deflected by the entanglements of his narrative from taking any very high advantage of his dénouement. But his people, all of them—Johnny, Bill Trapp, David Diggs, Edith, the Negro ladies who are the pillars of local religious enterprise, their unctuous parson ("the Reverend"), the habitués of Tolley's barbershop—are beautifully realized. And they are not enlisted in the service of the sort of *roman à thèse* in which Negro writers have tended to make their chief investment. Nor does Demby envisage the human community as immitigably split into two opposed camps, the one black and the other white. It is said, for example, of Bill Trapp that, years earlier, when he had been in the employ of a traveling carnival, as he secretly watched Negroes hanging about the big tents and whispering as if they were in church, "he felt close to them," felt that in their powerlessness and vulnerability "they were the same breed as he." And though the novel makes its full acknowledgment of all the bitter social realities that are the consequences of racial animus, these are realities which at last make only a kind of frame for that with which the book is most essentially engaged—namely, the terrifying capacities for violence and cruelty that are resident in the human heart. Demby asks in effect: why do we, black or white, live like this, and when will the thoughts that prompt us so fearfully to bruise one another be replaced by other thoughts? No doubt the kind of moral interrogation behind which his book lines itself up would have been immeasurably strengthened had he hovered longer and more intently over (in Conrad's famous phrase) "the outstretched ground of the case exposed." But his general design bespoke a quality of intelligence promising a new maturity in Negro fiction, and, viewed retrospectively, it may now be thought to have been a modest foretoken of the great event of 1952.

It was, of course, in the spring of that year that Ralph Ellison's novel *Invisible Man* burst upon the scene, and the astonishing authority of its art and of the systematic vision of the world which this art expressed immediately won for the book a preeminence which in the intervening years, far from being in any way diminished, has so consolidated itself that it is today universally regarded as an established classic of modern American literature. In a period when, no doubt under the influence of the new vogue of Henry James, so many representative American writers—Jean Stafford, Jane Bowles, Frederick Buechner, Isabel Bolton, William Goyen—were choosing to seek their effects by the unsaid and the withheld, by the dryly ironic analogy and the muted voice, Ellison, like Faulkner and Penn Warren, seemed notable in part for being unafraid to make his fiction howl and rage and hoot with laughter over "the complex fate" of the *homo Americanus*. And surely it is the uninhibited exhilaration and suppleness of his rhetoric that is a main source of that richness of texture which so distinguishes his great book. But sheer verbal energy alone does not guarantee any sort of large triumph for a work of fictional art: there must also be the gift for conveying, as James called it, "the direct impression" of the human world; and, in this, Ellison is superbly talented. Indeed, one of our keenest satisfactions in reading *Invisible Man* comes from the sense it gives us of being immersed in all the concrete materialities of Black experience: one hears the very buzz and hum of Harlem in the racy, pungent speech of his West Indians and native hipsters; one sees the fearful nonchalance of the zoot-suiter and hears the terrible anger of the Black nationalist on his street-corner platform; and all the grotesquery in the novel's account of a dreary little backwater of a remote Southern Negro college has in it a certain kind of empirically absolute rightness. The book is packed full of the

acutest observations of the manners and idioms and human styles that
constitute the ethos of Black life in America, and it gives us such a
sense of social fact as can be come by nowhere in the manuals of
academic sociology—all this being done with the ease that comes from
enormous expertness of craft, from deep intimacy of knowledge, and
from love. The late Delmore Schwartz exultantly declared shortly
after its appearance: "Reality (hear! hear!) is not mocked . . . as long
as such a book can be written."[5] And it has been the constant reitera-
tion of a similar verdict, over now a quarter-century, that has given
Ellison's novel a celebrity enjoyed perhaps by no other single text produced by any American writer since the time of Faulkner.

His protagonist is a young black man (unnamed) who, in the tradition
of "the American Adam," starts from a point outside the world. But he
is filled with "great expectations," for, in the beginning, he is what the
white masters of the Southern world in which he grows up were once
in the habit of calling a "good Negro": he has cheerfully accepted
all the promises of that Establishment, so much so that the oily-tongued
and cynical president of his college, Dr. Bledsoe, has singled him out
as his special ward. But, unhappily, on a certain day he unintentional-
ly exposes a visiting white trustee from the North to the local Negro
gin mill and to the incestuous entanglements of a Negro farmer's family in the neighborhood—and, as a result, is ousted from the college,
as a punishment for his having allowed a donor of the institution to
see what white folks are not supposed to see.

He then moves on to New York, there to pick his perilous course
through the treacherous byways of an infernally labyrinthine world,
as he seeks to make contact with whatever it is that may authenticate
his existence. The executive powers ordain that, being black, he shall
be "invisible," and thus his great central effort becomes that of wrest-
ing an acknowledgment, of *achieving* visibility. He gets a job in a Long
Island paint factory, and there he becomes involved—again, inadvertently—as a scab in labor violence. Soon afterward, however, he is
taken up by "the Brotherhood" (that is, the Communist Party), after
he is heard to deliver an impassioned and a quite spontaneous speech
one winter afternoon, as he finds himself part of a crowd watching the
eviction of an elderly Negro couple from their Harlem tenement flat.
The assignment he is given by his new confreres is that of *organizing*
the sullenness of Harlem. But he soon discovers that the Negro's cause
is but a pawn being used by "the Brotherhood" to promote its "line."
So, after a furious race riot in the Harlem streets, he in utter disillu-

5. "Fiction Chronicle: The Wrongs of Innocence and Experience," *Partisan Review*, 19, no. 3 (May-June 1952), 359.

sionment dives through a manhole, down into a cellar, for a period of "hibernation." He has tried the way of "humility," of being a "good Negro"; he has tried to find room for himself in American industry, to become a good cog in the technological machine; he has attempted to attach himself to leftist politics—he has tried all those things by means of which it would seem that a Negro might achieve visibility in American life. But, since none has offered a way into the culture, he has now chosen to become an underground man. All his reversals have been due to the blackness of his skin: so now, at last, he decides to stay in his cellar, where, by way of a tapped line, he will steal the electricity for his 1,369 bulbs from Monopolated Light and Power and dine on sloe gin and vanilla ice cream and *embrace* "The Blackness of Blackness."

Yet Ellison's protagonist, unlike so many of his counterparts in Negro fiction, is in the end by no means one *merely* wounded. True, he twice tells us, in the accent of Eliot's *East Coker*—first in the Prologue, and again at the end of his narrative—that his "end is in . . . [his] beginning." And so it is, for his last state—since it is an underworld, a place of exile, of dislodgment and expatriation—is in a way his first. But it is an underworld that *he* has *illuminated*. "Step outside the narrow borders of what men call reality and you step into chaos . . . or imagination," he says. When, that is, you step outside the domesticated and the routinized, you may step into chaos, since the definition of the world, as he has discovered, is possibility—the very infiniteness of which may be defeating, unless by dint of a feat of imagination some transcendence can be realized. And since, as it would seem, the protagonist-narrator conceives art itself to be the definition of such a transcendence, he—amidst the misrule and confusion of a demented world—has undertaken to form the lessons he has learned into a story, to "put it [all] down," and thereby (like another young man who became an artist) to forge in the smithy of his own soul the uncreated conscience of his native land. His story ends in a cellar, because, having constantly been told that it is in some such hovel that he belongs, this *eiron* has chosen mockingly to descend, then, into a Harlem basement, where, if he cannot have visibility, he can at least have *vision*— and where he can produce out of his abysmal pain a poetry that, "on the lower frequencies," may help to redeem all those, black and white, who, in refusing to *see* their neighbors, profane the sacrament of the brother. Nor does the voice of this monologist fail to indicate—in its urgency, its vibrant eloquence, its subtle alternations between outrage and hilarity—that he, far from being merely a wounded Adam, is indeed, even after all his searing encounters with the world, a winner

297

and a master of the field. But not only is he in the end triumphant: so too is the book in which he "puts it [all] down." *Invisible Man,* says Alfred Kazin, "is about the art of survival,"[6] and, as such, it is, in its brilliant minglings of comic and tragic modalities, something close to a masterpiece.

Though in the nature of its dramatized material it lacks the breadth and richness of Ellison's novel and though it is uncomplicated by his tough kind of dialectic ("dialectic," that is, in the sense of developing *argument*), James Baldwin's *Go Tell It on the Mountain,* coming out as it did only a year after the appearance of *Invisible Man,* seemed at the time indisputably to confirm the Negro writer's having at last become a central force; and we can now see it also to have marked the beginning of one of the major careers in American literary life of the past generation. Baldwin, like Ralph Ellison, was clearly aiming to produce, as he did, something very impressive; and, fortunately, both were in full possession of the truth than which there is none it is more important for the writer to have grasped—namely, that he can "step out into the universal only by first going through the narrow door of the particular."[7] Moreover, James Baldwin was also determined, like Ellison, to forswear that passionate incoherence which in the past had so frequently distinguished the conventional formulas of protest in Negro fiction. In an essay at the end of the forties called "Everybody's Protest Novel" he, in what was virtually his first major declaration, had very brusquely described and registered his disesteem for that fear of the rich, complex particularity of the human individual which he took to be a defining characteristic of "protest" fiction, from Harriet Beecher Stowe's *Uncle Tom's Cabin* to Laura Hobson's *Gentleman's Agreement* (a then popular novel dealing polemically with anti-Semitism). Here, he had argued, is a literature that moves wholly within the bloodless abstractions of ethical rhetoric, a literature asserting at least by implication that "it is [the human being's] categorization alone which is real and which cannot be transcended." And, as he had maintained, for all the simplicity of its good intentions, it is a literature which is mischief-making, in the insidiousness with which it persuades its victims to accede to the dehumanization it practices upon them. Indeed, though this twenty-five-year-old young man had just a few years earlier, when unaided and without connections, been befriended and helped by Richard Wright to win a Saxton Fellowship,

6. *Bright Book of Life: American Novelists and Storytellers from Hemingway to Mailer* (Boston: Little, Brown, 1973), p. 246.

7. Cleanth Brooks, "Irony as a Principle of Structure," in *Literary Opinion in America,* ed. Morton Dauwen Zabel (New York: Harper and Bros., 1951), p. 729.

he had not hesitated in this essay to cite the work of his benefactor as his culminating example of the special kind of *trahison* which he was rejecting: Bigger Thomas, he had said, "is Uncle Tom's descendant, flesh of his flesh."

So, when his own first novel appeared in 1953, it was not surprising that, instead of the "raging, near-paranoiac"[8] kind of recusancy which he considered to be a chief mark of Negro fiction, Baldwin should have chosen such a form as that of the *Bildungsroman*. And that "narrow door of the particular" through which he moved was nothing other than his own Harlem boyhood in a family presided over by his father, David Baldwin, a dour storefront preacher, whose religion was a narrow, fanatical pietism made absurdly stern and exacting in its ethic by what was neurasthenic in the experience of black proletarians living amid the wilderness of New York City.

The theme of *Go Tell It on the Mountain* concerns, then, the formation of a boy's character, a sensitive Negro boy who has to find his way toward some liberating sense of his own human possibilities in the repressive atmosphere of a primitive religion of Jesus and Satan which is fervently celebrated in his Harlem storefront church (The Temple of the Fire Baptized) and fiercely administered in his family. Indeed, as he faces the onerously restrictive world of his family and its dogmatical religion and the terrible backwater of Harlem, there comes a time when the young hero of the novel, John Grimes, decides that he must revolt. "He would not be like his father, or his father's fathers. He would have another life." He is standing one day in Central Park before a slope which "stretched upward, and above it the brilliant sky, and beyond it, cloudy, and far away, he saw the skyline of New York. He did not know why, but there arose in him an exultation and a sense of power, and he ran up the hill like an engine, or a madman, willing to throw himself headlong into the city that glowed before him . . . For it was his; the inhabitants of the city had told him it was his; he had but to run down, crying, and they would take him to their hearts and show him wonders his eyes had never seen."

The dream by which he is stirred that day in Central Park never comes to fulfillment, however, or at least not to a fulfillment so simple as that which the boy first imagines. For John is finally swept by his great need for reconciliation with his family and with his ancestral community, by his guilt over his awakening sexuality, by the unsubduable propensity for religious hysteria implanted in him by his nurture—he is finally hurled by all these forces onto the Threshing-Floor

8. Baldwin, *Partisan Review*, June 1949, pp. 585, 584, 578.

and swept into a high fever of spiritual convulsion in The Temple of
the Fire Baptized. And though in his moment of seizure an "ironic
voice insisted . . . that he rise from that filthy floor if he did not want
to become like all the other niggers," and though he feels himself, as
it were, in a grave, he beholds in this grave "the despised and rejected,
the wretched and the spat upon, the earth's offscouring." In this moment of awful transport the trouble-laden history of his father and
mother, of Aunt Florence, of Praying Mother Washington and Sister
McCandless and Sister Price, becomes as never before a living reality:
"their dread testimony" and "their desolation" become his, and he
knows that only as he passes through their darkness will he find his
right course. So, at the novel's close, after the fearful night of his conversion experience is over, he walks at dawn through the squalid
streets of Harlem with his mother and father, with Aunt Florence and
Brother Elisha and Sister Price—"among the saints, he, John . . . one
of their company now." His soul is filled with gladness, for he has
sworn to fight the good fight. And what is implied is that the vista he
beheld that day from his "mountain" in Central Park will finally be
achieved only by way of a pilgrimage involving an ascent of that Mount
of Primal Pain that has been immemorially trodden by Hager's children.

The book—which is one of the most tightly constructed and beautifully written novels of our period—is not, to be sure, a "protest novel,"
but it does become for Baldwin, finally, a passionate gesture of identification with his people. And it can now be seen in retrospect as fore-
shadowing the path he was increasingly to follow in the years to come.
It was succeeded, of course, by the essay in the morally fancy punctilio
of Paris homosexualism which formed his novel of 1956, *Giovanni's
Room*; but, despite Baldwin's deep engagement with the homosexual
life, this is a book that strikes us as a deflection, as a kind of detour.
Yet, throughout the 1950s, he was busily employed in journalism, writing about books and the theater and his travels and various aspects of
the American scene. And in all these various pieces—collected in *Notes
of a Native Son* (1955) and *Nobody Knows My Name* (1961)—as he
probed more deeply the meaning of Negro experience, his own chosen
role came more and more to be that of racial ideologue and of Chief
Barrister for the Black multitudes at the bar of the American conscience. It is such a commitment that, very clearly, was guiding his
performance in the deeply flawed novel of 1962, *Another Country*,
which, though surveying that special region of improvisings in sexual
life and probative ventures across racial barriers embraced by New
York's Greenwich Village, wants to summon us into the uncolonized

world of "another country," of *agape* and *philia*—but which is yet more filled with the passions of hatred and contempt than perhaps any other memorable American novel of our time. And the play of 1964, *Blues for Mister Charlie,* is, in all its angry polemic, similarly supervised by the interests of one whose primary intention is that of bringing forward a great arraignment, in the name of the overburdened Black commonalty.

Indeed, it is a penchant for spokesmanship in behalf of an increasingly aggressive racialism that defined the central tendency of James Baldwin's testimony through the 1960s, and it is the corrosively eloquent book he published in 1963, *The Fire Next Time,* which represents his finest work in this mode. The book opens with a brief "Letter to My Nephew on the One Hundredth Anniversary of the Emancipation" which says to this "tough, dark, vulnerable, moody" boy who is his namesake that, though he was set down by his country in a ghetto where he was intended to perish or at least "to make peace with mediocrity." he must never accept the official valuation placed upon his life by white America. But it is the remarkable essay forming the remainder of the book—the "Letter from a Region in My Mind"— that constitutes its principal statement. Indeed, its first appearance in the issue of *The New Yorker* for November 17, 1962, made a kind of thunderclap that was itself a most rare event in American cultural life: immediately it began to be talked about everywhere—on campuses, in pulpits, in political forums, in the corridors of federal Washington—with an intensity that seemed to promise a very profound reshaping of the national consciousness. It is not, of course, a coolly analytic essay on "race relations" but a moral manifesto whose extraordinary power resides in the grave, evangelical eloquence with which it enunciates a great immovable wrath. And, in the days following that late autumn week of 1962 in which William Shawn published the piece in his magazine, the nation knew itself to have been submitted to a most stringent judgment.

Much of the "Letter" is devoted to a brilliantly rendered chronicling of the indignities and humiliations that make up the common experience of the black multitudes in the American metropolis of our time; and no bit of harshness is spared as Baldwin takes us into the "wine-stained and urine-splashed" hallways of urban tenements and cites the bulletins of disaster daily brought to families, as he describes the bewildered despair with which adolescents settle into "the long, hard winter of life" and the murder of all hope that occurs as young people begin to discover that one shall "never defeat one's circumstances by working and saving one's pennies, [since] one . . . [shall]

301

never, by working, acquire that many pennies." The world he describes—with a great and terrible anger—is one in which all the effective power is in the hands of whites, so that there is no real possibility for the black proletarian of offering any resistance to a system which tells him where he may go and what he may do, where he can live and whom he can marry. And thus black children, supposing, since the world is white and they are black, that they must themselves be inferior, grow up in a culture which confers upon them—as soon as consciousness dawns—a sense of being hopelessly fated to exclusion and alienation. Ours, says James Baldwin, is a society tragically lunatic and demented, yet infinitely ingenious in the arrangements it devises for the abuse and oppression of people whose great offense is none other than that of being black.

His major purpose, however, ranges beyond the mere tabulating of grievance and sorrow, for what he wants finally to declare is that, *nevertheless,* the salvation of America, if there is to be any—if it is *ever* to be transformed into "another country"—is in the keeping of its Negro minority. For Negro Americans have "the great advantage of having never believed that collection of myths to which white Americans cling: that their ancestors were all freedom-loving heroes, that they were born in the greatest country the world has ever seen, or that Americans are invincible in battle and wise in peace, that Americans have always dealt honorably with Mexicans and Indians and all other neighbors or inferiors, that American men are the world's most direct and virile, that American women are pure." And thus, never having been captive to these great national superstitions about America's innocence and virtue and having been given by his own experience a profound sense of what is fateful and tragic in the general human condition, the Negro, if he will consent to *love* his white brother, may succeed in educating his mind and heart—into a new maturity and decency. By "love," however, Baldwin means no cheap grace, no easy forgiveness, for there is no forgiving the cruel chastisements white America has administered to black people for nearly three hundred years—"rope, fire, torture, castration, infanticide, rape; death and humiliation; fear by day and night, fear as deep as the marrow of the bone." He means, rather, when he invites his black brothers to "love" their white brothers, that their great mission, their great duty, is that of ruffling the common peace and of forcing the nation to see itself as it really is. Yeats, in his poem "Meditations in Time of Civil War," says: "We had fed the heart on fantasies, / The heart's grown brutal from the fare." And it is a similar testimony Baldwin makes, that the people who are soothed and comforted by "the American dream" have fed their hearts on terrible fantasies, that their hearts have grown brutal from the fare—and that, standing where he stands in relation to this dream, the Negro possesses a kind of wisdom which the country desperately needs. Indeed, he says, if ways are not found of releasing into the common life of the nation what has been learned amidst the unhappiness and travail of places like Harlem, we may well get *the fire next time!*.

In the moment in which James Baldwin's powerful indictment was issued, the pace of events in the field of racial politics was, of course, accelerating with a prodigious rapidity. Substantial gains in the correction of old inequities had been realized in the post–World War II period, but each advance had been bitterly opposed by white segregationists, and it was difficult to discern any large improvement of the general condition of American Negroes, in its daily actuality. Since the spring of 1954, when the Supreme Court had outlawed racial segregation in the nation's schools, not only had massive resistance to the ruling been officially offered by all the states of the old Confederacy, but Negro children, after being taken to local schoolhouses by their parents, had been submitted again and again to cruel harassments and intimidations by white schoolmates and their parents. And though the enactment by Congress of the Civil Rights legislation of 1957 and 1960 enabled the Attorney General's office more actively to safeguard persons whose constitutional rights were being violated (particularly in the area of the franchise), the judicial process seemed at best to be something cumbrous and dilatory. So, given the continuing intransigence of traditional racism, it was natural that impatience within the Negro community should begin, as it did, very greatly to intensify.

In 1956, in its effort to win more equitable seating regulations on local buses and to force the employment of a fair number of Negro drivers, the Negro populace of Montgomery, Alabama, under the leadership of a young Baptist clergyman, Martin Luther King, had mounted an extraordinarily impressive and, finally, a successful boycott of the city transit company. And, with the advent of the 1960s, enthusiasm for the techniques of direct action was beginning to be widely contagious. Negro college students throughout the South were staging sit-ins at lunch counters and in restaurants where they had been refused service. The Congress of Racial Equality, an interracial group working in the field of civil rights, was dispatching "freedom riders" throughout the region in an attempt to break segregated arrangements in interstate transportation, and in this effort CORE was being valiantly supported by such organizations as the Student Nonviolent Coordinating Committee (SNCC), the Southern Christian Leadership

Conference, and the Nashville Student Movement. The year 1963 marked, of course, the hundredth anniversary of the Emancipation, and it was a year made notable by many vast demonstrations mounted by Negro groups in the streets of cities in the North as well as in the South, as they pressed forward their demands for the desegregation of public facilities and for the extension of fair employment opportunities. And, as Congress debated President Kennedy's proposal of a new Civil Rights Act, this flurry of activity was brought to a kind of climax on the twenty-eighth of August by the March on Washington for Jobs and Freedom, when more than two hundred thousand people, black and white, from all over the land gathered on the mall extending from the Washington Monument to the Lincoln Memorial, in the largest outdoor mass meeting in the history of the nation's capital. The event was sponsored by hundreds of groups with national constituencies, and many of their leaders—A. Philip Randolph, Roy Wilkins, Walter Reuther—delivered speeches before the enormous throng assembled on the mall that hot August afternoon, but, more than anything else, the rolling periods of Martin Luther King's great culminating address ("I have a dream . . .") have now fixed immovably the whole occasion in the national memory.

Less than a year after the March on Washington, in the spring of 1964, under the goading of President Lyndon Johnson, Congress enacted the most comprehensive civil rights legislation in the country's history, the Act giving to the Attorney General effective power to defend all citizens against any deprivation of their free access to public facilities, of their exercise of the ballot, and of their use of the nation's public educational resources. But the strength of "white backlash"— as exemplified in the national following that soon gathered round the virulently segregationist Governor of Alabama, George Wallace—convinced many Negroes that, whatever the formal statutes of established law might say, theirs was still a very scrubby purse. And since legislative advance, while bringing satisfaction to those Negroes whose pocketbooks enabled them to reserve a table in a good restaurant or accommodations in a respectable hostelry, had not—forthwith, *mirabile dictu!*—substantially altered, though apparently promising to do so, the unhappy circumstances of black proletarians in the major centers of the urban North, their restiveness steadily increased and finally exploded in those thunderous riots that marked the "long hot summers" of the middle and late sixties, in New York and Los Angeles and Philadelphia and Chicago and Detroit and numerous other cities.

Amidst all this ferment, however, perhaps the most decisive event, at least as regards the shaping of a new Black sensibility, was the cry for "Black Power" that began to be sounded in the summer of 1966 by the young chairman of SNCC, Stokely Carmichael. Immediately it had a mesmerizing effect on the young, though this betokened not so much their illusions about the power (political and economic) Negroes had or were likely to win as the new sense of their own humanity that had been gradually forming over the previous decade—to which the stirring homilies of James Baldwin had contributed in no small measure. They had been profoundly enheartened, through all the perilous and exhausting civil rights battles in the South that followed the Montgomery boycott, by the discovery of the heroism of which they themselves were capable. Nor had they been untouched by the new vitalities that seemed to be at work south of the Sahara, in the achievement of independence by Ghana and Tanganyika, by Kenya and Zanzibar, by Sierra Leone and Uganda: Africa—the Land of their Fathers—was at last beginning to be free of European colonialism and to be in charge of its own destiny. So, as they looked back at their own past—"rope, fire . . . humiliation"—and at that of their brothers of "Mother Africa," they were wanting to affirm with the force of a newly strengthened certitude that here, in this saga of suffering and struggle, there is (as *The Fire Next Time* says) "something very beautiful"—and something which, as they began to feel, stands to be betrayed by any vision of the future as involving nothing more than their assimilation into the world of white America. And thus once Stokely Carmichael raised his cry of "Black Power," it, in animating these passions, was instantly captivating: the immediate response was, yes—let us have Black Power, let us consolidate that which is distinctly *ours,* for (as the watchword soon began to be) "Black is beautiful"; and, overnight, the semantics of self-definition made it *de rigueur* amongst the young that the term "Negro" be supplanted by the term "Black."

The rapidly increasing assertiveness of this new mood in the late sixties had, of course, certain consequences in the political arena—in the occasional disturbance of old alliances between Negroes and liberal whites and in various abortive programs of "Black nationalism." But its most telling result was observable in the changed tonality of cultural enterprise which found its most vigorous expressions in the new literary situation. In 1968 the young Black writer Julius Lester said: "I'm an Afro-American. This implies that I'm an amalgam. It is my responsibility to reflect the Afro side of the hyphen. The other side has been too much reflected."[9] But such an intention as Lester was expressing had always tended to distinguish the Negro writer, and the

9. Julius Lester, "The Arts and the Black Revolution," *Arts in Society,* 5 no. 2 (Summer-Fall 1968), 229.

new element that came to the fore in the sixties was an affair of the degree to which this old commitment was elaborated into a radically separatist ethnicism proposing to disengage itself not only from the larger world of American literature but also from the funded bequests of the entire Western tradition (which were conceived to be indelibly "white").[10] The program was gradually worked out in such magazines as *Freedomways, Negro Digest* (later *Black World*), *The Black Scholar* —and in the scores of writers' conferences that were convened on campuses and in community centers all over the North (in New York, Chicago, Detroit, Cleveland, Los Angeles, San Francisco) through the sixties and early seventies. Those who emerged as the chief strategists of this insurgency were the poet and playwright LeRoi Jones (who now calls himself Imamu Amiri Baraka), the novelist John Oliver Killens, the ideologue John Henrik Clarke, the poets Larry Neal and Don L. Lee, and the editor of the now defunct *Black World*, Hoyt Fuller; and what they brought into being is now generally spoken of as the Black Arts Movement—whose basic emphasis Larry Neal has set forth in the following way: "The Black Arts Movement is radically opposed to any concept of the artist that alienates him from his community. Black Art is the aesthetic and spiritual sister of the Black Power concept. As such, it envisions an art that speaks directly to the needs and aspirations of Black America. In order to perform this task, the Black Arts Movement proposes a radical reordering of the western cultural aesthetic. It proposes a separate symbolism, mythology, critique, and iconology."[11]

The major expression of this attempt at "a radical reordering of the western cultural aesthetic" has been an aggressive advertisement of "the Black Aesthetic," and its numerous definitions are as various as the manifold company of its ardent proponents. The Black nationalist Ron Karenga says: "Black art must expose the enemy, praise the

10. Again, in this, James Baldwin may be seen to have played a propaedeutic role, for, in one of the essays ("Stranger in the Village") he had collected in his book of 1955, *Notes of a Native Son*, he had spoken of himself as "strangely grafted" onto the West and of how distant from the roots of Negro experience he considered the world of "Dante, Shakespeare, Michelangelo, Aeschylus, Da Vinci, Rembrandt, and Racine" to be. "Out of . . . [the] hymns and dances [of European peasants] come Beethoven and Bach. Go back a few centuries and they are in their full glory—but I am in Africa, watching the conquerors arrive." Given what has come to be Baldwin's manifest chariness, however, with respect to the whole phenomenon of Black separatism, his having himself made some contribution to its development presents a kind of irony.

11. "The Black Arts Movement," in *The Black Aesthetic*, ed. Addison Gayle, Jr. (Garden City, N.Y.: Doubleday, 1972), p. 257.

people and support the revolution. It must be like LeRoi Jones' poems that are assassins' poems, poems that kill and shoot guns and 'wrassle cops into alleys taking their weapons, leaving them dead with tongues pulled out and sent to Ireland.' "[12] LeRoi Jones says: "The Black Artist's role in America is to aid in the destruction of America as he knows it. His role is to report and reflect so precisely the nature of the society, and of himself in that society, that other men will be moved by the exactness of his rendering and, if they are black men, grow strong through this moving, having seen their own strength, and weakness; and if they are white men, tremble, curse, and go mad, because they will be drenched with the filth of their evil."[13] Adam David Miller maintains that a literature responsive to the Black Aesthetic is one whose task is that not so much of "telling it like it is" as of telling it " 'like it needs to be' . . . [if a black man is] to make sense out of his experience."[14] John O'Neal says that a truly Black art is "Affirmation of the Black reality . . . Affirmation of Black potential, not trying to take black dreams and paint them white till even we don't know the difference any more."[15] Addison Gayle conceives the Black Aesthetic to be "a corrective—a means of helping black people out of the polluted mainstream of Americanism."[16] And a large anthology might be compiled of similar statements that have been a part of the many peppery declarations issued in recent years.

The manifest inchoateness of the whole ideology is perhaps best reckoned with in the terms advanced by the novelist Julian Mayfield, who, in an essay charmingly entitled "You Touch My Black Aesthetic and I'll Touch Yours," insists that he knows "quite definitely what Black Aesthetic is not" but admits that he is hard pressed to present a coherent account of what it positively comprehends within itself, for, as he candidly says, it "is easier to define in the negative."[17] And so, at the present time, it would seem to be. But the negatives behind which it lines itself up are by no means in question, and foremost amongst these is the infuriate veto registered against any and all hints that may appear in the work of Negro writers themselves of "cultural integrationism." Nothing, indeed, is more anathematized by the partisans of the Black Aesthetic than the kind of treason which they conceive to be represented by the Negro writer who says in effect that

12. "Black Cultural Nationalism," in *The Black Aesthetic*, p. 32.
13. *Home: Social Essays* (New York: William Morrow, 1966), p. 251.
14. "Some Observations on a Black Aesthetic," in *The Black Aesthetic*, p. 380.
15. "Black Arts: Notebook," in *The Black Aesthetic*, p. 56.
16. "Introduction," in *The Black Aesthetic*, p. xxii.
17. *The Black Aesthetic*, p. 23.

307

he is a writer who only happens to be a Negro and whose testimony in this regard is borne out by his wariness about the Black Aesthetic itself. So the fiction of William Demby and James McPherson and Leon Forrest is simply ignored. Or the poetry of Robert Hayden is viewed coolly, and with more than a little mistrust. In the estimate of LeRoi Jones, James Baldwin's work may be thought to be serious only "in the sense that, say, the work of Somerset Maugham is 'serious' writing";[18] and Addison Gayle finds it to reflect an "ignorance of black history and culture, [a] . . . condescending, negative criticism of the ancestral home, [and a] . . . contempt for Blacks based upon the same criteria as that [*sic*] used by whites."[19] But the large irony will not go unremarked, that the harshest acerbity is reserved for the most distinguished Negro writer on the American scene, Ralph Ellison, who cannot be forgiven for his own impatience with that "easy gesture of militancy" which he considers to be little more than a "con-game for ambitious, publicity-hungry Negroes." Nor can he be forgiven for the quiet steadfastness of his conviction that the Negro writer, like all other writers, must go it alone, "must suffer alone even as he shares the suffering of his group, and . . . must write alone and pit his talents against the standards set by the best practitioners of the craft, both past and present."[20] So he is said by many of the spokesmen for the Black Arts Movement to have been simply duped by the white Establishment, to have "bought the propaganda of the academic critics, accepted the image of the faceless, universal man."[21] And though some would doubtless want to modulate to a degree the violence of invective expressed by Ernest Kaiser's lengthy attack in *Black World* in December of 1970,[22] the animus in Kaiser's essay is, if not in its extremism at least in its basic tendency, fairly typical of that harbored by those of his general persuasion toward the author of *Invisible Man* and *Shadow and Act*.

The climate, then, which the new Black separatism has generated is one bristling with a partisanship more combative and recalcitrant than anything in this mode since the commotions occasioned in the name of the Proletariat by Michael Gold, Edwin Seaver, Granville Hicks, and their confederates more than forty years ago; and the En-

18. *Home,* p. 107.

19. *The Way of the New World: The Black Novel in America* (Garden City, N.Y.: Doubleday, 1975), p. 214.

20. *Shadow and Act* (New York: Random House, 1964), pp. 124, 139.

21. Gayle, *The Way of the New World,* p. 212.

22. See "A Critical Look at Ellison's Fiction and at Social and Literary Criticism by and about the Author," *Black World,* 20, no. 2 (December 1970), 53-59, 81-97.

glish observer Christopher Bigsby is not wide of the mark in suggesting that, though "the dialectic is no longer Marxist but ethnic," the skirmishings today on the American scene of the Black separatists against the "cultural integrationists" are strikingly reminiscent of "the virulence of the Stalin-Trotsky factions"[23] of the 1930s. Indeed, Ernest Kaiser's fulminations against "the weak, kicked-around-by-whites hero"[24] of *Invisible Man* carry us, in a strange way, directly back to Michael Gold's attack in the autumn of 1930 on Thornton Wilder's brooding with "tender irony" on his "little lavender tragedies."[25] And the reductionist formulas of the literary Marxism of that period—which espoused, of course, an economic determinism—are by way of being reinstated under the form of the new ethnicism, when it ordains, in Addison Gayle's formulation, that "a Negro community daily confronted by the horrors of the urban ghetto" represents a reality too much under stress to be liberated by any exploration of such questions as "Who am I? What is my identity? What is my relationship to the universe, to God, to the existential other?"[26] As a critic of Gayle rightly says,

> The vision of Negro American life implied in this dismissal of psychological, theological, and existential questions is shuddering to contemplate. It reduces the Negro to the role of merely victim of white brutality. It conceives of all Negroes as Bigger Thomases—mindless, inarticulate, totally determined, sub-human creatures incapable of experiencing creative freedom, intellectual curiosity, or liberating self-consciousness. The spectacle of the black critic thus circumscribing the range of black writing is full of pathos indeed, for it lulls the black writer into believing that any kind of careless, undisciplined craftsmanship is acceptable— as long as it voices the outraged Negro sensibility.[27]

But not only do the guardians of the Black Aesthetic carry on a rigorous policing action with respect to the reputations of Negro writters—pushing some down and others (most principally, Richard Wright) up—and with respect to the territory that Black literature may and may not explore: they are also eager, with a fury almost

23. "The Black American Writer," in *The Black American Writer,* ed. Bigsby (Baltimore: Penguin Books, 1971), p. 18.

24. Kaiser, *Black World,* December 1920, p. 82.

25. "Wilder: Prophet of the Genteel Christ," *The New Republic,* October 22, 1930, p. 267.

26. "Preface," in *Black Expression: Essays by and about Black Americans in the Creative Arts* (New York: Weybright and Talley, 1969), p. xi.

27. James W. Tuttleton, "The Negro Writer as Spokesman," in *The Black American Writer, p.* 255.

equal to that called forth by "integrationists" within the Negro community, to denounce those white critics who risk any public discussion
of Black literature. In his book *The Crisis of the Negro Intellectual*
Harold Cruse, for example, insists that "criticism of Negro writing is
mainly the Negro's responsibility."[28] Or, again, John Oliver Killens
says: "White critics are totally—and I mean totally—incapable of criticizing the black writer . . . They don't understand Afro-American-
ese."[29] So vociferously, indeed, has this dictum been laid down that
general discussion of Negro writers in the literary community—which,
even in an earlier time, had always been scandalously careless and
neglectful—has (excepting the work of Ellison and Baldwin) now
virtually ceased. And the unhappy result, of course, is that much
work deserving of wide attention—such as the fiction of John A.
Williams, Ishmael Reed, and Leon Forrest, or the poetry of Robert
Hayden and Michael Harper—is less well known than it ought to be
and too infrequently incorporated into the data with which American
criticism feels obliged to reckon.[30] But, as it would seem, many have
reached Richard Gilman's sad conclusion, that, in this late time, blacks
and whites can only look at one another "across a gulf of . . . speeches,
gestures, intentions, hopes." Gilman is very probably somewhat pleased
with that sensitivity in himself which leads him to discern that whites
can simply "no longer talk to black people . . . in the traditional humanistic ways," that Black literature is therefore "beyond . . . [their]
right to intrude on."[31] But, when his abdication begins to be writ large
amongst his white confreres (as it now does), it would seem surely that
a profound collapse of faith in the indivisibility of the human family

28. *The Crisis of the Negro Intellectual* (New York: William Morrow, 1967), p.
182.

29. Quoted in *The New York Times,* March 2, 1969, in an account of a seminar on
Black culture at Columbia University.

30. In 1969 Richard Howard published his survey of American poetry since 1950,
Alone with America (Atheneum): it is a huge book, running to nearly six hundred
pages, and is the most comprehensive estimate of the immediately contemporary
scene that any student of recent American poetry has produced. A substantial chapter is devoted to each of forty-one poets, who are ordered alphabetically, from A. R.
Ammons to James Wright. Yet, despite the breadth of his canvas, Howard chose to
treat not a single Negro writer (not even Gwendolyn Brooks or Robert Hayden,
both of whom have been doing impressive work over now the span of a generation).
And this remissness makes a large but quite typical instance of what is, unfortunately, the customary procedure of American criticism. Which leads one to feel that
no doubt in part the refusals of Black writers holding separatist ideologies are
prompted by the refusals which they themselves have suffered.

31. Richard Gilman, *The Confusion of Realms* (New York: Random House, 1969),
pp. 20, 19, 12.

and in the unity of culture has everywhere become a notable feature of the period.

So the weathers of American cultural life today, when viewed at least in relation to the role of the Negro writer, are distraught and ill-fated; and it is not a time in which bench marks can be easily descried. Yet, despite the confusions rife on all sides, there can be no failing to remark the unprecedented vitalities at work amongst Black writers, who, since 1960, have been more numerous and more active than at any previous point in our literary history.

In fiction, of course, the magnitude of Ralph Ellison's achievement in *Invisible Man* makes him the most distinguished presence, and his next book is one than which no other unbegotten novel has been more eagerly awaited in our time. Portions of the work in progress have occasionally appeared in journals since the early sixties, and they promise an important performance. But, meanwhile, his only major publication since the appearance of his first novel in 1952 is the brilliant book of 1964, *Shadow and Act,* which is a collection of his essays on diverse themes and topics concerning modern fiction, various aspects of American culture, and his interests in Negro music (jazz and the blues).

James Baldwin's major work since *Go Tell It on the Mountain* has been done in his essays—in *Notes of a Native Son* (1955), *Nobody Knows My Name* (1961), *The Fire Next Time* (1963), *No Name in the Street* (1972), and *The Devil Finds Work* (1976). He is one whose gifts as a fictionist are no doubt uncommon, but, in the writing that has followed his superbly constructed book of 1953, they are to be seen only fleetingly, in *Another Country* and in *Tell Me How Long the Train's Been Gone* (1968); and the novel of 1974, *If Beale Street Could Talk,* is something close to a disaster, in the sentimental automatism with which it reduces to hortatory banality the stunning insights of his nonfictional prose. Baldwin is, however, a man of immense talent, and one whose mercurial passions and intelligence make us think of him as a primary force in the country's literary life: so—like a figure in many ways so different as Norman Mailer—he is one whose future, though unpredictable, is felt to be filled with promise, not only for his own fulfillment but also for that of this late phase in American literature of the present century.

But who, then, after these *éminences,* are those to be made out as the figures nearest the center of the stage, in the field of the novel?

The special costs and preclusions that for Negro writers often belong to a literary vocation—most especially the discouragements occasioned by the indifference or condescension of the critical community and the difficulty of obtaining many of the customary forms of patron-age—are no doubt reflected in the unfortunate inactivity over a long period of certain of the more promising novelists who first appeared in the decade or so following the close of World War II. Though William Demby, for example, has at various intervals been said to be at work on one or another project, we have received no book from him since his impressive novel of 1965, *The Catacombs.* Here, he had moved a great distance from his book of fifteen years earlier (*Beetle-creek*)—from the American scene and from the conventions of realistic narrative; for, now, his setting was contemporary Rome (in which by the mid-sixties he had long been resident), and—by way of an elaborate artifice involving techniques of montage whereby the mythical and the historical, as well as personal and public dramas, are complexly inter-mingled—he was very ambitiously initiating an inquiry into what the existentialist jargon of the period called "the human condition." His chief personages are an American Negro novelist, "William Demby" (who is, of course, an invention); a young Negro actress and dancer named Doris, who is working in the film *Cleopatra,* in which Elizabeth Taylor and Richard Burton are being starred and in which she has a very minor role as one of Cleopatra's handmaidens; and an Italian count who is employed in Rome as a public relations consultant for a British airline. In the two years extending from March of 1962 through March of 1964, these three—against the background of the Algerian war, the Cuban missile crisis, and the Second Vatican Coun-cil—enact a little drama of love and deception, of death and rebirth, in which they at once interrogate and are themselves in turn cross-questioned by the forces of cruelty and violence sweeping across the Western world. But, however irrefutably all the powers and princi-palities ranged against life may seem to attest to the reign of the Demonic, the dialectic of the novel appears to be proposing that the perduring reality of life itself, in its essential holiness, attests to some-thing (or Someone?) more ultimate than the hosts of Satan; and thus, in the accents of Teilhard de Chardin, Demby finally steers his whole conception toward a radically sacramentalist vision of the world. It is, in the complex meditation it conducts, such a novel as might have been written at once by the Englishman Graham Greene and the Welshman David Jones, and the remarkable growth of intelligence and art which *The Catacombs* represented, when considered in relation to his first book, cannot fail to make William Demby's subsequent silence a cause of much regret.

Nor has anything substantial come from Owen Dodson over a long period. In 1951, five years after the appearance of his first collection of poetry (*Powerful Long Ladder*), Dobson published his first novel, *Boy at the Window.* Though quiet and modest in its manner and not calculated to make any sort of large gesture, it is a beautifully composed account of a year in the life of Coin Foreman, a Negro boy growing up in Brooklyn, who is just on the threshold of puberty and who, after his mother's death, being bereft of her gentle protection, is suddenly plunged into the tribulations afflicting a child without a parental champion and defender. The basic narrative vehicle is doubtless somewhat hackneyed, but to the endeavor of dramatizing how the difficulties of life in the months following the death of his mother gradually make this boy like "a boat baptized for a brave journey" Dodson brought an acuteness of psychological insight and an adroitness of exposition that at last quite redeem the novel from the banalities of novelistic *rites de passage* and make it, indeed, a memorable book. In 1977 the Popular Library issued in a paperback edition his second novel (*Come Home Early, Child*), again with Coin Foreman as its protagonist. But it quite lacks the stylistic poise and cogency of construction that distinguished *Boy at the Window,* and it is not an impressive piece of work. One hopes, however, that his gifts may once again succeed, for their dormancy over nearly a generation has surely impoverished the literature of Negro experience.

Or, again, the death of William Gardner Smith in Paris in November of 1974 ended a career that had earlier held promise but that, in its last years, had somehow miscarried. His first appearance as a writer was signalized by the uncommonly precocious performance marked by his first book, *Last of the Conquerors* (1948), which had been completed when he was barely twenty years of age. The central figure in the novel is a young Philadelphia Negro, Hayes Dawkins, who, as a member of the Army of Occupation after the collapse of Germany, finds, for the first time and to his great surprise—in the heart of Europe—a social polity in which the color of his skin prompts no denial of his essential humanity: which occasions the novel's pronouncing a very severe judgment on "the land of the free and the home of the brave." And it was a similarly insistent moralism that was controlling Gardner Smith's work in the mid-fifties (*South Street,* 1954), as he continued his effort at publicizing the bitter penalties and encumbrances to which a black man is fated by the system of life ordained by American racism. His book of 1963, *The Stone Face,* expressed, however, a certain change in the basic tenor of his writing, for, here, though his protagonist, Simeon Brown, is a Philadelphia Negro living in Paris as an expatriate, his real subject no longer is the cruel disadvantages enforced upon black Americans by their white compatriots but is,

313

rather, the mistreatment of the Algerians by the French. And Brown discovers that the "stone face"—"of antiman, of discord, of disharmony with the universe"—is not merely an American reality, that it in truth is what one beholds wherever one encounters those who violate and profane the human image. Thus, for example, the experience of taking an Arab friend into a Parisian restaurant where he himself, though black, is welcomed but where the Arab is refused service reminds him that "a Negro if he thinks and feels" has far more to resist than merely color-prejudice. For, as he comes finally to see, "Wherever . . . [the stone face] was found, it was his enemy; and whoever feared or suffered from or fought against this face was his brother." So strengthened is he, indeed, by this deepened sense of the true amplitude of the human community that, by the end of the novel, he is at the point of returning to America, where, presumably, his role may be something more than that just of protestant in behalf of the disenfranchised Negro. And one feels that the whole moral drama undergone by Simeon Brown was by way of expressing William Gardner Smith's having himself arrived at the point of being prepared to turn from the routines of "protest" fiction toward a wholly new direction. So it is a sad disappointment that, given his proficiencies in the arts of story, his early death should have prematurely blotted out the interesting prospect held forth by his last work.

The recent career of Julian Mayfield also represents a strange and regrettable stoppage. Though his last novel, *The Grand Parade* (1961), in its recital of how a white reformist politician seeks to bring racial peace to a troubled city, was a somewhat leaden and unfocused performance, his first books—*The Hit* (1957) and *The Long Night* (1958)—were spirited and tightly knit accounts of the human scene in New York City's Harlem. The book of 1957 presents a wonderfully funny and poignantly sad narrative of a crucial day in the life of Hubert Cooley, a middle-aged Negro building superintendent, whose yearnings for a new life involve the dream of escaping the dreariness of Harlem, of leaving his frumpy wife and taking a paramour out West for a fresh start. And at last, on the day which the novel chronicles, there comes a great piece of good luck: he hits the numbers for a little better than four thousand dollars, and immediately he is filled with a large, happy vision of the territory ahead. But then the numbers king holding his bet absconds, so that the dream which for one blessed moment seemed reachable proves in the end to be only an embittering mirage. And the same close, exact knowledge of Harlem life that Mayfield revealed in *The Hit* was also very much in evidence in *The Long Night,* where, again, the decisive event is an affair of the outcome of a numbers lottery, though the prize this time is far more modest. Little Steely Brown's mother hits the numbers for twenty-seven dollars, and she sends him to collect her windfall, with the stern warning that "if you lose that money, boy, don't you come back at all." In due course, however, the money, though not lost, is taken from the child by a street gang: so the novel's main burden becomes that of recounting "the long night" he spends circling about through the labyrinthine world of Harlem—which is teeming with cheats and rascals of every stripe—as he tries to beg or filch the money he must hand over to his mother, if he is to be saved from her ire. The nightworld through which the child moves is, in its chaos and violence, a world bereft of any kind of moral order, and the novel's way of juxtaposing this lunatic turmoil and little Steely's fear makes for a kind of Gothicism that is memorable indeed. The book, like its predecessor, is the work of a gifted writer, and one hopes that his long silence entails no permanent retirement from a literary vocation.

Among those Negro writers who came to the fore in the 1940s, it is Chester Himes, of course, who has produced the largest body of work. After his early novels—*If He Hollers Let Him Go* (1945), *Lonely Crusade* (1947), *The Third Generation* (1954), *The Primitive* (1955) —which were fairly conventional essays in angry reportage of the costs and hurts making up the staple of Negro experience in the American racial climate, Himes turned to the detective thriller; and in this genre he has produced a long series of books (such as *The Real Cool Killers*, 1959; *All Shot Up*, 1960; *Run Man Run*, 1966; *Blind Man with a Pistol*, 1969) which have won for him a considerable reputation in France, where, since the time of André Gide, there has been a sizable public devoted to that hard-boiled detective fiction coming from the States which is in the tradition of Dashiell Hammett and Raymond Chandler. In 1961, however, the Olympia Press in Paris published a book by Chester Himes that, in its mildly pornographic and broadly comic emphasis, represented his taking quite a new sort of tack. Indeed, far from wanting grimly to mount another indictment of the American racial system, *Pinktoes* proposes instead a waggish satire of the ventures across racial boundaries that are sometimes clumsily undertaken by middle-class Negroes and liberal whites—presided over in the novel by Mamie Mason, a wily Harlem hostess who brings together at her parties "establishment" types, black and white, ostensibly for the purpose of advancing interracial understanding. But Mamie's strong conviction is that race relations are most happily ameliorated in bed, and Himes's tale is largely given over to an account of the various complex machinations whereby the people at her soirées are enticed into liaisons irrespective of racial considerations. The narrative occasionally involves a bawdy hilariousness that has a certain charm, but, for all its high jinks, the book is unmarked even by the subtleties of Terry Southern's *Candy,* under whose influence one suspects it was in part written; and its ribaldry often palls. Himes is, however, an energetic practitioner of his trade, and, since he has mined something of this same sort of vein in his campy thriller, *Cotton Comes to Harlem* (1965), it may be a matter of some speculation as to the degree to which in his future work he will be inclined to specialize in the modes of a boisterous kind of comedy.

In some measure, if only very slightly, the Chester Himes of *Pink-toes* points forward to some of the most interesting Negro fictionists of recent years, to such novelists as Henry Van Dyke, Charles Wright, Clarence Major, and Ishmael Reed, who are also specialists in waggery and who, far more radically than Himes, are bent on rendering the world "in terms of the toe-nail." On a certain occasion the alcoholic protagonist of Malcolm Lowry's *Under the Volcano* is asserting that tequila wonderfully clarifies his thoughts and perceptions: which prompts the friend whom he addresses to respond that, if this is so, the things that are seen more clearly are surely not those "on which the balance of any human situation depends," that the seeing of drunkenness is like Christopher Marlowe's seeing "the Carthaginians fighting on his big toe-nail"—where everything is perfectly clear *because* it is seen in terms of the toenail. But this, one feels, is what these writers would want to urge that fiction really comes to—life rendered in terms of the toenail. Which is to say that, like such contemporaries as Thomas Pynchon and John Barth and Donald Barthelme and Ronald Sukenick, they conceive the world of the literary imagination to be something absolutely figurative and metaphorical. For, as it seems to be reasoned, given the well-nigh infinite distance separating the apparatus of human sensibility from the world of fact, literature cannot hope to deal with things "out there," except by way of fantasy and conceit, by way of farce and parodistic joking. The Henry Van Dyke of *Blood of Strawberries* (1969), the Charles Wright of *The Wig* (1966), or the Clarence Major of *All-Night Visitors* (1969) would seem to take it for granted that, as feigned history, the novel "has by this hour of the world just about shot its bolt": so theirs is a fiction radically insistent on its own fabulism, on the fictive character of its own constructions, and they turn out "novels which imitate the form of the Novel, [as if they had been written by authors imitating] . . . the role of Author."[32] *As novelists,* they say *credo quia absurdum est.*

Amongst these innovating experimentalists, Ishmael Reed presents the largest and what is perhaps the most representative case. Reed's acknowledgment of the decisive role played by Nathanael West's *The Dream Life of Balso Snell* in shaping his sense of the possibilities of fiction[33] is not surprising, for, like West, the author of *The Free-Lance Pallbearers* (1967) and *Yellow Back Radio Broke-Down* (1969), of *Mumbo Jumbo* (1972) and *The Last Days of Louisiana Red* (1974), is, clearly, one who considers mockery to be an essential office of the novelist; and his evident commitment to an aesthetic of *collage,* his penchant for the grotesque, his boisterous scatology, and his zany lyricism do, indeed, put us in mind of the West of *Balso Snell.* "Whoever called him Ishmael," says Robert Scholes, "picked the right name. His hand is against every man's."[34] And so it is, for the hilarious warlockry of his strange brand of hoodoo is directed not only against the demented bigotries of white America but frequently also against those canting *apparatchiks* of the Black Mafia who in their own way represent a special sort of betrayal. In his book of 1967, for example, after Bukka Doopeyduk is lynched for his efforts to overturn the totalitarian state of Harry Sam, the Free-Lance Pallbearers who attend to his burial include both white liberals and blacks of the kind whose avowal of loyalty to their own outriders comes always tardily and too late. Or, again, in *Yellow Back Radio Broke-Down,* the black cowpoke Loop Garoo gives short shrift to Bo Shmo and his gang, who want the novelist to aim at "liberating the masses" and to arrange things so that, finally, "the oppressor [will be] hanging from a tree": Loop knows that straitjacketing fiction within the protocols of any sort of racial or political ideology must inevitably spell its death, and with such a program he will not cooperate. Indeed, Reed stands absolutely opposed to any and all forms of what the patois of *The Last Days of Louisiana Red* designates as Moocherism. And Moochers are sometimes white and sometimes black. A president "who uses the taxpayers' money to build homes all over the world where he can be alone to contemplate his place in history when history don't even want him" is a Moocher. Or "people who, when they are to blame, say it's the other fellow's fault for bringing it up" are Moochers. "Moochers don't re-

32. John Barth, "The Literature of Exhaustion," *The Atlantic,* August 1967, pp. 32-33.
33. See "Interview with Ishmael Reed," in *Interviews with Black Writers,* p. 167.
34. Quoted from Robert Scholes's review of *The Last Days of Louisiana Red* in *The New York Times Book Review,* November 10, 1974, p. 2.

turn stuff they borrow. Moochers ask you to share when they have nothing to share." Moocherism, in fact, is in this lexicon the comprehensive name for all those rackets that hustle fraudulent accounts of the human reality, of whatever kind. And one suspects that, for all his passionate dedication to the Black Experience, the aesthetic commitments on which Reed's brilliant cartoons are based prompt him toward very imperfect sympathies for those formulas of "protest" that commonly regulate Black fiction. For, as Robert Scholes suggests, "beneath . . . [the] funky facade [of his fiction there] beats the heart of a preacher"[35] who, through the *drôlerie noire* of his merry and plotless (though deeply engrossing) comic strips, wants to do battle with all simplistic versions of experience.

Such writers as Ishmael Reed and Clarence Major and Charles Wright constitute, however, a minority amongst Negro novelists of our period; for, apart from John Wideman (*A Glance Away,* 1967; *Hurry Home,* 1970; *The Lynchers,* 1973) and Leon Forrest (*There Is a Tree More Ancient Than Eden,* 1973; *The Bloodworth Orphans,* 1977) and William Melvin Kelley (in such books as *Dem,* 1967, and *Dunfords Travels Everywheres,* 1970), black fictionists—John Killens, Ronald Fair, Nathan Heard, Margaret Walker, Cyrus Colter—are generally to be found committed to ways of construing the world that require to be placed at one or another point on the traditional continuum of realism and naturalism. And, of this large group, John A. Williams[36] and Ernest Gaines[37] would appear to be the most impressive figures. But the contemporary situation is one of great fluidity, for many highly talented novelists—Paule Marshall, Al Young, Kristin Hunter, Toni Morrison, Alice Walker—are currently at work, and it cannot now be foreseen how the scales of precedence may shift, as they undoubtedly will, in the coming years.

Certainly it would be a miscalculation to suppose that the relative standings of these writers have suddenly been altered by the extraordinary recent phenomenon of Alex Haley's *Roots.* For Haley's vocation is more nearly that of journalist than of novelist, and the future course of his career is likely to be shaped by his primary interest. But the appearance of his book in the early autumn of 1976 did present the American public with a work of historical fiction so captivating as to

35. Ibid.

36. Williams's major books are *Night Song* (1961), *Sissie* (1963), *The Man Who Cried I Am* (1967), *Sons of Darkness, Sons of Light* (1969), and *Captain Blackman* (1972).

37. Gaines's books are *Catherine Carmier* (1964), *Of Love and Dust* (1967), *Bloodline* (1968), *The Autobiography of Miss Jane Pittman* (1971), and *In My Father's House* (1978).

have occasioned a kind of cultural episode such as a piece of writing rarely prompts. Overnight, hundreds of thousands of copies were in the hands of vast numbers of people who do not normally buy any kind of book at all in hard covers; the big, expensive Doubleday edition even found its way into drugstores and supermarkets—whose stocks were then frequently raided, in large cities, by young hoodlums who would hawk their commodity at cut-rate prices in buses and on street corners. Everywhere—in the press and in the daily conversations of all classes of people—*Roots* was being talked about; and, during the last week of the following January, the nation was gathered each night before its television screens for the greatly affecting dramatic version of the narrative that the American Broadcasting Company had prepared in serialized form. Indeed, the whole affair made a remarkable attestation not only to the passionateness with which black Americans prize their own ancestral memories but also to the depth at which the moral imagination of white Americans is still challenged by "the peculiar institution," as it is by no other fact of our national history.

The huge, sprawling family saga that Haley had produced is not, of course, on the level of genre easily spoken of in a univocal way. He himself speaks of it somewhat oddly as a mode of "faction"—which is a term wherewith he intends to acknowledge that his narrative unites elements of "fact" and "fiction"—and it is no less muddling than "nonfiction novel," the term Truman Capote designed for the description of *In Cold Blood,* his book of 1965 on the slaughter by two brutal psychopaths of an entire family in Holcomb, Kansas. But though Capote's rigorously formal documentary is no more a new form of fiction or of nonfiction than is Oscar Lewis's *The Children of Sánchez* or André Malraux's *Anti-Memoirs* or George Orwell's *Homage to Catalonia,* it is an intensely stylized book. His account of the destruction of Herbert and Bonnie Clutter and their children is drenched in all the attendant facts, and it is a meticulously researched work of reportage: yet, in the patient cunning and sympathy with which it explores and renders the human reality of both the victims and the murderers, it manages to give its "facts" a resonance that enables them so to illumine a range of alienation and unhappiness that, finally, these facts assemble themselves into a work of art no less fascinating for not being in any way at all truly "novelistic."

Haley's book, on the other hand, presents a narrative that, throughout more than six hundred closely printed pages—until he at last begins to recount how he proceeded to trace out his family's history—has indeed the form and feel of a novel. But, apart from the long, beautiful opening pastoral (which is devoted to the growing up of his African forebear, Kunta Kinte, in the village of Juffure, not far from the Gambian coast), the one principle controlling Haley's novel might be said to be *additive,* for his procedure hardly involves anything more complicated than the adding of incident unto incident and of character unto character. True, his chronicle is supported by an immense amount of research over a dozen years in libraries and archives on three continents and by extensive reading in history and anthropology; and his manifest integrity of purpose elicits immediate credence when he says: "To the best of my knowledge . . . every lineage statement within *Roots* is from either my African or American families' carefully preserved oral history, much of which I have been able conventionally to corroborate with documents." But, after the finely crafted opening section on Juffure, the book turns out to be little more than an inordinately protracted series of anecdotes which, powerful and moving though many of them are, seem quite unsupervised by any imperatively systematic vision—and this may be to say that Haley's novel, in its subservience to a merely circumstantial realism, proves at last to be not fictive enough, to the extent that even a work of historical record needs to be if it is in some measure to allay the kind of unrest that lies behind the question raised by the Australian novelist Patrick White, "Why is the world which seems so near so hard to get hold of?"

Haley's whole project began in the early 1960s, as he found himself newly stirred by the family lore that had been handed on to him by his grandmother in the years when he was growing up in Tennessee. She had over and again related to him the story of how the American branch of their family had been founded in the Colonial period by "the African"—one calling himself "Kin-tay"—who, after the difficult Middle Passage, arrived in America aboard a ship that cast anchor at " 'Naplis," whence in the fetters of a slave he was taken into the Virginia plantation country. There, this proud young man was renamed "Toby," and, after numerous attempts at escape, he at last despairingly resigned himself to his servitude on the Waller plantation in Spotsylvania County, where he mated with "Bell, the big-house cook." To them in due course was born a daughter whom they called Kizzy, and, as soon as this little girl was old enough to have a retentive memory, her father was at pains to fix in her mind not only stray bits of his own inherited dialect but also his account of how back in Africa he had been captured by white slavers on a certain day when he had wandered beyond his village into a neighboring forest. Then, in her sixteenth year, Kizzy, according to family tradition, was sold to a small North Carolina planter whose child she bore, a boy named George; and to her own son she transmitted all that she could recall of her father's testimony about his origins. By dint of circumstances, rare indeed in the antebellum South, that permitted continuous residence in one region over a long stretch of time, the family—George's children and their children—remained an organic unit and did not leave North Carolina until George, after the Emancipation, formed a great wagon train embracing all his progeny and many other black families, and then led the entire band westward to Henning, Tennessee. And each generation of George's line learned the story (about "the African," about "Kin-tay") that he had received at his mother's knee—till finally it was handed on to the boy Alex Haley in the late 1920s and early 1930s by his grandmother Cynthia Palmer, who was Kunta Kinte's great-great-grandchild. By then, of course, the family story was not only a sketchy tale about "the African" but a rich and weighty narrative about a black House whose origination antedated the nation itself.

Now it was after he had completed the writing of *The Autobiography of Malcolm* X that Haley, with a freshened sense of the values subsisting in oral history, began to put in order and to seek to ratify the accounts of his family's experience that had been handed down through six generations. A Belgian scholar at the University of Wisconsin identified the handful of strange phonemes preserved by the family memory ever since the time of Kizzy as sounds belonging to the Mandinka tongue, a dialect spoken by the Mandingo people dwelling along the Gambia River. Shortly thereafter, Haley traveled to the Gambia, where he discovered the village "Kinte-Kunda," the sound of whose name was strikingly like that of his ancestor's name, "Kin-tay." Moreover, it was in the Gambia that for the first time he heard of those "old men, called *griots,* still to be found in the older back-country villages, men who were in effect living, walking archives of oral history." And it was on a subsequent trip to West Africa, after Gambian friends had located a *griot* who was particularly knowledgeable about the Kinte clan, that he organized a safari and headed for the village of Juffure, where this *griot* lived and where at last he heard a recital of the long, tangled history of the clan, down to the time of Omoro Kinte, whose eldest son, Kunta, born in the middle years of the eighteenth century, had strayed away from the village one day and never been seen again—"about the time the King's soldiers came." As Haley says, his mind "reeled" as he listened to the story, for he was convinced that "the African" was none other than the son of Omoro Kinte. And, indeed, a few months later Haley's researches in London disclosed that "the King's soldiers"—a force sent out from London to guard the Fort James Slave Fort on the Gambia River—*had* arrived in 1767; and then, one lucky day, his researches amongst slave-ship records in the Maryland Hall of Records in Annapolis ("'Naplis") disclosed that a ship named *Lord Ligonier* had sailed from the Gambia River, its destination Annapolis, on July 5, 1767. Deed-searches amongst Spotsylvania County records soon turned up evidence of one "Toby" having been purchased by the Waller family in early September of 1767—and, from that point on, the job of detection was relatively easy, being essentially a matter of carefully perusing census records of the family's movements from Virginia to North Carolina to Tennessee.

In its parts, the story that Haley has woven—of black roots and lineage, and of a remarkable capacity for suffering and prevailing—may well be the most moving that it will ever be the privilege of American literature to chronicle. The account he gives of the unspeakable horrors of the Middle Passage, of the gritty anomalies of day-to-day relations between slaves and "Massas," of the huddled warmth within slave families, and of the absolute human ambiguity of the total economy of life in the antebellum South—this is all set forth with a smooth sort of journalistic competence, and along an ever-rising tide of success that says in the end "and they all lived happily ever afterward." The whole yarn, as he says, is "a novelized amalgam of what I *know* took place together with what my researching led me to plausibly *feel* took place." And, indeed, for all the skeptical marginalia specialist scholars may append to the details of his reconstructions, the various anecdotes that the book stitches together do, in their broad outlines, have historical plausibility. But though Kunta Kinte's grave dignity hovers, strangely and memorably, over the entire narrative and though the extraordinary brio of Chicken George is a wonderfully bursting force that makes him unforgettable, Haley risks so little in the way of psychological exploration that his personages rarely manage to be barely adequate; they are so flat, so unorganized, that they never astonish us by their conduct and aspiration and eccentricity: we never get what E. M. Forster called "the sideway view." And thus, though Haley's book has scenes and people and actions, it—despite the occasional power of its parts—has (as the English critic John Bayley somewhat unjustly remarks of Joseph Conrad) "no myth with a view to insight."

Yet, its imperfections notwithstanding, the book is an impressive performance: the example of the stern resoluteness with which this man sought to repossess his own history does itself make one of the most inspiriting dramas in the literary life of our period, and the nation which once officially disowned his humanity is the richer for it.

The turbulent ethnic passions of recent years that have prompted many black literary strategists to search for a new Black Aesthetic have found their most intense expression in much of the poetry that has been ascendant since the early 1960s. Here it is, indeed—in the work of such writers as Imamu Amiri Baraka (LeRoi Jones) and Don L. Lee, Dudley Randall and Conrad Rivers, Sonia Sanchez and Nikki Giovanni, Mari Evans and Etheridge Knight—that we encounter the bluntest, the most intrepid and fervidly assertive, statements of the pride in racial heritage and the implacable disallowance of any kind of absolution for white America that define the position of the new Black radicalism. It is, as the black poet and anthologist Larry Neal says it ought to be, a poetry "loud, gaudy and racy" that addresses itself to the circumstances of life in Harlem and Watts, in Detroit and Chicago and Philadelphia: which is to say that it is a predominantly urban poetry wanting to record the hopes and joys and tribulations of Black experience in the jungles of the American metropolis of our time. Its jazzy rhythms are those of John Coltrane and Ray Charles, of Aretha Franklin and James Brown; and, as its virtuosos seek to invigorate the morale of their people and to deepen their confidence in Black enterprise and Black ideals, they are, as Neal says, like black magicians who are by way of "working juju with the word on the world."[38]

In its militant advocacy of Blackness—or of what Negro-American intellectuals for a brief time in the 1950s were calling (after Aimé Césaire of Martinique and Léopold Sédar Senghor of Senegal) *Négritude*—the new Black urban poetry is, of course, a product of the rising expectations and the terrible stresses felt in the ghettoes of the sixties and seventies. Yet its literary ethos reaches back to Negro traditions of an earlier time. It is Richard Wright—the Wright most especially of *Native Son,* of *Black Boy,* and of *White Man, Listen!*—who is the presiding genius of the whole movement, for the stringency of his expostulations and the immoderateness of his anger are by the generation of Etheridge Knight and Carolyn Rodgers felt to be the great type and example of how a matured black sensibility will reckon with the larger realities of American culture. But though the general tone and emphasis of this new verse derive from the legacy of Wright, it

· 38. "Afterword: And Shine Swam On," in *Black Fire: An Anthology of Afro-American Writing,* ed. LeRoi Jones and Larry Neal (New York: William Morrow, 1968), p. 655.

is in the work of two older Negro poets, Langston Hughes and Sterling Brown, that writers like Don L. Lee and Nikki Giovanni and Mari Evans find a kind of ratifying authority for their distinctively poetic stratagems.

Hughes's publishing career began, of course, in the mid-1920s and, as it stretched into the late sixties, represented, in the constancy of work it exemplified—from *The Weary Blues* (1926) and *Fine Clothes to the Jew* (1927) through *Shakespeare in Harlem* (1942) and *One Way Ticket* (1949) to *Montage of a Dream Deferred* (1951) and *The Panther and the Lash* (1967)—remarkable fidelity to a literary vocation. And though it was the prose tales about his marvelously engaging figure of Jesse B. Semple (spoken of most commonly as "Simple") that constituted his most impressive work of the years just prior to his death in 1967, the large accomplishment made by his ten volumes of poetry was, despite the sizable *oeuvre* (nine volumes) of his novels and stories, the canon whose pressure was most immediately felt by young Negro writers in the 1960s. Sterling Brown, on the other hand, who only recently concluded a long and distinguished career of more than forty years as a professor in the English faculty of Howard University, has produced only one volume of poetry, and that a book (*Southern Road*) which Harcourt and Brace published in 1932. But, as a senior professor over a long period in the leading Negro university in the United States and by reason of his great persuasiveness as a formal scholar of Negro literature, he has held an enormously influential position amongst younger Black writers. And what the new people coming to the fore in the 1960s were quickened by in the poetry of both Langston Hughes and Sterling Brown was their deep persuasion of the dignity of folk tradition and folk experience.

The folk realities addressed by Hughes, the poet laureate of Harlem, were, of course, those of the black proletarian in whose music (jazz, ragtime, swing, blues, boogie-woogie, be-bop) he found the great validating paradigm of his own way of orchestrating the experience of his people—by, as he said, "conflicting changes, sudden nuances, sharp and impudent interjections, broken rhythms, and passages sometimes in the manner of the jam session, sometimes the popular song, punctuated by the riffs, runs, breaks, and distortions of the music of a community in transition."[39] The poetry of Sterling Brown, on the other hand, has its fulcrum not in the world of the black proletarian but in that of the Southern peasant, and it is drenched in this lore and language: indeed—though to the scandalous discredit of American

39. Preface to *Montage of a Dream Deferred* (New York: Henry Holt, 1951); the pages of the Preface are unnumbered.

criticism it has been unstudied and remains virtually unknown outside Negro circles—it is, apart from the work of the Scots poet Hugh Mac-Diarmid, the one major example to be cited in modern poetic literature of the Anglo-American tradition in disproof of our commonly accepted notion that no subtly nuanced and deeply sophisticated poetry can be written in a folk dialect.

Now it is the accents of Langston Hughes and Sterling Brown that are to be heard over and again in the poetry of Imamu Amiri Baraka and Larry Neal, of Don L. Lee and Etheridge Knight, of Nikki Giovanni and Sonia Sanchez. And Brown is as influential as Hughes, for, though the scene of his verse is generally rural ("Long days beneath the torrid Dixie sun / In miasma'd riceswamps . . . / Wintry nights in mud-daubed makeshift huts"), whereas the new Black poets are urban, he, like Hughes, has in effect persuaded his younger contemporaries that, "whenever Black poetry is most distinctly and effectively *Black,* it derives its form from two basic sources, Black speech and Black music."[40] Indeed, whether it be a matter of "rapping" about "the Man" or celebrating some phase of racial experience or recording some motion of the individual heart, the sounds one hears in much of the poetry of recent years by Negro writers are those of the jazzily elegant Black patois of "the streets"—as when, for example, Mari Evans declares:

> i'm
> gonna make it a
>   crime
>   to be anything BUT black
> gonna make white
> a twenty-four hour
> lifetime
> J.O.B.[41]

Standing somewhat aside from the new "street" poetry, however, are certain gifted writers of the present and the recent past—Owen Dodson, Margaret Danner, Bob Kaufman, Curmie Price, Michael Harper—whose work, even when deeply fecundated by folk idioms, does not have its origin in the ideologies controlled by the Black Aesthetic, and of these the most distinguished poets are the late Melvin Tolson, Gwendolyn Brooks, and Robert Hayden.

40. Stephen Henderson, *Understanding the New Black Poetry* (New York: William Morrow, 1973), pp. 30-31.
41. "Vive Noir!" in *I Am a Black Woman* (New York: William Morrow, 1970), p. 73.

Though Tolson's first book, *Rendezvous with America,* appeared in 1944, in his forty-fourth year, it was not until the early 1950s, with the publication of *Libretto for the Republic of Liberia* (1953), that he won some bit of attention; and in the years since his death in 1966, despite the impressiveness of his final book, *Harlem Gallery, Book I* (1965), he has remained a figure obscure and unregarded, withal the high praise that has occasionally come from such poet-critics as Allen Tate and Karl Shapiro. Like many other American poets of his generation, he was deeply influenced by the Metaphysicals of the English seventeenth century, by the Symbolists of modern France, and by the classic *avant-garde* of the present century (Yeats, Eliot, Pound, Apollinaire, Pasternak, Crane)—which makes the general neglect of his work but another instance perhaps of the profound reluctance of the literary-intellectual community to reckon seriously with the Negro writer who asks to be considered as something other than merely a special case of ethnic ferment. And, of course, it is precisely the largeness of Tolson's response to the literary world of his time that has guaranteed his disfavor amongst those espousing the aesthetic doctrines of Black separatism—who are inclined to render something like the verdict of Sarah Webster Fabio, that his complex and difficult rhetoric represents only a "bizarre, pseudo-literary diction" that he misguidedly took over from "the American mainstream where it . . . belonged" and where it should have been allowed to remain.[42]

Yet, though a kind of casualty of his country's literary politics (black and white), Melvin Tolson's achievement is one deserving of some honor. The heavily declamatory fustian of his early writing had, by the time he undertook his remarkable *Libretto* (commissioned in 1947 by the Republic of Liberia as its centennial poem), given way to a language which, at its best, is marked by an extraordinary richness and intensity. True, the brilliance of the *Libretto,* like that of *Harlem Gallery,* is—in a way that recalls Pound's *Cantos*—an affair of arresting fragments: the *effort* to which Tolson committed himself may remind us of *The Waste Land* and of *Paterson* and of *The Anathemata,* but he had not the kind of systematic intelligence that sustains the long poem; yet, again and again, in the poems on Liberia and Harlem —which are great grab bags of vignettes and historical commemorations, of speculations and independent lyrics—one meets evidences of a gift that justifies Tolson's being spoken of in relation to the major poets of his time who used the English tongue. In *Harlem Gallery,* for example, he says:

42. "Who Speaks Negro?" in *Negro Digest,* 16, no. 2 (December 1966), 55.

The school of the artist
            is
the circle of wild horses,
        heads centered,
as they present to the wolves
    a battery of heels . . .

Or at another point in the same poem he asks:

Why place an empty pail
            before a well
            of dry bones?
Why go to Nineveh to tell
the ailing that they ail?
Why lose a golden fleece
        to gain a holy grail?

And one could quickly compile a modest anthology of similar passages that make it something of a puzzle that this poet has not long since been commonly acknowledged to represent the genuine distinction that he does.

Unlike Melvin Tolson, Gwendolyn Brooks has won many awards (among them, the Pulitzer Prize for poetry in 1950) and gained much recognition for what is now a very considerable body of work. As one looks at her progress from *A Street in Bronzeville* (1945) and *Annie Allen* (1949) through *The Bean Eaters* (1960) to *In the Mecca* (1968) and *Riot* (1969) and her more recent books, her special métier would seem to be that of the ordinary, day-by-day scene of black American life—which is for her not an object of research but something felt along the pulses, in the veins; and, in her recording of this sector of things, she, in the variousness of her perspective, in her avoidance of sentimentality, in the immaculate precision of her speech, is unsurpassed, even by Langston Hughes. "The Sundays of Satin-Legs Smith," for example (*A Street in Bronzeville*), makes a quite typical instance of the deftly turned comic ironies in which her earlier books abound. Satin-Legs is a gorgeous black dandy who, of a Sunday morning, "wakes, unwinds, elaborately: a cat / Tawny, reluctant, royal." After shedding his pajamas and bathing in lavender, he meticulously inspects the vaults that contain his glory, a glory not of diamonds and pearls but of

. . . wonder-suits in yellow and in wine,
Sarcastic green and zebra-striped cobalt.
All drapes. With shoulder padding that is wide
And cocky and determined as his pride;
Ballooning pants that taper off to ends . . .

> Here are hats
> Like bright umbrellas; and hysterical ties
> Like narrow banners for some gathering war.

And once he has selected his outfit for the day and his "kneaded limbs" have received "the kiss of silk,"

> He looks into his mirror, loves himself—
> The neat curve here; the angularity
> That is appropriate at just its place;
> The technique of a variegated grace.

Then he dances out into the morning to loiter along avenues down which comes "not the shapely tender drift of Brahms" but the lonesome, long-lost music of the blues; and his Sunday is given over to the movies and to squiring "his lady to dinner at Joe's Eats" for chicken and "coleslaw, macaroni, candied sweets, / Coffee and apple pie." Yet this young black *élégant,* for all his flamboyant princeliness, can retain his poise only by not hearing and not seeing and not remembering much of that which constitutes the immediate actuality of his world. Indeed, it is the subtly placed hints of his "fogged-out" identity that carry the remarkable power and pathos of the poem. And it is in such close readings of the human realities defining Negro life —the realities of frustrated desire and broken hope—that the special magnetism of Gwendolyn Brooks's poetry lies.

Brooks's book of 1968, *In the Mecca,* marked a new turning, however, in her poetic work. In this book and in those that have followed it, she continues to find her principal focus in the life that is daily lived in the country's black ghettoes, but, no doubt deeply affected by the terrible despairs expressed by the holocaustal riots that erupted in numerous cities in the mid- and late sixties, she has been writing in recent years in tones far more exigent than those characterizing her work of the forties and fifties. And, in this regard, she has very probably been much encouraged by her lately developed comradeship with the prime movers of the Black Arts Movement. There is a passage in *Annie Allen* which says: "Grant me that I am human, that I hurt, / That I can cry . . . Admit me to our mutual estate." But nothing resembling such a plea, says Miss Brooks, could she imagine herself voicing today, for hers is now a poetry that wants increasingly simply to listen "to Blackness stern and blunt and beautiful"—and to take up arms.

It is Robert Hayden who is perhaps the most consistently interesting Negro poet on the American scene of the present time. In the anthology of Negro poetry which he published in 1967 under the title

Kaleidoscope: Poems by American Negro Poets, he said in the brief introduction which accompanies those of his own poems appearing in the collection that he "sees no reason why a Negro poet should be limited to 'racial utterance' or to having his writing judged by standards different from those applied to the work of other poets." And though the conventions of literary discourse unfortunately prevailing today make it inevitable that his career should first of all be associated with nothing other than a special tradition of "racial utterance," his true peers, indeed, are such poets as William Stafford and James Wright and Galway Kinnell. Predictably, of course, the urbanity of his writing and his refusal of the easy exemptions claimed by the ideologues of Black separatism have made him a figure to whom the devotees of the Black Arts Movement respond chillily and, at times, with outright hostility. True, he has been offered occasional preferments (most notable of which have been the Russell Loines Award of the National Institute of Arts and Letters and his appointment in 1976 to a term as Poetry Consultant of the Library of Congress), but, though regularly anthologized in the numerous collections of Negro writing of the past decade, he remains one who, in the larger forums of American literary life, is untalked about and little known.

In part, Hayden's not yet having made any large impress on the literary community is perhaps a consequence of the slenderness in size of his total *oeuvre.* Though born in 1913 and thus now in late middle age, he—if we discount a slim volume of apprentice-work (*Heart-Shape in the Dust*) that appeared in 1940, and two small brochures that were privately published between 1949 and 1955—has produced only six small books (*A Ballad of Remembrance,* 1962; *Selected Poems,* 1966; *Words in the Mourning Time,* 1970; *The Night-Blooming Cereus,* 1972; *Angle of Ascent,* 1975; and *American Journal,* 1978). Yet, taken altogether, it is a body of work generally marked by a quiet felicity of verbal gesture that expresses the sort of authority won only by the most exacting discipline. Much of his poetry is comprised of occasional verse called forth by various personal memories and experiences. But Charles Davis, in a fine essay on his work, reminds us of what no careful reader will fail to discern, that in the most truly central statements of his career he shows himself to be a poet haunted by the burdens and promises of history.[43] Indeed, again and again—in, say, "The Ballad of Nat Turner" and "Runagate Runagate" in the *Selected Poems,* or in "On Lookout Mountain" and

43. See "Robert Hayden's Use of History," in *Modern Black Poets,* ed. Donald B. Gibson (Englewood Cliffs, N.J.: Prentice-Hall, 1973), pp. 96-111.

"El-Hajj Malik El-Shabazz" (Malcolm X) in *Words in the Mourning Time*—he is seeking to illumine the nature of those circumstances in the remote and the recent past that have steeled the spirits of Black people in America and offered them some hope of finally holding their ground. And, in this vein, perhaps the key exhibit to be cited is Hayden's "Middle Passage," which (based in part on the insurrection of 1839 on the Spanish slave-ship the *Amistad*) is devoted to the horrors aboard those "dark ships"—with "their bright ironical names / like jests of kindness on a murderer's mouth" (*Jesús, Estrella, Esperanza, Mercy*)—that transported slaves to this continent: it is, this account of "Voyage through death / to life upon these shores," one of the great long American poems of our time, and its lack of general renown is a marvel.

In the years following the close of World War II, though the great spate of activity by Negro writers in the field of fiction had not so large an analogue in the field of drama as it did in poetry, a very considerable amount of enterprise was under way there also. Expectably, New York City, with its large corps of gifted Negro actors and actresses—Frederick O'Neal, Ossie Davis, Ruby Dee, Hilda Simms, Canada Lee, Leigh Whipper, to mention only a few—was the center of ferment, even if most of the plays produced by Negro playwrights in the late forties and early fifties were presented either in Harlem or in downtown theaters "off Broadway." And in the decade coming after the close of the war in 1945 much work of a genuinely creditable sort —by Theodore Ward (*Our Lan'*), Oliver Pitcher (*Spring Beginning*), Alice Childress (*Just a Little Simple; Florence*), William Branch (*A Medal for Willie*), Julian Mayfield (*A World Full of Men; The Other Foot*), Loften Mitchell (*The Cellar*), and others—was done through the agency of such organizations as Harlem's American Negro Theatre, the Harlem Writers Club, the Council on the Harlem Theatre, the 115th Street People's Theatre, and the Henry Street Settlement.

The first large success of the period was that won by *Take a Giant Step* (1953), which was the work of a young black dramatist, Louis Peterson, who had been a protégé of Clifford Odets. The play was a sensitive, if somewhat conventionally developed, exploration of the difficulties experienced by a Negro youngster who, as he moves into adolescence, is increasingly shut out from the circles in his Philadelphia neighborhood of the white friends with whom he has grown up and who, temperamentally unfitted for the rude camaraderie of the local Negro taverns, is thrown back on a grandmother wonderfully affectionate but unable to offer the kind of companionship for which the boy yearns. It was a "well-made" play well received, and, though its initial Broadway run closed after only seventy-six performances, it was revived in the 1956-57 season and has since fixed itself in the minds of the theater-going public as a worthy vehicle of the contemporary stage.

In 1954, the year after the initial run of *Take a Giant Step,* the Greenwich Mews Theatre presented William Branch's *In Splendid Error,* which movingly dramatized the difficult decision Frederick Douglass had finally to reach, to withdraw his support of John Brown, after Brown resolved to attack Harper's Ferry. This highly successful effort was followed by two equally impressive productions at the Greenwich Mews, of Alice Childress's comedy about Negro actors, *Trouble in Mind* (1955), and Loften Mitchell's *A Land beyond the River* in 1957, a stirring account of a Negro clergyman's attempt to upset racial segregation in his South Carolina school district (based on one of the actual cases that had eventuated in the Supreme Court's ruling against school segregation in 1954). And Langston Hughes's *Simply Heavenly* had a short Broadway run in 1957.

It was, however, a play by a young Negro writer out of Chicago, Lorraine Hansberry, that captivated the public imagination at the end of the fifties as the work of no previous black playwright had quite managed to do. Indeed, by the time *A Raisin in the Sun* had completed its trial runs in Boston and Philadelphia and Chicago and had opened in New York at the Ethel Barrymore Theatre in March of 1959, it was clear that, with its shrewdly wrought design and magnificent cast (Sidney Poitier, Ruby Dee, Claudia McNeil, Diana Sands, Ivan Dixon, Louis Gossett), it was destined to be the great hit of the season, and so it was. Though its rivals were such works as Archibald MacLeish's *J.B.* and Tennessee Williams's *Sweet Bird of Youth* and Eugene O'Neill's *A Touch of the Poet,* it won the Critics Circle Award for the 1958-59 season; and, at twenty-eight years of age, Hansberry found her first major undertaking in the theater being talked about by many of her critics in relation, on one level, to Chekhov's *The Cherry Orchard* and O'Casey's *Juno and the Paycock* and, on another, to Odets's *Awake and Sing!*.

Hansberry's account of the struggle of a Negro family (the Youngers) to escape the daunting dreariness of the black ghetto on Chicago's South Side was not, of course, without its detractors (many of them black), and Harold Cruse's verdict represented one line of argument frequently voiced, that, against the background of the stony indifference with which the politicians of the New York theater had for so long faced the Negro playwright, her "play provided the perfect opportunity to make it all up, or at least assuage the commercial theater's liberal guilt . . . What obviously elated the drama critics was the very relieving discovery that what the publicity buildup actually heralded was not the arrival of belligerent forces from across the color line to settle some long-standing racial accounts on stage, but a good old-fashioned, homespun saga of some good working-class folk in pursuit of the American Dream" (*The Crisis of the Negro Intellectual,* p. 278). In short, as Cruse wanted in effect to say, the play is nothing more than a piece of soap opera, well made and (piquantly) in black face but essentially stale.

Not much time was to elapse, however, before the American theater was to see the arrival on the stage of "belligerent forces from across the color line to settle . . . long-standing racial accounts." These forces, to be sure, were not very much in evidence in Ossie Davis's hilarious folk comedy of 1961, *Purlie Victorious,* or in Langston Hughes's affecting play about Harlem storefront-church life, *Tambourines to Glory,* which opened at the Little Theatre in New York in the autumn of 1963. But, in March of 1964, they all of a sudden burst upon the scene, when *Dutchman,* the first major work of the gifted young black playwright LeRoi Jones, was presented at the Cherry Lane Theatre in New York City under the auspices of The Playwright's Unit Workshop of Richard Barr, Clinton Wilder, and Edward Albee. Here, indeed, for the first time was an earnest of something like a revolutionary Black theater, and this in fact, as subsequent developments have revealed, is what it was. Though Jones (now, of course, Imamu Amiri Baraka) acknowledged no indebtedness to Bertolt Brecht and though his dramaturgy is unmarked by the stratagems of Brecht's *Verfremdung,* the basic vision controlling this play and his subsequent work for the theater will, inevitably, put one in mind of Brecht's own mission, for, as Baraka—in something like a Brechtian accent—was later to say (and as he might have said by way of introducing *Dutchman*), a truly Black theater must "show victims so that their brothers in the audience will be better able to understand that they are the brothers of victims . . . And what we show must cause the blood to rush, so that pre-revolutionary temperaments will be bathed in this blood, and it will cause their deepest souls to move, and they will find themselves tensed and clenched, even ready to die, at what the soul has been taught."[44]

Neither in theory nor in practice does Baraka stand in the line of Antonin Artaud, but, if the term *le théâtre de la cruauté* may be re-

---

44. Quoted in Neal, *The Black Aesthetic,* p. 264.

leased from the special meanings it carries in Artaud's classic manifesto of 1938, *Le Théâtre et son double,* it may be said perhaps that here, indeed, is what *Dutchman* was calling into existence, a new Theater of Cruelty, a theater which seeks violently to cross-question American culture out of its sluggishness of conscience and, at the same time, to quicken in the Black community a new power of self-affirmation and a fresh resoluteness of purpose in its quest for justice. The action of the play takes place down in "the flying underbelly of the city," in a New York subway car where Clay, a decorously dressed young Negro, is accosted by Lula, a voluptuous white slut: "Boy, those narrow-shoulder clothes come from a tradition you ought to feel oppressed by . . . What right do you have to be wearing a three-button suit and a striped tie? Your grandfather was a slave, he didn't go to Harvard." And she persists in thus taunting him, while at the same time—in a somewhat absent-minded way—inveiglingly flinging at him the allurements of her saucy sexuality. "You look like death eating a soda cracker," she says—this kind of mockery being prompted, it seems, by nothing other than her vexation at being faced by a well-mannered, college-educated, middle-class Negro from New Jersey who is devoted to the poetry of Baudelaire. "The black Baudelaire! Yes! . . . My Christ. My Christ." So, since he does not conform to her dark, disordered notions of the inflamed eroticism that a black man ought to represent, she goads and prods ("You middle-class black bastard . . ."), ever more malevolently, until at last Clay explodes and spews forth in a long tirade the murderous angers toward whites that he carries in his heart. "Don't you tell me anything! If I'm a middle-class fake white man . . . let me be . . . I'll rip your lousy breasts off! Let me be who I feel like being. Uncle Tom . . . Whoever . . ." Then, when he is finished and is about to leave the train, she plunges a knife into his chest—after which she orders the other passengers in the car to throw the body off the train, and this they do. At the next stop, another young black man enters the car and takes a seat, whereupon Lula begins invitingly to stare at him in the way she had initiated her encounter with Clay; and, as the curtain falls, it is clear that the drama is becoming a kind of sinister roundelay that figures forth the pattern with which black men are ever and again confronted by the American reality—of seduction and insult and then of destruction, when they dare to offer any resistance. The play is a brilliant stage-piece which, in the tension-charged climate of the early sixties, detonated one of the major episodes of the period.

Shortly after *Dutchman* went into production at the Cherry Lane Theatre in Greenwich Village, Baraka withdrew from downtown New

York to establish (with Clarence Reed and William Patterson and a number of other Black theater people) the Black Arts Repertory Theatre and School in Harlem, on 130th Street near Lenox Avenue. And, during its brief life, it was from this bastion (to which whites were denied admission) that he—through productions of his own work and that of others, as well as through the tutelage he offered young writers—exerted a profound influence on the shaping of contemporary Black theater. James Baldwin's play of 1964, *Blues for Mister Charlie,* along with his earlier play *The Amen Corner* (1954), caught the imagination of young Black playwrights in the early sixties, but it is chiefly from the author of *Dutchman* and *The Toilet* (1964) and *The Slave* (1964) and *A Black Mass* (1968) that they feel today that they have learned how to address their people and to exercise in the world of American culture a radically prophetic vocation. Such playwrights as Ed Bullins, Adrienne Kennedy, Ron Milner, Douglas Turner Ward, Charles Gordone, and Lonne Elder—who represent, collectively, an extraordinary body of talent, on which, indeed, any hope for the renewal of the American theater must in large part rest—exhibit a very considerable diversity of viewpoint and emphasis. But, though they are not all committed to policies of cultural separatism, theirs is a vision of the theater which, like that of Imamu Amiri Baraka, conceives it to be an agency of truth-telling, of enlightenment, of social change, and possibly even of revolution. Moreover, whatever the pitch of their militancy, they, each of them, under the pressure of Baraka's example, consider their primary business to be that of "a black man talking to other black men, not talking simply to an audience of middle-class, credit-card-carrying whites."[45] And, if taxed with the charge that theirs is a racial particularism which fragments the human community, their reply will be to the effect that (in a word of Cleanth Brooks's quoted earlier on) one can "step out into the universal only by first going through the narrow door of the particular."

Finally, no account of the Black presence in American writing of our time can scant altogether one of the most remarkable strains in this line of work—namely, the testimony lately brought forward by the literature of Black autobiography. This very prominent element of the contemporary picture does not, of course, represent any sort of recently sudden influx into the American tradition, for, over a great stretch of years, one of the unacknowledged glories of this tradition

45. Louis Phillips, "LeRoi Jones and Contemporary Black Drama," in *The Black American Writer,* vol. II (*Poetry and Drama*), ed. C. W. E. Bigsby (Deland, Fla.: Everett/Edwards, 1969), p. 205.

has been the absorbing testaments that have come from not a few singularly gifted and incisive black autobiographers. Indeed, though not often so recognized, *The Life and Times of Frederick Douglass* presents a deposition at least as weighty as Thoreau's *Walden*—just as, in any truly objective balancing of the scales, the importance of Benjamin Franklin's *Autobiography* (as a classic statement of our distinctly American type of high-reaching earnestness) could hardly be conceived to exceed that of Booker T. Washington's *Up from Slavery*. Then, from the generation of W. E. B. DuBois to that of Richard Wright—to say nothing of the great nineteenth-century slave narratives of Noah Davis, Josiah Henson, Samuel Ringgold Ward, Henry Bibb, William Wells Brown, Moses Grandy, John Thompson, and J. W. C. Pennington—there came a long series of immensely interesting memoirs from James Weldon Johnson, Claude McKay, Angelo Herndon, J. Saunders Redding, Langston Hughes, and various others; and, in this range of literature belonging to the present century, if anything like Matthew Arnold's game of "ranking" is to be risked, it is doubtless Richard Wright's extraordinary book of 1945, *Black Boy*, which will generally be accorded priority of place. But the rising Black insurgency of the 1960s seems to have released the autobiographical impulse to a degree by far surpassing that which any previous development in Negro experience made for, and the result has been the emergence in recent years of a literature of personal testimony so rich and multifaceted that the merest profile of it—which is all that may be charted out in such an essay as this—can barely suggest its full interest.

One will think perhaps first of all of those searing documents—Malcolm's *The Autobiography of Malcolm X* (1965), Eldridge Cleaver's *Soul on Ice* (1968), H. Rap Brown's *Die, Nigger, Die!* (1969), Bobby Seale's *Seize the Time* (1970), George Jackson's *Soledad Brother* (1970), Donald Reeves's *Notes of a Processed Brother* (1971), Angela Davis's *Autobiography* (1974)—that have issued forth from the inner turbulence of the "Black revolution," coming directly from the center of the maelstrom. Here it is that we have what is perhaps the most striking literary evidence of the angers engendered in the hearts of black Americans by the iniquities of white racism. And the resulting militancy is something so radical that it furnishes by itself an entire *Weltanschauung*. The world is seen to be a harrowing jail (actual prison experience, of course, lying behind much of this literature), and it is assumed, therefore, that taking hold of one's full human stature will entail for a black man a truly revolutionary form of action. Integral selfhood, it is felt, can be won only by way of what Camus called

335

résistance, for the world at large—at least on the American scene—is conceived to be a vast combine intending to rob blacks of the natural autonomy belonging to their essential manhood and to foist upon them the identity of slaves. As Rap Brown says, "America's a bitch. Being Black in this country is like somebody asking you to play white Russian roulette and giving you a gun with bullets in all the chambers. Any way you go, jim, that's your ass" (*Die, Nigger, Die!*). And thus great impatience is expressed with those Blacks who buy the official promises of the culture and seek plus-marks for their tractability and cooperativeness, or who, after contracting out of the struggle, simply "sit in a fucking armchair and try to articulate the revolution while black people are dying in the streets" (Bobby Seale, *Seize the Time*). What is taken for granted is that the Black reality is something in essence organic, so that the *trahison* of one inevitably diminishes the prospect open to the people as a whole; and the selfhood that is in process of definition in these pungently written personal histories is one in every respect formed under the pressure of the conviction that "to *be*" is to be in-relation-*to* one's brothers. There is, of course, in some of this literature more than a little of attitudinizing; but the eloquence and the purity of sentiment and the formidable intelligence that mark *The Autobiography of Malcolm X* and *Soledad Brother* make them two of the great books of our time.

Many recent Black autobiographies are, of course, not surprisingly, devoted to accounts of childhood and adolescence and to the chronicling of the difficult passage into maturity, and, of these, the most impressive are Claude Brown's *Manchild in the Promised Land* (1965), Anne Moody's *Coming of Age in Mississippi* (1968), and Maya Angelou's *I Know Why the Caged Bird Sings* (1970). Claude Brown's narrative of his growing up as the child of black proletarians on the streets of Harlem and Maya Angelou's story of her own early years in the rural South are not primarily controlled by the intentions of any kind of political preachment—nor is Anne Moody's book so designed, though her recountal of her experiences as a standard-bearer in the civil rights movement of the early sixties in Mississippi is drenched in the passions of that heroic venture. But, even if these writers are not professional polemicists, they do, nevertheless, advance a severe interrogation of the American conscience, in their way of rehearsing without any recourse to cheap sentimentality how great was the cost of winning through to a chance at a decent life, given the disadvantages which were their birthright as Blacks; and the wide reception of their books, by both black and white readers, had no doubt a considerable influence on the nation's moral climate at the end of the 1960s.

There are, however, two notable books in this field—Vincent Car-
ter's *The Bern Book: A Record of a Voyage of the Mind* (1973) and
All God's Dangers: The Life of Nate Shaw (1974)—which stand some-
what apart from the prevailing ethos of recent Black autobiography, for
Carter's book presents the record of his experience as an expatriate in
Switzerland, and Nate Shaw's story—committed to a tape recorder by
Theodore Rosengarten—comes from an illiterate Southern peasant
(who, at the age of eighty-eight, died in 1973).

Vincent Carter (who was born in Kansas City, Missouri, in 1924)
went to Europe in the early fifties, settling in Paris for a brief time in
1953 and then moving on to Munich, to Amsterdam, and finally to
Bern, where he has remained ever since. And his brilliant book of
1973 relates the "voyage" he has steered in this "clean, polished, ship-
shape city," where, thousands of miles away from his native land, in
"the dead center of Europe," he has found, even here, that an American Negro may not escape "the language of scorn and ridicule," the
word *Neger* being felt to be "a sort of Satan of words." Yet, having
stayed on now in this ancient Swiss city for many years, he has become,
as *der Neger,* as *rara avis*—as "the only American Negro in a city of
over one hundred thousand people"—something of a Bernese institution. He is "Herr Carter" the writer, with a circle of friends and
tenuous attachments of various kinds to the fabric of the city's social
life; and, with the briskness of an unfailingly ironic humor, he has
produced a splendidly intelligent and engaging record of the collisions
and friendships he has experienced with the locals—to whom he has
occasionally had to shout "I am not a freak" and against whose clumsy
probings he has sometimes had to protect himself by huddling down
into the dark, secret underworld of his own interior. There have been
days, he says, when he has indulged "in orgies of beard-wagging and
laughing out loud, of much singing in the streets, satisfying himself
with the excuse that the Bernese have forgotten how to sing in the
streets and how to laugh with wide-open mouths." Yet he "walks
proudly and swings his arms and bears his head high and enters public
places like a rich Texan." Life here is no less real and no more fantastic than that which he knew in his native Kansas City: indeed, as he
tells us, "I have found it to be just as earnest and just as dangerous."
And the remarkable poise and sinuousness of the bright, vivid prose
which this black expatriate commands makes one hope that his as yet
unissued novels, *The Long Green Way* and *The Primary Colors,* may
soon find an enthusiastic publisher.

All God's Dangers: The Life of Nate Shaw is something quite different from *The Bern Book.* For Carter is an immensely sophisticated

literary intellectual the map of whose mind bears the incisions of Spinoza and Hegel, of Nietzsche and Rilke, of Gogol and Joyce and Stravinsky and Paul Klee and of the whole Western tradition; whereas Nate Shaw was a tough, cunning, infinitely resourceful and intelligent (but quite illiterate) black tenant farmer in Alabama whose magnificent *Life* would never have been set down had he not been discovered one January morning in 1969 by a young white man, Theodore Rosengarten, whose attempts at digging up the story of the Alabama Sharecropper Union of the 1930s had brought him into a little hamlet in the eastern sector of the central part of the state, where he found this extraordinary old black man, then eighty-four years of age. Rosengarten was accompanied by a friend and fellow graduate student, Dale Rosen, and on this icy winter morning they met Nate Shaw (whose real name was Ned Cobb) across the road from his house in the home of his half-brother TJ. "We asked him right off why he joined the union [back in 1932]. He didn't respond directly; rather, he 'interpreted' the question and began, 'I was haulin a load of hay out of Apafalya one day—' and continued uninterrupted for eight hours. He recounted dealings with landlords, bankers, fertilizer agents, mule traders, gin operators, sheriffs, and judges—stories of the social relations of the cotton system. By evening, the fire had risen and died and risen again and our question was answered." And by evening Rosengarten knew that, though he "had come to study a union," he "had stumbled on a storyteller" the range and fecundity of whose memory and expressive gifts endowed him with a very rare kind of genius. So he returned to Alabama two years later with a tape recorder to propose to Nate Shaw that he record his life; Shaw agreed, and the result is the great book Rosengarten issued in 1974—edited, to be sure, with a marvelous grace and tact, but essentially Nate's (all the words having come out of *his* mouth).[46]

"I never tried to beat nobody out of nothin since I been in this world, never has, but I understands that there's a whole class of people tries to beat the other class of people out of what they has. I've had it put on me; I've seen it put on others, with these eyes. O, it's plain: if every man thoroughly got his rights, there wouldn't be so many rich people in the world—I spied that a long time ago . . . O, it's desperately wrong . . . I found out all of that because they tried to take I don't know what all away from me." It is with such unblinkered clarity that the old man looks back over his long life, with

46. Though all the persons in the narrative are real, Rosengarten chose, except for historical figures, to give them fictitious names, in order to protect the privacy of the principal character and the members of his family.

its unremitting struggle for dignity and independence. Early on, he had resolved to wrest himself loose from the terrible bondage of tenant farming, from the system whereby the white landlord, for seed and fertilizer and flour and molasses and beans, takes a "mortgage" on the black tenant's crop and (since he sets the price on the cotton) ends up by arranging things so that, year in and year out, the black vassal is in his debt. By dint of the most arduous labors over many years, Nate Shaw managed at last to win ownership of his own land and house and barn and livestock, and succeeded even in acquiring mules and horses, a blacksmith's shop and an automobile, and a small bank account. But his modest prosperity was not rejoiced in by neighboring whites. So when, in the Depression of the early thirties, he chose to join the Alabama Sharecroppers Union, it became certain that trouble for him was not far off. And in December of 1932 it arrived. On a certain day armed deputies of the sheriff, on the basis of a trumped-up mortgage note from a white landowner in the vicinity, presented bills for the attachment of the property of one Virgil Jones, a neighbor of Nate's and, with him, a member of the Sharecroppers Union. Shaw vigorously, angrily protested, telling the deputies: "if you take all his stuff you'll leave his folks hungry. He aint got a dime left to support em if you take what he's got." And when the deputies declared that they, nevertheless, had their orders, Nate's indignant reply was, "Well, if you take it, I'll be damned if you don't take it over my dead body." After many heated exchanges, one of the deputies walked up to him and said: "You done said enough already for me to be done killed you." And, indeed, that night they returned, but, despite being shot three times in his back, Nate returned their fire and sent them off running—after which he fled to nearby Tuskegee; but, in due course, he was apprehended, and, after the kind of trial a Negro was regularly offered by Alabama justice, he was sentenced to a term of twelve years in the penitentiary. But, as he says, "I went through prison quiet as a plank of wood," persistently refusing parole as a reward for betraying the Sharecroppers Union. And, when released at fifty-nine years of age, he picked up again his farming and the care of his land and his family of ten children, and remarried following the death of his first wife ("I'd stayed with her 40-odd years, and that was short, short")—still intact, and filled with a decent pride in his own manhood, with devotion to the land and affection for his numerous children: a wonderfully observant and sensitive peasant who, in the hard polity to which he belonged, had never possessed an iota of any kind of power as the world normally reckons it, but who—like "many thousands gone" in the world of

Southern Negro life—yet commanded that awesome authority which any man has when, with a proper modesty, he *insists* on the dignity of his person, despite all the contradicting adversities.

Indeed, Nate Shaw's story—of the hundreds of persons (black and white) with whom he had dealings in the tangled and perilous world of the deep South over the first three-quarters of this century; and of how a black man, situated as he was, kept himself together and watched over his wife and children, and managed to be able to say to any and all comers, "If you don't like me for the way I have lived, get on off in the woods and bushes and shut your mouth and let me go for what I'm worth"—Nate Shaw's story is, in its anecdotal richness and profundity of cultural implication, one of the few narratives in our literature that deserves to be thought of as a truly American epic.

So it is a literature large and various and often representing considerable distinction that black American writers have produced over the past generation. Moreover, in a period in which the literary imagination begins to suffer a great crisis of confidence in the dignity of *l'écriture* and in the capacity of the Word to deal with the realities of "postmodern" experience, it is a literature not least remarkable in its assurance about the value of the verbal arts—and this is so, of course, because its practitioners are, most of them, rhetoricians who believe it to be within the power of a disciplined language to alter consciousness and thus to redeem the human reality.

Nor is this a body of writing, despite the foolish testimony of some of its apologists, which is in any way shut off from the main currents of the contemporary movement in American literature (and thus requiring that recourse be taken to special standards of criticism and appraisal). True, the plays of Imamu Amiri Baraka and the poetry of Robert Hayden and the fiction of Ishmael Reed are drenched in Negro experience, and inevitably so. But, ultimately, the true province of these writers is that not of the black ghetto but of the whole national community, for they want most essentially to complicate and deepen the American *conscience* (in the French sense at once of "conscience" and of "consciousness"). The world which they most thoroughly know is, of course, a world from which white America has withdrawn, but this retreat has entailed an immense cost, for so deeply involved with one another have been the lives of black men and white men on this continent for three hundred years that he who refuses to acknowledge the identity of the black man is by way of losing his own. And thus for the black writer to explore and exhibit the rich complexity of Negro life is for him not only to assist his own people toward a deeper understanding of themselves but is for him also to be an agent of self-discovery for the nation at large. Which means that the fiction of Ralph Ellison and James Baldwin, the poetry of Melvin Tolson and Gwendolyn Brooks, and the drama of Ed Bullins and Lonne Elder *belong* not just to a special ethnic tradition but to the integrally American achievement in the literature of the present time; and thus, finally, there is an insurmountable impropriety involved in the discussion of black American writers under a special rubric reserved for them alone. But, for the moment, given the carelessness with which the critical community generally canvasses their work, they must, as it would seem, be so treated, if any assessment of their accomplishment is to be guaranteed at all.

8

Women's Literature

Elizabeth Janeway

T HE first concern of anyone writing about Women's Literature must be to establish that it exists at all. A number of women who write would declare that they are writers who happen to be women and that the accident of their sex does not influence either the subject matter they treat or the forms they use. In the past "women's literature" has been a pejorative term and its rejection by women writers today is a reaction against automatic disparagement of their work. Serious professionals in any field do not welcome assignment to a subcategory, out of the mainstream and yet measured by mainstream standards. If an entity that can be called women's literature exists, it will have to be defined in a way that is mindful of its authentic value as a creation with its own laws and essential identity, not as a dialect version of high culture.

Any literature, that is, must have a base. If there is a women's literature, it will derive from an area of experience, worthy of exploration, which is known pretty exclusively to women and largely overlooked by men or, at the best, described in terms of alien standards. Female patterns of living and dealing with the world have produced in women a point of view different from that of their brothers. This point of view will not be easily accessible to men because it is conceived by them as being either odd or unimportant, since the norms of our culture are based on masculine experience and adapted to male roles and behavior. Even when the literature of revolt attacks, or condemns, orthodoxy, it does so in a masculine voice, using male formulations to express ideas grounded in male experience. Significant areas for discussion and study are thus always perceived in masculine terms, the assumption being that truly important subject matter and truly important literary forms will be found in their purest state only in literature created by men or attuned to male norms. An unnoticed exclusion of female lives and female judgments results.

Literary production by women and women's literature are not, of course, coterminous. It is quite possible for women to write successfully, by masculine standards, just because these standards are omnipresent in our society and so are part of the cultural background of women as well as of men. Still, doing so demands an adjustment for women. In some fields, certainly, the substitution of other experience for one's own as a basis for literary creation must hamper the process. (Analogously, though on a smaller scale, homosexual writers have had to transmute their erotic experience into heterosexual terms.) In a much-quoted text, from *A Room of One's Own,* Virginia Woolf commented on difficulties of composition at a basic level: "All the great [nineteenth-century] novelists like Thackeray and Dickens and Balzac have written a natural prose, swift but not slovenly, expressive but not precious, taking their own tint without ceasing to be common property. They have based it on the sentence that was current . . . at the beginning of the Nineteenth Century . . . It is a man's sentence; behind it one can see Johnson, Gibbon and the rest. It was a sentence that was unsuited for a woman's use."

This unsuitability, Woolf held, was owing to the fact that "the weight, the pace, the stride of a man's mind are too unlike her own for her to lift anything substantial from him successfully." This is untrue; women authors have of course learned much from the great male tradition. It is not, however, what the tradition has sought to teach them: they have been subjected, Woolf notes, to the "perpetual admonitions of the eternal pedagogue . . . now grumbling, now patronising, now domineering, now shocked, now angry, now avuncular." She supplies a few examples: "Women rarely possess men's healthy love of rhetoric . . . a strange lack in a sex which is in other things more primitive and materialistic." Again, "Female novelists should only aspire to excellence by courageously acknowledging the limitations of their sex." Two generations later this sort of condescension seldom surfaces so overtly, but the scholarly estimate of women's writing does not grant it full equality, for a glance at the canon of literary works judged as excellent and significant by today's critics reveals it as very largely masculine.

This may be a correct judgment. If that is the case, revaluation will not alter it; but works once deemed major do drop out of the mainstream or find themselves placed in new relationships. New genres appear, marginal at first, but some of them move toward the center, often gathering existing works to themselves as they go by a sort of gravitational force. Where individual writers used to appear, one can discern a new entity. This essay, then, attempts to discover what can be included in a field called women's literature if it is defined *not* as an adjunct to normal, masculine writing, but as an equally significant report from another, equally significant, area of existence.

Various guidelines have been used. A most helpful one is supplied by T. S. Eliot in his discussion of a similar question, the identification of something called American literature. Eliot changed his mind about this matter. In 1924 (*Transatlantic Review,* January issue) he held that "there can only be one English literature . . . There cannot be British literature or American literature." Later, however, in "American Literature and the American Language" (1953), he found himself able to observe "what has never, I think, been found before, two literatures in the same language." He went on to provide some identifying marks of a definable literature: "Strong local flavor combined with unconscious universality." Such a literature "comes to consciousness at the stage at which any young writer must be aware of several generations of writers behind him, and amongst these generations, several writers generally acknowledged to be of the great."

It is possible to discern Eliot's criteria in the case of women's literature. For some generations women novelists and poets, following on an earlier tradition of diarists and memoirists, have drawn their material from the local experience of the female sex, as the writers of a native vernacular did in other times and places. Among these authors are some "generally acknowledged to be of the great." A sense of "unconscious universality" is perhaps less easily seen, but its locus lies in the steady growth of importance and centrality attached to women's activities, which, in turn, encourages women to take knowledge gained here as emblematic of common experience. It is not the specialness of women's lives that is being sought in the explorations undertaken by many contemporary writers. The intent is, rather, to enlarge our understanding of the human condition by adding to it what has been excluded in the past, namely, women's experience, which is now perceived as humanly, "universally" valuable. On this point we might recall Henry Adams's observation, in *The Education of Henry Adams,* that "the study of history is useful to the historian by teaching him his ignorance of women. The woman who is known only through a man is known wrong."

These analogies and suggestions must be pulled together into some sort of core definition of women's literature, preliminary though it may be. The women writers treated here, then, will be those who deal with women's experience from within; but clearly not all writing by women, about women, can be called women's literature. The touchstone used is the author's vision of the experience treated. Is this experience described and judged in terms which can be various and individual but which are inherently the product of women's lives, or is it judged by masculine principles and values? This system of evaluation may sound arbitrary; in fact, anyone mapping new territory must be arbitrary. In practice it is easy enough to sense the difference between a study of women which regards them and their activities from the standpoint of an objective, supposedly neutral outsider, and one that rejects the assumptions on which such neutrality is based as being false.

An advantage in this approach is that it gets rid of such "political" considerations as the conscious, stated views of any writer on the position of women today. I would (for example) reckon Jean Stafford as an author of women's literature while noting with respect her rejection of the tenets of the women's liberation movement. I would exclude Lillian Hellman's plays and Mary McCarthy's fiction because these writers base their interpretations of women's needs and desires on standards that are essentially masculine even if they are not conventionally so. In the same way, the literary criticism of Susan Sontag and the political thinking of Hannah Arendt use traditional criteria with great force, but do not call on that special existence of women which feeds women's literature. The authors of this literature sense that women's lives run a different course from those of men, and they want to investigate the differences. Subliminally, at least, they know that one needs a different lens to see them clearly and a different semantic set to express them truly. The task seems worthwhile because it identifies unknown areas and seeks to relate them to the total human condition.

The effort to determine new values by which to judge any area of life is sometimes seen as a rejection of existing values, and by extension, of values per se. This need not be the case. It is not the idea of standards that is being questioned, but current limitations in orthodox standards. Imagine, if you will, that Western composers had been confined to writing music in a major key. What would happen when they suddenly discovered the minor? Not a rejection of major harmonies, but an extension of the range in which composition could take place.

The sources of women's literature stretch back in time, but the period from 1945 to the present is certainly that in which it has begun to come together as a coherent body. The impulse to create an identity, however, draws on a wide context that is not only literary, but also historical. An authentic literature reflects actual life. It pulls events together into comprehensible processes and patterns, and the patterns reach back, for the question "Who am I?" implies another, "Where did I come from?" In the same way, women's literature finds useful clues to identity in psychology and the social sciences: reports on behavior in the real world diminish the restrictive force and the misdirections of old ascribed images of femininity. A new literature is open to influences. It will try out ideas and images and ways of speaking, and its practitioners may write in several forms, or graft one form onto another. It is characteristic of women's literature, then, to be open and rather fluid. Common female experience can all but obliterate national lines, so that European writers like Simone de Beauvoir, Virginia Woolf, and Doris Lessing seem genetically related to contemporary American women's literature.

Another tendency is a concentration on lived experience, often presented confessionally, or, better, as a testament to "the way things are." Women poets report on bouts of madness and on suicide attempts. Men have written in this vein too, but in rather a different emotional tone. There is more distance between the male poet-as-writer and the suffering human creature whose experience is being discussed; artistic control is stressed. Women poets of madness and suicide give an impression of being raped by life, drowning in an overwhelming sea of sensation, though they do not welcome this fate in self-pitying, masochistic fashion. They appear, rather, to make a choice—and a daring one—not to resist. They seem to be putting themselves at risk purposively, *in order* to penetrate to the heart of the mystery of being, as if this were one way to discover the origin and meaning of their lives. Powerlessness means something different for women; it has been a constant and profound part of their lives, not chosen but assigned.

For a woman to look at her life, she must look at powerlessness; she must, that is, choose decisively to confront what has been happening to her as a passive creature and try actively to understand what it means and has meant. Often she must choose to give up known means of control and the accepted logic of causality in search of the inner reality of her experience. If this is a choice of madness, it is a special kind of choice. The closest analogy to such a quest is the mythic or legendary journey to Hell of the hero of the epics, taken from the role of the shaman of primitive religion, who puts himself and everyday

346

sanity at risk in search of healing truth that lies behind accepted structures of belief. It is possible to see this kind of interior journey, which
is very much part of contemporary women's literature, as a counterpart to the masculine drive to physical journeying, to "the road" of
Kerouac and the Beats.

Very often these interior journeys turn up annals of victimization.
These stories are confusingly familiar. They form the traditional matter of "women's literature" in the pejorative sense, where betrayed heroines abound. How does such present-day documentation of deception
and suffering differ from the illegitimate Gothic descendants of nineteenth-century romances? Here again, standards of judgment are arbitrary. The depth of involvement of the writer cannot in itself extend
her skill, but it can increase the daring with which she explores the
territory of terror. Then, having chosen this area for study, she is
prepared to judge it, not to accept its existence uncritically. Looking
at a faded convention in a new way can revivify it. The trivialization
of women's lives has been typified by the judgment that writing about
them is trivial. Much of it has been, but if the same material is written about seriously, it yields a different result. Charlotte Brontë has
been faulted for the soap-opera element of that mad woman in the
attic who concludes *Jane Eyre* by setting the mansion afire and hand-
ing Mr. Rochester over to Jane. Jean Rhys, in *Wide Sargasso Sea*
(1966), turned her into an unforgettable tragic figure. She is still "seduced and abandoned," in the conventional mode, but she is significant. A trivial form is being used to convey something important.
Such a development is not unique, but it is always confusing to the
critic, just as the use by serious writers of science fiction forms has been.

The form may in the end strangle the content, or squeeze it back
toward triviality, but contemporary novels of victimization are too
various and lively to suggest such a fate. Still, the close involvement
of many women writers with their material seems to minimize their
interest in form itself. The novelty in this work lies in a new vision
of experience, not—or rarely—in its expression. The innovation most
often seen is a mingling of fiction and autobiography. This is a dangerous combination in traditional work, but intensity of emotion and
involvement holds it together more effectively than might be expected.
In addition, the need for women to exchange information about their
lives and thus to arrive at shared judgments and conclusions gives such
reportage a particular interest in this period of growing awareness of
identity.

These special characteristics of women's literature mean that orthodox standards of evaluation do not quite fit. Familiar material—the

347

experience of powerlessness, betrayal, and victimization—which was once presented to show how limited were the lives of women and how vulnerable, is now being used for a quite different purpose, as notes from an underground. The fragile creatures who once lived there have decided to get up and leave, en masse, and as they do, they express some quite violent opinions about the experience. A great deal of what they have to say concentrates on mundane details, which they appear to find at least as important as metaphysical hypotheses. They are, moreover, personally involved with the material of their books and poems to the detriment of aesthetic distancing, as well as objectivity. Even Virginia Woolf was worried about the way that Charlotte Brontë's "indignation" at the narrowness of her own fate "deformed and twisted" her work and "interfered with the integrity of the woman novelist." Orthodox criticism would normally condemn the reworking of familiar, trivial material, the absence of serious reflection about abstract principles, and the failure to set one's work off from one's own emotions; and yet these books speak with great force to their audience. Is it not, then, the duty of the critic to try to see past the orthodox criteria to whatever new elements this writing brings to light? Perhaps in time women's literature will produce changes not only in literary forms of creation, but in forms of criticism as well. After all, the Romantic revolt against the standards of the Classicists did something of the kind.

Any survey of contemporary women's literature will be somewhat subjective. As yet we have no standard canon and no accepted measures for judging this writing. Later, more refined, studies will certainly alter some of the views expressed here and add to the authors considered. This is not an apology, but a necessary statement of fact, inviting the reader to disagree and to supplement the writers discussed. Changing social circumstances will also influence this literature more strongly than other fields because changes in the position of women and in the importance attached to their experience will produce shifts in point of view. In 1945, thus, America was at war, a war that was drawing to a close. Not surprisingly, the vision of woman projected in some contemporary writing was of a mother-figure who might, by her "selfless love . . . inspire the leaders of nations to forget their own political ambitions, petty hatreds, and selfish interests," and lead the world toward peace (quotation cited in Mary R. Beard, *Woman As Force in History,* 1946). The social questions that publishers felt to be of general interest dealt with returning war veterans. What happened to Rosie the Riveter when she went back to woman's place at home was of as little moment as what happened to the blacks who had moved from the rural South to the industrial cities of the North.

Predictably, the best-selling book of the year by a woman about women's experience was *The Egg and I* by Betty MacDonald (1945). It is a long, humorous dissertation on putting up with things, in this case life on a chicken farm with an inarticulate and self-centered husband; in short, a traditional study of female victimization which is deliberately stamped "Not to be taken seriously" by its humor. It is quite good humor: "According to Mother," writes MacDonald—the book is presented as a memoir—"if your husband wants to give up the banking business and polish agates for a living, let him. Help him with his agate polishing. Learn to know and to love agates (and incidentally to eat them.)" One may see this as an underground statement on the plight of women, distress made bearable by the laughter which declares it to be unimportant. Such an attitude is the ground-bass from which a serious and considered women's literature has had to detach itself.

Gertrude Stein's *Wars I Have Seen* (1945) is a very different study of powerlessness. It abstracts from the feminine situation (Stein recalls her life history in terms of wars she remembers) to that of a civilian population in occupied territory. Powerlessness invites boredom and lethargy: if one cannot change anything, one does not plan a future. It invites treachery and distrust. It produces a sense of unreality, when decisions are forced upon one. With distrust at large in the world, on what bases can judgments be taken? The feminine/civilian view begins to surface, contradicting an orthodoxy that no longer predicts events in a trustworthy way: "I have said so often between 1939 and 1943, I cannot understand why men have so little common sense why they cannot understand when there is no possibility of their winning that they will lose, why they cannot remember that two and two make four and no more." They "have nothing to do with the business of living," she adds, "because they believe what they are supposed to believe." In such a situation a tart contradiction to received ideas is welcome, as this from Alice B. Toklas in reply to some conventional statement about forgiving but not forgetting: "I cannot forgive," said Miss Toklas, "but I do forget." We might also note how effectively the tendency of women's literature to use banal, everyday events is demonstrated here. By reproducing these details Stein comments continually, though seldom explicitly, on the ways that war, repression, and the abandonment of political common sense distort existence. *Wars I Have Seen* illustrates the positive force of women's literature at the opening of the postwar era, just as *The Egg and I* embodies the negative tradition of self-deprecation that this literature has been determined to overcome.

Two books of nonfiction from the immediate postwar period offer a much more explicit confrontation between positive and negative images of women. Mary Beard's *Woman As Force in History* appeared in 1946, *Modern Woman: The Lost Sex,* by Ferdinand Lundberg and Marynia Farnham, in 1947. Beard was anxious to disprove the idea that "women had been nothing or next to nothing in the long course of history" prior to the rise of feminism in the nineteenth century. Her data have been challenged in part by recent feminist historians, who believe that she overestimated the status and the activities of women in the Middle Ages and Renaissance. But her thesis was advanced at a time when the public estimate of the value of women's efforts, in spite of their record of wartime employment, could be expressed (in *Life* magazine, January 29, 1945) as "simply ridiculous." *Life*'s proposal for the reform of women was to draft them, in order that they could be taught responsibility by the men who would exercise authority over them. More respected figures avoided such discourteous suggestions, but found it easy to overlook the contributions made by women and even, it might seem, their existence. Allan Nevins and Henry Steele Commager, for example, discussed the settlement of the American continent as if it had been effected by the male sex alone, while Christian Gauss of Princeton considered the possible future of civilization on a similar premise.

Beard's questioning of received historical tradition must itself submit to being questioned, but it points toward the reexamination of the past which is now so central to feminist work in the social sciences and the humanities.

The collaboration of Farnham and Lundberg, *Modern Woman: The Lost Sex,* embodies another trend in thinking about women which has produced some recent examples. Women are here seen as a problem—indeed, "as one of modern civilization's major unsolved problems . . . on a par with . . . crime, vice, poverty, epidemic disease, juvenile delinquency, racial hatred, divorce, neurosis and even periodic unemployment." Not only that, because they live "in an emotional slum," they are themselves "principal transmitting media of disordered emotions," which then affect others. Neurotic mothers create neurotic children.

Although (in the view of Farnham and Lundberg) history is largely responsible for the plight of these unfortunate women, they cannot be absolved of guilt because their own response has been destructive, not positive. They have listened too readily to the siren songs of the women's movement, learned to hate men while, at the same time, they seek to achieve maleness. A dizzyingly bitter attack on feminists—grim-faced and sadistic, they are moved by a deep, raging hostility that leads them to seek to castrate men and go back to primitive promiscuity and communal ownership—does not spare other women who may have shunned these carryings-on, but have "acted out their discontent in the home, with disastrous consequences to the rising generation." In addition, by "denying their femininity" the poor creatures have sentenced themselves to frigidity.

The diagnosis suggests the cure: "Women who experience sexual difficulties, with some exceptions [but we hear no more about these], are women who consciously or unconsciously reject the idea of motherhood." Let them, then, select a new goal, that of The Feminine Mother, who "accepts herself fully as a woman [and] knows . . . she is dependent on a man. There is no fantasy in her mind about being an independent woman, a contradiction in terms." Once cured of neurosis, she "can tell, without reading books on child care, what to do for the children by waiting for them to indicate their need." Indeed, much of formal education should be returned to her, while spinsters should be barred "from having anything to do with the teaching of children on the ground of theoretical (usually real) emotional incompetence." At the same time, negative propaganda should direct women away from "male areas of exploit or authority—law, mathematics, physics, business, industry, and technology." With such measures taken, the nation may yet be spared the fate of ancient Rome.

It is worth dwelling on this intemperate treatise in order to make clear some of the popular assumptions about woman's role that were prevalent as our period opens. *Modern Woman: The Lost Sex* was widely read and discussed. The malice of its attack on women's natural aspirations is masked throughout by pietistic assertions that it supports true femininity, which is equated with passivity and subordination. Still relevant is the technique of argument which awakens self-doubt and guilt in the reader by suggesting that inevitable mischances or occasional disabilities are her own fault, thus promoting the fear of autonomous action and so reinforcing its thesis. Later volumes of feminist philosophy should be seen against a background of this kind of propaganda, which masquerades as analysis. Statements from the women's movement are often emotional and tendentious, but it is this manipulatory sermonizing that provokes such reaction. We should not imagine that it has ceased to exist.

351

The period under consideration is sharply divided by the rebirth of conscious feminism in the 1960s, a process which has had the general effect of shifting the view of women's intentions and accomplishments even among those who have reacted very little personally to its advent. It seems best, therefore, to treat the topic of this essay historically rather than simply by sorting out the work and careers of individual authors. The break is not complete. Distinguished women writers at work in the two decades following World War II did much to express the matrix of feeling and judgment from which sprang the renewed self-consciousness of women which is typical of the later sixties and seventies. Katherine Anne Porter, Eudora Welty, Christina Stead, Jean Stafford, Zora Neale Hurston, Caroline Gordon, Kay Boyle, and Hortense Calisher were all publishing fiction as the era opened. None of them, of course, was dealing consciously with feminist issues, but in their work can be found a steady, unromantic concentration on the immediate lived experience of women.

This was, in fact, the continuation of earlier trends; as T. S. Eliot suggested, a literature needs roots. Kate Chopin, Emily Dickinson, and Edith Wharton have supplied recent women writers with a sense that they have indeed been preceded by some authors "generally acknowledged to be great" who wrote out of feminine experience. Though Dickinson's sensibility was confined, for its data, to the private world of women, it reached far beyond this in its expression. Chopin, long overlooked and reclaimed only recently by feminist critics, touched a note that has become increasingly significant when she described the heroine of *The Awakening* as a family prisoner. Not just her husband but "the children appeared before her like antagonists who had overcome her; and sought to drag her into the soul's slavery for the rest of her days." Edith Wharton, placing her women in society, still found a major theme in the limitations that society laid on them as prisoners of a slightly larger world. Willa Cather and Ellen Glasgow continued the serious exploration of women's lives, extending the range covered both socially and geographically. The contribution of women writers of the forties was a reinforcement and an enlargement of the realization that what women know and do and think, of and by themselves, is worth writing about.

Certainly moving and vital female figures are not absent from the work of men, but there they seem to serve different purposes. They create crises for male protagonists. They illustrate aspects of life in a symbolic fashion. They are instruments for social criticism. What distinguishes women's literature is that the everyday existence of women is being investigated for its own significant value. This examination of unexamined lives may well have been influenced by the proletarian novels of the thirties; but whereas these were laden with a political message, serious women writers of the forties and fifties were not trying to convey an explicit moral. The romantic love story does not vanish, but it becomes increasingly problematic. There is little suggestion that any couple lives happily forever after a wedding. Much more frequent is the assumption that couples do not. Indeed, some of the characters in these novels were already making statements that would be echoed in the later writing that reflects the conscious feminism of the sixties and seventies. As early as 1937 Christina Stead had already caught the festering, ingrowing fury of frustrated housebound women. *The Man Who Loved Children* (1940) precedes the period dealt with here, but it was reissued and read later as a forerunner in much the way that Kate Chopin's *The Awakening* has been, though to a lesser extent. Here is its heroine: "Henny was one of those women who secretly sympathize with all women against all men; life was a rotten deal, with men holding all the aces . . . Against [her husband] the intuitions of step-mother and step-daughter came together and procreated, began to put on carnality . . . This creature that was forming against the gay-hearted, generous, eloquent goodfellow was bristly, foul, a hyena, hate of woman the house-jailed and child-chained against the keycarrier, childname, riothaver." Later when Henny is thinking about her children, it is only in her sons that she can take pleasure: "About the girls she thought only of marriage, and about marriage she thought as an ignorant, dissatisfied, but helpless slave did of slavery."

Caroline Gordon, in *The Women on the Porch* (1944), gives us a softer heroine, less brutal in her condemnation of marriage, but far from content with it:

> I was married young, [Catherine] thought. Maybe I've only begun to live now and it seemed to her, looking back, that her marriage had been only a long straining to live up to what her husband demanded of her. She recalled evenings when she had sat silent for hours while two men, or half a dozen, conducted a conversation of which only an occasional phrase was intelligible to her. It had always been like that. When she had the opportunity of making new friends—and she rarely had that opportunity nowadays—her first thought was not whether she liked the new acquaintances or whether they liked her but whether they would be acceptable to her husband. Even now, after fifteen years of married life, she could not tell what would bore him.

Zora Neale Hurston, in *Their Eyes Were Watching God* (1937), has moved beyond personal introspection to generalize: "De white man throw down de load and tell de nigger man to pick it up. He pick it up because he have to, but he don't tote it. He hand it to his woman folks. De nigger woman is de mule uh de world so far as Ah can see."

Again and again in women's writing of this era we note, first, descriptions of the dependence of women on men; second, their anger at their situation and, at the same time, their acceptance of their lot. Rebellion is private. Sometimes, as with Katherine Anne Porter's heroines, it gives women inner strength. They endure their fate because they are capable of separating their inner selves from it sufficiently to judge it, as with the Grandmother in *The Old Order* (1944). They acquiesce in what seem to them demands of necessity but hold back some part of themselves from complicity in the bargain. The condition of Jean Stafford's heroines is influenced by their age. Her tomboys enjoy their freedom; so do her domineering old women who have lived past the years when they are expected to submit to the traditional role of Happy-Wife-and-Motherdom. Young women fall in love, and their emotions push them toward the conventional (the only normal) choice, though this is not all that happens to them, nor is it all that is possible. But the area outside the conventional role is bleak. Those who do not accept it must expect to experience varying forms of disaster, running from social disability to the death by fire of the heroine of *The Catherine Wheel* (1952). If happiness still goes with marriage, there is nothing automatic about it.

Eudora Welty's heroines are more likely to find happiness following on conventional marriage in the conventional way; but when they do, they either belong to an earlier period or they live in a time-warp that casts back to an older system of life. The mistress of a large Delta plantation is "happy" because she is so engaged in multifarious activities that she has no time to reflect on her emotional state. Those who live narrower lives in less affluent conditions cast doubt on the validity of the conventional role by their tendency toward the eccentric. There seems to be some connection between feminine contentedness and the preservation of the life-style of an earlier day.

Two other southern women writers go further in presenting characters whose oddity dissociates them from contemporary values and norms of behavior. In the work of Carson McCullers and Flannery O'Connor eccentricity is so general a state that it can no longer be seen as odd. Instead, these oddities merge to express a state of alienation that breaks through any gap in the accepted pattern of life. Another reality is being reported on: isolation, a frantic search for relatedness without any real knowledge of relatedness. McCullers still gives us innocence embodied in children and occasionally in adults who carry some stigma or handicap. O'Connor's people have moved further away from any settled structure of belief and behavior, to live like weeds in a stony desert. Innocence has been distorted by ignorance and malice; but ignorance and malice are the result of a bad fit between the inner experience of life and the symbolic actions available to express it publicly.

The interest of southern writers of both sexes in eccentric characters corresponds to the social and economic circumstances of southern life at this time, "backward" in material matters and still shadowed by memories of defeat, occupation, and powerlessness. An analogy can be drawn between these conditions and the normal subordination that has been the ordinary lot of women and that was becoming, increasingly, the subject of literature. It was natural for southern women writers to feel this connection. The idea of another sort of life, tangent to that of the mainstream, but running its course according to different rules, is familiar to literature: pastoral offers an example in which such a different life is idealized. It would seem that the life black people led might have presented itself for such use, as peasant life was used by the novelists of nineteenth-century Russia; and indeed, Faulkner did attempt to employ blacks as a means for commenting on the norms of white society. But black existence was less amenable to manipulation for aesthetic purposes than were the peasants of Tolstoy, Turgenev, and Chekhov, because it possessed a structured "other" culture of its own that resisted the effort. Eccentrics and misfits, however, were merely individuals who could be exploited as examples critical of the standards of white middle-class society.

Flannery O'Connor and Carson McCullers, while in no way specifically feminist in their work, are critics not just of society but of its premises. Thus they help to legitimize a fundamental challenge to mainstream values and to orthodox roles, including gender roles. They have moved further from the past than did Faulkner, for whom the old myth of honor still colors the sky, still provides a contrast to the dislocation and disorder of life in the present. For O'Connor and McCullers, this order is not there at all, might never have existed. The lens through which their books present a world to the reader is set to a different focus from the expected. The distortion of view is expressed through the disturbing characters who swim before our eyes —crazy curios of old men and women, obsessed children, young people inappropriately in love or devoting their lives to impossible endeavors—but this material could not be seen at all if not for the distortion of the lens. Their writing authenticates the use of this skewed view, just as Gertrude Stein's writing-as-speech pattern put forward the legitimacy of using repetitions and hesitations to get under the skin of formal communication.

In poetry the forties and fifties sometimes seem to be reversing expected gender roles, which assign the personal voice to women and the abstract idea to men. Perhaps the attention to classic craftsmanship found in Marianne Moore, Elizabeth Bishop, and Babette Deutsch represents a reaction against the personal poetry of Edna St. Vincent Millay and Elinor Wylie with its emphasis on romantic love in a fairly familiar mode, which the previous decades had taken as prototypically feminine. In any event, while the Beats plunged into self-exploration, Moore created brilliant tesselated surfaces which seem composed by utmost adult skill married to the intense ageless vision of a child, but which offer no guidelines to an interior world. These poets hardly say "I," and it is rare for them to speak of particular experience and its intimacies. Their poetry reinforced a growing acceptance of serious writing by women into the critical canon, but it did not challenge the canon.

The experience of passion and attachment between men and women does not disappear from the work of women poets in these years any more than it does from fiction, but certain changes take place. First, it is deemphasized, becoming one among other themes. Then it is abstracted and subjected to questioning. What does the experience of passion mean for a woman? writers are asking. They find it less and less possible to accept the traditional significance of romantic passion as a supreme and unique emotional event.

One way of dealing with these personal storms of feeling is to generalize them by sinking them into myth so that they may be identified as more than individual, as part of "what happens to women" typically and recurrently. Sometimes (as with the novelists) mythic symbols are introduced to reject traditional feminine virtues of gentleness and passivity in an oblique way. Louise Bogan puts the intenser forms of female experience into mythic figures under the names of Medusa or Cassandra or The Sleeping Fury, while still assuring us that this "wilderness" is not to be found in women, that is, "normal" women living ordinary lives. The split between life-as-woman and life-as-a-creator-of-literature is clearer in her work than in that of the novelists then writing, no doubt because the demands of poetry on the author are more intense and less easily diffused. Writers of fiction can turn a double awareness into different, disputing characters; poets need a single eye. In Bogan's work the most powerful emotion is found in poems that use myth or dream as mask: "Tears in Sleep" and "The Dream" can be added to the mythic figures used, as cited above. A woman's consciousness, it seems, must put on fabulous form before it can speak fully and openly. In some poems this pursuit of outward symbol illuminated by inner passion becomes so intense, its meaning knotted so tightly, that we receive the impact with a kind of magical force. Nothing is explained. The words are utterly simple and yet profoundly mysterious, falling on us like a spell. Who is it speaking in "The Crossed Apple"? Is she Eve, who offers temptation with fruit from her orchard, the "lovely apple" that can breed "wood for fires, leaves for shade, apples for sauce"? It is the product of a new cross, "a tree yet unbeholden," and thus is represents the promise of an unknown, unpredictable future. Certainly some power of enchantment sounds through the female voice!

> Eat it; and you will taste more than the fruit:
> The blossom, too,
> The sun, the air, the darkness at the root,
> The rain, the dew,
>
> The earth we come to, and the time we flee,
> The fire and the breast.
> I claim the white part, maiden, that's for me.
> You take the rest.

Something is being said here that we feel with an intimate frisson, but it is masked behind the conscious verbal form like a dream message behind the dream work. A female voice is speaking, but to whom? Is it to a lover or, perhaps, to an apprentice sorceress whose turn it is to learn both to use and to hide her power at a time when committing the act of poetry is held to turn a woman into a fabulous monster since in humans the split between woman and poet remains unhealed?

The use of myth, archetype, and dream by women poets may create new symbols, but it also revivifies the old ones. H.D. (Hilda Doolittle) seized on the apocalypse of destruction which overtook wartime London, where she was living, to probe the meaning of catastrophe as a recurrent event in human life. In the opening lines of "The Walls Do Not Fall" (1944, reissued in *Trilogy*, 1973) she is asking why humankind still survives although the flesh "was melted away, the heart burnt out," and the "husk dismembered." Now that we have "passed the flame: we wonder / what saved us? what for?"

To answer her question she sieves through myth and history looking for instances of wholeness and continuity in dismemberment and fragmentation, and finding symbols of rebirth which are archaic but protean. These she reproduces with the force and intimacy of dream. Indeed, she incorporates dreams in her work. They are bits of experience that our minds have tied up into symbols for our private selves, ordinary everyday touches of myth:

> this is no rune or riddle,
> it is happening everywhere.

Among these dreams is an explicit figure of the New Eve, seen first in terms of the past, as coming to "retrieve what she lost the race," but then discovered to partake of the nature of Demiurge, genetrix of a new future, a vision found again by later women writers. This Eve will bring with her a book not "of the ancient wisdom" but containing "the blank pages / of the unwritten volume of the new." She can no longer be seen imprisoned "in a cave / like a Sibyl"; she is instead "Psyche, the butterfly / out of the cocoon" ("Tribute to the Angels," 1945; reprinted in *Trilogy*).

At the opening of our period Muriel Rukeyser is already demanding self-determination in "Beast in View":

> I want to speak in my voice!
> I want to speak in my real voice!

But the images of women that exist in men's eyes, and have been accepted as limiting definitions, cannot be ignored; they can only be transcended. In "Wreath of Women" (from *Beast in View,* 1944), she explores the process as it takes place among the "women in my time," for whom "Choice is [the] image; they / Choose the myth they obey," a myth that had limited choice to "Whores, artists, saints and wives." The best that could be hoped for was some composite life, whose diversity might at least give the spirit some inward, motive, vitality, but whose task was always "to give / Weakness its reasons / And strength its reassurance." Each of us, and the poet too, have taken gifts of life, grown in the narrow gardens where these women have had to live. To honor these gifts is to see clearly the choice they now offer: to accept the past of "interminable girlhood," or to venture on "the free pain and terror" life truly imagined and lived in full.

The enlarged possibilities of life are reflected in a loosening of the rhyme scheme as Rukeyser looks toward a future where reconciliation of the self with the undertaking of a vocation is finally feasible. Even so, it has not happened yet and the landscape retains a tinge of the fabulous, a dream scene where our gaze finds:

Three naked women saying Yes
Among the calling lakes, the silver trees,
The bird-calling and the fallen grass,
The wood-shadow and the water-shadow.

The use of myth to express the condition of women is ambiguous, incorporating both the image that has been imposed from without and the aspirations that stir within. As feminist awareness dawns and grows, myth and fable are more and more intertwined with the everydayness of women's lives, which is now coming to symbolize a connection to reality instead of the triviality of their existence. In the title poem of her book *With Eyes at the Back of Our Heads* (1959), Denise Levertov writes of a mountain "not obstructed with woods but laced / here and there with feathery groves." Before we can reach it, however, we must find our way through "a facade / that perhaps has no house back of it" and where in any case the doors "are too narrow, and one is set too high / with no doorsill." What is to be done, faced with this mean entrance to a desired future? Instead of accepting a distorted facade as a barrier, one remakes it:

> The architect sees
> the imperfect proposition and
> turns eagerly to the knitter.
> Set it to rights!
> The knitter begins to knit.

Fairy tale or parable, the passage through the distorted "house" of the present is made possible by means of an ordinary female skill, the knitting that corrects proportions at the behest of the architect-professional.

A movement toward common speech that is yet charged with symbolic significance can be seen in the poetry of Adrienne Rich during the decade of the fifties. Like Rukeyser, who interpreted the few roles allowed women as condemning them to an "interminable girlhood," Rich sees masculine protectiveness turning them into spoiled children and chronic invalids. They are granted the "blight" of a "sinecure" in which their work is judged by degrading standards, so that "mere talent is enough for us— / glitter in fragments and rough drafts." By such condescending judgments, "we hear / our mediocrities overpraised . . . / every lapse forgiven." Things change, however, if masculine protection is refused. Then those "who cast too bold a shadow / or smash the world straight off" face another fate: "solitary confinement, / tear gas." Writing in 1960, Rich remarked wryly that there were "Few applicants for that honor."

But she too foresaw a future of change, mediated by a female creator even though "she's long about her coming, who must be / more merciless to herself than history." At her advent, when she plunges "breasted and glancing" through the air, we shall see her "beautiful as any boy / or helicopter"

>   poised, still coming,
>   her fine blades making the air wince
>   but her cargo
>   no promise then:
>   delivered
>   palpable
>   ours.

During these years the earliest instrument of women's writing, the journal, was being put to exhaustive use by Anaïs Nin. Though not published till the sixties and seventies, Nin's experiment in seeing the world through the network of her own nerves and emotions gives us invaluable news of how, in the thirties and later, a sensitive female consciousness perceived the messages that reached it from life. The use of oneself as a measuring stick leaves the writer open to charges of egocentrism and self-aggrandizement, and Nin, like Norman Mailer, has not been spared. Indeed, the reader sometimes feels that one more reported compliment on the author's unique sensibility from one more great man will be the last straw; but there is something else at work here which contradicts, or overrides, the impression of vanity or silliness that swims off Nin's pages at times. This is a commitment to honest and to full, complete revelation of lived experience in the conviction that this experience is not that of a special, treasured, rare female creature but that of someone whose quirks and faults and insights and joys and dislikes are of value because of what they show that is common to other human beings. Like Whitman, Nin is not afraid of contradicting or making a fool of herself, and as a result we get from her fresh, salty tides from a wide sea, even if rubbish sometimes floats on the surface.

Other conventional volumes of memoirs by women of course appeared at this time, usually by those who had attained some degree of distinction in one field or another and whose lives could thus be seen as examples of success within society-as-it-is. But these chronicles all include some difficulties, and almost always they are those of women forced to choose between the accepted pattern of femininity and whatever it is that brings them to success. Most widely read was Eleanor Roosevelt's simply written story of growing up an ugly duckling in a famous, if uneasy, family, and of her life-long struggle to find a mode of life that accorded with her own standards and her own moral imperatives.

Two autobiographies by close contemporaries of Eleanor Roosevelt may be cited to indicate the tensions inherent in the lives of success ful women. In *Many a Good Crusade* (1954) Virginia Gildersleeve documented (with circumspection) the life of an early career woman in academia. Unrivaled administrative skills and single-minded dedication to her work established her as dean of Barnard College of Columbia University, one of the "Seven Sister" schools, a post she held for nearly forty years, retiring in 1945 to become the only woman on the American delegation to the San Francisco conference which set up the United Nations. The cresting of the first feminist wave was played out in the everyday events of Gildersleeve's life. Very much part of the New York Establishment, she accomplished political feats which thwarted the conventions of the Establishment: the admission of women to Columbia's graduate professional schools is one that she notes with carefully repressed pleasure. In her life we see one aspect of the split between old roles and new realities.

Ellen Glasgow's very different story of the life of a highly successful woman writer appeared in the same year, 1954. *The Woman Within*, being a posthumous work, could afford to be more intimate and revealing, though even so names of the men closest to Glasgow are suppressed. Here, the emotional crises almost overwhelm the literary success that Glasgow enjoyed. This is the account of a desperate, indeed an unrelenting, struggle with the context of life, outwardly pleasant and inwardly murderous. She was the ninth of ten children, with a patriarch worthy of Roman antiquity for a father, and her every effort to reach autonomy required the courage to attack, not simply the stamina to endure. "Looking back on my life," she wrote (and it was a life marked by milestones of tragedy), "I can see that a solitary pattern has run through it from earliest childhood. Always I have had to learn for myself, from within . . . To teach oneself is to be forced to learn twice." The family romance that she lived out in an old-fashioned extended household was a Senecan tragedy, where death and desertion became commonplace. She and her sister, she records, "lived and breathed and moved for months at a time in the atmosphere of despair. The very bread we ate tasted of hopelessness . . . And then, in the midst of it all . . . I was seized . . . by a consuming desire to find out things for myself, to know the true from the false . . . I flung myself on knowledge as a thirsty man might fling himself on a desert spring. I read everything in our library . . . I was devoured by this hunger . . . to discover some meaning, some underlying reason for the mystery and pain of the world. [She was only in her teens but] I had ceased to be a child . . . I had entered the long solitude that stretches on beyond the vanishing point in the distance."

This stoic determination to outlive tragedy—and the catastrophes that befell her included the early death of her mother, of her favorite brother, of the brother-in-law who had become a friend and mentor, of the lover she could not marry, plus the advent of deafness that increasingly cut her off from the world—was not unique to her in her time. But of all her generation of writers—and it included Colette and Willa Cather as almost exact contemporaries as well as Virginia Woolf, eight years younger—Glasgow speaks most forcefully of the saving grace to be found in work, work as a continuing, demanding presence that bestows an identity on an individual even while it stretches her past known limits. Women had certainly lived such lives from the beginning of time; now they were looking at them consciously.

Other kinds of nonfiction were being written beside the diaries and memoirs that have long been occupations of women. Lillian Smith took up the century-old concern among southern women for an end to black oppression, which she saw (like the Grimkes before her) as causing a self-inflicted distortion of white identity and moral ideals. In her novel *Strange Fruit* (a best seller in 1944 as our era opens) and in the essays collected as *Killers of the Dream* (1949), she described the pain and the crippling of human relationships which our society has suffered as a cost of racial bigotry. Her condemnation of prejudice was based on a moral stand and did not challenge the social and economic structure of which discrimination was a part. In this way it was both limited and made acceptable by its fit with the old female image, where womanly concern for others was felt to be proper. But in a period when few black voices could yet speak strongly for themselves, her work, insisting on the moral obligation to live out actively a commitment to equality, affirmed the old connection that women have felt between their own position and that of black people from the days of Abolition on.

This connection, very naturally, is more readily seen by women than by black writers, whose experience of oppression by all whites does not invite sympathy for those who are perceived as belonging to the oppressors, even if oppressed themselves. But as an element frequently found in women's literature, it extends the realization of one's own experience toward metaphoric universality. Older southern women writers, like Katherine Anne Porter, Eudora Welty, and Caroline

Gordon, could, on occasion, draw black characters who are far from being stereotypes. Though the everyday events of experience recorded in women's writing often reflect the traditional submission and outward humiliation of blacks as facts of the life then being lived, there is also evidence of respect for emotional qualities that are not the banalities of the black stereotype: endurance, stamina, wit, and deep resources of strength and dignity.

We see examples in Eudora Welty's story "A Worn Path" (in *Selected Stories*, 1954), a spare report on the arduous trip to town made by "an old woman with her head tied up in a rag" determined to get her grandson the medicine he needs, but also to beg, borrow, or steal the few coins that will buy him a toy, a trip made on the knife edge of physical strength. It is not just Granny's compassion but her cunning that Welty admires. In *The Women on the Porch* (1944), Caroline Gordon moves into the mind of Maria, a black cook, and establishes her commitment to grief for her son, jailed for two murders. She is able to make comprehensible the black woman's conviction that the crippling and distorting restrictions of the white world have produced black violence, and will continue to do so. Black fury is seen (and it was a rare vision at the time) as the product of a society that maintained the logic of white law at the price of violence among its black subjects. Katherine Anne Porter describes the surfacing of true identity, hidden for a lifetime but still alive, in the old black woman Nannie, who insists, in her old age, on moving into a cabin of her own away from the white family she has raised and tended. To their astonishment "she was no more the faithful old servant, Nannie, a freed slave: she was an aged Bantu woman of independent means, sitting on the steps, breathing the free air."

Authentic black experience from within was coming from Gwendolyn Brooks in the forties and fifties, in poetry and in autobiographical fiction. It is interesting, and typical of a new literature, to note how we find a continuing loosening in Brooks's work of the elegant and rather formal style used at first, as if it were necessary to prove her mastery of Mandarin before she could feel free to use demotic language. This kind of breakthrough indicates not only the growing courage of the first substantial writers in a new field, but also their sense of having an audience tuned to a new idiom. These writers discover that they are speaking not just for a people, but to them. Brooks has emphasized her consciousness of race above sex, but the content and the feeling of her writing fall within the bounds of women's literature. We see black aspiration and women's use of everyday experience combined in part II of "The Womanhood" (in *Annie Allen,*

363

1949), a poem on her small son. In it she describes how "we both want joy of deep and unabiding things, / Like kicking over a chair or throwing blocks out of a window." But this transitory delight symbolizes something more: the courage to experiment, reach out and try new experience. The chair may fall with "a beautiful crash," but the child "has never been afraid to reach. / His lesions are legion. / But reaching is his rule."

Other women writers combine the experience of working-class backgrounds in ethnic and minority groups with that of growing up female. Tillie Olsen uses the minutiae of obscure lives to pose and reflect on major metaphysical questions. Such abstract questioning, as has been noted, is rare in women's writing of this period. When it occurs it is apt to be associated with the socialist or anarchist doctrines that were very much a part of working-class life among immigrants. Olsen goes far beyond ideology, however. What meaning can be found in life at the end of life? she asks, in the prose of *Tell Me a Riddle* (1961), as Yeats asked in his poems of old age. Here, these are questions put in a female voice, questions that value the high creeds of revolutionary self-sacrifice in terms of "one pound soupmeat, one soupbone . . . bread, day old" and "cheap thread." These cares are what an old woman remembers in her mortal agony, and they overwhelm memories of dedication to the Movement, marriage, children born and laboriously raised. Love, anger, frustration, hope, the fellowship that endured poverty—all fall away before the inescapable chores of living, relieved only by a sudden echo from music heard in childhood. To her husband the old woman becomes an astonishing, disturbing stranger: "It seemed to him that for seventy years she had hidden a tape recorder, infinitely microscopic, within her, that it had coiled infinite mile on mile, trapping every song, every melody, every word read, heard and spoken—and that maliciously she was playing back only what said nothing of him, of the children, of their intimate life together." He is right. What she had hoped for was a patch of life of her own, completely to herself; and then death intervened.

The full weight of consciousness is present and expressed in the simple events of life for Olsen's women. "I stand here ironing," begins a woman in the story of this title (in *Tell Me a Riddle*) and weighing out the inescapable failure of her care for her oldest child, raised without her father, passed to a neighbor in order that the mother could earn enough to keep them both, a little girl who had to be good and was; of whom too much was demanded. Reflection can find no cure, no solution, only note again how childhood loneliness was matched with adult anguish and balanced against what the other chil-

dren needed, "that terrible balancing of hurts and needs I had to do
. . . and did so badly, those earlier years." Awareness of what we
owe each other and cannot give, of what humanity might become if
love could be unrestricted, shapes this story, though "I will never total
it all now," the mother tells herself. "My wisdom came too late . . .
Let her be. So all that is in her will not bloom—but in how many
does it? There is still enough left to live by. Only help her to believe—help make it so there is cause for her to believe that she is
more than this dress on the ironing board, helpless before the iron."

Grace Paley's short stories come out of much the same background,
but they are told with wild humor. It is not the humor of earlier
women's writing, which served to trivialize the experience recorded,
but a humor of attack and mockery. Life is absurd and Paley's wom-
en are caught in its irrational trickery, but they may well be less deceived about events and causation than the men who work so hard to
fit these tricks into the patterns of received wisdom. These women
are swinging into a future. Like Gwendolyn Brooks's little boy, they
are "not afraid to reach." They are moving beyond victimization, acting out changes in ordinary relationships that underlie the conscious
revaluation of women's experience which appears in the latter part
of our period.

These observations of life, like the notations of eccentricity that
appear in the work of Flannery O'Connor and Carson McCullers, differ from the eccentric symbols used by such male writers as Pynchon,
Barth, and Barthelme in being less willed and worked, more *objets
trouvés,* odd pebbles turned up on the path of one's daily walk. Certainly as women writers begin to turn into feminist writers, a systematic criticism of the orthodox structure of ideas manifests itself. But
it stems from, and often harks back to, the contradictory details of
"what the woman lived," to use the title given to Louise Bogan's published letters. Like the diaries of Anaïs Nin, this and other collections of casual writing by women authors serve to validate for other
women the commonality of their experience. Such validation is a central purpose of feminist writing, as it is for any national or ethnic
literature in its first, formative stages. Those who are shaking off
old standards of judgment need to compare what they have in common, and so establish an essential indwelling identity, which will give
coherence and vitality to the negative identity defined by differences
from the past model that is in process of being replaced.

In the early sixties, two major nonfiction works illustrated the
growing ability of women to criticize cogently the taken-for-granted
approaches to methods of modernizing our society. Jane Jacobs's *The*

Death and Life of Great American Cities (1961) attacked the mindless acceptance of "urban renewal" which destroyed old neighborhood patterns of life and networks of community support for families and individuals. In her view, a commitment to architectural design and essentially academic (therefore masculine) principles of development was winning out over the intimate knowledge of human interaction, which only those who lived by these interactions could value properly. Even more influential, Rachel Carson's *Silent Spring* (1962) attacked the suicidal use of technological methods for controlling the natural environment by pesticides, with little or no prevision of the results. Both books can be seen as examples of an extension into the public sector of the kind of care for individual human creatures that is traditionally assigned to women. Both testify to the dangers of downgrading "housekeeping," in these cases social and ecological housekeeping, in favor of uncontrolled experiment. In a strict sense these books may not be countable as "literature," but they evidence a growing breadth of mind among women writers as to the subject matter on which they felt themselves able to speak with serious weight. Thus they contributed to the increasing confidence that women were feeling in their capacity to judge not only their own lives, but also the dynamics of social process. It is another step toward the "unconscious universality" that T. S. Eliot noted as a prerequisite to a true literature.

Betty Friedan's *The Feminine Mystique,* published in 1963, is the document that is most often taken to signal the appearance of a new wave of feminist self-consciousness. Friedan's book is important as a social statement rather than as a literary text; but its anger and its enthusiasm evoked a response from a widening circle of readers that has made it a classic of Movement writing. Ten years before, the American edition of Simone de Beauvoir's *The Second Sex* had received praise from critics (some as unlikely as Philip Wylie) and had been widely read; it is still a source of intellectual stimulation, but it did not produce the public reaction that welcomed Friedan's examination of the frustrations plaguing American middle-class women. Readers of *The Feminine Mystique* found their own malaise tellingly described, and identified as originating in a social context, not in private neurosis.

Previously, orthodox wisdom had been assuring them that happiness and fulfillment were to be found only in self-abnegation, nurturance of others, and the acceptance of a subordinate role, a doctrine put forward overtly in such works as *Modern Woman: The Lost Sex,* but also implicit in much other writing, both serious and popular. Talcott Parsons, for example, took it for granted, in his studies of the function of the family, that the most important choice of a woman's life—almost the only important choice—was her selection of a husband. Once married, she took her status in society from him, as she had previously done from her father. Independent action on the part of a woman was conceded to be possible, but neither frequent nor significant enough to offset the influence exercised by the "male head-of-household." This assumption was now being challenged. Friedan's achievement was to assert convincingly that female reactions which had formerly been seen as "deviant" were, in fact, signs of normal resentment against disabling restrictions. For any woman, social permission to respect one's own opinions and rely on the validity of one's own perceptions was liberating, but surely for none more than for those who undertook creative work.

During the late sixties and, even more, the early seventies, feminist polemical writing began to proliferate. Much of it was ephemeral, but a considerable body of serious literature and valuable scholarship was accumulating. It is beyond the scope of this essay to consider the latter in any detail, but its purpose and its approach parallel that of women's literature and thereby provide scholarly support. Indeed, the underlying premises of what can and should be studied and taught in the humanities and social sciences have been altered as the women's movement extended the range of material deemed worthy of study. Historians, sociologists, anthropologists, psychologists, theologians, and students of comparative religion, critics, philosophers, and theoreticians have found their disciplines linking themselves to form a new area of women's studies. Mary Daly, in *Beyond God the Father* (1973) explores the significance to Christian thought of the absence of a female principle. Jean Baker Miller (*Toward a New Psychology of Women,* 1976) and Dorothy Dinnerstein (*The Mermaid and the Minotaur,* 1976) discuss sociopsychological changes in family structures, both past and potential, and the profound impact on social values they are having and will have. Elizabeth Janeway in *Man's World, Woman's Place* (1971) and *Between Myth and Morning* (1974) has taken women's lives as a field in which the effect of shifts in social and cultural directives on behavior patterns can be observed. How does the experience of women reflect and respond to historical trends? How does it illustrate the process of psychological adjustment forced universally by major alterations in the context of life? Historical research into women's lives has enlarged and enriched the fund of information available to economic historians and demographers. The tendency in sociology and anthropology to concentrate on material dealing only with males and to base general conclusions on these observations has been to some extent countered by research that draws on feminine experience as well: Man the Hunter is now granted a partner in prehistory, Woman the Forager. Such activity, quite apart from the information it turns up, points to the increased importance attached to women's perceptions and judgments. It thus authenticates the trend, already noted in women's literature, to take seriously what women think and do. Since this has seldom been the case in the past, such authentication adds to women's confidence and enlarges the area of study or of literary endeavor that they feel is open to them. Thus recent polemical writing and continuing scholarly research have had direct and indirect effects that cannot be ignored on the range and the seriousness of women's writing.

Scholarship in the novel field of women's studies has of course added breadth to common knowledge, with the result that more of women's lives can be taken for literary material. In addition, the exaggeration typical of polemics has functioned in a positive fashion in this new area. To think or to say the unthinkable may be absurd or false in a period enjoying great homogeneity of style and culture; but when the "thinkable" becomes stale—or false to reality—exaggerated, angry questioning can initiate productive thought about alternatives. Thus when Kate Millett, with *Sexual Politics* (1970), and Germaine Greer, with *The Female Eunuch* (1971), set out to attack on a dozen fronts what they saw as outmoded patterns of patriarchal thought, they might be faulted here or there, but they were providing evidence that received ideas were ripe for rethinking. Polemical writers also showed up the irrational connections contained in accepted systems of thought about the sexes. Even when these radical attacks have little literary value in themselves, they act as manifestoes which diminish the force of obsolescent assumptions attuned to an old system, but becoming alien to the growing structure of thought which informs a new literature.

More closely related to enduring literary style than to exaggeration is an element widely present in feminist writing of the sixties and early seventies: the resort to immediate autobiographical experience, which is not, however, offered as merely individual. Rather, "what happened to me" is presented as a parable of what has happened, or may probably happen, to other women. Sometimes this reporting is fictionalized, but it does not detach itself entirely from the writer's impressions nor from her didactic purpose. It does not aim at true fictional distancing but keeps a connection with fact and a handhold on personal emotion.

This intrusion of the "I" as both author and character is typical of any movement literature in its early stages, when a need to testify to newly discovered truths looms larger than aesthetic rules. We find it, during the early seventies, in *Combat in the Erogenous Zone* (1972), where Ingrid Bengis reports not only on her experience of male/female relations, but also on what she has learned from them in a general, philosophic sense. We find it in the rather more conventional reportage (of a high order) in Vivian Gornick's *In Search of Ali Mahmoud* (1973). Gornick's journey into Egyptian middle-class life was set off by the sensation, disturbing to a woman conscious of her Jewish background and its valued culture, that she and her Egyptian lover have a great deal in common. To discover what this is she undertakes a journey to his country and a visit to his family, which must at all times be checked against her own sensibility, so that her book gains value from both objective reporting and subjective feeling. Kate Millett's *Sexual Politics,* passionately felt but presented within a conventional scholarly frame, was followed by *Flying* (1974), an intimate report of the crises and interior tensions created by her unexpected rise to fame as a heroine of the women's movement. Such writing can be called confessional, but the guilt usually associated with that term is seldom present. The intention is, rather, to bear testimony to aspects of life that have been overlooked, or misinterpreted.

The impulse to report on personal experience is clearest in the work of poets. The earlier use of mythic or fabulous figures does not disappear, but its purpose begins to shift. These figures cease to serve as a mask for profound feelings and become, instead, a setting-off place for an examination of ordinary experience; or they are used as metaphors to identify the significance of an emotional event. Old symbols may be retained, but they are given a new content that grows out of daily existence. In *To See, to Take* (1970) Mona Van Duyn responds to Yeats's poem "Leda and the Swan" with two of her own, "Leda" and "Leda Reconsidered." Yeats makes the moment of union between god-bird and woman an epiphany of transcendence and terror, taking place outside imaginable life. Van Duyn, on the contrary, introduces the rest of life. In her "Leda" we are given a vision of Leda grown old, not so much rejecting as never having conceived the "men's stories [in which] her life ended with his loss." This Leda "was not, for such an ending, abstract enough . . . She married a smaller man with a beaky nose, / and melted away in the storm of everyday life."

But this picture did not exhaust the possibilities of the scene for Van Duyn. In "Leda Reconsidered" she replaces it with that of a woman who can anticipate the future and imagine the reality of others, even of the god:

> She had a little time to think
> as he stepped out of the water . . .
> She sat there in the sunshine . . .
> watching him come,
> trying to put herself
> in the place of the cob, and see
> what he saw . . .

To see what he saw, she looks at herself and finds a woman with a sense of the context of life; indeed, one whose presence and emotional force influences the mythic encounter. She is an accepting participant who considers the meaning of what happens and chooses to be chosen.

> She waited for him so quietly that
> he came on her quietly,
> almost with tenderness,
> not treading her.

Yeats's Leda is overcome:

> How can those terrified vague fingers push
> The feathered glory from her loosening thighs?

But Van Duyn's is present and conscious:

> Her hand moved into the dense plumes
> on his breast to touch
> the utter stranger.

In this recent poetry, myths are constantly transformed by the content of everyday life that is poured into them. When Carolyn Kizer declares herself to be "Hera, Hung from the Sky" (*Midnight Was My Cry*, 1971), she is not masking emotion, but illustrating it:

> In an instant of power, poise—
> Arrogant, flushed with his love,
> Hypnotized by . . .
> . . . the dream
> That woman was great as man—
> I threw myself to the skies
> And the sky has cut me down
> I have lost the war of the air:

Half-strangled in my hair,
I dangle, drowned in fire.

In "A Voice from the Roses" (*Halfway*, 1961), Maxine Kumin
takes an old myth, that of Arachne, transformed into a spider by an
angry Athene for her impudence in challenging the goddess to a
contest of weaving, and uses it to illuminate the ambivalence of a
mother-daughter relationship; but she can also, in "The Appointment" (*Halfway*), cast up a new anonymous symbol for some as yet
unnamed disturbance: a wolf, "my wolf," who settles like a pet at
her bed's foot to watch the night through,

breathing so evenly
I am almost deceived.

The nightmare-wolf, calmly in possession of his accustomed place,
looming out of dream into daylight, increases further the uneasiness
his presence causes because he arrives with no mythic identity, has
slipped loose from any established order of myth or folk tale. Similarly, Sylvia Plath's "Disquieting Muses" (*The Colossus and Other
Poems*, 1962) gain no reassurance from bearing a familiar name.
"Mother, mother," asks the poet,

what illbred aunt
Or what disfigured and unsightly
Cousin did you so unwisely keep
Unasked to my christening, that she
Sent these ladies in her stead
With heads like darning eggs to nod
And nod and nod at foot and head
And at the left side of my crib?

Like Levertov's knitter, setting things to rights with her needles,
Plath's muses with darning-egg heads translate us to a world of female
perceptions and skills. Each illustrates the trend toward altering the
effect of symbols by shifting their content and replacing stale references
by others that are immediate and intimate.

Plath's poetry, and her life, were completed before the new feminist
consciousness had begun to find expression, but her work has become
a touchstone for the women's movement and is best considered in this
context. She and Anne Sexton represent a poetic current that is central to the cultural identity of the first phase of the movement. Both
women use personal material which is at once the stuff of daily life
and the expression of despair and dislocation. The exhaustive exploration of this material should not be misunderstood as masochistic

or narcissistic. Its readers do not find it so. They are not looking for Gothic horrors but, first, for reassurance that their own similar sensations have been shared and, second, that someone has faced them and struggled to understand them.

It is difficult for critic, as well as reader, to separate this literature from its experiential context. On purely critical grounds, one cannot judge this writing successfully without understanding that part of its impact comes from its intimacy, and that this impact derives also from a shared moment in time. To say that this poetry deals with pain and frustration is not enough. One must add that it could not have been written at all, and this novelty is part of its force, unless a particular kind of pain and frustration *could now be perceived as ending*. The ability to look openly at humiliation and degradation, and to testify to the profound emotional confusion that arises when the presence of these emotions is first brought to light, depends on a sense that such a state need not continue. If there is no choice open but pain or numbness, the human creature will try to be numb, and shield the pain with self-deprecatory laughter—as we have seen. Even when earlier writers of fiction expressed resentment at the fate of women, it was tempered by awareness that there were few alternatives. Plenty of bad marriages and disorientated wives can be found in novels, but as long as marriage remained a prerequisite for normal female life, it was seen, perforce, as something that women had to put up with; and the worst and most crippling of its disorders went unmentioned or were disguised. When a life without marriage, or without the traditional form of patriarchal marriage, became socially and emotionally feasible, what had been hidden began to emerge. The atmosphere of exposé increases the impact of these revelations.

Plath and Sexton function not just as authors but also as exemplary figures for their readers. They act out familiar scenes, but they carry the action beyond what is expected. Both of them married and had children. Both of them went through episodes of madness. Marriages broke up. Each killed herself, succeeding in this act after earlier attempts had failed. Their struggles and tensions are recorded in their work, and their lives reinforce their words. Each endeavored to combine a life in the traditional mode with a career as a writer, and each broke down. For their devotées, reality gives the writing a weight that goes beyond merely literary statement.

This is not meant to belittle the value of their work. Plath's novel, *The Bell Jar* (1963), is episodic and uneven, but that could be said of many poets' novels. From a rather formal beginning, her poetry grows steadily in intensity and power. In "Edge" (*Ariel*, 1965) we see her death previsioned, but the strength of the poem lies not in our knowledge of the soon-to-be-accomplished event but in her transformation of the simple data of life into chilling symbol:

> The woman is perfected.
> Her dead
>
> Body wears the smile of accomplishment,
> The illusion of a Greek necessity
>
> Flows in the scrolls of her toga . . .
>
> Each dead child coiled, a white serpent,
> One at each little
>
> Pitcher of milk, now empty.
> She has folded
>
> Them back into her body as petals
> Of a rose close . . .
>
> The moon has nothing to be sad about . . .
>
> She is used to this sort of thing.

Sexton's poetry, like Plath's, is much involved with the tensions between rules about motherhood and daughterhood and the realities of obligatory relationships. These poets are constantly forced to consider such noble symbols in terms of dailyness. Plath, both in imagining her death and in actually going to it, thought of her children. Though she saw them dead in the poem, drawn into "perfection" with her, in real life she left them sleeping with bread and milk beside them. Sexton, put to writing her first poems as a therapeutic task set by her doctor, dates the bout of madness that hurled her out of normal life by remembering the illness of one of her children and times her return to sanity by encounters with the child, and with her own mother. These poets need and use immediacy, taken (writes Sexton) from the "narrow diary of my mind / [and] the commonplaces of the asylum."

For Plath and Sexton and for other women writers as well the experience of madness is neither shunned nor sharply divided from the rest of life. It is, rather, seen as a metaphor for the absurdity of the rest of life, absurdity brought to light in newly felt contradictions and frustrations. In literature of this period, madness becomes a limit toward which victimization and powerlessness push women; but there is also a sense in which madness is chosen as a revolt against normality when normality can no longer support a life that includes joy, freedom, and imagination. Like the eccentric characters of O'Connor and McCullers, those who have fallen into madness measure and criticize the values of orthodoxy.

In one year, 1970, several books by women writers made serious attempts to understand situations of alienation and madness that seemed to grow out of traditional roles. (Toni Morrison's powerful *The Bluest Eye* appeared at this time but will be discussed later with the novels and memoirs of other black writers because the experience called on differs from that used by white women.) In *Play It As It Lays,* Joan Didion chronicles the disintegration of her heroine, Maria, into numb despair. Maria has been separated from her small daughter, who is institutionalized for some mental or emotional disturbance. She takes this as evidence of total personal failure and incapacity to act in any way that can produce a positive result. She is hopelessly at odds with what is required of her by social expectations: if they are right, she must be wrong. But if they are right, there is no impulse of hers that she can trust; and that must mean that she is evil, beyond redemption. It is a vision of Hell after Judgment Day, when no remorse, no penance, can buy salvation. There is no help for Maria; Didion is not, however, directing us to drown in fruitless pity for her heroine, but to consider the unbearable weight that a traditional role can lay on an ordinary person.

Gain Godwin, in *The Perfectionists,* gives us a heroine, Dane, who has not just fallen into a traditional role, but has chosen a particularly difficult version of it. Dane is determined on the self-abnegation and denial of will that have been celebrated as female virtues because she sees them as something more: doors to transcendence of selfish involvement in the world. She marries an unorthodox psychologist and takes on his strange, probably autistic, little son. The marriage choice she makes is a bid not for safety, but for the challenge of a demanding existence. It is not, however, an existence over which she can exert control: ordinary life continues to make its own ordinary demands for proper behavior and day-to-day management, even though this behavior runs counter to her own emotions. It is not enough to devote herself to the silent, secret child; she must cope with him. She is not very good at it, and begins to see him as an antagonist. Her affection does not reach or alter him, and Dane then finds herself striving to penetrate his identity by force, whether that hurts him or not. The role of nurturing, self-denying woman, even when chosen by the woman herself, turns out to be inappropriate and ineffective. It offers guilt instead of the promised fulfillment.

In the same year Nancy Milford published her biography of Zelda

Fitzgerald, where we find a close reading of the advent of madness in real life. A talented woman lives out a role of subordination to a talented man. Zelda too made a daring marriage choice which preferred challenging experience to safety, and unfortunate results followed. This marriage takes on aspects of a *folie à deux,* but it is Zelda who is judged as mad, not Scott. His talent is admired and exploited, insofar as his drinking and eccentric behavior permit. Her talent is actively discouraged. Scott feels her writing as competition so unfair that it amounts to betrayal, and her attempt to become a dancer is dismissed as utter foolishness. There is no way to tell, now, who should be "blamed" for these conclusions, and Milford is not really trying to do this. Like Didion and Godwin, she is describing the rules of the game. But all these books point out how the rules can work to move women, by way of powerlessness and victimization, into a state that is then diagnosed as madness.

During the seventies a revaluation of traditional marriage proceeded apace. Different aspects are examined: marriage may be repudiated entirely, it may become the scene of a struggle, it may be left behind and life alone tested, but it ceases to be taken for granted as inevitable in and/or necessary to normal life. The equation of marriage with fulfillment is rejected, but the rejection is still seen as difficult. Heroines do not leave or refuse marriage and go calmly on to some other sort of average living. Having feared flying, they burst out of wedlock and try to soar on their own. Divorce leaves them threatened as well as isolated: who is friend, who is enemy? Familiar figures change shape; loss of status (no male head of household to define one now!) plunges ex-wives into vulerability. Alternative relationships must be improvised, and within them even accepted friends may become strangers. Autonomy carries a component of loneliness: these women lie alone at night thinking about unmarriageable lovers, or they take on partners whom they would, in earlier days, have reckoned highly unsuitable. There is little or no disposition to return to the orthodox matings they found crippling, unless, as in Alison Lurie's *The War between the Tates* (1974), the tone of the novel is satiric. But there is not much joy offered these departing heroines. Their lives are fragmented.

And yet the old bargain has become impossible. The wives who go back feel themselves to have redefined their identities so completely that the marriage will be taken up at a new point, in a new way. This will include the details of living; it is not simply an abstract aspiration. For these heroines, whether they try to salvage an old relationship or hang on to the new status of woman alone, it is often the strand of dailiness that holds things together. The shift within the self is endured and made permanent by keeping in touch with a chain of minute-to-minute sensations. One of the most dramatic moves into isolation is described by the Canadian author Margaret Atwood in *Surfacing* (1972). Having broken with her lover and escaped from the friends who had come to share some time on a wilderness lake where she had lived as a child, this heroine undertakes an explicit and conscious reenactment of the mythic journey to the interior, including a deliberate search for sacred images painted by Indian shamans and a repetition of their imagined ritual of denial and destruction. But the fantasy is embedded in the immediate. We are given minute details of the ritual: what is to be worn, what can be eaten, what must be destroyed and thrown away. There is no blurring of experience in these books: when the past is rejected and the future not yet invented, one holds fast to the present.

There appear, then, to be two major elements at work in women's literature as it moves beyond the phase in which it is simply in search of an identity. First is the insistence on looking at the data of ordinary life and on using the occupations of women, overlooked by high culture, as trustworthy evidence in which some kind of significance can be sought. While a structure of values that was formed elsewhere, by others, and matched to other needs is being abandoned, one clings to felt reality, even if this reality can be described as mad, under the old system. Second, there is an urge to create a new set of values that will suit the lives and purposes of women as seen by women: a system of authentic emotional relations and interconnected beliefs drawn from lived experience that will develop the force of social myth, and thus explain the workings of the world and direct appropriate behavior.

At first blush, this grandiose program may seem to conflict with the emphasis on minutiae of living; and, indeed, some feminist writing does rush toward utopia, indulge in fantasies, and imagine future societies so doctrinaire as to be hardly habitable by human beings. But this is typical of any movement writing in its early days. Generally in women's literature, and certainly in the most effective writing, whether it is fiction or nonfiction, the drive to create a new world of symbols does not separate itself from dailiness. Instead, it works within everyday experience, looking there for clues to a new interpretive paradigm which is already taking shape. Its first manifestations may be felt merely as disturbances in orthodox theory; but as they increase, they point to the existence of an alternative world view which will in time stand forth in its own essential identity. This quest for a new symbology respects the real and refuses to assign an arbitrary value to it, preferring to let its own significance illuminate it from within. We can even find a description of this search in women's writing. Adrienne Rich's image of a future female explorer, quoted above, seen to "plunge breasted and glancing through the currents" recurs a decade later as the poet "diving into the wreck," not only for herself, but as a being who is more than a single individual:

> We are, I am, you are
> by cowardice or courage
> the one who find our way
> back to this scene
> carrying a knife, a camera
> a book of myths
> in which
> our names do not appear.

And in "The Long Distance Runner" (*Enormous Changes at the Last Minute,* 1974) a fantasy that is held down to earth by immediate details of objects seen and scenes traversed, Grace Paley writes of a woman revisiting the neighborhood where she spent her childhood, and feeling the changes that have taken place by living them out. In the end this "Long Distance Runner" sums it up: "A woman inside the steamy energy of middle age runs and runs. She finds the houses and streets where her childhood happened. She lives in them. She learns as though she was still a child what in the world is coming next."

The future can best be foreseen by looking at what goes on under our noses, these writers say. Ideas of a different world—and if this literature rages at the past, it is hopeful about the future—tug us toward imagining new systems. Nonetheless, they declare, all our lives remind us that one cannot make bricks without straw or a society without considering who gets meals, cares for children, looks after the old, mourns the dead, and keeps the wheel in motion. In the past and still in the present, these tasks were and are done by ubiquitous, irreplaceable female creatures, loving, marrying or not marrying, earning as well as spending, and always tending to the recurrent, necessary processes that go on below the level of attention and bind communities together.

The work of Joyce Carol Oates, a writer both prolific and wide-ranging, illustrates a number of these themes and the devices used to communicate them. The eccentricity of Oates's characters is sometimes as great as those of Flannery O'Connor, but they are always placed within the framework of society. Sometimes they are part of an elite whose actions show up the workings of a shaky and inhumane social

377

structure. Sometimes they are conscious rebels struggling for change even though they are not certain that any change is really possible. Or they may be puppets of social forces, but if so they are feeling puppets. They may reject the whole world as it is, and be defined as mad. Oates refuses to vouch for any alternate system of morals even as she discloses the immorality of the one that exists. Her protagonists are not conventionally good, though some of her rebels try uneasily to be. But her central characters have been too mishandled by life for goodness. They are selfish, if not greedy, and yet they are conscious that something has gone very wrong. They do not, like the rebels, aspire to make a better world of community and connection, they are concentrated on saving themselves; but they tend to posit a better world, or at least to hope for one because they sense that it is only in such a place that they could be saved. They differ from the manic, driven automata who have achieved fame, success, and money in the artificial world of the present, because they are still capable of natural feeling. Oates's protagonists may try for the goals that are held up to them as desirable, but they sicken on the way.

"Success," then, is equated with sickness. Oates's rebels know that, they appreciate the overwhelming need to substitute a healthy society for the way we live now, but they cannot imagine a substitute that is persuasive to those who are infected with sickness. As with Mered Dawe in *Do with Me What You Will* (1973), the attraction they exert is lunar, spectral. Typically, Mered is victimized—arrested, beaten, declared mad, driven mad. But he is simply the most obvious victim. The society described here is a madness-inducing machine. No fully human relationships are possible within it, though the rebels somehow keep the hope of them alive in others. These people are fetishists, they can love only in part, feverishly. They are themselves only present in part, able to exist only by not looking at the world, like Elena in this book, or, like her mother, Ardis, able only to leave an earlier persona behind like a snake shedding its skin. We come to know Ardis quite well before she marries off Elena (beautiful, biddable, dreaming) to the famous, monstrous lawyer, Marvin Howe. When Ardis reappears later she is someone quite different, a television personality with a new name and a new appearance. She is not just willing to deny her past identity, she insists on it. Her motherhood, she tells her daughter, must be a secret between them.

To be successful, says Oates, one must give up any stable identity, which implies giving up the ability to establish authentic relationships with others. But this demand creates a great malaise in the bulk of Oates's folk, for though they long to be successful they want an identity too, and shrink from the sacrifice of self made by the great. Who am I? they ask. What can I believe? They stare at minor events, trying to assess them, Are they important? There is no way to be sure. Without continuing identities there can be no sharing of experience, no validation by others of what has taken place; and so there is no assured causality. Oates's characters are tossed about, their lives out of control, whether they come from the working class, as in *them* (1969), whose dreams and hopes are token gifts from advertisements and commercials, or have climbed to be the amazing powerful men of *Expensive People* (1968) and *Do with Me What You Will,* whose wives, nevertheless, run off with other men, whose children turn against them, and whose powers wane with age like those of anyone else. Desperately they attempt to find their way into the alternative reality that must exist somewhere, in a universe of truth—or why do we live? Why do we dream up such a word as "truth"? The hero of the short story, "An American Adventure" (in *The Seduction,* 1975) walks uneasily through a familiar neighborhood: "What worries me is that there is a world beyond the world I see that is simultaneous with it." But it is a world where "nothing is human. There are no rules or laws or chemical 'truths' . . . [It is] a hard, vivid world emptied of people and therefore permanent."

Such alienation slips into madness. Again, it is a condition conceived of not as essentially different from the state in which we live most of the time, but as a limit, or a metaphor, for our present case. Oates's characters are pulled two ways, looking for a natural identity in a permanent world (though then it would have people in it), but bemused by injunctions from the chaotic present that hold up to them the gaudy goals which authority tells them to value. At the same time, their natural sense assures them that these goals are irredeemably false. Caught in this tension, they move easily to violence, which has its own validating force, so that murder becomes a kind of reassurance: if one could do something as extreme as to kill, one must surely be in possession of a truth important enough to kill for. Action authenticates meaning. Or does it? Murder is not difficult at all, Marvin Howe assures Elena. He could have had her lover killed at any time, it would have been cheap, since the man is so unimportant. He is rather astonished that he did not.

It is an unwelcoming, indeed a terrifying, world. And yet these characters, confused, obsessed, on the verge of slipping from one persona to another, rage through it in so violent and lively a fashion that they redeem it. Against its expressed pessimism they assert the value of life: a life that refuses to accept falseness as truth, that searches for something better, is fobbed off with a new falseness, recognizes it, and goes on searching. "If you woke up one morning and ran outside and ran away from your life, wouldn't you come into a new one?" asks a young girl in the story "Where Are You Going, Where Have You Been?" (*The Wheel of Love,* 1970) "Only into a life that is worse!" says the author, already laying out the trap into which the girl is to run. But the hope and the question are not presented as foolish. An active drive toward something better is everywhere; it is what these people live by. Oates will not hand us a positive answer about the future, show us that simultaneous universe where we could find new lives and understand their meaning. What she does is report an omnipresent urge to discover or make such a universe. Her characters look for clues to such a place in the events of their lives, desperate to find a world with a coherent structure, where human beings can live with dignity.

Such an assessment of humankind is nothing new: Dostoevsky offers a familiar example. What Oates adds is the flavor of women's testimony on their experience, whether she writes of their interior lives or of the actions of men in a world deficient in feeling. Her women feel themselves directed from outside. They lose spontaneity and autonomy and take on instead tasks of consumption that they are instructed to find central to their lives. The maintenance of art and high culture is assigned to them, and because they are subordinate, art is trivialized and loses its power to heal and communicate. These are failures of the overall system of our society, but they are acted out by women. These women, like those of Dostoevsky, tend to hysteria; but where Dostoevsky takes this for granted, Oates shows us how and why this happens. Typical of women's literature is her analysis of what even the great male writers have presented as simply "female traits of character." Women writers are splitting open the atom to show us the mechanism inside. It is not a mechanism special to women. Understanding it enlarges our knowledge of psychological causation: another contribution to universality.

The process of discovering new symbols in everyday life is apparent in Oates's work. She is, for example, vastly interested in houses: in how they are furnished, what they cost (usually in rent; her characters are too mobile to buy property), and what sort of neighborhood they occupy. Her restless, formless people are defined by the living space they settle in briefly; they establish a temporary stability for their uncertain identities in terms of monthly rent or social position of neighbors. But houses, like personalities, are subject to cooption: Marvin

Howe, a lawyer whose fees can bankrupt the clients he represents, owns houses all over the country, taken in part payment from those he has "saved." He fattens on these legitimate victims like a fairy tale ogre, and the social approval he enjoys suggests that in the world Oates portrays, this ogre-victim relation is central.

The telephone has long been a symbol in women's writing. Stubbornly silent, it signifies a lover's rejection, and its rings will as often as not be deceptive, nursing false hopes. Even so, it speaks of the possibility of communication and connection with another. In Diane Johnson's novel *The Shadow Knows* (1974), however, the telephone is a channel for inchoate, violent intrusion. Her heroine, N., has left her husband—the change in her life is symbolized by a change of housing, moving herself and her four children from a comfortable middle-class home to a unit in a housing project—and the telephone sometimes brings her a call from her lover, one of those unmarriageable men, married to someone else. But more often the message is menace: from an anonymous phantom; from an ex-nursemaid raving vengefully of terrors to come; from an ex-husband, her own or that of her current baby-sitter, expected but ambiguous. If there is a connection via phone, it is with a world that is no longer understandable, a world where tires are slashed, doors bashed at, and women attacked in the dark. "You are vulnerable," says the telephone. N. knows that is true, but feels it is a price she is willing to pay, for vulnerability is how one stays human and responsible. The toughness she hopes to achieve is that not of a hardened surface, but of interior survival strength.

Relationships too are reassessed for their symbolic significance. Marriage is one, as we have seen: Is it a necessary part of life? If it is undertaken, what weight should be allowed each partner? What demands should be accepted? How can it be enlarged, if it can be? What is the place of children and their needs? Less explicitly stated, but running through memoirs, poetry, and fiction, is an effort to take this last question by itself and rethink the parent-child relationship, especially that with the mother. Sylvia Plath's furious attack on "Daddy" is one of her best-known poems, but in "The Disquieting Muses," cited above, she blames her mother for the disturbing presences that shape her work and haunt her life. Her mother "meant well, [her] witches . . . always got baked into gingerbread," and she saw that the proper arts were taught her daughter. But the daughter found herself unteachable in these disciplines. She learned from other muses, and if they were "unhired by you, dear mother," still, "this is the kingdom you bore me to."

Here, and in much other writing by women, the mother is seen not

381

only as source of life but as source of knowledge. Even when life is good, the knowledge that women have had to learn has been painful: an awareness of secondary status and limited living space. Yet within this process of learning, one has learned oneself how to deal with the world and to engage oneself with others. When women begin to question traditional truth about such arrangements, they find themselves questioning what their mothers taught them. No wonder, then, that painful and ambivalent attacks on mother-figures are so common in women's literature, and not only in the writing that comes out of a white middle-class background.

In *The Woman Warrior* (1976) Maxine Hong Kingston remembers her growing up in California as "a girlhood among ghosts." Strictly speaking, the "ghosts" are the white Americans as seen by the Chinese community, but the confrontation of cultures affects her Chinese family too. The force of their beliefs and behavior is drained away by the society they have come to live in. Kingston's mother, who had qualified as a doctor at home and lived independently, still followed her husband overseas when he sent for her, and she tries to preserve old ways and to raise her daughters in proper submission. The girls, caught between the California in which they go to school and the "talk-stories" that strive to preserve the Chinese past, hardly know whether their fate directs them to leave the whole ancient tradition behind or to conform to the role of daughter-slave, according to the harsh rules laid down by their mother. Kingston rebels. Yet, returning home years later, she hears the driven tyrant of a mother moan, "How can I bear to have you leave again?" and herself feels the tug to return to her roots, even though "my mother would sometimes be a large animal, barely real in the dark; then she would become a mother again." It is only when her mother allows affection to show, and gives permission for her to go, that she feels free of a weight of obligation that matches her anger. The book itself is the gift given in return for this freedom. It is not grateful, expected affection that it offers, however, but a strict analysis of what can be preserved and what must be left behind in order that affection may be possible between mother and daughter.

Black women writers have produced some of the most intense and revealing studies of the strains that a madness-inducing society puts on its members. History is always present in these books, fiction or no; and it is a history of daily inescapable assault by a world which allows so little room for a continuous coherent self to grow that one wonders how survival is possible at all. In *The Bluest Eye* (1970) Toni Morrison weaves together scenes from an underground whose inhabitants suffer as much from confused social directives as they do from abysmal poverty. The exploration of this world of victimization gains from the fragmented form of the book, for life there is essentially fragmented when seen through the eyes of any single individual. Bad as oppression was in the rural South (and other writers, like Sarah Wright in *This Child's Gonna Live*, 1969, tell us about that), life there had some sequence. In the northern cities, powerlessness is made worse by the unpredictability of events: anything can happen, and those who have climbed a step out of chaos fear nothing so much as falling back into it.

The seductive tug of white standards and values adds to the disorder of mind. A black woman servant will find the only safety and order she can expect while she is at work in a white woman's home, will taste power there, find tradesmen polite, and her work valued. She will also, before the eyes of her own child, seem to prefer the white child she looks after: society tells her the latter is more valuable. Morrison's stunning insight reveals the disrupted emotions produced by living in a world where white standards and goals are presented to blacks as uniquely important and, at the same time, impossible for them to achieve.

In Morrison's work and in that of other black women writers we find examples of how women's literature can extend itself beyond women's experience. A life without power, known to black women ("Everybody in the world was in a position to give them orders," Morrison writes, echoing Zora Neale Hurston a generation before), produces an astonishing capacity to see into other, similar conditions. Morrison, Toni Cade Bambara, and Nikki Giovanni not only write of women, proud of their vigor and ability to survive, but also understand the frustrated fury of black men, whose identities are falsified and torn apart because the masculine ideal of power and control is both presented to them and denied. Morrison does not excuse, but she comprehends, the inverted desperate rejected search for affection and closeness that can produce violence, even violence as extreme as the rape of a man's own daughter. To communicate such understanding leads us, again, toward universality.

In writing of their own lives these women both question and affirm the importance of the mother-link to the past and of the knowledge that society directs and permits a mother to pass on to her children. Maya Angelou's memoirs, beginning with *I Know Why the Caged Bird Sings* (1969), give us a split mother-figure: her own, and her mother's mother, Momma. Momma was a storekeeper and a proud landholder in a small Arkansas town who knew her place and kept it with disdain but defended it with fury. Maya's mother was a sophisticated woman, on her own in great cities. When the child, at seven, was sent to her, she decided that her mother was "too beautiful to have children, that's why she sent us away." The care she gave seemed to demand gratitude in return, and Angelou, like Maxine Kingston, found she had to rebel. Reconciliation came only years later, when seventeen-year-old Maya, having concealed her pregnancy until the last moment, turned to her mother for help and the help was given.

Other black women writers cast back to strong women through a matrilineal connection. In *Generations* (1976) Lucille Clifton recalls the legend of her great-great-grandmother Caroline, born free in Dahomey in 1823, captured and enslaved as a child, and at age eight marched from New Orleans to Virginia. She survived to raise a great-grandson and assure him that he could be proud of coming from "Dahomey women." A strong and intransigent grandmother, Louvenia, lives in Nikki Giovanni's memory, a trouble-maker who had to be smuggled out of Georgia in the dead of night to the comparative safety of Knoxville, Tennessee. Giovanni and Toni Cade Bambara bring the tradition of autonomous black women up to date, remembering themselves as tough, fighting little girls, though both see the deliberate undermining of the self in black men by white society as a hateful part of the causes for women's strength. But though they deplore the pressure on black men, they still celebrate the daring and the adventurous spirit of black women. Some of this celebration creates icons: the legend of Harriet Tubman makes her a fabulous figure. Indeed, Tubman and Sojourner Truth are cited as myths to be honored by white as well as black women. The spirit of these myths is re-created in images of black women who invent and labor for change in the present.

Alice Walker, in *Meridian* (1976), gives us a black heroine who has some of the strangeness and even the physical disorders that mark significant figures in Flannery O'Connor's work. Meridian, however, has a conscious purpose in her life that is presented as both realistic and hopeful; she is not merely an eccentric instrument for criticizing the deficiencies of society. Meridian has a long journey to make out of privacy and ordinary life, out of early marriage and motherhood, that seems like a dream, out of an existence that hardly belongs to her to a large involvement with the world. If she becomes a figure of myth, she does it before our eyes, not in the memory of some descendant. Instead, she carries and transforms the weight of the past, for her awkward choice of independence distresses a mother who has accepted, and been broken by, ordinary life, though Meridian's choice also expresses the ambition her mother could not fulfill herself.

384

It is Meridian's destiny to act out, and to analyze for herself and for us, the social forces that produced the civil rights movement of the early sixties and the revolutionary violence that succeeded it among the urban guerrillas of the North. Meridian cannot give herself over totally to this violence: she is willing to die for the changes she believes in, but she cannot state her willingness to kill for them. Disowned, she returns to the South alone, to gestures of confrontation that seem minor and a bit ridiculous—to a dailiness of struggle. Yet we feel that something profound is working itself out within her. She too has undertaken an interior spiritual voyage, searching for essential meaning by exploring the data of life, present and past. At the end of the book Meridian is emerging as saint and heroine. She stands inescapably askew to contemporary life, very much as Dostoevsky's Myshkin does in *The Idiot*; but Meridian, we guess, will not end in complete madness and withdrawal, as Myshkin does. Meridian, says Walker, has imposed on herself the sentence of bearing the conflict of our time in her soul. She has lived through it. Now this sentence "must be born in terror by all the rest of us." Not privately but publicly Meridian becomes a progenitor. Perhaps the creation of a figure through whom we are invited to look to a future society that is no longer a madness-inducing machine points to still another sort of universality of imagination that has grown out of the experience of black women.

The passage of women from daughterhood to motherhood, whether it is private and actual or, as in the case of Meridian, symbolic, appears to be replacing the rite of marriage as indicator of maturity in women's writing. No doubt, union with a male is the symbol most apparent to male writers and is naturally the one chosen by a male-oriented society. The act of sex that transforms a virgin into a woman will take precedence in masculine literature, as it necessarily does in time. Women's experience, however, suggests that the more essential change is from the role of daughter to that of mother, and that the two conditions illuminate each other. Anne Sexton struggles with her "desertion" of her daughter during her stay in an asylum by matching it with her mother's "desertion" of herself by death. "The Double Image," in which this comparison is made, refers less to individuals than to relationships. Sexton remembers how her mother had her portrait painted soon after she had left the asylum. It seemed to the poet that the image of herself was to replace the reality, the actual daughter whose attempt at suicide could not be forgiven. At the same time, in the same poem, she finds herself doing something similar. When her own daughter was born, she recalls, she had hoped for "a small milky mouse of a girl," not a boy; for she, too, needed an image:

> I who was never quite sure
> about being a girl, needed another
> life, another image to remind me . . .
> I made you to find me.

When we extrapolate from Sexton's words, we find her private search for an image to explain herself to herself reproduced in women's literature, where the quest for a new image with which to explain life is central. Women are writing in order to assess what life has taught them, what it has made of them; and, indeed, the work of any new literature concentrates on forming a new identity out of an overlooked, or misunderstood, past and a turbulent present. The search covers many areas, the images are various, the voices that describe them diverse, but always a grasp on daily life supplies both continuity and commonality. Susan Griffin gives us poetry, in *Like the Iris of an Eye* (1976), where unfinished phrases express the disjunction and interruptions of everyday life. She also writes a minute-to-minute, nursery-level account of experience that is shorn of obvious feeling. Yet out of this building-block architecture is constructed the shape of a life.

> This is the story of a day in the life of a woman trying
> to be a writer and her child got sick. And in the midst of
> writing this story someone called her on the telephone . . .

There follows a record of interruptions, some of them interesting, and concerns, many of them traditionally a part of women's lives in the age-old mode: fixing meals, sewing curtains and pillows, watering plants, and, pervasively, anxiety over the sick child, all mingled with exasperation at one's inability to center on one's work. The whole conveys the flavor and scent of a representative, even symbolic, life by means of bits of commonplace brilliantly selected and joined together to make a coherent statement. Of course, it is an old story. Very few women have not lived through such a day, whether they were trying to write a story or to complete any other undertaking. But Griffin is not simply living this, she is thinking about it; thinking about it not angrily nor with self-pity, not as an irritating example of how women's lives are trivialized—though humanly speaking all these factors are there—but fundamentally as a clue to the nature of life itself. One's identity is precious, one's work demands to be done, and yet one exists in a network of relationships, there is no way out. They cannot be denied any more than Diane Johnson's N. can refuse the vulnerability that goes with keeping herself open to the world.

Naomi Lazard's "ordinances" (1978) have something of the same flat tone, but the irony is overt. These are direct messages from Authority in a madness-inducing society. They direct the reader to stand in one line or another, which should be chosen with care, and which will then move, or not, toward a goal that will be the opposite of what is desired. Or they offer

Congratulations.
The suspense is over. You are the winner.

But of what dubious contest the reader, and the winner, too, are completely unsure, while the prize may or may not turn up, in which case "do not bother to inform us."

A more passionate view of dailiness declares the need to transcend it. Marge Piercy in *Woman on the Edge of Time* (1976) both describes details of living and provides a visionary future with which to contrast the present. Piercy is imagining an alternative reality, a science fiction utopia. She is offering it not as an escape from the present, a fantasy into which we can retreat, but as an injunction to invent a future that will meet our needs better, both emotional needs and social urgencies, a way of living not guaranteed to drive us crazy. In *Speedboat* (1976) Renata Adler holds tight to the present, but she abstracts from its flow moments of strong feeling that seem to belong to another pattern, clues in a different language. The current pattern is disintegrating; and if we are to construct another, we need material with which to work. Adler's flashes of "found" meaning judge the present and its ridiculous associations by setting themselves off from it, while at the same time they ask to be joined in new ways that will create new styles of living, serious and feasible. They speak of true feeling and relational reality that can still be found and preserved in the surrounding falseness.

Other novelists use more conventional techniques, but one finds in them the same major themes: exploration of the experience of powerlessness in an effort to understand the past and its effects, revaluation of familiar relationships, both that of marriage and sexual connection and that between parent and child, and a search for symbols expressive of authentic present reality which can be joined together to build a new structure of beliefs that will match contemporary human needs and show us the way to a livable future. Paula Fox's sharp eye and daring mind rummage through recent history, reviewing our path to the present. Like Alice Walker (and Doris Lessing, in England), she considers the movements of rebellion and revolution that have engaged Americans during the last generation, seeing them as another

387

sort of attempt to establish an alternative reality; they are failed attempts, but they indicate a need. The Communists of the thirties and forties furnish a model that, in *The Western Coast* (1972), is interwoven with the California culture, so different from that of the more rooted East. Annie Gianfala comes to a hard-won maturity in the years of World War II, moving from a passivity almost as complete as that of Oates's Elena, in *Do with Me What You Will,* to a considerable command of her actions and judgments. Again, the immediacy of experience provides Annie with learning tools: Poverty, violence, unpleasant ailments, hunger, grubby jobs, a succession of men who are in some way deficient and who see Annie as an answer to their problems but not as a person whose autonomy must be allowed for. Only Max sees her so, and Max, who loves her, is another unmarriageable married man, committed to other responsibilities. Max and Annie avoid a traditional love affair, but a larger relation between them supports them both in trust and respect, disproving easy, belittling judgments on human life.

The complicated tugs of motherhood and daughterhood, which have to do with the passage of values as well as with the establishment of identities, are absent in this novel, but they are dwelt on in Fox's *The Widow's Children* (1976), where we see women so overwhelmed by the disruption of patterns of living through social change that they are unable to pass on values. Raising children is itself a process of inventing a future, a process long handed to women as obligation and vocation. The weight of this responsibility is central to female feeling. Consequently, the stunting of growth by a disturbed society is felt in a personal way by women and expressed in their writing with immediate anger. Men may see, and detest, the loss and distortion of human potential, but they are usually spared the burden of dealing with the details. In *The Abduction* (1970) Maxine Kumin gives us the example of a black man, Dan, who is truly concerned for the deprived "inner city" children that a government program is trying to help; but it is the white woman, Lucy, who acts at a moment of crisis. By Dan's lights, and indeed in the reality shown here, she is wrong to flee the riots that follow the assassination of Martin Luther King, taking with her the small, brilliant black boy, Theodore, who stands as a symbol of hope for black and white teachers alike. Dan knows that Lucy is in the grip of fantasy, imagining a new sort of family, with Theodore as her son and Bey, the head of the project and her lover, as the father. Lucy does indeed feel herself a failed mother in her own marriage, one beloved daughter dead in a car crash and the other abandoned to an unsympathetic German lover, while she nurses a guilty sense of delinquency because she has not "given" her husband a son.

But though Lucy's action is irrational and Dan is right to step in and reclaim Theodore, we are seeing here a new sort of heroine. If the absurdity of our world has driven her to unacceptable action, at least it is action, not passivity. And her dream of a kind of family connected by conscious affection that is broader than blood kinship is noble. It may perhaps point to some sort of future where isolated individuals reach out to each other and where true concern and mutual help extend past orthodox family bonds to a wider community. The madness-inducing machine has caught sensible, capable Lucy, but the fantasy with which she reacts points to a felt need—one that is widely seen in women's fiction of the seventies as an urgency to find better ways to raise children, not just because this is part of women's traditional occupation, but as a matter of grave social policy.

Adrienne Rich turns her attention to this question in *Of Woman Born: Motherhood as Experience and Institution* (1976). The shift of genres in which a poet discusses the social machinery that directs maternal behavior and shapes emotions is not unusual in contemporary women's writing. Rich sees the current mother-role as one of collaborator and coconspirator with patriarchal society. Women's vital need to remake images of themselves can begin here in reality, as well as in literature. Explicit in the book is evidence that feminists are far from rejecting motherhood, as some propagandists claim. What they reject are inhumane distortions of the affectionate pride in and hope for one's children that should be allowed to nourish the process of mothering. Says Rich: "If I wish anything for my sons, it is that they should have the courage of women . . . who, in their private and public lives . . . are taking greater and greater risks, both psychic and physical, in the evolution of a new vision . . . acts of immense courage [which can involve] moments, or long periods, of thinking the unthinkable, being labeled, or feeling, crazy; always a loss of traditional securities . . . I would like my sons not to shrink from this kind of pain, not to settle for the old male defenses . . . And I would wish them to do this not for me, or for any other woman, but for themselves, and for the sake of life on the planet Earth." Once more we come on an expression of a drive toward universality which will be achieved by allowing the female experience its place in human concerns.

Critics of women's literature are still few, but in some recent books we begin to find the sort of reexamination of old texts that can provide a basis for thinking about the human condition in a way that includes women's situation. The mid-sixties shift in their perception of themselves shows up later in critical writing than in poetry, autobiography, or fiction, as is only to be expected: writing criticism demands the existence of a structure of beliefs on which judgments can be based, and such a structure is formulated slowly for any genre in any art. Without it, criticism tends to be anticriticism, which takes the existing apparatus and reverses it, pointing out how falseness has engendered defects in insight and failures of discrimination; but without a doctrinal system there can be no positive statements.

We see this effect in such a preliminary work as Mary Ellmann's *Thinking about Women* (1968). Ellmann's title is misleading, perhaps purposely. Her topic is male thought about women, with masculine criticism of women writers as the field of study. Women's writing is thus at a remove from Ellmann's text, which is mainly an analysis of how the acceptance of stereotyped views of women has distorted masculine perceptions of their work, their worth, and their very nature. Ellmann documents a history of what must be called massive male stupidity, if we define stupidity as the deliberate choice of ignorance and comfortable prejudice. Her insight is penetrating. The chapter on phallic criticism is a graveyard where can be found generations of self-deceptive, self-congratulatory opinions on women writers, still not unknown, but increasingly embarrassing to read. It is worth being reminded of how widespread and how respectable has been the unquestioned assumption of women's inevitable, innate, and significant "otherness," and Ellmann here collects utterances on the subject not only from those we might expect (Norman Mailer, Leslie Fiedler, Anthony Burgess), but from Robert Lowell, Malamud, Beckett, and Reinhold Niebuhr.

Useful as this is, however, Ellmann, writing in the middle sixties, had little to go on in offering an alternative. Her own style is not free from the self-deprecation she deplores in other women writers, and she is put to it to point to creators of women's literature whom she can really admire. She finds no continuing tradition in women's writing and her recommendations are limited and limiting: reliance on wit and mockery and the rejection of a tone of authority, which she sees as a masculine trait, thereby confusing, it would seem, social and political authority with knowledgeable force derived from lived experience. But she perceives well how the attention women writers pay to details of existence contributes to their strength, and that such interaction is not trivial but evidence of their engagement with reality.

Another transitional work is Patricia Meyer Spacks's *The Female Imagination* (1975). Though Spacks does not limit her observations to male thinking about women, she seems uncertain of what her material does consist in. The first task of criticism is to frame relevant questions, and that is hard for early practitioners to do: the old questions still distract them. Spacks gives us a number of sharp insights on particular writers. She is sensitive, for example, to the special quality of outlook shared by Lillian Hellman and Mary McCarthy that sets them somewhat apart from ordinary female experience and legitimizes for them the use of masculine standards. However, her exclusively literary criteria do not allow her to see how women involved in left-wing political thought of the thirties became able to use these alternative realities, which broadened orthodox standards for a time. Overall, Spacks is uncertain about major themes to be explored and major questions to be asked in approaching the work of women writers.

Elizabeth Hardwick's *Seduction and Betrayal* (1974) stands by itself. It does not need, nor take, a place in a historic transition of thought, but comes straight from a critical and imaginative intelligence of such a high order that one feels it stands outside of history. Of course, this is too sanguine a reaction. A serious examination of writing by, or about, women undertaken in the fifties would have had to excuse or justify itself in some way. Writing in the seventies, Hardwick manages to reconcile the sound standards of the old critical canon with the insights given women by shared experience that differs from that of men, and to explicate in a straightforward way the effect that living as a female has had on those who also wish to live as writers.

Seduction and Betrayal includes essays on male writing about women, on women writing about their lives both as fiction and biography, and on women who were not authors but who stood close to the careers of men: Jane Carlyle, Dorothy Wordsworth, Zelda Fitzgerald. At first view, this looks like a heap of material without structure, but Hardwick knows the right questions to ask. This is a book about relationships: How can men and women live together? What have they felt about this, and how have they expressed their opinions and hopes? Where have things gone wrong, where do misfit images fail to match reality? Hardwick is quite as aware as Ellmann (or Kate Millett, for that matter) of the indignities that have been the lot of women writers, but she is not just calling angry attention to them, she is considering how they have affected the work of these women. This is a central part of the essential business of criticism, and when it can at last be undertaken, rancor falls away.

Her short essay on the Brontës, for example, draws far-reaching conclusions from the familiar details of the restrictions laid on poor and talented women. It is, so to speak, a sequel to Virginia Woolf's famous vision of what would have happened to a sister of Shakespeare who possessed his genius. The Brontës lived on a cresting wave of change when it was just becoming possible for women to write seriously as professionals, but when the social disabilities of doing so were still high.

> The worries that afflicted genteel, impoverished women in the nineteenth century can scarcely be exaggerated. They were cut off from the natural community of the peasant classes. The world of Tess of the D'Urbervilles, for all its sorrow and injustice, is more open and warm and fresh than the cramped, anxious, fireside-sewing days of the respectable. Chaperones, fatuous rules of deportment and occupation, drained the energy of intelligent, needy women. Worst of all was society's contempt for the prodigious efforts they made to survive. Their condition was dishonorable, but no approval attached to their efforts to cope with it. The humiliations endured in the work of survival are a great part of the actual material in the fiction of Charlotte and Anne Brontë.

Hardwick sees her subjects as figures in a landscape, and she understands what this landscape offers and requires if one is to exist there by using the view as material for fiction. What one sees, of course, is individual: Emily Brontë gazed at a lonelier, stonier, more dramatic range of country than that of her sisters. Perhaps truth was more important to her than survival. Charlotte and Anne reworked the drab humiliations they had known as teachers and governesses to suggest that defeat was not absolutely necessary, even though the suggestion was not entirely justified; defeat had to be expected. Hardwick understands well the process of making heroines out of sour scraps of memory, so that survival could at least call on imagination for the right to hope: "Most governesses in fiction are strangely alone, like sturdy little female figures in a fairy tale. They walk the roads alone, with hardly a coin in their pockets; they undergo severe trials in unfamiliar, menacing places and are rescued by kind strangers. Shadows, desperations, and fears are their reality, even if they go in for a litany of assurances of their own worth and sighs of hope that their virtues will somehow . . . stand them in good stead."

Hardwick's comprehension of what it is that authors are doing is equally helpful in her chapters on men writing about women. The title essay in *Seduction and Betrayal* deals with ravished heroines, from Clarissa on. It is the heroism of these female figures, Hardwick finds, that is essential in the minds of their creators. Their moral stature and human dignity must be beyond question. For such a character, "her fall or her fate can only be truly serious if a natural or circumstantial refinement exists." Indeed: "In the novel, when the heroine's history turns about a sexual betrayal, it matters whether she is the central figure in the plot or a somewhat less powerfully and less fully considered 'victim' on the periphery. If she is the central figure, psychological structure seems to demand a sort of purity and innocence. Not physical innocence, but a lack of mean calculations, of vindictiveness, of self-abasing weakness. Sexual transgression loses its overwhelming character as a wrong or as a mistake when the persons have virtues of a compelling sort, or spiritual goodness, or the grandeur of endurance. The inner life of the woman matters, what she feels and has felt, the degree of her understanding of the brutal cycles of life."

Hardwick lays her finger here on one of the perennial problems that rise when we compare the female figures of classical literature with what we know from history about women's actual lives: how can Antigone or Lysistrata be derived from the uneducated, housebound women of Perichlean Athens? These grand heroines, projected from men's minds, are clearly designed to inhabit an alternative reality: they reflect a male need to value women as equal and worthy, in order to authenticate an order where honor and dignity rule. There is surely nothing wrong with such projections, if we see that the question they pose (social, not literary) becomes how to alter current reality toward this ideal. If we assume that these heroines typify existing reality, we are guilty of a literary blunder: we are falsifying what exists. The impulse of women writers to immerse their characters in a soup of everyday annoyances is an effort to avoid this falsification.

The decade of the seventies saw a growing acceptance of the idea that a women's literature exists and is a proper field of study. Two solid critical works illustrate the change that has taken place since Mary Ellmann, scouting about for exemplary authors, found them thin on the ground. Ellen Moers in *Literary Women* (1976) concludes with a fifty-page bibliography (and there are still omissions). Elaine Showalter provides one nearly as long, combining primary material and critical estimates, in *A Literature of Their Own: British Women Novelists from Brontë to Lessing* (1977). Both books do much more than list and describe. Some of the themes which have been touched on in this essay are examined in depth. Moers opens with an example of dailiness in a writer's life that more than matches Susan Griffin's: a letter from Harriet Beecher Stowe to her sister-in-law, dated 1850, where cooking, cleaning, negotiations with a plumber, a long bout of household sewing and the birth of a child ("I was really glad for an excuse to lie in bed") are supplemented by the report that "I have employed my leisure hours in making up my engagements with newspaper editors"; that is, she met her deadlines. Perhaps the most valuable product of Moers's researches is the sense she gives us of a conscious continuity in women's literature: the influence of Jane Austen on George Eliot; the admiration that Emily Dickinson felt for Elizabeth Barrett Browning's poetry and its effect on her own work; the use Gertrude Stein made of George Eliot.

Relevant to this continuity is Elaine Showalter's remark: "Criticism of women novelists . . . has ignored those who are not 'great,' and left them out of anthologies, histories, textbooks and theories. Having lost sight of the minor novelists, who were the links in the chain that bound one generation to the next, we have not had a very clear understanding of the continuities in women's writing, nor any reliable information about the relationships between the writers' lives and the changes in the legal, economic, and social status of women." The effect of this, Showalter notes, is that "each generation of women writers has found itself, in a sense, without a history, forced to rediscover the past anew, forging again and again the consciousness of their sex."

Women's literature is at last developing the history and traditions that validate it as an entity. It is doing this by questioning time-hallowed assumptions which grow both from literature and from life: Showalter's analysis of Virginia Woolf subjects her marriage to scrutiny for the light that it throws on her work. Like Hardwick, but in greater detail, Showalter explores the opening up of a literary career as an alternative to governessing for nineteenth-century women. The price that the copyright of a pot-boiler could bring tells us something about the reasons why talented women wrote pot-boilers. In male criticism of women writers of the period we discern an element of financial fear: May they not drain off the audience that supports the male boiler of pots? All this insistence on seeing literature in its social context is typical of current critical writing by women. It is another mode of hanging on to reality.

Carolyn Heilbrun in *Toward a Recognition of Androgyny* (1973) goes beyond the (much needed) effort to establish definitions of women's literature and to examine its origins. Heilbrun is looking toward a future in which the old tradition and the new will have become one: "androgynous" in her terminology can be equated with "universal" as used in this essay. Heilbrun looks back to myth for examples of common feeling between men and women, for fully shared and valued experience. She takes the heroines of Greek drama as expressions of a male need for women who can act with full human responsibility, and traces this hope through the works of the accepted critical canon. It surfaces in unexpected places, not simply in the heroines of

Henry James and Ibsen, but in D. H. Lawrence's *The Rainbow*. These women heroes are removed from immediate life, but, in Heilbrun's view, they represent models which can facilitate the coming together of male and female ways of looking at the world. Such writers as Virginia Woolf and Colette, Heilbrun suggests, give us a preview of an androgynous literature that could help to create affectionate understanding between the sexes.

This is hopeful; perhaps it is also true. Still, one feels that the range and power of women's writing is growing and deepening in a way that will, and must, send it scouring through the experience that has lain unexamined until now. If this happens, it will pour into the mainstream, bearing its full freight. There is a body of women's literature still to be written and a tradition still to be forged before this segment of human existence will be open to exploration by all.

9
Drama
Gerald Weales

TASTES change so rapidly in this country that yesterday's avant-garde becomes tomorrow's old hat. Intellectual and political fashions become outmoded, then quaint, finally historical—all within a few years. Inevitably, this fact of American ideational life is reflected in its literature, particularly in its plays—perhaps because the theater is so public, so social an event. Poets may occasionally be unacknowledged legislators of the world, but even the best of playwrights (see William Shakespeare) is more likely to give form and flesh to ideas that are already in the air. The staying power of any dramatist depends not on the ideas he dresses, but the dressing itself, on the dramatic vitality of his vehicle and the cross-cultural validity of his characters—on his creation of a container into which any century, any decade, any year can pour its temporary eternal truth.

The history of drama is a parade of great names who manage to escape the limitation of their own time, but the true history of any national drama is a recognition that the theater at any moment provides an intellectual and artistic milieu—call it religious ritual in the Middle Ages, call it show business in the United States in the twentieth century—in which the dramatists work and by which most of them are defined. Recognizing both the power and the slipperiness of popular ideas, the critic as literary historian tries to tidy up the past, patting things into shape, fastening on labels. In the United States, where until recently critics have pretended that American drama was born in the Provincetown Playhouse one dark O'Neillian night in 1916, they have had less space in which to work and, as a consequence, the

American drama finds itself divided into decades, each bearing its own identification mark: the psychological 1920s; the political 1930s.

Such tags are not inaccurate, simply incomplete. Plays do have a family look about them but, faced with perennial devices, recurrent ideas, a play may resemble its ancestors or its descendants as much as it does its siblings. Take Lorraine Hansberry's *A Raisin in the Sun* as an example. It was unusual in 1959 to have on Broadway a play about a black family written by a black playwright. If the Hansberry play is new and surprising on that score, it is very much of its time in its questioning of a favorite American myth, that success is not only possible but inevitable. Although Hansberry goes her own way in treating the subject, *Raisin* begins in doubts that are also reflected in plays as different as Arthur Miller's *Death of a Salesman* (1949) and the musical *Do Re Mi* (1960) by Jule Styne and Garson Kanin.[1] Stylistically, *Raisin* reaches farther back. Its plot, hinging on accident (the theft of the insurance money), suggests the realism of the 1920s and 1930s—George Kelly's *Craig's Wife* and Clifford Odets's *Awake and Sing!* to take two very different examples—in which an artificial plot device becomes a valid mechanism for the testing of the protagonist. Technically, the reach goes still farther back, at least to David Belasco. The play is set (or it certainly was in production) in a very realistic Chicago apartment with a stove at which Ruth seems really to be scrambling eggs. *A Raisin in the Sun* is, then, a turn-of-the-century play, a 1930s play, a 1950s play, and a signpost pointing into the future.

The paragraphs above, carefully designed as an essay in the socio-aesthetics of genre criticism, in fact constitute an apologia. In the discussion that follows I will pat out shapes and hang labels with the diligence that belongs to my trade, but the reader—who almost certainly has guessed that American drama since World War II did not begin on August 14, 1945—is advised to look behind the labels and to check the untidy edges of the shapes from which dangle strings that reach into the past and the future.

Critic-cataloguers are beset not only by plays like *A Raisin in the Sun* and Jason Miller's *That Championship Season* (1972), which, but for the easy obscenity of the language, might pass for a 1920s play in the dusk with the light behind it, but by playwrights who refuse to stay in place. We can call George Kelly a 1920s dramatist and

1. Throughout, the dates represent the first production or first publication of the finished play, whichever is earlier, unless the context within the sentence calls for another date.

Clifford Odets a 1930s one, and be correct in doing so. But we can hardly expect either man to honor the designation. Build a stout critical barricade around a decade and playwrights will come scrambling over the wall, new scripts in hand, as Kelly did with *The Fatal Weakness* (1946), and Odets with *The Big Knife* (1949), *The Country Girl* (1950), and *The Flowering Peach* (1954). An account of American drama since World War II would be incomplete if it did not include mention, however casual, of playwrights, like Kelly and Odets, who belong to earlier periods of American theatrical history; the years since 1945 have seen productions of new plays by Eugene O'Neill, S. N. Behrman, Howard Lindsay, Russel Crouse, Elmer Rice, George S. Kaufman, Marc Connelly, Moss Hart, Maxwell Anderson, Philip Barry, Thornton Wilder, Robert E. Sherwood, Lillian Hellman, Sidney Kingsley, William Saroyan. The list is hardly a complete one.

The phenomenon among this group is O'Neill. Most playwrights' careers come to an end; O'Neill's came to a culmination. After a quarter of a century as America's major playwright, with an international reputation crowned with the Nobel Prize in 1936, O'Neill turned his back on the grandly symbolic, excessively literary experiments of the 1920s and 1930s and, returning to the naturalism of his first plays, wrote the most distinguished work of his career. Perhaps a discussion of these plays has no place in this volume, since they were written in the late 1930s and early 1940s, but they were not performed until after the war, most of them posthumously. They may thus be considered part of the American theater of the 1950s, a tough, bleak, uncompromising voice which, oddly enough, reached a wide audience in a decade when the more conventional successful playwrights were looking for easy solutions to sometimes bogus problems. Although *The Iceman Cometh* opened on Broadway in 1946 with much fanfare, it was not until the celebrated off-Broadway revival in 1956 that the stature of the play became obvious to a great many more people than the handful of O'Neill specialists who had always championed it. *Iceman* was followed by *Long Day's Journey into Night* (1956); *A Moon for the Misbegotten* (1957), which had closed on the road in 1947; *A Touch of the Poet* (1958); *Hughie* (1964); and *More Stately Mansions* (1967), an almost stageable excavation from an unfinished O'Neill manuscript.

The Iceman Cometh and *Long Day's Journey into Night* are O'Neill's finest plays. *Iceman* is a dark philosophic comedy about the necessity for illusion. Built on a classic dramatic situation, the invasion of a placid environment by a disrupting outside force (as in *Uncle Vanya*), *Iceman* brings Hickey, the truth-peddling traveling salesman, into Harry Hope's bar, where the customers, the inmates, exist on cheap whiskey and their expectations for tomorrow. After almost destroying the people he has come to save, Hickey, who has illusions of his own to protect, abets the re-formation of the Hope-sustained community. Only Larry Slade, the protagonist of the play, fails to escape Hickey's message, finds himself forced from the safety of uncommitted observation to pity, to pain. Since *Long Day's Journey into Night* is based on O'Neill's own family, too much initial attention was paid to its presumed autobiographical revelations, particularly by those people who prefer biography to art. The play has since escaped those limitations and stands as one of the most frightening family plays since *Oedipus Rex. Journey,* defying conventional geometry, is at once linear and circular. As the play moves along a descending line—morning to night, light to dark, sunshine to fog, possibility to despair—the action comes full circle; this is a process the four principals have gone through before. The cyclical sense of the play is reinforced by the pattern of emotional involvement among the four Tyrones, who obviously love each other even more than they hate one another; with each of them, love leads to suspicion leads to hate leads to cruelty leads to guilt leads to protectiveness leads to love leads to . . . and the Tyrones take the audience down and around with them into the fog-filled night, where the only glimmer of light turns out to be a patch of biography in the sky. In some fashion, Edmond (who is Eugene) did escape the trap he re-creates with such anguished affection, but that is outside the play. If there is consolation in the play itself, it lies in the perfection of a work that is relentless in its refusal to sacrifice artistic necessity to the sentimental needs of the audience.

None of the postwar work of the other playwrights from the 1920s and 1930s approximates the power of *Long Day's Journey into Night,* and most of it is less impressive than the plays by which those dramatists earned their reputations in earlier decades. There are a few exceptions. Thornton Wilder's *The Matchmaker* (1954), a revision of *The Merchant of Yonkers* (1938), uses the devices of standard farce to celebrate—as he did in *Our Town*—the endless excitement of the ordinary. Lillian Hellman's *The Autumn Garden* (1951) may hammer its points home a bit too insistently—a familiar Hellman shortcoming—but it is a perceptive treatment of the consequences of inaction. Her much maligned book for Leonard Bernstein's *Candide* (1956) is spare and sardonic, the proper vehicle for a musical so clever, so uncompromising that, when it first appeared, the critics and the musical comedy fans stumbled over one another in their unseemly haste to escape into banality (*Li'l Abner* was a hit that year). For the most part, even the best of the older playwrights, the most contemporary sounding, seem to be glancing over their shoulders at an earlier era. Postwar American theater was taking shape somewhere else.

Anyone who chose to go to a Broadway theater on August 14, 1945, would have found a mixture of the familiar and the unfamiliar. There were musical comedies, new style (*Oklahoma!*) and old (*Follow the Girls*). There were exercises in nostalgia, like John Van Druten's *I Remember Mama* and the Lindsay and Crouse adaptation of Clarence Day's *Life with Father*. There were comedies that ranged from the fey (Mary Chase's *Harvey*) through the clever (Van Druten's *The Voice of the Turtle*) to the naughtily innocent (Norman Krasna's *Dear Ruth*). That soldiers figure in the last two of these plays is a reminder that American theater, as usual, was trying to reflect its time. There were even serious war plays—Ralph Nelson's *The Wind Is Ninety* and the adaptation by Paul Osborn and John Hersey of the latter's *A Bell for Adano*—but this was a genre which was never really to develop on the American stage. William Wister Haines's *Command Decision* (1947), for all its stereotypes, is a reasonably effective examination of decision making at the upper level, and *The Girl on the Via Flaminia* (1954), adapted by Alfred Hayes from his own novel, is a touching treatment of the conflict of cultures through the love affair of an American soldier and an Italian girl; but for the most part the theater left it to the novel and the poem to deal artistically with the war and its social implications. Topicality aside, the available fare that August night was mostly standard Broadway. One genuinely unusual play was *Dark of the Moon,* by Howard Richardson and William Berney, an attempt to make lyric theater of folk material, daring in its time for a simulated copulation on stage which would seem tenderly naive now that *copulation* has ceased to be an operative word in dramatic dialogue. The other unusual play was *The Glass Menagerie*.

Unlike *Dark of the Moon,* an attractive anomaly, *The Glass Menagerie* was a beginning—perhaps of the postwar American theater, certainly of Tennessee Williams's career. He began writing plays in the mid-1930s, and in 1940, after having won a Group Theatre contest, he had his first important commercial production, *Battle of Angels*. The Theatre Guild withdrew the play after a disastrous Boston opening; so it was not until 1945 and *Menagerie* that Tennessee Williams found his voice on the American stage. Since then, he has averaged better than a play every two years. He was a critical and a commercial success for fifteen years—with *A Streetcar Named Desire* (1947), *Cat on a Hot Tin Roof* (1955), and *The Night of the Iguana* (1961), prize winners all, as his greatest hits—but during the 1960s, his work began to do less well. He was still considered one of America's most important playwrights—and rightly so—but his new works failed to draw audiences, and critics tended to see in the pallid echoes of his early plays simple repetition rather than the restatement of familiar Williams themes. It was during this period that he suffered the mental and physical collapse that he describes so coyly in *Memoirs* (1975), with much more venom in "What's Next on the Agenda, Mr. Williams?" (*Mediterranean Review,* Winter 1971). There has been a new burst of creativity in the 1970s, although much of it involves the reworking of earlier material; even *Small Craft Warnings* (1972), the best received of the more recent Williams plays, is a very slight revision of *Confessional,* which he had published in a collection of short plays, *Dragon Country,* two years earlier. The *although* and the *even* in the sentence above may suggest a criticism that I do not intend. Although I find the later Williams plays less interesting, less theatrically exciting than the early ones, the fault does not lie with the fact that he has been trying to reshape materials already at hand. His art has always been as much revision as vision. *Battle of Angels* was turned into *Orpheus Descending* (1957) and *Summer and Smoke* (1948) was rewritten as *The Eccentricities of a Nightingale* in 1951 although it did not reach the stage until 1964, the New York stage until 1976. *Camino Real* (1953), the film *Baby Doll* (1956), *Sweet Bird of Youth* (1959), and *Kingdom of Earth* (*The Seven Descents of Myrtle*) (1968) were all based on earlier short plays; *Kingdom,* in all its forms, stems from a Williams short story, as do *Cat on a Hot Tin Roof, The Night of the Iguana,* and *The Milk Train Doesn't Stop Here Anymore* (1962), which has been produced in several versions. Williams's most recent plays—*Red Devil Battery Sign* (1975), *Vieux Carré* (1977), and *A Lovely Sunday for Creve Coeur* (1978)—testify more to the playwright's artistic persistence than to his dramatic vitality. For the latter, there are the Williams revivals; it is almost impossible to move around the country without encountering Blanche DuBois or Alma Winemiller or another of the Williams heroines. "I just don't want to be a total has-been during my lifetime," Williams told a *Playboy* interviewer (April 1973); instead, he has become a classic.

There is something about *The Glass Menagerie*—a softness, a sweetness—that sets it apart from the other Williams plays. Still, it is a good place to begin to understand the devices, the characters, the themes that run through all of Williams's work. He has always been a playwright in the American realistic tradition who insists on writing nonrealistic plays, and *The Glass Menagerie* shows this most clearly. The realism lies in the characters, in a psychological validity that is revealed in a gesture, a reaction, a turn of phrase. When Amanda comes home at the beginning of the second scene of *Menagerie* to accuse Laura—mutely at first—of having dropped out of business college, Williams provides her with "a bit of acting," business with gloves, hat, purse which defines both her exasperation and her concern, helps establish her as monster and mother. Think of Blanche in *Streetcar* trying desperately to be amusing as her birthday celebration dissolves around her; Gooper's sudden outburst in *Cat on a Hot Tin Roof* that uncovers a lifetime as the unfavored child; Maxine's tempting Shannon with a rum-coco in *The Night of the Iguana*—conventional character definition, but presented with a skill more impressive than that practiced by many rigidly realistic playwrights. More Dickens than Howells, Williams has created a gallery of characters who, even when they are larger than life—grand grotesques like Archie Lee in *Baby Doll* or Alexandra Del Lago in *Sweet Bird of Youth*—climb out of their plays, trailing a truth, however tatty, with which audiences identify.

There are unrealistic characters, too, standard stereotypes such as the clergyman in *Cat on a Hot Tin Roof* who exist primarily as functions. Sometimes, such characters are variations on ancient theatrical devices—Flora and Bessie, for example. Williams uses the "two female clowns" to taunt the heroine of *The Rose Tattoo* (1951) and—perhaps to reward them for a comic turn well done—he gives them a one-act play all their own, *A Perfect Analysis Given by a Parrot* (1958). As Beulah and Dolly, they are information givers in *Orpheus Descending,* and as Molly and Polly they provide the verbal stream on which *The Gnädiges Fräulein* (1966) runs. Watching them perform in the last play, mixing dialogue with direct address to the audience, one is aware of a presentational mechanism Williams has always used, for his realistic characters as well as their cartoon cousins. Since Tom is the narrator of *The Glass Menagerie,* he can be expected to speak to the audience, but Amanda—in her telephone scenes—also uses dramatic monologue that dispenses with other characters, a device that Williams polished in later plays—Maggie's opening speech in *Cat on a Hot Tin Roof,* the soliloquies of Alexandra and Chance in *Sweet Bird,* the confessions of the bar customers in *Small Craft Warnings.*

When the characters in *Sweet Bird* do their set pieces, Williams calls for a spotlight on them, heightening the artificiality of the presentation. It is bringing unreality to the unreal, for the set of *Sweet Bird* is intended not to suggest a real hotel room in a real Gulf town, but a momentary resting spot in a significantly named St. Cloud with Easter morning hovering in the wings. After *The Glass Menagerie,* in which he asks for projections—words or pictures—to be flashed on a screen (a device that is ordinarily not used in production), Williams never again went so far toward antirealistic devices, but he has always described lights and sets in ways that emphasize their artificiality—asking us to compare them with the work of a particular painter or to see how they feather out at the top, fingering into a stage sky. The reality of place in Williams has less to do with verisimilitude than it does with the mood, the theme of the play.

This discussion of technique has barely scratched the surface of Williams's work, leaving untouched his ritual use of costume (see *Iguana*); his excessive fondness for symbol (those roses in *The Rose Tattoo*); his use of names as labels; the demanding rhythm of his speeches, by which his characters live and his scenes take shape—a rhythm so unmistakable that when a leading performer, even a good one, misses it, the production is likely to collapse. It might be tempting to expand on these points, but some space has to be saved for what the plays are about.

"Tennessee Williams, for example, is total sensibility," Truman Capote told a *New York Times* interviewer (December 28, 1975). "Absolutely no intelligence." There is the expected note of Capote bitchiness in the remark, but variations on it have been repeated, often by admirers of Williams, all through his career. His compulsive return to the same themes—the outsider faced with an antagonistic society or an indifferent universe, the struggle for survival, and the search for temporary comfort—suggests that his themes are more visceral than intellectual in their origins. His autobiographical comments, from "The Catastrophe of Success"—his introduction to the 1949 New Classics Edition of *Menagerie* ("the monosyllable of the clock is Loss, loss, loss, unless you devote your heart to its opposition")—to *Memoirs,* seem to confirm this suggestion. Yet, continue to dress feelings in theatrical form for thirty years and they begin to look like ideas.

Williams's "fugitive kind," particularly in his early plays, can be identified by those physical or spiritual differences which set them off from the rest of the world. They are artists or pseudo-artists (like Tom in *Menagerie*); they are nervous to the point of insanity (like Blanche in *Streetcar*); they are cripples (like Laura in *Menagerie*), although it is sometimes difficult to decide at what point the physical defect, the illness becomes imaginary; they are sexual specialists, too virginal or too priapic; they are foreigners (like Serafina in *The Rose Tattoo*). Their differences bring them abuse, violent (the rape in *Streetcar*) or genteelly malevolent. In the plays of the late 1950s, the outsiders are visited by excessive horrors—the lynching of *Orpheus Descending,* the cannibalism of *Suddenly Last Summer* (1958), the castration of *Sweet*

Bird. At about this time, however, particularly with Alexandra in *Sweet Bird,* it becomes difficult to tell the monsters from the victims; but read *Streetcar* as Stanley's attempt to save his home from an invading Blanche, and it becomes clear that this ambiguity has been with Williams from the beginning. The real enemy for Williams has always been time, as Chance says at the end of *Sweet Bird* and as Williams emphasizes in plays like *Suddenly Last Summer* and *The Night of the Iguana,* in which, showing his characters struggling against a murderously indifferent God, he almost turns theological. Survival, then, emerges as Williams's primary subject, and we realize that many of his presumably fragile heroines are tough mixes of the indomitable Amanda and the crippled Laura. Surviving, however, is a cruel and lonely process—and an impossible one—and from Tom's search for temporary companions in *Menagerie* to the huddling brother and sister of *Out Cry* (1973), Williams's characters have reached for the brief comfort of coupling, touching, supporting, depending "on the kindness of strangers." There was a time when prim critics used to go out of their way to separate their neat worlds from Williams's visionary one, but the persistence of the best of his plays, despite the clucks of disapproval, suggests that the general audience recognizes and identifies with a fear of dying and a longing for life, however exotic the circumstances. The fugitive kind turns out to be mankind, after all.

"But everyone has agony," the playwright said. "The difference is that I try to take my agony home and teach it to sing." A self-fashioned epigraph for Tennessee Williams? No, it is Arthur Miller, speaking to Joe McGinniss in *Heroes.*

Miller and Williams, Williams and Miller. The two playwrights have been the major representatives of American drama since the 1940s, an odd coupling that has more to do with quality than with similarity. Miller reached Broadway first with *The Man Who Had All the Luck* (1944), an unsuccessful play about a man who expects disaster until his wife teaches him that everyone makes his own luck. There are echoes of *The Master Builder* in *Man* (Solness, like Miller's hero, distrusts his success "because some time my luck must change"), but it was *All My Sons* (1947), Miller's first important play, that fastened on him the Ibsenite label which stayed with him even after the appearance of *Death of a Salesman.* Perhaps Miller's adaptation of *An Enemy of the People* (1950) had something to do with the persistence of a comparison that is as unfair to the Norwegian playwright as to the American. Audiences, less concerned with critical categories than either Miller or his commentators, responded warmly to both *All My Sons* and *Death of a Salesman*. The first spoke directly to its time, a note of hope and high-mindedness that in some sense overrode the pain with which the play ends; the second slipped its temporal bounds and remains the most commanding play written for the American stage since the war. Looking backward in the pages of *New York* (December 30, 1974 / January 6, 1975), Miller sees 1949 as "the last postwar year," the halcyon moment before he recognized as illusory his "oneness with the Broadway audience." There was probably less illusion in that oneness than he now believes; but his next two plays—*The Crucible* (1953) and *A View from the Bridge* (1955)—could hardly have been expected to touch so central a nerve as the one reached by *Death of a Salesman*. Still, *The Crucible,* once it could be seen as a play and not as an argument in the political battles of the McCarthyite 1950s, has become almost as much a staple in American schools as *Salesman* is—but then Miller (and with more justice in 1975 than in 1949) would not confuse that audience with the one he once wrote for on Broadway. In 1957, Miller published *Collected Plays,* with a long, analytical introduction sitting, like a headstone, on the corpus. He then turned his back on the New York stage and did not return until 1964, when both *After the Fall* and *Incident at Vichy* were presented.

Miller's early plays form a cohesive group, although at first glance they seem very different. *All My Sons* is conventional realism, Ibsenite only in that Miller—as Ibsen so often does—starts in the middle of things and spends most of the play uncovering the facts of the past so that the audience can see the last-act consequences in the present. *Death of a Salesman* plays a similar truth-and-consequences game, but the realism here—as in Williams—is contained in individual scenes and in the psychology of character. Originally called *The Inside of His Head,* the play is expressionistic in its structure, as Willy Loman moves between past and present, stepping through the dissolving walls of his home, his life; and in some of its devices, such as Ben, the cartoon robber baron, less character than function. *The Crucible* is a romantic history play, fitted out with slightly archaic language and graced with a theatrically effective mass hysteria scene; it is closer to *Sons* than to *Salesman* in its presentation of character, an exercise in social psychology that is buttressed (in print) with the carefully edited notes of Miller as researcher. *A View from the Bridge* is operatic realism making a bid to be classic tragedy; the playwright provides a chorus figure, a narrator who insists on the inevitability of the force that drives the protagonist—a device that weakens the play by making it less show than tell.

Whatever the differences of technique and tone, the four plays share a common theme. Each of Miller's heroes is involved, in one way or another, in a struggle that results from his acceptance or rejection of an image that is the product of his society's values and prejudices, whether that society is as small as Eddie Carbone's neighborhood in *A View from the Bridge* or as wide as the contemporary America that helped form Willy Loman. This pattern is evident in Miller's work from the beginning, in *The Man Who Had All the Luck,* for instance, and in his novel *Focus* (1945), in which the anti-Semitic protagonist finally accepts the Jewish label his neighbors force on him. In a more conventional didactic play than *All My Sons,* Joe Keller would be a capitalist villain and nothing more. In Miller's play he is a man who has built his own business and learned the ethics of self-protectiveness in the process, a loving husband and father whose concerns stop "at the building line." When his son Chris demands that he be a good citizen as well, he says, "I'm his father and he's my son, and if there's something bigger than that I'll put a bullet in my head!" When Joe kills himself, destroying the image of success that his society has offered, that he has accepted, his story takes on the patness of the moral tale, complicated only by Chris's attraction to some of the goals that formed his father. Miller's next hero, Willy Loman, is a much more interesting victim of the American success myth because when he dies the *Death of a Salesman* he still embraces the dream that is killing him. Unlike Joe Keller, for whom success is the result of hard work and selective chicanery, Willy Loman sees it as a birthright—at least for those Americans who have good looks, personality, "the old humor, the old confidence," the ability to be not liked, but well liked. That Willy is a failure who has been dumped by the company for which he worked all his life and that he has never been much of a success, as his persistent lying in the flashback scenes indicates, does not lessen his faith in the magic of "personal attractiveness." When his son Biff tries to comfort him by getting him to recognize his failure and to see that success is neither inevitable nor necessary, Willy hears only what he wants to hear, takes Biff's declaration of love as a testimonial to his beliefs, and dies assuming that the dream can be transferred, that his insurance money will make Biff a winner.

Joe Keller and Willy Loman find ready-made societal images to attach themselves to, and both become victims of the attachment. Society is not so passive in the next two plays. In *The Crucible,* Salem tries to force John Proctor to confess to being a witch. In *A View from the Bridge,* Eddie Carbone's neighborhood lives by a code which makes him an informer. "It is not enough any more to know that one is at the mercy of social pressures," Miller wrote in "On Social Plays," the introduction to *View*; "it is necessary to understand that such a sealed fate cannot be accepted." Both John Proctor and Eddie Carbone die rejecting the labels society wants to hang on them because both of them believe, as Proctor says, "a man will not cast away his good name." Proctor, guilty of lechery, almost succumbs to an atmosphere in which a different guilt is rampant, but in the end—moved in part by the author's need to defy the accusers—he dies a hero's death. Carbone's heroism is more ambiguous, more ironic, the grand gesture of a man who is indeed an informer and who wants a lie to cleanse his name; he is unusual among the protagonists of the early plays in that he accepts the rules and prejudices of his society and dies because he violates them.

The basic premise of these plays is that the individual has little choice, that he can conform and be destroyed or refuse to conform and be destroyed. Yet the plays are not pessimistic because inherent in them is a vague faith in man, a suspicion that the individual may finally be able to retain his integrity. This appears in its purest form not in the words of Chris Keller or in John Proctor's final decision, but in the artistic fact of Willy Loman; he is a character so complex, so contradictory, so vulnerable, so insensitive, so trusting, so distrustful, that he forces man on us by being one. Ironically, when Miller returned to the stage, it was the playwright, not society, who was forcing the images, who was demanding a *mea culpa* more universal than the one that Proctor escapes in *The Crucible*. "The first problem is not what to do about it," Miller wrote in "Our Guilt for the World's Evil" (*New York Times Magazine,* January 3, 1965), "but to discover our relationship to evil, its reflection of ourselves." Quentin in *After the Fall* and Von Berg in *Incident at Vichy* make the mandatory discovery and are presumably rescued from the stasis that holds them; Quentin is free to live again, to marry Holga, and Von Berg to die, a willing sacrifice. Miller intends that his characters should find release by discovering within themselves the capacity to commit the greatest evil of which man is capable ("no one they didn't kill can be innocent again," says Holga in *Fall*), but he somehow conveys the idea that where everyone is guilty, no one is. Given the autobiographical elements in *After the Fall*, the play suggests an apology no one asked the playwright to make. However personal the impulse that brought Miller to his new subject matter in the 1960s, he continued to be preoccupied with the post-Freudian variation on original sin in *The Price* (1968) and in *The Creation of the World and Other Business* (1972), in which Cain rejects both God and the Devil, but carries the Fall with him into exile. Although the characters in *The Archbishop's Ceiling* (1977) suffer from a certain amount of political and sexual guilt, the play, in its concern with intellectual and personal freedom and with the relationship between homeland and art, suggests a new emphasis in Miller's work, a return to the public-private balance of the early plays, colored now by a complex of motivations left behind by the doctrinaire reading of human behavior implicit in the 1960s plays.

The difficulty with the later Miller plays lies not so much in their ideas as in what those ideas do to Miller as dramatist. *After the Fall* and *Incident at Vichy* present not struggle but analysis. More didactic than the early Miller plays, which used to be criticized on those grounds, both *Fall* and *Vichy* are peopled with characters who seem motivated only by the need to illustrate the playwright's ideas. Nor can the heavy-handed Jewish comedy in *Creation* mask the fact that the borrowed biblical figures are simply points of view. Only *The Price* escapes the thematic trap. Also a discussion play, it is saved by a family quarrel in which the shifting tides of argument are strong enough to exert an emotional pull on the audience—and by Miller's only successful comic figure, Gregory Solomon, the aged furniture dealer as life-force. Besides, the play is as much about talk as it is talk, and the doubt it throws on the therapeutic discussion spills across Miller's other plays of this period as though the playwright were questioning work in which agony natters when it ought to sing.

Miller and Williams are special cases, but for every William Wycherly there has to be a crowd of Aphra Behns. It is the latter—honest hacks and aspiring artists alike—who give a period its peculiar character, although the leading dramatists reflect the texture of the time, directly or obliquely. The 1950s was a psychological decade, a period in which the playwrights solved problems with the assurance and the profundity of syndicated columnists. Its dramatists focused on the personal—family difficulties, loneliness, the uncertainties of adolescence—and if they lifted their eyes to the social, the political, the universal, the wider vistas were somehow domesticated, reduced to problems in how to relate. "Make Love, Not War" was a 1960s slogan, but if the young people who shouted it had had a better sense of recent history, they would have known that Broadway audiences a decade earlier really believed in such a possibility or responded as though they did. Love was a pervasive solution, taking many forms, crossing all barriers. It appeared most often as therapeutic sex, as in Robert Anderson's *Tea and Sympathy* (1953). At the end of the play, the understanding wife of the headmaster sits on the edge of the bed and begins to unbutton her blouse, offering herself to the sensitive adolescent so unsure of his masculinity. That famous last scene is more than a perfect curtain for a neat theater piece; it is almost an embodiment of the worst fears and the best hopes of a cautious decade. If love, as tea and sympathy, is at one end of a spectrum, at the other is love at its most portentous, one grand abstraction among many, as in these lines from Arch Oboler's *Night of the Auk* (1956): "Give *yourself* a name! / Reach to heaven for it—in final understanding—in love!" A philosophical melodrama, a lyric cry in a science fiction setting, *Auk* has a 1950s feel for cliché ("We are all alone, / Each to himself"), and its best ambitions (who does not want to avoid an atomic war?) remind us that there were good intentions abroad in that decade. Between these two extremes stand most of the playwrights of the 1950s, singing, with the chorus at the end of *Do Re Mi,* "Make someone happy. Make just one someone happy."

Tennessee Williams has his own touch of 1950s orthodoxy in his sense of sex as a kind of comfort station in the apocalypse, but he is too sardonic or too clear-sighted to take his salvation straight, as *Period of Adjustment* (1960) shows. Coming at the end of the decade, Williams's play is an even more merciless comment on the reigning platitudes than the Gore Vidal essay "Love, Love, Love" (*Partisan Review,* Fall 1959), which is sometimes taken as the venomous last word on the subject. When *Adjustment* appeared, it was received, with some bewilderment, as Williams's attempt to write a standard Broadway marital comedy. It concerns two couples, one of them newly married, beset by loneliness, incompatibility, impotence, even a touch of angst, and the play ends—as such comedies always do—with the two couples solving their problems in bed. As one might expect in a play subtitled "High Point over a Cavern," the happy-ending blackout is less than it seems. There are tremors as the suburb in which the play is set sinks still farther into the ground, and the audience is left with the image of an erection over the abyss. Unlike Williams, Miller earnestly succumbed to the love ethic. This can be seen in the introduction to *Collected Plays,* in which, retroactively, he finds in *Death of a Salesman* "an opposing system which, so to speak, is in a race for Willy's faith, and it is the system of love which is the opposite of the law of success." There is no such thing in *Salesman,* but *The Misfits* (1961) does borrow the 1950s anodyne. At the end of the film Miller wrote for Marilyn Monroe, then his wife, Gay drives off with Roslyn, saying: "Just head for that big star straight on. The highway's under it; take us right home." Not a tremor, but the Fall was not far up that road.

The representative playwright of the period was neither Williams nor Miller. It was William Inge. He arrived on Broadway in 1950 with *Come Back, Little Sheba,* a modest critical and popular success. Then came *Picnic* (1953), *Bus Stop* (1955), and *The Dark at the Top of the Stairs* (1957), commercial hits which were taken seriously by some critics and which certainly did touch, soothe something very basic in the Broadway audience. The tentative happy ending of *Come Back, Little Sheba,* in which Doc and Lola stay together, each cross and support for the other, becomes more positive, less artistically acceptable in the later plays. That Cherie and Bo get together at the end of *Bus Stop* is understandable, since they are a country-music variation on Beatrice and Benedick, but they are only icing on a loss-and-loneliness cake. When Madge follows Hal to Tulsa in *Picnic,* a Broadway ending not in the early drafts of the play nor in the revision, *Summer Brave* (1962), her romantic gesture is supposed to be a cure for the restlessness of the two attractive but not very bright young people, and the reconciliation of Cora and Rubin in *The Dark at the Top of the Stairs* not only erases their obvious incompatibility but presumably solves their economic problems as well. That last scene, when Cora goes up the stairs, "like a shy maiden," to Rubin's feet above is an even more compelling image of the softness in 1950s drama than the unbuttoned blouse in *Tea and Sympathy.* Despite the success of *The Dark at the Top of the Stairs,* it was the beginning of the end of Inge as a popular playwright. His best qualities as a dramatist lay in characters, like Lola, whose self-revelation is unknowing, and in what Harold Clurman in *Lies Like Truth* called his "lyric realism." With *Dark* Inge began to put his characters through extended self-analysis, a relentless flow of words that was to inundate his next play, *A Loss of Roses* (1959), which did not even give the audience the therapeutic happy ending it had come to expect. More plays followed, and films, novels, television, but Inge had become a historical figure. He died on June 10, 1973, an apparent suicide. It would be simplistic to suggest that his career had brought him his last unhappy ending, but it is difficult not to remember Tennessee Williams's preface to *Dark,* in which he recalls Inge's telling him, back in 1945, "that being a successful playwright was what he most wanted in the world for himself."

So far as the 1950s are concerned, Robert Anderson, unlike Inge, is a one-play playwright. Neither *All Summer Long* (1953), his interesting adaptation of Donald Wetzel's novel *A Wreath and a Curse,* nor the bromidic *Silent Night, Lonely Night* (1959) reached the large audiences that *Tea and Sympathy* did. In his more recent work he has used a variety of ways to express his continuing concern with marriage and loneliness. *You Know I Can't Hear You When the Water's Running* (1967) is a related group of four one-act plays that range from gags to schmaltz; *I Never Sang for My Father* (1968) breaks the realistic dramatic frame to let the narrator-protagonist consider the prickly old man who is the play's reason for being; *Solitaire/Double Solitaire* (1971) is a further manipulation of theatrical convention but in the service of conventional ideas.

More interesting than Anderson's work is that of Arthur Laurents, another Broadway regular who tried to bring serious plays to the 1950s stage. His first play, *Home of the Brave* (1945), an effective drama about a psychosomatically paralyzed veteran who has to be shocked into walking again, reflects prewar concern with social themes in its depiction of anti-Semitism, but, as an essay in psychological treatment, it points toward the 1950s; toward *A Clearing in the Woods* (1957), for instance, in which Laurents appears to be using expressionistic technique as psychoanalysis. Between these two plays appeared *The Bird Cage* (1950), a commercial disaster that is still one of Laurents's most intriguing plays, and *The Time of the Cuckoo* (1952), a rueful comedy about an American innocent abroad which occasionally lapses into sentimentality. With *West Side Story* (1957), Laurents turned to musical comedy, and, although there have been plays since then, his best work has been the books for the Leonard Bernstein musical and for Jule Styne's *Gypsy* (1959). Musical comedy has been good for Laurents as a dramatist because the demands of the libretto have forced him to work more austerely, cutting away a tendency, obvious in even his best plays, to explain too much, too often.

During the 1950s, a number of playwrights moved from television to the stage—Paddy Chayefsky, Horton Foote, Tad Mosel, Robert Alan Aurthur—bringing with them themes very like those with which their brothers on Broadway were already preoccupied. Chayefsky's *Marty*, on television (1953) and in film (1955), is a touching illustration of peer-induced loneliness, but when the same theme was treated on stage in *Middle of the Night* (1956), adapted from an earlier television play, Chayefsky's neat, small effects stood exposed as clichés of character, language, situation. After attempts to deal with more ambitious material—*Gideon* (1961) and *The Passion of Joseph D* (1964)—Chayefsky seems to have moved permanently to the movies, where in *The Hospital* (1971) and *Network* (1976), he is working a sardonic vein that he never touched on stage. N. Richard Nash probably does not belong among the television transplants since his Broadway career goes back as far as *The Young and Fair* (1948), but his best play, *The Rainmaker* (1954), is an expanded television script. Another case of therapeutic sex, this one somehow escapes the confines of the label by suggesting a cross between romantic comedy and the Cinderella story. Shimon Wincelberg's *Kataki* (1959) is the most unusual of the plays adapted from television; essentially a monologue, it shows the mutual suspicion and growing friendliness of two men—an American and a Japanese soldier—trapped on an island together, neither knowing the other's language. Perhaps because the American, who does the talking, is as hateful as he is attractive, the play was a failure both on and off Broadway.

The strangest, the grandest, perhaps the most pretentious of the love plays in the love decade is Archibald MacLeish's *J.B.* (1958). Celebrated in the 1930s for radio plays like *The Fall of the City* and *Air Raid* and still struggling with dramatic form in 1971 with *Scratch,* MacLeish, as a playwright for the stage, reached a wide audience only with *J.B.*, triumph enough in a theater in which verse is let in only on sufferance. MacLeish's inventiveness—in choosing contemporary plagues for his Job to suffer, in making an upper-echelon vaudeville turn of the debates between God and the Devil, in putting modern clichés in the mouths of his false comforters—dissolves at the end when all he can offer is J.B.'s "Blow on the coal of the heart." Two other visitors from neighboring genres were much more interesting in their treatment of the pervasive themes of loneliness and separation. Carson McCullers's *The Member of the Wedding* (1950) is a highly effective adaptation of her own novel, and Jane Bowles's *In the Summer House* (1953) is an eccentric play which escapes being a psychological drama by hiding behind speeches that are often as funny as they are oblique. Truman Capote's *The Grass Harp* (1952), a softer, sweeter version of his novel, probably belongs with the work of McCullers and Bowles, but his book for the Harold Arlen musical *House of Flowers* (1954) is at once stronger and more characteristic.

With rare exceptions, the plays of the 1950s confirm William Gibson's remark that "the theater, in this country, in this decade, was primarily a place not in which to be serious, but in which to be likeable." The statement appears in *The Seesaw Log*, in which an account of the production is printed with the text of Gibson's *Two for the Seesaw* (1958). A likeable play.

When Louis Kronenberger made his choices for *The Best Plays of 1953-1954,* two of them—*The Girl on the Via Flaminia* and the Jerome

Moross–John Latouche musical *The Golden Apple* (1954)—were unusual in that they had begun theatrical life in off-Broadway theaters. By the early 1950s off-Broadway was being taken seriously by theater enthusiasts and entrepreneurs alike, but success was still being measured by the move from off-Broadway to Broadway even though—as with both these shows and with Calder Willingham's *End As a Man* (1953)—the transplants tended to wither in theaters too large for them. Since New York had a tradition of little theaters—artistic in the 1920s, political in the 1930s—there was nothing unusual about a postwar return to an alternative means of production. Groups would form, have an exciting few seasons, and then disband, although some of them flourished and then went on to other things. Julian Beck and Judith Malina began by producing conventionally avant-garde plays, but their Living Theatre went on to become America's most celebrated—most notorious—theater collective; by way of contrast, the Circle in the Square moved into its own Broadway home in 1972. In the beginning the greater part of the off-Broadway repertory consisted of modern classics, new European drama, and the revival of Broadway plays—such as *Summer and Smoke* and *The Grass Harp*—which were thought to need more delicate handling than they had received first time around. Underlying all this activity was the assumption that off-Broadway would be the breeding ground for new American playwrights, although many of the works that attracted attention—James Lee's *Career* (1957) is a good example—were conventional plays which are now little more than statistics. There were unusual productions, such as *Uniform of Flesh* (1949), the Melville adaptation by Louis O. Coxe and Robert Chapman, which later, in a stronger, prose version, reached Broadway as *Billy Budd* (1951). Poets such as James Merrill, John Ashbery, and Frank O'Hara worked with Herbert Machiz's Artists' Theatre in the mid-1950s, but none of their work had the theatrical vigor of O'Hara's later play, *The General Returns from One Place to Another* (1964). Robert Hivnor's *The Ticklish Acrobat* (1954) is the best of the Artists' Theatre plays, an imaginative and remarkably good-humored comedy about a Dalmatian village which withstands the invasion of an American archaeologist, just as it has absorbed so many other invasions over the years. Verbally and visually inventive, *Acrobat* is far superior to and a great deal funnier than many plays which have reached wider audiences, but then Hivnor, from *Too Many Thumbs* (1948) to *A Son Is Always Leaving Home* (1971), has always worked on the periphery of the American theater.

By the end of the decade, off-Broadway had become simply another producing mechanism, not that different from Broadway. Producers, directors, performers moved comfortably from one arena to the other, depending on the nature of the material, and a new group of playwrights had emerged to take their places in the mainstream of American theater. Jack Gelber's *The Connection* (1959) was selected as one of *The Best Plays of 1959-1960,* the first play to stay off-Broadway and still be included in the collection, although the abridgment was confined to a section by itself.

Gelber's play, which received a great deal of praise from critics who damned William Inge, is an extremely efficient theater piece with an antirealistic frame that helps mask the conventionality of plot and idea and a sentimentality almost as strong as Inge's. To make the scarcely startling point that we are all addicted to something, Gelber offers a play within a play, a melodrama about addiction which—since the play is supposed to be acted by real addicts—goes to pieces during production as the actors ignore the script, and both the playwright and one of the cameramen who are supposed to be filming the play decide to turn on as well. *The Connection,* however, ends as the melodrama it pretends not to be and proves—as George Axelrod did when he adapted expressionistic techniques to a standard Broadway comedy in *The Seven Year Itch* (1952)—that antirealism is another tool for the conventional playwright. None of the later Gelber plays had either the control or the immediate appeal—the subject matter, the jazz band on stage—of *The Connection,* and the large following that he built with his first play quickly melted away. He stays committed to antirealistic devices and structural games, as *The Apple* (1961), *Square in the Eye* (1965), *Sleep* (1972), and *Jack Gelber's New Play: Rehearsal* (1976) all show.

Jack Richardson is the most intellectually engaging of the playwrights to emerge in the early 1960s, which does not necessarily mean that he writes the best plays. All of his work—however different in setting, subject matter, style—offers variations on a single theme. For Richardson, life is a confusion, a constant surprise, an unpredictability, which man, if he is to be truly alive, must embrace; it is a struggle in which inevitable defeat and loss (mortality is, after all, part of the bargain of life) is balanced against "the sense of possibility," as he called it in "Grace through Gambling" (*Esquire,* April 1967). In *The Prodigal* (1960), Orestes, who rejects both Agamemnon and Aegisthus, runs away from the knowledge that power always leads to violence; at the end, he returns to Argos to commit his murders—forced there by Electra's, by society's, by his audience's need for heroes. *Gallows Humor* (1961) is a pair of short plays in one of which the compulsively tidy Walter chooses to go to his execution from a cell in which erotic irrationality has reclaimed him, while in the other his executioner, rejecting the call of chaos, declines to kill his wife— absurdist comedies about dying alive and living dead. In *Lorenzo* (1963), the titular hero, who believes his actor's world the real one, a refuge from the chaos of war, finally dons a helmet—knowing that, win or lose, he has lost—and is quickly killed. The protagonist of *Xmas in Las Vegas* (1965), an even more unlikely Broadway comedy than *Period of Adjustment,* plays a savage Santa Claus scene in which each of his family—himself included—is given a symbolic death-in-life gift, but his son, rejecting the offered pistol, chooses to follow in his father's gambling footsteps, to be "next up at the table." Single-sentence descriptions of these plays can give little sense of the complexity of idea in them and say nothing about their shortcomings as plays. In one of his drama reviews (*Commentary,* March 1967), Richardson wrote that "once the curtain goes up, and there is a revelation of what the evening's metaphor is to be, the audience may grow restive unless the ensuing play adds some intelligent, humorous, or tragic flesh to that metaphor." That is his own difficulty as a playwright—a failure to put flesh on his metaphors.

Arthur Kopit, fresh out of Harvard and trailing clouds of undergraduate glory, came to the New York stage in 1961 with *Oh Dad, Poor Dad, Mama's Hung You in the Closet and I'm Feelin' So Sad.* A clever play, a witty play, it is more serious than its pastiche of parody and nonsense sometimes lets it seem. It is both having fun with the cliché of the emasculated American male and presenting the theme dramatically through its stuttering wreck of a hero and the two women in his life, his mother and his girl, those complementary types, the iron maiden and the child seductress. The plays that followed *Oh Dad—The Day the Whores Came Out to Play Tennis* (1965), for instance—confirmed the cleverness but suggested that Kopit lacked the substance needed to balance his playful invention. With *Indians* (1969), one of the most ambitious plays to come from this group of dramatists, Kopit fulfilled his initial promise. There are some problems with *Indians*—jokes almost too broad for their context, scenes that edge a complex play toward didactic statement—but for the most part the play is up to the major theme which Kopit has chosen. Kopit uses Buffalo Bill to explore the familiar American phenomenon in which a man's achievements are converted into a marketable public image, or, as Buffalo Bill puts it, "I'm simply *drawin'* on what I was . . . and raisin' it to a higher level." This transformation is accompanied, as it so often is, by the conviction that self-advertisement is a public service, that doing well is doing good: "Givin' 'em somethin' t' be *proud* of!" Mythic creations have practical consequences, and Bill, who discovers that as neither man nor myth can he save Sitting Bull and his people, ends as the rationalizing voice for the destruction which he deplores. All this in a play that slides easily from show business to history, from parody to dream—antirealistic drama not as protest but as art. Neither *Secrets of the Rich* (1976) nor *Wings* (1978) is conceived on the scale of *Indians,* but *Wings* is a very impressive short play in which a cluster of aural and visual images menace or comfort a woman who has suffered a stroke and who accepts the final adventure of death as the play moves "from fragmentation to integration."

Among the other playwrights who came from the off-Broadway theater at about the same time as Gelber, Richardson, and Kopit are Arnold Weinstein, Murray Schisgal, William Hanley, and Frank D. Gilroy. Weinstein has worked on musicals with William Bolcom (*Dynamite Tonite,* 1963, and *Greatshot,* 1969) and has adapted Brecht (*Mahagonny,* 1970) and Ovid (*Metamorphoses,* 1969), but his most impressive play is still his first, *Red Eye of Love* (1961), a cornucopia of parody, blackouts, language games, and running gags. At his best, he has a strong satirical imagination, at once horrifying and funny, as when the blinded soldier in *Dynamite Tonite* sings about how he will miss the movies or the hero of *Red Eye* tries to invent a doll that will get sick and die: "Kids would love that. Real live death to play with." Murray Schisgal's talent, at least at the beginning of his career, was to catch and mock the psychological and sociological clichés of the urban middle class. He can be seen at his best in the one-act *The Tiger* (1963) and in *Luv* (1963), but in some of his later work— *Fragments* (1965) and parts of *Jimmy Shine* (1968)—he seems to be taking seriously attitudes that he laughed at in the earlier plays. William Hanley's most ambitious play is *Slow Dance on the Killing Ground* (1964), a three-character discussion play in which each of the principals is given a revelatory set piece and in which all of them are presented as victims of the societal violence to which they contribute; still his best play, the one-act *Mrs. Dally Has a Lover* (1962) is a post-coital conversation between a middle-aged woman and her eighteen-year-old lover which—despite some excessive literary decoration (references to Donne, Cellini)—provides an effective portrait of a difficult woman, warm and sensitive, demanding and self-preoccupied. Frank D. Gilroy's first two plays, *Who'll Save the Plowboy?* (1962) and *The Subject Was Roses* (1964)—the one about a failed life, the other, a failed marriage—are small, thin, naturalistic plays that go for simple character points and sentimental effects; however fragile, they have a theatrical validity absent in his soap-opera reworking of the Phaedra story, *That Summer—That Fall* (1967) and his attempt at Broadway comedy, *The Only Game in Town* (1968).

"The new generation's knocking at the door. Gelber, Richardson, Kopit . . . (*Shrugs*) . . . Albee." The speaker is FAM in Edward Albee's *Fam and Yam* (1960), "An Imaginary Interview," a trifle that apparently grew out of his having been designated as one of the newest great hopes of the American theater. Albee was the first, perhaps the only one of his theatrical generation to move from YAM (Young American Playwright) to FAM (Famous American Playwright). It was *Who's Afraid of Virginia Woolf?* (1962), coming hard on the heels of his successful short plays—*The Zoo Story* (1958), *The Sandbox* (1959), *The Death of Bessie Smith* (1959), *The American Dream* (1961)—that signaled his new status. In the decade that followed, Albee—good professional that he is—worked diligently at his craft, alternating adaptations from Carson McCullers (*The Ballad of the Sad Café*, 1963), James Purdy (*Malcolm*, 1966) and Giles Cooper (*Everything in the Garden*, 1967) with original plays—*Tiny Alice* (1964), *A Delicate Balance* (1966), *Box-Mao-Box* (1968). His pace slackened at the end of the 1960s. When *A Delicate Balance* opened in New York in 1966, there was talk of a double bill, *Life and Death,* scheduled for production during the same year. It was five years and several plays later before *All Over,* the play about death, was finished, and it was 1975 before the other half of the proposed double bill emerged as *Seascape.* Despite all this theatrical activity, Albee never had a critical or popular success to equal—or even to approach—that of *Who's Afraid of Virginia Woolf?* "The critics set somebody up, maybe too soon—underline *maybe*—and then they take great pleasure . . . in knocking them down," Albee told the *New York Times* (April 18, 1971) in the familiar mixture of hurt and hatchetry that he has aimed at critics ever since *The Zoo Story* opened in New York in 1960. It is understandable that a playwright who is not content to do the same thing over and over should become impatient with critics who he feels do not pay proper attention to his present work. (It is a familiar lament; see Tennessee Williams's *Memoirs*). In Albee's case, the fault lies less with the critics than with *Virginia Woolf.* It is so good that his later plays—some of them impressive after their own fashions—seem dim by comparison. It is possible that Albee came to see the play as an albatross of sorts and tried to get it off his neck with *Box-Mao-Box.* Long-Winded Lady in that play would be at home in *Virginia Woolf,* verbally and emotionally; yet she uses her rhetoric as a way of avoiding the human situation with which she seems to be dealing, as do the other characters—Mao with his quotations, the old woman who recites "Over the Hill to the Poorhouse." If Albee was passing a dismissive judgment on his earlier work with *Box-Mao-Box*—clearly his most experimental play—by 1976, as director of a revival of *Virginia Woolf,* he seemed to accept the play as the contemporary classic it has become.

In the *Times* interview quoted above Albee managed to dismiss most of American drama, past and present, to say that the genre became serious only with Williams and late O'Neill and to imply that he is their successor. Albee has probably done more kidding around in interviews in the last fifteen years than anyone his artistic age and weight, but this inflated sense of his work is a joke only to someone who does not know that a hawk is sometimes a handsaw. I am tempted to follow Albee's self-evaluation—at a respectable distance. Not only has he written a number of one-act plays that have become standard dramatic fare on American campuses and *Who's Afraid of Virginia Woolf?*—his crown and his cross—but he has produced a body of work more substantial than any of the 1960 crop of YAMs. Material enough, reason enough to take a more extended look at his themes, his techniques, the underlying assumptions of his work.

Most of the Albee plays lack specific settings, real towns located in real states; all of them take place in the existential present so dear to contemporary writers in which life is measured in terms of loss, love by its failure, contact by its absence. The pervasive metaphor in his work is the zoo, as Jerry describes it in *The Zoo Story,* "with everyone separated by bars from everyone else." Even though Albee's zoo provides suites for two people (*Virginia Woolf*) or more (*A Delicate Balance*), they are furnished with separate cages. Even the speeches, particularly in *A Delicate Balance,* break into fragments tenuously connected on the page by ellipsis, on stage by anticipatory pauses. Restless, uncomfortable in their own skins, most of his characters are like the Nurse in *Bessie Smith*: "I WANT OUT!" Violence is one way of trying to slip the cages—physical in *The Zoo Story,* verbal in *Virginia Woolf.* The other possibility is love (that, too, a form of penetration), but the Albee plays are full of characters who cannot (Nick in *Virginia Woolf*) or will not (Tobias in *A Delicate Balance*) make that connection. The persistent images are of withdrawal, the most graphic being the one in *Balance,* the information that Tobias in fact withdrew and came on Agnes's belly the last time they had sex. Jerry's story about his landlady's vicious dog—although he over-explains it—is still Albee's most effective account of an attempt to get through the bars (so effective that Tobias uses a variation on it when he tells about his cat). Accepting the dog's attacks on him as a form of recognition, Jerry tries first to win the dog's affection (with hamburger) and, failing that, to kill him (with poisoned hamburger: it is difficult to differentiate between the tools of love and hate). In the end, he settles for an accommodation, one in which he and the dog ignore each other. His leg remains unbitten, but he feels a sense of loss: "We neither love nor hurt because we do not try to reach each other." Most of the Albee characters make their accommodations, find the delicate balance, learn, as Lawyer says in *Tiny Alice,* to "face the inevitable and call it what you have always wanted."

Implicit in the separateness of the Albee characters and the bogus forms of community they invent to mask the fact that they are alone (in *Box-Mao-Box,* for instance, the silent auditor allows Long-Winded Lady to see monologue as conversation) is the assumption that this is Albee's view of the human condition. Yet in much of his work there is a suggestion that the problem is a local one, somehow the result of a collapse of values in the Western world in general, in the United States in particular. *The American Dream,* Albee says in the preface to the play, is "an attack on the substitution of artificial for real values in our society." When *Virginia Woolf* was new and critical hubris rampant, Diana Trilling (*Esquire,* December 1963) came up with the suggestion that George and Martha are the Washingtons, a bit of symbol making that seemed too cute to be true, but in the *New York Times* (March 28, 1976), Albee confirmed the labels and described the play as "an examination of whether or not we, as a society, have failed the principles of the American 'Revolution." It is obvious, within the text of *Virginia Woolf,* that Albee intends his sterility tale to have a cultural point, but—unless he is having his little Bicentennial joke—his new reading of the play turns Arthur Miller's later imposition of a "system of love" on *Death of a Salesman* into very conservative exegesis.

The Washingtons aside, there is a residue of social criticism in Albee's work, forming an unstable mixture with the underlying assumptions about the human condition. If the lost and lonely Albee character is an irrevocable fact—philosophically, theologically, psychologically—his plays must necessarily be reflections of that situation; any gesture of defiance is doomed to failure. If the Albee character is a product of his societal context and if that context is changeable (not necessarily politically, but by an alteration of modes of behavior between one person and another), then the plays may be instructive fables. Albee has often disavowed solutions without denying the possibility that they exist; in the *Atlantic* (April 1965), he said

that "one of the responsibilities of playwrights [is] to show people
how they are and what their time is like in the hope that perhaps they'll
change it." Albee, then, shares with most American playwrights an
idea of the utility of art, but the strain of didacticism in his work
(*Seascape,* for instance), is balanced by an ambiguity about the nature
of his dramatic parables. There are critics who find affirmation in
the stabbing at the end of *The Zoo Story,* who assume that George
and Martha are off to face the dark at the top of the stairs (the last
act is called "The Exorcism"), even that Tobias's operatic attempt
to put real meaning into the word *friendship* has significance beyond
the gesture. To me, these are balance-tipping events that conventional
theater says are positive but that the Albee material insists are negative.
The latent reformer in Albee may side with the yea-sayers against his
nay-saying self, and the more recent plays seem to confirm this
possibility—*All Over* in its acceptance of death, *Seascape* in its acceptance of life. I take refuge in Albee's answer to a question about the
meaning of *Seascape* (*New York Times,* January 26, 1975): "It is
about a series of events and their resonances."

That answer can lead to a discussion of Albee's method as well as
his matter. At his best (*The Zoo Story, Virginia Woolf, A Delicate
Balance*), the playwright puts an action on stage—an encounter in a
park that becomes a suicide-murder, a night-long quarrel that ends
in the death of an illusion, an invasion that collapses before the defenders can decide whether to surrender or to fight—which has dramatic
vitality in its own right and from which a meaning or meanings can
emerge. The central situation—the encounter, the relationship implicit in the quarrel, the state of the defenders and the invaders—is
defined in verbal terms. There is business, but it is secondary. Jerry's
poking and tickling Peter is only an extension of what he has been
doing with words; George's attempt to strangle Martha is a charade
not far removed from their verbal games. When events get more
flamboyant—the shooting of Julian in *Tiny Alice*—they tend to become ludicrous, as do the words when (again, *Tiny Alice*) they are
asked to carry too much symbolic or allusive freight. Since *Virginia
Woolf,* Albee's language has become more elaborate, intricate—arid,
some would say—but, however idiomatic, it has always been an artificial language, built on three main devices: interruption, repetition,
and the set speech. Its strength as theatrical language is that it is
never simply a container, a means to carry information; it is a dramatic
device in its own right, a mechanism for revealing character, even
embodying theme. "What I find most astonishing," Agnes begins as
A Delicate Balance opens. Albee's grandest interrupted speech mean-

ders through Tobias's practical attempt to get the after-dinner drinks, and we are fifteen speeches into the play, past two reappearances of the "astonishing" phrase, before the opening sentence ends; seems to end, really, for the phrase recurs just before the final curtain, as Agnes goes her placidly relentless way—"to fill a silence," as the stage direction says—in a speech which defines, by its shape more than its content, the steady flow of nonevent which sustains the delicate balance.

Late in 1958, the year in which Albee wrote *The Zoo Story,* Joseph Cino opened a coffeehouse in Greenwich Village where staged readings and, later, full productions of plays could be held; by 1961, Caffe Cino had a regular program of plays—usually new works by new playwrights—that ran for a week or two. By the time the first generation of off-Broadway playwrights began to emerge, then, off-off-Broadway had begun to take amorphous shape as a producing alternative to—yes—the commercialism of off-Broadway. Productions of all kinds multiplied rapidly, and whether it was the call of art or the longing for recognition that brought so many determined people into so many lofts, churches, and coffeehouses, it is generally conceded that, while much of the work was very bad, the idea was fine. It was a chance for new performers, new directors, and—most important from the standpoint of this chapter—new playwrights to be seen. Off-off-Broadway quickly developed its own Establishment—Cino, La Mama Experimental Theatre Club, Judson Poets' Theatre, Theatre Genesis—which developed not only its own audiences and its own voices but reputations that quickly reached uptown and abroad. During the 1960s, a young playwright had a better chance of getting his work produced than at any time since the end of World War II because a hearing was no longer confused with a Broadway—or even an off-Broadway—production. Off-off-Broadway is now a great deal less chaotic than it was in its infancy; it has a producers' organization and rules that Actors' Equity helped define. Yet, the changes in off-off-Broadway are less important than those on the American theater scene as a whole. Although off-off-Broadway has fed talent into the commercial theater, it has not been remade in the Broadway image. In fact, it is the Broadway image that has changed.

During this century at least, Broadway (or the New York commercial theater for which that word stands) has been the center not only of American show business but of American drama. There have always been little theater productions scattered around the country and a handful of well-established regional theaters, but new playwrights were introduced (or their existence confirmed) by New York production. In the last fifteen years, regional theaters have grown in number and in quality, and although most of them stick to proven works—bearing the imprimatur of either New York or history—there is a new sense of independence in the air. While new playwrights— Lanford Wilson, Megan Terry, Sam Shepard, Leonard Melfi, Rosalyn Drexler—were moving from off-off-Broadway production to print, proving that one can bypass Broadway on the way to recognition as an American dramatist, some of the same playwrights and a great many others were learning that a reputation as an American playwright can begin in Washington, New Haven, Minneapolis, Louisville. It is true that Tennessee Williams and William Inge were performed at Margo Jones's theater in Dallas back in the 1940s, but their plays somehow did not exist until they reached Broadway; *Farther Off from Heaven* (1947) had to wait and be born again ten years later as *The Dark at the Top of the Stairs*. Today—to take another Dallas example—things have changed. When Preston Jones's *A Texas Trilogy* came to New York in 1976, the three plays had already been performed as a group for an extended run in Washington and one of them, *The Last Meeting of the Knights of the White Magnolia,* had been done widely around the country. When they were received, somewhat coolly, as standard if clever examples of traditional American regional drama, the *Trilogy* quickly closed. This was presumably disappointing to Jones and his admirers, but it was not a failure in the 1940s or 1950s sense of the word; Preston Jones is still a playwright with a national reputation. Except for an occasional musical, Broadway has almost ceased to exist as an initiator of new work. It is now a merchandiser of pretested goods.

What the new look in American theater means is that it is no longer possible to write the history of American drama by consulting the list of productions in the *Best Plays* series, a fact that the series itself realized in 1964-1965, when it began to include an extended listing of productions in theaters all over the United States. It also means that it is less easy than it once was to get a handhold—thematic or technical—on American drama; ideas still cluster, movements still flourish and die, but the comforting labels mentioned at the beginning of this essay offer less security than they once did. A great many new American playwrights have emerged in the last decade and a half, and a number of them have bodies of work large enough and interesting enough to attract loyal audiences, wary critics, and the writers of dissertations. I am going to have to be very selective—no, arbitrary— in dealing with these dramatists and, since I have to begin somewhere, I will start with Ronald Ribman, whose work I particularly like.

Ribman's first two plays, *Harry, Noon and Night* (1965) and *The Journey of the Fifth Horse* (1966) introduced a remarkable dramatic talent into the American theater. The former is a strange comedy in which each of the acts is a two-person confrontation, an elaborate game in which one is victim, the other victimizer—a difficult, allusive play which has a frightening edge to its funniness and an essential sadness at its core. *Journey* is an intricate work, based in part on Turgenev's *The Diary of a Superfluous Man,* which moves from reality to dream to an amorphousness—the staging of scenes from *Diary*—which lies somewhere between; Ribman's superb invention is the publisher's reader, whose story is told alongside that of Turgenev's Chulkaturin, another superfluous man who unwillingly identifies with the author he is reading and finally throws the manuscript aside, trying, painfully, to disown the identification. Very dissimilar in style, the plays are related through their treatment of failure clowns, to take a phrase from *Harry*; of fifth horses, to use *Journey*'s borrowing from Turgenev. With the television play *The Final War of Olly Winter* (1967) and the pacifism implicit in the historical play *The Ceremony of Innocence* (1967), Ribman moved into direct social comment, but the movement was neither as abrupt nor as complete as it at first seemed. All his plays, early and late, deal with characters who are trapped by their circumstances, by societies in which the range of possibilities is limited by fixed attitudes, and to which the characters, however rational (see Ethelred in *Ceremony*), respond with an irrationality which is at once a protest and a confirmation of the imprisoning cast of mind. The central figure in *Fingernails Blue as Flowers* (1971), who is perhaps intended to be an old man active only in memory, is Ribman's best image of entrapment *in situ,* fixed as he is in a beach chair, unacknowledged by those around him; Ribman's most vigorous struggler is the hero of *A Break in the Skin* (1972), a play that has gone through several versions under various names without ever quite pleasing its author or his audiences. *The Poison Tree* (1973) is a prison drama which—behind the explicit comment on prison conditions and racial bigotry—develops its titular metaphor by showing the manipulative guard as his own victim, all the characters as creatures of the situation. In *Cold Storage* (1977), the relentless and often very funny garrulity of one of the main characters forces the other to break out of the guilty shell which has been trap and comfort to him since his family helped him escape the Nazi holocaust, which destroyed them; set in a cancer ward, the play is a celebration of life at the door of death.

Ribman reached his first audiences through the American Place

Theatre, one of whose activities on behalf of new American drama was an attempt to bring practicing poets and novelists into the theater. The happiest product of that program is Robert Lowell's *The Old Glory* (1964). Earlier Lowell had done an adaptation of Racine's *Phèdre* (*Phaedra,* 1961) and he was to do a version of Aeschylus's *Prometheus Bound* (1967), but his reputation as a dramatist rests on *The Old Glory,* a group of three short plays—more often played separately than as a trilogy—which are held together by a common theme and by the image of the flag. The culminating action of *Endecott and the Red Cross* is Endecott's rejection of the Red Cross of England; of *My Kinsman, Major Molineux* is Robin's choice of the Rattlesnake over the Union Jack. *Benito Cereno* is, implicitly, a three-cornered struggle among the American flag, the Lion and Castle of Spain, and the pirate's skull and crossbones, and all three—particularly the last two—are used dramatically in several scenes. Lowell's persistent flags are not literary imposition; they have no intrinsic meaning beyond that which the characters bring to them. They are used as flags are in reality, as symbols of an abstraction worth fighting for (freedom) or against (authority). *The Old Glory* is about revolution—Endecott initiates one, Robin joins one, Delano puts one down—and the process by which the oppressed become the oppressors; freedom, as Babu demonstrates in the victory ritual in *Benito Cereno,* can be reached only by walking across the fallen flag and kissing the skull of the former tyrant. The American implications of this complicated subject (Lowell returns to it in *Prometheus Bound*) are emphasized by his having gone to Nathaniel Hawthorne and Herman Melville for his material. Of the three plays, *Benito Cereno* is the richest in language. In it, metaphor and allusion do not exist simply for the word's sake, but have a dramatic function; they emphasize Captain Delano's inability to hear what he says, to see what is around him. Among other poets turned playwright, William Alfred made a splash with *Hogan's Goat* (1965), a serious play as popular fustian; Kenneth Koch wrote some funny neo-Dada pieces—*Bertha* (1959) and *George Washington Crossing the Delaware* (1962); James Scheville moved from the conventional verse drama of *The Bloody Tenet* (1956) to the explorations in theatricality of his recent work. Yet Lowell—for *The Old Glory* in general, *Benito Cereno* in particular—is the poet with the strongest claim on a place among American dramatists.

When Irene Oppenheim asked Sam Shepard (*The Village Voice,* October 27, 1975), "How do you want people to approach your plays?" he answered, "Any way they can." A line that would have been a wisecrack in Neil Simon's mouth was a steppingstone to Shepard's now familiar distrust of interpretation, about which he is more re-signed than he apparently was when he asked the American Place Theatre not to invite critics to the production of his first full-length play, *La Turista* (1967). Three years earlier, when Shepard was twenty-one he wrote *Cowboys* (1964), the first of a number of one-act plays that quickly established him as an off-off-Broadway playwright of great promise. Rightly so, for Shepard has developed in ways much more interesting than most of his off-off-Broadway associates and now—still in his early thirties—he has produced an impressive body of work. In the early one-acts, he puts a number of not very well differentiated characters into a situation in which an undefined something seems to be going on and lets them talk, either in long monologues or in exchanges that tend toward single-sentence lines. It is possible to find meaning, in the traditional sense, in these works, but, as Shepard told a *New York Times* interviewer (March 5, 1967), he is interested not in the communication of ideas but in "theatrical event." A suspicious mind with a fondness for ideas might find more coyness than commitment in Shepard's remarks, but the best of the one-acts justify him. Although *Red Cross* (1966) is never intellectually or emotionally satisfying in a conventional sense, its central action is somehow complete in a way that resolves the tension within the piece. Besides, the visual images are startling, and the verbal quality provides an early instance of Shepard's fine talent for stage language, his intricate use of American idiom. The full-length play seemed to defeat Shepard at first; *La Turista* is like a string of his one-acts insecurely stapled to-gether. With *Operation Sidewinder* (1970), *The Tooth of Crime* (1972), *Geography of a Horse Dreamer* (1974), *Curse of the Starving Class* (1976), and *Buried Child* (1978), his control of the longer form has become sure, and the works are suggestive in a more serious way than the one-acts, which seem often to tease. *The Tooth of Crime*, for instance, is a confrontation between some kind of superstar, a "killer" in a metaphorical profession compounded of rock music, guns, and automobiles (familiar Shepard images), and a young man with a new style. The challenger will replace the older man, with the blessings of the star's own staff and the amorphous trade association which seems to control the business/art game. As theatrical event, *The Tooth of Crime* is compelling, as contests often are, but meaning does seem to have been sneaking up on Shepard over the years and the play is all the more rewarding for what it appears to be saying about success, American style. The weakness of the play lies in the specific references to performers, some of whose names may need footnotes in a few

years, but the central dramatic metaphor is as perennial and as powerful as it was when Ibsen called his version *The Master Builder*.

A playwright who clearly does not shy away from ideas is Jules
Feiffer, although, as his work as a cartoonist indicates, he understands
how easily an idea can become a psychological, social, or political
cliché. His characters, who resemble the people in his cartoons, are
animated attitudes, whose success as stage figures has less to do with
verisimilitude than it does with theatrical shtik. Feiffer's virtue as a
playwright is that he creates unified dramatic structures in which
apparently disparate material is held together by a controlling assumption, about violence—*Little Murders* (1967) and *The White House
Murder Case* (1970)—or commitment—*Knock, Knock* (1976). In *Little
Murders*, still his best play, the random violence that is the ostensible
subject is simply the most obviously theatrical evidence of a general
collapse reflected in technological malfunction (the failed electricity)
and the impotence of traditional authority figures—the judge, the
detective, the priest. *Little Murders* and *The White House Murder
Case* (as well as a great many of the Feiffer cartoons) suggest a dark
view of American society and of human possibility, but in *Knock,
Knock* Feiffer sounds an overtly positive note which may have been
implicit all along in the impulse that sent him to satire.

When Lanford Wilson catapulted into the show-business bigtime
with *The Hot l Baltimore* (1973)—the first off-off-Broadway play to
become a situation-comedy series on television—he already had a
list of produced plays as long as Sam Shepard's, including one unsuccessful try at Broadway—*The Gingham Dog* (1969)—and a host of
well-known off-off-Broadway plays, such as *Balm in Gilead* (1964),
The Rimers of Eldritch (1966), *This Is the Rill Speaking* (1965) and
The Madness of Lady Bright (1964). The last, a portrait of an aging
homosexual, broke the unwritten rule about short runs off-off-Broadway and became one of Caffe Cino's most successful plays; presumably
an acting tour de force, on the page *Lady Bright* is a collection of
clichés about loneliness. Wilson works more often in large-cast plays
in which he wishes to convey some sense of community, of environment. Whether he violates conventional form (*The Rimers of
Eldritch*) or works in straightforward naturalism (*The Hot l Baltimore*), whether his settings are rural (*This Is the Rill Speaking*) or
urban (*Balm in Gilead*), he dresses standard theater stereotypes in
the kind of mannerisms that passed for truth in the heyday of dramatic
realism. His theatrical virtue is that he provides an occasion for interesting ensemble playing; his chief weakness—as *Serenading Louie*
(1970) shows—is that his characters so easily dissolve into soap-opera

figures. In *The Mound Builders* (1975), set at an archaeological dig in southern Illinois, the Wilson strengths and weaknesses are again on display, but he gives his familiar material greater resonance by sending echoes of the earlier culture through the contemporary setting.

David Rabe's *The Basic Training of Pavlo Hummel* (1971) opened in New York at about the time sentiment against the war in Vietnam found a firm foothold in the mainstream of American opinion; it was shortly followed by *Sticks and Bones* (1971). Since the former was about a young man who dies in Vietnam and the latter about a blinded Vietnam veteran who comes home to a television situation-comedy family which must destroy him, Rabe was welcomed as a propagandist in the cause of peace; there is something skeletal about the early works—frames on which a message might be hung—which helps explain this initial response. When the plays were published in 1972, Rabe used his introduction to reject the label "antiwar" because it implied both a kind of play ("the thin line of political tract") which he never intended writing and an assumption about the political effectiveness of theater which he does not believe. Unlike Megan Terry's *Viet Rock* (1966), which came at a more difficult time, *Pavlo Hummel* was never simply pacifist; its use of basic training as ritual—like the prison routine in Kenneth H. Brown's *The Brig* (1963)—provides an immediate theatrical intensity which is supposed to open up metaphorically. As though to make clear his larger intentions, Rabe—a Vietnam veteran himself—put the war behind him with *The Orphan* (1973) and *In the Boom Boom Room* (1974). By the time *Streamers* (1976) appeared, it was clear that the army barracks in which the action takes place is the setting, not the subject; Rabe is once again involved with themes which he has been concerned with in all his plays. In a letter to the Russian producers of *Sticks and Bones,* printed in the *New York Times* (March 18, 1973), Rabe complained about the way his play was produced in Moscow, insisting that "it is about distortion of perception for the sake of personal need." All the plays are about that distortion and about its consequences—violent usually, destructive certainly. Rabe's sense of things suggests that he is a naturalist in the strict sense of the word, working O'Neill territory but, as yet, without O'Neill's equipment.

There was a moment of shock during the unctuous interview with the Vietnam veteran in Jean-Claude van Itallie's *TV* (1966), at least when one first saw it, but compared with *Sticks and Bones* it seems now to have been an easy satiric point to have scored. Since Rabe's play is a sustained theatrical metaphor, it is unfair to compare it with van Itallie's work, most of which consists of short plays that are little more than satiric or parodistic sketches. This is particularly true of early work, such as *It's Almost Like Being* (1964), which, whatever its larger intentions, comes across as a nicely done parody of a standard movie musical which would not be out of place in a clever Broadway revue (if such a thing still existed). Even *America Hurrah* (1966), a trilogy which brought van Itallie a wider audience, is only an extension in fact and in spirit of his earlier off-off-Broadway work; two of the three pieces—*TV* is the new one—had been done a year earlier as individual plays. Although van Itallie says in a note in *Contemporary Dramatists* (1973) that *America Hurrah* is an example of a play he wrote alone—contrasting it to his work as scenarist with a group—one of the sections, the platitudinous *Interview*, suggests an actors' exercise called the transformation, used regularly by Joseph Chaikin's Open Theatre, with which van Itallie became associated in 1963. In the exercise, a performer, with no formal transition, becomes a new character (as in *Interview*) or the same character in a new situation or at another time. Not simply a training device, the transformation is a way of questioning the conventional idea of reality. Much of the early work of Megan Terry—certainly the pieces collected in *Four Plays* (1967)—reflects both the technical and the philosophical implications of the transformation. If *Interview* is the Open Theatre filtered through van Itallie, his most impressive play, *The Serpent: A Ceremony* (1969), is a direct product of his work with the group; ironically, to anyone who has seen the Open Theatre perform *The Serpent*, van Itallie's words are the least imaginative contribution to the total theatrical event. For a writer to cease to be the controlling voice in the preparation of a script, to become one person within a creative group—as van Itallie did in the Open Theatre—was not at all unusual toward the end of the 1960s, when the theater collective emerged as an alternative theater. Since, for such groups, texts were starting points at best, only a few pieces, of which *The Serpent* is one, have been printed. Other examples include The Living Theatre's *Paradise Now* (1971) and The Performance Group's *Dionysus in 69* (1970).

Moving from groups back again to individuals, one finds such a flood of plays and playwrights that there is danger of drowning in a sea of names. Martin Duberman. When his very effective documentary play *In White America* (1963), a history of the American black in which the demand for freedom is regularly stifled for the sake of the status quo, opened in New York, Duberman was taken as a history professor who had lost his way and stumbled into the theater; he stayed, continued to write plays, and recently, as in *Visions of Kerouac* (1976), he has begun to use the theater, as a gay writer, to ex-

plore the crippling effects of American sexual attitudes. Israel Horovitz. An inventive and prolific playwright, Horovitz has been oddly
burdened by his early success with *The Indian Wants the Bronx*
(1968); for all the imagination running loose in the later plays, he
has not been able to come up with a dramatic action as compelling
as the one in *Bronx,* in which two young toughs tease, then torture an
East Indian who speaks no English and can judge their intentions
only by their shifting tones of voice. David Mamet. Consistently
praised for his ear for American speech, Mamet shows—in *Sexual
Perversity in Chicago* (1974), *A Life in the Theatre* (1977), *The Water
Engine* (1977), and *American Buffalo* (1975), his finest play to date
—that his concern with language is social as well as aesthetic, that
he is fascinated by the way words dictate ideas and ideas, action. Ronald Tavel. Julie Bovasso. Tom Eyen. A. R. Gurney, Jr. Marsha Norman. Playwrights of all persuasions, working in any number of forms.
But I have to stop somewhere, and I keep thinking of those playwrights from earlier decades with a single interesting play or a free-
floating talent for dialogue or a feel for dramatic event who have
somehow been shaved away in the process of compression. It will
be another ten years before we know who really demands a paragraph
in the pocket history of American drama in the 1970s.

The line above has the look of a curtain line about it, but—as so
often happens in recent American drama—it is only a teaser. Any
reader equipped with a color code will have noticed that Lorraine
Hansberry, who serves an exemplary function at the beginning of
this essay, is the only black dramatist mentioned so far. I have saved
a discussion of the black playwrights until this point not because
I think they should be confined in a critical ghetto, but because the
changing place of the black dramatist in the American theater forms
a story in its own right. In recent years, historians in search of roots
have worked their way back through American drama listing black
theaters, black playwrights, black performers who have flourished at
one time or another. The impulse is sound, but the lists cannot mask
the fact that, with rare exceptions, blacks have never been (perhaps
"have never been allowed to be" would be more accurate) a part of
serious theater in the United States. Even the songs of Noble Sissle
and Eubie Blake, which are finding new audiences today, were in musicals not far removed from the caricature of the minstrel show. There
was not a noticeable change in the years just after the war, no rush of
black playwrights to Broadway. Louis Peterson, whose *Take a Giant
Step* (1953) is an occasionally touching but completely conventional

play about adolescence, was an exception; Langston Hughes, who had written plays in the 1930s, adapted some of his Simple stories in the off-Broadway *Simply Heavenly* (1957), a romantic comedy set against the background of a bar, filled for the most part with sweet eccentrics. It was Lorraine Hansberry and *A Raisin in the Sun* which marked a real change.

A play about a black family in a Chicago ghetto, *Raisin* has a protagonist who learns, painfully, that being a man is not the same thing as being a success. As I indicated at the beginning of this chapter, the play shares themes and its realistic style with much of the rest of the American repertory. Hansberry was deeply concerned with what it means to be black, particularly to be a black writer, as so many of her letters and speeches attest—those in *To Be Young, Gifted and Black* (1969), the play-portrait of the dramatist compiled after her death by her husband, Robert Nemiroff. What being a black writer did not mean for Hansberry was a limiting of her subject matter. Her second play, *The Sign in Sidney Bruslein's Window* (1964), set in Greenwich Village, depicts a representative group of Villagers, only one of them black; her middle-class Jewish hero passes from self-protective indifference to commitment to despair before he comes again, tentatively, to social and personal possibility. When Hansberry died in 1965, she left an unfinished play about contemporary Africa, *Les Blancs*. In the form we have it, finished by Nemiroff and Charlotte Zaltzberg, it shows both Hansberry's continuing attraction to protagonists who must work through their own confusions to a sense of self and her growing interest in the techniques of nonrealistic drama which had already surfaced in *Sidney Brustein*.

Hansberry's work marked not only a beginning but an end. By the time *Sidney Brustein* opened, two other plays—James Baldwin's *Blues for Mister Charlie* and LeRoi Jones's *Dutchman*—had carried the new black militancy to the stage. Both plays are more sophisticated than they were sometimes thought to be in the excitement that surrounded them in 1964, but Baldwin and Jones did herald a new group of playwrights who—unlike Hansberry—put the emphasis on the adjective, not the noun, in the label "black dramatist." *Blues for Mister Charlie* is a complicated play, working in several times at once and trying, through the various stories, to make a number of points, both ideational and dramatic. The trial which sits at the center of the play is both a comment on the black and white communities that try to use it and are used by it and an occasion for self-revelation for the play's white liberal and its black Christian moderate. The central figures are the angry young black man and the poor white who kills him, attempts by Baldwin to give flesh to his concept of the fatal interrelationship of black and white in America, an idea he treated at length in *The Fire Next Time,* which was published the year before *Blues* was produced. The difficulty with *Blues,* as a play, lies in the failure of that flesh. Although Baldwin supplies his characters with a wealth of biographical data, presumably to give them sound naturalistic motivation, they never escape a tendency toward abstraction. After the production of *Blues,* Baldwin's early play, *The Amen Corner* (1955), a fairly standard maturation story which in setting, subject, and tone suggests his first novel, *Go Tell It on the Mountain* (1953), was resurrected—produced and printed. Despite the incidental virtues of both plays, they indicate that the dramatic form is not a congenial one for Baldwin; there were no plays after *Blues.*

Dutchman is a much better play than *Blues for Mister Charlie.* It works on two levels at once. Lula and Clay are real people, confronting one another on a real subway. At the same time, the setting —the black as well as the white riders—becomes a metaphor for an acquiescent society, accepting a situation which creates the black desire to kill, provides the masks to stifle it, and, when those masks are insufficient, permits a murderous white reaction. It is not the suggestion of ritual in the killing nor the ideational point of the play that gives *Dutchman* dramatic strength; it is the frightening vitality of Lula—and, to a lesser extent, Clay—that makes it so effective. Jones presumably wants to give similar force to Walker in *The Slave* (1964), but he is all racial identity with none of the concreteness of Lula and Clay. The protagonist of *The Toilet* (1964), a boy who reluctantly joins the other blacks in beating a white friend, is more interesting; and the play, despite its tearful ending, is the only one of Jones's other works that approaches the quality of *Dutchman.* Shortly after the success of that play, Jones turned his back on the theater, on the white world in which he had functioned as poet and editor. As the essays in *Home* (1966) indicate, Jones moved from "Cuba Libre" (1960), in which he can still use "we" to mean "we Americans," to the work of 1964 and 1965, in which his identification is purely black and the prospect is destruction. Newly named Imamu Amiri Baraka, he began to write solely for black audiences, to use the play as a weapon or a teaching tool. Criticism—particularly white criticism—has no way of judging a play's effectiveness in such terms; it can only shake its head in the face of a work like *A Black Mass* (1966) with its unpleasant amalgam of mysticism and racist propaganda. Of Baraka's plays, only *Slave Ship* (1969) has reached the mixed audience that admires *Dutchman.*

In the mid-1960s, as Jones turned into Baraka, the black theater began to divide into those—like the Negro Ensemble Company—who wanted to reach as wide an American audience as possible, and those —like the New Lafayette Theatre in Harlem—who saw themselves as black voices in a black community. Douglas Turner Ward, one of the founders of NEC, Lonne Elder III, and Adrienne Kennedy—three very different playwrights—are representative of the first group. The two short plays that make up Ward's successful double bill, *Happy Ending* and *Day of Absence* (1965), are little more than extended jokes, almost as broad as Ossie Davis's *Purlie Victorious* (1961). Elder's *Ceremonies in Dark Old Men* (1969) is a Negro family play which, like *A Raisin in the Sun,* has its aesthetic roots in traditional American realism. Kennedy's work—*Funnyhouse of a Negro* (1964), the two 1965 one-acts published as *Cities in Bezique* (1969)—is complex and allusive, putting the techniques of the traditional avant-garde to work in the service of the author's pained sensibility.

Although the American Place production of *The Electronic Nigger and Others* (1968), a bill of three short plays, gave Ed Bullins his first wide recognition as a playwright, he was—for a time at least—the strongest voice for the separatist theater, both as editor of *Black Theatre* and through his work with the New Lafayette. He did continue to have plays produced for general audiences, but when *The Duplex* (1970) was performed at Lincoln Center in 1972, he complained that white hands had turned his black material into a minstrel show; anyone who saw the 1975 roadshow production of *The Fabulous Miss Marie* (1971), in which black hands did the shaping, knows that it is easy for the Bullins material to come across as comic caricature, not far removed from that in the popular Melvin Van Peebles shows—*Ain't Supposed to Die a Natural Death* (1971) and *Don't Play Us Cheap* (1972). Bullins has written a number of overtly political plays, such as those collected in *Four Dynamite Plays* (1971), but the bulk of his work is not revolutionary, ideationally or technically. Perhaps most representative of his drama are those plays— *In New England Winter* (1967), *In the Wine Time* (1968), *Miss Marie, The Duplex*—part of a projected cycle of twenty, in which, through recurring characters, he explores black society, celebrating the vigor of the people and at the same time showing their acquiescence in their own situation.

During the 1970s the pattern of play-going among blacks changed. In increasing numbers, they began to attend the commercial theaters in large cities. The result has been not a sudden blossoming of serious black drama, but—as one might have predicted from the history of

432

Broadway—the emergence of Melvin Van Peebles as a celebrated show-business giant and an increase in musicals like Charlie Smalls's *The Wiz* (1975) and the anthological *Bubbling Brown Sugar* (1975). Some serious plays, such as Joseph A. Walker's *The River Niger* (1972) and Ron Milner's *What the Wine-Sellers Buy* (1974), have done well with this new audience. Among the newer black playwrights, the two attracting the most attention are Philip Hayes Dean, whose *The Sty of the Blind Pig* (1971) has a remarkable scene depicting religio-sexual ecstasy, and Charles Fuller, who has turned to one of the uglier incidents in American history for *The Brownsville Raid* (1976).

It would be inappropriate to write an essay on American drama and not give at least a nod to two popular genres—farce and musical comedy—in which Americans have excelled. I will not attempt an elaborate generic definition for farce, but simply assume that it is a recognizable form in which the characters are types, identified by their compulsions or their tics, and in which the action is an exterior one and the business frenetic. French farces tend to be about sex and English farces about the unlikelihood of sex, but American farces have more variety, often growing out of the occupation of the main characters—advertising farces, racetrack farces, show-business farces. Their tone is generally irreverent and, at their best, when the playwright can control American idiom and use the wisecrack without letting it upstage the dramatic context, they are more interesting verbally than a great many more serious, more literary plays. They exist often in an impure form, having been infested by satire or character comedy or, alas, sentiment. Farce has flourished on the American stage since the early nineteenth century, but it was toward the end of the century that it found its American voice most clearly. Its best decades were the 1920s and 1930s. In recent years, acting companies have discovered that there is more theatrical vitality in 1930s farces like *Boy Meets Girl*, by Bella and Samuel Spewack, and *Three Men on a Horse*, by John Cecil Holm and George Abbott, than in the once respectable artistic endeavors of the period—the verse tragedies of Maxwell Anderson, say, or even the more lugubrious myth-making experiments of Eugene O'Neill. And probably more truth about America, too.

Farce fell on evil days in the postwar years. Some of the verbal quality can be found in the plays of Garson Kanin, who worked for years with George Abbott, but *Born Yesterday* (1946) is essentially a didactic political comedy—a very good one—and *The Rat Race* (1949) and *The Live Wire* (1950) are satiric character comedies. Even 1930s farceurs like Samuel Spewack, in *Two Blind Mice* (1949), and Howard

Lindsay and Russel Crouse, in *State of the Union* (1945), turned to the kind of political comedy popular in the late 1940s before the witch hunters came along to stifle even the mildly satiric impulses in commercial theater. During the 1950s, Broadway comedy went soft and sentimental, ran to marital plays with happy endings which seemed less an inheritance from classical comedy than testimony to the status quo. This cannot be laid completely to the repressive political atmosphere of the period because the seeds of this kind of comedy had already been planted in the 1940s with the liberal political variation on the mushy final curtain in *State of the Union* and Fay Kanin's *Goodbye, My Fancy* (1948). For whatever combination of reasons, farce disappeared from Broadway in the 1950s. Its tone was certainly antithetical to that of a decade famous for its blandness, its spirit of conformity. The comedies were the equivalent of the conventional serious drama of the period—the light at the top of the stairs. The only genuinely irreverent comedy of the decade is Samuel Taylor's *The Pleasure of His Company* (1958), in which the heroine chooses her father and fun over "the dull comfort of marriage"; since Taylor's work runs to elegance—see *Sabrina Fair* (1953)—rather than farce, the 1950s audiences, pleased with the feel of the play, tended to overlook the implications of the heroine's choice and to miss altogether the gentle incestuous note in the father's flirtatiousness.

Farce, as I describe it at the beginning of this section, is almost as much an attitude as it is a dramatic form, an American way of responding to situations which is so pervasive that it is difficult to imagine its withering away. Of course, it did no such thing. It went underground and began to pop up in odd places. One of the oddest is the theater work of Saul Bellow. It can be seen most clearly in the three one-act plays that make up *Under the Weather* (1966), although Bellow does mix comic pathos with his slapstick. Perhaps because Bellow is the author, one expects the plays to have "meaning," but a farce's meaning lies in its dramatic action, and with these plays Bellow follows tradition, keeps all messages implicit. He could not do that with *The Last Analysis* (1964), that strange blend of farce and philosophical comedy; a patchwork quilt of borrowings from all genres, *Analysis* may not belong in a discussion of farce, but it is such a fascinating play, with a marvelously vital central character, that it was certain to elbow its way somehow into this chapter.

There are farcical elements in the work of Neil Simon, one of the most successful playwrights ever to grace the American commercial stage, but farce seems as ill at ease in his company as it does with Saul Bellow. There are almost enough doors opening and closing in

Come Blow Your Horn (1961) to earn it a cross-cultural listing as a French farce, but it is really a Jewish family comedy about growing up. That Simon is a playwright who dresses character comedy in wisecracks became increasingly clear with *Barefoot in the Park* (1963) and *The Odd Couple* (1965). With *Plaza Suite* (1968) a note of desperation appeared, and his vision of impotent people in a malevolent society—*Last of the Red Hot Lovers* (1969), *The Prisoner of Second Avenue* (1971)—became so oppressive that he turned to the story of Job—*God's Favorite* (1974)—presumably to lighten his work. Audiences who would not have touched black comedy with asbestos gloves presumably found screamingly funny his slow descent into contemporary hell. With *Chapter Two* (1977) a new positive note has appeared in Simon's work, but the tedious discursive quality of the play suggests what may have been implicit in all his work—that Simon is Willian Inge with one-liners.

Farce also found its way into the work of the off-Broadway and then the off-off-Broadway playwrights. In retrospect, it is clear that much of the appeal of plays like Arthur Kopit's *Oh, Dad* and Murray Schisgal's *Luv* lay in their use of standard farce devices; the meaning we extracted from the plays—and it was there to be extracted—was only the intellectual dressing that masked a sigh of relief at having an old friend back on the American stage where he belonged. Some of these playwrights discovered that they were farceurs in earnest and have embraced the form without apology. In *Jimmy Shine* and the lamentable double bill *The Chinese, and Dr. Fish* (1970), one could see Schisgal trying to get out of his significance cocoon, and with *All Over Town* (1974), he finally gave Broadway a farce, contemporary in setting and subject matter, with the look, the sound, the rhythm of the pure American genre. After beginning his dramatic career with an interesting destruction parable, *And Things That Go Bump in the Night* (1964), Terrence McNally wandered across off-off-Broadway stages, sampling a variety of genres, until—with *Bad Habits* (1974) and *The Ritz* (1975)—he came home to farce.

Unlike farce, which had to pick its way through the postwar theater, finding a resting place where it could, musical comedy grew richer, stronger, more powerful—until, bloated, it stumbled over its *hubris* and had to begin again. The last part of that story was not to come until the 1960s; the possibilities for the musical comedy seemed boundless in the years right after the war. *Oklahoma!* (1943) was where it all began, theater historians would say, the show that brought musical comedy to its first maturity. A neat formulation, not necessarily a true one. At least since *The Black Crook* (1866), which is sometimes called the first American musical comedy, the genre has been trying to pull its pieces together—its songs, its story, its comic turns, its dances. Its history is a movement toward integration. *Oklahoma!* is important in a consideration of postwar theater because it was the first show that Richard Rodgers wrote with Oscar Hammerstein II and its success helped set the taste for musical comedy immediately after the war. Romantic shows in which the sentiment is moist, the comedy broad, and the corn as high as an elephant's eye, these very American relatives of the operetta flourished in the 1940s. Harold Arlen's *Bloomer Girl* (1944) and the Frederick Loewe–Alan Jay Lerner *Brigadoon* (1947) are examples, but Rodgers and Hammerstein are the ones who perfected the product with *Carousel* (1945), *South Pacific* (1949), and *The King and I* (1951). *The Sound of Music* (1959) is a late-blooming example of the phenomenon, but it shows all the signs of mechanical breakdown that were apparent in earlier Rodgers and Hammerstein shows like *Pipe Dream* (1955) and *Flower Drum Song* (1958).

While *Oklahoma!* and *Carousel* were bringing tears to the eyes of honest men, Leonard Bernstein's *On the Town* (1944), with a book by Betty Comden and Adolph Green, was doing justice to the other tradition in musical comedy, the one that reached back to vaudeville and farce rather than operetta. The story of three sailors on a one-day leave in New York City, it is witty, tough, irreverent. It is also tender—about young love and New York City—but its allegiances are with a genre that wears its heart on a wisecrack. Although they are usually set in a musical-comedy world which vaguely resembles contemporary America, shows like *On the Town* are no more realistic than the romantic ones. Frank Loesser's *Guys and Dolls* (1950), one of the best of the genre, is a Damon Runyan fairy tale. The two varieties of musical are sometimes identified according to setting—the romantic taking place in the American past or an exotic present, the other on the immediate urban scene. Yet when Jule Styne used pre–World War I America in *High Button Shoes* (1947) and the 1920s in *Gentlemen Prefer Blondes* (1949), he was clearly working the nonromantic side of the musical-comedy street, and it becomes clear, when one listens to the philosophy of Lorelei Lee in *Blondes,* that it is tone more than setting that differentiates the two kinds of show. In any case, neither form stays within its bounds. The book that Bella and Samuel Spewack wrote for Cole Porter's *Kiss Me, Kate* (1948) mixes a standard backstage romance with *The Taming of the Shrew,* and Porter's lyrics, studiously naughty, refuse to let any part of the musical be taken too seriously. For *Candide,* Leonard Bernstein created a superb operetta score which the lyrics—by Richard Wilbur, John Latouche, Dorothy Parker, Bernstein himself—and Lillian Hellman's book tinge with acid; in *West Side Story,* with the help of Arthur Laurents, Bernstein put *Romeo and Juliet* among the street gangs of New York.

In whatever tradition, the musicals of the 1940s and the early 1950s came increasingly to depend on a heavy book, one that was more than an excuse for song and dance numbers. Plots were more complicated than they had been in the simple days of boy meets girl; characters were presented with more psychological validity (see Rose in the Jule Styne–Arthur Laurents *Gypsy*); social reform took center stage (see the Kurt Weill–Maxwell Anderson *Lost in the Stars,* 1949). It was a time of great vitality and variety in the musical, and the general quality of the work was high all along a line that reached from opera— Marc Blitzstein's *Regina* (1949), Gian-Carlo Menotti's *The Medium* (1947) and *The Consul* (1950)—to revue—Harold Rome's *Call Me Mister* (1946), Charles Gaynor's *Lend an Ear* (1948). This swarm of names does not begin to identify all the solid work of the period, but it does give some sense of a flourishing that was shortly to be crushed under gigantism. As shows became larger, more lavish, more earnest, more expensive, they became less imaginative, less witty, less tender. By the 1960s, Broadway was a cage for singing pachyderms. It was rare for a show to appear—Frank Loesser's *How to Succeed in Business without Really Trying* (1961) is a happy exception—in which the goal of integration was reflected in consistency of idea and tone rather than in excess of stuffing. At about this time, the musical went off-Broadway and found success working small; *The Fantasticks* (1960), by Harvey Schmidt and Tom Jones, is the long-running example. Or smaller still, off-off-Broadway, as with James Wise's *Dames at Sea* (1966), which began at Caffe Cino. Every season there are monsters lumbering toward Broadway to be born, but fewer and fewer of them each year, for Broadway has come to realize that it is a controlling idea, not size, that gives finished form to a musical. Stephen Sondheim, who was lyricist to Styne for *Gypsy,* to Bernstein for *West Side Story,* has become the most respected composer of the 1970s, partly because—with the too sentimental *Company* (1970) and the innovative *A Little Night Music* (1973)—he has begun to develop small-chorus shows, chamber musicals on a large stage. Fred Ebb and John Kander, with *Cabaret* (1966), *70, Girls, 70* (1971), and *Chicago* (1975), have developed the toughest new satirical voice in American musical comedy. As mehitabel used to say, "there's a dance in the old dame yet."

It is now more than thirty years since *The Glass Menagerie* opened on Broadway, and that is more years than fell between *Bound East for Cardiff* and the Williams play. It should be a segment of time large enough to build a neat summary on, but it remains open ended, and conclusions, judgments, have a way of oozing out of the opening, sinking into the porous ground of the future. I have described real changes and real achievements, but changes have a way of ringing changes on changes, and I have also described real achievements that looked not so real ten years after the fact. Everything about the period still seems tentative to me.

10

Poetry:
After Modernism
Daniel Hoffman

A great disorder is an order.
STEVENS, "Connoisseurs of Chaos"

I am the man—I suffer'd—I was there.
WHITMAN, "Song of Myself"

P OETS," as Ezra Pound wrote long ago, "are
the antennae of the race." The violent disjunctions characteristic of late twentieth-cen-
tury life—the breakup of established economic, political, and social
institutions, the accelerated separation of the contemporary self from
the history of the race, the alienation of the individual in a cosmos felt
to be a field of force rather than a divinely ordered harmony—all these
disruptions were recorded, as though on seismographs, in Eliot's *The
Waste Land* (1922), Stevens's *Harmonium*, Williams's *Spring and All*
(both 1923), and Pound's *A Draft of XVI Cantos* (1925). Each American poet who has come of age since then has had to face his situation
in the terms these early modernist masters have disposed. There would
seem to have been three main choices. Some, like Frost (who ante-
dates all this) and those who chose to be influenced by Eliot's *Poems*
(1920), tried to adopt conventional meters and modes of versification
to the exigencies of contemporary themes; inevitably, the tension between their traditional poetics and their content points toward ironic
lyricism, as in the work of John Crowe Ransom, Allen Tate, and the
other Fugitive poets. Opposed to them were poets who continued the
impulses of the modernist movement—among them George Oppen
and Louis Zukofsky with their Objectivist movement of the 1930s,
Kenneth Rexroth in the 1940s, and, in the 1950s, Charles Olson. Later
in time and greater in number are those younger poets who, starting
their careers under the aegis of conventional versification (with all
its implications for the continuity of both history and literature),
break rebelliously with tradition, allying themselves with one or an-

439

other of the early modernists or their disciples; some work out a personal aesthetic, an individual style by which to declare independence from all poetry hitherto.

American poetry is always, at its best—as Whitman said of *Leaves of Grass*—"a language experiment." Our poets of first intensity are by definition bold and individual stylists. There is not so much a period style as many styles in the period; how many of these embody "a change of heart," as Auden wrote a new style must, remains to be seen. Pound had early written that "technique is the test of a man's sincerity," and American poets, like their fellow countrymen in other fields, are tinkerers; much of their energy has gone into refining or devising poetic contraptions that work on new principles, hence open up untested possibilities to the imagination intent on making verbal models of states of feeling.

By 1945 it was hard to think of Robert Frost as an innovator; one forgot how unfamiliar his monologues of seeming Yankee talk had looked to readers before and after World War I. Frost found his metier at forty and stayed with it for another forty years. He had promised, in the first poem in *A Boys Will* (1913), "They would not find me changed from him they knew— / Only more sure of all I thought was true." Consistency was his special virtue. To the end his lines, in what he called "loose iambics," were marked with his characteristic tension between verse meter and speech rhythms. If he took no part in the modernist break-up of formal verse, he still laid the foreground for a new aesthetic of poetry as speech. He was an intermediary between Wordsworth and William Carlos Williams.

Drink and be whole again beyond confusion.

So ends the last major poem of Frost's long career. The poem is "Directive," the year 1947, the injunction a solace against a time of "all this now too much for us," the draught proffered in a Grail cup hidden in childhood among the roots of a cedar—no doubt a New Hampshire Cedar of Lebanon. Frost's entire *oeuvre* was a search for such a draught, which, when found, offered, as he says in the preface to his *Collected Poems* (1939), only "a momentary stay against confusion." Few of his contemporaries and none of his successors have been able to resist confusion with the wholeness Frost advises, but could not embody, in his poems.

He does, however, discover, over and over, the brevity of achieved moments of poetic vision—and that vision proved increasingly stoical as the poet acknowledged the forces of darkness and chaos in human experience (as in "Design" and "Provide, Provide"). In the

440

years before his death in 1963 Frost became the most widely acclaimed poet in America since Longfellow. Much of his popular fame rested on a widely held misapprehension about his work: he was regarded as a simple pastoral poet, a New England local colorist whose early dramatic poems distanced suffering by making it remote in place, time, and circumstance. Randall Jarrell (in *Poetry and the Age,* 1953) and Lionel Trilling, in a controversial lecture first published in *Partisan Review,* 1959, pointed to the cosmic and personal desolation at the heart of Frost's snowbound bucolics.

Rather than his late writings, it was Frost's living presence as a Great Stone Face, with his deep roots in Thoreau's ruggedly individualistic New England (*Walden,* Frost wrote, was his "favorite poem"), which made him seem a dominant figure in the years after World War II. *A Masque of Reason* (1945) and *A Masque of Mercy* (1947), his only efforts at extended composition, ventured into poetic drama without conquering the stage. *Steeple Bush* (1947) and *In the Clearing* (1962) complete his legacy of some four hundred briefer poems, but his best work had been done. It was not given to Frost in old age to buttress his stays against confusion with a world-ordering system of thought like that of Yeats or with a religious certainty like Eliot's. If there is lacking in his work the amplitudes of poets such as those, if Lawrance Thompson's three-volume biography reveals the white-headed sage to have been often a vain, ruthless, and selfish man, still none can deny that *Complete Poems,* his complete works (1967), contains several score of poems essential to the American imagination. As Galway Kinnell writes in an affectionate tribute to Frost,

> we think of a man who was cursed
> Neither with the mystical all-lovingness of Walt Whitman
> Nor with Melville's anguish to know and to suffer,
> And yet cursed . . .

In illuminating his own sufferings, Frost leavened ours.

Wallace Stevens, like his contemporary Frost, did not publish a book of poems until he was past forty. He, too, achieved in his late flowering a prospect of the poetic enterprise to which the remainder of his career stayed true. Born in 1879, Stevens before the turn of this century attended Harvard, where he heard the lectures Santayana incorporated into *Interpretations of Poetry and Religion* (1900), a debt everywhere implicit in Stevens's work and specified in "To an Old Philosopher in Rome" (in *The Auroras of Autumn,* 1950). Stevens had not the pastoral mode of Frost to disguise his sense of desola-

441

tion; his early poems "The Snow Man" and "Domination of Black" (*Harmonium,* 1923) create a soulscape, the vacancy of which it was Stevens's self-chosen task, until his death in 1955, to fill with structures of imaginative invention, hence with delight. His entire enterprise can be seen as heroic, a brilliant attack against *le malaise du fin de siècle,* against the emptiness of Heaven, where "the death of one god is the death of all." The withering away of traditional religion leaves the poet of the twentieth century with only the impoverished earth and "the gaiety of language" as his patrimony. So it is that Stevens's poems are all elaborations of the theme of Coleridge's dejection ode: how to make poetry, how to invent joy, in the absence of a consoling sacred text or a divine being. (Frost, too, had asked, in his little poem "The Oven Bird," "what to make of a diminished thing.") Stevens's "Sunday Morning" (1915) finds his protagonist not at church but questioning the certainties no religion can give her, finding, at the end, "Ambiguous undulations" in the flight of "casual flocks of pigeons." Three decades later, in "Esthétique du Mal" (1944), although we are "Natives of poverty" in this "terra infidel," nonetheless "The greatest poverty is not to live / In a physical world." In "Angel Surrounded by Paysans" (*Auroras of Autumn*), "the necessary angel of earth" is "only . . . A figure half seen, or seen for a moment, a man / Of the mind." Divinity itself, insofar as we can know it, is "of the mind," a fleeting knowledge of a part of our own humanity. The poet who began with "a "mind of winter" ("The Snow Man") in old age writes "Credences of Summer" (in *Transport to Summer,* 1947): confronting the unmitigated energy of the sun "Without evasion by a single metaphor," with "clairvoyant eye" he beholds "its essential barrenness" and says, "this is the centre that I seek." In poem after poem Stevens sought this unmediated power at the center of experience, sought to define "The essential poem at the centre of things" —which proves to be "something seen and known in lesser poems," since "One poem proves another and the whole" ("A Primitive like an Orb"). Thus the act of imagining is its own validation; each discrete poem is a part of the created universe the poet imagines and makes possible for the imagination of his readers to share. Not for nothing did this celebrant of the poetic process itself, of meta-poetry, call his first collection *Harmonium,* or entitle his longest exploration of his constant theme "Notes toward a Supreme Fiction."

Yet it must be acknowledged that Stevens's virtues have the defects of their merits. He proclaims the redemptive possibilities of language in a body of poetry more hermetically concerned than any hitherto in America with the power of the imagination to free the mind from what Yeats called "the desolation of reality"—and yet not to do so in a cloud of Neoplatonic idealism but rather, as Santayana advises, to make the mind's constructs from the detritus of the real. Or as Stevens puts it, "To picnic in the ruins that we leave." This enterprise is noble, yet his repudiations, whether conscious or temperamental, are a measure of the desolation that his work must fill. In that work there are no relationships between the poetic speaker and other persons, no passions, neither human love nor hatred, no sense of the self as a member of any society save the select company of abstract characters the poet has imagined. Of course there is no God, and neither angels, priests, sin, sinners, nor suffering mankind.

Tocqueville, describing the effects of democracy upon poetic tradition, had written in 1837 that "when skepticism depopulates heaven . . . in the end democracy diverts the imagination from all that is external to man, and fixes it on man alone." Stevens takes this course to a further conclusion than had anyone earlier in his generation. Heaven being empty, Stevens attempts to fill its "dividing and indifferent blue" with an imagined hero whom, among his many guises, he calls "major man": a hero of capable imagination. In "Notes toward a Supreme Fiction" he limns this figure:

> The major abstraction is the idea of man
> And major man is its exponent, abler
> In the abstract than in his singular

—since the quality he celebrates is the imagination of man, larger than that of any individual. Time and again Stevens attempts to conceive and define this "difficult, inanimate visage." In "A Primitive like an Orb" he personifies this divine yet human efflatus comprised of the qualities of creative mind writ large:

> Here, then, is an abstraction given head,
> A giant on the horizon, given arms,
> A massive body and long legs, stretched out,
> A definition with an illustration, not
> Too exactly labelled, a large among the smalls
> Of it, a close, parental magnitude,
> At the centre on the horizon, concentrum, grave
> And prodigious person, patron of origins.

Such texts confirm the contention of the critic Harold Bloom, among others, that Stevens fulfills Emerson's prophetic essay "The Poet." If in some respects Stevens's themes are continuations of those of the Romantic movement, in others he is in thought as well as style one of the masters of modernist poetry. He gives the illusion of the

443

self's autonomy, of the imagination's spinning redemptive fables out of its own "clairvoyant eye," independently of place, time, or history. In this, his work resembles post-Symbolist French poetry, such as that of René Char and Pierre Reverdy, both influences upon a later generation of American poets. Like them, Stevens was immersed in the late nineteenth-century tradition of French Symbolism which helped also to form the poetic method of T. S. Eliot. It is inexact to say that Stevens carried out in in English *l'esthétique de l'art pour l'art,* but it would be untrue to deny that it stayed with him.

Although Stevens lived in Hartford, Connecticut, and worked as a vice president of an insurance firm, taking little part in the New York literary scene, it had not always been so. Reclusive though he was, he began as a fellow contributor to the magazines that published Eliot, Pound, Williams, Marianne Moore, and the other poets of *l'entre deux guerres.* Now that we have become accustomed to his "gaiety of language," we can see that in poetic method he is much more conventional than any of these contemporaries. His rhythm, true, is a highly personal variation upon blank verse, freed from metrical constraints, pulsing to a drummer deep within the ear of the poet who writes with such accuracy of phrasal or clausal lineation. But few poets of this century are as true as he to the intellectual architecture of the poem: no renunciations here of paraphrasable argument, or structural balance, or the engagement of mind as a maker of the poem. Sometimes the imagery in Stevens works with the surprising logic of dream, but usually it is the conscious, not the unconscious, mind that manipulates his ideas of order. The unconscious manifests itself more likely in his "lingua franca et jocundissima"—which becomes "the imagination's Latin," embodying the delight and the value he seeks, and finds.

Stevens died only a decade after the postwar period began, but his reputation has risen ever since. His *Collected Poems* appeared in 1954, followed three years later by *Opus Posthumous* (fugitive poems, short prose pieces, and his seminal *pensées.* "Adagia"), then by *Letters* (1966) and his journals, entitled *Souvenirs and Prophecies* (1977), the last two edited by his daughter Holly Stevens. *The Necessary Angel: Essays on Reality and the Imagination,* the poet's effort to define his aesthetic assumptions, had appeared in 1951. Stevens's influence on other poets has been pervasive and independent of the critical fashions of writing about his work. On the one hand, his *Harmonium,* with its pure play of language, its ecstatic hullabaloos, altered the possibilities of diction in American poetry. On the other, his late, long meditative poems, in which the autonomous imagination creates a world "to take the place / of empty heaven and its hymns," have been models for A. R. Ammons and John Ashbery, among others, in their explorations of the perceptible world. Which is to say that many have joined the chorus in Theodore Roethke's affectionate tribute, "A Rouse for Stevens (To Be Sung in a Young Poets' Saloon)":

> Roar 'em, whore 'em, cockalorum,
> The Muses, they must all adore him,
> Wallace Stevens—are we *for* him?
> Brother, he's our father!

The most admired work of poetry published during the war was T. S. Eliot's *Four Quartets* (1943). Here was the mature achievement of a great poet who, in a time when the world itself was in jeopardy, found more than "momentary stays" in the contemplation of the timeless moments in which the soul experiences eternity. These moments are poised against the surrounding catastrophe, most explicitly evoked in the final quartet, "Little Gidding," when the speaker meets "a familiar compound ghost"—his guide, compounded of the shades of Virgil and Yeats, who leads him through the inferno of the air raid patrol in London: "From wrong to wrong the exasperated spirit / Proceeds, unless restored by that refining fire / Where you must move in measure, like a dancer." The authority of *Four Quartets* resides, of course, not in paraphrasable meanings of its contemplation of mortality intersected by moments of timelessness, but in the artistic perfection of a philosophic work of magnitude. The effect of Eliot's achievement upon his successors was overpowering. It is as visible in the intensity of the rebellions against what Delmore Schwartz (who had earlier praised him) in 1949 called "The Literary Dictatorship of T. S. Eliot" as in the prevalence, until his death in 1965, of modes of writing modeled on his example and the tenets of his influential essays.

In the end it was his essays more than his poems which carried his influence into the country he had left so long before. Although Eliot, from *Prufrock* (1917) through *The Waste Land* (1922), had, along with Pound and Joyce and Lawrence, been a prime mover of the revolutionary aesthetic of modernism, after *Ash Wednesday* (1930) and his proclaiming himself a "classicist in literature, royalist in politics, and anglo-catholic in religion," he stood, in the minds of most contemporaries, for the preeminence in literature of a traditional culture outside the self, a European culture on which the poet must draw and to which his work may contribute. The authors about whom he wrote in *Selected Essays* (1932, 1950) became the monuments in college curricula: Dante, the Elizabethan dramatists, the Metaphysical poets, Baudelaire. Although recent criticism of Eliot has emphasized the covert Romantic and autobiographical themes of his poetry, it is hard to overestimate the effect on American poets in the 1940s and 1950s of Eliot's self-protective tenets concerning the need for impersonality in poetry (promulgated first in "Tradition and the Individual Talent," 1919).

The emotion of the time, just after our alliances during the war, when a whole generation of young Americans had intensely experienced foreign cultures after the long years of American isolationism during the Depression, favored the rapid spread of Eliot's dogmas about the poet's need to participate in "the mind of Europe." It was the metaphysical strain in Eliot's poetry, especially strong in *Poems* (1920), that offered the mold into which much American poetry was poured—first in the work of John Crowe Ransom, Allen Tate, and the other Fugitive poets in the 1920s, then after the war, in a whole generation whose early work continued in this vein—among them Robert Lowell, Theodore Roethke, W. S. Merwin, John Hollander, and Adrienne Rich, all of whom later burst out in freer forms. Others, however—Howard Nemerov, Richard Wilbur, Howard Moss, and John Frederick Nims among them—have stayed fairly constant to the aesthetic with which they began.

The few poems Eliot published after *Four Quartets* were slight. Yet a posthumous publication in 1971 made possible the revaluation of his early achievement and a better-informed understanding of the relationships in his poetry between conscious intention, the seemingly spontaneous expression of materials from the unconscious, and subsequent revision. Valerie Eliot, the poet's widow, oversaw publication of a facsimile of the manuscripts of *The Waste Land,* with Ezra Pound's annotations and Eliot's cuts and transpositions. The rejected passages make surprising reading: thin social satire, parodies of Pope, adaptations of Dryden, and a focus upon the modern city which would have obscured the ultimate structure of the poem. (See the essays by Hugh Kenner and others in *Eliot in His Time,* ed. A. Walton Litz, 1973.) Pound showed great intuitive comprehension of the poem's true intentions, as yet unperceived by Eliot himself. Pound's executive editing helped turn a bundle of fragments into the poem we know, with its powerful concision, resonance, and hidden structure, virtues only intermittently evident in his own analogous *Cantos.*

We may take as an emblem of the beginning of this period "now too much for us" another aging American poet as he watches the swallows

446

swoop in the Tuscan sunlight and perch like notes of music on the stave of telephone lines outside the cage in which he is imprisoned at Pisa. The year is 1945, and Europe, like the Troy he had imagined a quarter-century earlier, is "a heap of smouldering boundary stones." Ezra Pound has been captured by the American military police and is in a maximum security jail, among rapists, murderers, and deserters. The charge against the poet is treason. During the war the expatriate Pound had made some hundred and twenty-five broadcasts for the propaganda bureau of the fascist government, aimed at persuading American soldiers and civilians to resist the machinations of President "Rosenfeld" and the "Jew bankers" who had tricked them into a war against Mussolini's virtuous and economically rational regime. How did the poet with the finest ear in our century for the English language come to be jailed for sedition?

Pound had taken history for his province, and being, as Gertrude Stein once said of him, "a village explainer," he had a preference for simplistic solutions to complex problems: "with one day's reading a man may have the key in his hands," he wrote in Canto 74. In matters of aesthetics his radical revisionism seemed on firm ground. If *ABC of Reading* (1934), his curriculum for young poets (Calvalcanti, the troubadours, Rihaku, Confucius) constituted a course of study entirely different from Eliot's, his admirable effort was to make poetry in this century as well written as prose. He accomplished more than anyone else in freeing poetry from "the emotional slither" of worn-out Victorian diction and an aesthetic that truckled to the pruderies and prejudices of the middle class. When his radical zeal spilled over from poetry to politics, however, his intellectual equipment proved tragically inadequate and betrayed the idealism of his view of a conceivably perfect society.

In his social criticism Pound is in the line of Shelley, Ruskin, and Morris, protesting the corruption of the spirit by materialism and industrialism. Pound's attack, mounted in the 1930s, presents, as an alternative to the industrial capitalism that had expressed its inner evil by bringing on World War I, not the revolutionary Marxism to which others were turning but the economic theory of Social Credit, promulgated by Major C. H. Douglas. Self-exiled to Rapallo, Italy, Pound saw in the planned economy of the fascist state what looked to him like a rational solution for the Western world; he failed to notice the fate of independent artists and thinkers under fascism. Pound's depiction of Hell in *The Cantos* is populated with contemporary warmongers, international bankers, and munitions peddlers, most of whom are Jews. Though widely read and deeply if erratically

447

learned in literature, history, and anthropology, Pound was inescapably attracted to a scapegoat theory of historical determinism. The decline of Western civilization is attributed, according to this view, to the corrosion of spiritual values by a gross materialism, which Pound attacked as "usury," and the chief conspirators who undermine civilization by their usurious practices are found to be the Jews. Although Pound was kind to individual Jews he knew, like the poet Louis Zukofsky, his hatred of Jews in the abstract led him to hold views like those in the vicious and completely discredited *Protocols of the Elders of Zion* and to make utterances indistinguishable from the rabble-rousing rant of bigots like Gerald L. K. Smith. As Eliot once remarked, Pound's Hell was for other people. True, his hatred was not confined to Jews—he had many hostilities—but it was this one which made him seem after his capture an ideological ally of the Nazis.

Brought to the United States for trial, Pound was declared mentally unfit and was remanded for an indeterminate term to St. Elizabeths, the federal insane asylum in Washington, D.C. While there he continued to write. By 1940 he had published seventy-one installments of his life work, *The Cantos,* begun in 1915. He now completed Cantos 74-84 (Cantos 72-73 were omitted from the canon). *The Pisan Cantos* appeared in 1948; the following year the Fellows in Poetry of the Library of Congress—Eliot among them—awarded this volume the Bollingen Prize. Their choice occasioned a public outcry. The Bollingen was swiftly separated by act of Congress from its nominal connection to the Library, and Pound remained, as always, at the center of controversy. As the years passed he was neither tried nor released; all others convicted of similar propaganda offenses against the Allies had served their terms and been freed. At last, in 1958, after intervention by Archibald MacLeish, Frost, and Ernest Hemingway, Pound was freed without trial on condition that he leave the country. He lived with his daughter in Venice until, at eighty-seven, he died in 1972.

Ezra Pound dominates the postwar period by his personal presence, by his personal tragedy, by the scope of his achievement in *The Cantos,* and by the several directions for succeeding poets which he first explored with unparalleled originality, energy, and self-consuming passion.

He is himself the embodiment of the *poète maudit.* His imprisonment, his sufferings, his confinement in a madhouse, and his indomitable continuation of *The Cantos* despite these circumstances, made Pound seem more than ever before, to his admirers, the Philoctetes whose poetic vision was the weapon which alone would redeem the times. As in the myth which Edmund Wilson had proposed years

earlier to represent the poet's role in our culture, along with his redeeming vision we had to accept his loathsome wound.

Whether *The Cantos* fulfill their promise seems as problematical
now as during Pound's lifetime. Early on, R. P. Blackmur had dismissed Pound's life work as being complicated without true complexity; the reader's interest, said Blackmur, moves from the poem
to its sources, and disappears in sand. But Allen Tate had praised
the sweep of the work, seeing in Pound's poem the conversation of
intelligent men. The question remains, is this conversation an
achieved work of art or the presentation of a creative process? What
is clear is that *The Cantos* has no overarching plan; even the provisional architecture which Yeats, in his preface to *A Vision,* recalls
Pound's having expounded to him seems applicable only to the first
thirty cantos. In the end, Pound's *Cantos* moves like an all-encom-
passing kaleidoscope from the Homeric world to Malatesta, from
the stability of Confucian Cathay to the execrable incantations against
contemporary warmongers and defilers of the arts, from details of
the presidencies of Adams and Van Buren to lives of the troubadours
and Pound's own recollections of Yeats, Joyce, Eliot, and other contemporaries.

The movement of Pound's verse in *The Cantos* replicates the fluidity of his thought and feeling, and dramatizes the flow of time. All
time is contemporaneous, hence the sudden veerings between the
present and any of several epochs of the past. All languages—that is,
all those which Pound chose for his purpose—are coterminous, hence
the macaronic character of the text, in which words or phrases
from Greek, Latin, Italian, Provençal, or French suddenly appear, as
do Chinese ideograms. Thus *The Cantos* ambitiously embodies the
sweep of historical knowledge within a single sensibility. Narrative,
although occasionally used to establish a character in an action, is
not the basis of presentation; we are given instead the flow of event,
character, thought, and feeling through the expressive being of the
poet. Along with Eliot's *Waste Land* and Joyce's *Ulysses,* Pound's
Cantos enacts into literature in English the modern rejection of lineal
time.

Concomitant with the obliteration of lineal time is the breaking-up
of sequential versification and of sustained decorum of style. Erich
Auerbach, in *Mimesis* (1946), demonstrates how epics, romances, and
novels of the past derived their stylistic decorum from the assumptions of the social class of their audience. Like his modernist contemporaries and successors, Pound had to write for an audience of his
own imagining, one that the force of his writings eventually created,

449

rather than for an extant readership. Unprecedented means of presentation were needed to embody experience which accepted verse conventions were inadequate to express. Among Pound's means of breaking stylistic decorum is the use of many levels of diction within the work, as the poem's language replicates the author's feelings, not the reader's expectations. In the first of *The Pisan Cantos* (74), for instance, the flow of association leaps and twists among several dictions, rhythms, styles. We find the terse clarity of Imagist phrasing in "olive tree blown white in the wind / washed in the Kiang and Han" succeeded by longer lines of allusive grandeur—"You who have passed the pillars and outward from Herakles / when Lucifer fell in N. Carolina." At times the cinematic cuts from epoch to epoch, from language to language, flicker like unedited rushes—

> Butterflies, mint and Lesbia's sparrows,
> the voiceless with bumm drum and banners,
>   and the ideogram of the guard roosts
> el triste pensier si volge
>   ad Ussel. A Ventadour
>   va il consire, el tempo rivolge
> and at Limoges the young salesman
> bowed with such french politeness "No that is impossible."
> I have forgotten which city

Interjected among such broken retrievals of the past are comments on present politics in flat and prosaic language: "and but one point needed for Stalin / you need not, i.e. need not take over the means of production." On occasion the diction attempts dialect speech and uses demotic slang, as when a Negro fellow prisoner says, "Hey Snag wots in the bibl'? / wot are the books ov the bible? / Name 'em, don't bullshit ME." Yet again the language is direct and lyrical when defining an aesthetic principle: "that the drama is wholly subjective / stone knowing the form which the carver imparts it / the stone knows the form." The tone is jerked in another direction by such lines as "the yidd is a stimulant, and the goyim are cattle / in gt/ proportion and go to saleable slaughter." The canto ends with Pound's allusive variation on a lyric of Ben Jonson's, and leaves us in the classical underworld of the dead, all memory obliterated:

> Hast 'ou seen the rose in the steel dust
>   (or swansdown ever?)
> so light is the urging, so ordered the dark petals of iron
> we who have passed over Lethe.

Syntax and lineation are as broken apart as levels of diction. There

450

is no normative beat or line length; rather, the poet's sense of phrasing determines the lengths of his lines, and indentations and spacing are used as visual orchestrations of the movement of the language. The flow of feelings supervenes the structures of conventional syntax, for feeling, unlike thought, may require expression in forms other than completed statements.

The Pisan Cantos stands among the finest sustained achievements in Pound's sprawling monument, the ultimate aim of which appears to be to define itself by becoming what it is: a poetry of perpetual process, in which the unities of beginnings and ends are purposely lacking because all is flux, all is middle. The first word of Canto 1 is "And"; to *The Cantos* there is in fact no ending. Pound published *Rock-Drill* (Cantos 85-95) in 1955, and *Thrones* (Cantos 96-109) in 1959. *The Cantos of Ezra Pound* (1970) contains his life's work, which trails off into incompleteness with fragmentary notes to Cantos 110-117. Pound never performed on his own poem such curative surgery as had articulated the inner structure of Eliot's *The Waste Land.* Or rather, Pound's work was based on a rejection of formal apriorism far more radical than Eliot's, as were Pound's other rejections more radical and far-reaching. I speak of his rejections of syntax and logic, of rationalism in all its modes. His poetry constitutes a heroic attempt to assert the primacy of an imaginative vision of wholeness by intuitive and metaphoric means, an effort to reproduce in verbal forms the energies of man feeling. Pound's efforts are deeply subversive of inherited modalities of thought.

The Pisan Cantos went further than any book of poems heretofore in controverting the dominance of Eliot's dogmas, by then widely accepted, about the necessary impersonality of poetry. The hero of *The Pisan Cantos* is Pound himself, the poet restored to his old Romantic role as the center of feeling, the suffering sensibility conferring moral authority as well as aesthetic integration upon the individual vision which it alone can formulate from the chaos we must all endure. Pound by his example lent authority to this recrudescence of the Poet as Visionary, as he did also to the Poet as Mad Seer. It would be hard to imagine what verses Robert Lowell, John Berryman, or Allen Ginsberg, among others, might have given us had not Pound helped make possible the poems they later wrote. Furthermore, the sheer scope and ambitious range of *The Cantos* have been the model for nearly every subsequent long poem in American literature: for Williams's *Paterson*, for Olson's *Maximus* and Robert Duncan's "Passages," which follow its example in ransacking history and myth, as well as for Lowell's *History* and Berryman's *Dream Songs*, influenced by

451

Pound's example of the self as the fulcrum of historical and personal experience.

Pound is thus at the center of widening rings of influence upon the poets of his time. With his polemical assaults upon established values and his early programs for the reform of literature (Imagism, Vorticism), he attracted allies and followers, who in turn founded yet newer movements.

"Criticism like Pound's is advocacy of a certain kind of poetry," Eliot wrote of his friend in *Poetry* (1946), at a time when nearly all of Pound's criticism was out of print. Within a few years Pound's influential prose was available as never before. *The Letters of Ezra Pound 1907-1941* appeared in 1950, his *Literary Essays* in 1954, and in 1973, an omnibus *Selected Prose 1909-1965*. Meanwhile new editions were published of most of his prewar books, among them *The Spirit of Romance* (1910, repr. 1968), *ABC of Reading* (1934, 1950), *Jefferson and/or Mussolini* (1935, 1970), and *Guide to Kulchur* (1938, 1968), as well as his writings on the Chinese ideogram, the Noh theater, and several volumes of his translations. This flood of Pound's critical advocacies and exemplary texts both nourished and enlarged the number of his disciples. As Pound's diagnostic views of poetry gained wider assent, so did those of his old friend William Carlos Williams and his younger admirer Charles Olson. Visiting Pound in St. Elizabeths, however, Olson was vexed by Pound's incorrigible social views (see *Charles Olson and Ezra Pound,* ed. C. Seelye, 1975); disavowing Pound's influence, Olson set out to make American poetry new yet again, although repeating many of his repudiations and proposing analogous solutions to similar artistic and cultural discontents. Williams, Olson, and the Black Mountain movement took strength from Pound's example.

To the later beneficiaries of Pound's influence I shall return; but priority in accomplishment, as well as in time, belongs to Williams. For forty years he worked, as it were, in the shadow of Pound, his voluminous body of poetry appearing in tiny editions from small presses; but at last, in 1946, with the appearance of the first book of *Paterson* (Books I-V, 1963), Williams emerged as a major poet and a major force on other poets. *His Collected Earlier Poems* and *Collected Later Poems* (1950-51) and the subsequent publication of his essays, plays, fiction, and autobiography mark out the extraordinary range of this obstetrician who lived all his life in Rutherford, New Jersey, except for two trips to Europe. He had studied pediatrics in Leipzig during 1909-10 and spent a few months abroad in 1924, joining Pound in London and meeting Yeats on the first trip, Joyce, Valery Larbaud, and Brancusi on the second; but Williams's imagination stayed firmly rooted at home. Where *The Cantos,* like *The Waste Land,* seems a steamer trunk into which a world traveler has stuffed his souvenirs, *Paterson* hoards the contents of the hometown doctor's roll-top desk. If the matter of *Paterson* is provincial, nonetheless it is one of the most attractive poetic works of the modernist movement. Williams made a successful fusion of the impulses of the local color movement with those of Symbolism. His Paterson, however, is not only a city, but also a man, a corporate person ("his mind is the telephone directory"). Thus *Paterson* is at once a continuation and a scaling-down of Whitman's vast identification of the self with America: not in the large, but in the particular place, with its own traditions, its history, its landscape. Crucial to that landscape is the Falls of the Passaic River, whose inarticulate roar the poet would translate into a language. The theme of the poem is the search for a language adequate to record the thoughts and feelings of Mr. Paterson, at once the poet and the people of his city and his time.

In his shorter poems (*The Desert Music,* 1954; *Journey to Love,* 1955; *Pictures from Brueghel,* 1962) Williams continued and extended his mastery of poetry as notation of the perception of experience in the instant of its happening. From his association in the twenties with the Philadelphia painters Charles Sheeler and Charles Demuth, Williams had developed his own brand of imagistic presentation; he was determined to grapple with the realities of industrial America and to use the rhythms of actual speech rather than what seemed to him the arbitrary metrics of poetic convention. Williams became our foremost practitioner of poetry as speech, in this going beyond even Pound, who never forswears, as Williams does, the rival aesthetic of poetry as song. But Williams defined his rhythmic principles—what he called "the American foot," a three-stepped line of no predetermined length, responsive to subtle shifts of emphasis—in opposition not to Pound but to Eliot. Wildly misreading *The Waste Land,* Williams considered it a step backward, a betrayal of the free-verse movement, a shackling of American poetry to the iambics of the English tradition. Every poet's poetics will be self-serving to some extent, and in Williams this is especially so. Perhaps, as the son of an Englishman, he had a stronger need than most American poets consciously to shuck off all the attributes of British poetry. In any event his demotic style is that of a master: it seems limitless in its appetite for experience, able to encompass wide ranges of feeling. Williams is a poet of renewal, of the power of imagination to re-create the life force in each of us. There is in his work awareness of suffering, but he is no tragic poet. Not even the withholding, after a scurrilous campaign of defamation by the right-wing tabloid press, of the Consultantship in Poetry of the Library of Congress, to which he had been appointed in 1952, nor subsequent strokes, defeated the man. His last years, though enfeebled, were productive, and his reputation and influence have continued since his death at seventy-nine in 1963. From many tributes, perhaps these lines from "To William Carlos Williams" by Richard Eberhart best express Williams's inimitable bequest:

> With gusto to toss the classics out, and with them
> The sonnet, you live yet in a classic Now,
> Pretend to advance order in your plain music,
>
> And even preach that Form (you call it measure,
> Or idiom) is all, albeit your form would mate
> The sprawling forms, inchoate, of our civilization.

Other poets whose careers were rounded out to honorable conclusions in the years after World War II include such formalist and conservative poets as Ransom and Tate, John Hall Wheelock and Mark Van Doren; experimentalists in private lyricism and public verse such as Horace Gregory and Archibald MacLeish; and first-generation modernists such as Conrad Aiken, e. e. cummings, and Babette Deutsch. Three women poets of that generation emerged from years of silence or neglect with publications that demand revaluation of their work: Mina Loy's *Lunar Baedecker & Time-Tables* was republished in 1958 with appreciative forewords by Williams, Kenneth Rexroth, and Denise Levertov; her work explores new freedom from both verse and sexual conventions. The *Selected Poems of H.D.* (Hilda Doolittle) appeared in 1957, but it was after the poet's death in 1961 that the appearance of *Hermetic Definition* (1972) and *Trilogy* (1973) made inevitable the reassessment of her achievement: no longer can she be seen merely as a cameo neoclassical Imagist, for these long philosophical poems represent a major effort in another direction, which the critical history of this period must acknowledge. The third poet of the twenties to reappear after a long, self-imposed silence is Laura Riding, whose *Selected Poems: In Five Sets,* issued in England in 1970 and in the United States in 1973, reprints poems last seen in her *Collected Poems* (1938). These strike a tone original in that earlier period, one which strongly marked both Robert Graves and W. H. Auden and, through their influence, many younger poets on both shores.

454

The Mind Is an Enchanting Thing

        is an enchanted thing
            like the glaze on a
        katydid-wing
                subdivided by sun
                till the nettings are legion.
        Like Gieseking playing Scarlatti . . .

So runs the title into the opening stanza of one of the six poems in a slender little booklet, *Nevertheless,* that appeared at the height of World War II in 1944. The piquancy of Marianne Moore's observations, the unexampled lurching lilt of her lyric flow through a complexly varied pattern of syllabic lines in each stanza, the oddness of her rhyming of stressed with unstressed syllables, the accuracy of her descriptions of natural facts, and the unexpectedness of her metaphors are all evident in these few lines. In this extraordinary poem, the mind is further compared to an "apteryx-awl," to "the / kiwi's rain-shawl / of haired feathers"; like the gyroscope, the mind is "trued by regnant certainty."

        Unconfusion submits
        its confusion to proof; it's
    not a Herod's oath that cannot change.

Other poems of Marianne Moore's are better known, but none with more grace embodies the qualities that characterize her work. Hers is a mind that *would* submit "confusion to proof," nor would she hold a demonstrably false idea or opinion, since truth is "not a Herod's oath." At the same time, mind, to her, is enchanting and enchanted. "Feeling and Precision" is the title of the first of her literary essays in *Predilections* (1955), and those two qualities are, in her best work, in symbiotic tension. "When writing with maximum impact the writer seems under compulsion to set down an unbearable accuracy," but such precision, she says, "is a thing of the imagination." Miss Moore, who studied biology at Bryn Mawr, respected the accuracy of scientific taxonomy and based her use of metaphor on similarly rigorous description; it was not casually that she called her second book *Observations* (1924). Her many poems in which creatures, often odd ones like the pangolin or frigate pelican, abound gave her repute as a fabulist—a misconception encouraged by her translation of *The Fables of La Fontaine* (1954). In her own poems, however, her interest is always as much in the reality of the creature observed as in its putative emblematic value. Yet her creatures are not only themselves but cunning disguises for her own reticent self, for whom "Feeling at its deepest . . . tends to be inarticulate." Ostensibly speaking of a snail, her observation that "If 'compression is the first grace of style,' / you have it" is both apt and self-reflexive; so is her comment (in "His Shield") on a salamander who "revealed / a formula safer than an armorour's: the power of relinquishing / what one would keep; that is freedom." Writing "about" creatures gave her the freedom to be articulate.

From the time her first booklet, *Poems,* appeared in 1920, Miss Moore had been a poet whose idiosyncrasies secured her only the most discriminating of audiences. Eliot had introduced her *Selected Poems* in 1935, but it was her *Collected Poems* (1951), published when she was sixty-four, that brought fame and, for the first time, a wide public. Her new poems, with all their angularities, now appeared in *The New Yorker* and *The Ladies' Home Journal. Life* magazine photographed the poet visiting animals at the zoo. The shy spinster who lived with her mother in a modest Brooklyn apartment had become a celebrity. Subsequent volumes—*Like a Bulwark* (1956), *O to Be a Dragon* (1959), and *Tell Me, Tell Me* (1966)—it must be admitted spread her gifts a bit thin. The best late poems have her customary grace, but lack the fierce intensity of the earlier work; she also wrote about the Brooklyn Dodgers and the racehorse Tom Fool, and published explicitly didactic verses. For *The Complete Poems* (1961) Miss Moore revised or truncated some of her long-familiar poems and, despite her title, left others out. (Her complete preface is characteristic: "Omissions are not accidents.") To a reader familiar with the original versions, this redesigning of her *oeuvre* does not improve them.

Marianne Moore's precision of observation and of thought, in metaphors as surprising as her rhythms and lineation, embodies the strength of feeling of this women who advised, "we must be clear as our natural reticence allows . . . we must have the courage of our peculiarities." Her courage and clarity are rock-ribbed by an old-fashioned Protestant ethic. Obedient to decorum, she is nonetheless strong-minded, strong-willed, uncompromisingly declaring her individuality. Despite the seeming preciosity of her sometimes exotic subjects and the incorporation into her poems of phrases culled from her curious reading, Marianne Moore's sensibility is democratic. Little though she resembles Whitman otherwise, in her early poem "New York" what she most praises in her city is " 'accessibility to experience' "—within quotes since the phrase is borrowed from Henry James. Her famous poem "Poetry" (which in *Complete Poems* she reduced to its first three lines) rebukes the "half poets" who fear to include in poetry the mysteries of experience and depths of feeling, "the raw material of poetry in / all its rawness and / that which is . . . genuine." As she wrote in another poem, "Ecstasy affords / the occasion and expediency determines the form."

Like the other major poets of her generation Marianne Moore extended the possibilities of poetry in her diction, subjects, and means of composition. Her individual combination of airiness with density, of probity with pleasure, was not lost upon certain of her successors, for whom, as for her, "art is but an expression of our needs; is feeling, modified by the writer's moral and technical insights."

Whitman, in *Specimen Days,* paid unexpected tribute to Longfellow for providing American poetry with "rich color, graceful forms and incidents . . . competing with the singers of Europe on their own ground . . . He is certainly the sort of bard and counteractant most needed for our materialistic, self-assertive money-worshipping present age in America . . . for and among whom he comes as the poet of melody, courtesy, deference—poet of the . . . past in Italy, Germany, Spain, and in Northern Europe." A far greater poet than Longfellow has provided contemporary America with many of the same civilizing values from the Old World. Emigrating here in 1939, W. H. Auden soon enough seemed a fair exchange for T. S. Eliot, who had long lived in London. In his early period, which expatriation from England brought to a close, Auden with bold precocity formed an original style in opposition to Eliot's dominating influence. This poetry alternates between the plangent lyricism of personal emotions and dark forebodings of the oncoming catastrophe of war in Europe. With its landscape of industrial waste, its dream images of ancient myths and schoolboy fantasies, and its commitment to leftist politics, Auden's poetry had become the voice of a whole generation's fears and hopes. Once in the States, however, where the stylistic revolution of the twenties was soon to gain a popular acceptance not to be paralleled in England for another twenty years, Auden, whose preoccupations shifted from Marxist to Freudian and later to Kierkegaardian thought, seemed more to represent an intellectual than a poetic avant-garde.

Reviewers and critics were much perplexed by what they termed his shifting allegiances, by his caprice in *The Collected Poetry of W. H. Auden* (1945) in arranging his poems alphabetically by the first letter of their opening words, and by his constant revision or excision of old poems. In retrospect, now that *The Double Man* (1941), *For the Time Being* (1944), *Nones* (1951), *The Shield of Achilles* (1955), *Homage to Clio* (1960), *About the House* (1965), and *City without*

Walls (1969) have been subsumed, first in *Collected Shorter Poems* (1967), then in *Collected Longer Poems* (1969), and finally in the posthumous *Collected Poems* (1976), it is the constancy of his poetic enterprise, rather than the early stages in his philosophical development, which mark this astonishingly extensive, lively, and varied body of work.

Auden is a dazzling virtuoso who remade poetry not by renunciations of convention but by his daring and original levies on tradition. There is hardly a form of English verse that Auden did not rekindle with new life for modern occasions: ballads, sonnets, sonnet sequences, odes, sestinas, elegies, verse plays, opera libretti, lyrics to be set to music, verse meditations (on, *inter alia,* each room of his house, each of the canonical hours), not to mention occasional poems, limericks, clerihews, and other light verse.[1] These poured from him in a nearly inexhaustible stream. Not until the last few years of his life—he returned to Oxford in 1972 and died the following year—did his inspired inventiveness flag, as the style became chatty, the verse line slackened, the diction turned more and more toward linguistic rarities culled from the *Oxford English Dictionary.* No sooner had Auden died than his work came under attack by younger poets—for being only versified essays, for telling us nothing that we needed to know. The facts, however, are surely otherwise.

Auden was a forceful presence in American letters, not only because (as Eliot had said a great poet must) in writing himself he wrote his time, but because he exemplified qualities of the poetic imagination without which our literature would have been much impoverished. In an age of madness he was a poet professing sanity. In a time of disbelief, after his leftist and psychiatric periods, he found spiritual haven in the Anglican Church; but his Christianity was grounded in existential theology, not, like Eliot's, in the sermons of Lancelot

---

1. Light verse, based on shared norms of conduct and of versification, has not fared well as the century advances. The impulses toward the breakup of established forms and a poetry of personal revelation mitigate against it. Auden, though he is the master, is not, however, the sole adept of light verse in this period. Theodore Roethke and Howard Nemerov, Reed Whittemore and X. J. Kennedy are others. Vladimir Nabokov's only venture into verse in English, *Poems* (1959), is satirical and literary. L. E. Sissman writes engaging social satire in *Pursuit of Honor* (1971). John Updike's title poem in *Midpoint* (1969) is at once a serious self-exploration and a spoof of the long poem, using stanzas from Dante and Spenser and the meters of Pope, the rhythms of Whitman and Pound, as well as the iconography of concrete poetry. Light verse of a more simplistic sort was popularized by Ogden Nash, whose one technical device—the comic distortion of the heroic couplet—had been long ago anticipated by Swift in "Mrs. Frances Haris's Entreaty."

Andrewes. In a period of endless experimentation and the deconstruction of artistic form, Auden believed in rules for poetry, in verse as a form of play in which originality and delight derive from bold refingerings of conventions. For him no form was dead beyond resuscitation. Auden is the only poet who not only masters the traditional accentual-syllabic meters of the Anglo-American tradition, but also domesticates with equal success the French syllabic meter and revives with colloquial ease and contemporary relevance the Anglo-Saxon alliterative line. He is always entertaining, whether his verse speaks, meditates, or sings. His delineations of our lot can be ironical, as in "Under Which Lyre": or told with full knowledge of history's tragedy in "The Shield of Achilles"; or he can thrust the light of his intelligence into the mysteries of the creative imagination ("The Cave of Making").

"Poetry is not magic. In so far as poetry, or any other of the arts, can be said to have an ulterior purpose, it is, by telling the truth, to disenchant and disintoxicate." So Auden defined his own anti-Romantic position, which placed him beyond the sympathies of readers for whom the confessional poem or the deep image represents the sole intensity of poetic experience. Auden's avowed rationalism impelled him toward satire in poetry, and toward a dialectical method in criticism in which all conceptions are discussed in terms of their opposites. This leads to the truly profound sometimes rubbing shoulders with the merely witty and, occasionally, the factitious, when comparisons are pursued for their own sakes. *The Enchafèd Flood* (1950), his only book-length critical work, Auden described as an "attempt to understand the nature of Romanticism through an examination of a single theme, the sea." The rest of his critical writings were essays, reviews, prefaces, and lectures, collected in three volumes. *The Dyer's Hand* (1962) contains his major essays, brilliantly describing the poet's task, his confrontation with the modern world, the artist's relationship to society. *Secondary Worlds* (1968) explores the types of the hero, the imaginative world of sagas, opera, and the relation of poetry to religion. A lively selection of other fugitive pieces appeared posthumously in *Forewords and Afterwords* (1973).

As critic and man of letters, Auden belongs in the select company of Edmund Wilson, Lionel Trilling, and Malcolm Cowley as well as Eliot, Pound, Ransom, and Tate—those whose commentaries on the literature of the past and the writing of the present help to give their times a consciousness of contemporary sensibility. As judge of the Yale Younger Poets Series, Auden wrote for each year's prize book a foreword examining the characteristic *donnée* of the new poet he had selected. In successive years (1952-1957) these poets and the subjects of Auden's introductions were Adrienne Rich and poetic form; W. S. Merwin and the uses of myth; Daniel Hoffman and the poet's relationship to the natural world; John Ashbery and the surreal imagination; James Wright and the subjects possible for poetry; John Hollander and the connections between poetry and music. Thus Auden both encouraged and defined the salient interest in the poetry of his young contemporaries.

In a period of under forty years during which nearly every poet alive is a contemporary of all of the others, chronology is an arbitrary maker of categories. The great events in this period, the events most operative upon its poetry, are World War II, the postwar period of seeming social and literary conformity, and the cultural revolution of the sixties occasioned by a whole complex of simultaneous social and political causes: the coming of age of the multitudes born just after World War II; the corrosive effects on American life of the decade-long Vietnam war (1962-1973); the civil rights struggle; an economy based on war production unable in peacetime to control its inflation; ever-increasing bureaucratization of industry and government; the undermining of public faith in the democratic process during several "imperial presidencies," culminating in the exposure and disgrace of President Nixon in 1973-74. In the midst of it all, it seemed to many that the institutional bulwarks of culture—politics, education, our traditional commitment to the work ethic—were being undermined. Most of the poets to be discussed in this chapter lived through all of these perturbations of American life. Only a very few survived them with the same aesthetic assumptions and poetic intentions with which they began. There has perhaps never been a generation of greatly talented poets who, whatever their individual proclivities, have so widely shared in a stylistic revolution.

In broad outline, that revolution involves the shift of the literary imagination from a conviction of the historical continuity of culture, which guarantees that the present is both a continuation of the past and a link to the future, to a sense of the discontinuity of history, which makes each moment, each act, each emotion experientially unique and therefore requires that style and form be provisional, experimental, reflective of the process of becoming self-aware rather than of the continuation of any familiar category of expression, thought, or feeling.

The foregoing construct defines the work of no single poet in all of its terms but sketches in a general way the work of nearly all the poets to be discussed. The divergences of each from this generalized model will be self-evident. So, too, will their accommodation or resistance to the shift of sensibility which became felt in the middle of the period. Of course, just as there were some poets who began and remained conservators of poetic tradition (Ransom, Tate, Yvor Winters, J. V. Cunningham), there were others (Louis Zukofsky, George Oppen, Kenneth Rexroth) who from the beginning were in the camp of deconstruction, improvisation, the poetry of process.

What was to be acted out across the decades was the old dichotomy between Classicism and Romanticism, between making and finding, already exemplified in the careers of the modernist masters. As has been indicated above, through the influence of his criticism Eliot came to represent the conservative impulses in modern poetry, tendencies buttressed by the formalism of Yeats, Frost, Stevens, and Auden. At the same time Pound and Williams had raised the flag of revolt against all that. If it seems odd that it took so long for either camp to consolidate its gains—the positions having been marked out in the twenties—we may reflect that cultural lag is a concomitant of all conquests, including literary ones. When I speak of a conservative or academic poetry, I refer to tendencies within the context of the modernist movement.

Three poets who began their careers before World War II and have survived to become the elder statesmen of American poetry in the 1970s illustrate how the general shift of sensibility described above may be seen in work of unmistakable individuality. Robert Penn Warren and Stanley Kunitz have moved from formality to more flexible styles, while Richard Eberhart has gone his own way, scarcely touched by the seismographic shifts in the work of others.

Warren's progress as a poet can be taken as a paradigm of the history of sensibility in this period. He was the youngest of the prewar Fugitives, and no poet in the country wrote with more fidelity to the assumptions of Ransom, Tate, and their fellow-southerners—belief in poetry as public discourse, in rational organization of the poem, in strict meters and formality of diction, in a stance of ironic lyricism. This poetic program derived from the conservative social views set forth in 1930 in *I'll Take My Stand,* essays by southerners concerned to turn back the tide of northern industrialism which had already torn forever the fabric of the old agrarian South they yearned to re-create. The poetics of Ransom, Tate, and Donald Davidson—and Warren in this period (until his *Selected Poems, 1923-1943*)—combine their dream of a hieratic, stable, preindustrial society with T. S. Eliot's conceptions of literary tradition and of historical continuity. The poems Warren

461

has preserved from these early years in his *Selected Poems, 1923-1975* (1976), however, are those whose narrative structure, brooding contemplation of time, and retrieval of a vanished Kentucky boyhood most nearly anticipate the later work (as in "The Ballad of Billie Potts," "Original Sin," "Kentucky Mountain Farm"); only a few, like "Bearded Oaks," remain to epitomize his early formalism.

Warren's achievement as a poet is a part—I believe it the major part—of his total *oeuvre,* embracing fiction, literary criticism, and social commentary. For over a decade after the war these other strands in his work were dominant. (*All the King's Men,* his best-known novel, appeared in 1946; *Segregation: The Inner Conflict of the South* in 1956; *Selected Essays,* including his magisterial studies of Coleridge and Melville, 1958). Warren, in collaboration with Cleanth Brooks, had published *Understanding Poetry* (1938), the most influential and popular formulation of the New Criticism, making analysis of texture and structure a commonplace in the teaching of poetry. Twenty years later, in the hands of some disciples, the New Criticism hardened into mechanical explication of texts in avoidance and sometimes in ignorance of their historical circumstances; but Brooks and Warren had long since moved from their polemically necessary position of the 1930s—Brooks in his biography of Faulkner, and Warren in a series of studies of Dreiser, Whittier, Melville. Together with R. W. B. Lewis they edited yet another text in 1973, *American Literature: The Makers and the Making,* in which their introductory essays fully restore to the discussion of literature the historical criteria of moment and milieu. Warren's *Democracy and Poetry* (1975) is his most succinct analysis of American literature as a tradition with a historical continuity. It is one in which the moral sense of the private self is seen as increasingly besieged, isolated, and endangered by the process of historical change. In this context Warren's later poems are to be read as fervent efforts, in the absence of religious certainty, to hold and embody personal values against the enemy of permanence, time. His poetry is thus a distillation of the troubled contemplation of history which characterizes his novels.

Between the selection from his early poems in 1944 and his next volume of verse, *Promises* (1957), there intervened not only the prose books mentioned above but also the publication of his most extended poetic work. *Brother to Dragons: A Tale in Verse and Voices* (1953) embodies many of Warren's abiding themes. In it he re-creates, dramatizes, and ponders the misadventures of Lilburn Lewis, a Virginian who had wantonly murdered one of his slaves. Since Lewis in actual life had been a nephew of Thomas Jefferson, this crime, the ultimate treatment of another human being as a thing, an extension of one's own self, becomes implicated in that larger matter, the historical guilt of the United States. Jefferson (who, like Warren himself, is a speaker in the closet drama), is appalled by his nephew's inhumanity; yet Jefferson's Enlightenment faith in the innate goodness of man proves as much an abstraction as Lewis's insane self-righteousness. In another direction, too, Lilburn Lewis's guilt is presented in a context larger than one man's miserable life, for his crime results not only from the inhumanity of slavery but from his fixation upon his own mother. Thus the Oedipal guilt of the human lot is implicated in the guilt of history.

In *Promises* and thereafter Warren excels in sequences, series of lyrics on a common theme in which we are compelled from one poem to another by unpredictable loopings of thought and slipknots of feeling. The mode is often narrative, the rhythm either a short colloquial line or bursts of long lines played off against the pauses of white space, a style that establishes tension between the spatial arrangements of its syntax and the visual appearance of the poetry which controls the tempo in which it is read. His ostensible subjects may be the sievings of memory in "Ballad of a Sweet Dream of Peace," his parents brought to life again after half a century ("Tale of Time"), a meditation on Emerson while taking a jet flight 38,000 feet above the America that Emerson regarded as "itself a poem." His most extended series is *Audubon: A Vision* (1969), a haunted extrapolation from a brief passage in the artist's journal. Warren re-creates the smoldering violence of the frontier. Audubon, spending the night in a filthy cabin, is about to be murdered for his gold watch by an old woman and her loutish sons (the scene is reminiscent of Warren's earlier "Ballad of Billie Potts"). At the eleventh hour three travelers arrive and administer frontier justice to the thieves. The woman, hideous in life, earns dignity in her hanging.

As Warren writes in *Or Else* (1974), "Time / Is the mirror into which you stare." His searching, compassionate poems explore both sides of that mirror, experience and memory, with their strangely syncopated rhythms of feeling. Experience itself is meaningless, a flux of random events, until clarified by memory's meditation upon it. It is the mark of Warren's achievement that the sort of experience that can so serve his poems is—or gives the impression that it is— without limit. Not only the great emotional events of a lifetime, but others seemingly dross and trivial, have the power to burst into the unabashed truths and mysteries by which his poems celebrate life and outwit the tyranny of time. Among them are his remembrance of a visit to a ranch where an Indian helper killed rattlers by dousing them with gasoline and flicking matches as they raced for their holes; character sketches of an old Negro driving a mule; a white supremacist unable to comprehend the history that has warped his soul; a lynching. Of these public and historical experiences as well as of the family ghosts in "I Am Dreaming of a White Christmas,' Warren could say,

> All items listed above belong in the world
> In which all things are continuous,
> And are parts of the original dream which
> I am now trying to discover the logic of. This
> Is the process whereby pain of the past in its pastness
> May be converted into the future tense
>
> Of joy.

This poet, with his eye, with his mind's eye and his knowledge of the depth of our experience in time, has followed the hovering hawk —to use one of his recurrent symbols—into "the infinite saffron of the sky," although "The hawk, in an eyeblink, is gone."

The two other leading poets of Warren's generation have responded differently to their fifty years' experience of poetry and of life in the twentieth century. Stanley Kunitz has published sparsely, with only four books of verse (*Intellectual Things*, 1930; *Passport to the War*, 1944; *Selected Poems 1928-1958*, 1959; *The Testing-Tree*, 1971). Richard Eberhart, a poet of profligate energy, gathers his fifteen books together in *Collected Poems 1930-1976* (1976).

"I keep reading the masters, because they infect me with human possibility," Kunitz has written (in *A Kind of Order, A Kind of Folly: Essays and Conversations*, 1975). "The vainest ambition is to want an art separated from its heritage, as though tradition were a cistern full of toads instead of a life-giving fountain." The masters he has read include the Jacobean poets, Blake, Yeats, and Hopkins, whose strains he has combined into a highly personal style. In his first three books that style was metaphysical and strictly formal; in *The Testing-Tree* his scansion has loosened. (The formality continues in his translations from Russian poets.) In meters strict or irregular, Kunitz's work is marked by a visionary intensity which renders experience at once dreamlike and mythic, as in "Open the Gates":

> The hinges groan: a rush of forms
> Shivers my name, wrenched out of me.
> I stand upon the terrible threshold and I see
> The end and the beginning in each others' arms.

464

In his later work apocalyptic images and archetypal structures are less abstract; the poems are rooted in such public events as Dietrich Bonhoeffer's plot against Hitler, or the first moon landing, or in family relationships. *The Testing-Tree* begins with a long poem addressed to his daughter (*"What do I want of my life? / More! More!"*); it ends with the title poem, re-creating a ritual of the poet's boyhood in Massachusetts that links him with shamans or Druids who cast stones at a tree to challenge the future. In such poems as these and "The Illumination," "King of the River," "The Mulch," "After the Last Dynasty" and "The Portrait," Kunitz has transformed feelings into fables in which "the heart breaks and breaks / and lives by breaking," in full knowledge that

> It is necessary to go
> > through dark and deeper dark
> > and not to turn.

Richard Eberhart, though born in Minnesota, has lived most of his life in New England. There is the stamp of transcendentalism upon his work. Like Kunitz, he responded early to both Metaphysical and Romantic masters; in Eberhart's poetry the influence of Donne, combined with that of Traherne and other seventeenth-century mystical poets, is yoked to the bequests of Blake, Wordsworth, and Emerson. While at Cambridge University, Eberhart was a student of I. A. Richards and a classmate of William Empson and Kathleen Raine; his own work veers between the rigor and the abandon of these contemporaries. For Eberhart is a strangely uneven poet: his besetting weakness is a too-easy leap into heady abstractions, the willed imposition of spiritual significance rendered in assertive syntax, Latinate diction. His strengths are the opposites of these flaws: poems of a lambent clarity at once simple and profound, such as "I Walked Out to the Graveyard to See the Dead." Some of these proceed with a rigorous logic, like that of Blake's "The Mental Traveller," reversing the terms of their own images. In his early redaction of the theme of Wordsworth's "Intimations" ode ("If I Could Live at the Pitch That Is Near Madness"), Eberhart sees mankind ranked in battalions, "demanding a moral answer":

> I gave the moral answer and I died
> And into a realm of complexity came
> Where nothing is possible but necessity
> And the truth wailing there like a red babe.

Eberhart's best poems grapple with realms of complexity, with the necessity of our facing death, with the need to transfigure suffering.

465

His brooding poems on death and transfiguration irresistibly take us from a *memento mori* to "Saint Theresa in her tent" ("The Groundhog"), from human grief to acknowledgment of death as "Mother, Great Being, Source of Life" ("The Soul Longs to Return Whence It Came"). As an elegist ("To Evan"; "As If You Had Never Been") Eberhart is compassionate, eloquent; "The Fury of Aerial Bombardment" rises above the rhetoric of most war poetry to sound its plangent lament. If "The Clam Diggers and Diggers of Sea Worms" is a modern instance of Wordsworth's "The Leech Gatherer," its empathy for "primitive simplicity" and "dignity beyond speech" is unassailable. Eberhart touches the bleak depths of experience in poems like "The Human Being Is a Lonely Creature" and "Despair," yet can exult, in "Great Praises," in the sensuous world of change, decay, and dying:

I used to hate the summer ardour
In all my intellectual pride,
But now I love the very order

That brushed me fast aside,
And rides upon the air of the world
With insolent, supernal splendour.

"The Groundhog" has made Eberhart famous for a poem about a dead creature, but his poems on the living—among them "Sea-Hawk," "Ospreys in Cry," and "Lions Copulating"—are animate with vital energies. So are his characterization of "A New England Bachelor" and "A Wedding on Cape Rosier." His "Meditation Two" invokes "the improbable advent of unity" to "triumph over the mocking dualisms" of life and of art. It is that improbable advent which Eberhart seeks and celebrates, and, in well over a score of memorable poems, finds.

In his poem to Delmore Schwartz, Robert Lowell has his late friend misquote Wordsworth's "Resolution and Independence"—

"We poets in our youth begin in sadness;
thereof in the end come despondency and madness."

These lines typify not only Schwartz but Lowell himself, and three other poets of the first generation after World War II, poets who, like Schwartz, were all too early lost after despondency, madness, alcoholism, suicide: such were the shared fates of Theodore Roethke, Randall Jarrell, and John Berryman. Theirs, however, was not the only way poets responded in their lives and work to the falling apart of their outer and inner worlds; Elizabeth Bishop, Richard Wilbur, Howard

Nemerov, and still others made their poetry a bastion of order against chaos. Whether that chaos is internalized in their work or exiled from it, the best poetry of the period is written under its pressure.

Yet Roethke could say, of his poems in *The Lost Son* (1948), "in spite of all the muck and welter, the dark, the *dreck* of these poems, I count myself among the happy poets." Creative joy is evident in his poems, which he described (in an essay in *On the Poet and His Craft,* 1965) as stages "in a kind of struggle out of the slime; part of a slow spiritual progress; an effort to be born, and later, to become something more." Just before the war, in 1941, Roethke's first book, *Open House*, had appeared. It is evident that the change from a formal style to an unconventional, freer, more experiential style, such as we have seen in Warren and Kunitz, was more accelerated in Roethke's case than in theirs. *Open House* was written under the influence, among others, of his tutorial muse Louise Bogan, whose lyrics, Roethke observes, reveal "a tragic personality . . . who shapes emotion into an inevitable-seeming, an endurable, form"—a judgment no one would contest who has read her "Medusa," "Women," or "The Dream" (*Collected Poems, 1923-1953*). In *Open House* Roethke imprints a personal voice upon lyric conventions—a voice already unmistakable in its simplicity of statement, as in the title poem ("I'm naked to the bone / With nakedness my shield"). This style is continued in *The Lost Son* (1948), a book whose originality startles in the presentation of the poet's *donnée*: son of a German-American greenhouse florist in Michigan, Roethke writes in "Cuttings" of "This urge, wrestle, resurrection of dry sticks"; in "Root Cellar," "Nothing would give up life: / Even the earth kept breathing a small breath." A whole series of poems dramatizes the primordial life-urge in this artificed garden, not of Eden, but of life and death, and re-creates with affectionate candor the adults who worked and the boy who played in its beds of carnations and orchids. Roethke has written of his "quest for identity" that he can be aided not only by the dead (he speaks of Yeats), but by "*all* living things, including the sub-human. This is not so much a naive as a primitive attitude: animistic, maybe. Why not? Everything that lives is holy."

Markedly different in form, his poems in *Praise to the End!* (1951) are still a consistent development of his search for identity, his reverence for "everything that lives." In these the persona is infantile: "A deep dish. Lumps in it. / I can't taste my mother," he muses of his weaning. In the short-line rhythms of nursery rhymes and children's game-songs the self evokes the id, speaker of truths felt before thought. "In this kind of poem," Roethke has explained, "the poet must be willing to face up to genuine mystery. His language must . . . telescope image and symbol, if necessary . . . speak in a kind of psychic short-hand when his protagonist is under great stress." The effect is of in-fantine babbling in which the rhythm compels one's attention (Roeth-ke said his poems "are written to be heard"), and attention discovers clues to a meaning the method at once hides and reveals. In "Give Way, Ye Gates," "O Lull Me, Lull Me," and "The Lost Son" Roethke seems to deal unmediatedly with the archetypes of consciousness, as Jung defines them. Later in the volume, in the title poem and in oth-ers such as "Unfold! Unfold!" the religious sensibility behind his reverence for even subhuman life becomes rapturously explicit:

> Sing, sing, you symbols! All simple creatures,
> All small shapes, willow-shy,
> In the obscure haze, sing! . . .
>
> > A house for wisdom, a field for revelation.
> > Speak to the stones, and the stars answer.
> > At first the visible obscures:
> > Go where the light is.

Here the Jungian archetypes have been subsumed into a mysticism derived from Blake and Evelyn Underhill.

Such affirmations proved an unstable fusion of the will-to-unify with the felt threat of the chaos of experience. Only two years later, in *The Waking* (1953), Roethke suddenly abandoned this experi-mental style for poems which either returned to the mode already explored in his first two books, or, as in "Four for Sir John Davies," introduced yet another turn in his work. Here he again invokes uni-fication of feeling, but this time to a different music:

> The great world turns its axle when it can;
> I need a place to sing, and dancing-room.

Unlike the Neoplatonic original, Roethke's improvisation on the Renaissance poet's *Orchestra* is an invocation of sexual unity and the redemptive joy thereof ("The flesh can make the spirit visible"). The spirit of Yeats as well as Davies informs these strictly rhymed pentameter stanzas, to which Roethke gives the unmistakable accents of his own end-stopped declaratives in other poems of various tones —the ecstasy of "The Renewal," the sophisticated lubricity of "I Knew a Woman Lovely in Her Bones," the dark night of "The Pure Fury."

Further sequences followed—"The Dying Man," "Meditations of an Old Woman," and "North American Sequence," the last published in *The Far Field* a year after Roethke's death in 1963. In the posthumous sequence, he achieves the symbolic equivalence of the self with the landscape of the continent, and his cadence shifts to a Whitmanesque cataloguing in a long, more casual line which is yet capable of intensity. Many of Roethke's brief poems, such as the haunting "Snake" and "The Beast," are among his lasting work.

Roethke has been criticized for undigested borrowings from Yeats and Eliot, but his handling of the language noticeably differs from that of his sometime models: the strongly stressed aphoristic line is a constant, whether the stanzas rhyme or no, or the line be short or long. The grace and strength of Roethke's style is such as to replace the intensity of suffering, self-doubt, or metaphysical anguish behind the poem with the very different intensity of the poem itself, and to infuse the *angst* with a sort of joyfulness. Where successful, his work does fulfill his aim of writing poems "which try, in their rhythms, to catch the movement of the mind itself, to trace the spiritual history of a protagonist (not 'I' personally but of all haunted and harried men)."

Like Roethke, who suffered from mental illness and alcoholism, Delmore Schwartz was a tormented man and a poet who could not rest content with an achieved personal style. His early work (*In Dreams Begin Responsibilities*, 1938), reprinted in *Summer Knowledge: New and Selected Poems* (1959), gave promise of brilliant intellectual lyricism. "In the Naked Bed, in Plato's Cave" and "Socrates' Ghost Must Haunt Me Now," with its plea, "Old Noumenon, come true, come true!" make moving poems from the mind's desire to know; in "Coriolanus and His Mother" (a closet drama) and *Shenandoah* (a verse play, 1941) Schwartz explored Freudian determinism of self-identity, a theme better handled in the stunning short story which gave its title to his first book of poems and fiction. Anyone reading such poems as "The Heavy Bear That Goes with Me" or "A Dog Named Ego, the Snowflakes as Kisses," or who responds to the acknowledgment in "The Ballad of the Children of the Czar" of the human lot ("Well! The heart of man is known: / It is a cactus bloom"), will understand the promise that these early poems held of greatness to come. But something went tragically wrong. *Vaudeville for a Princess* (1950) was a misfired effort, nearly all its poems omitted in the *New and Selected Poems*. In the late poems in *Summer Knowledge* Schwartz seems desperately to have wrapped himself in vatic robes, chanting in slack long-lined poems his insistence that "The heights of poetry are like the exaltation of the mountains. / It is the consummation of consciousness in the country of the morning!" Only in a very few poems does the new style inform its own rhetoric with a convincing inner structure. "Seurat's Summer Afternoon along the Seine" succeeds, perhaps because the painting offered Schwartz an escape from subjectivity. Schwartz was an editor of *Partisan Review,* taught at several universities, wrote brilliant and generous criticism (posthumously collected in *Selected Essays,* 1970), but this greatly gifted man gave way to drink and despair. In 1966 he was found dead in a dingy hotel in Greenwich Village. His friend Saul Bellow based *Humboldt's Gift* on Schwartz's unfulfilled life.

Another poet whose great gifts did not quite deliver their promise before his untimely death in 1965 was Randall Jarrell. Graduating from Vanderbilt University before the war, after service in the air force he carried on the tradition of poet as critic established by Ransom, Tate, and Warren. Jarrell's *Poetry and the Age* (1953) is a prose paean to the primacy of the poetic imagination. The essays demonstrate with conviction and power the "dazzling originality" of Whitman's language, the depth of Frost's acquaintance with the night, and, with equanimity leavened by wit, discuss the lot of the modern poet in a society of philistines ("The Obscurity of the Poet"), many of whom have Ph.D.'s and write for the literary quarterlies ("The Age of Criticism"). In an age of such criticism, Jarrell was a poet-critic at his best; later essays appear in *A Sad Heart at the Supermarket* (1962) and the posthumous *The Third Book of Criticism* (1969). He was author also of *Pictures from an Institution* (1954), which raised the genre of the academic novel to a comic satire without peer. From this distinguished prose one infers a man of unusual intelligence, compassion, and wit.

In his poetry Jarrell speaks of losses, fear, the numbed terror of men at war, the irretrievability of the past. In *Little Friend, Little Friend* (1945) and *Losses* (1948), armed with his knowledge of both the techniques and the psychology of air war, Jarrell preserves as in a time capsule what it felt like to live in the midst of destruction, to survive when "Men wash their hands, in blood, as best they can"— or, as in "The Death of the Ball Turret Gunner," not to survive:

> I woke to black flak and the nightmare fighters.
> When I died they washed me out of the turret with
>   a hose.

Jarrell's sensibility was attuned to childhood—his own, and that of the race; many poems recapture the world of *Märchen* from the Brothers Grimm, tales from which, he asks, had we not learned "of our own hearts, the realm of death— / Neither to rule nor die? to change, to change!" This refrain is repeated in the title poem of *The Woman at the Washington Zoo* (1960): "change me, change me!" Yet it is change itself that makes the past irrecoverable and tinges Jarrell's poems with inconsolable sorrow for the loss of experience. His *Complete Poems* appeared in 1969, three years after he was killed by a car as he walked through a highway underpass, an apparent suicide. Lowell has called Jarrell "the most heartbreaking poet of his generation," and this is true. Part of the heartbreak is the reader's sense that Jarrell had not yet quite achieved a truly personal rhythm which would have given his poetry the power his gifts and his vision deserve.

The generation of poets who, like Jarrell, came of age in the early forties arrived just when the modernist masters were beginning to be taught in graduate seminars, and when the New Criticism had come to establish not only how Donne or Keats should be read but what the reader and poet might expect of contemporary poetry. Such criticism encouraged, if not enforced, the Metaphysical development of imagery in stanzaic forms and regular meters; the avoidance of the Romantic ego, as advised by Eliot, which—after his example and those of Yeats and Pound—led to the use of masks or personae; and the implicit assumption that poetry is a form of public discourse (however personal the poem), referential to the history of the race, the language, and the art. So it is that the poets of the forties, who before V-J Day had been called the War Poets, soon became known in literary journalism as the University Wits. This was a label most of them would eventually repudiate.

These poets included John Malcolm Brinnin, John Ciardi, John Frederick Nims, Howard Moss, William Jay Smith, and Winfield Townley Scott, as well as Howard Nemerov and Richard Wilbur. But none more fully conformed to the group identity at first, or later cast off the labeling influences with greater vehemence, than Karl Shapiro. His first two books, *Person, Place, and Thing* (1942) and *V-Letter* (1944) have many superbly written, memorable poems, sometimes Audenesque in diction ("Drug Store") or boldly Metaphysical in conceit ("Fly"), with themes from peace as well as war reflecting the implacable violence of life and the poet's humane sympathy for the suffering of his fellows ("Auto Wreck," "The Leg"). Shapiro felt the empathy of the outsider for the victim everywhere, as evidenced in his poem "University": "To hurt the Negro and avoid the Jew / Is the curriculum." After near-conversion to Catholicism, Shapiro found his own identity as a Jew, a subject about which he wrote directly, as though already casting off the New Criticism. Other hints appear in his *Essay on Rime* (1945), a blank verse *ars poetica* of over two thousand lines composed while Shapiro was in the medical corps in the Dutch East Indies. In this learned yet conversational treatise he says, *inter alia,* "in the prosody of prose / Mines of new rhythm lie"— mines he would soon explore. But first came two books in which, though hewing to conventional forms and meters, he burst the bonds of impersonality. "Recapitulations" (in *Trial of a Poet,* 1947), using quatrains as strict as those in Eliot's Sweeney and Bleistein poems, like the poems of Delmore Schwartz at this time anticipates the later confessional mode. The prosody of prose first appears in "The Dirty Word" that "hops in the cage of the mind . . . stomping with its heavy left claw on the sweet meat of the brain . . . And out of the worn black feathers of the wing have I made these pens to write these elegies, for I have outlived the bird, and I have murdered it in my early man-hood." We are not here told what this word is, but from the poem's reappearance at the beginning of *Poems of a Jew* (1958) its meaning is inferrable. In the introduction to that book Shapiro says that the Holocaust "revived the spiritual image of the Jew . . . as man essentially himself, beyond nationality, defenseless against the crushing impersonality of history. He is man left over, after everything that can happen has happened."

This thoughtful, impassioned, and talented man found himself in a dilemma. The modernist movement in poetry was dominated by Pound and Eliot, whose denigration of Jews Shapiro could neither forgive nor ignore. No more could he separate their aesthetics from their prejudices. (He alone on the 1948 Bollingen Committee voted not to give Pound the prize.) Yet Karl Shapiro had won his place in poetry, it must have seemed to him, through acquiescence in Eliot's conceptions of poetry, tradition, and literary decorum. Shapiro's se-lected essays, *The Poetry Wreck* (1975), document his polemical re-jection of what he saw as the poetry establishment. "T. S. Eliot: The Death of Literary Judgment" (1960) articulates a rejection of Eliot's critical authority already widely felt among younger poets. At this time Shapiro's own poetry took a vehemently anti–New Critical twist: in *The Bourgeois Poet* (1964), he took license to explore his own feel-ings in prose poems. Although at the time Shapiro was reviewed as imitating Allen Ginsberg, he had been considering "the prosody of prose" for twenty years. Nothing if not volatile, Shapiro, who now attacked the use of rhyme as decadent, next, in *White-Haired Lover* (1968), wrote love sonnets in the mode of Millay. In *Adult Bookstore* (1976) this style in turn gives way to strophic free verse. In prose, too, Shapiro has come out upholding a position not even he could have predicted a dozen years earlier—the final essay in *The Poetry Wreck* bemoans the illiteracy of the young who accept the likes of Rod Mc-

Kuen as poets; what they lack is familiarity with the discipline of the sort of poetry Shapiro himself has been trying so hard not to write, and scorns as

> Frozen poems with an ice-pick at the core,
> And lots of allusions from other people's books.

Despite his gifts and intelligence, after his early books Shapiro never settled upon a personal rhythm, an unmistakable individuality. Perhaps his rejections, felt as inescapable, have been made at too great a cost.

Four poets of this generation who have not felt Shapiro's impetus to cast off their former selves but rather have developed by processes of ripening are Richard Wilbur, Howard Nemerov, William Meredith, and Elizabeth Bishop. Not for them Roethke's descent into the primordial id, or the attempts to navigate such troughs and crests as swamped Schwartz and Jarrell. The poets of their generation who dominate the second half of this period were of course Robert Lowell and John Berryman; compared to them, with their intensities and stylistic veerings, these poets seem to operate at lower keys, treating more restricted ranges of feeling from the security of an aesthetic grounded upon assumptions Lowell and Berryman felt they had to abandon. The taste of the seventies has veered toward extremes of self-revelation and the forsaking of verse conventions for improvisatory poetics. Yet the poets named above have not been swayed by fashion, and each in his own way has helped to temper the prevailing romanticism with the virtues of discipline, restraint, and poise.

Wilbur, the youngest (he was born in 1921), leapt to instant preeminence with the finished, controlled lyricism of *The Beautiful Changes* (1947). Just as pastoral poetry is written only in a complex urban culture, only a time of such violence and spiritual uncertainty as our own could encourage the writing of poems like Wilbur's, which hold the dark impulses of the self and the age at bay with civility of outlook and stylistic grace. His early work reflects the linguistic delicacy of Marianne Moore, the contemplative aestheticism of Wallace Stevens. "Cigales," "Water Walker," and "The Beautiful Changes" and, in his next book, *Ceremony* (1950), poems such as "Juggler" and "The Death of the Toad" evoke the poise of aesthetic design in the handling of experience: small in scale, Wilbur's subjects become the springs from which metaphors flow. This is an objective, contemplative poetry, ribbed by the invisible rigor of its exclusions. His range is extended in *Things of This World* (1956), yet the very virtues of

"Mind" are indicative; in this poem, the mind is compared to a bat, flitting faultlessly in a cavern (a beautifully functional allusion to Plato's myth of the Cave):

> And has this simile a like perfection?
> The mind is like a bat. Precisely. Save
> That in the very happiest intellection
> A graceful error may correct the cave.

Mind, so described, is intelligence, the principle of light in an outer darkness. That mind might in part be made of the darkness whose hazards Wilbur's bat so skillfully avoids is not a possibility his poems entertain.

Perhaps as a result of his making superb translations of Molière, Wilbur more recently has moved from meditative to dramatic lyrics. His themes continue through *Advice to a Prophet* (1961), *Walking to Sleep* (1969), and *The Mind-Reader* (1976). He has said that his poems "incline to favor a spirituality which is not abstracted, not dissociated and world-renouncing. A good part of my work could, I suppose, be understood as public quarrel with the aesthetics of Edgar Allan Poe." The pull of that pure poetry advocated by Poe is strong in Wilbur, and is strongly resisted. A particularly fine example of his spirituality which does not renounce the senses is "Love Calls Us to the Things of This World." Yet Wilbur writes, as Poe could not conceivably have written, a poem "For the Student Strikers" at Wesleyan in 1970; true to his conviction that decorum and reasonableness are the necessities of civilized life, Wilbur advises the dissident students to knock on the doors of the hostile townspeople and "Talk with them, then," for "the people are not unlike you." Such advice to the young prophets of radical change may go unheeded, as they, and others, if they turn to poems at all, crave expression of the violence they feel in themselves. Wilbur's work, they may conclude, is not for them, yet such a poetry keeps alive the uses of decorum, the possibilities of civil discourse, of combining mind and feeling in forms and language evocative of delight.

Explaining the title of his first book of poems, *The Image and the Law* (1947), Howard Nemerov wrote that it alluded to "the ever-present dispute between two ways of looking at the world, the way of the eye and that of the mind . . . The mind, operating through images, derives moral laws which are the results of art." Nemerov's poems have remained true to these distinctions, though they do not account for all of his virtues. Gifted with an easy-seeming (though doubtless hard-won) formality, Nemerov excels in three among the many varieties of poems he has written. These are the metaphysical, or speculative, poem; meditative landscape poems—perhaps his most personal note is struck in these; and what may be called light verse, a term here intended to touch on the satiric, the ironical, the genuinely funny. With typical modesty he has written of his own work, "Brought up to a poetry of irony, paradox, wit, as primary means of imagination, brought up to a view that did not always sharply divide the funny from the serious and even the sorrowful, I continue so, and have sometimes found it a strain to suffer critics gladly upon this issue in particular." Not having swerved very far from the aesthetic of his youth, this accomplished poet has had often to suffer critics, gladly or otherwise. Of his development he writes that it was "away from . . . technical devices; I now regard simplicity and the appearance of ease in the measure as primary values, and the detachment of a single thought from its ambiguous surroundings as a worthier object than the deliberate cultivation of ambiguity" (*Poets on Poetry,* 1965).

The metaphysical poems of this voluminous writer of nine books of verse are legion; perhaps none succeeds better than "The Goose Fish" (from *The Salt Garden,* 1955), which in the rational development of its images and the controlled irony of its grotesque elements (lovers, embracing on a moonlit beach, find themselves observed by the skull of a dead fish) triumphantly creates in us the delight in ambiguity which Empson (another of Nemerov's early models) praised. A later example, simpler in structure though no less complex in feeling, is a dramatic monologue, "Death and the Maiden" (*New and Selected Poems,* 1960).

Two of the most remarkable nature poems of this generation are surely Nemerov's "A Day on the Big Branch" and "The Pond." In blank verse, clearly American though suggesting Wordsworth more than Frost, Nemerov in the first explores the incompletion of our recurrent desire for merger of ourselves into an unassimilable wilderness; and in the second, the round of the natural year is melded into the round of life and death in a lyrical meditation of great strength and delicacy. Nemerov's satiric-comic mode begins, memorably enough, in his first book with "History of a Literary Movement" and continues with such later poems as "Mousemeal," "To the Governor & Legislature of Massachusetts," "A Modern Poet." In *Gnomes and Occasions* (1972) and *The Western Approaches* (1975), the comic, serious, and sorrowful are evident, alone and entwined, in epigrams and lyrics which record the observations of an intelligent man of feeling.

Nemerov's work is characterized, even unified, by its discursive syntax and the logical development of imagery—which of course in comedic circumstances becomes true wit. His is a middle style, capable of giving pleasure across a wide band of observations and touching many points on the compass of emotion. Though not attuned to the vehemence of Lowell, Nemerov has his own way of sounding the depths, as in "Mud Turtle," his portrait of the clumsy yet menacing and indomitable creature with a "swollen leech" attached to its soft skin—

> Nobody wants to go close enough
> To burn it loose; he can't be helped
> Either, there is no help for him
> . . . .
> Bearing his hard and chambered hurt
> Down, down, down beneath the water,
> Beneath the earth beneath. He takes
> A secret wound out of the world.

In *Earth Walk: New and Selected Poems* (1970), William Meredith surveys his own work in three earlier volumes, and, in "Reading My Poems from World War II," he writes,

> The poems are not narrative, you never find out
> how they end. Rather, they seem impelled
> by a moral purpose: we are asked not to blame the men.

Meredith's sailors and airmen have been, he says, "transformed into beasts in a stylized chase / . . . as they ride across this tapestry." Indeed, the seascape in his poems of naval warfare appears to him as "a blue meadow" dotted with ships, and "Airplanes, like shoals of tropical fish, / swim in a thin upper sea." These observations are just to the emphasis of those poems, their arrangements of details into patterns which project upon the appearance of the world an internally necessary order. "Certainly," the poet concludes of the men in his war poems, "they have been seen by accountable eyes." The accountability of course is that of the poet, whose "moral purpose" informs the "tapestry" he has designed from the chaos of a world at war. Meredith's forms and rhythms have loosened considerably in his later work, but he has remained a formal poet whose view of experience is that it implicitly contains the forms the poet must discover. He has dealt with the most implacable of themes, the threat of death and the vast loneliness of the sea; his service as a naval aviator lends the perspective from which the struggles of individual men are seen at a distance, ships become figures in a pattern, and the poet's pictorial imagination responds at once to the design and the need for "accountable eyes."

476

There are many such poems in his early books (*Love Letter from an Impossible Land,* 1944; *Ships and Other Figures,* 1948; *The Open Sea,* 1958; *The Wreck of the Thresher,* 1964). He has expressed the modest hope that these poems imply the presence of "a candid man paying steady, scrupulous attention to the events of his life"; that is as close as Meredith has wished to come to autobiography.

Thus it is typical of him that while adopting the freer rhythms prevalent after Lowell's *Life Studies* and Berryman's *Dream Songs,* Meredith has resisted the often concomitant tendency to write directly autobiographical or confessional verse. His book-long portrait, *Hazard, the Painter* (1975), is a third-person study; "Resemblances between the life and character of Hazard and those of the author are not disclaimed but are much fewer than the author would like." This is a novelistic presentation, sixteen vignettes localized in time—the time is 1972, when "Nixon's the One" and Hazard "cannot shake his unpopular conviction / that his nation has bitterly misspoken itself." Hazard feels "He is in charge of morale in a morbid time." The painter for two years has been trying to render a "human figure dangling safe," a man in a parachute "full of half-remembered instruction / but falling and safe." Poems about his wife, children, neighbors, the futile hopes of liberal politics, and his knowledge that he is no Titian or Renoir flesh out the sketch of Hazard, who, at the end, "shapes up":

> Gnawed by a vision of rightness
> that no one else seems to see,
> what can a man do
> but bear witness?

Without raising his voice, in a modest style modeled on speech rhythms, Meredith embodies in his work the artist's quest for order in a shattered world.

Another painterly poet is Elizabeth Bishop. Her early work in its dexterous objectivity, its delight in curious though ever-accurate observations, and its delicacy and restraint carries on the tradition of her friend Marianne Moore. Miss Bishop, beginning as a poet of sight, as she moves from the painter's aesthetic distancing of her subjects to subjecting herself to the reality of what is observed, becomes a poet of vision. The emotions the observed things arouse in her become themselves the structuring principle of her poems, in language always pellucid, plangent, a medium of such transparency that we cease to be aware of the objects in the poems as objects but know them as the terms of our being, inextricable from our experience of them. The

477

relation of this process to painting may be inferred from "Poem" (in *Geography III*, 1976). Seeing a little painting by her great-uncle, she exclaims, "Heavens, I recognize the place, I know it!"—and so shares with her long-dead uncle its memory:

> art "copying from life" and life itself,
> life and the memory of it so compressed
> they've turned into each other. Which is which?

Art, whether "on a piece of Bristol board" or in a poem, is a form of life itself, a bequest of

> —the little that we get for free,
> the little of our earthly trust.

The deepening in Miss Bishop's work from objectivity to the imaginative interiorization of observation is evident in such early poems as "Roosters" and "The Fish" (*North & South*, 1946). In the first the reality of roosters is emblematic, external to the observer whose imagination plays so sportively over barnyard and Gallic steeple with metaphors and associations based on fidelity to the actual and on religious imagery lightly invoked. In "The Fish," however, the caught creature is immediately seen as a mysterious mirror image of the self, its sufferings her sufferings, its wounds felt as hers, its affirmation of life force therefore experienced as a sacred "earthly trust" that makes her cut the line and let it go. All this is rendered in diction of great immediacy, no self-conscious literariness interposing between participant, object, and reader. This poem looks forward to Miss Bishop's later style, fully matured in *Poems: North and South— A Cold Spring* (1955).

"Over 2000 Illustrations and a Complete Concordance"—a poem about looking through a Bible—describes a world with "Everything only connected by 'and' and 'and,'" an experiential chaos which would have been saved by "this old Nativity," could we but have seen it "—and looked and looked our infant sight away." This too concerns "the little of our earthly trust," and how we can bear even that little unredeemed by a transcendent faith. The trope of this poem is to compare the exotic scenes in the illustrated Bible with the way our travels "should have been." Travels are significant to this poet, who grew up in Nova Scotia, lived for fifteen years in Brazil, and called her third book *Questions of Travel* (1965). The contrasts between north and south, austere coasts and verdant tropics, striate her works. (Her first three books are gathered with some new and uncollected poems and translations in *The Complete Poems*, 1969.)

The Nativity we might have seen is followed by several poems of her own "infant sight" and childhood in Nova Scotia—"The Bight," "A Summer's Dream," "At the Fishhouses," and "Cape Breton." These luminous evocations of *what is there,* with exquisite fidelity to the reality observed, move almost imperceptibly from sight and sound to the very depths of consciousness, of being. "At the Fishhouses" begins, casually enough, with the speaker observing an old man mending his nets amid the silvering "layers of beautiful herring scales . . . There are sequins on his vest and on his thumb." The poet shifts her gaze over the wharfside to the water,

> Cold dark deep and absolutely clear,
> element bearable to no mortal,

bearable only to fish, to seals; and she recalls one seal that came nightly, being "curious about me." This seal "was interested in music; / like me a believer in total immersion," and acknowledged her singing him such Baptist hymns as "A Mighty Fortress Is Our God." Whimsical yet believable, this passage ever so lightly dips us into the truth that total immersion, required for resurrection, may be beyond mortal bearing. One cannot escape the folk memory of seals as the souls of lost fishermen—which brings us back reflexively to the old man with whom the poem began, mending nets to catch fish from the cold dark sea. The sea is both "bearable to no mortal" and the redemptive element. "At the Fishhouses," which commenced with a secular image suggestive of Saint Peter, concludes with this meditation upon the depths in which we must be lost to become found:

> If you would dip your hand in,
> your wrist would ache immediately,
> your bones would begin to ache and your hand would burn
> as if the water were a transmutation of fire
> that feeds on stones and burns with a dark gray flame.
> If you tasted it, it would first taste bitter,
> then briny, then surely burn your tongue.
> It is like what we imagine knowledge to be:
> dark, salt, clear, moving, utterly free,
> drawn from the cold hard mouth
> of the world, derived from the rocky breasts
> forever, flowing and drawn, and since
> our knowledge is historical, flowing, and flown.

Religious meaning is wholly implicative, thoroughly immersed in the secular experience of merging with the sea and of knowing. For with knowledge derived from suckling at "rocky breasts," the image of the sea engulfing the person has become reversed, as the person gulps the sea. But such knowledge, being "ours," is perforce "historical," and must therefore be both "flowing, and flown"—a process of acquisition which escapes us in our act of achieving it.

In this poem depths are arrived at through the clarity of invocation, the truths at first hidden revealing themselves through the inner nature of language itself rather than by any conscious manipulation of puns in search of ambiguities. Miss Bishop, true to her own reticent persona, never makes personal revelations or, even when introducing herself as a character, exploits her own feelings. She rather is there, in the poem, as the one to whom happens the experience the poem records more of its own volition than of hers; this objectivity places her in the way of receiving the most particular of experiences which turn themselves into the most universal of meanings. We see such growths of metaphor out of actuality deepened by the play of dreamwork upon the workaday in the three chief poems of her later book, *Geography III*: "In the Waiting Room," "Crusoe in England," and "The Moose."

In the last-named poem, a busload of passengers, traveling from a little Nova Scotian village toward Boston, are drawn together by "Moonlight as we enter / the New Brunswick woods, / hairy, scratchy, splintery." Their conversation is "Grandparents' voices . . . in Eternity"—who said what, who was lost at sea, who took to drink or went mad, answered with the half-uttered syllable "that means 'Life's like that. / We know *it* (also death).' " The pilgrimage jolts to a sudden stop as the bus driver turns the headlights off:

> A moose has come out of
> the impenetrable wood
>
> . . . .
> Towering, antlerless,
> high as a church,
> homely as a house
>
> . . . .
> Why, why do we feel
> (we all feel) this sweet
> sensation of joy?

The moose ("It's a she!") is Miss Bishop's totemic creature, an apotheosis like the buck in Frost's "The Most of It" or Faulkner's bear, which represents the natural order of creation and is therefore sacred, a source of joy. Her totem arrives on the human highway in the middle of the dark wood, and as her governing imagery so often is (like the "rocky breasts" in "At the Fishhouses"), it is female, here suggesting home and church. As she has told us is the nature of such knowledge, "flowing, and flown," when the bus driver shifts gears, "there's a dim / smell of moose, an acrid / smell of gasoline."

When Robert Lowell desired to change his style from its early grandiloquence to the colloquial intensity of *Life Studies,* one of his most cherished models was the work of his friend Elizabeth Bishop. Her poems are always modest in their overt claims on us, but rich and deep, tinged with the strangeness of things and the mystery of knowledge.

The two strongest poetic personalities of this generation were Robert Lowell and John Berryman. Lowell arrived earlier with *Lord Weary's Castle* (1946); Berryman's early work was able but derivative. In *Homage to Mistress Bradstreet* (1953), however, he emerged as a major poet. The two were friends, and rivals, their careers curiously parallel. They were the most ambitious, accomplished, dense, and idiosyncratic poets of their generation, and did more than any others to change sensibility and extend the possibilities of their art. With the death of Berryman in 1972 and of Lowell in 1977 an era was ended. Among their survivors are several extraordinary poets, but none dominates the climate of contemporary poetry as these had done.

With his first, privately printed book, *Land of Unlikeness* (1944), introduced by Allen Tate, Lowell burst upon the scene with his furious energy, learning, and lust for apocalypse. Two years later *Lord Weary's Castle,* containing some poems rewritten from the earlier volume and much new work, announced the arrival of a poet of unmistakable power. His sensibility was steeped in the great tradition, his lines rolled with Miltonic grandeur, in ambitious poems that adapted to personal uses stanzas modeled on Donne or borrowed from Matthew Arnold. The poet so well armed felt violent conflicts, both personal and cultural, with great intensity. Indeed, it was the assimilation of the cultural to the personal that gave Lowell's poems their urgency, their universality.

Robert Lowell had already expressed in his life his vehement need for self-delineation, putting the greatest distance possible between himself and the Brahmin caste of his family. A grandnephew of the late president of Harvard, he left Harvard for Kenyon College, where he studied with Ford Madox Ford and John Crowe Ransom. This scion of Old Boston sought out the two leading men of letters of the South, Ransom and Tate, and made himself an heir to the Fugitives, adopting their views on the centrality of what Eliot had termed "the historical imagination" as well as their criticism of industrial and urban society. What is more, Lowell, descendant of Episcopal ministers, became a convert to Roman Catholicism. This was a break both religious and secular, since, in Boston, Catholicism associated him with the faith of the Irish and other immigrant stocks. And in wartime this son of a naval officer went to prison as a conscientious objector. Yet each of these rebellions expressed the very values from which it was intended to separate him. At Kenyon, Lowell continued the classical education for which he was destined.

If no poet of the period so fully assimilated history to his own sensibility as Lowell, none so deeply felt the need to transcend historical reality. Not even Eliot in "Ash Wednesday" or *Four Quartets* renounced the world with the intensity of Lowell in "As at a Plane Tree by the Water," "In Memory of Arthur Winslow," or "Christmas Eve under Hooker's Statue." Many of the poems in *Lord Weary's Castle* contrast the spiritual desolation of earthly time with the almost impossible hope of eternity. The poet's visionary Catholicism is used as an instrument of accusation and judgment of his American—and specifically his New England—inheritance. Boston becomes the City of Dis in the iconography of these poems, and the condition of our life is represented by the war. In "Children of the Light," he writes, "Pilgrims unhouseled by Geneva's night . . . planted here the Serpent's seeds of light." The light of their heresy has now become the "pivoting searchlights" of the Air Defense Command, whose shining shocks "the riotous glass houses" of those who let candles gutter by deserted altars,

> And light is where the landless blood of Cain
> Is burning, burning the unburied grain

—an allusion to the disposal of surplus wheat while postwar millions starved abroad. In poem after poem Lowell fired his dense metaphorical charges against the "riotous" secular culture in which even observance of the Puritans' pieties would be bootless, since their inheritance is corrupted by acquisitiveness and stained with blood of "the Redman's bones."

Lord Weary's Castle is filled with hints of directions Lowell would explore in later books. The translations from Rimbaud, Valéry, Rilke, and Sextus Propertius, already called "imitations" in a prefatory note, look ahead to his versions on themes from other poets from Homer to Pasternak in *Imitations* (1961). The tetrameter line in stanzas of couplets modeled on Marvell's "The Garden," which would become the chief structure in *Near the Ocean* (1967), is powerfully used in the poem "The Drunken Fisherman." Ten poems (including several imitations) in *Lord Weary's Castle* are in sonnet form (sometimes irregularly metered or rhymed); the form, handled more freely, would become the stanza for nearly five hundred poems in five books from *Notebook 1967-1968* (1969) through *The Dolphin* (1973).

His being a New England Lowell, not in itself an artistic advantage, he made the center of his poetic identity. In *Lord Weary's Castle,* his own personality speaks individually but indirectly in poems like "In Memory of Arthur Winslow," distanced by historical and mythological reference to fulfill Eliot's dictum that the poet himself not be the subject of the poem. The high baroque style of the elegy on Arthur Winslow contrasts to the style of "Mary Winslow" (another elegy), which is closer to Ransom's light ironic tone; with diction almost colloquial, as in Eliot's "Cousin Nancy," this is a faint precursor of *Life Studies* (1959). When Lowell deals with his family romance at yet a further remove, inventing masks, his strategies are least successful. It was such flawed, complicated poems, however, as "Between the Porch and the Altar" and "The Death of the Sheriff" which pointed his immediate way to his next book, *The Mills of the Kavanaughs* (1951).

Here he wrote self-revelations resembling Browning's most contorted psychological dramatic monologues but versified in pentameter couplets of sonorous gravity. The tales Lowell felt compelled to tell were all too ingenious, too arcane. His personae include the widow of a Catholic naval officer stationed at Pearl Harbor whose mansion in Maine has a garden-statue to Persephone; a Canadian nun stationed in New Brunswick; the widower of a German-American Catholic suicide. The verse is supple, the characterizations obscurely vivid, but the sensibility behind the poems is obsessed by personal problems these masks neither clarify nor resolve. The title poem, half again as long as *The Waste Land,* gleams with sharp images and rich evocations of the Maine setting—some to be resurrected in later poems; but in style as well as content this is an intricate monument at the dead end of a trail.

In the next eight years Lowell published no book, perhaps because his life was so disoriented. The last poem in *Mills of the Kavanaughs* implied the loss of his belief in Catholicism; he was by then divorced from Jean Stafford and married to Elizabeth Hardwick. On a reading tour in the mid-fifties, Lowell arrived in San Francisco, where Allen Ginsberg's *Howl* and Gary Snyder's *Myths and Texts,* not yet published, were being declaimed in coffee houses in North Beach.

Lowell found his own poems ponderous, stilted, weighed down with the armor of their conventions; reading them aloud, he made impromptu revisions toward more colloquial diction.

At this time Lowell had, or felt that he had, exhausted what his training thus far made it possible for him to say. Now he turned to the rival tradition in American poetry. "Williams enters me but I cannot enter him . . . I am almost saying that I cannot enter America," Lowell wrote in 1962. "It's as if no poet except Williams had really seen America or heard its language." What Lowell most values in Williams's free forms are his inimitable qualities, "quick changes of tone, atmosphere and speed." It is these which Lowell will now adopt and perfect in his own work, foregoing "the full armor of the past." "The times have changed. A drastic experimental art is now expected and demanded. The scene is dense with the dirt and power of industrial society." The verse line is no longer an inheritance cloaked with allusion, heavy with reference, but a fresh invention or discovery; its rhythm is inherent in the expression of each particular experience or emotion. And the poem's structure is no longer an *a priori* architecture of stanzas; it is improvisatory, implicit but inchoately present in experience, which it is the poet's task to clarify by expressing in its intrinsic form. The qualities in Williams that Lowell calls "American" give this illusion of expression without precedent, the freedom of the individual confronting life not on his fathers' terms but on his own. Lowell also said at this time that he wished to recover for poetry the territory it had surrendered to the novel—by which he meant the presentation of actuality. He had in mind the concrete particularity of Flaubert and Chekhov.

These were the chief stylistic influences that served the change in Lowell's way of treating his subjects. Only in "Rebellion" had he spoken out directly, and there aesthetic distance is imposed by nightmare. But now, after the examples of *The Pisan Cantos* and *Howl*, as well as of Baudelaire, Rimbaud, and Rilke, in *Life Studies* (1959) Lowell comes close to Poe's prediction of the theme that would revolutionize poetry: *My heart laid bare.* Shapiro and Schwartz had preceded him, prematurely in the event, in grappling with personal demons. By the time Lowell undertook to write free-associating poems about "the anarchy of my adolescent rebellion against my parents," the times had prepared an audience to receive his revelations. Middleclass Americans were now familiar with psychotherapy, and the direct expression of Oedipal conflicts would soon be welcomed; the poet's obligation would be felt to be that of telling the undisguised truths about his most intimate relationships, rather than cloaking these in masks, allusions, or allegories. In fact, it was Lowell's therapist who suggested he write a journal of his childhood experiences. The result was the prose section, "91 Revere Street," of *Life Studies*: this provided the context for the succeeding poems, some of which were first written as prose, some as formal verse.

Another *donnée* of this new psychological frankness was that in his poems Lowell now unabashedly "faced the kingdom of the mad." Where Roethke had written of this aspect of his own suffering, "What is madness but nobility of soul / At odds with circumstance? "—restating the Romantic assertion that in madness is wisdom—Lowell, in such poems as "Waking in the Blue," "Home after Three Months Away," and "Man and Wife," dramatizes his mental illness not as divine revelation but as mortal suffering. When he writes, "We are all old-timers, / each of us holds a locked razor," his illness is extended beyond the walls to the rest of society. From his poems on the world about him we can infer that society itself is mad; the suffering poet in a mental hospital looms as a Promethean hero for our sick age.

Life Studies is the fulcrum of American poetry after the war, the turning point not only in Lowell's own career but also in the work of many younger poets. What he had accomplished here—the breakthrough from received to provisional rhythms and forms—corresponded to a widely sensed change in feeling, in the expectations of readers of poetry. Lowell's new subjects placed the poet's personality at the center of his art and at the center of his audience's interest in his work.

From the first Lowell had built his poems outward from inward experience, but had done so by mythologizing experience, as in the early elegy for his grandfather Winslow. But now, in another family elegy, "My Last Afternoon with Uncle Devereaux Winslow," there are no rhymes, no regular stanzas, no religious or classical or historical allusions, as the five-year-old boy regards his doomed uncle:

> While I sat on the tiles
> and dug at the anchor on my sailor blouse,
> Uncle Devereux stood behind me.
> He was brushed as Bayard, our riding horse.
> His face was putty.
>
> . . . .
>
> He was dying of the incurable Hodgkin's disease . . .

What are given are the bare facts of experience, not a bill of lading of High Culture: bare facts chosen with so sharp an eye to their inherent reflexive meanings that a pattern of associations develops from their mere report—the anchor on the sailor blouse, for example,

relates to his uncle's and aunt's desire to sail away on a last honeymoon. The passage above, the conclusion of the poem, goes on,

> My hands were warm, then cool on the piles
> of earth and lime,
> a black pile and a white pile . . .
> Come winter,
> Uncle Devereaux would blend to the one color.

Throughout the poem the little boy playing in the summer farmyard
is contrasted to the hieratic family life and the twenty-nine-year-old
victim. The child's innocent eye is a dramatically neutral recorder of
the pathos of his uncle's fate. In this improvisatory structure the experience is inseparable from the form, and the structure inheres in
the experience itself—or rather in its presentation. The lines are in
no regular or predictable rhythm, but find in their own phrasing the
dynamics of their division. Nor is there an extractable argument
from this poem.

The mode of poetic thinking in this section of *Life Studies* was to
be developed further in *For the Union Dead* (1964). But it is worth
noting that the innovative features of *Life Studies* account for only
part of that book, and in the long run for Lowell the other part would
be just as significant. The poems in that other part include the four
in the opening section ("Beyond the Alps" is the most notable of these)
and the four in section three addressed to other writers (Ford Madox
Ford, Santayana, Delmore Schwartz, Hart Crane). Most of these are in
meters and stanzas, developed flexibly from his mode in *Lord Weary's
Castle*. Four are sonnets. In Lowell's work there is a continuing tension between the metrical tradition of referential poetry and the free
verse of provisional structure. Successive books would veer toward
one or the other, sometimes embracing both. The iambic pentameter
line proved not so readily dispensable; it had become the natural
vehicle for Lowell's poetic speech, sometimes abandoned and replaced
but never for very long. He can "enter America" through Williams's
rival tradition, but he cannot give up either Europe or history.

It is when Lowell yokes these contrary tendencies together, in poems
whose stanzaic structures contain irregularly metered lines that de-
part from but retain the resonance of their iambic base, that he most
successfully combines personal experience with public significance.
Such poems as "Skunk Hour" in *Life Studies* and the title poem in *For
the Union Dead* exemplify this style at its most piercingly personal,
most far-reaching. In "Skunk Hour" the "subject" is the poet's fear of
the onslaught of madness; this is specified in a line at the center of

the poem, "My mind's not right." But leading up to that are five stanzas in which the range of vision, concern, and association relentlessly narrows from the world of the "hermit heiress," hierarchic and ancient, to that of the *arriviste* "summer millionaire," to that of the "fairy decorator," whose work, like his love, is fraudulent. At the center of these concentric circles, the poet, cut off from the lovers parked near the town graveyard, feels his "ill-spirit sob in each blood cell . . . I myself am hell." His survival finds a surprising image in his recognition of kinship with a skunk rooting in garbage, who "will not scare." This poem is filled with strengths and subtleties which resist summary or analysis (though see John Berryman's essay on the poem, reprinted in *The Freedom of the Poet*, 1976). The falseness of the "real" world, the pain of alienation from it, and the strength of the poet's identification with the life force represented by the skunk come through with the combined poignance and gravity that give this poem its force. The skunk stays in one's mind as a natural image, at once indulgent and grotesque, of the poet as Philoctetes.

"For the Union Dead" (the style of the poem epitomizes that of the book) extends the associative freedom of "Skunk Hour" to themes simultaneously public and personal, as the public dimension is made importunate by the pressures of personal feeling. The time is 1963, the civil rights movement is juxtaposed to Boston's monument for Colonel Shaw, who led a troop of Negro soldiers in the Civil War. As St. Gaudens's statue commemorates their heroism in their time, Lowell's poem is a monument to our time, when "a savage servility / slides by on grease." The poem swallows history (the Negroes' monument "sticks like a fishbone / in the city's throat"), and, through the interplay of its subterranean and reptilian imagery, judges ourselves. Where the judgments in *Lord Weary's Castle* had been rhetorical and denunciatory, ordained by the poet's looking down from his lofty platform of visionary dogma, here the speaker is implicated in the world he observes. The conclusions flow from his observations. This poem has set its seal upon a turbulent decade.

During this troubled time, with the aid of his new flexible style, Lowell strove to assimilate both history and Europe. In *Imitations* he did not merely translate Homer, Sappho, and fifteen poets from Villon to Montale; he virtually absorbed them. His versions are frequently original Lowell poems based on their originals, heightened to a violence of language and act often absent from the foreign texts. The centers of this book are Baudelaire and Rimbaud, the Symbolists for whom poetry was a self-created world. In the same year, 1961, appeared Lowell's translation of *Phaedra*, treating Racine with as much liberty as Racine had taken with Euripides. Here was a fable from two earlier cultures which probed the conflicts of love, lust, and loyalty within a family. It was as though the Greek and French tragedies validated the plots of Lowell's tangled dramatic monologues.

Already steeped in his American predecessors, Lowell proves the one writer since Hawthorne who has most thoroughly assimilated Puritanism and its burdens. With political passions stirred by opposition to the Vietnam war, Lowell wrote a trilogy of one-act plays (*The Old Glory*, 1965) based on tales by Hawthorne and Melville. "Endecott and the Red Cross" combines Hawthorne's tale of the Puritan who ripped the Red Cross from the British flag with his story "The May-Pole of Merry Mount"; a second play dramatizes "My Kinsman, Major Molineux"; while the third is developed from Melville's novella *Benito Cereno*. In these plays Lowell treats, respectively, rebellion against the Established Church; rebellion against the State; and the revolt of slaves against their masters. In "Benito Cereno," the most notable verse play since the death of Yeats, although the immediate victims are the Spanish captain and his crew, the focus of Lowell's irony is the American sea captain who tries to rescue them. A morally obtuse Yankee, he blunders into evil without recognizing what is under his nose. Contemporary application of Melville's fable was not far to seek.

In the sixties Lowell became more involved in public events. He accepted President Johnson's invitation to attend a cultural fête, then publicly rejected it to protest continuance of the Vietnam war. He marched on the Pentagon in company with Norman Mailer and several thousand war protesters. When Senator Eugene McCarthy announced his candidacy in the 1968 Democratic presidential primary, Lowell became his supporter and friend. During the student uprisings at Columbia that year Lowell was present. All of this was to penetrate his poetry; the problem would be how to manage public symbolic action and personal feeling.

Pound's *Cantos* provided the model, perhaps the negative model, for such a mixture of motives, experiences, and themes. But Lowell could not commit himself to a *vers libre* epic. Perhaps it was his long partiality to the sonnet, combined with the example of his psychoanalyst, Dr. Merrill Moore, a literary disciple of the Fugitives and author of *M* (1938), a book of one thousand very freely written "autobiographical sonnets," that led Lowell to choose the unrhymed sonnet as his stanza for *Notebook 1967–1968* (1969). The stanza became a machine for the minting of poems. "Accident threw up subjects, and the plot swallowed them—famished for human chances," Lowell wrote, calling his book "one poem, jagged in pattern." It is neither chronicle, almanac, nor diary, but his response to the times, interspersed with flashbacks to his own past and the larger past of history. "I lean heavily to the rational, but am devoted to surrealism."

Once committed to his rational-surreal stanzas, Lowell seemed compelled to recycle into them all of his life, works, and readings. "One poem" inevitably suggests the sonnet sequences of the past, although his fourteen-liners are perhaps more unlike sonnets than like them. In place of the conventional sonnet's devices Lowell provides a freer rhythm, a more open flow of association, sudden alternations between close observation and slashing images that render states of feeling. But scarcely any of the stanzas coheres as a single poem. The effect is of occasional flashes of lightning in a dark wood—"words meat-hooked from the living steer." The original *Notebook 1967–1968* outgrew its own diaristic design, and the following year, 1970, an expanded edition, called simply *Notebook*, appeared. Three years later this work-in-progress was metamorphosed yet again in the simultaneous publication of three books: *History, For Lizzie and Harriet,* and *The Dolphin.*

In the first version of *Notebook,* stanzas on contemporary events alternated with ruminations on historical types and analogues; for example, grouped under the heading "Power" were poems on Allah, Attila, Clytemnestra, Roland, Tamerlane, Richard III, Charles V, the Duc de Nemours, Bishop Berkeley, Andrew Jackson, Admiral Onishi; in *History* these, some retitled or rewritten, appear chronologically, dispersed between pages 35 and 132. *History* is half given to Lowell's meditations on and re-creations of such figures, from biblical times through the early twentieth century; the remainder of the poems are snatches and sketches of his own life and times, particularly his reworking of the matter of *Life Studies* and his quick, vivid sketches of the writers he has known. These last are the most memorable. The "rationality" toward which Lowell leans is suggested by the chronological arrangement, implying that *History* will offer the incorporation of the usable human past into one contemporary sensibility. The "surrealism" enters in the disjunction of design, both of the individual stanzas and of the whole. Thus the work replicates the chaotic flux of life itself. As Lowell writes in *For Lizzie and Harriet,* "I'm learning to live in history. / What is history? What you cannot touch." Here, the question just asked and answered is preceded by the phrase, "You're gone." In this book Lowell abstracted from and added to the *Notebook* stanzas about, or addressed to, his divorced wife and daughter. The third volume, *The Dolphin,* constitutes yet another quasi-sonnet sequence on his attachment and subsequent marriage to Caroline Blackwood, the English novelist. Thus these two smaller books continue the unsparing self-revelation begun in *Life Studies*.

History, for all its incidental brilliancies, seems too much an act of will, a conscious effort to write the equivalent of an epic poem. It may be that its disordered rationalism, its surreal glintings, require—as each of Lowell's earlier books required—that we learn to read it on its own terms; perhaps the sheer bulk of the work demands that we live with it until, as with Pound's *Cantos*, it becomes assimilated to contemporary sensibility. The two more personal books are more accessible, for Lowell had already taught us to embrace confessional poetry, and the obscurities of their individual stanzas seem only incidental to the design of the wholes.

The title of his next, and last, book of poems, *Day by Day* (1977), suggests a drastic scaling down of the grandiloquent implications announced by *History*. Now, taking as his subjects middle age, his third marriage, the birth of a son, residence in England, illness and hospitalization, his return to the United States, and memories of his earlier life, he writes autobiographical poems of the most painful honesty. At last freeing himself from the obsessive stanzas of the past decade, he returns to an irregular free verse reminiscent of *For the Union Dead*, but more baffled and exhausted in tone and rhythm. Poems end equivocally: "Is getting well ever an art, / or art a way to get well?"; "if we see light at the end of the tunnel, / it's the light of an oncoming train." Yet even this joyless view of life Lowell makes the grounds for the affirmation of a new style, thus a kind of deliverance, as he tells us in "Epilogue":

> Those blessèd structures, plot and rhyme—
> why are they no help to me now
> I want to make
> something imagined, not recalled?
>
> . . . .
> All's misalliance.
> Yet why not say what happened?

He would invoke "the grace of accuracy" found in Vermeer—the choice of this painter of homely detail is appropriate to the scale of local truths Lowell aches to record with absolute fidelity:

> We are poor passing facts,
> warned by that to give
> each figure in the photograph
> his living name.

Torn by the conflicts of his personal life, in which "choice itself is wrong," Lowell, returning to New York from a visit in Ireland to his son and his now-estranged third wife, suffered a fatal heart attack. "My eyes flicker, the immortal / is scraped, unconsenting, from the mortal." His turbulent autobiography remains what he made it in his poems, a life study of his time.

"John, we used the language as if we made it," Lowell wrote in a sonnet addressed to his contemporary (*History*, p. 203). The line is tribute, and it is true: Berryman's poems seem written in a dialect the reader must learn to read. At first, though, that was not the case. Until he found his own voice, or rather voices, Berryman was an adept, promising writer of intellectualized verses. His early work (*Poems*, 1942; *The Dispossessed*, 1948) echoes Yeats and Auden; the tone is objective, lacking personal intensity. His subjects are the crises of the times. Not until the crises in the poems became those of the poet himself did the work speak, shout, laugh, or moan with authenticity and power.

This new style was first revealed in the work that is its most perfected expression, *Homage to Mistress Bradstreet*, published in *Partisan Review*, 1953, and as a book in 1956. The fifty-seven eight-line stanzas were modeled, Berryman has said, on Yeats's "In Memory of Major Robert Gregory," though repeating a more varied metrical pattern than those stanzas. The alternation of longer and shorter lines gave a pulsation to the movement of the verse. But what brought its power to the poem was the conceit on which the whole is based, and the discovery of voices which made possible the expression of that conceit. In *Homage*, Berryman communes with, speaks to, and merges with Anne Bradstreet, the Puritan poetess. She is invoked as his Muse and soon enough becomes, in an amazing passage, his imaginary mistress, whom he would love across the centuries. Meanwhile she has told, in greatly apocopated and syncopated stanzas, of her voyage to America, her marriage, her childbearing, her faith, her griefs, her isolation and alienation from the world in which she wrote what he calls "all this bald / abstract didactic rime I read appalled." The astonishing passage in which she endures childbirth in the wilderness (stanzas 18-21) becomes a paradigm of the pain of all creation, a theme Berryman would expatiate upon in the later *Dream Songs*.

At the time he wrote *Homage* he was also writing, or had just written, *Berryman's Sonnets*, not published until 1967. This sequence of 115 Petrarchan sonnets anatomizes an adulterous love affair. "The original fault was whether wickedness / was soluble in art," he says in a dream song prefatory to the sonnets. "History says it is," he rather dubiously concludes, and so published the sequence. In these poems, too, he had made stylistic advances over his early work, chiefly in the direction of idiosyncrasies of syntax, quick changes of tone, of rhythm. The sonnets are so personal, indeed so *confessional,* it is hard to realize that they were written in the early 1950s, before *Life Studies.* Clearly much of the libidinous energy of the sonnets, or rather of the affair they record, enters *Mistress Bradstreet.* In these two long poems Berryman had used extremely demanding regular stanzas with the greatest possible stylistic and syntactical freedom. He was bursting the bonds of form while retaining the intensity of form's restraints.

Berryman also began publishing his dream songs, as he called them, in magazines in the mid-1950s; *77 Dream Songs* appeared in 1964, *His Toy, His Dream, His Rest* (containing Dream Songs 78-385) in 1968; the two books were combined the next year as *The Dream Songs.* The dedication of the second volume "To Mark Van Doren and to the sacred memory of Delmore Schwartz" obliquely hints at clues to the inception of these strange threnodies. Van Doren had been Berryman's teacher, encourager, and friend; unlikely as it seems, the younger poet may have found, if not a model in Van Doren's conservative, delicate lyrics, at least an instigation toward his innovative enterprise. It was Van Doren's "Dunce Songs," a series of irregular rhymed poems in the Tom o'Bedlam tradition, that Berryman particularly praised, calling them "beautiful and weird," though in the event they were not so weird and beautiful as his own dream songs would be.

Berryman admired his contemporary Schwartz to idolatry, for Schwartz, already a confessional poet before the war, had dared, or had been doomed, to make the exploration of his own inner life the subject of his poetry. Hailed, as we have seen, as a great original before either Lowell or Berryman had published at all, Schwartz was never able to surpass or repeat his early achievement. ("I'd bleed to say his lovely work improved / but it is not so"; Dream Song 150.) At last, his talent destroyed by paranoia and alcohol, Schwartz died a ruined poet. Berryman, also an alcoholic and sufferer from depression, had the luck, however, to have his gifts survive these afflictions. *The Dream Songs* may be seen as the fulfillment of what Schwartz had attempted with less sustained success.

As was true in the earlier *Mistress Bradstreet* and *Sonnets,* Berryman required a stanza against which to forge the rhythms of his feelings. The form he devised was at once as tight and as loose as could be desired: the dream song consists of three six-line stanzas, containing rhyme—usually the third and sixth lines rhyme, sometimes others do, or do not. Metrically, too, the line is elastic, the normative pentameter stretching or shrinking as emphasis requires. Often the third and sixth lines are sapphics, but not always, and other lines may be brief as well.

The Dream Songs derive poignant power from the interchanges between seemingly autonomous voices who speak or sing in them. One of these is Berryman's voice, often grave, sometimes literary (as in his opening lines "O journeyer, deaf in the mould, insane . . ."), yet quickly shifting to the demotic ("Goodbye, sir & fare well. You're in the clear."). Sometimes syntax is wrenched, and the strong accentual rhythm displaced for emphasis, as in this concluding stanza from Dream Song 1:

> What he has now to say is a long
> wonder the world can bear & be.
> Once in a sycamore I was glad
> all at the top, and I sang.
> Hard on the land wears the strong sea
> and empty grows every bed.

Sometimes opposed to, sometimes in concert with this voice is another, that of a persona called Henry (the "he" of the stanza above). He is addressed by an unnamed friend as Mr. Bones, Henry Pussycat, Henry Hankovitch, and by other familiar nicknames. On investigation, Henry proves to be "a human American man" whose sufferings, lusts, griefs, and memories are the burden of his "sad wild riffs." Henry and his end-man sometimes speak as in a minstrel show, white men in blackface using a darky dialect in which Berryman could unbutton libidinous fantasies (Dream Song 26):

> The glories of the world struck me, made me aria once.
> —What happen then, Mr. Bones?
> if be you cares to say.
> —Henry. Henry became interested in women's bodies,
> his loins were & were the   scene of stupendous achievement.
> Stupor. Knees, dear. Pray.

Many are the losses Henry mourns and moans—the deaths of Roethke, Frost, Jarrell, Schwartz—but in especial this loss (Dream Song 76):

> in a modesty of death I join my father
> who dared so long agone leave me.
> A bullet on a concrete stoop
> close by the smothering southern sea
> spreadeagled on an island, by my knee.
> —You is from hunger, Mr. Bones.

Berryman's father in fact committed suicide when the poet was eleven. As a lapsed Catholic Berryman seems abandoned also by his Father: "God's Henry's enemy." *The Dream Songs* has no narrative or chronology; the poems are arranged thematically as Henry tries through his art to cope with his despairs, undergoes again and again a kind of dying from which there is a sort of resurrection. This psychic pattern dominates the poems. Inevitably they suggest comparison with Lowell's decade-long immersion in *Notebook* and *History*. In his last book Lowell addressed the dead Berryman, saying "really we had the same life," the experience of their generation ("Les Maudits"). And Lowell confesses he has at last "discovered how we differ—humor." This indeed is so. Many of the dream songs are wonderfully comic, laughter making bearable Henry's "wonder the world can bear & be." But although *The Dream Songs* and *History* share much of these poets' generic life, each containing poems to or about the older master poets and their own doomed generation, Lowell's effort to embody the world's history and the public events of his time is not paralleled in Berryman's book. True, there are dream songs such as "The Lay of Ike" and a few others about events of the 1960s, but Berryman's songs and dreams all exfoliate from his wounded self.

Despite the dream songs about his father's suicide, in his posthumous, unfinished novel *Recovery* (1973), about his struggle with alcoholism, the problems of the author-surrogate devolve from his relationship with "an unspeakably powerful possessive adoring MOTHER." That an Oedipal problem might be a root of Berryman's anxieties could be inferred from his one sustained critical study, *Stephen Crane* (1950), a brilliant, empathetic, complexly Freudian analysis of the earlier writer's personality as well as his work. Berryman's choice of "Henry" as the name of his mask in *The Dream Songs* is intricately related to Crane's obsessions in *The Red Badge of Courage,* whose hero is called Henry Fleming, and in *The Monster,* in which the mutilated Negro is also named Henry.

After Berryman's suicide in 1972, many further dream songs were found among his manuscripts (over forty appear in the posthumous collection *Henry's Fate,* 1977). But after choosing 385 for the canonical *Dream Songs,* Berryman in his next book, *Love and Fame* (1970), and in *Delusions, Etc.* (1972), completed just before his death, abandoned the dream song stanza and its counterpointed voices for prose-textured, rhythmically ragged quatrains. The material of these poems is his own life, reconstructed or exploited without the intervention of masks or interlocutors. Among loving evocations of his student literary life at Columbia and Cambridge universities in the 1930s and, in the later book, an anguished series of poems on the canonical hours, his effort at total truth telling includes a compulsion to boast of sexual conquests. Some of the confessional poems are both explicit and unattractive. But these, like poems of Baudelaire, may be intended to define the poet's subjection to life without spirit. Berryman had arrived at that sump of spiritual exhaustion from which Lowell would write *Day by Day*. In a poem in *Delusions, Etc.* entitled "He Resigns," "Hosts / of regrets come & find me empty."

> I don't feel this will change.
> I don't want anything
> or person, familiar or strange.
> I don't think I will sing
>
> any more just now;
> or ever. I must start
> to sit with a blind brow
> above an empty heart.

Like Lowell, like his idol Schwartz, like Pound, like Wordsworth, Coleridge, and Keats before them, Berryman confronts and grapples with his despair by making it the burden of his art. In the great Romantic tradition the poet is at the center of the poem: replacing the public man as hero, the poet, as the man of feeling, tells us how it is to live in this world. His sorrows and his sufferings are not only personal disasters, they define the emotional climate of our age.

11

Poetry:
Schools of Dissidents
Daniel Hoffman

Now if ever it is time to cleanse Helicon . . .
POUND, "Homage to Sextus Propertius"

"What are all those fish that lie gasping on the strand?"
YEATS, "Three Movements"

BY the time that Lowell and Berryman had broken away from the period style of the 1950s, several other revolts were well under way. One of these, the confessional movement, so called by literary journalists, was in fact instigated by the two poets just named and by Lowell's former writing students W. D. Snodgrass, Anne Sexton, and Sylvia Plath. Other epicenters of resistance to what was perceived as the effects of the New Criticism on current writing emerged almost simultaneously all around the country: in San Francisco, where the Beat Generation suddenly burst into public notice in national magazines (not so much for their writings as in outraged accounts of their divergent life-styles); in North Carolina, where Charles Olson at Black Mountain College led the movement in the arts to which that college lends its name; in the work of W. S. Merwin and other existential poets whose pessimistic view of the world could no longer support their use of extant poetic conventions; in Minnesota, where Robert Bly and James Wright delved into their own psyches—with the help of Spanish surrealism—for "deep images" revelatory of fundamental truths; in New York, where several poets associated with French surrealism and action painting—Frank O'Hara, John Ashbery, Kenneth Koch—introduced a solipsistic aestheticism almost new to American poetry.

Each of these poetries attracted disciples, publicists, and interpreters. New magazines and publishers sprang up to proclaim their messages of deliverance from the tyranny of the iamb: *San Francisco Review* and Lawrence Ferlinghetti's City Lights Press for the Beats; *The Fifties* (later *The Sixties,* then *The Seventies*) magazine and press of Robert Bly; for Black Mountaineers, Robert Creeley's *Black Mountain Review,* Cid Corman's *Origin,* Clayton Eshleman's *Caterpillar,* and many more fugitive organs. The confessional poets and the New York School needed no special presses—they were taken on at once by trade publishers.

This balkanization of contemporary poetry has produced an acrimonious spirit of discussion in which partisans of each splinter group make exclusionary claims for their own aesthetic against what they presume to be the literary establishment and, sometimes, against each other. (A congeries of these poets, who share little but their rebellion against the period style of the fifties, are gathered together under one roof in Donald Allen's anthology, *The New American Poetry,* 1960; their respective prolegomena appear in his *Poetics of the New American Poetry,* 1973.) Few are the contemporary critics or poets who can express admiration for, say, Frank O'Hara without feeling compelled to disparage the achievement of, say, Richard Wilbur; O'Hara himself could not abide Lowell; the master of Black Mountain and denizens of his subordinate foothills have put forward their claims by attacking those of their contemporaries. Kenneth Rexroth, as will be seen, introduced the Beat Generation with intemperate diatribes against all poets east of San Francisco. At any rate the Establishment —The Enemy—are perceived as nearly all poets not of the persuasions just enumerated, comprising the elders discussed in the previous chapter and a group of younger poets as individual in accomplishment as James Merrill, Anthony Hecht, John Hollander, Richard Howard, David Wagoner, Theodore Weiss. But the Establishment, as established by those who oppose it, does not include Galway Kinnell, Louis Simpson, James Dickey, A. R. Ammons, or William Stafford, who, without carrying cards in any of the aforementioned literary parties, march to their own drummers against the alleged academicism they, like the other rebels, reject.

The fratricidal intensity of these quarrels reflects a peculiarly American situation. Poetry has become the most private, least accessible of the arts in a mass society in which universal literacy, for most, has offered the gift of tongues to Caliban. In a culture in which Rod McKuen and Kahlil Gibran sell millions of books while Pulitzer prize-winning volumes of verse are quickly remaindered at Marboro's, poets, as James Dickey once said, scuffle for the scraps. A nation of over two hundred

497

million requires, as in politics, boxing, rock music, and all else, that a poet be king of the cats, or be ignored. Hence the shrill attention-seeking for movements and their leaders, the publicity and bloated propaganda which are often offered in lieu of critical discussion. A further incentive to the incivility of much of the writing about poetry is the fact that each school with missionary zeal puts forth its reformist scheme for poetry in full belief that it has indeed made everything written heretofore obsolete. At what cost to the range of possibilities for the art of poetry these claims are made and exercised it remains for each reader to determine for himself.

Despite all this, the poets to be discussed here reflect a period undoubtedly the most lively, the most varied, the most pleasurable, and also the most anguished in the history of American poetry, as I trust this survey of several examplary careers will show.

Although the impulse to restore the poet's self to the center of his song clearly received its greatest impetus from Pound's *Pisan Cantos*, Lowell avowed that it was the poems written in his Iowa poetry workshop by his student W. D. Snodgrass and later published in *Heart's Needle* (1959) that crystallized for him the possibilities he explored in *Life Studies* in the same year. The first forty pages of Snodgrass's book are formal, allusive poems with the wry irony that is this poet's thumbprint. "While civilizations come down with the curse, / Snodgrass is walking through the universe." His "April Inventory," much anthologized, records the wistful rebellion of an aging college instructor ("The sleek, expensive girls I teach / . . . Bloom gradually out of reach"); although he hasn't "read one book about / A book or memorized a plot," his plaint is enshrined in perfectly balanced stanzas. The breakthrough into something new is in the title sequence. Here too the form is conventional, as reminiscent of Housman as of Ransom, teetering sometimes on the brink of sentimentality, but the subject is unprecedented. There had been many a sequence of love poems, but in these ten lyrics Snodgrass explores the emotional consequences of his divorce and separation from his three-year-old daughter. Such a laying bare of personal intimacies, such unembarrassed self-exposure, opens the way for Lowell, and through him for many others, to the expression of the suffering inner man or woman, subjects hitherto avoided or masked by discretion and unquestioning acceptance of a decorum which when once breached would never again assert its sovereign rule.

Lowell, as we have seen, struggled to free himself from the very tradition Snodgrass was learning at Iowa. He passed on the method of his new style to later students of his at Boston University, particularly to Anne Sexton and Sylvia Plath. Both shared with Lowell the affliction of mental illness; both, after repeated attempts, succeeded in taking their own lives. These deeply troubled women tried to write as though poems flowed out of their nerve-ends. Not even the traditional structures of verse convention lent the illusion of stability to their best work, whose expression of unmediated anguish bespoke not only the poets' personal lack of balance but, it seemed, the malaise of their times.

The title of Anne Sexton's first book, *To Bedlam and Part Way Back* (1960), announces a further extension of this uninhibited self-exposure, in which she "had to learn / why I would rather / die than love" in a life in which "The world is full of enemies. / There is no safe place." In seven succeeding books her subjects are her own mental breakdowns; her strained relationships with parents, husband, children; her amatory experiences; her need for, and inability to find, religious faith. There is a searing tension between her death wish and her desire to find life rewarding enough to justify the struggle to live (*All My Pretty Ones,* 1962; *Live or Die,* 1967). She wrestles these private demons in a style close to speech that attempts to trace her sudden shifts of feeling. In the end, despite wide acclaim and many honors, Anne Sexton took her own life at the age of forty-six in 1974.

Obsessive themes like those of Sexton became for Sylvia Plath both the fuel and the all-consuming fire that flares with frightening intensity in her poems. Plath was the daughter of a distinguished emigré German biologist who died when she was nine, leaving her with an unbearable sense of having been abandoned, as well as with an unassuageable guilt that she might somehow have been responsible for his death (see "Daddy"). Brought up by her hard-working mother, she became a super-competent winner of academic and literary honors at Smith College, including a summer editorship on the College Board of *Mademoiselle* magazine. This experience became the *mise en scène* of her novel, *The Bell Jar* (1963), the first half of which reads like a comedic satire akin to the college novels of Randall Jarrell or Mary McCarthy. But this is only the setting for the real subject, the emotional breakdown of the protagonist, her unsuccessful suicide attempt, and the ominously successful suicide of her doppelgänger in the book. Art was imitating life, for Plath had taken overdoses of pills while in high school and again at college. Psychiatrists advise that such attempts are desperate cries for help; yet between suicide attempts Plath seemed outwardly able to cope. Her first book of poems, *The Colossus* (1960), showed an expertise in the poet's craft that was widely praised, but only in retrospect did it seem to forecast the fearful asymmetry of her later work. Robert Lowell, whose Boston University poetry classes she occasionally attended without being an enrolled student, recalled, in his foreword to her posthumous second book, *Ariel* (1965), "I sensed her abashment and distinction, and never guessed her later appalling and triumphant fulfillment."

On a fellowship to Cambridge University Plath met and married the British poet Ted Hughes. He too had published a first book (*The Hawk in the Rain,* 1957) in which formality of stanzas barely concealed a fiercely unremitting sense of raw power at the heart of things, the vengeful energy of a Calvinist confronting a world of tooth and claw from which God is absent. The reciprocal influences of these two poets—and of both with W. S. Merwin, their neighbor in the late 1950s on Primrose Hill in London—just as all three were breaking away from stanzaic, conventional forms into new improvisatory styles, were incalculable, though difficult to specify. Two children were born to Plath and Hughes; they lived awhile in the country in Devon, then returned to London. The triple roles of Muse, Mother, and Poet cannot have been easily filled by Sylvia Plath (as may be inferred from "Three Women" in *Winter Trees*). For whatever reasons the couple separated, Plath caring for the babies. She was living on the very edge, as though breathing a wild intoxicant in the very air. Poems poured out of her in a torrent, poems of fierce rhythms and violent images that had the stamp of inevitability about their jagged shapes and searing themes. In the midst of this unparalleled and successful expression of the destructive element within, Sylvia Plath put her head in the oven. Her friend A. Alvarez maintains (in *The Savage God,* 1971) that she had planned another cry for help, counting on being discovered a few minutes later by her char. But the cleaning woman that day was unaccountably late, and when she arrived Sylvia Plath was dead.

Ariel, edited by Ted Hughes, proved but a part of Sylvia Plath's legacy; the subsequent publication of *Crossing the Water* (1971) and *Winter Trees* (1972), in which nearly all of the poems date from the last nine months of Plath's life, extended the achievement of *Ariel* but did not greatly alter its scope. In that book, as Lowell wrote, "Everything . . . is personal, confessional, felt, but the manner of feeling is controlled hallucination, the autobiography of a fever . . . Suicide, father-hatred, self-loathing—nothing is too much for the macabre gaiety of her control. Yet it is too much; her art's immortality is life's disintegration." In one of these poems the moon "drags the sea after it like a dark crime"; in another the moon "would drag me /

Cruelly, being barren. / Her radiance scathes me." As for the sun, "The sun's poultice draws on my inflammation." She imagines herself an elm tree, inhabited by a bird of prey: "Nightly it flaps out / Looking, with its hooks, for something to love." In "The Applicant" she describes herself as a candidate for love, an automaton made of hooks, false teeth, "Rubber breasts and a rubber crotch." Two poems in *Ariel*, it is true, treat of her children with clear-eyed affection ("Morning Song"—"Love set you going like a fat gold watch"; and "Nick and the Candlestick"); but those that have etched themselves into the veins of all readers of that book are nightmarish presentations in a Gothic mode of a masochistic seeking of suffering, as in "Cut," where she thrills to the slice of the knife through "My thumb instead of an onion," and imagines her own beheading. In "Lady Lazarus" she is a suicide expert: "Dying / Is an art, like everything else"; she will arise from her own ashes a witch and cannibal who will "eat men like air." "Daddy" is her litany for her betrayal by her dead father, the nursery rhythm and jingling rhymes making weird contrasts to her hateful vision of father as a Nazi, herself as a Jew in "Dachau, Auschwitz, Belsen." In a series of Poems—"The Bee Meeting," "The Arrival of the Bee Box," "Stings," "Swarms," "Wintering"—this daughter of the author of a treatise on bumblebees becomes the queen and victim of the hive, in terrified dreams of alienation and death. The achievement of these extraordinary poems is at once technically marvelous and profoundly shocking; no contemporary poet had so devastatingly revealed the self's immitigable fascination with sado-masochism, with the ecstasy of its own destruction. Plath's poems move by sharp thrusts and slashes of apocalyptic imagery; the lineation is phrasal, managed with the firm hand of inevitability. These poems whose themes are of a life dangerously out of control are always themselves in control; but in the end, as Lowell said, "it is too much." There is a tale of Poe's, "The Oval Portrait," in which the perfection of the artist's portrait is achieved at the cost of the subject's life. Sylvia Plath made herself the subject of her own art, its energy, its achievement nourished by her will to self-destruction.

Discussing her work, M. L. Rosenthal has written that "a genuine confessional poem has to be superbly successful artistically if it is to achieve [its] fusion of the private and the culturally symbolic." The poems of Plath have this power. Inevitably, however, her work and that of other "confessional" poets has been attacked for their exclusive concentration on abnormally exacerbated states of feeling, and some critics denigrate the times in which such poems are taken as the measure of our society's dis-ease. Surely the best of such poetry has the undeniable authenticity of the poet's emotional life, disordered as it is; and such authenticity is so rare that we must receive it gratefully wherever found. Yet it is bootless to see poetry of this kind as universal in meaning, as has been claimed by some enthusiasts. Plath's work is genuine, authoritative, but extremely narrow in the range of experience, feeling, and human possibilities it can embody.

A further confusion engendered by the popularity of confessional poetry has to do with the nature of the creative act. A Romantic and misleading identification of creativity with madness, nourished by the work of Pound, Lowell, Roethke, Berryman, Ginsberg, Sexton, Plath, and still others, became widespread. The notions that madness is sanity and its cognate—that the rationalism required by social behavior is really institutionalized madness—were popularized by R. D. Laing and other glorifiers of unconscious impulse. In his essay "Freud and Literature" (*The Liberal Imagination,* 1950), Lionel Trilling had tried to dispose of the simplistic folly of confusing artistic creativity with neurosis: "The illusions of art are made to serve the purpose of a closer and truer relation with reality." Trilling alludes to Charles Lamb's essay "Sanity of True Genius," and it is those few pages written at the beginning of our two centuries of Romanticism that would best, if heeded, save readers from this indiscriminate confusion: "The greatness of . . . poetic talent . . . manifests itself in the admirable balance of all the faculties. Madness is the disproportionate straining or excess of any one of them . . . The true poet dreams being awake. He is not possessed by his subject, but has dominion over it . . . Where he seems most to recede from humanity, he will be found the truest to it."

The distinction between what Rosenthal (in *The New Poets,* 1967) called confessional and what David Kalstone (in *Five Temperaments,* 1977) termed autobiographical poetry involves subject, range, and tone: the autobiographical poet, not trapped by emotional illness in sufferings brought on by unresolvable crises, may be able to use more of his life in his work, and even when the poem's subject is similar to the confessional poet's, that subject may be viewed with perspective, detachment, humor. One poet whose work centers on the direst personal crisis, yet makes a telling contrast to Plath's and Sexton's Gothic anticipations of their own deaths, is L. E. Sissman. In *Dying: An Introduction* (1968), in the title sequence and in many other pages of *Hello Darkness* (1978), his posthumous collected poems, Sissman faced the knowledge of his own oncoming death from cancer. For Sissman the blank verse monologue, among other conventions, served, as conventions have always done, to reinforce the continuities of his own experience with those of other men and women who have suffered pain and treasured life as he did. These quietly meditative and often wryly humorous poems are the testament of a brave man.

Where Sissman was compelled by circumstance to face death, Adrienne Rich meets life on the most honest terms she can. The burden of her poems is the making, hence the discovery, of her self. Over the years since *A Change of World* appeared in 1951, her sense of who she is and what terms of living are possible to her has changed considerably; all her work is marked with the integrity Auden praised in his preface to that precocious prize-winning book, written while she was a college student. She has enumerated her early models ("Frost, Dylan Thomas, Donne, Auden, MacNeice, Stevens, Yeats") for those poems which Auden said "respect their elders but are not cowed by them." Rich has pointed to "Aunt Jennifer's Tigers" as embodying deeper themes than she then knew would possess her, themes she would teach herself to deal with directly, at first hand. Here she presents a persona in a vignette that dramatizes the tension between Aunt Jennifer's imaginative life (the vehement tigers she embroiders) and her actual circumstances ("The massive weight of Uncle's wedding band / Sits heavily upon Aunt Jennifer's hand."). Even in death her hands will be "Still ringed with ordeals they were mastered by."

In *The Diamond Cutters* (1955) and *Snapshots of a Daughter-in-Law* (1963) Rich feels her way through dramatic monologues and referential poems that dramatize her inner life as a wife and mother increasingly aware that

> A life I didn't choose
> chose me: even
> my tools are the wrong ones
> for what I have to do.

"Was it worthwhile to lay— / With infinite exertion— / A roof I can't live under?" she asks ("The Roofwalker," *Snapshots*). In her second book several dramatic poems synopsize the tone and method of Lowell's *Mills of the Kavanaughs* with the bleak monologues of Frost's in which the loneliness of women in New England is spoken to uncomprehending men. The wife of a professor in Rich's "Autumn Equinox," weeping at night, can't be comforted by his "Are you ill, unhappy? / Tell me what I can do." In "The Perennial Answer" the woman is married to a violent brute but loves a Bible-beating Puritan who, after the husband's death, still dares not requite her. In "The Insomniacs" the speaker's malaise fits all too snugly into the rhymed

503

tetrameters ("My pillow sweats; I wake in space, / This is my hand before my face"); Rich's energy and anguish would soon crack apart such neat versification. In the title sequence of *Snapshots* Rich alternates between Eliot-like invocations of echoes from poetic tradition, ironically deflated ("When to her lute Corinna sings / neither words nor music are her own") and a harsh and brave directness of vision and speech—

> *Dulce ridens, dulce loquens,*
> she shaves her legs until they gleam
> like petrified mammoth-tusk

and again,

> The argument *ad feminum,* all the old knives
> that have rusted in my back, I drive in yours,
> *ma semblable, ma soeur!*

The crux of the matter is explored in a manner barren of such allusions but compelling in its truth in "A Marriage in the Sixties":

> Two strangers, thrust for life upon a rock,
> may have at last the perfect hour of talk
> that language aches for; still—
> two minds, two messages.

Such isolation is the doom of a marriage in which "pieces of the universe are missing."

In "Snapshots" she poses the question of the *donnée* that from now on her work will explore: "has Nature shown / her household books to you, daughter-in-law, / that her sons never saw?" Woman's sense of the truth of her life may reveal a world of feeling unthought of in men's philosophy. Rich invokes a series of predecessor women—Anne Hutchinson, Emily Dickinson, Mary Boykin Chesnut (whose journal evokes the Civil War), Caroline Herschel, the astronomer denied her brother's fame because of her sex ("Planetarium"). From the often balked careers of these women she draws sustenance to remake her own life. "Piece by piece I seem / to re-enter the world," she writes in "Necessities of Life," in which her life was "like kneading bricks in Egypt," a slavery she escapes, first through the minimal comfort of sensuous response,

> What life was there, was mine,
>
> now and again to lay
> one hand on a warm brick
>
> and touch the sun's ghost
> with economical joy,

then, when "practice may make me middling-perfect,"

                 I'll
dare inhabit the world
trenchant in motion as an eel, solid

as a cabbage head.

Helen Vendler (*Parnassus,* 1973) remarks on the beauty of the first
passage above, the ambiguity of the second. As the poem ends ("I
have invitations: . . . houses along the road stand waiting / like old
women knitting, breathless / to tell their tale") Vendler observes,
"acquiescence and rebellion compete." That the girl who earlier had
"dreamed of being Wittgenstein should join the garrulous crones"!
She had come just so far in 1962 (this poet dates each of her poems).
Six years later, in "Planetarium" (*The Will to Change,* 1971), she
saw herself in a more positive and active light:

> I am an instrument in the shape
> of a woman trying to translate pulsations
> into images   for the relief of the body
> and the reconstruction of the mind.

This enterprise allies her with the radical feminist movement (see
her prose tract *Of Woman Born,* 1976), yet in her poems Rich seldom
subordinates the integrity of her poetic means to the oversimplifica-
tions of a manifesto. Indeed, her poetic means have developed toward
ambiguity and complexity of feeling. Influenced by motion-picture
technique (in such poems as "Images for Godard" and "Shooting
Script"), she has also written adaptations of ghazals by the Urdu poet
Mirzā Ghālib, of which she says, "The continuity and unity flow
from the associations and images playing back and forth among the
couplets in any single ghazal." Her later work resembles both the
disjunctive associations of Lowell's style in his last books and the
free composition advocated by Charles Olson. These various free-
flowing techniques make her work evocative of feelings experienced
before the mind has categorized them.

> Pain made her conservative.
> Where the matches touched her flesh, she wears a scar.
>
> . . . .
>
> Sometimes I dream we are floating on water
> hand-in-hand; and sinking without terror.

The title poem of *Diving into the Wreck* (1973) shows Adrienne
Rich making from her own circumstances, from her sense of her situation, a fable of the condition of her time:

I came to explore the wreck.
The words are purposes.
The words are maps.
I came to see the damage that was done
and the treasures that prevail

. . . .

The wreck and not the story of the wreck
the thing itself and not the myth
the drowned face always staring
toward the sun . . .

We are, I am, you are
by cowardice or courage
the one who finds our way
back to this scene
carrying a knife, a camera
a book of myths
in which
our names do not appear.

Her *Poems Selected and New, 1950-1974* appeared in 1975.

It is odd that the direct use of autobiographical material, which has always been a staple of fiction (especially of first novels), should have required a virtual aesthetic revolution in poetry. Perhaps this fact is one measure of the strength of the anti-Romantic poetics of the 1940s and 1950s, now battered by this and several other movements. The immediate result of the work of the poets just discussed was of course the opening up of subjects hitherto taboo and, further, the exploration, in a less exacerbated manner than that of the confessional poets, of personal history. The latter could lead in several directions, for example, A. Poulin, Jr.'s, probing of his French-Canadian and Catholic heritage (*In Advent,* 1972), or William Heyen's *The Swastika Poems* (1977), a painful coming to grips with his German family—uncles in Hitler's Luftwaffe—hence with the guilt of modern history. Closer to the confessional enterprise is the work of Frank Bidart, where, as Richard Howard points out in his introduction to *Golden State* (1973), "it is Bidart's tactical decision to open with an 'autobiographical' narrative which is not his own, thereby preparing us to accept his ulterior revelations . . . as fictions, as mythological identities, not confessions." Thus Bidart begins this book with the "confession" of "Herbert White," who has murdered a girl and masturbated over her decomposing body ("Hell came when I saw / MYSELF"); and he ends his second volume, *The Book of the Body* (1977), with the "confession" of "Ellen West," who so hated her body that she starved

506

herself to death. Between these fictive identities, Bidart presents, in a prose-textured rhythm as unlike as possible "the lies / of mere, neat poetry," poems in which "I sensed I had to become not merely / a speaker, the 'eye,' but a character." Then he can realize how "the past in maiming us, / makes us," as he re-creates the father who couldn't comprehend him and whom he could not accept (in *Golden State*); in *The Book of the Body,* the mother he cannot forgive, and the confusions of his life, "terror at my own homosexuality," which "evaporated slowly with 'Gay Liberation.'" In these poems Bidart has effectively dealt with some of the most painful crises of selfhood.

Crises sometimes equally painful are dramatized in James Merrill's poems, but in them the panache of style, the graceful symmetry of forms, and the ironic or comic view of the protagonist's predicament displace our attention from the sufferings of the self. Merrill's auto-biographical poems have a glitter, an elegance *con brio,* not seen in American poetry since Wallace Stevens's fictive imaginings. Their settings—a childhood of great wealth, residence abroad in maturity— are suggestive also of the *donnée* of Henry James's novels, but this material serves as the background of memory, whose labyrinthine thread unspools in a narrative mode leavened by the imagination of comedy. Merrill's poetry is at once profoundly conventional and adventurous, even experimental; the adventurousness resides in the nature of the sensibility which uses traditional modes for its expression.

The three decades of his practice as a poet have seen a perhaps un-exampled breakup of traditional verse-making, but none of this has had the least effect upon Merrill. From *First Poems* (1951) through *Divine Comedies* (1976) in his seven volumes he has not swerved from the perfecting of his own style. His verse, always glistening with the patina of a highly worked finish, has developed from a marmoreal surface often obscuring his themes to a subtle and sophisticated instru-ment for clarifying the depths of feeling and discernment beneath its shapely flow. Merrill found his metier in his third book, *Water Street* (1962). He unfashionably favors meters (pentameters, usually), form (he is given to blank verse, the sonnet sequence, and the envelope rhymed quatrain). And, as noted above, in opposition to most poetry of the time, all of these forms present narratives. As he writes in *Divine Comedies,*

> Take, for that matter, my beanstalk couplet, above,
> Where such considerations as rhyme and meter
> Prevail, it might be felt, at the expense
> Of meaning, but as well create, survive it;
> For the first myth was Measure . . .

507

What is subjected to measure, then, is transformed; experience, actuality itself, is not the meaning of the poet's art but the ground from which meaning is created, as memory—or fiction—is transfigured into myth. The myth may be that of the classical pantheon, or something like it, or the mythic autobiography of the poet. These modes, the mythic and the autobiographical, alternate in his earlier books; *Divine Comedies* brings them together.

Merrill's two longest poems before "The Book of Ephraim" in *Divine Comedies* were mythic inventions, one private, the other, in its lighthearted way, cultural. "From the Cupola" (*Nights and Days*, 1966) is a densely allegorized psychomachia in which Psyche, "the classic, New England old maid," seeks "the unfamiliar, the 'transcendental,'" while Eros takes his sweetheart to a drive-in movie where "The love goddess his mother overflows a screen . . . You can feel / lust and fulfilment Eros no more than / ocean its salt depths or uranium its hot / disintegrative force or I our fable." More readily accessible is "The Summer People" (*The Fire Screen*, 1969), a minor masterpiece of ironical comedy. Where the earlier myth explored the nature of love, this long ballad anatomizes friendship under the aegis of Time and Tenderness, "the past masters / of rime, tone, overtone." Into the bored lives of a quartet of amiable, idle friends in a decaying seaside village comes a perfect host, Jack Frost, who, in his disused church remodeled as a folly, gives wonderful parties and altogether embodies the pleasure principle. (This character may emanate, at a distance, from the now-forgotten H. Phelps Putnam's "Ballad of a Strange Thing," *Trinc*, 1927). Pure pleasure, however, is prelapsarian, unearthly. Jack has a familiar—a white cat. Jack's dalliance in mere human society palls at last, and in a trice his spell is broken: his cat bites one of the friends, who lets the SPCA destroy it. The cat's ghost summons Jack from afar. Abandoned by their master of revels, the four friends fall into their former life of bickering and ennui, now shadowed by encroaching Time. Mere summary can scarcely suggest the delights of "rime, tone, overtone" in this graceful *conte moralisé*.

The poet who can so effectively dramatize imaginary lives is no less telling with the givens of his own. Unlike such exacerbated poets as Lowell, Berryman, and Plath, Merrill deals with the troubling *donnée* of his strained relationships with parents and the effects of these early dispositions upon his mature identity not in the revelation of breakdowns and suicidal urges, but in narratives in which the situation, remembered from a perspective that invites the ironic glint, the comic aside, is but one of the elements revealing the inner meaning of his experience. This is exposed—to him as to us—as much through his searching observation of things, gestures, words, as through the plots which are often but the occasions of these. Merrill's is a triumph of style. His verse moves with a deftness, an ease, a grace lent by his light, colloquial diction, a play of imaginative associations, irradiating its surfaces. If Merrill stands out among his peers by his devotion to verse-making, he is also unlike them in the novelistic action of his verses. This body of work pays occasional homage to the great memorialist under whose aegis it is begotten, as when Merrill writes in "For Proust" (*Water Street*), "What happened is becoming literature."

The novelistic imagination, in verse as in prose, is one to which meaning is ultimately revealed through social interactions. Only a few of Merrill's poems have the self-enclosed, self-limited action of dreamwork, or surrealism—"The Mad Scene," "Part of the Vigil," "Nike," and "Getting Through," where "Everything is cryptic, crystal-queer." More normally, more naturally, his images arise from a plausible situation, as in "Scenes of Childhood," where he and his mother watch a home movie made thirty years before in which "The man's / Shadow afflicts us both," the film "Catches fire," after which "I gradually fade and cool . . . Father already fading— / Who focused your life long / Through little frames." Each of these verbs and nouns resonates with redoubled meanings as the family's Oedipal tensions are at once summoned and controlled by Memory, this poet's muse. Other poems in *Water Street* which resurrect, explore, and dramatize these tensions are "The Water Hyacinth" and "The Midnight Snack"; in *The Fire Screen*, "Mornings in a New House"; in *Braving the Elements,* "Up and Down," a better controlled and dramatized treatment of the earlier poem "Childlessness."

Another poet of memory is invoked by Merrill's titles (*Nights and Days,* "Days of 1964," "Days of 1935"), reminders of the series "Days of 1910" by the chief poet of modern Greece, Constantin Cavafy. This allusiveness results from choice, not chance, since Merrill has for years lived part of the time in Greece and many of his later poems are set there. But "Days of 1935" (*Braving the Elements,* 1972) reflects his own childhood. Unlike Cavafy's, Merrill's sense of the past does not open up antiquity to him; his past is the Proustian vista of his own life. In "1935" the boy, hearing of the Lindbergh kidnapping on the servants' radio, imagines himself—*wishes* himself—abducted by a hard yet vulnerable pair named Floyd and Jean. In their easy intimacies (banging each other on the creaking bedsprings in their hideaway shack) and their appearance ("A lady out of Silver Screen"; "The man's face . . . / Lean, sallow, lantern-jawed"), they are the opposites of the boy's view of his parents, whose photos appear beneath a tabloid headline, "FIEND ASKS 200 GRAND":

> My mother gloved,
> Hatted, bepearled, chin deep in fur.
> Dad glowering—was it true he loved
> Others beside her?

Left alone with their captive while Floyd telephones their ransom demand, Jean asks, "Do you know any stories, Kid?" The boy "stared at her—*she* was the child!"—and like Scheherazade (in the later poem "The Thousand and Second Night") puts her to sleep with his fairy tales of Bluebeard and the Sleeping Beauty. He knew already "That life was fiction in disguise." Rescued at last, he is about to testify, condemning them to "the Chair," when he falls out of bed and awakens his old nurse, who

> took me in her arms. I pressed
> My guilty face against the void
> Warmed and scented by her breast.
> Jean, I whispered, Floyd.

In his waking life "The child is bored" in the kitchen while his parents entertain "Tel & Tel executives, / Heads of Cellophane or Tin." His dream of the forbidden life of passion, daring, adventure—the low life—is over, for "Floyd and Jean are gone."

The first nine poems in *Divine Comedies* do most of the things Merrill has done elsewhere, often better than before. But it is his ninety-page extravaganza, "The Book of Ephraim," which opens new territory, though developed out of what he has previously explored. Ephraim speaks to JM (Merrill) and DJ (David Jackson, his friend and housemate) through their Ouija board, from an astral plane instructing them on the transmigration of souls, and bringing them news of the dead, answers to their queries, and prophecies for the living. The two seekers are initiated into these mysteries by their tutelary spirit, "A Greek Jew / Born AD 8 at XANTHOS"; Ephraim speaks only in the Ouija board's capital letters. This fantastic apparatus inevitably suggests that of Yeats's *A Vision*, although Yeats had no comparable sense of humor and insisted upon a rigid systematization of both psychology and history not emulated here. The purpose of Merrill's wacky machinery is similar to his: to bring him images for his poems.

Among the spirits living, dead, and imagined who figure in these pages are various friends, relatives, poets (Auden, Yeats), obscure men of letters, characters in JM's abandoned novel. The poem is made up of unnumbered sections each as formal as Merrill's earlier work, sometimes combining within one section blank verse with rhymed quatrains or sonnets in sequence; but the structure of the whole seems aleatoric. Through Ephraim JM and DJ help souls transmigrate; their friend Maya Deren, filmmaker and enthusiast of voodoo, has visions; with Ephraim's intervention, the past is made coterminous with the present, freeing the poet from subjection to time (the undoing of "The Summer People"). The tone varies from farce to the Dantesque gravity of JM's encounter with his young artist-nephew, whose view of human nature is more cynical than his own—but even here the gravity is lightened by Merrill's comedic perspective. Page by page, "The Book of Ephraim" is a virtuoso performance. At times its direction, its shape and purpose seem obscure, but ultimately it proves to be an open-ended encyclopedic contraption, the invention of which—like Lowell's *History*, Berryman's *Dream Songs*, or their common ancestor, Pound's *Cantos*—makes possible to the poet the expansion of his work to include well-nigh everything that memory or invention casts up into the nets of his craft. Merrill's supernatural device, then, is a way of liberating the self to extend the domain of the imagination. But unlike Pound or Lowell, Merrill, in freeing his imagination from time, does not plunge into History: history, for him, is always rooted in the personal life, as was true of Berryman. Unlike Berryman, however, Merrill is a most sanguine poet. His gravest pages are tinged with melancholy, but his melancholy seldom threatens him, since even on his saddest days he views his own—and our—situation wryly, with a smile, sustained by the Art he had invoked—

> Won't you help us brave the elements
> Once more, of terror, anger, love?

The poem of Merrill's from which those lines are taken is called "Dreams about Clothes." The trope of clothing or costume as the facilitating disguise by which Art allows us to confront our selves was used by Richard Howard in his preface to Frank Bidart's first book. There, Howard spoke of the tactic by which the younger poet presents his revelations "as fictions, as mythologized identities, not confessions." This process is carried still further in Howard's own poetry, for Howard has met his own need to deal with the crises of the self and its confrontations with history by avoiding the direct confrontation of confessional or autobiographic means, and by reaching back past the personae of Pound, the masks of Yeats, to their great predecessor who wrote, "I'll tell my state as though 'twere none of mine." These words of Robert Browning Howard quotes in the dedicatory epigraph of his third book, *Untitled Subjects* (1969), in which his method is for the first time displayed at its full range.

If the dramatic monologue seems an avoidance of the fragmented bequest of modernism, Howard's versification also has the look of being a departure from the givens of the time: neither formal in the accentual-syllabic mode of Anglo-American tradition, nor free in the fashions disposed by Black Mountain or Paterson, New Jersey, Howard's lines have a free formality of another kind. These monologues appear in differing stanzas, some of considerable intricacy, all written in syllabics, a mode which only Auden had hitherto pursued with such consistency and success. In adopting syllabics Howard responds to another, perhaps deeper influence than Auden's. Richard Howard is an accomplished lexicographer and linguist who has translated over a hundred books from the French. Syllabics have not appealed to most poets in English, being based upon the nonaccentual character of French versification. But a few poets—Auden, Marianne Moore, Hollander, and Howard principally—have gladly undertaken this alien method of structuring their own language and made it seem as homegrown as the pentameters of Merrill or Anthony Hecht, or the phrasal strophes long or short of Bly, Levertov, or Creeley.

Richard Howard was assuredly aware of what these other poets were doing while he was doing something different from any of them, for in the same year as *Untitled Subjects* he published his six-hundred-page *Alone with America,* essays on forty-one contemporary poets he has read with close attention and empathy. In keeping with his title, borrowed from Perry Miller's description of the plight of the Massachusetts settlers ("They looked in vain to history for an explanation of themselves"), Howard treats each of these contemporaries as though he were indeed alone with America; each poet's work is read hermetically, discussed in terms of its own premises and accomplishments, but with scarcely any linking of one lonely poet's enterprise with another's.

Howard's own enterprise slowly discovered itself in his first book, the Audenesque *Quantities* (1962) and its surer successor, *The Damages* (1967). Howard from the first has been a poet of great facility, writing with an easy expansiveness that threatened to overwhelm his poems' sometimes modest draughts on emotional necessity. Several poems in *The Damages* may illustrate Howard's exploration of his own *donnée* and discovery of how most effectively to use it. "Seeing Cousin Phyllis Off"—aboard the S.S. *France*—touches on Merrill's world of the traveling well-to-do (though to be sure she sails second class), a portrait both affectionate and ironical. "Private Drive: Memorial for a Childhood Playmate," the longest poem in the book, uses autobiographical material to dramatize childhood introduction to sexuality, but the treatment is diffuse compared with the more distanced, better controlled rendering of the theme in "Seferiades." This too is long—nearly three hundred lines alternately in eight or seven syllables. Part I presents the ultimate untranslatability of poetry, as a visiting Greek poet waves off his American translator, seizes the podium and speaks, in Greek, about Helen and the gods, "something about a myth." Part II abruptly shifts to a dock at a summer camp, to which six young boys have returned after their two-mile swim across the lake and back. On the other shore they had been met by a "weirdo in the woods," a woman who fed them mushrooms and jasmine tea: " 'The cup,' she said, 'drink this, it will / make you immortal . . .' " The initiation, for at least one of them, touches on sexual identity. Their waterfront counselor, a balding Nestor, interprets to these American boys the age-old myth in which they have been unwitting participants, as perhaps were Helen and the other personages in the Greek poet's untranslatable lines.

It is, however, in "Bonnard: A Novel" that Howard discovers the means best to make use of Browning's example. Here the speaker, both observer of and participant at such a tea party as Bonnard might have painted, is not Howard himself but an invented character. Both manner and subject anticipate the dramatic monologues in *Untitled Subjects* two years later, in which Howard presents fifteen moments in the history of sensibility in the nineteenth century. There, the stance is often peripheral, the communication often epistolary, as Howard's spokesmen (sometimes minor figures, sometimes the great themselves) comment upon or disclose the characters, loves, failings, and artistic principles of the painters, novelists, critics, and composers of the century. With a sure sense of the dramatic angle, the apposite moment, and a command of intimate period detail (the product of what, if put to other uses, would be called extensive scholarship), Howard offers his series of Jamesian vignettes: scenes from the life of Rossini; Lady Trevelyan's letter to her son George about her brother, Macaulay, subject of the son's lifeless biography; Gladstone's secretary characterizing his master; Strauss proposing to Schoenberg, after seeing Debussy's defective opera, that he compose *Pelléas und Mélisande*. These reveal the spirit of the age: our own as well as theirs. The Victorians' heroizing of the artist, their personal inhibitions, mismarriages, ambitions, all are brought to a kind of double life, revealing both the subjects of the poems (whose heroes are artists, not noblemen; untitled also in that only the dates of their occurrence identify them) and aspects of our own, indeed of the poet's own, character.

The applicability of these brilliantly imagined moments to autobiography is not always as clear as the inscription to Browning promises, for intimate personal materials are distanced and transformed by objectification and the glamor of being expressed through the lives of famous others. Thus such material is relieved of the emotional pressure of its origins. One such subject is presented as an illusion of the last century through which we can see, as the conductor Hermann Levi writes to Sir Moses Montefiore, the early Zionist, to justify his participation at Bayreuth; he attributes Wagner's anti-Semitism merely to envy of Meyerbeer, and confidently predicts a future there when all may "enjoy an art no more for Gentile / than for Jew." In "1889," an expatriate Englishman writes to counsel a friend against replying to Havelock Ellis's intrusive questionnaire; the letter conveys a vivid sense of the homosexual aestheticism of the time and its attendant feeling of expatriation from society ("We are all and everlastingly / alone").

Ruskin, writing to his father, says,

> My own power, if it be that,
>   Would be lost by mere
> Fine Writing. You know I promised no Romance—
> I promised them Stones. Not even bread.

Howard's subjects, too, would be lost in "mere Fine Writing," but that the writing offers masks, or masques, in which his own sensibility is revealed through his engagement of self with history. Lowell, in *History*, engorged his sensibility with images of power ransacked from the Old Testament, Herodotus, the Renaissance, as well as with memoirs of his own encounters with the great modernists of our time, but Howard's personae are exclusively drawn from the realm of sensibility itself; and, being a modern, his reaches back no further than that of Turner in "1801." His book concludes with William Morris's widow instructing her daughter during a Zeppelin raid on London in 1915—the destruction of the Victorian world—to throw away none of her memorabilia: "These are mine. Save them. / I have nothing save them."

514

Where Merrill is novelistic, Howard inclines toward dramatic form. The method of *Untitled Subjects* is carried on in *Findings* (1971) and *Fellow Feelings* (1976), the monologues expanded in *Two-Part Inventions* (1974) into dramatic dialogues similarly based on fictive elaborations of the lives of writers and artists: the visit of Oscar Wilde to Walt Whitman in Camden; Edith Wharton's ride to the cemetery with her lover's ashes, beside a companion who intimates that he had been her lover's lover; Ibsen's revisiting Capri in old age, encountering an early love, and through her finding the theme of his last play. It is in the imaginative energy, inventiveness, depth of character, and the language—at once conversational, lyrical, and dramatic—in such "fictions, mythologized identities," rather than in his occasional directly personal poems, that Howard most successfully realizes his own gifts. None of his fellow poets in *Alone with America* has explored the life of Art with such a fine, Jamesian sensibility as he; Howard's fashion of being alone with America is to find himself in his explorations of British and European Romantic art. Yet even his seeming avoidance of American life in the presentation of an American life is itself in the tradition of our contemporary poetry, a continuation of one thread in the fabric of *The Cantos* of Ezra Pound and an enactment, as it were, of Eliot's conviction that the poet must have in his bones a sense of the history of Europe and his art.

The various rebellions against the aesthetic of the fifties, as we have seen, involved rejections of poetic tradition and literary decorum. Along with the casting off of strict meters came abandonment of received structures, a new demotic diction, rejection of narrative or sequential organization and paraphrasable content, and the reintroduction of personal subjects—Oedipal tensions, sexual confessions, suicidal urges, madness—presented without the mediation of masks or historical analogues. To many poets the past seems unalterably fractured, no longer usable (as with Frank O'Hara and John Ashbery); or the poet is so overwhelmed by private anguish that the past is primarily personal and oppressive (the confessional poets, Ginsberg); or, attempting to comprehend what history has made of us, the poet has recourse to bits and pieces of hermetic and mystagogic machinery, while rejecting the anti-intellectual intellectual organization of such a construct (as in the private sacred books of Ephraim by Merrill or *The Book of Nightmares* by Galway Kinnell).

But these rebellions, inevitably, had their own precedents and relied upon the examples of notable ancestors. In the early part of the period

Pound is the energizing force, but by the late 1950s his influence is modified or replaced by that of Williams and, by the 1970s, by that of Whitman. To be sure, Whitman had been present all along, ever since Pound made his famous "Pact" with the "pig-headed father" he had "detested . . . long enough": "We have one sap and one root—/ Let there be commerce between us." Williams established *his* commerce with Whitman in "An Essay on *Leaves of Grass*" in *Leaves of Grass One Hundred Years After,* edited by Milton Hindus (1955). Along with their debts to Williams and Pound, the confessional, Beat, and Black Mountain movements are all based to some extent on Whitman's vision, though each draws from his copious bequest a different line of inspiration. "I am large, I contain multitudes": Walt, the suffering Self; Walt the leaner and loafer at his ease, going against the grain of materialistic America; Walt the visionary who finds the pismire equal in wonder to the journeywork of the stars; Walt the democratizer of sensibility—glorifying pokeweed, mullein, the blab of tires in the city, opening up prohibited subjects ("Through me forbidden lusts . . ."); Walt who, like his acolyte Ginsberg, "put his queer shoulder to the wheel"; Walt, "An American, one of the roughs," who "contains a kosmos" and throws all the conventions of many genteel traditions on the ashheap while seeking the freedom of his own innate psychic rhythms in his verse.

All of this, as Whitman has said, "was seething, seething, until Emerson brought me to a boil." And Emerson's "The Poet" is rightly regarded as the seminal text for a critical understanding of where our poetry has gone in the past century. Emerson is crucial for the critic, but for the poets, who are more concerned with techniques embodied in poems than with ideas stated in essays, it is Whitman who incarnates nearly all of Emerson's often self-contradictory tenets and is therefore the more seminal figure.

Reliance on Whitman's autochthonous example made possible a broader, more demotic poetry than had been aroused by the Promethean rebelliousness of Pound. To follow the Ezratic bequest required an immersion and a belief in history and tradition after all—albeit a different tradition from that of university wits—and by the end of the 1960s few among the younger poets were moved to emulate the mastery of a bibliography even so idiosyncratic as Pound had advised. By then it seemed that science itself no longer believed in its own absolutes. The universe is now "known" to be expanding toward infinity, and our solar system is not only perceived but felt to be an insignificant bundle of flecks whirling for a few eons as an aftermath of a primal explosion. The space it inhabits is filled with dying red giants and dead black holes—and a whirling junkyard of manmade satellites. It is harder now than ever before to maintain the verities which necessarily underlie any viable, stable attitude to history. Society itself, especially in an industrial democracy, is subject to congeries of conflicting centers of power, few or none of which offer the individual the security granted him by the traditional institutions they have destroyed or replaced. Man is inexorably thrown back on his own devices: his own sensations, his own bodily rhythms, his own tactile experiences, his own dreams, his own sense of the archetypal experience of the psyche within him—these, having lost their anchors, their supports in religious belief or a sense of life as participating in a historical continuity, are what is left to the poet who tries in his medium—language, verbal rhythms, the presentation of the truth of his experience—to define and embody what he feels as the human condition. Our condition has seldom seemed more desperate. Yet poets—who attend more carefully than writers in other forms to that most traditional of human devisings, their language, and whose work achieves intensity by condensations, simplification—create in their poems relative, provisional truths. The resemblances between their works reflect these general conditions; the differences, the specific ways each deals with these.

In the second number of the new *Evergreen Review*—the year was 1957—Kenneth Rexroth, indomitable anarchist poet and literary streetfighter, wrote that "Poets come to San Francisco for the same reason so many Hungarians have been going to Austria recently." It was not to escape Stalin's tanks, however, but to flee from "the world of poet-professors, Southern Colonels and ex-Left Social Fascists" that Allen Ginsberg, Gary Snyder, Lawrence Ferlinghetti, Gregory Corso, Jack Kerouac, and others had come to the Golden State. For good measure Rexroth described the editors of "The *Vaticide* [*Partisan*] *Review*" as "Brooks Brothers Boys who got an overdose of T. S. Eliot at some Ivy League fog factory," and repeated his denunciations of the old and his praises of the new writers in *New Directions 16* and *New World Writing 11* in the same year.

Rexroth, whose work (see *Natural Numbers*, 1963) had been undervalued by those he attacked, could well hail this group of young rebels as his heirs, for he had been at odds with both American capitalism and the Eliotic aesthetic for twenty years. Soon his acolytes were christened "the Beat Generation," and quickly they outgrew their champion's avuncular partisanship. Their opposition, in the decade that Lowell later called "the tranquillized fifties," to the Establishment—in which poets joined the university, the university served the industrial consumer society, and the politics of conformity ruled both the public and personal life of suburbia—was expressed not only in their declamatory, unmetered verses, but in their life-styles. It may be said that the Cold War and Senator Joseph McCarthy's roughshod persecution of supposed Communists engendered such dissent as theirs. In California, traditional home of refugees from the burdens of tradition, they became the bards of the cult of complete personal freedom, of the nascent drug culture, of beatific visions and Oriental religions, of communal living. They were the vanguard and Pied Pipers of the Hippie movement a decade later. Two of these rebels—Allen Ginsberg and Gary Snyder—were poets of expansive talent and personal charisma who became influential prophets to the disaffected young.

On his trip to the West Coast in 1956, Robert Lowell found at his readings that audiences grew restless, for they had been hearing a very different kind of poetry chanted and declaimed:

> I saw the best minds of my generation destroyed by madness, starving hysterical naked,
> dragging themselves through negro streets at dawn looking for an angry fix,
> angelheaded hipsters burning for the ancient heavenly connection to the starry dynamos in the machinery of night . . .

Thus begins Allen Ginsberg's then-unpublished "Howl," with its long litany of denunciation of America for what it has done to his contemporaries

> who studied Plotinus Poe St. John of the Cross telepathy and bop kaballa because the cosmos instinctively vibrated at their feet in Kansas . . .

—the zeal of the prophetic Whitman and the prophetic Blake leavened by spurts of zany humor—

> who demanded sanity trials accusing the radio of hypnotism & were left with their insanity & their hands & a hung jury,
> who threw potato salad at CCNY lecturers on Dadaism and subsequently presented themselves on the granite steps of the madhouse with shaven heads and harlequin speech of suicide, demanding instant lobotomy . . .

The second part of "Howl" is a rhythmic attack on "Moloch whose mind is pure machinery"; the third alternates the refrain "I'm with you in Rockland" (a mental asylum where Ginsberg's friend Carl Solomon was confined) with gradually lengthening phrases beginning "where" (as the lines in part one had begun "who . . ."). "Footnote to Howl" asserts that "The world is holy! The soul is holy! The skin is holy! The nose is holy! The tongue and cock and hand and asshole holy!"

These thirteen pages in the little square pamphlet published by City Lights in 1956 became the most widely sold, read, and discussed poem of the decade. The fervor of its denunciation of all the pieties of the Eisenhower period, the vehemence of its demolition of accepted literary standards, and the violence, for the times, of its language brought widespread attack on the work, the author, and the tribe of Bohemian rebels who acclaimed "Howl" as the testament of their generation's despair and Ginsberg as the prophet of their future. So many restraints upon feeling and expression have been abandoned since the 1950s that it is difficult now to imagine the outrage caused among the nonliterary public by this now-familiar poem. *Howl* was quickly prosecuted for obscenity, and through the San Francisco courtroom trooped a host of academic critics to defend it on grounds established twenty-five years earlier in the case of Joyce's *Ulysses:* the work had redeeming value as a serious criticism of society. This widely reported trial of course did little to impede the popularity of the work in question.

It is hard to reconstruct the dismay felt in literary circles at the emergence of Ginsberg. That the poems in *Howl* are literary constructs is clear indeed, but they are constructed in a poetic and aesthetic tradition different from those in force at the time. Ginsberg does not hide his debts, he celebrates them, as when he finds Walt Whitman "poking among the meats in the refrigerator and eyeing the grocery boys" in "A Supermarket in California." In *Kaddish and Other Poems* (1961) further allegiances appear: Max Jacob, Tristan Tzara, Blaise Cendrars, Jean Cocteau, André Gide, Vladimir Mayakovsky are invoked in "At Apollinaire's Grave," while in "Death to Van Gogh's Ear" the pantheon is of the American underground poets, the damned, the suicides, the homosexuals—Hart Crane, Vachel Lindsay, and Poe contribute to this Poundian attack on money-mad materialism. Ginsberg clearly sees himself in the Romantic tradition of the *poète maudit,* as a demonic, inspired, mad, revelatory voice attacking the corrupt underbelly of smug society and proposing an alternative way of feeling, way of saying, way of life.

How did a shy, bespectacled college boy, a student of Mark Van Doren and Lionel Trilling who had won prizes at Columbia for his lyrics modeled on Donne and Shelley (see *The Gates of Wrath,* 1972), suddenly become this bard of "bop kaballa"? From the title poem in *Kaddish* a reader may infer the circumstances behind his transformation, which occurred, Ginsberg has said, when a vision of Blake appeared to him from a Harlem rooftop. Indeed, everything in Ginsberg's private life seemed to make unlikely his becoming one of the "Brooks Brothers Boys . . . at an Ivy League fog factory." He was from a family of Russian immigrants, a Jew, his family had ties to the Communist labor movement, his mother was insane, and he was a homosexual: five prescriptions, in the 1940s and 1950s, for a sense of deep alienation from postwar America. Trilling's Arnoldian values at Columbia seemed an Anglophilic veneer that had nothing to do with the life of feeling. Ginsberg, meeting the novelist-to-be Kerouac at the West End Bar, seceded from all that, as *Howl* proclaimed. "Kaddish," however, is his masterpiece, a heart-wrenching evocation of his boyhood, the life of his desperate family, the anguish of having to play the hand life dealt him, and his transcendence of sordid circumstance through the power of his visionary imagination. The paranoia of his poor mother becomes, in strophes at once wildly comic and fearful, a trope for Hitler's persecution of the Jews; her madness is an intolerable affliction yet the source of *her* mystic vision. The poem is written in long strophes, with image wildly piled on image, the onrush of imaginative ingestion of experience creating the rhythm of the work. In thirty pages Ginsberg has written his surrealistic evocation of what a naturalistic novelist might struggle to express in a thousand—and not capture, as the poet does, the depth of feeling in his life.

By the early 1960s Ginsberg was a public personality with a huge following—as much for his voluble partisanship for all of the libertarian movements of the time (civil rights, gay liberation, opposition to the Vietnam war, the life of impulse achieved by any means—through drugs, transcendental meditation, Oriental religions)—as for what he actually wrote. In fact, on his tours around the world Ginsberg became a guru to the disaffected and was welcomed by huge throngs of admirers in India, Japan, London. In *Allen Ginsberg in America* (1969) Jane Kramer has chronicled this chapter of sociological history. Such fame, in which acolytes hung on his every word, taping and transcribing his conversations and lectures, perhaps inevitably led to a loosening of the texture of his actual writings. Maybe with approaching middle age he no longer felt the nearly unbearable tensions of his youth. At any rate, the poems in *Reality Sandwiches* (1963), *Planet News* (1968), *The Fall of America* (1972), and *Mind Breaths*

(1977) on the whole either lack the intrinsic structure of those in the earlier books or repeat their gestures without their intensity. Where his best poems had discovered the rhythms of the experiences they expressed, Ginsberg later simply annotated what happened to him, making texts from what he saw through the window on bus or plane trips. The onrush of images is intended to break up received perceptions, to transform sensibility. Sometimes the effect is that of an over-stuffed hoagie made by a mad short-order cook, but when Ginsberg discovers the inherent form of his expression the results are both original and effective.

At a time when poetry was chiefly a craftsman's written art, Ginsberg took it out of the study and onto the podium. He became a skilled public performer of his rhetorical and oratorical poems, preceding his readings with lengthy chantings of Buddhist prayers. That Ginsberg would see himself as a religious seeker is not surprising: in him are combined the revolutionary transcendental strophes of such visionaries as Christopher Smart, Blake, and Whitman as well as the denunciations and annunciations of the prophetic books of both Testaments. Ginsberg has absorbed and internalized, too, the Hebraic strain of visionary prophecy; where Berryman rather exotically invokes Bal Shem Tov in one of his dream songs, Ginsberg's work is striated with the joyous energies of Hasidic mysticism. At the same time this latter-day Jeremiah has also absorbed the example of Pound's attacks on materialism and his presentation of the suffering self. (After Pound's release Ginsberg visited him in Italy, and reported that the aged poet now repented the error of his anti-Semitism; but as far as I know, Pound never wrote anything to this effect.) Although Ginsberg reflects, among other sources, his Jewish background, it is to Tibetan Buddhism, with its willed withdrawal from the body and the world, that he has turned in a way that oddly resembles Eliot's search for the changeless moment. (Eliot has said that when he wrote *The Waste Land* he was on the point of becoming a Buddhist.) Now in his fifties, Ginsberg has at last achieved a plateau of relative tranquillity. Once the arch-rebel against all things academic, he has become part of a new academy: the Naropa Institute of Buddhist Studies and the arts in Boulder, Colorado, where, with such other poets as Gregory Corso, Lew Warsh, Michael McClure, Robert Duncan, and Ted Berrigan (all either ex-Beats or Black Mountain poets), Ginsberg conducts The Jack Kerouac School of Disembodied Poetics.

Other poets appeared in San Francisco in the fifties and sixties—among them Ferlinghetti, Corso, McClure, Jack Spicer—but the only one whose work has been as ambitious and as influential as Ginsberg's is Gary Snyder. Few poets would seem to have as little in common as these two, yet such was the direction of their cultural rebellion that they have been gurus to analogous, if not identical, bands of followers. Ginsberg's immigrant radicalism is paralleled in Snyder's commitment to social justice through his affiliation (shared with his early mentor, Rexroth) with the native IWW rebel-reformers of the western lumber camps. Where Ginsberg is an urban poet, however, Snyder seeks transcendent knowledge in Nature, experienced often in solitude. The landscape is western, the theme a heritage from Thoreau. The title of his first book is *Riprap* (1959), defined as "a cobble of stone laid on steep slick rock / to make a trail for horses in the mountains," and the poetic set forth in the title poem is determinedly utilitarian, a life-preserving stratagem in a hard place.

> In the thin loam, each rock a word
>   a creek-washed stone
> Granite: ingrained
>   with torment of fire and weight
> Crystal and sediment linked hot
>   all change, in thoughts,
> As well as things.

Pound and Williams pointed the way to his valley, but Snyder climbs the steep rock and drinks the cold mountain water on his own terms.

While at Reed College Snyder had studied anthropology and lived among an Indian tribe, ever since sharing their reverence for the land and the life it nurtures, as well as their need to mythologize not only the marvelous and the transcendent but also the coarse and lusty energies of life, as he does in *Myths and Texts* (1960) and in "The Berry Feast," written before 1955 (*The Back Country*, 1968):

> Fur the color of mud, the smooth loper
> Crapulous old man, a drifter,
> Praises! of Coyote the Nasty, the fat
> Puppy that abused himself, the ugly gambler,
> Bringer of goodies.
>
>> In bearshit find it in August . . .
>> Bear has been eating the berries.
>>   high meadow, late summer, snow gone
>> Blackbear
>>   eating berries, married
>> To a woman whose breasts bleed
>> From nursing the half-human cubs . . .

Like many West Coast artists and writers Snyder turned to the Orient for alternatives to Western traditions. Here, too, Rexroth had preceded him with skillful translations of Chinese and Japanese poetry. Pound, whose Cathay poems had invented China for modern poets, was an early influence too, as Snyder's broken lineation and sharp imagistic shifts suggest, but where Pound's and Rexroth's Orientalism had been exclusively literary the younger poet immersed himself much more deeply in Japanese culture. Snyder, who had worked as a logger, forest ranger, and deckhand on a tanker, got off the boat in Japan and spent three years in a monastery as acolyte to a Zen master. Unlike many who tripped out on exotic religions in the 1960s, Snyder was as serious in this as in his other commitments. His journals and essays, collected in *Earth House Hold* (1969), record his travels and seekings. Snyder is at once a syncretist and a revolutionary; like earlier transcendentalists he grafts Oriental mysticism on American optimism.

In a note called "Buddhism and the Coming Revolution" he would "move toward a free, international, classless world . . . respecting intelligence and learning, but not as greed or means to personal power." He quotes the Wobbly slogan, "Forming the new society within the shell of the old," as he would replace "the Judeo-Capitalist-Christian-Marxist West," and combine "social revolution" from the West with the East's "individual insight into the self/void."

In another essay, "Why Tribe," Snyder evokes the "small but influential heretical and esoteric movements" which have expressed a mystical continuity "that runs without a break from Paleo-Siberian Shamanism and Magdelanian cave-paintings; through megaliths and Mysteries, astronomers, ritualists, alchemists and Albigensians; gnostics and vagantes, right down to Golden Gate Park." Others may be less willing to link the Great Love-In of 1969 with "peasant witchcraft in Europe, Tantrism in Bengal, Quakers in England, Tachikawa-ryū in Japan, Ch'an in China," or agree that these are indeed connected. For Snyder, however, they comprise "the Great Subculture . . . ecstatic positive visions of spiritual and physical love." His later essays, in *Turtle Island* (1974), are more pragmatic and show that Snyder is a rationalist with a well-founded program for survival in a time of political and ecological oppression. These ideas became the foundation of his poetry.

Already in *Myths and Texts*, Amerindian myth is interwoven with Oriental meditation, and these strands are twined together in *The Back Country* (1968), *Regarding Wave* (1970), and *Turtle Island*. Snyder is a sophisticated Romantic Primitive, seeking the mythic patterns of original archetypes to which all human life, whether knowingly or not, conforms, as does the rest of the natural world. For him, poetry is "a riprap on the slick rock of metaphysics." He has said, "I hold the most archaic values on earth . . . the fertility of the soul, the magic of animals, the power-vision in solitude, the terrifying initiation and rebirth; the love and ecstasy of the dance, the common work of the tribe." If the poems on those problems for which his prose outlines solutions are sometimes marred by didacticism, his best work is characterized by its openness to sensuous pleasure, to humor, and to abiding human concerns. In his poem "What You Should Know to Be a Poet," he advises knowledge of "animals as persons," the names of trees, flowers, weeds, stars; "the movement of the planets / and the moon. / your own six senses, with a watchful and elegant mind," mastery of one tradition of magic, and "dreams. / the illusory demons and illusory shining gods." He advises the acolyte to "kiss the ass of the devil and eat shit," to "love the Human," and seek

> the wild freedom of the dance, *extasy,*
> silent solitary illumination, *entasy*
> real danger. gambles. and the edge of death.

When Snyder began to write in the early 1950s, the oral literature of the American Indians had been examined and translated chiefly by linguists and anthropologists; since then, in large part thanks to his opening up the territory, other poets have become interested in such material, and in the past decade a new generation of American Indian poets themselves have written of their situation as inheritors of their ancestral culture. The most egregious collections of Amerindian poetry appear in Jerome Rothenberg's copious anthologies, *Technicians of the Sacred* (1968) and *Shaking the Pumpkin* (1972). The texts are translated or reworked by many hands from ethnologists' versions. Rothenberg's prefaces and practice propose that archaic and primitive texts "intersect" with visionary poetry like Blake's—in short, he enlists the verse of preliterate and oral cultures to undermine and replace the values of allegedly rational, higher culture. In this enterprise he joins hands with many Black Mountain poets. Such may be a function of Amerindian chants for contemporary white Americans, but so to interpret oral literatures out of the contexts of their uses in their own cultures can be misleading, as Karl Kroeber trenchantly suggests in "Poem, Dream, and the Consuming of Culture" (*Georgia Review,* 1978).

A poetically successful and historically responsible use of such material has been made by David Wagoner, like Snyder a poet from the Pacific Northwest. He has drawn on American Indian ritual and imagery in poems which re-create in English the cultural values of the original texts. A suite of "Seven Songs for an Old Voice" concludes his book *Sleeping in the Woods* (1974) with invocations of First People, Beaver, Bear Mother, while the section of new work in his *Collected Poems 1956-1976* animates such natural forces as Ice and Stump as well as Raven, Hawk, and the Dream Catchers. Wagoner has collected and retold tales of the Northwest Indians in *Who Shall Be the Sun* (1978), from which the poems just mentioned are drawn. A series in which Stump is the central character is comparable, in the archaic energy of its mythic figure, to Ted Hughes's *Crow,* though requiring less supension of disbelief because Wagoner has remade an actual legend. His versions of Indian tales, like Snyder's, are believable recreations of primitive mythopoesis.

Most eminent among the Native American poets is N. Scott Momaday, whose poems appear in *Angle of Geese* (1974); he is best known for his novel, *House Made out of Dawn* (1968) and his history of the migration of the Kiowa in *The Way to Rainy Mountain* (1969). He and over a dozen younger poets appear in Duane Niatum's anthology of contemporary American Indian poetry, *Carriers of the Dream Wheel* (1975). Unlike the tribal chants in Rothenberg's collections or the legends retold by Snyder or Wagoner, the work of most of these poets is not to translate ancestral rituals but to explore their own loss of cultural continuity. As Simon J. Ortiz puts it, "The prayers of my native selfhood / have been strangled in my throat." These poets of Native or mixed descent are contemporary American graduates of university writing programs who, in styles characteristic of their generation, make poems of the experience, unique to themselves, of being descended from tribal cultures that seem irrelevant to most of their countrymen. Joseph Bruchac's "Winnebago Brave," in a midwestern bar, "speaks in Winnebago & / they answer in German. / I'm Sioux, man, he says . . ." but "They do not understand warriors." How could they, when the name of his tribe is known to most Americans now only as a trademark on recreational vehicles?

While the Beat writers were achieving notoriety for their divergent life-styles, a more philosophical rebellion had already been launched at an experimental campus in North Carolina. When Charles Olson was Rector of Black Mountain College from 1951 to 1956, he collected on his faculty and among the tiny student body such innovators as the composer John Cage, the dancer Merce Cunningham, and, in addition to himself, the poets Robert Duncan, Robert Creeley, Edward Dorn, and John Wieners. Others who became affiliated with the Black Mountain school of poetry (as it was termed by the anthologist Donald

525

Allen) include Cid Corman, Joel Oppenheimer, Theodore Enslin, John Logan, Jonathan Williams, LeRoi Jones, and, most accomplished of all, Denise Levertov. These poets differ much in style and range and subject, but they do share attitudes first clarified and promulgated by Olson in his aggressively polemical essays. His effort is to disabuse American poets of their dependence upon their past, and to discover in the unmediated self all the necessary principles of inherent form in a time when the breakup of traditional culture, as he felt it, made obsolete the conventions not only of the arts but of rationalism itself.

Olson's Black Mountain was an academy of the avant-garde, set up, it would seem, to wrest command of Olympus from its rivals, such as John Crowe Ransom's Kenyon College, where the Fugitive tradition continued with Randall Jarrell as well as Ransom on the faculty, and successive students included Lowell, Anthony Hecht, James Wright, and Robert Mezey. Other rival colleges of bards included Yvor Winters's Neo-Augustan establishment at Stanford; Paul Engle's graduate writing seminars at Iowa; and Mark Van Doren's more catholic and casual tutelage at Columbia, where poets as diverse by their own lights but, except for Ginsberg, as academic by Black Mountain's as Thomas Merton, Berryman, Louis Simpson, Daniel Hoffman, John Hollander, and Richard Howard were all encouraged by the resident poet-professor. Olson himself was a poet-professor too, but a guru of a different sort from any on tenure at universities more conventional than Black Mountain College. He was an antiacademic academician who had prepared for a Ph.D. in American Civilization at Harvard but left without the degree, publishing instead of a footnoted dissertation his provocative, rhapsodic *Call Me Ishmael* (1947), a personal, visionary interpretation of Melville, and later, after a Guggenheim grant, *Mayan Letters* (1953), deciphering the Indian hieroglyphs of Mexico.

Olson in 1950 brought out his essay "Projective Verse." This has the tone of a manifesto from an exiled political party. Its opening gesture is designed to baffle the opposition, attract the faithful, and embody its central dogma concerning the need to cast aside old forms, old syntax, old meters:

(projective   (percussive   (prospective

vs.

The NON-Projective

(or what a French critic calls "closed" verse, that verse which print bred . . .)

Verse now, 1950, if it is to go ahead, if it is to be of *essential* use, must, I take it, catch up and put into itself certain laws and possibilities of the breath, of the breathing of the man who writes as well as of his listenings.

Projective verse, then, will free poetry from dependence on mechanical forms derived from printed type, and will also free it from a metrics grounded solely on the sound of the language. Poetry will find new forms based on breathing, the natural rhythm. Olson formulates "the two halves" of poetic composition as "the HEAD, by way of the EAR, to the SYLLABLE" and "the HEART, by way of the BREATH, to the LINE," and speaks of "the dance of intellect" among the syllables, "the PLAY of a mind . . . that shows whether a mind is there at all."

In the same essay, however, he calls also for poetry to be composed upon the typewriter as an instrument capable of scoring "exactly the breath, the pauses, the suspensions even of syllables, the juxtapositions even of parts of phrases." The poet can now, "without the convention of rime and meter, record the listening he has done to his own speech and by that one act indicate how he would want any reader, . . . to voice his own work." That the typewriter may impose a mechanical disposition of form just as print had done is not foreseen, nor is the possible contradiction between the desired breath-line and the desired eye-breaks made accessible by the use of the space bar.

The theory of Projective verse is phrased in terms of "the *kinetics* of the thing": "A poem is energy transformed from where the poet got it . . . by way of the poem itself to, all the way over to, the reader. Okay. Then the poem itself must, at all points, be a high energy-construct and, at all points, an energy-discharge." In using the vocabulary of physical science to define poetry Olson continues in the vein of Pound and Ernest Fenellosa (*The Chinese Written Character as a Medium for Poetry,* 1920) and the Objectivist statement of Louis Zukofsky in 1931 (reprinted in *Prepositions,* 1967). Poetry is at the same time kinetic energy and organic process, like breathing. What this invocation of biology and physics implies is the validation through natural laws of a poetry which rejects intellection, abstraction, the entire inheritance of formal furniture. Olson's essay "Human Universe" carries the attack forward: "The harmony of the universe, and I include man, is not logical, or better, is post-logical, as is the order of any created thing." The enemies of order are therefore the inventors of logic: Socrates (for his "willingness . . . to make a 'universe' out of discourse"); Aristotle, whose "logic and classification . . . have so fastened themselves on habits of thought that action is . . . abso-

527

lutely interfered with"; and Plato, for "his world of Ideas, of forms as extricable from content."

It is the intellectual mold of abstraction, the habitual subordination of the particular to the general category into which it is formed by typological and analytical thinking, which in our culture makes necessary a new stance to experience if poetry is to render the truth of reality. Olson's revulsion against the cognitive tradition of Western culture dramatizes his dismay at what he diagnoses as the proof of its failure. That tradition and that culture have culminated in the social inequities intrinsic to modern capitalism; the fruits of rational thought are nationalism and industrialism, both of which express their natures in war and devastation. Like Pound's, Olson's poetry and aesthetics are based upon an extensive, even heroic, effort to substitute for the entire mental set of a defective civilization a new principle of responding to and expressing reality. Like Pound, Olson assumes that poetics can have the power to alter perception, to change sensibility and hence affect the behavior of men and of nations. The prophetic hopes of Walt Whitman echo through the pronouncements of both of these revolutionaries of the word.

Olson desires an alternative culture to ours, one in which the fingertips rather than the brains are the organs of knowing. Having lived in Mexico, he finds that the Mayan Indians embody such values. Their myths, their hieroglyphs are more retentive of the reality of experience than are our abstract ideas, our post-Socratic syntax. Here too Olson is in the line of Pound, who preferred the Chinese ideograph to the English sentence as a medium for poetry.

Olson's program of Romantic Primitivism has been enormously influential upon poets younger than he, partly through his capacity for inspiring discipleship but also because his conceptions, expressed with all the defiance of the iconoclast, are deeply rooted in the discontents of the American character. The effect of his program is to liberate the self from subjection to history. Confronting the past, the self is freed from its behests to reexamine the particularities of its bequests. None of the generic categories into which experience of the past has been squeezed by our Greco-Judaic-Christian intellectual tradition retains or transmits the truth, as the self would experience it, of any events, past or present. Such self-reliance, it will be inferred, reinforces that Emersonian strain in American feeling which Quinten Anderson has characterized as the Imperial Self. Thus the Projective poet is set free to use the rhythms of his own body's breathing as the measure, the perceptions of his own fingertips as the recording instruments, and the resources of his typewriter as the scoring device for confronting experience head-on, as though for the first time—indeed for the first time, since none of the conventions used by his predecessors will discover or enact the forms of his own experience, which only he can create.

These are heady prolegomena; what comes of them in poems written under their rule? Olson's work has been collected under two titles: *The Archaeologist of Morning* (1971) contains all of his shorter poems, and *The Maximus Poems,* published in several installments between 1953 and 1975, comprises his improvisatory epic, intended to countervail such predecessors as *The Waste Land, The Bridge, Paterson,* and especially, *The Cantos.* At its best, Olson's is a polemical poetry designed to demonstrate and validate the propositions upon which it is based. Writing in 1951 to a friendly German critic, he speaks as the American poet instructing the European reader:

> . . . come here
> where we will welcome you
> with nothing but what is, with
> no useful allusions, with no birds
> but those we stone, nothing to eat
> but ourselves, no end and no beginning, I assure you, yet
> not at all primitive, living as we do in a space we
>   do not need to contrive . . .

The style of his poetry, Olson assures his readers from abroad (in a phrase reminiscent of Williams), is "our anti-cultural speech, made up / of particulars only."

The look of Olson's poems on the page illustrates his felt need to break up expected forms. Availing himself of the typewriter, he sometimes stretches his lines across the page in proselike, Whitmanic, occasionally rhapsodic periods; elsewhere, lines are brief fragments. He will orchestrate two or more voices by indentation. He may intersperse prose passages among the verse. Many of his devices have been anticipated by e. e. cummings, by Apollinaire (in "Un coup de dés"), by Pound and Williams, but even the last-named maintain a rhythmic base to strengthen and counterpoint their irregularities. Olson, though capable of this, rarely aims to do so. "The Kingfishers" is perhaps his most widely admired poem; it well illustrates the discontinuity characteristic of his method of "composition by field." This meditation on value systems juxtaposes the trade among the Mayans in the feathers of this bird with, among other elements, quotations (in French, for some reason) from a revolutionary and apocalyptic speech by Chairman Mao. The effort is to incorporate by association the contrast between a hieratic, ancient culture and a mercantile, modern one. The result is a poetic process ultimately similar to Symbolism, achieved by means designed to reflect the seemingly unstructured subliminal flow of feeling, embodying rather than bypassing or regularizing its leaps, halts, incompletions. Where successful, the result is moving and powerful:

> with what violence benevolence is bought
> what cost in gesture justice brings
> what wrongs domestic rights involve
> what stalks
> this silence
>
> what pudor perjorocracy affronts
> how awe, night-rest and neighborhood can rot
> what breeds where dirtiness is law
> what crawls
> below

Other poems which notably orchestrate the flow of feeling include "The Moebus Strip," "In Cold Hell, in Thicket," "The Death of Europe," "As the Dead Prey upon Us," and "The Librarian." But all too often Olson's work pays the penalty his theories exact in incoherence, and suffer from a texture essentially unrhythmic, from a diction lacking in density.

Eliot's *The Waste Land* appropriated "the mind of Europe"; Pound's *Cantos* ransacked world history; Whitman in *Song of Myself* made America the measure of his soul; Williams, in *Paterson*, fused a modern industrial city and its past with his personal sensibility. But in *The Maximus Poems* Olson focuses upon the present and the past of the fishing village of Gloucester, Massachusetts, where he grew up. His character Maximus, unlike Paterson, does not embody his town, but participates by absorption in the history of its founding and by responding to what the poet feels and thinks in its present life. The sequence begins with an extended and petulant attack upon another Gloucester poet, Vincent Ferrini, who had started a literary magazine in contravention of Olson's principles. Soon Maximus re-creates the founding by the Puritans of Gloucester as a center of the fishing trade: "I would be an historian as Herodotus was, looking / for oneself for the evidence of / what is said," and accordingly the poem reproduces raw data, lists from bills of lading, newspaper clippings describing ships and fishermen lost at sea. Compared with Lowell's apocalyptic indictment of the greed of New England whalers in "The Quaker Graveyard at Nantucket," Olson's approach to his documentary evi-

530

dence of the seventeenth-century fishermen is seemingly objective. He doesn't hand down condemnations based, as are Lowell's, on religious values outside the experience in which his poem participates. Olson's attitude to history is exemplified in Maximus: this persona plunges into the seventeenth century's adventure seemingly without preconceptions, though of course in his immersion in the particulars of the place and time, as well as in his objectivity, are implicit the very modern freedom from abstraction Olson requires. Yet in the end, regarding the past, like Pound and Lowell he finds all bleared with trade, smeared with materialism:

one's forced,

considering America,
to a single truth: the newness
the first men knew was almost
from the start dirtied
by second comers. About seven years
and you can carry cinders
in your hand for what

America was worth. May she be damned
for what she did so soon
to what was such a newing
. . . .
We have the gain. We know
. . . that no one
knew better
than to cash in on it. Out,
is the cry of a coat of wonder.

So the promise of the New World is once more betrayed; the probing of our beginnings discovers that all was "Stiffening, in the Master Founder's Wills."

Olson's two principal disciples are Robert Creeley and Robert Duncan. Both, especially Creeley, have been instrumental in promoting Olson's influence, editing his writings, spreading his doctrines among younger poets (see *A Quick Graph: Collected Notes and Essays*, 1970). Superficially, these two poets seem not to resemble each other very much, despite their affiliation and shared enthusiasms, for Duncan's work is ambitiously large-scale, romantic, mythic, and prolix, while Creeley's is almost a minimal art in which economies of intention, form, and language are the virtues of a resolutely stringent aesthetic. Yet in his own way each carries out Olson's attack on apriorism of form, language, and institutions.

Duncan's major effort has been the writing of two intertwined long poems, cantos of which are interspersed among other poems in his books (*The Opening of the Field,* 1960; *Bending the Bow,* 1968). These are titled "Passages" and "The Structure of Rhyme" (which is of course mostly unrhymed). Their discontinuous composition derives from *The Cantos* and *Maximus,* but Duncan is much more lushly romantic than Olson or Pound. By turns sensuous, transcendental, ecstatic, occult, and Orphic, Duncan has a deep sense of the poem as "a ritual referring to divine orders." With his affinities to Blake and Whitman this San Francisco poet seems more like Ginsberg than like Creeley. His aesthetic is elaborated in "Beginnings of the H.D. Book," of which thus far only excerpts have been published (see *A Caterpillar Anthology,* 1971). For Duncan, the work of H.D. leads to an exploration of the primitive and mystical roots of poetry.

Creeley's longest poems are briefer than Duncan's shortest, and where Duncan uses a bardic, long, incantatory line, Creeley's lines are minimal indeed: often a word or two, a syllable, surrounded by columns of blank space in which the evocative concision of statement reverberates as in an echo chamber. In a poem called "The Figures" he describes the organic process of creating forms inherent in his material by analogy to a wood-carver who feels the pieces of wood "moving into / the forms / he has given them." So with Creeley's forms, and with his language. Creeley's style is an instrument of exclusions by means of which he is enabled to trace the immediacy of his feelings. Where Duncan, like Olson and Pound, reaches outward from the self to grasp the mythico-historical sweep of experience, Creeley's cameo-like carvings present only fragments of experience, the quintessential *now* of his feelings, rarely with reference to any ritualistic or literary past. In *For Love: Poems 1950-1960,* containing his most accomplished work, there is a slantwise reliance on the most minimal forms—quatrains, tercets, couplets—and rhyme is used ironically. Irony is the tone, too, when his work, rarely, is openly referential, as in his "Ballad of the Despairing Husband," in which a marital argument— its fleers and jabs in the earthy language of intimacy—suddenly becomes an invocation of the Muse. Poems in *For Love* dramatize feelings of alienation ("I Know a Man," "La Noche"), and the egocentricity of a drug trip is exposed with wit in "A Wicker Basket." But the most memorable of these often sharp, amiable, and honest-speaking lyrics are those exploring the tangles of erotic feeling. As a poet fated to speak of love's exactions, Creeley is comparable to Robert Graves, his opposite in every formal respect. Yet in Creeley's rigorously crafted poems each word bears its full stress of implication, and the arrangement, though improvisatory and unlike the repetitions of conventionally formal verse, achieves a formal structure of its own.

The very titles of his subsequent books indicate the increasing fragmentation of experience in Creeley's work: *Words* (1965), *Pieces* (1969). With *A Day Book* (1972) and *Hello: A Journal* (1978) the subject matter has become not so much the poet's inner life as a record of his observations and the shards of reflection these observations evoke. By a different route from that of Ginsberg, lacking the latter's Buddhist tranquillity, Creeley, in these nervous, disjointed, and desperate fragments, writes his parallels to the rambling, vatic journal-poems of his friend. Creeley has never included ideas, or commitments to social issues, in the repertoire of his work; his stripped-down poems have been, as it were, a proving of Pound's belief in "technique as the test of a man's sincerity." He has given up everything that a poet might be armed with save his commitment to the shapes and sounds of words and the truth of his own feelings. His accomplishment is admirable, the renunciations he must make, costly. Since Creeley's individual style is a learnable technique, he has had a great influence upon younger poets, who in many cases borrow the manner without having struggled through the rejections and discipline that made his style not merely possible but inevitable for him. So in the end Creeley's recognizable style turns up in imitations in every new magazine, one of the dozen or so period styles now fostered in the academic writing workshops, opposition to which was one of the instigating and cohering elements among the original poets at Black Mountain.

"I think of Robert Duncan and Robert Creeley as the chief poets among my contemporaries." So wrote Denise Levertov in Donald Allen's *The New American Poetry, 1945-1960,* the anthology that mobilized Black Mountain, Beat, and New York School poets against the myrmidons of Academia. Levertov had been born in London to a Welsh mother and a Russian-Jewish father who had converted and become an Anglican minister. On both sides she is descended from mystics of the turn of the nineteenth century: one the founder of a Hasidic sect, the other a Welsh tailor called Angel Jones of Mold, as Levertov tells in "The Sense of Pilgrimage" in her collected essays, *The Poet in the World* (1973).

Her first book, *The Double Image,* published in London in 1946, reflected the rhetorical romanticism of postwar British verse. A year later she married Mitchell Goodman, the American novelist, and emigrated to the United States. She published no books for eleven years, during which time this British Neo-Georgian transformed herself into a new-style Romantic American poet. She discovered the America she sought in the rejections of tradition and convention that characterized the Black Mountain poets and, behind them, in Pound, in H.D., and in the example of another American poet who, like herself, was born of a British father and had chucked out tradition to write with immediacy. William Carlos Williams is Denise Levertov's principal master, as the title of her second book suggests.

Here and Now (1957) showed that these new enthusiasms had been accommodated to an individual style. Levertov's work—she is a voluminous poet with another ten books in the succeeding twenty years—is more accessible than Duncan's, not being studded with mystical arcana. And she is open to a greater range of experiences than is Creeley. She writes in as close fidelity as she can to the principles of what she has defined as "organic form," her own adaptation of the Black Mountain group's development of the Pound-Williams-Imagist-Objectivist aesthetic: "The metric movement, the measure, is the direct expression of the movement of perception . . . And the sounds . . . imitate . . . the feeling of an experience, its emotional tone, its texture. The varying speed and gait of different strands of perception within an experience (I think of strands of seaweed moving within a wave) result in counterpointed measures." And again, "Form is never more than a *revelation* of content."

As Levertov is the historian of her feelings, her books are documentaries of the quotidian. Each moment's evocation of emotion is memorialized in the shifting rhythms, the wayward patterns of sound, the widening ripples of imagery that best embody this poet's fleeting realizations of felt meaning. Lowell, Berryman, and Elizabeth Bishop, even while seeming to free themselves from formal conventions, yet write from a metrical base and, as it were, sculpt their lines into hoped-for permanence; but Levertov, like Williams, Olson, and Creeley, writes a poetry of process whose achieved forms are improvisations revealed by the occasion of each poem. Few are buttressed by the recurrence of the familiar. She is all but completely committed to the present, the ever-renewing revelations of her own capacity to feel, as each passing instant impinges upon her sensibility. With the exception of certain mythical prototypes in her poems of sexual love, the past does not figure much for her. The history she records is what is happening, interpreted on its and her own terms, with neither such enrichments nor such burdens of allusion as lift or weigh the work of poets like Bishop, Berryman, or Lowell.

As her essay "A Sense of Pilgrimage" suggests, she sees at the center of her own work a quest figure on an archetypal journey through life. Of her many volumes one might take *O Taste and See* (1964) as indica-

534

tive of her work. The opening poem, "Song for Ishtar," invokes the moon, immemorial symbol of both love and inspiration, but here both creativity and love are inextricable from the body, from the poet's sexual nature, from her self-awareness as a woman. "The moon is a sow / and grunts in my throat," she writes in a poem reminiscent of the nearly forgotten Mina Loy's "Pig Cupid" (Levertov in her preface to the republication of Loy's work, 1958, wrote, "The value is—indivisibly—technical and moral"). In such poems as "The Ache of Marriage," "Love Song," "Eros at Temple Stream," "About Marriage," and "Hypocrite Women" in this book, and many others elsewhere, Levertov transcends the physicality of sex not by idealizing or mysticizing love but by giving reverence to the bodies that "In the black of desire," like herself and the moon, "rock and grunt, grunt and / shine." Other poems in *O Taste and See* lament the deaths of Pound, Williams, and H.D. ("the old great ones / leave us alone on the road"), seek solace in rebirth first in nature, then in the image (in a film) of a tribal ritual; she invokes the Muse, then celebrates the replenishment of nature ("A Turn of the Head," "The Victors"). "In Mind" and "A Prayer" define the mystery of creativity in which a part of the self is possessed by a power beyond the power of will. The lineation of these poems is both strong and delicate, reminiscent (sometimes explicitly so, as in "Grey Sparrow Addresses the Mind's Ear") of Japanese imagist poetry.

The other major aspect of Levertov's work is her enunciation of public themes, such as Creeley abjures. Her husband, Mitchell Goodman, became an early opponent of the Vietnam war and on this account a defendant, with Dr. Benjamin Spock, in one of the most celebrated political trials of the sixties. Denise Levertov was an active participant in this antiwar movement, which generated a moral passion reminiscent of Abolition before the Civil War. The parallel seems apt because to the antiwar activists the enemy was not Vietnam but those in the power structure of our own country who waged and abetted an unforgivable war in which the victims numbered a whole generation of Americans as well as the soldiers and civilians of another country. Levertov writes in later books (*The Sorrow Dance*, 1966; *To Stay Alive*, 1971) as *poète engagée*, her protest poems of the Resistance stirred by fervor. Yet these, although fiercely recording the anguish of their decade, lack the authority of her personal lyrics because their polemical, denunciatory, and rhetorical force is ultimately sentimental, pitting an "us" endowed with grace against a "them" who are hateful, stupid, and wicked. However true to her—and our—perception of the times, these poems lack the complexity of feeling of

535

those on the death of her sister ("The Olga Poems") or, in *Footprints* (1972) and *The Freeing of the Dust* (1975), poems on other personal themes.

In her range of themes—her lyrics of personal emotion, her expression of eroticism, her impassioned political outcries—Denise Levertov is the voice of the sixties in much the way that Muriel Rukeyser gave and continues to give articulation to an earlier generation of radical, feminist, and personal feeling.

In the midst of poetic movements determinedly contemporary or futurist, movements which deny the relevance of earlier traditions, there has been an unparalleled interest in the poetry of other cultures, other languages, both ancient and modern. Homer has been twice remade for our generation, as Richmond Lattimore's *Iliad* (1951) and *Odyssey* (1967) and Robert Fitzgerald's translations (1974 and 1961) have kept alive the father of epic and romance for readers with little Greek. Those without Latin have relied on C. Day Lewis's *Aeneid* (1952); no American poet of comparable stature has translated Virgil's epic since, though David R. Slavitt rendered his *Eclogues and Georgics* in 1972. The period has been perhaps the most prolific in verse translations of distinction since the Renaissance, with British as well as American poets exploring and reinterpreting classics of every past age and language. All of this activity suggests that American poets as never before were participating in what Eliot called "the mind of Europe" (as well as, in truth, the mind of Asia, of Africa, of South America). Yet for many who rebelled against the very traditions Eliot had advised poets to master, it was "the mind of Europe" itself—contemporary Europe—that contributed to their searches for new means of self-expression. In the period *l'entre deux guerres* and since, the mind of Europe rebelled against its own heavy burdens, as poets who felt the present as irrevocably broken from the past devised new means to express the anguish, alienation, and self-absorption made inevitable by their predicament.

These means, this rebellion, took shape in the Dada and surrealist movements on the Continent during and after World War I. Curiously, these movements had no counterparts at the time in either the United States or Britain; except for such minor and exotic voices as Edouard Roditi and Charles Henri Ford, who seemed to American readers like Parisian *fleurs de mal*, and, in Britain, the equally alien work of David Gascoyne, poetry in English was virtually innocent of surrealism. Forty years later, however, the examples of French surrealist poets after both world wars were being followed by Americans in their defiance or evasions of the Anglo-American tradition. Spanish surrealism, too, entered the American sensibility. These two anti-rationalist movements each had a recognizable tone. In France the poetry of absurdity and subjectivity, which developed out of the Symbolist movement it succeeded, came into being as a protest literature, a means of maintaining the hegemony of the individual against the threat of a centralized society, a bourgeois culture. With the world exhibiting its madness in orgies of destruction, the poet expresses his own authenticity by exploring personal feelings no social law can touch; here the Id is First Citizen, the dream more actual than quotidian reality. Joy and wonder striate the solipsistic oneirism of such poets as André Breton, René Char, Robert Desnos, Jules Supervielle, while a tone of more somber introspection informs the lyricism of Yves Bonnefoy.

In Spain and Latin America, poets faced the repressive politics of dictatorships in which open dissidence invited arrest, imprisonment, the truncheon, the firing squad. Subjectivity, the revelation of unconscious impulses, the trajectory of images in dreams both express the individual existence of the beleaguered poet and make possible his attack—as it were in code—upon the way things are. Poets in Spain (among them Federico García Lorca, Vincente Aleixandre, Rafael Alberti, Blas de Otero) and in South America (Pablo Neruda and Nicanor Parra in Chile, Octavio Paz in Mexico, César Vallejo in Peru) in varying ways combined social themes with the expression of private sensibility. An Iberian fatalism gives Spanish surrealist poetry a gravity of its own. Where French surrealist verse is likely to be wayward, devolving from a personal *esthétique,* each poet seeking to "donner un sens plus pur aux mots de la tribu," the aspects of Spanish poetry most influential upon Americans have been its expression of pure emotion, its search for archetypal images, and its examples of a non- or antirational aesthetic in the service of an art committed to social causes.

While Eliot and Stevens had introduced Symbolist practice into American poetry in the twenties, it was not until the Vietnam war of the sixties that surrealism became naturalized here. When American poets came to see their society as Continental poets saw theirs, as the impersonal force, the oppressor of their freedoms, the domestication of surrealism as a poetry of both escape from and attack on the oppressive, dehumanizing society of the time became possible. This influence appeared first in the work of poets as different from one another as W. S Merwin, Robert Bly, and the so-called New York School—Frank O'Hara, John Ashbery, Kenneth Koch. Each would soon have many disciples; surrealist subjectivity swept American poetry with the rapidity of fast-food franchises popping up on interstate highways.

Nowhere is the effect of these influences more dramatically shown than in the later work of W. S. Merwin. The contrast in method, language, tone, and versification between what he has written since the early 1960s and his first four books (between 1952 and 1960) is startling indeed. Merwin began as a virtuoso of literary tradition, a linguistic and formal tradition more European than Anglo-American. His first volume, *A Mask for Janus,* Auden's choice for the 1952 Yale Series of Younger Poets, arrived in a swirl of cansos, ballads, sestinas, carols, anabases, odes, and songs, used with a great—even a self-regarding—skill, and exhibiting the poet's ear for sound and measure calculatedly offbeat, as well as his predilection for archaic diction. His insistence on forms proclaimed the necessity for form; what else was proclaimed a necessity by this determined display of ancient fingerings was the continuity of literary expression, of the language itself, therefore of feeling, of experience.

Merwin's sensibility is attuned to fable, legend, myth; quest figures wander through his pages, as in "The Ballad of John Cable and Three Gentlemen," his reworking of *Everyman cum* Ransom's "Captain Carpenter," a final journey without the consolations of redemption. The immediate sources of this work lie in Merwin's fusion of two rival but complementary influences from earlier twentieth-century poetry. Of all poets of his generation, Merwin, who studied languages at Princeton, most nearly emulates the range of the young Ezra Pound, whose first book was *The Spirit of Romance.* For years Merwin made his living as a translator, giving us superb modern versions of medieval epic, ballad, and romance (*The Poem of the Cid,* 1959; *Some Spanish Ballads,* 1961; *The Song of Roland,* 1963), as well as of *The Satires of Perseus* (1961). After college Merwin had spent two years on Majorca as tutor to the children of Robert Graves. In such a poem as "December: Of Aphrodite" (*The Dancing Bears,* 1954) the intertwining of the Poundian with the Gravesian strands in Merwin's work is evident.

In these first two books Merwin explored his poetic inheritance. His fullest expression of what could be accomplished with his literary, linguistic, and intellectual equipment is the long poem in *The Dancing Bears,* "East of the Sun and West of the Moon," his dazzling rendition of the tale of Cupid and Psyche, borrowed from Apuleius's *The Golden Ass* (see Graves's chapter on this tale in *The White Goddess,* and his translation of the whole); Merwin combines this myth with the ancient folktale motif of the woman who takes a bear for her lover. In writing an extended mythological poem in 1954, Merwin was responding to the intellectual and emotional climate of the decade, expressed critically in Northrop Frye's *Anatomy of Criticism* (1957), as it had been poetically by Lowell's "The Mills of the Kavanaughs" and by Olson's and Williams's epics in progress. Behind this tendency to mythologize experience lay the weighty examples of *The Waste Land, The Cantos, The White Goddess,* and Yeats's *A Vision.*

In Merwin's hands this fable—of the white bear who conveys the willing maiden away to a strange, deathlike land of silence, where he comes to her by darkness as a young man bound by a wicked stepdame's enchantment that forbids her to see his face—is elaborated in thirty-nine thirteen-line blank verse stanzas. Glimmering cloud-castles of imagery and description enwrap the narrative, with its folktale reiterations. After the girl disobeys the bear-lover's injunctions and, heeding her mother instead, holds a dripping candle over his sleeping face, he disappears, and she must seek him in the land "East of the sun and west of the moon . . . There no one comes." Along the way she must find the three hags on three horses and receive three gifts and ride the three winds to the enchanted castle and three times match wits with the hideous princess with a nose "three ells long."

> Neither a solar nor a lunar story
> But a tale that might be human

the tale begins, shifting from the skeptical pronouncement "All magic is but metaphor" to the words of the lady, triumphant at last in her harrowing of the enchanted castle, "All metaphor is magic." Then, and only then, "the lucid moon, turning / Her mortal guises in the eye of man, / Creates the image in which the world is." Merwin's intricate fable combines with the need for absolute mutual confidence in love the epistemological quest for the meaning of experience itself, discovered in the transforming, lunar power of metaphor, of imagination. Without this power there is but the void of lovelessness, the nothingness of "a trope of Death" in the land of silence which this extended cadenza attempts with its strange music to fill and thus transform.

In *The Dancing Bears* Merwin had extended his mannerist style as far as it would take him. Like Lowell, he had come to the end of something; a change was necessary. The poems in *Green with Beasts* (1956) are mostly stychic: no more intricate stanzas, no more borrowings of tradition from Troubadour to Pre-Raphaelite. The language, too, is relatively purged of inkhorn terms, as Merwin leans toward a bestiary described in a commoner tongue. This is clearly a transitional book, pointing the way toward *The Drunk in the Furnace* four years later. There the blank verse is further roughened, especially in a series of ten family portraits at the end of the book. These no doubt are Merwin's response to Lowell's *Life Studies*; hitherto none of his subjects had been personal, or identifiably American. The first dozen poems in this book are meditations on sea voyaging, continuing the persistent theme in Merwin of the archetypal seafarer who is ever, like Pound's figure in *The Cantos*, making landfall at a new *periplum*. These poems are starker, less elaborate than hitherto, but their diction, though plain, is still elegant, as in the poem about Odysseus, who cannot remember which among his islanded women, "improbable, remote, and true, / Was the one he kept sailing home to." His poems on his forebears—eccentric uncles, straight-laced grandmother, wild riverboat-pilot grandfather—are not figures of myth or legend, but memorable portraits of themselves in an actualized Pennsylvania landscape. This American milieu is judged in "Pool Room in the Lion's Club": insulated from "the whole world" by "their gainless harmless pastime," the villagers at their one table remain "Safe in its ring of dusty light / Where the real dark can never come." Merwin will undertake the exploration of that real darkness, limned in "Burning Mountain" by the underground fire that "riddles the fissured hill," a hellfire like the earth's "molten core." In the concluding title poem a stray drunk inhabits an abandoned furnace, banging out a musical din "with poker and bottle" when in his "spirits"; the villagers "In their tar-paper church . . . / nod and hate trespassers."

> When the furnace wakes, though, all afternoon
> Their witless offspring flock like piped rats to its siren
> Crescendo, and agape on the crumbling ridge
>   Stand in a row and learn.

This is the poet's figure of the poet, a drunken outcast whose clangor breaks the silence and from whom the children of his people may "learn."

Silence, singing, exile, ignorance, learning: these are among the tokens of Merwin's poetry henceforth. With his next book, *The Moving Target* (1963) Merwin commences yet another phase of his career. Now great stylistic changes disturb the reader as they compel him to a closer attention: abandonment of regular and repetitive forms, the gradual erosion of syntax and punctuation, of the whole shebang of poetic conventions as Merwin had used them hitherto. He writes an "Inscription for a Burned Bridge" that can apostrophize his attitude to the bridges of tradition he had thus far erected over the chaotic flood of his stream of consciousness: "I have gone in with the river. / I will serve you no longer but you may follow me."

For his new bare, stripped style in *The Moving Target,* luminous and musical yet stark and haunted by the existentialist dissociation of feeling from perception, there had been anticipations in the sparc language of Merwin's medieval translations. Merwin had lived for years in France and had been translating many modern poets (among them Lorca, Neruda, Parra; Jean Follain, Pierre Delisle, Philippe Jacottet; Sergey Esenin, Osip Mandelstam, Iosip Brodsky—see *Selected Translations, 1948-1968*), thus schooling himself in the methods of surrealist and postmodern poetry. The nearest models for his new style, however, may be inferred from his contributions to *Hypnos Waking* (1956), the work of René Char translated by several hands, and, as Richard Howard suggests, in the poetry of Jorge Guillén. The luminous epigrams of the French poet, the sievings of silence of the Spaniard, helped to define Merwin's way. But his combination now of linguistic austerity with an oneiric vision reflects sources deeper either than these models or than the exhaustion of his elegant fabrications hitherto. In three prose reports written in 1962 for *The Nation* he deals directly, as seldom in his poems, with the political texture of contemporary life. One of these (June 16) reports the arrest, trial, and imprisonment of a group of Quakers who, protesting the escalating arms race, held a sit-in on the steps of the White House. They were charged with *violating the peace.* The entire issue of December 29 is given to Merwin's account of the voyage of the *Everyman,* a yacht manned by a Quaker crew who tried to sail into the atomic testing zone in the Pacific but were intercepted by the navy and placed under arrest. These reportorial pieces suggest the utter futility of the Western—particularly the American—tradition of individual freedom, of intelligence as a protection against the organized brutalities of the status quo. The diagnosis for life in America was dismal: an oppressive government of soulless bureaucrats was crushing the free spirits, the good souls, among us.

Merwin's other prose article (February 24) introduced his translations of several poems by Agostinho Neto, the Angolan insurgent then imprisoned by the ruling Portuguese. Merwin identifies his own aims as a poet henceforth with those of this beleaguered freedom-fighter:

> The decision to speak as clearly and truthfully as possible for the other human beings a poet finds himself among is a challenge to obscurantism, silence, and extinction . . . He finds a sufficient

triumph in the decision itself, in its deliberate defiance . . . and in any clarity which it helps him to create out of the murk and chaos of experience . . . He will not have been another priest of ornaments.

The renunciation of "ornament" by the poet as spokesman for "other human beings" may seem to promise a poetry at once political and popular, but Merwin moved in just the opposite directions: toward the discovery and definition of the authentic self in a world devoid of objective meaning. Neither historical, social, nor cultural institutions have the power of sustaining the contemporary self—they have not the power of truth; the self must reconstitute the very terms of its being from its own experience, which is, as it were, without precedent. Merwin henceforth abjured the ornament of an elaborate syntax—for is not syntax the imposition upon language of abstract logical relationships?—and worked toward a more and more fragmented expression of the actual gropings of consciousness. By a route quite different from Olson's Merwin, too, reached back to the pre-Socratics (the epigraph of his book, *The Lice,* is from Heraclitus), as he tried to live in a post-Socratic world where Reason is the carcass of a dethroned king.

In the opening poem in *The Moving Target,* "Home for Thanksgiving," he writes,

I bring myself back avoiding in silence
Like a ship in a bottle.
I bring my own bottle . . .

Common objects bespeak unexampled significations. Like the witless offspring in "The Drunk in the Furnace," the reader stands agape, and must learn how to read. The odd image just quoted, combining a return home (like that of Odysseus) with silence and an aborted voyage, is made clearer by a later poem addressed to his stillborn brother: "Born into death like a message in a bottle." *The Moving Target* reads like the grammar of a new dialect; its vocabulary, unlike Merwin's earlier far-flung raids on the *Oxford English Dictionary,* is severely limited. Certain nouns recur: bottle, shoe, knife, mirror, window, lock and key, door, hand, glove, feet, cup, ticket, dial. These concrete terms seem animate with a life of their own, a mysterious life which it is the poet's fate and mission to observe, express, interpret. The oddness of the disembodied actions, the seemingly arbitrary combinations of things, suggests surrealism; but this is a poetry that does not merely surrender to the destruction by dreamwork of the sensible order of things. Instead it asserts a new order, perceptible in its oneiric images, which is truer to our feelings than the timeworn relationships the poem's reordering replaces.

Like Merwin's other books, *The Moving Target,* despite its stylistic innovations, has the shape of a quest; commencing with "Home for Thanksgiving," it concludes with these lines from "Daybreak": "I join the procession / An open doorway / Speaks for me / Again." Like Whitman—or El Cid—the speaker follows the endlessly receding open road of the future, but without Whitman's ebullient hopefulness. Between homecoming and departure, the speaker, under the sign of an epigraph from Christopher Smart ("Let Lemuel bless with the wolf, which is a dog without a master, but the Lord hears his cries and feeds him in the desert"), discovers that like the wolf he has no home. Themes from earlier books recur, with the contrast between hope then (as in "Dictum: For a Masque of Deluge") and despair now ("Noah's Raven"). "Sire" recalls the poems about Merwin's grandfather in *The Drunk in the Furnace;* the interest, however, is no longer in his ancestor as an individual but as a metaphysical extension of the speaker's self ("Which of my many incomprehensions / Did you bequeath me . . . ?"). In the eviscerated universe of *The Moving Target* the poet "puts out the light / The better to see out into the dark." There, "The lightning has shown me the scars of the future." He invokes "My dread, my ignorance, my / Self . . . Bring / Integrity as a gift." In his voyage through ignorance, "all shores but the first have been foreign, / And the first was not home until left behind." His quest figures had traveled through the earlier books either not knowing the way ("The Bones of Pallurnus . . ."), or retracing the fated steps of Everyman ("The Ballad of John Cable . . ."), or, as in "When I Came from Colchis" and "You, Genoese Mariner," exploring the mysterious bourne of love, as did the lady who journeyed east of the sun and west of the moon. The journey now is toward a still more unknown destination than love, the everyday itself transfigured into the unfamiliar, as is revealed in "Second Sight":

> It's the old story.
> Every morning something different is real.
> This place is no more than the nephew of itself . . .

Here "Memory is my city / Hope my city Ignorance my city," as a voice wanders among the children of "Division, mother of pain." In this joyless prospect, it is yet the poet's obligation to define what is true, and, like the characters in the bleak landscape of Samuel Beckett's world, to make of these circumstances the grounds for discovery:

> Here I am once again with my dry mouth
> At the fountain of thistles
> Preparing to sing.

In *The Lice* (1967) he continues to sing, perfecting a brief Imagist lyric perhaps modeled on haiku, which he had used to good advantage in *Target,* in such poems as "Dusk in Winter," "How We Are Spared," and "For the Anniversary of My Death." The impulse toward concision leads to the crystallization, in other, longer poems, of lines of epigrammatic clarity, such as these:

Now all my teachers are dead except silence

Everything that does not need you is real

What you do not have you find everywhere

The gods are what has failed to become of us

If you find you no longer believe enlarge the temple

Whatever I have to do is not yet begun

A complementary tendency toward expansiveness informs several poems. Merwin writes "The Last One"; based on the inversion of a South American Indian creation legend, this limns the world's destruction by an atom bomb. In "The Unfinished Book of Kings" and in four psalms in his next book, *The Carrier of Ladders* (1970), he offers what might be sacred texts of the tribe, if there but were a tribe.

Not only is there no tribe, no community, in Merwin's poems, there are no persons. Not even the speaker is a person: what we hear is a disembodied voice obsessed by the desolation it so resolutely explores, the silence it so prolifically fills with broken song. For this reader, at least, the great imaginative excitement of Merwin's discovery of this existentialist *donnée* and of his exploration of its seemingly shriveled possibilities in *Target* and *The Lice* diminishes as he continues to use the same style in succeeding books (*Writings to an Unfinished Accompaniment,* 1973; *The Compass Flower,* 1977), and as he still further elaborates his solipsistic view of existence in prose parables derived from the work of Beckett, Kafka, and Jorge Luis Borges (*The Miner's Pale Children,* 1970; *Houses and Travellers,* 1977). In both verse and prose this style has become as mannerist as had his earlier one before he renounced being "another priest of ornaments." The passivity of his poetic persona has become stylized, as the disarrangement of objects and actions has become habitual. Whether the work, at once seminal and prolix, of this poet now in his early fifties may take yet another turn—perhaps toward the inclusion of the felt presence of others that could assuage his cosmic isolation and leaven his wonder with accessible human ties and a wider range of feelings—will of course depend upon what the ripeness of age may bring to him.

544

Meanwhile, he has inscribed on the empty slate of the heavens several score of luminous poems. His work is of first importance in its introduction into the American sensibility of the methods of surreal and existentialist poetics. Postmodernist poetry has become an international idiom, and Merwin has done much to bring American poetry and the mid-century "mind of Europe" together.

When their manifesto, *The Lion's Tale and Eyes,* appeared in 1962, Robert Bly had not yet published his first book; his collaborator James Wright was author of *The Green Wall* (1957) and *Saint Judas* (1959), books whose formal stanzas modeled on Frost, Robinson, and Hardy evoked compassion for poor Ohio villagers, a lost love, the outcast and abandoned of American life. Bly, in his preface, rejected "the poetry of direct statement" that describes "the outer world," for, he says, "The poem expresses what we are just beginning to think, thoughts we have not yet thought." This presages a radical rejection of rhetoric, of description, of the confessional mode; what is sought is the strippeddown realization, in the most direct, simple language, of the inner self's moments of transcendence. The most famous poem in this collection is Wright's "Lying in a Hammock at William Duffy's Farm in Pine Island, Minnesota." A dozen lines observe the scene in clear, visual images—a butterfly on a tree trunk, cowbells, the luminescent flare of year-old horse droppings, a chicken hawk floating overhead. The poem concludes, "I have wasted my life." The implication is the stronger for being stated indirectly—never before has the poet so vividly seen and felt his surroundings; he abandons rhetoric to lean and loaf at his ease. If Wright's poetry suggests Whitman, Bly's poems (reprinted in his first book, *Silence in the Snowy Fields,* 1962), similar in the passivity of their speaker, suggest Thoreau.

Bly's American transcendentalism is reinforced by Jacob Boehme's revelation that "according to the outward man, we are in this world, and according to the inward man, we are in the inward world . . . generated out of both worlds, we speak in two languages, and we must be understood also by two languages." (Bly quotes this passage as an epigraph in *The Light around the Body,* 1967.) Bly's effort has been to discover or devise a language adequate to the revelation of the inward man, who speaks in sleep, in dreams, in moments rich with illumination, in the acknowledgment of what Jung describes as the archetypes of the unconscious. In Continental Romantics and surrealists and in Oriental image-poets Bly found models for this enterprise, publishing between 1961 and 1974 his translations of Georg Trakl and Rilke; Vallejo, Neruda, Jiménez, and Lorca; the Swedish poets Tomas Tranströmmer and Gunnar Ekelöf; Issa Kobayashi and Basho. He praises the "magnificent silence" of Trakl's poems, in which the poet rarely speaks himself but "allows the images . . . of silent things" to speak for him. "Jiménez does not write of politics or even his own opinions, but only of solitude, and the strange joy that comes to a man in solitude." In his work "emotion after emotion" is "called out with great force and delicacy." To this method of evoking strong feelings Bly has given the name "Deep Image." His intentions in *Silence in the Snowy Fields* are similar to those of the poets he praised for their inward imagination, passivity of will, and depth of imagery. Compared with other American poets until then, Bly, through a triumph of renunciation, achieves a remarkable consistency of tone. In "Waking from Sleep,"

> . . . we sing, and do tiny dances on the kitchen floor.
> Our whole body is like a harbor at dawn;
> We know that our master has left us for the day.

But by the end of this book, some aspects of the outward world intrude upon the sleeper: "The human face shines like a dark sky / As it speaks of those things that oppress the living." These lines look ahead to *The Light around the Body* (1967), in which the active principle of American transcendentalism breaks in upon the plangent dream-life of Bly's passive narrator. Thoreau, who attacked social institutions in *Walden* and defined his country's conscience in "Civil Disobedience," seems a living presence behind Robert Bly's poems protesting and attacking the brutalities of the Vietnam war.[1] Bly's poetry of simplest statement, so effective in plumbing the silences of the spirit, proves less effective as an instrument for expressing moral outrage:

> These suggestions by Asians are not taken seriously.
> We know Rusk smiles as he passes them to someone.
> Men like Rusk are not men:
> They are bombs waiting to be loaded in a darkened hangar . . .

In Bly's next book, *Sleepers Joining Hands* (1973), however, his *poésie engagée* is artistically more successful. "The Teeth Mother Naked at Last" restores rhetoric to the poetry of denunciation; surrealistic juxtapositions of images from the luxurious American con-

---

1. With David Ray, Bly founded American Writers against the Vietnam War in 1966, a group that soon included Kinnell, Ginsberg, Levertov, and many more; their readings and rallies helped to influence public opinion, especially among the young, during the next half-dozen years. The poetic record of the war's effect on the men who waged or witnessed it is most effectively told by Michael Casey, *Obscenities* (1972), and John Balaban, *After Our War* (1974).

sumer economy against those from the murderous war among the Asian peasants give the poem its bitter black humor:

> It's because we have new packaging for smoked oysters that bomb
>   holes appear in the rice paddies
>
> It is because we have so few women sobbing in back rooms
> because we have so few children's heads torn apart by high-
>   velocity bullets,
> because we have so few tears falling on our own hands
> that the Super Sabre turns and screams down toward the earth.
>
> It's because taxpayers move to the suburbs that we transfer
>   populations.
> The Marines use cigarette lighters to light the thatched roofs of
>   huts
> because so many Americans own their own homes

In this book Bly provides also a prose essay ("I Come Out of the Mother Naked") that enlarges his Swedenborgian division of inwardness and outwardness to explain the history of the race. Drawing on the nineteenth-century ethnologist Bachofen (*Mother Right*, 1861), Bly proposes an original matriarchy from which the present patriarchal religions and states are deviations. In his search for the beginnings of consciousness, Bly finds Mother consciousness the source of deepest truth, and schematizes four states (the Good Mother, Death Mother, Ecstatic Mother, and Stone Mother). In twenty pages Bly attempts what Robert Graves had already accomplished in his encyclopedic *The White Goddess* (1948). Romantic Primitivism leads toward acknowledgment of what Jung terms the anima, the feminine principle, as the source of spiritual energy. With the end of the war Bly has returned to writing of the rewards of solitude: "I can't tell if this joy / is from the body, or the soul, or a third place."

The poetics of the deep image transformed the work of its other early protagonist, James Wright. In *The Branch Will Not Break* (1963) Wright, like Bly at this time, purifies his verse of everything but those images that evoke or define his feelings. For instance, in "A Blessing," a description of a pony grazing leads to this unexpected epiphany:

> . . . the light breeze moves me to caress her long ear
> That is delicate as the skin over a girl's wrist.
> Suddenly I realize
> That if I stepped out of my body I would break
> Into blossom.

Such emotive images, summoned in sinewy rhythms and pellucid language, illuminate many moments in this book. Sometimes, however, Wright's images seem forced or inauthentic and the resultant feelings sentimental, as when "Blind hoboes sell American flags / And bad poems of patriotism / On Saturday evenings forever in the rain." The lyrical release from selfhood into ecstasy occurs again, though less often, in *Shall We Gather at the River* (1968). In his first two books, mentioned earlier, formal poems proclaimed the worth of deprived, wounded persons and solace was sought in the bleak landscapes of his home town of Martins Ferry, Ohio. These themes recur in the new work in *Collected Poems* (1971) and in *Two Citizens* (1973), where, concomitant with sympathy for the beaten-down, are self-doubts tinged with despair. The rhythm of Wright's free verse is often enervated by the depression it expresses. His work utters the painful truths that the public world is almost too hard to bear, that such joys as the experience of love may give us are wrenched from a life that for the most part negates the possibility of happiness. In *To a Blossoming Pear Tree* (1977) Wright seems closer in mood than he has been in years to the accessible transfigurations of *The Branch Will Not Break*, but his poetic means no longer depend on the deep image in these discursive poems.

The influence of Bly and Merwin upon their contemporaries has been pervasive, for they led American poets to the divided streams of surrealist method as an available alternative to the intellectual and formal conventions of Anglo-American poetic tradition. The turn in Merwin's career, like that of Warren, Lowell, and Berryman before him, is repeated again and again in other poets who, like these, abandoned their early mastery of received practice for a more associative, less cognitive exploration of feelings. We have seen this in James Wright; it is observable also in Louis Simpson, James Dickey, and Galway Kinnell. And there is a whole generation of poets younger than these who plunged immediately into surrealist modes, rejecting formal tradition without having practiced it, as we see in Charles Wright, C. K. Williams, Mark Strand, Charles Simic, Stephen Berg, and others. For them all sorts of new raids on the unconscious now seemed possible, new expeditions into feelings hitherto unexpressed because American poets had been limited by using received maps of the territories language had already explored. The poets of the surrealistic mode repeated in a new way the Promethean gesture of seizing directly the fires of Vision. Charles Wright, in *Hard Freight* (1973), defines "The New Poem":

It will not reveal its name.
It will not have dreams you can count on.
It will not be photogenic.

It will not attend our sorrow.
It will not console our children.
It will not be able to help us.

Wright's personal variation on the mode, evident in his two long skeins of interconnected poems, "Tattoos" and "Skins" (*Bloodlines*, 1975), combines surrealism with the autobiographical impulse, a reconstitution of events as memory transforms them to reveal the mystery that inheres in the inner life.

The new poem that Charles Wright anticipates may be found in the work of his contemporaries who separate or recombine in various ways the several directions in the work of Merwin, Bly, and James Wright—the solipsism of the alienated self on the one hand, on the other an oneiric poetry of direct response to social forces. C. K. Williams writes desperate outcries against the monolithic injustices of life after the Holocaust, of life during the threat of atomic annihilation, as in "A Day for Anne Frank" (*Lies*, 1969); and in his poem "In the Heart of the Beast" (*I Am the Bitter Name*, 1972), attacks the brutality of the Green Beret cast of mind in America that led to the shooting of student demonstrators at Kent State University, Ohio, in 1970. In *With Ignorance* (1977), using a long, prose-textured line, Williams writes fables that usually begin with some ordinary encounter but move from reality through surrealism toward a revelation, as in "Bob," in which the speaker's meeting an underworld hit-man at a bar becomes, in retrospect, a vision of a hidden "self in myself."

Mark Strand is an elegist of the deepest alienation. His second book, *Reasons for Moving* (1968), bears as epigraph this sentiment by Borges, so like Bly's aphorisms from Boehme: "while we sleep here, we are awake elsewhere and that in this way every man is two men." Strand, in lyrics distinguished by their syntactical simplicity—which itself results from an ultimate clarity of perception—explores, in all its oddness and sadness, this doubleness, this duplicity which is characteristic of life itself. In a typical gesture, a man tells how he is obsessed by someone standing immobile on his front lawn; in desperation he digs a tunnel into the neighbor's yard, comes out "in front of a house / and stand there . . . / I feel I'm being watched / . . . I have been waiting for days" ("The Tunnel"). In the poem from which the book takes it title, Strand writes, "In a field / I am the absence of field . . . Wherever I am / I am what is missing." The entitling poem from his next book, *Darker* (1970), is similarly an invocation of that book's enterprise:

> I have a key
> so I open the door and walk in.
> It is dark and I walk in.
> It is darker and I walk in.

Strand's commitment will be to walk into the darkness of his life. "Time tells me what I am. I change and I am the same. / I empty myself of my life and my life remains." From the bleakness of that life he wrings a minimal consolatory lyricism from which false hope has been strained away: "We have no heart or saving grace, / no place to go, no reason to remain."

The Story of Our Lives (1973) extends through eight long poems Strand's two besetting themes, the evacuation of the life of the senses and the doubleness of consciousness. His moving "Elegy for My Father" speaks in accents suggestive of Merwin:

> You folded your arms over your chest and you dreamed of the
>   world without you,
> Of the space under the trees,
> Of the space in your room,
> Of the spaces that would now be empty of you,
> And you went on with your dying.

"The Story of Our Lives," "Inside the Story," and "The Untelling" elaborate the trope that "We are reading the story of our lives / as though we were in it, / as though we had written it." The interchangeability of the life imagined with the life lived, the entranced confusion as to which is the cause and which the effect, is an accomplished entelechy in this extended meditation in which the primacy of imagination is at once questioned and embodied. Strand's method of approaching experience has been reinforced by, if not derived from, his immersion in Spanish surrealism; he edited the translations by himself and others of *New Poetry of Mexico* (1970) and translated Rafael Alberti (*The Owl's Insomnia: Selected Poems*, 1973).

In *The Late Hour* (1978) Strand has returned from his explorations of darkness: "Even this late it happens / the coming of love, the coming of light." The light in these poems is likelier that of the moon than sunlight, as Strand—still an oneiromancer—explores the chances of happiness with a wonder similar to that with which he peered into the dark.

In his first book, *What the Grass Says* (1967), Charles Simic speaks of living as "a gift / Which I am no longer afraid / To open." In

Dismantling the Silence (1971) he is no longer so confident: "I leave you with / A door you don't wish to open / A key you are afraid to possess . . ." His stance and style show derivations—from Merwin (in the passage just quoted); from Roethke ("The snail gives off stillness. / The weed is blessed."); from Bly ("There is a smell of damp hay, / Of horses, of summer sky, / Of laziness, of eternal life"); from Strand (in "The Inner Man": "We cast a single shadow. / Whose shadow?")— but already Simic, with the help of French surrealism, has found a tone of his own: cryptic, wry, inward, and mysterious. Here is a complete poem, "The Wind": "Touching me, you touch / The country that has exiled you." He tells us "I'm like a cold glass of milk / The stars will drink before going to bed." In another poem made of equally disconnected images, he declines to interpret: "This is a tale with a kernel. / You'll have to use your own teeth to crack it."

Simic's poems have a structure of extended metaphor or the bones of a narrative showing through the imagery that develops sideways from one's expectations. "Hang the meat on the hook / So that I may see what I am," he counsels; in a poem called "Axe,"

> Whoever swings an axe
> Knows the body of man
> Will again be covered with fur.

His gift is for the epigram, as of a new wisdom literature: "It's not only its own life that man's body has to endure." "I am whatever beast inhabits me." And for images as startling as they are appropriate; whether bleak or lyrical, the tone is poignant, as though reaching for some meaning just beyond what the images reveal:

> A man who was to be hanged went along the road,
> His head was bent, his face was dark and twisted
> As if death meant a straining to empty one's bowels.
>
> . . . .
> The stars will come into the autumn sky
> Like boats looking for survivors at sea.

Simic, who was born in Yugoslavia (he came to this country in 1949 when eleven years old), has translated several leading Yugoslav poets, including Ivan V. Lalic and Vasko Popa (1970). In his next book, *Return to a Place Lit by a Glass of Milk* (1974), he uses riddles and nursery rhymes as well as the methods of *Silence* to probe such abstractions as "the enigma of the invisible," and what it is that "goes without saying." Sections of this book are determinedly jokey; the best such performance is the long poem "The Chicken without a Head," which reads like a sendup of the apocalyptic posturings of Ted Hughes's *Crow*. Prefaced by the aphorism "There's nothing more serious than a joke," this, like his other surreal fantastications, is offered as an epistemological exploration. Despite his evident philosophical interests, Simic's surreal technique in this book risks being more a means of minting imagistic surprises than a way of revealing a vision of life. In a recent interview (*Manassas Review,* 1978) Simic speaks of his newest poems as containing "no jokes or surrealistic images . . . the poems are much more autobiographical than they used to be . . . the impulse is away from embellishment and towards a greater economy of means." His hope, in his poetry, he says, is "to restore strangeness to the most familiar aspects of existence . . . for the sake of living more intensely. I think poetry's banner says 'More Life.'" His work thus far is at once playful and serious, uneven, sometimes excessive in its arbitrariness and cleverness, but his talent and purpose are securely demonstrated. What the new turn in his style produces will be awaited with interest.

Intellect as an organizing agent is all but banished from Stephen Berg's poetry. Berg is above all an emotive poet, his feelings flowing across the page in bursts of spontaneous phrases, often plotless, resistant to summary or brief quotation. The occasions of his poems are the daily occurrences of life—"I squeeze the edges of my chair / and hear 'This is happening! This! This! This!'"—as intensity of feeling ennobles the ordinary with wonder, joy, fear, grief.

> I hear
> . . . the silence
> I fear somewhere inside me lift its tiny
> cry to the name,
> because how can I eat love know death die and be someone's other
> unless I'm a poor breath chanted into the air through rotted teeth
> on the songs of old men?
> Well, here I am outside, a man
> who can neither share wine nor dance.
> Clouds pass, cars pass, people
> I haven't seen in twenty-five years speak to me.
> Through hard green prongs on a branch, one
> yellow and blown with leukemia, dips his face
> to my face.

As in this poem ("On the Steps," *The Daughters,* 1971), there is in Berg's other work a strain of the Hasidic "joy-crazed worshippers / whose hands woke God." Berg, too, has learned to tap unconscious energies, in part by his translations and adaptations of European Symbolists and post-Symbolists; he published the Hungarian poet Miklós Radnóti's *Clouded Sky* in 1973; I. F. Annensky, Anna Akhmatova, and Blas de Otero are among those rendered in *Grief* (1975), a book which begins and ends with meditations based on Chekhov's stories. In Berg's own poems what structure exists is the result of unanticipated inner coherence in the flood of images released by strong emotion. In brief lyrics the experience of the poem can have concluded before the feelings have clarified their own direction, but in the best of these, as in longer poems such as "In the Monument Works" and "Dark Lords" (*The Daughters*) and "Why Are We Here?" (*Grief*), the innate structure of feeling reveals itself without diminution of the surging energy that characterizes this poet's work.

A different strain of surrealism—more satirical, absurdist, parodistic, self-absorbed and detached from external reality—made its way into the mainstream of contemporary American poetry through the work of a group of poets who shared influences from French poetry and painting. The New York School, so-called, actually began in Cambridge after the war, when several poets came together in the Poet's Theatre. In her memoir prefacing V. R. Lang's *Poems & Plays* (1975), Alison Lurie affectionately describes this milieu in which Frank O'Hara, John Ashbery, and Kenneth Koch—all then at Harvard—were first to work together. Fulbright years in Paris (a decade's residence there for Ashbery as an art critic) followed, then they reassembled in New York, where Ashbery was curator at the Museum of Modern Art and O'Hara an editor on *Art News,* both in association with Jackson Pollock, Larry Rivers, and other artists active in abstract expressionism and action painting. Ashbery took an M.A. and Koch a doctorate at Columbia, where the latter remained to teach. These poets share an aesthetic based upon the practice of Dadaists of the twenties (André Breton, Tristan Tzara) and postwar French surrealists (Pierre Reverdy, Jules Supervielle, St.-John Perse, Robert Desnos) combined with the deconstructive energies translated from painting into poetry. Each in his own fashion attempts to cram into each poem a whole universe —not of experience, but of the associations his own sensibility reaches or confects in response to almost any given stimulus. The result is an aestheticism often all but divorced from any given reality, a solipsistic presentation of personal fantasy arranged in long lines often with neither syntactic organization nor punctuation to guide the reader. Much though they share in their general approach to poetry, however, each has an unmistakably individual way of disposing language and rhythm.

Frank O'Hara, who died in 1966, published little during his life, but his *Collected Poems* (1971) revealed a huge corpus of poems—and since then still more have been discovered. His tone is unique: a lighthearted gaiety, an improvisational quickness which accurately catches both the exact course of the poet's feelings and the aesthetic of action painting, or the cuts, the shifting visual textures, of motion pictures. This is a poetry in which the art is in the act of writing, immediate, sensory, nonreflective, yet marked by the poet's personality and, in a different context from the confessional kind of poetry—quite without its deep anxieties and dark tinges of mental instability—is frankly homosexual in its erotic orientation.

Although the self is necessarily at the center of O'Hara's poems—indeed, is the only center—it exists without a past, without history, without any nonparodic references to cultural paraphernalia or any burden of anxieties. The self is all sensibility, a kind of autonomous instrument for the recording of its own sensuous responses to the stimuli around it. Its environment is New York, the modern city, as in "Music" or "The Day Lady Died." His poem "In Memory of My Feelings" is a disjunctive cadenza upon the capacity of his divided selves to swallow up and become what their perceptions bring them:

Grace
to be born and live as variously as possible. The conception
of the masque barely suggests the sordid identifications.
I am a Hittite in love with a horse. I don't know what blood's
in me I feel like an African prince I am a girl walking downstairs
in a red pleated dress with heels I am a champion taking a fall
I am a jockey with a sprained ass-hole I am the light mist
in which a face appears
and it is another face of blonde I am a baboon eating a banana
. . . .
And now it is the serpent's turn.
I am not quite you, but almost, the opposite of visionary.

If these lines are typical in their arbitrariness, it is not that O'Hara does not strike graver tones. His elegy for Billie Holiday ("Lady Day") seems a similarly random pile-up of impressions as he walks down the street, but these are juxtaposed to the knowledge, from the front page of an evening paper "with her face on it," that—as he tells it in the neutral tone of the foregoing description—makes him sweat and lean "on the john door in the 5 SPOT"

while she whispered a song along the keyboard
to Mal Waldron and everyone and I stopped breathing

This is something new among elegies: not an invocation of the deceased, none of the apparatus of *Lycidas* or the like, but an absolutely objective recounting of what really happened to the poet at the moment of his knowledge of loss. "The Day Lady Died" is more accessible to the uninitiated than most of O'Hara's poems.

The spirit of *épater les bourgeois* is enacted over and over with a winning good-humoredness, as in his mock manifesto for "Personism, a movement which I recently founded and which nobody knows nothing about." This put-on is directed against such pompous declarations, as they seemed to O'Hara, as Olson's essay on Projective verse:

> Personism has nothing to do with philosophy, it's all art. It does not have to do with personality or intimacy, far from it! But to give you a vague idea, one of its minimal aspects is to address itself to one person (other than the poet himself), thus evoking overtones of love without destroying love's life-giving vulgarity, and sustaining the poet's feelings toward the poem while preventing love from distracting him into feeling about the person. That's part of Personism. It was founded by me after lunch with LeRoi Jones on August 27, 1959, a day in which I was in love with someone (not Roi, by the way, a blond). I went back to work and wrote a poem for this person. While I was writing it I was realizing that if I wanted to I could use the telephone instead of writing the poem, and so Personism was born. It's a very exciting movement which will undoubtedly have lots of adherents. It puts the poem squarely between the poet and the person, Lucky Pierre style, and the poem is correspondingly gratified.

O'Hara wrote for private circulation among his friends, but John Ashbery, a voluminous poet, has published a dozen books since his Yale Series volume *Some Trees* in 1956. Although that book clearly grows out of the poetic traditions it rejects, Ashbery's motivation, indeed the source of his artistic energy, is not the continuation of an art but the effort to create an autonomous anti-art, to obliterate the art of the past by parody, by assertions of its absurdity and irrelevance, by the substitution of a new set of relationships for art and for the reality of which received art is thought to be the mirror. Images of the familiar world are juxtaposed in unexampled ways to present a self-created universe—not so much a universe of discourse as a world of feeling. Like O'Hara, Ashbery was for years at the center, in Paris and New York, of avant-garde painting. Its deconstructive energies consorted well with similar tendencies in the French poetry Ashbery became immersed in during his ten years' residence in Paris. Unlike Merwin, Ashbery has followed the same aesthetic from the beginning of his career. Private, obscure, purposely lacking in logic, this work, it would seem, is designed to alienate readers; and for years, despite his frequent publications, Ashbery's poems were the enthusiasm of only a small coterie. The appearance of *Self-Portrait in a Convex Mirror* in 1975, however, evoked the highest acclaim. The book was given all three major prizes the following spring—the Pulitzer, and the National Book Critics Circle and National Book awards. Harold Bloom, long his champion, hailed Ashbery as "joining that American sequence that includes Whitman, Dickinson, Stevens, and Hart Crane," thus fulfilling the Emersonian prophecy of the autonomous imagination. No less uncompromisingly obscure than hitherto, Ashbery's work suddenly became widely admired and much imitated. I hope, in this brief space, to sort out its qualities and discriminate among them.

From so copious a poet I choose several exemplary texts. His early book *The Tennis Court Oath* (1962) seems designed to outrage any possible readers; a more concerted effort to *épater les bourgeois* would be hard to find. One would imagine his title poem might have some relationship to the French Revolution:

> You were not elected president, yet won the race
> All the way through fog and drizzle
> When you read it was sincere the coasts
> stammered with unintentional villages the
> horse strains fatigued I guess . . .

What is being proclaimed here is indeed the overthrow of an old order, the order of cognitive knowledge, the assumptions of reality which our entire past has bequeathed us. In place of these heavy burdens we are given this poet's arbitrary and solipsistic reveries. The title "Rain" suggests to him "The spoon of your head / Crossed by livid stems . . ."; a poem called "Measles" begins, "There was no longer any need for the world to be divided / Into bunny, when he had chased the hare . . ." The effect is determinedly whimsical; with no authority to support such meanderings save the poet's own self-regarding voice, the reader is likely to resist these particular assertions as being no likelier than any others the poet, or the reader, might choose to substitute for them. The vices of such a sensibility—and they persist into his later books—are whimsy, narcissism, a solipsistic aestheticism; as no less a fantasist than Wallace Stevens had observed of surrealism, its besetting flaw is that it presents "invention without discovery, like a clam playing the accordion."

The sestina "Faust" is a more rewarding performance, which better suggests Ashbery's underlying aesthetic. Everyone else writing a sestina has taken the challenge to be how to create intelligible action and a forward movement in so constricting a rhetorical corset as this, with the six end-words recurring in their draconian pattern of shifting sameness. Ashbery turns this problem inside out. He accepts the wholly arbitrary pattern as an abstract structure against which to counterpoint his associative verbal cadenzas. The pattern is absurd, the poem joins it in the formal assertion of non sequiturs. This poet has stated, "I feel I could express myself best in music. What I like about music is its ability of being convincing, of carrying an argument through successfully to the finish, though the terms of this argument remain unknown quantities. What remains is the structure, the architecture of the argument, scene or story. I would like to do this in poetry." He hopes, also, to reproduce the persuasive power in dreams, which assert meanings "not logically connected" to events, or propose "a hidden relation among disparate objects." Then, typically, Ashbery adds that he isn't really sure he wants to do these things. "I often change my mind about my poetry. I would prefer not to think I had any special aims in mind." Thus would he confound his earnest explicators.

Two poems from a later book, *Rivers and Mountains* (1966), embody the peaks and the pratfalls of this aesthetic. The practitioner of Dada never tires, as his readers may, of the jejune; in a poem of 150 lines we are given the names of 150 rivers, as though to propose that poetry can be made from anything—this time the index of an atlas, next time perhaps a laundry list or errata slips from a dictionary. If such perpetrations tell us anything, it is that the pleasure principle can be indulged only by strangling the intellect. "The Skaters," however, is something else: a thirty-page reverie in which the epistemological questionings of appearances which underlie the serious purpose of Ashbery's poetry are made explicit. Of course the poem isn't *about* skaters; it is while the poet watches the skaters that the images and questionings he lets us overhear pass through his consciousness:

> It is this madness to explain . . .
>
> What is the matter with plain old-fashioned cause-and-effect?
> Leaving one alone with romantic impressions of the trees, the sky?
> Who, actually, is going to be fooled one instant by these phony
>   explanations?
> Think them important? So back we go to the old, imprecise
>   feelings, the
> Common knowledge, the importance of duly suffering and the
>   occasional glimpses
> Of some balmy felicity. The world of Schubert's lieder. I am
>   fascinated
> Though by the urge to get out of it all, by going

Further in and correcting the whole mismanaged mess. But am
  afraid I'll
Be of no help to you. Goodbye.

The entire poem comprises his effort to discover "some balmy felicity"
independent of "old-fashioned cause-and-effect": "I propose a general house-cleaning / Of these true and valueless shapes which pester
us with their raisons d'être." He is tempted delectably "by the urge to
get out of it all," yet paradoxically, since this solipsist has no Platonic
or Plotinian perfection to propose beyond the experience of his senses
(absurd though their evidence appear), the way out of his subjection
to "these true and valueless shapes" is "by going / Further in," by absorbing the appearances about him, as it were, "and correcting the
whole mismanaged mess." Thus follow pages of his corrections.

"At thirty-two I came up to take my examination
  at the university.
The U wax factory, it seemed, wanted a new general manager.
I was the sole applicant for the job, but it was refused me.
So I have preferred to finish my life
In the quietude of this floral retreat."

The tiresome old man is telling us his life story.

Trout are circling under water—

Even in this autonomous universe in which consciousness is suspended
from a purposeless sky by the five threads of its sensuous perceptions,
"Nature is still liable to pull a few fast ones." Hence the poet ad-
monishes himself, "back to dreaming, / Your most important activity."

In *Self-Portrait in a Convex Mirror* Ashbery continues his "study-
ing . . . the art of distilling / Weird fragrances out of nothing," as he
perceives, or avoids perceiving, "the teasing outline / Of where we
would be if we were here." Such poems as "Scheherezade," "Grand
Galop," "Mixed Feelings," and "Lithuanian Dance Band" offer these
teasing outlines and fragrances, with Ashbery's characteristic bright,
visual evanescence, as in daydreams. It is all reverie conceived exclusively on the right side of the brain, attractive in texture; but toward
structure it is seditious, hence few of these poems hold together as unified experiences and their profusion of imagery, however dazzling, is
fatiguing. The prevailing emotions are pleasure and wonder in a
seemingly endless substitution of an arbitrary *pointillisme* for reality.
Occasional shadowings of apprehension reflect the potentially desperate
plight of a consciousness unable to accept what is, required to provide from its own imagination that whole universe of the familiar

which until this morning both art and mankind had been able to comfort themselves by believing in; but these apprehensions are swept away by the kaleidoscope of further associative images. Ashbery is usually observant of syntax, since it is the pattern of completed sentences which permits the poet to make nonstatements in the form of statements, repeatedly tripping the reader who expects that content may correspond to form. His style favors a long, relaxed line, which rarely has the rhetorical and rhythmic structure of Whitman but has more in common with the floating strophes of St.-John Perse, the impish juxtapositions of Desnos, the antilogical *jeux d'esprit* of Reverdy.

The title poem, "Self-Portrait in a Convex Mirror," is Ashbery's masterpiece. Purged of the willed obscurity that makes nearly impenetrable the prose-poems in *Three Poems* (1972) and the aimless noodling that fatigues and exasperates the reader of *Houseboat Days* (1977), Ashbery in "Self-Portrait" finds the image and occasion for the perfecting of his art. This is a fifteen-page reverie on Francesco Parmigianino's portrait of himself, copied upon a semiglobe of wood from such a convex mirror as barbers use. In his contemplation of this Renaissance image, "Glazed, embalmed," yet "lively and intact in a recurring wave / Of arrival," Ashbery brings into play his own sensibility in all of its inventiveness, creating out of his musings upon it and his knowledge as an art critic a meditation in which, like Francesco's portrait, "The whole is stable within / Instability." The tone throughout is grave; the absurdist put-downs of surrealism are foregone as he sees

> only the chaos
> Of your round mirror which organizes everything
> Around the polestar of your eyes which are empty,
> Know nothing, dream but reveal nothing.

From this nothingness the poet intuits that

> The forms retain a strong measure of ideal beauty
> As they forage in secret on our idea of distortion
> Why be unhappy with this arrangement, since
> Dreams prolong us as they are absorbed?
> Something like living occurs, a movement
> Out of the dream into its codification.

The emotional force and feeling of Ashbery's poetry is markedly different from Merwin's. In the surreal world of Merwin's work we are given to apprehend that reality is not what we had thought, it is otherwise; his existential surrealism results from a profound despair at the possibility of holding together the things of this world as they have hitherto been accounted to be held. His dissociations of language from inherited meanings, of affect from observation, of his art from its traditional forms express his sense that culture itself has fallen apart and the individual is now cast back upon the desperate shores of his own consciousness. Merwin's work at its best thus participates in the disjunctive art of René Char, the bleak lyricism of Samuel Beckett, the strange epiphanies of Borges. Ashbery's practice seems closer in motive to that of Breton and Cocteau, in its emphasis on art as play ("Today has no margins . . . / . . . 'Play' is something else: / It exists, in a society specifically / Organized as a demonstration of itself"), on pleasure, and on dreamwork. Ashbery tells us that reality is an illusion and art the illusion of an illusion whose true subject is not what that art makes it seem, but whatever he discovers or proposes it to be. Thus he obliterates both the realism of art and the validity of objective experience; all is dominated by subjective response. This method is both daring and self-indulgent. Its results are either the exfoliations of an aesthetic narcissism or the creation—as in "Self-Portrait"—of a fluidity, a beautifully associational stream of consciousness which creates its own structure as it reveals itself:

> . . . Is there anything
> To be serious about beyond this otherness
> That gets included in the most ordinary
> Forms of daily activity, changing everything
> Slightly and profoundly, and tearing the matter
> Of creation, any creation, not just artistic creation
> Out of our hands, to install it on some monstrous, near
> Peak, too close to ignore, too far
> For one to intervene? This otherness, this
> "Not-being-us" is all there is to look at
> In the mirror, though no one can say
> How it came to be this way. A ship
> Flying unknown colors has entered the harbor.

Thus Ashbery's work is an extreme instance of that dissociation of sensibility from intellect which Eliot diagnosed as the condition of Romantic excess inherited by early twentieth-century poetry. The past is wholly irrelevant to present experience: the Parmigianino portrait is observed not as a Renaissance object, nor even as a historical analogue to the present, but as the occasion for the meditations on the tenuous nature of experience which occur to its present observer. Lacking a history, self-consciousness revels, as it must, in the appearances of things, yet finds life itself to be beyond understanding—since understanding is not a part of the self's equipment. Hence the poignant mingling of delight in its own dreaming with sadness that all is evanescent, nothing will stay. Because Ashbery abnegates the structure of observed reality, he has been hailed as a poet fulfilling Emerson's behest that the creative imagination discover that world within the world which shows us the innate architecture of spirit. The surrealist method of his art, however, proposes no such universal and therefore joyous hieroglyph as Emerson foretold. Compared with Emerson's Romantic affirmations that within Nature herself dwell the immutable symbols which language represents and which themselves are evidence of the Beauty, Truth, and Virtue at the heart of things, how hedged about by doubts, how cut off from all but aesthetic satisfactions are this poet's convex reflections of what the self can see—a disruption and rearrangement of surfaces, a palimpsest that erases with its reorderings the reality of both experience and all predecessors' art. Yet the fact that it is his poems which are the occasion of such efforts at discrimination as this testifies to their vitality and to their contribution to the poetic experience of our generation.

It is not as paradoxical as may appear that Ashbery's work has received such wide acclaim although he remains, as ever, a poet of private vision: just the opposite of what the public might be thought to value in group-oriented, other-dominated America. This art of withdrawal from the "real" world and substitution of a solipsistic immersion in the pleasure principle was hailed just when the end of the Vietnam war, Watergate, and the decade of civil rights activism found Americans—even, perhaps particularly, those sensibilities among us who seek in the work of our poets images of their own concerns—ready and eager to put behind them all the strains of those anguished commitments and to plunge into a *poésie pur* unentangled by any guilts, responsibilities, or relationships to painful realities of which the country had grown weary. Fortunately, at such a moment Ashbery, with his marvelous fecundity and his individuating rhythm appeared to fulfill the need his work made evident.

Ashbery's stance and style are paralleled in the work of James Schuyler (see the title poems in *The Crystal Lithium*, 1972, and *Hymn to Life*, 1974), and extended by such younger poets as David Shapiro and Ron Padgett. Ashbery himself, after all his years attacking academicism, has, like Ginsberg and Creeley, joined the enemy, at least to the extent of giving up his museum work and art journalism to become a teacher of poetry workshops at Brooklyn College.

Unlike his friends O'Hara and Ashbery, Kenneth Koch has been an English professor rather than an art critic, but his poetry began with

561

antiacademic and antirational gestures similar to theirs. His early work flaunts the near-incoherence of surrealism; later, a reasonableness, even a Horatian didacticism lacking in the other productions of the New York School, appears. Koch is one of the few truly comic poets of his generation. In his first poems he was intent upon repudiating "the midterm, the myth, and the missus," putting down with many a flourish the academic pieties, as he saw them to be, of the fifties. *Ko, or A Season on Earth* (1959) is a long poem in ottava rima stanzas, Byronic in tone as well as derivation: an absurdist novel in verse in which are interwoven four completely discrete stories. These take place mostly during one baseball game between the Dodgers and the Cincinnati Reds (Koch comes from Cincinnati) in which the pitcher is a Japanese named Ko with a wicked fast ball. While this is going on, in a rival plot reminiscent of Auden's early plays a dog-infatuated financier perpetrates a near-murder of one Huddel, and is the subject therefore of a search by a secret agent involved with the daughter of an "action poet" who changes himself and the young couple into the images of his poems. This is all lighthearted spoofery, in rhymes as daft as "half-whispered," "A crisp bird," and "want to lisp herd / on herd of fleecy warm and white-lines syllables." Beneath the zaniness is the depiction of a world so disjunctive it has no order other than what the poet's caprice imposes upon these plots of his own choosing. A sequel, *The Duplications,* similarly Byronic, appeared in 1977. In "The Art of Poetry" (from *The Art of Love,* 1975), Koch wrote,

> The epic is particularly appropriate to our own contemporary world
> Because we are so uncertain of everything and also know too much.
> A curious and seemingly contradictory condition, which the epic salves
> By giving us our knowledge and our grasp, with all our lack of control as well.

Perhaps because the derivations of his later work are so much more literary than are O'Hara or Ashbery's, Koch's poetry, while receiving respect among avant-garde readers, has not generated quite the same enthusiasm as theirs. Yet Koch may prove to have a much greater influence than either a decade or two hence. His *Wishes, Lies and Dreams: Teaching Children to Write Poetry* (1970) has become an unofficial teacher-training manual for the Poetry in the Schools Program, funded by the National Endowment for the Arts. Koch's method does away with traditional poetry with its rhymes and meters, and substitutes for these other ways of organizing verbal structures: repetitions ("I wish I was . . . ," "I used to be . . . / But now I am . . ."), concentration upon the suggestibility of colors, music, or other sensory experiences. To conquer initial shyness or embarrassment he has adapted to pedagogy the Dadaist put-down of individual inspiration by having a class compose a poem made of a line contributed by each child. These and other devices succeed in liberating the imaginative energy of his young pupils, whose poems are touched with a charming wonder but, being all derived from a set of initial formulas, have a structural resemblance to one another. In the hands of a poet like Koch this is doubtless a fine way to teach children to find joy in expressing their emotions; it makes available to them their own pleasure in wordplay, in nonsense, in nonlogical expression, all essential to the experience of poetry. But the method can become banal, and has, in the hands of instructors without Koch's talent or inherent taste. Koch has extended this teaching experience in *I Never Told Anybody: Teaching Poetry Writing in a Nursing Home* (1977), with results equally surprising, equally predictable. Writing poetry is increasingly recognized as a therapeutic measure of great worth, making valuable to the individual his own expression of his own experience, whether or not the results contribute to literature.

12
Poetry:
Dissidents from Schools
Daniel Hoffman

> . . . the object in writing poetry is to make all poems
> sound as different as possible from each other . . .
> FROST, "The Figure a Poem Makes"

> . . . all these phenomena are important . . .
> MARIANNE MOORE, "Poetry"

NEITHER confessional nor autobiographical, Beat nor Black Mountain, Deep Image nor surrealist poetry enumerates all of the ways that American poets broke apart the seeming fetters of conventions. Among those not primarily allied with any of the foregoing schools are some of the most ambitious, original, and interesting poets of the latter part of the period. For the most part they are as different from one another as they are from the schools they have not joined, or from the formalism most of them—after patiently mastering it when young —have abandoned. Although none has been as imperious as Lowell, Berryman, or Olson in writing the history of the self as the history of his time, several, among them Louis Simpson, Galway Kinnell, James Dickey, A. R. Ammons, and William Stafford, in writing of themselves have given us works of magnitude.

In such early poems as "American Preludes" and "Mississippi" Louis Simpson seems to be discovering America, as though for the first time. For him, born and raised in Kingston, Jamaica, coming to the United States to attend college, serve in the infantry in the European theater during World War II, then take a doctorate at Columbia and hold professorships on both coasts, discovering America was a literal truth as well as a metaphor. He brought to that discovery a sensibility well schooled in the poetry of wit and the pastoral mode, and a sharp, uncompromising view of the quality of life he would measure against the elegant formality of the verse tradition he had early assimilated. If his wry ballads suggest Auden, his haunted lyrics de la Mare, his

564

erotic poems the Cavaliers and Graves, Simpson nonetheless had strongly established his individual style, absorbing these influences and that of Ransom in lines of great tensile strength and heightened language.

In his first three books (*The Árrivistes*, 1949; *Good News of Death*, 1955; *A Dream of Governors*, 1959) he offered some of the most memorable poetry of World War II, comparable in authority to that of Jarrell and Shapiro. Simpson's theater was Europe, and his is the Jamesian theme of juxtaposition of the culture of the Continent—"A siren sang, and Europe turned away"—with "this America, this wilderness," where "grave by grave we civilize the ground" ("To the Western World"). He caught the malaise of his contemporaries of the postwar decade in a brief poem that gave it, and them, a name: "The Silent Generation."

In *At the End of the Open Road* (1963) the direction of this ambitious and accomplished early work took a new turn. Many of the poems in this book are unrhymed and unmetered; the dominant spirit now is Whitman rather than, as earlier, the aesthetic of Eliot and the other models I have suggested. Simpson does not, like Ginsberg and so many other Whitman enthusiasts, adopt Whitman's bardic pose or incantatory line; instead he takes Whitman's brave hopes for American life a century earlier as the measure against which to set the present, and so reveal what our past has given us. Simpson had moved to California, a new territory he discovers to be indeed the end of the open road; as his book begins he says, "Here I am troubling the dream coast / With my New York face." He bids Whitman "Lie back! . . . / Let the realtors divide the mountains, / For they have already subdivided the valley." In another poem, "Walt Whitman at Bear Mountain," he asks, "Where are you, Walt? / The Open Road goes to the used-car lot." Clearly, the challenge is to face this reality, this life of junk, and in it, or out of it, somehow discover or recover the transcendence that Whitman had announced as our birthright. To do so, Simpson now feels, requires the abandonment of formality in his verse and in its diction; henceforth he would write verse that sounds like speech. Simpson, like Lowell, Berryman, Roethke, Merwin, and so many others of the period, moves from poetry as song to poetry as speech, from formality to an effort spontaneously to trace the movement of feeling. In a brief poem that quickly became an emblem of the times, he defines "American Poetry";

Whatever it is, it must have
A stomach that can digest
Rubber, coal, uranium, moons, poems.

Like the shark, it contains a shoe.
It must swim for miles through the desert
Uttering cries that are almost human.

America itself is the Waste Land, yet her poets, whom Whitman had so confidently invoked, are, as Merwin wrote in the same year, "Walking at night between the two deserts, / Singing."

In his next book such poems as "Sacred Objects" and "Doubting" are under Whitman's aegis, but *Adventures of the Letter I* (1971) points to a more personal poetry than Simpson had written hitherto. The first seven poems are sketches of his mother's ancestors in the province of Volhynia—Russian Jews sketched in Chekhovian narratives that may have been suggested by the recently translated poems of Andrei Vosnesensky (*Antiworlds,* 1966). The use of his family's and his own biography for subjects continues in *Searching for the Ox* (1976) with poems about his Jamaican boyhood and later life in New York and California. Yet Simpson is not a "confessional poet." Along with these are poems on other subjects, almost all with a narrative base; for Simpson, although sharing the flattened style of Bly and James Wright, does not surrender narrative to the sole intensification of the deep image. These recent books have been much admired for their evocations of feeling from plain speech and commonplace situations, but they seem to this reader to show losses as well as gains, compared with Simpson's earlier work collected in *Selected Poems* (1965). Where he had once brought his "New York face" with its formalities of speech and feeling to the littered freedom of "the dream coast," now he had returned to the East a California poet, his muscular lines relaxing into the texture of prose, the fierce concision of his language flattened. Still, in *Adventures* he could yet embrace the largeness of theme of his most effective earlier poems—

I myself am the union of these states,
offering liberty and equality to all.
I share the land equally, I support the arts,

I am developing backward areas.
I look on the negro as myself, I accuse myself
of sociopathic tendencies, I accuse my accusers . . .

Galway Kinnell, like most of his contemporaries in the 1950s, began under the formalist aegis. In his case the proximate model was Yeats, to whose work he was introduced by his Princeton roommate, W. S. Merwin. But Kinnell soon discovered that the Yeatsian virtues of balance, design, intellectual conception of the poem's development and the reiterated regularities of meter, rhyme, and stanzaic form impeded, rather than expressed, his own apocalyptic sense of what his poems must say. From the first Kinnell went out of his way to avoid the New Critical pieties favored by the instructors in the Princeton writing program, R. P. Blackmur and John Berryman. Instead he found early encouragement from another poet then on the faculty, Charles G. Bell, who has written that Kinnell's early work "foreshadowed in volcanic latency all his later long poems." Kinnell soon moved away from the rather conventional work in his privately printed *First Poems 1946-1954* toward a fiercer, more uncompromising style.

In *What a Kingdom It Was* (1960), still vestigially in the Yeatsian mode except for his Whitman-like poem of teeming New York Life, "The Avenue Bearing the Initial of Christ into the New World," and in *Flower Herding on Mount Monadnock* (1964), in loosening rhythms, we find a phenomenology of flame. The fiery imagery neither is purgatorial, as in Eliot, nor presages the phoenix, but expresses the self-consuming intensity of life, the life that, in Yeats's phrase, "man's own resinous heart has fed." Kinnell begins as religious sensibility unassuaged by his inherited faith. In "First Communion" he tells Jesus he finds it "disappointing" that they merely "drink juice and conjure / Your person into inferior bread," and he "would not go again into that place." In the poem "To Christ Our Lord," the title ironically referring to one by Hopkins, the boy whose love had been stirred by "wings beating into the hushed air" has nonetheless shot the Christmas goose, as he was bid, and "Now the grace praised his wicked act . . . he ate as he had killed, with wonder." In "Seven Streams of Nevis" Kinnell blocks out a stanza to a persona embodying each of the seven traditional virtues; in the last of these, since "fire brings out the best / In things," Sir Henry decides that whoever "Has cooked his eyes at the sunrise / Of the beautiful, and thumbed himself blind, is *wise*." How is life to be experienced fully and transcended but by immolation?

Even the Statue of Liberty is on fire, "her hand, burning, / Hair, flesh, blood, bone." Robert Frost is praised because he "dwelt in access to that which other men / Have burnt all their lives to get near." Kinnell's "Tillamook Journal" resembles Gary Snyder's sympathetic and accurate notations of natural things, but praises the "intolerant" Douglas fir which "breeds best in the open / As in the aftermath of fire," and concludes beside the tempestuous shore where "It is only steps to the unburnable sea." In "Middle of the Way," Kinnell writes, "I lie on earth the way / Flames lie in the woodpile." This Thoreauvian meditation ends, "I know I live half alive in the world, / I know half my life belongs to the wild darkness."

In *Body Rags* (1968) he pushes further into that wild darkness which is within him. Parts of this book record Kinnell's imprisonment in Plaquemines Parish, Louisiana, for his active part in the civil rights movement ("The Last River"). In "Vapor Trail Reflected in the Frog Pond," his parody of Whitman's "I Hear America Singing" articulates his revulsion at our destruction of Vietnam. But it is the last poem in the book, "The Bear," that penetrates deepest into the "wild darkness." Here the poet becomes the shaman-hunter of the bear. In its primitive energy and sense of the magical identity of hunter and beast this is the American poem closest to Faulkner's "The Bear" and to the work of the British poet Ted Hughes. Kinnell's poet-shaman lays out a wolf's rib whittled "sharp at both ends" and dipped in blubber, then he tracks the bloody turds of the bear who swallowed it. On the third day, "I . . . hesitate, and pick it up, / and thrust it in my mouth, and gnash it down." When the bear dies of its internal wound,

> I hack
> a ravine in his thigh, and eat and drink,
> and tear him down his whole length
> and open him and climb in
> and close him up after me, against the wind . . .

As he dreams of becoming, of being, the bear "stabbed twice from within," he dreams of his own bear-death. Awaking into the rebirth of his own life, he wonders

> what, anyway,
> was that sticky infusion, that rank flavor of blood, that poetry,
> by which I lived?

Few of his contemporaries have a conception of the source of poetry as primitive, as powerful, as untameable as this. It was Kinnell's gift, or part of it, from the beginning, as such poems in *Kingdom* as "Burning" and "The Wolves" suggest.

In these poems there is a phantasmagoria, an intuitive slash of imagery ripping apart the blocked-out premises of the rational life; but this is not surrealism. Kinnell, who has said that his favorite non-English poet is Neruda, and who published in 1968 his translation of Yves Bonnefoy, is truer in his own work to the other subject of his major work as translator, François Villon. Kinnell's Villon (1965; revised 1977), rendered in avoidance of either meters or rhyme, aims at a style "factual, harsh, and active." Distinguishing his own method, Kinnell replied to an interviewer, "The mystery of the world isn't apprehended only by surrealist poets . . . The use of the term "inner life" means that one is not quite whole, that one has an inner life and an outer life, and they don't quite come together. In the purest poem the inner and outer meet. If a poem remains at a surrealistic level, possibly it means that no integration takes place, that the inner and the outer world do not come together." He noted, too, that "in our country we have a rich tradition of evoking physical things . . . If the things and creatures that live on earth don't possess mystery, then there isn't any." To gain access to their mystery we must "go out to them so that they can enter us." Only in this interpenetration of the self and the not-me can we achieve the "integration" of our "inner and the outer world."

The Book of Nightmares (1971) is Kinnell's most ambitious poem, a series of ten sections, each in seven parts, modeled on Rilke's *Duino Elegies*. Where Rilke, writing before World War I, inscribes a paean to the angels of joy, over half a century later Kinnell writes of first and last things seen in darkness. The Nightmares are framed by poems on the births of his daughter and son. In "Under the Maud Moon" occurs the most physical and mystical description of birth since Berryman's *Mistress Bradstreet*:

> and she skids out on her face into the light
> this peck
> of stunned flesh
> clotted with celestial cheesiness, glowing
> with the astral violet
> of the underlife . . .

And as the umbilical cord is cut "she dies / a moment," then, at her first breath, there are "the slow / beating, featherless arms / already clutching at the emptiness."

The succeeding poems explore the speaker's relationship to living and dead creatures, and to men who are dead; an aborted, hopeless love affair is recorded; he imagines himself a drunk who has died in a hotel room; he writes his Villon-like testament bequeathing his body-parts to his fellow men, who have wrought the violence of the world upon each other. The sufferings in these poems are cut through with moments of tenderness, with humor, with love for his wife, her pregnancy, the birth of their children. These glints are twisted into the dark strands; all is tinged with a sense of visionary and prophetic insight into the center of reality. The vatic air is enforced in the poem by the introduction of such hermetic properties (the Crone, the sign of the Bear, the Sothic year) as Yeats would have drawn from the "harsh geometry" of *A Vision*. But here they are simply brought in, from no extrinsic source, as though the reported moments of private anguish and exaltation participate in some unstated larger context.

In this respect, and in respect also of the rather arbitrary symmetry of the ten sections each divided into seven parts, *The Book of Nightmares* implies a more systematic philosophy than it employs or demonstrates. Passages throughout are tinged with the excitement of a vision that penetrates the husks of experience, but these do not depend upon the structure of the whole. This is a work of considerable power in which the exigencies of feeling carry the reader over occasional obscurities. Kinnell's poem is a great chance-taker, a daring effort, a defiance of death-in-life in which he offers what consolations he can in the menaced world of nightmares into which his children have been born. Ultimately it is not in its grandiloquent astrological gestures, or in its chthonic invocations, but in the resurgent life-force itself and in the human resilience of humor that *The Book of Nightmares* transcends its nightmares. The poem ends as the speaker urges his newborn son,

> On the body,
> on the blued flesh, when it is
> laid out, see if you can find
> the one flea that is laughing.

"The belief in the value of one's personality has all but disappeared from our verse. Yet the inexhaustible vitality and importance of writing are there, and nowhere else." Growing up in the South and attending Vanderbilt after the war, James Dickey began his work with this assumption, so set against the grain of Eliot's and the Fugitive's notions of impersonality. In his discriminating yet aggressive first collection of reviews, *The Suspect in Poetry* (1964), he pushed aside the Beats, Black Mountaineers, and confessional poets, as well as the academics, to make room for his own poetry of Romantic afflatus. He sunk his roots into Roethke's cellar, calling Roethke "the greatest poet this country has yet produced," but although, as in the title poem of his first book, *Into the Stone* (1960), the verse shares Roethke's sense of the transcendence of life, the accent and emphasis are Dickey's own:

> I see by the dark side of light.
> I am he who I should have become.
> A bird that has died overhead
> Sings a song to sustain him forever.

Dickey came to poetry relatively late, in his middle twenties, and has said that he "knew nothing whatever of poetic technique, of metrics, prosody, stanzaic construction," which to "a certain extent" he still subordinates to "the individually imaginative or visionary quality" of poetry. Over the next dozen years he learned these techniques, his first book appearing when he was thirty-seven. It was quickly followed by *Drowning with Others* (1962), *Helmets* (1964), *Buckdancer's Choice* (1965), and *Poems 1957-1967* (1967), in which the foregoing are excerpted and over fifty new pages are added. Dickey's poetry poured over the 1960s in a tidal wave with its assertive energy, its personality, its distinctive subjects. In a later gathering of reviews, *Babel to Byzantium* (1968), Dickey recalled that he had things he wanted to write about, "and certain ways of feeling about them: about war, about love and sex, about being a Southerner, about hunting and flying and canoeing, about the flight of birds and the movements of animals." Soon his poems would indeed express each of these experiences, but his initial impulse was to subsume the possible realism of such subjects in a visionary, ritualistic response to the occasions of life. In this respect his early work shares the impulse toward the search for archetypes and the uses of myth we have seen in the poetry of Snyder and Merwin, and in that of their common precursors from Eliot to Lowell and Olson. In "The Vegetable King," the speaker of the poem, who camps out on his lawn each April, says, "From my house and my silent folk / I step, and lay me in ritual down" as he becomes "part of the acclaimed rebirth / Of the ruined, calm world, in spring." In their secular fashion other poems in *Into the Stone* sacramentalize the poet's encounters with night, time, natural forces, and creatures; his sense of an identity participating in time-transcending rituals is reinforced by the presence of his dead brother. Yet the nature in which he finds himself is threatening; in "Walking on Water," as the speaker, a boy, poles a floating plank across the bay, a shark follows at his heels. It is not the onlookers who are transfigured by the image of a boy walking on water, but "under their place of enthrallment, / A huge, hammerheaded spirit / Shall pass, as if led by the nose into Heaven."

Images of water, creatures, and an insistence upon transfiguration recur in *Drowning with Others*. Dickey's lifeguard, unable to save a drowning child, has a vision of being, like Christ, "The savior of one / Who has already drowned in my care"; but his efficacy is equivocal, since at the end he holds "in my arms a child / Of water, water, water." In "The Heaven of Animals," predators and victims are alike "in full knowledge / Of what is in glory above them . . . They fall, they are torn, / They rise, they walk again." With his bow and arrow, Dickey, the hunter, in "Fog Envelops the Animals" and "The Summons" becomes a part of nature transcending its own processes, and a part of the immutable order of the universe in "For the Nightly Ascent of the Hunter Orion." In the final poem of this book, "In the Mountain Tent," the speaker merges "Into the minds of animals, / I am there in

571

the shining of water / Like dark, like light, out of Heaven," his voice one with "the God-silenced tongue of the beasts. 'I shall rise from the dead,' I am saying."

What Dickey aims for, he has said, is "a fusion of inner and outer states, of dream, fantasy, and illusion where everything partakes of the protagonist's mental processes and creates a single impression." He would "incarnate . . . those moments which in memory are most persistent and obsessive." He wants his readers to be "not at all sure where the danger and repose separate, where joy ends and longing begins," in poems that seem to be "one emotion, impure and overwhelming." In *Helmets* and thereafter such moments occur more and more in experiences in human time, rather than in the timeless cycle of nature; the visionary element is sought in desecrated life, as in "Drinking from a Helmet" and in "Cherrylog Road." In the first of these the speaker is a soldier who, in the midst of combat, finds someone else's helmet and uses it to drink from instead of his own. But then he replaces his own helmet with the one inherited from the dead soldier. He would become the dead man whose helmet he wears. The narrative element, always present in Dickey, predominates as his subjects move toward untransfigured life, with reliance upon novelistic detail whether the experience be from memory, dream, or fantasy. In "Cherrylog Road" the speaker describes a forbidden liaison with a girl; the rendezvous is in the seat of an abandoned car in a junkyard. He leaves on his motorcycle, "fleshed / With power . . . Wild to be wreckage forever."

The two principal poems in *Buckdancer's Choice* deal with questions of guilt. In "The Firebombing," a former air force pilot, "twenty years overweight" in his suburban "half-paid-for-pantry," remembers his napalm raid raining fire on Japanese householders. This is recalled as "The greatest sense of power in one's life / That must be shed in bars, or by whatever / Means." In the end, though, he cannot "say to any / Who lived there, deep in my flames: . . . Come in, my house is yours." He can "imagine . . . Nothing with children of ashes, . . . nothing I haven't lived with / For twenty years, still nothing not as / American as I am, and proud of it." There is no absolution.

Where "The Firebombing" deals with the moral dilemma of the American forced by history to become a mass killer, in "Slave Quarters" Dickey treats the special problem of the South:

> How take on the guilt
>
> Of slavers? How shudder like one who made
> Money from buying a people . . .

His persona imagines himself fathering on a slave woman a son he cannot bring himself to acknowledge; what happens, he asks, when "two hundred years are turned back / On with the headlight of a car? / When you learn that there is no hatred / Like love in the eyes / Of a wholly owned face?"

Even more reminiscent of Faulkner is "The Sheep Child." But where the novelist in *The Hamlet* gave us Ike Snopes's rhapsodic love for a cow, in Dickey's poem the speaker is the pickled body of an infant monster produced when a farm boy coupled with a ewe. This sensational subject is rendered with pathos and sadness ("My hoof and my hand clasped each other, / I ate my one meal / Of milk and died"); the sheep child incarnates the inescapable body of love, "In the minds of farm boys . . . Dreaming of me / They groan   they wait   they suffer / Themselves, they marry, they raise their kind."

These new subjects, so different in feeling from the rhapsodic incantations of natural and supernatural forces in the early poems, Dickey found required a different rhythm, a different line. He devised what he calls a "split line," several short lines or bursts of words on one line, with blank space between them instead of punctuation. The resulting movement is at once sweeping and stuttering, a reflexive movement that carries along the narrative flow yet records the often halting, baffled emotional progress of the persona trying to define an experience while it happens. In "The Shark's Parlor," the feral fish does not—as in "Walking on Water"—lead the way to Heaven, but represents instead a tremendous but self-sufficient life-force. The poem is almost a tall-tale account of how a shark, caught from a seaside cottage, and by great effort hauled into the parlor, wrecked the house. "The Fiend" is the breathless re-creation of a voyeur. The split line style at its most extensive, however, appears in "Falling." This narrative of an airline stewardess who fell from a plane over Kansas uses the long staccato lines to invest the poor girl's fearful, fatal fall with her transformation into a momentary goddess of love and fertility

                            while farmers sleepwalk without
Their women from houses   a walk like falling toward the
    far waters
Of life   in moonlight   toward the dreamed eternal
    meaning of their farms
Toward the flowering of the harvest in their hands

The very title of *The Eye-Beaters, Blood, Victory, Madness, Buckhead and Mercy* (1970) makes importunate claims on the reader. These poems are almost all of extreme situations, and in most the rhythm is a lurching alternation between irregular short and long lines, with neither the incantatory clarity of Dickey's early work nor the narrative clarity of poems like "Falling." The vestigial influence of Roethke has all but disappeared; some of the more successful poems, like "Looking for the Buckhead Boys," in their sievings of memory suggest the work of Robert Penn Warren, but without Warren's lyric impulse. Since this book Dickey has published two other long works, his novel *Deliverance* (1970) and a poem, *The Zodiac* (1976), which suggest that the strands hitherto knotted together in his best poems have come apart. *Deliverance* is a fable of four men's initiation into the wilderness—a canoe trip down a torrential river in Georgia—in which are dramatized such themes from Dickey's poems as testing the self in nature, hunting, guitar playing, in short the vigorous outdoor life at once manly and menaced by brute force and evil impulse. The most sensitive of the four is killed in the white water, and a stranger is shot—deaths in which the survivors are implicated. The novel, made into a successful film (Dickey played a bit role as a redneck sheriff), proposes no spiritual transcendence of its dangers; the deliverance promised by the title is survival.

The Zodiac, however, is a desperate search for such transcendence, now divorced from specific actions. Its persona, a Dutch seaman, reputedly a poet, is Hendrik Marsman—his given name suggesting the explorer Hudson, his surname an explorer from outer space—whose journal Dickey claims to have translated so freely that the resulting poem is his own. Marsman is at once an alcoholic and infatuated with the design of the heavens (as is Dickey—see "Reincarnation (II)" in *Poems 1957-1967*). Marsman's search is for nothing less than the meaning of the universe, sought not in human interactions but in the revelation of divine purpose in the very heavens. The work is only vaguely structured; its division into twelve unequal sections has little evident relation to the qualities of the zodiacal signs. Along with much incoherent flailing about, however, there are passages that express this poet's need for affirmation:

> Oh my own soul, put me in a solar boat.
>   Come into one of these hands
>   Bringing quietness and the rare belief
> That I can steer this strange craft to the morning
> Land that sleeps   in the universe on all horizons

He prays for the instrument

>   Which at a touch reveals the form
> Of the time-loaded European music

That poetry has never really found,
Undecipherable as God's bad, Heavenly sketches

. . . .

So long as the hand can hold its island
    Of blazing paper, and bleed for its images:
    Make what it can of what is:

      So long as the spirit hurls on space
    The star-beasts of intellect and madness.

A. R. Ammons is above all else a poet of particulars, resisting abstraction, unification, categorizing, as he makes explicitly plain in the title poem of his third book, *Corsons Inlet* (1965):

the walk liberating, I was released from forms,
from the perpendiculars,
    straight lines, blocks, boxes, binds
of thought
into the hues, shadings, rises, flowing bends and blends
      of sight:

      I allow myself eddies of meaning:
yield to a direction of significance
running
like a stream through the geography of my work

The gesture as well as the sentiment is typical of Ammons, his visionary moment occurring during a walk along a tidal inlet where what impinges upon his consciousness—and functions as a paradigm of all such impingements—are his close observations of the "disorderly order of bayberry; between the rows / of dunes, / irregular swamps of reeds." Ammons hardly ever meets anyone else on his walks or in his musings. In this isolation of the perceiving self he demonstrates a vein of the American sensibility, a Thoreauvian attention to the minute particularities of nature where a poet of less provincial interests might, like Yeats, attend instead "the minute particulars of mankind." But it is chiefly Whitman who has set his mark upon Ammons's mind, as in "Still," where the poet says, "each day I'll wake up / and find the lowly nearby . . . everything is / magnificent with existence." This democratic sensibility exults in "moss, beggar, weed, tick, pine, self," as had Whitman before him in "mossy scabs of the worn fence, heaped stones, elder, mullein, and pokeweed."

In another respect Ammons resembles Whitman too—in his effort to incorporate into his poetry the natural science of his time. Ammons's book-length poem, *Sphere: The Form of a Motion* (1974), in effect his "Song of Myself," draws astronomy, botanical observation,

575

and biology into its wide net of association as the poet meditates on the flux of life and its still center, tracing, in a single sentence 1,860 lines long (Ammons uses colons throughout as connectives) the wayward coursing of his mental and emotional life, inquisitively thrusting into the underleaves of his observations, pitting things and notions against their antinomies, embodying in his work the three-dimensional circularity promised by his title. In this poem the whole is contained, very loosely, within a form, 155 stanzas each of four tercets, the rhythm a seven-stress line. This patterning differs from his earlier book-length meander, *Tape for the Turn of the Year* (1965), typed on a roll of adding-machine tape; hence this month's meditations are in short, irregular lines. In *Sphere,* Ammons's other chief dependence is specifically invoked: where Stevens had written "The Man on the Dump," Ammons's protagonist says, "I want to be the shambles, / the dump, the hills of gook the bulldozer shoves . . . / I want to be named the area where charlatan rationality comes / to warp." Stevens is at once invoked and rejected as Ammons borrows another of his own striking images for a proposal with which the earlier poet would scarcely agree: "if the abstract poem goes out and never / comes back, weaves the highest plume of mind beyond us, it / tells us by its dry distraction, distraction."

Juggling the contradictions of the abstraction and the rationality he would dismiss, Ammons invokes both his readers and his principal mentor:

> they ask why I'm so big on the
>
> one:many problem, they never saw one: my readers, what do they expect from a man born and raised in a country whose motto is *E pluribus unum:* I'm just, like Whitman, trying to keep things
>
> half straight about my country: . . .
>
> I figure I'm the exact
> poet of the concrete *par excellence,* as Whitman might say:

But in fact it is the tension between abstractions, "the one:many problem," that leads Ammons to his reliance upon particulars in his repeated demonstrations that reality is too multitudinous to be contained within any form or plan the mind proposes. His loose forms have the advantage of a capaciousness, an appetite for ingesting and expressing both experiences and thoughts, observations and theories. While expressing his distrust of theories this poet is among our most assiduous theorists of poetry, though the poetry to which his theories pertain is primarily his own.

Ammons excels in three sorts of poems, each of his own devising. Two of these I have mentioned, the meditative ramble and the long investigation of the qualities of life and thought. The third is the brief fable, in which a rather Orphic speaker holds colloquies with mountains, rivers, winds. Ammons's method leads to a voluminousness (*Collected Poems 1951-1971*, published in 1972, is four hundred pages long) that, like Wordsworth's, diffuses his moments of intensity in floods of words, sometimes in aerated gab; for a poet so distrustful of "forms . . . binds of thought" is likelier to let his pen run on in hopes that it will lead him somewhere than he is to blot out half a line. At his best he is refreshing; his characteristic mode is the free-formed expression of a modern skepticism imbedded in a nineteenth-century, Romantic capacity to find and acknowledge "magnificence."

The poetry of William Stafford is equally innocent of foreign entanglements. Stafford did not publish his first book (*West of Your City*, 1960) until he was forty-six and had developed his characteristic style; in the five successive collections gathered in *Stories That Could Be True* (1977), his poems accumulate, reiterating their characteristic virtues, but one cannot say that they show much change or development. Stafford is a poet of the sharply felt moment, and accordingly his poems are brief, their occasions numerous. He does not provide the structuring of experience an extended work would require; it is as though by producing innumerable blades of grass or leaves, he can infer the existence which he does not state of the landscape or the tree from which they grow. Stafford's diction is consistently simple, his syntax conversational, as though to intrude as little as possible of willed artifice into the experiences his poems embody.

He writes with a westerner's sense of open spaces—"Pioneers, for whom history was talking through dead grass, / and the main things that happened were miles and the time of day." His perspicuous diction makes the imaginative leap from the concrete to the spiritual seem immanent and accessible, as when

> We think—drinking cold water
> water looking at the sky—
> *sky is home, universe is one place.*

Seeking such moments of expansiveness and truth, Stafford does not confuse or substitute aesthetic delight for a higher purpose. Along with the modernity of his offhand style, his casual symbolism, he is committed—as were such nineteenth-century poets as Whittier and Emerson—to moral responsibility, as in "Glimpse between Buildings," where he writes of that image of the imagination itself,

Now that the moon is out of a job
it has an easy climb these nights,
finds an empty farm where a family could live,
slides wide over the forest . . .

Moon, you old unsinkable submarine,
leaf admirer, be partly mine,
guide me tonight along city streets.
Help me do right.

Yet Stafford typically shuns city streets, traveling, as the title poem
of his first book in 1960 has it, "west of your city, outside your lives /
in the ultimate wind." In "By the Snake River," he must seek himself
to find himself apart from others,

> because what I tried to carry in my hands
> was all spilled from jostling when I went
> among the people to be one of them.

Where the river "comes down with a wilderness of power," he can
find what he seeks "among rocks, while the deep sturgeon move / in
this water I lift pouring through my hands." The poet thus finds
himself through immersion into the "wilderness of power" in nature
—a dominant theme in earlier American literature, spoken in our
poetry only by such poets versed in country things as Frost, Snyder,
Kinnell, Dickey, Ammons, and Stafford. In the latter's work the image
of the river, wild, changeable yet ever constant, recurs nearly twenty
years later, still an emblem of the poet's self-discovery, in "Ask Me":

> Some time when the river is ice ask me
> mistakes I have made. Ask me whether
> what I have done is my life . . .
>
> You and I can turn and look
> at the silent river and wait. We know
> the current is there, hidden; and there
> are comings and goings from miles away
> that hold the stillness exactly before us.
> What the river says, that is what I say.

If the wilderness—and the Indians—in Stafford's poems reflect Oregon, where he has lived since 1948, his sense of space, the plains, the
farm and the small town as centers of human relationships comes out
of his Kansas boyhood. Stafford's midwestern sensibility speaks to
our generation as had Sandburg's to his, half a century before. Though
they lack any program of ideas, Stafford's modest and occasionally

domestic poems do provide coherence of feelings and of images in their responses to experience, as each of the blades in a wheatfield bends in a patterned design when blown by the same strong winds.

> They speak in tongues, no doubt;
> High glossolalia, runic gibberish . . .
>   Some come in schools, like fish.
> These make their litany of dark complaints;
>   Those laugh and rejoice
> At liberation from the bonds of gender,
>   Race, morals and mind,
> As well as meter, rhyme and the human voice . . .

Thus Anthony Hecht, writing as conservator of tradition, rejects *all* of the foregoing experimentalists. In doing so he is not entirely alone. Among those who write determinedly as though the breakup of form and meter had not occurred, or had happened in some distant place like Bulgaria, are several poets whose work, though formal, is distinctive and diverse. Clarity and strength striate the poems of Charles Edward Eaton. The poems of Robert Fitzgerald and Richmond Lattimore are intensely poised between lyricism of feeling and classical restraint. David Slavitt's work is ironic and forceful. Peter Davison's elegiac and bucolic poems are both formal and contemporary in feeling (*Walking the Boundaries: Poems 1957-1974*). Josephine Jacobsen (*The Shade-Seller*, 1974) and Barbara Howes (*The Blue Garden*, 1972) ring changes upon form and cadence.

The quietly independent poems of Theodore Weiss, learned and quirky, reach back past modernism to the example of Browning, especially in such impressive verse monologues as "Caliban Remembers" (*The Last Day and the First*, 1968). The other abiding influence on Weiss is Wallace Stevens, whose sense of "the gaiety of language" he emulates in the wordplay of many of his lyrics. Weiss's conviction of the possibilities and the intractability of his medium are suggested in "The Cure" (*Fireweeds*, 1976): "And what can you appeal to / if you have nothing but this language / to handle your feelings . . ." he asks, concluding,

> . . . it is, like rain,
> a vernacular that nothing can translate
> because it refuses to relate, its own
> nature all that it relates.

David Wagoner has a less ambiguous view of the possibilities of language:

Each word a rock
The size of a fist—
I throw them one by one
At the dark window.

So reads his "Note from Body to Soul" (*Collected Poems 1956-1976*). If there is no equivocation as to the ability of words to break the dark window, in reading Wagoner's other poems we come to feel more fully what he sees the function of language to be: letting in the light. Wagoner is a poet of clarity; aware of the darkness behind the window, he is confident of its penetrability, hence his poems are built on normal syntax, formal regularities (whether stanzaic or stychic), and the tone of a man of good sense, neither vatic nor self-obsessed. Roethke's influence—they were colleagues at the University of Washington during Roethke's last decade, and Wagoner has edited the elder poet's notebooks, *Straw for the Fire* (1972)—appeared in Wagoner's early poems, since dropped from his collected work. The most lasting effect of Roethke upon him, as X. J. Kennedy has suggested (in *Parnassus,* 1977), was to bring him west from Ohio to Seattle, for Wagoner has become a poet of the western landscape, the wilderness, reflecting the realistic, open-minded sense of possibilities held by people in a rugged land not yet ruined by industrialism.

A prolific novelist, Wagoner has no need to abjure narrative in his poems, and he has the novelist's capacity for imagining what it is like to be other persons. Even when being autobiographical, Wagoner, striving to break the dark window, does not feel compelled toward confessional gestures. The first page of *Collected Poems* establishes a tone that pervades the rest of the book: Wagoner's selection from his own work presents us with constancy rather than radical change. That tone, in "To My Friend Whose Parachute Did Not Open," is of a voice for whom experience is both mysterious and comprehensible, its understanding of tragedy making tragedy bearable. Wagoner writes in a middle style, not as likely as Stafford to break into a burst of lyrical revelation, but perhaps more patiently exploring the crannies of his experiences. In several poems that treat of survival in the wilderness—"Staying Alive," "Slow Country," "An Offering for Dungeness Bay"—the wilderness is a metaphor for our life, in which survival is possible, as in the first-named poem, to the man without illusions, or, as in the others, a state of grace may be achieved through love, or through the acknowledgment of the life-force in all living things. In "The Shooting of John Dillinger outside the Biograph Theatre" and "The March of Coxey's Army" Wagoner gives ironic celebration to events in the popular consciousness. His retelling of myth, fairy story, and folktale in "The Labors of Thor," "Beauty and the Beast," and "The Death of Paul Bunyan" make a winning fusion of the comic with the fantastic—qualities prefiguring his masterful treatment of American Indian legends, discussed earlier. A recurring trope in Wagoner's work is the figure of the Magician (this poet is himself an amateur sleight-of-hand performer), and in many other poems besides "The Inexhaustible Hat" and "The Extraordinary Production of Eggs from the Mouth" the elements of surprise, humor, drama, and the transformation of reality are accomplished with zest. Wagoner's abiding style is conversational, his rhythm a loose accentual-syllabic beat, his style the flesh and bone of his thought.

Anthony Hecht is the strictest metrist of them all. Superficially he would seem to have continued unchanged the Eliot-Ransom line in which he began, for even in his latest book he continues his characteristic use of intricate metrical organization and crossed rhymes that make his stanzas look like seventeenth-century poems. Although he has remained true for the most part to the New Criticism's conception of what poems should be, Anthony Hecht is not, and never was, merely a conventional versifier. He combines a metaphysical style with a keen sense of the play of language and an attitude to experience which sets him apart from most of his contemporaries. The ironies in his superbly crafted poems are not merely verbal. For Hecht is a modern man who actually believes in God and whose view of American life is not, like those of the Whitman-inspired, optimistic. In the midst of inescapable discrepancies between what we expect of life and what experience gives us, Hecht is open to sensuous pleasures; the very texture of his versing is a play of sound, a search for aural consonances that doubly delight the mind and the ear. But at the core of his poetry there is a Hebraic stoicism in the presence of immitigable fate. This quality is suggested by the title of his second book, *The Hard Hours* (1967).

From the beginning Hecht's work has been implicated in history: he is not one to confront experience *ab ovo*. In his earliest book (*A Summoning of Stones*, 1954) he declared his commitment to the life of society, ergo taking history as his province, rather than being an artist who dwells in the isolation of the self. This is implied in "Alceste in the Wilderness": Hecht's poem places Molière's misanthrope in the solitude he had claimed, at the end of the play, was preferable to society's corruption, but that solitude proves at once savage and ravaged by death and desiccation. "Versailles shall see the tempered exile home, / Peruked and stately for the final act." Yet in another referential poem Hecht declares his own freedom from a slavish conformity, poetic as well as social: "Samuel Sewall, in a world of wigs, / Flouted opinion in his personal hair"—the metrical variation of that last half-line flouting regular iambics.

In another respect *A Summoning of Stones* resembles the early work of Hecht's friend Louis Simpson; as did Simpson in *The Arrivistes* and *A Dream of Governors,* Hecht writes of an American's discovery of Europe, for instance, in "The Gardens of the Villa d'Este," which begins, "This is Italian." But Hecht's poem is an exploration of the aesthetic bequest of Europe, not of the terror or pity history had exacted in such places during the recent war; that darker theme will emerge in *The Hard Hours.* Here, in a stanza characteristically baroque in rhythmic and metrical pattern, Hecht uses the occasion of beholding a formal garden to define, analogically, the intentions of his own formal art:

> For thus it was designed:
> Controlled disorder at the heart
> Of everything, the paradox, the old
> Oxymoronic itch to set the formal strictures
> Within a natural context, where the tension lectures
> Us on our mortal state, and by controlled
> Disorder, labors to keep art
> From being too refined.

In *The Hard Hours,* much control of much disorder. The poems embody anarchic emotions yet allow their expression with a shaping consciousness, as of grief in "The Vow," or madness in "Bird-Watchers of America" and "Third Avenue in Sunlight." At times Hecht's dramatic lyrics armored in biblical allusions remind one of the diction and vehemence of Lowell ("These eyes, which many have praised as gay, / Are the stale jellies of lust in which Adam sinned"). But in poems that dramatize the hard hours of his generation's history, Hecht speaks with a tragic irony that is his own unmistakable voice. "More Light! More Light!" plays out against the implications of Goethe's dying cry two episodes from history: the burning at the stake of an accused heretic in the Middle Ages, and this:

> We move now to outside a German wood.
> Three men are there commanded to dig a hole
> In which the two Jews are ordered to lie down
> And be buried alive by the third, who is a Pole.
>
> Not light from the shrine at Weimar beyond the hill
> Nor light from heaven appeared. But he did refuse.
> A Lüger settled back deeply in its glove.
> He was ordered to change places with the Jews.

582

In the absence of the light of either Goethe's humanism or the Word, the Pole's refusal may suggest that he, like their Nazi captor, is too scornful of Jews to kill them himself. As for them, "Much casual death had drained their souls away," and they obey the order to bury the Pole. But then the Nazi makes them dig him out and get back in. The gravity of Hecht's quatrains mold this fable of "casual death" as unassuageable, without transcendence.

World War II made young Americans unwitting participants in the inexorable action, whether chaos or design, of history. Some, like Jarrell and Simpson, recorded their pity and fear at imminent death; some, like Dickey, brooded years later on the destruction and killing that had been their duty. For the American who is a Jew, the war had a meaning even more fraught with terror, pity, and guilt. It was supposed that Germany, next to the United States, had the most assimilated Jewish community in the world, yet those Jews were the victims of genocide. So horrifying are the facts of the Nazis' extermination policy, managed as a murder-industry with death camps organized like factories, that one might think the bare recital would make trivial any imaginative elaboration. The effect of the Nazi era on the consciousness of Jewish American poets was to cast a threatening shadow over the presumed security of life itself. Hecht, thinking of his own children, says that he "could not, at one time, / Have saved them from the gas," as though his forebears had never left Germany for America. Just as soldiers spared in combat feel irrationally guilty when they think of their luckless buddies, many American Jews felt guilt at having been spared the fate of their brethren in Belsen. For instance, Irving Feldman, in the title poem of *The Pripet Marshes* (1965) imagined his Jewish friends, Americans all, whom he would "seize as they are and transport . . . in my mind to the *shtetlach* and ghettos," where "in a moment the Germans will come." All Jews are potential victims; in "The Six Million" Feldman writes a *kaddish* for those who were killed. Stephen Berg, too, cannot escape the menace, the suffering, the guilt of this unforgivable tragedy. In *The Daughters* he writes a poem based on the report "that the French poet, Robert Desnos, broke out of a line of naked prisoners on their way to the gas chambers at Buchenwald and went from prisoner to prisoner reading palms, predicting good fortune and happiness." The victim of history's insanity offers in this surrealistic gesture the transcendent consolation of the release from suffering in death, for "The lovely season is near."

In "Rites and Ceremonies" Hecht, who as a soldier twenty years earlier had seen the death camps, the survivors, and the dead, writes a ten-page meditation not only on the ovens of Buchenwald, where they "are perished as though they had never been," but on the historical roots of persecution. The present agony, evoked in the first section ("The Room"), is set against earlier examples: in part two ("The Fire Sermon"), the burning alive of Jews in the Middle Ages who, during the plague, confessed after torture to poisoning the wells; and in part three ("The Dream"), a redaction of Du Bellay's account of a pre-Lenten Festival of Misrule in which Jews were scourged as scapegoats. These sufferings, contemporary and historical, lead, in the final section, "Words for the Day of Atonement," to a moving, austere prayer for forgiveness of "the whole Congregation of the Children of Israel, and the stranger dwelling in their midst. For all the people have inadvertently sinned." This long poem, by its structure as well as its language, makes possible the transcendence of its painful subject. In its length the design, in its deployment of varied forms and rhythms suggesting *Four Quartets,* as well as in the title of the second part and in liturgical phrases taken from "Ash Wednesday," Hecht's "Rites and Ceremonies" repeatedly evokes Eliot. This homage to the preeminent religious poet of our time is intentionally double-edged. Hecht is the most accomplished poet younger than Wilbur to perpetuate in his own practice the aesthetic Eliot's influence had dominated. But like Karl Shapiro he doubtless felt dismay that this principal maker of modernism, despite his public professions of Christian piety, had never made any attempt to suppress his early poems with their crude caricatures of "Bleistein with a Cigar" and "Rachel *née* Rabinowitz," nor had he ever repented of his exclusion of Jews in *The Idea of a Christian Society* (1940) and *Notes Toward the Definition of Culture* (1949), as though Buchenwald had no relevance to the conditions of his own salvation. Unlike Shapiro, who as we have seen rejected Eliot's aesthetic, Hecht remains true to the innate formalism of his own poetic character, writing a major poem which rivals the work of the predecessor to which it avowedly refers. Its further effect is by inference to implicate in the enormity of genocide—the great sin of history—those social attitudes expressed and made to appear respectable by Eliot, who spoke them from pulpit, from university chair, from the columns of eminent journals: attitudes in which the deeper, more violent prejudices of the masses are always grounded; hence they are as blameable as the cruder rantings of Pound, whose vulgar anti-Semitism was a strand of his insanity. "For all the people have inadvertently sinned."

In other poems in *The Hard Hours* Hecht writes of personal themes such as were the burdens of confessional poems by many contempo-

raries. But Hecht characteristically makes of private tensions statements of the human condition rather than revelations of his own
anxieties. "Three Prompters from the Wings" is at once reminiscent
of Auden's tone and trimeter movement, and, in its structure, of Ransom's "Spiel of the Three Mountebanks," as the three Fates tell by
turns the tale of Oedipus, seen by the Future, the Present, and the
Past. "Behold the Lilies of the Field" is indeed a confessional poem—
the speaker is on a couch, telling his story to his therapist; but in this
dramatic monologue the confessor is a character in the poem, by no
means necessarily the poet himself. The patient's mother's phone
calls merge into a dream of the humiliation of a conquered king who
is stripped, exhibited naked and in chains, and finally flayed alive and
stuffed by his enemies. The father-figure subjected to these punitive
fantasies proves to be the emperor Valerian, the dream transposed from
the tenth chapter of Gibbon's *Decline and Fall*. For Hecht, private
fantasies recapitulate history, and history is personal suffering writ
large.

Millions of Strange Shadows (1977), only the third book by this
scrupulous poet, is committed to the formalism of his earlier work, with
its elegant and slightly elevated diction and sinuous syntax in rhymed
stanzas or blank verse. But some new poems are more directly personal than hitherto, in particular "Apprehensions." This long autobiographical monologue recounts boyhood memories of a brother's
illness, his father's ruined investments in the Crash and subsequent
attempted suicide (as the Depression caused depression), and the presence throughout of Fräulein, the "teutonic governess" whose "special
relish for inflicted pain," savored in tabloid accounts of horrible murders and dismemberings, will a few years later be inflicted by her race
upon the world. In the midst of such apprehensions the speaker has
an epiphanic moment when, before a storm, the visible world of city
streets and apartment house walls becomes numinous (as in the opening poem of *The Hard Hours*, "The Hill"). But this transcendence
is only momentary, "to be put away / With childish things" in a
world where "sex was somehow wedded to disaster, / Pleasure and
pain were necessary twins." He meets his Fräulein "By secret assigna-
tions in my dreams . . . As the ghettos of Europe emptied." She merges
into the Nazi woman *kommandant* who had parchment lampshades
made from the skins of her victims in Belsen.

How different in tone is the self-ironical wryness of "The Ghost in
the Martini," in which the middle-aged poet, asked by a voluptuous
admirer of twenty-three what he was like at her age, hears the inner
voice of the awkward, genuine self he has outgrown. This poem, so-

phisticated and lubricious at the same time that it uncovers—and covers—inner wounds, gives unstintingly of those pleasures of cadence, plays of words and thought, that are Hecht's thumbprints. In this and in many other poems (among them "Sestina d'Inverno," "A Birthday Poem," "Coming Home," and "The Feast of Stephen"), some comedic, some ironical, some deeper in tone, Hecht's style, "by controlled disorder," gives artistic coherence to a world in which, as he tells his son Adam, "there will be many hard hours, / As an old poem says . . . I cannot ease them for you, / They are our common lot."

In a time when intelligence is so widely distrusted among poets and readers, John Hollander has never failed to engage his polymathic mind in the enterprise of his poetry. This makes for both the difficulties and the delights of reading his poems, which cunningly carry an overload of learning whatever their intrinsic forms. Yet it is bootless to call a poet of such originality academic. Hollander's work results from the fusion of a curious, wide-ranging intelligence—equally a familiar of traditions in literature, philosophy, and myth, and of speculative psychology and science—with the skills of a virtuoso versemaker. In his book-length poem, *Reflections on Espionage* (1976), sportively embodying his *ars poetica,* the secret agent Cupcake (who "worked for an altogether inconvenient little republic") writes, "Steampump is gone . . . He taught me, as you surely / Know, all that I know." These ruminations properly commence by acknowledging the tutelage of "Steampump"—Auden, recently dead—who, as all his readers have recognized, Hollander from the first resembled in the qualities I have enumerated, as well as in his sense of poetry as a kind of serious play replicating life itself. In *Reflections on Espionage* this play is presented as the encoding of experience into the secret messages transcribed by the agent-poet, whose "cover" is his employment in a museum (the university). In this work, all too truly, Cupcake communicates only with his fellow agents.

> One comes, I suppose, to love the ciphers as
> One loves the messages lurking inside them . . .
> That code itself, the purest form of language,
> Thrills the enciphering mind; putting the plain
> Sense into travelling garb is a kind of
> Singing. And until They change the codebook my
> Eleven seems a kind of measure fit for
> Reaches of feeling as wide as any mode's
> (Even hendecasyllabics, the darling
> Of blatant, or of tenderer Catullus).

Unlike Henri Coulette's *The War of the Secret Agents* (1966), another Audenesque fantastication that limned the moral squalor of double agents in World War II in a cleverer plot than any in the novels of John Le Carré, Hollander's book is about the inescapably subversive nature, not of military intelligence, but of poetry ("the work") in relation to the everyday world ("We all find / It hard to live with the work, work with the life"). *Reflections* uses the apparatus of an espionage network—a code, cover identities—but does not emulate popular spy fiction in that it lacks an adventurous plot. (It is, however, a *roman à clef* of literary life: many of the agents are identifiable.) The allusion in the passage above to "my Eleven" names the "measure" that Cupcake uses to "encode" experience: a line of eleven syllables which is, he says, "fit for / Reaches of feeling as wide as any mode's."

From even this brief excerpt it may be inferred that the line divisions of syllabic verse differ markedly in feeling from those of either accentual syllabics or phrasal free verse. Hollander wrote in accentual syllabics with characteristic virtuosity until, in *Tales Told of the Father* (1975) he shifted to the syllabic line, thereby substituting for the verbal music he had mastered a more prose-textured and speculative movement, though capable of delicate modulation of tone. As will be seen, this shift in the fingering of the language is appropriate to the content of Hollander's recent work.

Auden's preface to Hollander's first book, *A Crackling of Thorns*, in the Yale Series (1958), praised the younger poet's expertise in writing poems as songs or "words for music perhaps." Hollander's early lyricism did not so much derive from the Eliotic mixture of knotty metaphysical style with Laforgueian irony then so prevalent as it harkened back to the Renaissance tradition of song from Campion to Marvell, and particularly to the work of that neglected poet, Ben Jonson. Hollander would explore this tradition critically in *The Untuning of the Sky: Ideas of Music in English Poetry, 1500-1700* (1961). In his preface in the same year to an edition of Jonson's poems, Hollander observes that "the separation of 'sense' from expressive content is the arch-heresy of orthodox reading today. Yet Jonson insists on in theory and demonstrates . . . in practice, a view of the nature of poetry depending on the notion of a 'core' of prose sense or even moral purpose, surrounded by an exterior added by art, rather than secreted by the poem's soul within." Insofar as this distinction applies to Hollander's own work as well, it sets it off from the practice of most of his contemporaries. Where, for instance, Kinnell's *Book of Nightmares* or Ammons's *Sphere* or Merrill's "Book of Ephraim" are poems embodying the process of discovering their own meanings, Hollander's comparable poems, "Visions from the Ramble" and "Spectral Emanations" (from the books of the same titles, 1965, 1978) seem to express and elaborate meanings already known to the poet. But Hollander writes in *Reflections,* in a coded message to Image (Merrill) that the root of the word *spy* indicates "a seeker, not a seer"; and in *The Head of the Bed* (1974) he sieves his unconscious phantasmagoria to work his way through nightmare images toward an understanding arrived at only by the end of the poem. Hollander's work seems to me divided between the creation of intricate and delightful cryptograms that encode "a 'core' of prose sense or even moral purpose" and equally intricate, perplexing, and rewarding works whose meanings are "secreted by the poem's soul within." That is, he is both a Neoclassicist and a Romantic Symbolist poet, as he is both a poet of intellection and a poet of "Reaches of feeling as wide as any mode's." Like his early master Auden he uses many modes, many voices, many forms; the challenge, which his late work most successfully meets, is the interiorization of content. Only covertly is Hollander autobiographical: the self in his work is not usually a suffering witness, but is intrinsic with the activity of mind.

Although his work from *A Crackling* through *Visions from the Ramble* (1965) is committed to rehearsals of the literary traditions we inherit, Hollander felt the condition of his modernity in a skepticism that curdles the milk of spiritual affirmation. Thus in his early poem "The Great Bear," children search the night sky in vain for the mythic image absent from experience. His drafts upon tradition include "Upon Apthorp House," a modern instance of Jonson's "Pennshurst," and an elegy ("Damoetas"), yet the sensibility of this poet, pastoral upon occasion, is deeply attuned to his native New York City in such works as the title poems of *Movie-Going* (1962) and *Visions from the Ramble.* He can summon up movies and movie-houses (in a catalogue like Homer's of the ships) to "invoke the colors of our inner life" and to "keep / Faith, perhaps, with the City." In "From the Ramble" (the Ramble is an imitation wilderness within Central Park), the speaker has a childhood vision of three Graces in the pools there, reminiscent, in supple hexameters, of Spenser's Garden of Delight; revisiting this spot in the heart of the city, he finds the pools dried, moribund, where "Glimpses out at the boundaries of all this ruined garden / Reveal a city to be achieved, the towers unreal," and he sees himself as "a tall fat man now I guess . . . thirty-five," whom he, still a child, feels bless him. The search for this transcending moment enriched by the interaction of the poet's dual identities as man and boy comprises the finest of Hollander's early poems.

Hollander's virtuosity has encouraged the impression that his work is disunified, but when it is considered as an *oeuvre* the tension between his opposing selves, each the master of its mode, reveals the integrated wholeness of his accomplishment. For instance, the wit of the lubricious daydreams invoking the sexual plenitude of Copenhagen and the loss of the same in Smyrna (*Town & Country Matters,* 1972) intentionally suggests the Earl of Rochester and the "blatant, or . . . tenderer Catullus," several of whose most licentious poems are translated. These abandoned romps are the obverse of the grave, haunting lyric nightmare, in *The Head of the Bed* (1974), in which the speaker is at first possessed by "A filthy myth of Lilith," his false muse who embodies a narcissistic love. But by the end of the poem, with growing self-knowledge, as "He opens all the seals of touch," he displaces Lilith with "Lady Evening . . . letting the night dawn"; in his "last waking to a trumpet of light," it is she who "Lay beside him as the lamps burned on." The meditative tercets invoke the tone of Stevens as Hollander embodies in his imagery of darkness and light his therapeutic conquest of regressive impulse by a more whole and sane vision of his muse. For Hollander, who can acknowledge (as in the title poem of *The Night Mirror,* 1971) "the bondage of horrors / Welling up only from deep within," uses his art not merely to express his neuroses but (as he says in *Reflections*) to master them:

> I have been concluding that our lives, fulfilled
> As they are by the work (so we must believe)
> Are uniquely free of terror. Terror is
> The condition in which we are disabled
> From doing what we must, and know we must, do.

In "Ad Musam" he had in elegant quatrains forsworn showering his muse with presents—now that they "are both of an age," he says he will "not spend it / Loving, but living / Your life, and you mine." This assumption of a more mature relation to his muse is followed in due course by *The Head of the Bed, Reflections on Espionage,* and "Spectral Emanations", the long poems in which Hollander's intelligence, vision, and craft are most convincingly blended.

In the midst of his encipherments Cupcake had murmured, parenthetically, " (Lamplight, after all, was supposed to / Be my main business this year)." The lamp is that which glowed in stanza 15 of *The Head of the Bed,* and is summoned as "A Poem in Seven Branches in Lieu of a Lamp" in the title poem of *Spectral Emanations* (1978, Hollander's selected poems). This, the most cryptic of Hollander's encipherments, in its structure derives from a Judaic legend, Gnostic and

589

apocryphal, which is glancingly mentioned by Hawthorne in Chapter 17 of *The Marble Faun*. As Hollander summarizes it in his prose preface, "The golden lamp of the Second Temple in Jerusalem, borne into Rome in the triumph of Titus, probably did not fall off the Milvian bridge when Constantine saw in the sky the sign by which he would conquer. The text which follows intends to hoist up another lamp from other waters than those of the Tiber. Lost bronze is silent, let alone gold; even the newest oil has no echo." So from the start the legend is equivocal—"probably did not fall . . . is silent . . . has no echo"; a salutary skepticism which opens the way for Hollander to do with his legend what he will. His preface is instructive: "I have here kindled the lights of sound, starting with the red cry of battle, followed by the false orange gold, true yellow goldenness, the green of all our joy, blue of our imaginings, the indigo between and the final violet that is next to black . . . Below each cup of color is a branch of prose, following and supporting it." Each "cup of color" is a syllabic poem (the line lengths varying from six syllables in the first and seventh, to eight in the second and sixth, ten in the third and fifth, and twelve in the central "Green"). These texts are supple in movement, opaque in meaning, as though protecting their revelations while bringing them before us in their monochromatic light. The meaning of each section, I presume, is best illuminated by the light of the whole of "Spectral Emanations," the fusion of all seven lamps burning with the white light of Truth. There is room in this dense text for humor—the character Roy G. Biv, whose name is an acronym for all the colors and whose surname means, in Hebrew, "sewer-pipe" —and for a narrative (the prose branch of "Green"), told by one of the seven secret agents seeking to raise the lost lamp. ("I am to embark not on a night journey but upon a pastoral cycle of magic and simplifications"). The method of the whole work seems to be at once an allegory of the seven qualities of the lamp and a Symbolist discovery of those qualities, as though embodying the knowledge that knowledge itself is only an abstraction until it has been won through experience, which is difficult. Hollander is a fecund allegorizer—he even wrote, in 1969, a masque in Ben Jonson's manner, inventing a mythic plot with such characters as Variety, Pattern, Chance, and Terpsichore (*An Entertainment for Elizabeth*, 1972). "Spectral Emanations," if I read it aright, is in its unique fashion a masque for our own time, with its "core" of prose sense or moral purpose embedded in verse and prose-poems at once mysterious, musical, perplexing, yet holding promise of a spiritual fulfillment for the agent who can crack its code.

Future readers, looking back on the 1960s and 1970s, may well conclude that after the deaths of Olson, Berryman, and Lowell—following
close as these did on those of Frost, Stevens, Williams, Eliot, Pound,
and Auden—American poetry was in a silver age, without commanding, dominant figures, but enriched by the work of many poets of
original accomplishment. If, among the score or so of poets still to be
named, few have as yet attracted the popular or even the critical acclaim of some of those discussed above, the work of these writers—and
that of others space precludes discussing—has nonetheless contributed
their individual accents to the clamor of competing styles and modes
which characterizes this period. In the midst of the social ferment and
the breaking up or transformation of institutions described in the foregoing chapters, the style, attitudes, intentions, and subjects of poetry
were, as we have seen, extended in many new directions. The poets
still to be mentioned here go off on tangents of their own devisings,
some responding to certain of the schools and individual styles already
discussed, others writing in opposition to these. It is difficult to categorize poets who resist being lumped together with others or with one
another.

Several of these, like many of the poets from Lowell and Berryman
on discussed above, began by mastering, with their individual imprints, the stanzaic style of metaphysical wit prevalent in their youth,
and then in middle life, responding to both the loosening of institutions and the effect on their poetry of new influences, transformed their
work, as we see by comparing the early and later poems of William Jay
Smith and Donald Justice. The first half of Smith's *New & Selected
Poems* (1970) displays his characteristic elegance and exotic subjects
("The Peacock of Java," "On the Islands Which Are Solomon's"), his
fascination with the circularity of dreamwork ("Galileo Galilei,"
"Dream"), and his demotic irony ("Amercan Primitive"):

> Look at him there in his stovepipe hat,
> His high-top shoes, and his handsome collar;
> Only my Daddy could look like that,
> And I love my Daddy like he loves his Dollar.

There is in Smith's work a lightness of tone and touch which points
back to Eliot's precursor Jules Laforgue, whom Smith expertly translated in 1956, and to Robert Herrick, whose poems he edited in 1962
and whom he described as "a master of understatement [who] knows
what to omit . . . nothing is too small for him to notice or too great to
reduce in size." A few years later, with *The Tin Can* (1966), Smith
abandoned his neat formality for a long, more shambling and inclu-

sive line. What that line includes in "The Tin Can" and "Northern Lights" is a sense of transport to a purer life ("as if the soul alone could speak, and having spoken, rippled, rubbed, and crossed, had been drained of speech / And shone forth new-clean, clear-cold, and white, with nothing within to hold or hide"); in "Fishing for Albacore" and "What Train Will Come?" Smith grasps the gritty particulars of modern life which his early style had often strained away. Smith's prose-textured line and nearly surreal movement owe less to other American poets making parallel experiments than they do to his own translation of Valéry Larbaud, *Poems of a Multimillionaire* (1955).

Donald Justice's *The Summer Anniversaries* appeared in 1960, the year after Lowell's *Life Studies* and Snodgrass's *Heart's Needle*; but although Justice, too, was at the University of Iowa at this time, there is little trace of the autobiographical or confessional breakout in his first book. Instead his lyrics, sonnets, and sestinas cast a glamor of stylistic grace upon the conventions of the Eliot-Ransom tradition. Even when Justice's material is personal, the allusive style and slightly archaic diction hold the subject at an aesthetic distance, as in "Tales from a Family Album." At the moment when many contemporaries were rejecting such conventions, Justice reconstituted them with an individual music, nostalgia, and irony, as though to demonstrate that a tradition thrives principally on the talents of its practitioners. By 1965 however, Justice had immersed himself in another tradition; in that year appeared *Contemporary French Poetry*, coedited by Justice and Alexander Aspel, a colleague at Iowa, where teachers and students in the poetry workshop made the translations of over a dozen surrealist poets from Pierre Reverdy to Jacques Dupin. "This poetry," wrote Aspel, "avoids apparent symmetries of form, but for that reason all the more intensely seeks broken and mobile patterns of stylization," using devices "based on a concentration of poetic power on images that aim beyond the conceptual limits of language so as to convey some unnamed intuition." The effects of his immersion in these broken and mobile patterns are evident in Justice's *Night Light* (1967) and *Departures* (1974). In these books Justice moves toward a phenomenology of absence, as the self dissolves into its perceptions and intuitions:

> In the distance,
> The whining of saws; and needles,
> Silently slipping through the chosen cloth.
> The stone, then as now, unfelt,
> Perfectly weightless. And certain words,

That will come together to mourn,
Waiting, in their dark clothes, apart.

On the other hand, a poet who has changed very little in the years between her first book, *Lines at Intersection* (1939), and *To All Appearances: Poems New and Selected* (1974) is Josephine Miles. Like the friend of a friend she describes in her poem, "Friend," her work is "A singular complex of idiosyncratic qualities." Her outward consistencies are stanzaic, rhyming, and tonal; her usual poem is in quatrains, her diction colloquial, her attitude to life unsentimental yet perceptive and tender. The wit in her poems is not mere wordplay but the inevitable outcome of a view of life that juxtaposes contraries in recognition of their contradictory resemblances. She can be wryly metaphysical, as in "Monkeys"; comment on cultural disparities ("Savages"); make pleasurable lyrics from the contemplation of life in its daily purposelessness ("Belief," "Ride") or as seen under the sign of an ancient determinism ("Oedipus"):

The gang wanted to give Oedipus Rex a going away present.
He had been a good hard-working father and king.
And besides it is the custom in this country
To give gifts on departure.

But we didn't know what to give Oedipus; he had everything.
Even in his loss, he had more than average.
So we gave him a travelling case, fitted, which we personally
Should have liked to receive.

Miles, who has published several distinguished studies of the language of poetry, is a celebrant of the quotidian. Her idiosyncracies seem an unexpected blend of the wit, moral steadfastness, and verbal inventiveness of Emily Dickinson and the contemporary British poet Stevie Smith; but nobody before her or since has made a style quite like hers, which can with such insouciance celebrate the most commonplace event, as she does in "Sale":

Went into a shoestore to buy a pair of shoes,
There was a shoe salesman humming the blues
Under his breath . . .

who, on hearing her say "please I need a triple-A," immediately "plucked from the mezzanine the very shoe."

Skill of the blessed, that at their command
Blue and breathless comes to hand
To send, from whatever preoccupation, feet
Implacably shod into the perfect street.

593

The poems of Josephine Miles often seem similarly plucked by an unfailing skill from the mezzanine of alternative choices.

Frederick Morgan's first volume, *A Book of Change* (1972), appeared when he was fifty, the poems wrenched from him by "pain and fear, / change after change releasing me to now." Among the changes recorded in this book, whose title suggests the *I Ching*, are grief for a son's death; the consolation of a God whose voice from the whirlwind tells him, "It's death to cling to me, but life to find me"; memories of his own youth recalled in middle age; and a fulfilling marriage. Morgan uses several modes and styles, veering from the gravity of his unrhymed sonnet meditations on death to the conversational plain style of love lyrics and autobiographical poems. The strongest vein is a visionary poetry based on ancient mythic images, which his second book will strengthen. In "The love of the jaybird for the rose" he makes a Rabelaisian paean to the lusty renewal of spring in the sort of hymn Stevens might have sung had he been willing, as Morgan is, to celebrate sexual energy directly. *A Book of Change* concludes, "this is ripeness, the golden fruit / of the great world-tree that dies, and lives." The theme of this book of changes is regeneration.

As though to catch up on his late start, Morgan has been a fecund poet. Dualities striate his *Poems of the Two Worlds* (1977), in which are played many variations on the title poem. There "the sordid clock-tower on east 94th street" and other quotidian facts are contrasted to "the second world where the dead walk arm in arm, / perfected ones garbed in their destinies." The interpenetration of these worlds is dramatized in "Woyzeck." Morgan is attuned to the fabulous, and his "Mirrors of Childhood" are animate with creatures from dream, nightmare, and folk memory—ogre, witch, torturer, an opposing self. In "Hideyoshi" the two worlds suggested are life and death, violence and contemplation, passion and tranquillity, as the triumphant general

> then with his bloody sword
> cut wild blossoms and grasses
> and in an hour's silence
> composed a subtle and delicate combination . . .
>
> Those whom he had conquered
> he now must judge:
> he wished a mind clean-purged
> of violence and ardor.

The two worlds we inhabit are also those of body and of mind, as appears in "Centaurs," one of several satiric poems in tight quatrains reminiscent of Robert Graves's treatment of similar psychomachia. Morgan writes with the verve of a young poet exploring for the first time the hitherto inarticulate selves his art permits him to discover. A brief book, *The Tarot of Cornelius Agrippa* (1978), develops the prose poem, used more tentatively in his first two volumes, to create fables akin to folktales and legends, a gnostic gospel.

In *A Probable Volume of Dreams* (1969) Marvin Bell confronts the disjunctions of life not by seeking their resolving unification but by savoring the absurdities of their contradictions. His poems speak with a winning humor. If Bell assumes vatic poses, it is only to deflate their pretensions. The clarity of his diction and syntax heighten the incongruities of what is perceived and recorded, as in "On Returning to Teach":

> But as the moon bears
> with great heaviness waters to itself,
> one tongue reissues for attention.
> It is mine. I have come back to win
> the National Book Award, but am locked in
> the English Department, let me out!
>
> . . . .
>
> In the second childhood, there are not more children.
> In the second semester, the teachers are older.

The Escape into You (1971) is a sequence of fifty-four poems, all in three six-line stanzas. One can't help being reminded of Berryman's *Dream Songs,* yet the humor tinged with sadness with which Bell explores his feelings is recognizably his own. A later series of thirteen poems in this form commemorate Bell's father, a recurring presence in his poems (*Residue of Song,* 1974). In *Stars Which See, Stars Which Do Not See* (1977) the metaphysics on which Bell's poems, with their inconsequent delights, are based is specified in such lines as these from "New Students":

> . . . there's a way in which you are loved,
>
> an anatomy of correspondences, and
> a shapeless universe disguised as time—
> which is not possible to understand.
> That is why this circumstance of energy
> is recorded as glory and passes into study.

Regionalism is no longer considered a literary force, yet when American life is at once so multitudinous and disorganized, so varied and

so resistant to summary, many poets reach out to the immediate realities of their own lives, their families, their towns, their regions. We
have seen this impulse inform the work of Frost and Williams's *Paterson*; Lowell's and Olson's treatments of their New England heritage;
Warren's memories of the Kentucky of his youth; and the western
themes of Snyder, Stafford, and Wagoner. Several southern poets
younger than Warren write from an imaginative conception of their
heritage, among them Dabney Stuart (*A Particular Place,* 1969), Miller
Williams (*Halfway from Hoxie,* 1973), and Fred Chappell (*River,*
1975). Where, for them, the rural South is re-created from boyhood
memories, for Wendell Berry the farmer's kinship with the land is the
matter of his daily life. The most determined Southern Agrarian of
his generation, Berry works a small farm in his native Kentucky, as
though to give modern currency to a belief of Jefferson which he quotes
as epigraph to one of his poems: "The small landholders are the most
precious part of a state." Berry is well aware that "Now the old ways
that have brought us / farther than we remember sink out of sight,"
trodden down by "strangers ignorant of landmarks." In *The Country
of Marriage* (1973) one of his more desperate masks is that of the Mad
Farmer; but the equanimity Berry seeks, in love and with the land—
these are mutual sacraments—is given as a hard-won alternative to the
desolation of industrial America, rural or urban, in such poems as
"A Marriage, an Elegy":

> They suffered as their faith required.
> Now their union is consummate
> in earth, and the earth
> is their communion.

Berry is an uneven poet, his work is sometimes slack, but at his best,
writing in a mode influenced by Denise Levertov, he achieves a
memorable, simple intensity: "O love, / open. Show me / my country. Take me home." Like Gary Snyder, he is a committed ecologist
and has become a hero of the counterculture.

Another poet whose tone and technique are contemporary but
whose subjects often derive from a rural setting is Philip Booth. A
lifelong resident of Castine, Maine, a coastal village where Lowell was
for years a summer neighbor, Booth takes his venue from the sea, its
islands, ships and creatures, and the woods around the village. His
is a poetry of space and solitude, of outward and inward weather perceived as his kinsman Thoreau perceived them. In *Letter from a Distant Land* (1957) Booth addressed Thoreau in leisurely and bucolic
blank verse, subsequently tightened, as his selected poems, *Margins*

(1970) demonstrates. He can write a tersely witty poem, "Maine," in which Yankee making-do is applied to old cars and their engines; but as Booth probes his own roots more deeply his verse becomes more pared-away and economical. In his best work he strongly dramatizes the laconic Yankee qualities of mind and speech. In *Available Light* (1976) this spare style permits him entry into other landscapes of dreamwork and fable ("Dreamscape," "A Dream of Russia") as well as opening out in taut, lean, granitic glimpses of authentic truths wrested from language as cold and clear as the weather:

> Given
> this day, none
> better, I try
> these words to
> quicken
> the silence: I
> break track
> across it
> to make myself
> known.

"I think we are the last true regionalists," Hayden Carruth writes in "Vermont" (*Brothers, I Loved You All*, 1978):

> Not local colorists, at any rate, not keepers
> of quaintness for quaintness's sake. We're realists.
> And realism means place, and place means
> where we are. We name it, with all its garbage
> and slaughter, and comeliness too, and then
> it is our center—where we are.

"We try," he adds, "to make it / a center of everywhere," for "Place is the now / which is eternal." Thus in this long poem, struggling to be not too much in debt to Frost, Carruth defines the local as the incidence of what is universal. In "John Dryden," "Marshall Walker," and "Crows Mark" he most successfully realizes the implications of the fully realized particulars of his subjects—a local wild man, a farmer neighbor, his own farmhouse—and continues the vein begun in such poems as "Homecoming" and "Concerning Necessity" in *From Snow and Rock, from Chaos* (1973). Yet Frostian regionalism is but one string to Carruth's bow; this prolific poet is tempted by other modes, other models; most successful are his sequences of fifteen-line stanzas: "Paragraphs" in *Brothers; Contra Mortem* (1967); and "The Asylum" in his first book, *The Crow and the Heart* (1959). The earliest of these skeins of near-sonnets was excerpted from a longer work,

The Bloomingdale Papers, not published until 1974, although written during Carruth's hospitalization twenty-five years earlier: Carruth's work deserves comparison with Roethke's and Lowell's on similar themes:

> And you, my crowd,
> My mad folk, here will you cry loud?
> And will you add beseeching to the wind?
> For on the curious blast
> Of punctured sorrows soughs the mind that sinned
> Inexorably across the past,
> And Troy, I think, sounds distantly and shrill.
> How hard the search here for the self at last!
> The loud wind comes to chill us and to kill.

In *Contra Mortem* the poet celebrates consciousness, "a being freeborn and intricate like the day" in his twenty-eight charms against death. In "Paragraphs" he defines his inner being in terms provided by Bakounine's anarchist manifesto, for "the real revolutionary is one who can see / all dark ahead and behind, his fate / a need without a hope: *the will to resist.*" The versification in this series is broken up, the method reminiscent of Pound or Olson. Carruth's sympathy with the Black Mountain forms of postmodernism may be inferred from the representation given such poets in his copious anthology, despite its title taken from Stevens, *The Voice That Is Great Within Us* (1970). In quite a different vein he has written also a long poem, *Journey to a Known Place* (1961), in four cantos, one for each of the traditional elements, the versification alternately suggesting Williams and Eliot in its treatment of his Dantesque theme. Despite the unevenness resulting from his veering between several styles, the body of this poet's work deserves respect.

Richard Hugo's characteristic theme and style appear in *The Lady in Kicking Horse Reservoir* (1973):

> Isn't this your life? That ancient kiss
> still burning out your eyes? Isn't this defeat
> so accurate, the church bell simply seems
> a pure announcement: ring and no one comes?
> Don't empty houses ring? Are magnesium
> and scorn sufficient to support a town,
> not just Philipsburg, but towns
> of towering blondes, good jazz and booze
> the world will never let you have
> until the town you came from dies inside?

"Degrees of Gray in Philipsburg" epitomizes Hugo's obsessed concentration upon the bleak, used-up industrial towns of the American West, where the defeated and the lost summon up the consolations of reality in supple blank verse. *31 Letters and 13 Dreams* (1977) uses this style for the dreams, a longer line for the letters addressed to other poets. These epistles are autobiographical explorations, pitched in the same gray key as the earlier work. Hugo strikes an authentic and original note in his blending, as it were, of the *donnée*s of Williams and Edgar Lee Masters—except that his speakers are not yet in the grave.

The harsh industrial landscape which Lowell singled out as Williams's special province and a necessary subject of American poetry is explored further by Philip Levine, as in "Coming Home, Detroit, 1968":

> . . . The charred faces, the eyes
> boarded up, the rubble of innards, the cry
> of wet smoke hanging in your throat,
> the twisted river stopped at the color of iron.
> We burn this city every day.

Here, and in other poems in *They Feed The Lion* (1972), the wasted landscape is interiorized as character becomes inseparable from environment. Residence in Spain provides Levine with his other recurring subject, and exposure to Spanish surrealism lends his work a harsh intensity (as in "Angel Butcher," "The Children's Crusade"). The title poem of *1933* (1974) is a Whitman-like incantation enumerating the terms of his childhood; other poems in this book and *The Names of the Lost* (1976) use a tautly controlled short line to explore the suffering and sacrifices of Spain during and after the Civil War and, from the disarray and losses of his own life in the industrial wasteland of the modern city, Levine reaches toward moments of insight, anger, and compassion.

The lure of writing a long poem about history, as Pound once described *The Cantos*, has afflicted American poets ever since Joel Barlow grounded his modest talent with *The Columbiad*. In the foregoing pages I have mentioned such excursions into contemporary equivalents or substitutes for the epic mode as *The Cantos, Paterson,* Lowell's *History*, Berryman's *Homage to Mistress Bradstreet*, Olson's *Maximus*, Duncan's "Passages," as well as those long poems which interiorize history, making it intrinsic with the self—as in *Song of Myself*, Berryman's *Dream Songs*, Merrill's "Book of Ephraim," and Kinnell's *Book of Nightmares*. Each of these poems has been experimental in form, breaking up narrative as the idea of continuous time has been replaced by a kaleidoscopic coterminousness of all experience. Yet in our period there have been several interesting though neglected efforts to write narrative poems on American history. In the case of Winfield Townley Scott's *The Dark Sister* (1958), the subject is American prehistory: for this is a saga of Freydis, half-sister to Leif Ericson, an exultant muse of greed and the desire for power. Taking his subject from the hints given in the opening chapter of William Carlos Williams's *In the American Grain* and using a long swinging line capable of including narrative, dialogue, and interpretive comment, Scott re-created the half-savage Vikings as images of modern men and women, their struggles paradigmatic of the history to come. Louis O. Coxe, in *The Wilderness* (1958), also treats of our beginnings. His twenty-page blank verse title poem dramatizes the effort of the seventeenth-century Jesuit Duclos to bring the true Faith and the flag of New France into New England, with the Abenaki Indians as sacrificed instruments of God's will. His expedition is disastrous, not least because instead of enlightening the Indians, Duclos emulates their savagery in his desire for power. Continuing the dramatic-narrative mode of Frost and Robinson, Coxe, in probing the corruption of power, comes near to Lowell's concerns; his poem shares its background with "The Mills of the Kavanaughs." In *The Middle Passage* (1960) Coxe wrote of the crossing of a slave ship, a subject treated in more experimental style two years earlier in a brief poem of the same title by Robert Hayden, and more forcefully later by Lowell in his play, "Benito Cereno," adapted from Melville's story. George Keithley, in a book-length narrative poem, *The Donner Party* (1972), uses the tale of those feckless pioneers snowbound in the Rockies, starving, reduced to cannibalism, as a paradigm of the settlement of the continent. Other narrative poems on American history are few. More provincial in subject than the foregoing is *Local Lives* by Millen Brand (1975), vignettes about the Pennsylvania Dutch, modeled on Masters's *Spoon River Anthology*.

Two of the strongest and most memorable long poems of the period are Donald Finkel's *Answer Back* (1968) and *Adequate Earth* (1972). Each is a book-length suite of poems extruded from a single executive metaphor: the exploration, respectively, of Mammoth Cave and of the Antarctic continent. (Finkel spent a summer at the naval station in Antarctica while at work on the latter book.) His poems are collages of quotations from a variety of sources interspersed with his own passages. "These precious scraps," he writes in *Adequate Earth*, "culled from sledging journals, memoirs, histories, technical articles, etc., are intended simply as lights in a constellation of which my own observations form

600

an integral part." In *Answer Back* the cave becomes transformed into images of birth, love, the cosmos, consciousness. In *Adequate Earth,* much of the "culled" material is taken from journals of the rival expeditions intent on being first to find the South Pole. Set off against these quotations and Finkel's own meditations are passages he has invented as "the gospels of the Emperor penguins," an animistic device that casts into perspective the desires, strivings, and heroism of his human explorers of what Scott called "an awful place." Here Finkel describes his Quonset hut as a Walden; like Thoreau, though in techniques more resembling Williams or Pound, he is testing the bedrock reality of life to discover whether it is good.

The rejection of the long poem, as well as of all other extant poetic conventions, can scarcely be more far-reaching than in concrete poetry, a genre which has also flourished in Europe. Its principal forerunner among modern poets was e. e. cummings. Concretism, however, is more closely allied to the aesthetic of avant-garde painting. Minimalism has paralleled, if not influenced, such poets as Creeley; its closer equivalent in poetry is concretism, the effort to marry word and image so as to beget the briefest of visual puns. In these the neck of rhetoric has been truly wrung, at the cost of a nearly nugatory content. The principal American concretists are Mary Ellen Solt and Richard Kostelanetz. Solt's "Sunflower" may be the most famous work in this genre. Held at arm's length, it seems a picture of a sunflower; inspected more closely, the flower proves to be composed of the word SUNFLOWER printed in a wavering vertical line to make the stem, repeated in a series of concentric circles to compose the head. Kostelanetz's "DISINTEGRATION" typifies his work—in this, the one word, in capitals, is repeated in a column, each line more pocked than the preceding. Variations of the mode by several hands appear in the anthologies *Concrete Poetry: A World View,* edited by Solt and Willis Barnstone (1968), and *Imaged Words and Worded Images,* edited by Kostelanetz (1970).

Concretism emphasizes the visual quality of poetic experience to the exclusion of all else, with results sometimes resembling the typographical logos of advertising art. More fruitful unions of image and word have been offered by less dogmatic poets. William Jay Smith's playful children's book, *Typewriter Town* (1960), anticipated concretism's avant-garde. John Hollander's *Types of Shape* (1969), in which poems are set in shapes as complex as a key or a reflected swan, is reminiscent of the seventeenth-century tradition of emblem poets, Francis Quarles and George Herbert.

The poet who has most consistently made the visual arrangement of lines on the page a constituent of the poem's feeling and meaning is

601

May Swenson. In her six books, from *Another Animal* (1954) through *New & Selected Things Taking Place* (1978), what is said is enlivened and embodied in the poem's shape. Sometimes, as in "Unconscious Came a Beauty," "The Lightning," or "Out of the Sea, Early," the typography pictorializes the subject—respectively, a butterfly, a lightning bolt (represented by a diagonal streak of white zipping through her lines), or a snail. But May Swenson also handles typographic appearance in less obvious, more abstract fashions. "The Shape of Death" is suggested by the irregularity of the white ribbon winding between the halves of her poem, in which the lines are flush right as well as flush left. In another poem on this grave theme, "Deaths," the lines are a Whitman-like catalogue of all those whom death will claim; the opening phrase in each is "One will die," separated from the rest of the line by white space and the indentation of runovers so that what we see is a column on the left repeating "One will die"; the inventory completing each line gives substance to this incantation. Meaning finds shape in "Survey of the Whole":

> World's lopsided
> >That's its trouble
> >Don't run in a circle
> >Runs in a loop

and again in "Camofleur":

> Walked in the swamp   His cheek vermilion
> >A dazzling prince
> >Neck-band white   Cape he trailed
> >Metallic mottled

The disarrangement casts into doubt the order in which the lines are to be read. Excerpts cannot do justice to these effects, which depend on the appearance of the entire poem for their force and their charm.

With keen intelligence Swenson has extended the examples of Williams and e. e. cummings and the precepts of Olson regarding typographical composition into a principle of poetic form. Her inventiveness is protean, yet this is but one of the charms and strengths of May Swenson's poems. She is equally attuned to the sounds of words, and her poems are often built on rhyme and near-rhyme, as in "The Blue Bottle" and many other poems. Her sensibility shares with Marianne Moore and Elizabeth Bishop a close and loving attention to the particulars of experience, the actualities of how things look, sound, or if animate, act; above all, how it feels to perceive and understand them. In "Painting the Gate" and "Blue," for example, there is replicated the pattern of action in the first, of perception in the second, in patterns of sound and rhythm which confer upon the reader the author's joy in her action, in her perception. The kinds of dissociation of experience which in Ashbery seem so often willful or tinged with melancholy appear in Swenson's "Written While Riding the Long Island Railroad" as kaleidoscopic impressions received—and given—with pleasure. "Night Visits with the Family" offers a surreal catalogue of a dozen relatives' dreams, then subsumes them all in the section titled "May's Dream." May Swenson's dreams, or poems, are tactile and sensuous evocations of reality which, through the wit and delight of their recognition of the patterns of feeling they embody, transcend the reality that is their nominal subject.

All of the poets named in these pages are my contemporaries, and I count it a privilege to have lived in the midst of such plenitude, conflict, variety and confusion, so many efforts to discover order and embody it, so many trials to "make it new." Since the persona through whom I have spoken in these chapters is neither confessional nor autobiographical, to speak of my own work here would scarcely be appropriate; I can, however, mention Richard Howard's chapter, "Daniel Hoffman," in *Alone with America,* and "A Major Poet" by Monroe K. Spears (*Southern Review,* 1975).

Each new generation of poets comes to self-consciousness by either rejecting or absorbing the work of its immediate predecessors. At the beginning of the period—there were giants in those days—young poets defined themselves in relation to Eliot, Yeats or Stevens, Pound or Williams, Auden or Marianne Moore, assimilating or repudiating the bequests of these modernist masters. Poets of the sixties felt their presences more remote, less inviting or intimidating than those of Lowell, Roethke, Berryman, Olson. When we turn to their still younger contemporaries, to poets who were scarcely born or were playing stickball when Eliot walked the fire patrol in London or Pound was imprisoned at Pisa, the seminal poets of the century, except for Williams and Pound, recede into history as large, distant, and monumental, like the heads of the presidents carved on Mount Rushmore. Lowell and his generation, too, look likely soon to join them, as the new young poets define their enterprise in relation not to these battalions of the dead but to the work of most of the movements and individual dissidents from movements discussed in the past two chapters. The history of the period is thus a series of repeated gestures of repudiation or assimilation, as poets absorb what they can transform and use, and reject from the poetry of the immediate past and the life of the present whatever they feel is false, tawdry, or threatening to their sense of self. The chief repudiations made by the younger poets repeat those made before them of what is perceived as the "tradition" of "rationalism." Because thought is thought to have made the mess the world is, they would cry with Keats, "Oh, for a life of Sensation rather than Thoughts." Despite their variations from decade to decade, the poets of postmodernism, like those of modernism, comprise ripples on the great groundswell of the Romantic movement which nearly two centuries ago established the oppositions of feelings to thought, of self to institutions, which separate modern man from his past. The chief difference between the contemporary and the Romantic and modernist generations is, we now recognize the past as lost.

Lost, except for Whitman: not lost for Whitman because he was the first American poet for whom the history of the self subsumed the history of the race. Whitman's living influence abides, whether directly, as in the work of Gerald Stern (*Lucky Life,* 1977), or combined with that of others such as Ashbery and the surrealists, as in the work of Norman Dubie (*In the Dead of the Night,* 1975).

The poets coming into their own after the Vietnam war appear to have absorbed most of the tendencies described in the foregoing pages. Expansion of subject toward confession and autobiography is widespread, as is an interest, often simultaneous, in the poetry of primitive peoples and in the translation of the latest contemporaries from France, Germany, Russia, indeed from all of Europe and South America. Surrealism predominates in the work of Stephen Dobyns, Michael Benedikt, and Bill Knott, while it has had a diffused effect on many other poets. (The names I cite here are illustrative only; this is not intended as a definitive list.) The breaking up of rhythm, stanza, and serial development, experimentally undertaken by Olson and the Black Mountain poets as well as by Merwin, Bly, Wright, Ashbery, and their respective followers, has now become the norm, or one of the norms, to which new verse conforms. This normative technique is explored, in all its latitude for individual differences, by such poets as Daniel Halpern, Larry Levis, William Matthews, Gregory Orr, Linda Pastan, and Stanley Plumly.

In their pursuit of unclosed forms and fluid structures and in their rejection of rhetoric, such poets as these, nurtured on surrealism and its American derivatives, have in common a turning away from the density of verbal texture in favor of diction more like ordinary speech than the artifice of a crafted style. Thus the original Romantic gesture of Wordsworth, seeking the language of ordinary men heightened by strong feeling, is re-created anew, after having been made again

604

and again by Frost, Pound, Williams, and their various followers. The processes are repeated without surcease by which poetic style forever rebels against what is considered an established artificiality, produces over and over in the name of naturalness a new diction which in time becomes habitual, to be in its turn regarded as an academicism against which still newer poets rebel by simplifying diction yet again.

The Tradition, whether its avatar be Yeats, Eliot, Stevens, Tate, Ransom, or Auden, is at once the ghostly presence against which the rebels rebel and a living body of work by the poets of the middle generation—Merrill, Wagoner, Hecht, Hollander, and others—whose influence is absorbed and modified again by the younger poets who continue to master the poetry of conventional forms, dense texture, and heightened diction. Those who write with conviction and inventiveness in this vein, bringing the new life of their modern occasions and the sensibility of their age to traditional verse-making—among their other accomplishments in other veins—include Marilyn Hacker, Judith Moffett, John Peck, Robert Pinsky, and Dave Smith. It is only in the necessary fantasy of its opponents (and in the lines of derivative verse writers whose work soon disappears) that a tradition stands still, fails to change, goes on repeating itself without embodying creative responses to changed circumstances. Ultimately, both the poetry of tradition and the poetry of revolt must be poetries of convention, for rebelliousness is itself a convention and art in any case is never created directly from life; as the taxonomies suggested in the foregoing chapters indicate, all art is an insider's game.

The foregoing names are but a few of the poets of this talented generation finding voices to assert the reality of their individual existence. If thus far their results seem more a development from than a violent deviating against the styles of their immediate predecessors, we may recall Auden's observation that there can be no great change of style without a prior change in sensibility, in feeling, in the conditions of life anterior to feeling, sensibility, or style. The last decades of the twentieth century may be a period of consolidation rather than one of bold innovation reflecting or predicting still further disruptions of the personal relationships, institutions, and attitudes that underlie literary expression.

In poetry as in fiction, drama, and the other arts, the centripetal forces of contemporary culture and contemporary anticulture are so strong that no single writer or poet has been able to yoke together a Modern Synthesis that could serve his art as the Medieval Synthesis served that of Dante. Our last successful syncretist was Yeats, and what a strained contraption of eccentricities he found necessary to

605

stem this modern tide that destroys all ancient verities! In the United States we not only inhabit the present, we invent the future, while with greater energy than other peoples we perfect the forgetting of the past—mainly because most of the human past seems to us Americans not to have been ours anyway. So the American poet is left with his self, his mirror convex or concave, his dictionary and thesaurus, his eyes sweeping a landscape of concrete highways, processed hamburger stands, conglomerated industries, glossy condominiums, and junk-strewn ghettoes, a middle-class population molded in the image of the TV consumer ads it spent half its childhood watching, a declining attention span, fewer and fewer readers of anything serious in a populous nation whose dreams are suckled on the vapid concoctions of popular entertainment. The isolation of Poe, Whitman, Dickinson, Melville—the great writers of our brief past—is scarcely alleviated by the passage of a century. For their successors, too, the continuation of their art must certainly depend upon the tenacious, impractical, foolhardy, stubborn commitment of the poets themselves, rather than on any visible public demand their work conceivably fills. The poet, as Emerson has told us, "is isolated among his contemporaries by truth and by his art, but with this consolation in his pursuits, that they will draw all men sooner or later. For all men live by truth and stand in need of expression. In love, in art, in avarice, in politics, in labor, in games, we study to utter our painful secret. The man is only half himself, the other half is his expression." However relegated now by their vision and their craft to the recognition of only a coterie of enthusiasts, our genuine poets will have bequeathed to a future they scarcely dare believe in the record of how it was to feel, to think, to live, in our time.

Index

Hyman, Stanley Edgar, 64

Inge, William, 410, 422
Innis, Harold, 40

Jacobs, Jane, 365–366
Jacobsen, Josephine, 579
James, Henry, 132, 140, 154, 177, 194, 202, 220, 233, 295, 456
Janeway, Elizabeth, 367
Jarrell, Randall, 60, 61, 131–132, 441, 466, 470–471, 526, 565, 583
Jiménez, Juan Ramón, 545, 546
Johnson, Diane, 381, 386
Johnson, Fenton, 288
Johnson, Georgia Douglas, 288
Johnson, James Weldon, 288, 289, 292, 335
Johnson, Virginia E., 25
Jones, James, 95, 96–100, 120, 122, 124, 138, 139, 228, 229, 245
Jones, LeRoi, *see* Baraka, Imamu Amiri
Jones, Madison, 185
Jones, Margo, 422
Jones, Preston, 422
Jones, Tom, 437
Jonson, Ben, 450, 587, 588, 590
Joyce, James, 1, 53, 74, 272
Jung, Carl, 241, 468, 545, 547
Justice, Donald, 591, 592–593

Kafka, Franz, 544
Kaiser, Ernest, 308–309
Kalstone, David, 502
Kander, John, 437
Kanin, Fay, 434
Kanin, Garson, 397, 433
Karenga, Ron, 306–307
Kaufman, Bob, 325
Kaufman, George S., 398
Kazan, Elia, 92
Kazin, Alfred, 72, 79, 194, 196, 287, 298
Keithley, George, 600
Kelley, William Melvin, 318
Kellogg, Robert, 69
Kelly, George, 397, 398
Kennedy, Adrienne, 334, 432
Kennedy, John F., 304
Kennedy, X. J., 458n, 580
Kenner, Hugh, 79-80, 446

Kerouac, Jack, 104, 109–111, 115, 125, 140, 144, 270, 347, 520
Kesey, Ken, 111
Keyes, Frances Parkinson, 85
Killens, John Oliver, 306, 310, 318
King, Martin Luther, 303, 304
Kingsley, Sidney, 398
Kingston, Maxine Hong, 382, 384
Kinnell, Galway, 329, 441, 497, 515, 546n, 548, 564, 566–570, 578, 599
Kinsey, Alfred, 22, 23–25
Kirk, Russell, 11
Kizer, Carolyn, 370
Klein, Marcus, 201, 224
Knight, Etheridge, 323, 325
Knott, Bill, 604
Knowles, John, 144
Kobayashi, Issa, 546
Koch, Kenneth, 424, 496, 537, 553, 561–563
Kopit, Arthur, 415–416, 417, 435
Kostelanetz, Richard, 601
Kramer, Jane, 520
Krasna, Norman, 400
Kroeber, Karl, 524
Kronenberger, Louis, 412
Kumin, Maxine, 371, 388
Kunitz, Stanley, 461, 464–465

Laing, R. D., 28, 252, 502
Lalic, Ivan V., 551
Landess, Thomas H., 178
Lang, V. R., 553
Larbaud, Valery, 592
Larsen, Nella, 288
Latouche, John, 413, 437
Lattimore, Richmond, 536
Laurents, Arthur, 411, 437
Lazard, Naomi, 387
Leavis, F. R., 11
Lee, Canada, 330
Lee, Don L., 306, 323, 324, 325
Lee, James, 413
Le Guin, Ursula, 275
Lerner, Alan Jay, 436
Lessing, Doris, 346, 387
Lester, Julius, 305
Levertov, Denise, 359–360, 371, 454, 512, 526, 533–536, 546n, 553, 596
Lévi-Strauss, Claude, 12, 73

Index